ROGET'S
21st CENTURY
THESAURUS

ROGET'S
21st CENTURY
THESAURUS

THOMAS NELSON PUBLISHERS
Nashville

Copyright © 1992 by Thomas Nelson Publishers

Published in Nashville, Tennessee by Thomas Nelson, Publishers and distributed in Canada by Lawson Falle, Ltd., Cambridge, Ontario.

Library of Congress Cataloging-in-Publication Data

Roget's 21st century thesaurus
    p. cm.
  ISBN 0-8407-6830-3 (PB)
   1. English language—Synonyms and antonyms. I. Thomas Nelson
Publishers. II. Title: Roget's twenty-first century thesaurus.
PE1591.R716 1992
423′.1—dc20   92–6946
                                                 CIP

1 2 3 4 5 6 7 8 — 98 97 96 95 93 92

Publisher's Preface

Leap into the future with Thomas Nelson's Roget's 21st Century Thesaurus. Our concise, modern edition is an abridged version of Roget's original work published in 1852. With more than 1,000 entries, this powerful reference is an essential part of every school, home and office library. Included is a "plan of classification" (following Roget's original format) and a tabular synopsis of categories to aid you as you search for the perfect synonym. To assure clarity, all antiquated and duplicated entries have been removed.

The publishers are certain that you will find this resource both beneficial and enlightening as you use it to explore the depths of the English language.

How to Use Roget's Thesaurus

PETER MARK ROGET (1779—1869) was a British lexicographer and physician. *Roget's Thesaurus,* a standard reference work for over a century, represents his highly personal view of how the English language reflects the structure of the universe. In some ways, that view is dated today; but the complex structure and breadth of the thesaurus still prove surprisingly helpful to the modern user.

For most users, the key to the synonyms in the body of the book lies in the alphabetical listing in the index. The uniqueness of Roget's original plan of classification provides the user with access to related words and requires nothing more than a near-synonym to help locate the word sought. *Roget's Thesaurus* is more than simply a synonym dictionary—both in the lists following individual headwords and in the grouping of headwords under the various sections, it is a diverse collection of associated and related words and phrases.

For example, suppose you are looking for a synonym for *lull:* a check in the index yields the reference number, 403; turning to that entry provides the synonyms *silence, stillness, quiet, hush, peace.*

But, suppose you are trying to find a verb meaning 'to feel very dissatisfied' and the synonyms listed under *discontent* are not "strong" enough for your purpose. A brief check of the related, contiguous headwords will lead you to the entry for *regret* which provides the synonyms *lament, deplore, bemoan, bewail, rue.*

This edition of *Roget's Thesaurus* has a number of other special features. Dictionaries of synonyms, unless they are of considerable size, rarely provide alphabetical listings of all the words in the book. In this edition, you will find every word listed in the index.

Larger books may provide more synonyms, but the user of a thesaurus is rarely looking for a rare or unusual word: he wants an equivalent word that is part of everyday language. This edition is the only abridged *Roget's Thesaurus* available. While retaining the original structure and all the 1,000 headwords, all antiquated words and phrases have been removed. In addition, the book has been modernized to include the most current usage and the newest developments in language.

In this abridgment, many duplications have been omitted to save space. For maximum usefulness, the user should look through other associated parts of speech for the word he is seeking, for adjectives and verbs can yield nouns and adverbs, and vice versa. For example, adverbs can be formed by adding -*ly* to some adjectives and nouns by adding -*ness* to some adjectives.

The Publisher

Caution: If the word selected is not completely familiar, check its meaning and usage in this volume's dictionary before risking its use in an incorrect or unidiomatic context.

The words shown in **boldface** *in the index indicate they are the title or heading of a category.*

Plan of Classification

(following the original Roget plan)

Tabular Synopsis of Categories

Class I. ABSTRACT RELATIONS
I. EXISTENCE

1. existence	2. nonexistence
3. substantiality	4. unsubstantiality
5. intrinsicality	6. extrinsicality
7. state	8. circumstance

II. RELATION

9. relation	10. nonrelation
11. consanguinity	
12. correlation	
13. identity	14. contrariety
	15. difference
16. uniformity	16a. lack of uniformity
17. similarity	18. dissimilarity
19. imitation	20. nonimitation
	20a. variation
21. copy	22. prototype
23. agreement	24. disagreement

III. QUANTITY

25. quantity	26. degree
27. equality	28. inequality
	29. mean
	30. compensation
31. greatness	32. smallness
33. superiority	34. inferiority
35. increase	36. decrease
37. addiction	38. deduction
39. adjunct	40. remainder
	40a. decrement
41. mixture	42. simpleness
43. junction	44. disjunction
45. link	

VIII. CAUSATION

Class II. SPACE
I. SPACE IN GENERAL

II. DIMENSIONS

Class III. MATTER
I. MATTER IN GENERAL

316. materiality

317. immateriality

318. world

319. gravity

320. levity

II. INORGANIC MATTER

321. density

322. thinness

323. hardness

324. softness

325. elasticity

326. inelasticity

327. tenacity

328. brittleness

329. structure

330. granularity

331. friction

332. lubrication

333. fluidity

334. gaseity

335. liquefaction

336. vaporization

337. water

338. air

339. moisture

340. dryness

341. ocean

342. land

343. gulf, lake

344. plain

345. marsh

346. island

347. stream

348. river

349. wind

350. conduit

351. air-pipe

352. semiliquidity

353. bubble, cloud

354. pulpiness

355. unctuousness

356. oil

356a. resin

III. ORGANIC MATTER

357. animate matter

358. inanimate matter

359. life

360. death

361. killing

362. corpse

363. interment

364. animality

365. vegetation

Class IV. INTELLECT
I. FORMATION OF IDEAS

450. intellect

450a. absence of intellect

451. thought

452. absence of thought

453. idea

454. topic

455. curiosity

456. incuriosity

457. attention

458. inattention

459. care

460. neglect

461. inquiry

462. answer

463. experiment

464. comparison

465. discrimination

465a. indiscrimination

466. measurement

467. evidence

468. counter-evidence

469. qualification

470. possibility

471. impossibility

472. probability

473. improbability

474. certainty

475. uncertainty

476. reasoning

477. intuition, sophistry

478. demonstration

479. confutation

480. judgment

481. misjudgment

480a. discovery

482. overestimation

483. underestimation

484. belief

485. disbelief, doubt

486. credulity

487. incredulity

488. assent

489. dissent

490. knowledge

491. ignorance

492. scholar

493. ignoramus

494. truth

495. error

496. maxim

497. absurdity

498. intelligence, wisdom

499. imbecility, folly

500. sage

501. fool

502. sanity

503. insanity

504. madman

505. memory

506. oblivion

507. expectation

508. nonexpectation

509. disappointment

510. foresight
511. prediction
512. omen
513. oracle
514. supposition
515. imagination

II. COMMUNICATION OF IDEAS

516. meaning
517. meaninglessness
518. intelligibility
519. unintelligibility
520. equivocalness

521. figure of speech
522. interpretation
523. misinterpretation
524. interpreter
525. manifestation
526. latency
527. information
528. concealment
529. disclosure
530. ambush
531. publication
532. news
533. secret
534. messenger
535. affirmation
536. negation, denial
537. teaching
538. misteaching
539. learning
540. teacher
541. learner
542. school
543. veracity
544. falsehood
545. deception
546. untruth
547. dupe
548. deceiver
549. exaggeration
550. indication
551. record
552. obliteration
553. recorder
554. representation
555. misrepresentation
556. painting
557. sculpture
558. engraving

Class V. VOLITION
I. INDIVIDUAL VOLITION

600. will	601. necessity
602. willingness	603. unwillingness
604. resolution	605. irresolution
604. perseverance	
606. obstinancy	607. recantation
	608. caprice
609. choice	609a. neutrality
	610. rejection
611. predetermination	612. impulse
613. habit	614. disuse
615. motive	615a. absence of motive
	616. dissuasion
617. plea	
618. good	619. evil
620. intention	621. chance
622. pursuit	623. avoidance
	624. relinquishment
625. business	
626. plan	
627. method	
628. mid-course	629. circuit
630. requirement	
631. instrumentality	
632. means	
633. instrument	
634. substitute	
635. materials	
636. store	
637. provision	638. waste

639. sufficiency

640. insufficiency	641. redundance
642. importance	643. unimportance
644. utility	645. inutility
646. expedience	647. inexpedience
648. goodness	649. badness

650. perfection	651. imperfection
652. cleanness	653. uncleanness
654. health	655. disease
656. salubrity	657. insalubrity
658. improvement	659. deterioration
660. restoration	661. relapse
662. remedy	663. bane
664. safety	665. danger
666. refuge	667. pitfall
668. warning	
669. alarm	
670. preservation	
671. escape	
672. deliverance	
673. preparation	674. nonpreparation
675. essay	
676. undertaking	
677. use	678. disuse
	679. misuse
680. action	681. inaction
682. activity	683. inactivity
684. haste	685. leisure
686. exertion	687. repose
688. fatigue	689. refreshment
690. agent	
691. workshop	
692. conduct	
693. direction	
694. director	
695. advice	
696. council	
697. precept	
698. skill	699. unskillfulness
700. expert	701. bungler
702. cunning	703. artlessness
704. difficulty	705. facility
706. hindrance	707. aid

708. opposition	709. cooperation
710. opponent	711. auxiliary
712. party	
713. discord	714. concord
715. defiance	
716. attack	717. defense
718. retaliation	719. resistance
720. contention	721. peace
722. warfare	723. pacification
724. mediation	
725. submission	
726. combatant	
727. arms	
728. arena	
729. completion	730. noncompletion
731. success	732. failure
733. trophy	
734. prosperity	735. adversity

736. mediocrity

II. INTERSOCIAL VOLITION

737. authority	738. laxity
739. severity	740. lenience
741. command	
742. disobedience	743. obedience
744. compulsion	
745. master	746. servant
747. scepter	
748. freedom	749. subjection
750. liberation	751. restraint
	752. prison
753. keeper	754. prisoner
755. commission	756. abrogation
	757. resignation
758. consignee	
759. deputy	
760. permission	761. prohibition

762. consent
763. offer 764. refusal
765. request 766. deprecation
767. petitioner
768. promise
769. compact
770. conditions
771. security
772. observance 773. nonobservance
774. compromise
775. acquisition 776. loss
777. possession 777a. exemption
778. participation
779. possessor
780. property
781. retention 782. relinquishment
783. transfer
784. giving 785. receiving
786. apportionment
787. lending 788. borrowing
789. taking 790. restitution
791. stealing
792. thief
793. booty
794. barter
795. purchase 796. sale
797. merchant
798. merchandise
799. market
800. money
801. treasurer
802. treasury
803. wealth 804. poverty
805. credit 806. debt
807. payment 808. nonpayment
809. expenditure 810. receipt

Class VI. AFFECTIONS
I. AFFECTIONS IN GENERAL

II. PERSONAL AFFECTIONS

918. forgiveness

919. revenge
920. jealousy
921. envy

IV. MORAL AFFECTIONS

922. right

923. wrong

924. claim

925. unrightfulness

926. duty

927. dereliction of duty
927a. exemption

928. respect

929. disrespect
930. contempt

931. approbation

932. disapprobation

933. flattery

934. detraction

935. flatterer

936. detractor

937. vindication

938. accusation

939. probity

940. improbity
941. knave

942. disinterestedness

943. selfishness

944. virtue

945. vice

946. innocence

947. guilt

948. good man

949. bad man

950. penitence

951. impenitence

952. atonement

953. temperance

954. intemperance
954a. sensualist

955. asceticism

956. fasting

957. gluttony

958. sobriety

959. drunkenness

960. purity

961. impurity
962. libertine

963. legality

964. illegality

965. jurisdiction

966. tribunal

967. judge

968. lawyer

969. lawsuit

970. acquittal

971. condemnation

973. reward

972. punishment
974. penalty
975. scourge

V. RELIGIOUS AFFECTIONS

976. diety
977. angel
979. fabulous spirit
981. heaven
983. theology
983a. orthodoxy
985. revelation
987. piety

990. worship

995. churchdom
996. clergy
998. rite
999. canonicals
1000. temple

978. devil
980. demon
982. hell

984. heterodoxy
986. religious writings
988. impiety
989. irreligion
991. idolatry
992. sorcery
993. spell
994. sorcerer

997. laity

ROGET'S THESAURUS

Class I

Words Expressing Abstract Relations

I. Existence

1 existence *n* being, entity, subsistence, reality, actuality, presence, fact, matter of fact, truth, science of existence: ontology.

v exist, be, subsist, live, breathe; occur, happen, take place; consist in, lie in; endure, remain, abide, survive, last, stay, continue.

adj existent, extant; prevalent, current, afloat; real, actual, true, positive, absolute; substantial, substantive; well founded, well grounded.

adv actually, in fact, in reality.

2 nonexistence *n* inexistence; insubstantiality, nonentity; blank, *tabula rasa,* void, emptiness, nothingness; potential, possibility; annihilation, extinction, obliteration, total destruction.

v not exist; pass away, perish, die, die out, disappear, dissolve; annihilate, destroy, obliterate, wipe off the face of the earth; nullify, void; take away, remove.

adj nonexistent, inexistent; blank, void, empty; unreal, baseless, unsubstantial, intangible, ineffable, spiritual, spectral; unborn, uncreated, unbegotten, unconceived; potential, possible; exhausted, gone, lost, departed, extinct, defunct; fabulous, visionary, imaginative, ideal, conceptual, abstract.

3 substantiality *n* materiality, corporality, tangibility, material existence, bodiliness, matter, stuff; creature, being, person, body, flesh and blood, substance; thing, object, article.

adj substantive, substantial, corporeal, material, bodily, physical, concrete, tangible, palpable, corporal, materialistic.

4 unsubstantiality *n* nothingness; nothing, naught, nil, nullity, zero; shadow, phantom, apparition, dream, illusion; fallacy, inanity, frivolity; hollowness, blank, void; flimsiness, thinness, slightness.

v vanish, evaporate, fade, dissolve, melt away, disappear.

adj unsubstantial, baseless, groundless, ungrounded, without foundation, fallacious, erroneous, untenable; insignificant, slight, thin, trifling, frivolous; imaginary, visionary, dreamy, shadowy, ethereal, airy, immaterial, spectral, illusory, incorporeal, intangible, bodiless, abstract; vacant, vacuous, empty, blank, hollow.

5 intrinsicality *n* ego, essence, quintessence, gist, pith, marrow, sap, lifeblood, backbone, heart, soul, core; principle, nature, constitution, construction, character, type, quality; habit, temper, temperament, personality, spirit, humor, grain, moods, features, peculiarities, aspects, idiosyncrasies, tendencies, bents; inbeing, inherence, essentiality.

v be intrinsic, be inherent.

adj intrinsic, inherent, implanted, innate, inborn, inbred, ingrained; essential, fundamental, basic, normal; inherited, congenital, hereditary, indigenous, in the blood, in the genes; instinctive, instinctual, internal, personal, subjective; characteristic, peculiar, idiosyncratic; fixed, set in one's ways, invariable, unchangeable, incurable, ineradicable.

adv intrinsically, at bottom, in effect, practically, virtually, substantially.

6 extrinsicality *n* extraneousness, externals.

adj extrinsic, extraneous, external, adventitious; collateral, accidental, incidental, objective.

adv extrinsically.

7 state *n* condition, case, circumstances, situation, status, surroundings, pass, plight, pickle; mood, temper, frame;

constitution, structure, form, phase, frame, fabric, stamp, set, fit, mold; mode, style, fashion, light, complexion, character; tone, tenor, turn.

   v be in a state.

8 circumstance *n* situation, phase, position, condition, posture, attitude, place, point; footing, standing, status; occasion, happening, event, juncture, conjunction; predicament, exigency, emergency, crisis, pinch, plight, pass; climax, apex, turning point.

   adj circumstantial, conditional, provisional; contingent, incidental, adventitious; critical, climactic.

   adv under the circumstances, under the conditions; thus, in such wise; accordingly, that being the case, since, seeing that, as matters stand; conditionally, provided, if, in case; if so, if it so happen, in the event of, provisionally, unless.

II. Absolute Relation

9 relation *n* connection, concern, bearing, reference; correlation, analogy; similarity, affinity, homogeneity, alliance, association, nearness; approximation, relationship; comparison, ratio, proportion; link, tie, bond.

   v relate to, refer to; bear upon, regard, concern, touch, affect, have to do with, pertain to, appertain to, belong to; bring into relation with, associate, connect, parallel; link, bind, tie.

   adj relative, relative to, relating to, referable to, with reference to; belonging to; related, connected, associated, affiliated, allied; in the same category, relevant.

   adv as regards, about, concerning, with relation to, with reference to, with regard to, with respect to, in connection with, under the head of, in the matter of.

10 [absence of relation] **non-relation** *n* irrelation, dissociation, lack of connection; disconnection, disjunction; inconsequence, irreconcilability, disagreement, heterogeneity; independence.

   v have no relation to, have no bearing upon, have nothing to do with, have no connection with.

   adj unrelated, irrespective, unallied, unconnected, disconnected, heterogeneous, independent; adrift, insular, isolated; extraneous, strange, alien, foreign, outlandish, exotic; irrelevant, inapplicable, not pertinent, beside the mark, off base; remote, farfetched, out-of-the-way, forced, detached, distanced; incidental, parenthetical.

   adv parenthetically, by the way, by the by; incidentally.

11 [relations of kindred] **consanguinity** *n* relationship, kindred, blood; parentage, paternity, maternity, lineage, heritage; filiation, affiliation, connection, alliance, tie; family, blood relation, ties of blood, kinsman, kinfolk, kith and kin, relation, relative, one's own, one's own flesh and blood; fraternity, sorority, brotherhood, sisterhood; race, stock, generation.

   v be related to, claim relationship with.

   adj related, akin, consanguineous, allied, affiliated, connected; kindred, familial.

12 [double or reciprocal relation] **correlation** *n* correspondence, reciprocity, reciprocation, interdependence, mutuality, interchange, exchange.

   v reciprocate, alternate, interchange, interact, interdepend; interchange, exchange; correlate, correspond, relate.

   adj reciprocal, mutual, correlative, corresponding, analogous, complementary; equivalent, interchangeable, alternate.

   adv reciprocally.

13 identity *n* sameness, exactness, equality, correspondence, parallelism, unity, convertibility, resemblance, similarity; self, oneself, name, personality; facsimile, duplicate, replica, copy, reproduction.

   v be identical, coincide, coalesce.

   adj identical, self, the same, selfsame; coincident, coinciding, coalescent, indistinguishable; one, equal, equivalent.

   adv identically.

14 contrariety *n* contrast, foil, antithesis, oppositeness, opposition, contradiction, antipathy, antagonism; the reverse, the inverse, the converse, inversion, subversion, reversal, the opposite, antipodes.

v be contrary, contrast with, differ from, oppose; invert, revert, turn upside down; contradict, contravene; antagonize.

adj contrary, opposite, counter, converse, reverse; opposed, antithetical, contrasted, antipodean, antagonistic, opposing; conflicting, inconsistent, contradictory; negative, hostile.

15 difference *n* discrepancy, disparity, dissimilarity, inconsistency, variance, variation, diversity, imbalance, disagreement, inequality, inequity, divergence, contrast, contrariety; discrimination, distinction, nice distinction, shade, nuance, subtlety.

v differ, vary; diversify, modify, change, alter; contrast, mismatch; discriminate, distinguish.

adj different, diverse, heterogeneous, unlike, divergent, altered, changed, deviant, deviating, variant, varied, modified; diversified, various, divers, miscellaneous, manifold; other, another, not the same, unequal, unmatched, wide apart; distinctive, characteristic, discriminative.

16 uniformity *n* homogeneity, permanence, continuity, consistency, stability, accordance, standardization, conformity, agreement; regularity, constancy, evenness, sameness; monotony, routine, invariability.

v be uniform, accord with; conform to, assimilate; level, smooth, even.

adj uniform, homogeneous, of a piece, consistent; consistent, regular, constant, even, level; invariable, unchanging, unvarying, unvaried, unchanged, constant, regular; undiversified, solid, plain, dreary, monotonous, routine.

adv uniformly; always, invariably, without exception; ever, forever.

16a lack of uniformity *n* diversity, irregularity, unevenness, inconsistency, nonconformity, heterogeneity.

adj diversified, varied, irregular, inconsistent, motley, patchwork, uneven, rough; multifarious, of various kinds.

17 similarity *n* resemblance, likeness, similitude, semblance, affinity, approxi-

mation, parallelism; agreement, correspondence, analogy; brotherhood, family likeness; repetition, sameness, uniformity, identity; the like, fellow, match, pair, mate, twin, double, counterpart; alter ego, chip off the old block, birds of a feather, like two peas in a pod; simile, parallel, type, image, representation.

v be similar, resemble, look like, bear a resemblance, take after, approximate, parallel, match, rhyme with.

adj similar, resembling, like, alike; twin; analogous, parallel, of a piece; allied to, akin to, corresponding; approximate, much the same, near, close, something like; imitative, mock, pseudo, simulating, representing, representative; exact, true, lifelike, faithful, true to life, identical.

adv as if, so to speak; as it were, as if it were; quasi, just as.

18 dissimilarity *n* dissimilitude, unlikeness, difference; diversity, disparity, divergence; novelty, originality, uniqueness.

v be unlike, differ from, bear no resemblance; vary, diversify, differentiate.

adj dissimilar, unlike, different, disparate; unique, new, novel, unprecedented, unmatched, unequaled; diversified.

19 imitation *n* copying; copy, duplication, reproduction, replica; mocking, mimicry, aping; simulation, impersonation, representation, semblance, approximation, paraphrase, parody; plagiarism, forgery.

v imitate, copy, mirror, reflect, impersonate, duplicate, reproduce, simulate, counterfeit; mock, take off, mimic, ape, personate, parody, caricature, travesty; follow, emulate, pattern after, model oneself on, parallel, follow, take after.

adj imitative, modeled after, modeled on, based on; fake, phony, counterfeit, false, imitation, mock; duplicate, second hand.

adv literally, word for word, to the letter.

20 nonimitation *n* originality, uniqueness.

adj unimitated, uncopied; unmatched, unparalleled; inimitable, original, unique, special, one of a kind, rare, exceptional.

20a variation *n* alteration, change, modification; divergency, deviation, aberration, innovation.

v vary, change; deviate, diverge, alternate, modify.

adj varied, modified, diversified, altered, changed.

21 [result of imitation] **copy** *n* facsimile, counterpart, effigy, form, likeness, similitude, semblance, cast, mold, model, representation, image, portrait; reflection, shadow, echo; transcript, transcription, reproduction, imitation, carbon, ditto, stencil, duplicate, reprint, transfer, replica; parody, caricature, burlesque, travesty, paraphrase; counterfeit, forgery, deception.

adj faithful, lifelike, exact, similar.

22 [thing copied] **prototype** *n* original, model, pattern, precedent, standard; type, archetype, exemplar, paradigm, module, example; text, copy, design; die, mold; matrix, mint, seal, punch, intaglio, negative, plate, stamp.

v be an example, set an example.

23 agreement *n* unanimity, harmony, accord, accordance, concord, union, unity, understanding, settlement, treaty, pact; uniformity, conformity, consistency, congruity, logic, correspondence, parallelism, apposition; consent, assent, concurrence, cooperation.

v agree, accord, harmonize; correspond, tally, *(informal)* jibe; meet, suit, fit, befit, square with, dovetail, match; adapt, fit, accommodate, adjust.

adj agreeing, accordant, correspondent, congenial, harmonious; reconcilable, comfortable, compatible, congruous, consistent, logical, consonant, commensurate; in accordance with, in harmony with, in keeping with; apt, apposite, pat, pertinent; agreeable, happy, felicitous.

24 disagreement *n* discord, dissonance, dissidence, disunion, discrepancy, nonconformity, incongruity, dissension, conflict, opposition, antagonism, difference; disparity, disproportion, mis-

match, variance, divergence, inequity, inequality.

v disagree, clash, jar, argue, quarrel, dispute.

adj disagreeing, discordant, dissonant, inharmonious; at variance, hostile, conflicting, antagonistic, clashing, disputing, factious, dissenting, irreconcilable, incompatible, inconsistent with; incongruous, disproportionate, disparate, divergent; disagreeable, uncongenial, mismatched; out of joint, out of step, out of tune.

III. Simple Quantity

25 [absolute quantity] **quantity** *n* size, mass, volume, amount, measure, measurement, substance, strength; mouthful, spoonful, handful; stock, batch, lot, dose.

adj quantitative, some, any, more or less.

26 [relative quantity] **degree** *n* grade, extent, measure, amount, ratio, standard, height, pitch; reach, range, scope, rate, caliber; gradation, shade, tint; tenor, tone, compass; sphere, station, rank, standing; point, mark, stage, level; intensity, strength.

adj comparative, gradual, shading off.

adv by degrees, gradually, step by step, bit by bit, little by little, inch by inch, drop by drop; in some degree, to some extent; up to a point.

27 [sameness of quantity or degree] **equality** *n* parity, symmetry, balance, counterbalance; evenness, monotony, level; equivalence, equipose, equilibrium; par, even keel, quits; identity, similarity; tie, dead heat, draw, drawn game, neck and neck race; match, peer, equal, mate, fellow, brother; equivalent.

v equal, match, reach, keep pace with, run abreast; come up to; balance, even the score; equalize, level, trim, adjust; strike a balance; restore equilibrium.

adj equal, even, level, monotonous, coequal, symmetrical, balanced; on a par with, on a level with, on an equal footing with, up to the mark; equivalent, tantamount, synonymous, quits, even, much the same, all one, one and the same; drawn, half and half, six of one and half a dozen of another.

adv equally, to all intents and purposes.

28 [difference of quantity or degree] **inequality** *n* disparity, dissimilarity, difference, odds; unevenness, imbalance; inferiority, shortcoming, deficiency, imperfection, inadequacy; mediocrity; superiority.

v be unequal, have the advantage, turn the scale, turn the tide; topple, overmatch; not come up to, fall short of, not come up to snuff.

adj unequal, uneven, imbalanced; disparate, partial, inferior, insufficient, deficient, inadequate, mediocre, short.

29 mean *n* medium, average, balance, middle, mid-point, center, median, golden mean; compromise, neutrality.

v split the difference, take the average, move to the center.

adj mean, intermediate, middle, average, standard, normal, neutral; mediocre, middle class, bourgeois, commonplace, run of the mill, egalitarian.

adv on the average, in the long run.

30 compensation *n* equation; indemnification, requital; compromise, measure for measure, tit for tat, eye for an eye, retaliation, equalization; setoff, off-set, counterpoise, ballast; indemnity, equivalent, *quid pro quo,* amends, reparation.

v compensate, indemnify, recompense, remunerate; counterbalance, counterpoise, countervail, offset, counteract, balance, balance out, make up for, square, even out, equalize; cover, neutralize, nullify; redeem, atone, make amends.

adj compensatory, compensating, equivalent, equal.

adv but, however, yet, still, notwithstanding, nevertheless, although, though, nonetheless; howbeit, albeit; at all events, at any rate, be that as may, even so, on the other hand, at the same time.

31 greatness *n* magnitude, size, bulk, dimensions, vastness; multitude; enormousness, immensity, might, strength, intensity, fullness; importance, distinction, eminence, renown; quantity, store, volume, mass, bulk, heap; abundance, sufficiency.

v be great, soar, tower, rise above, transcend; enlarge, increase, expand.

adj great, large, considerable, big, huge, mammoth, gigantic; ample, abundant, sufficient; full, intense, strong; widespread, extensive, wholesale; goodly, noble, precious, mighty; utter, uttermost, arch, profound, intense, consummate; extraordinary, important, unsurpassed, supreme; complete, total; vast, immense, enormous, extreme, inordinate, excessive, extravagant, exorbitant, outrageous, monstrous; towering, stupendous, prodigious, marvelous; unlimited, infinite; absolute, positive, stark, decided, unequivocal, essential, perfect; remarkable, notable, noteworthy.

adv [in a positive degree] truly; decidedly, unequivocally, absolutely, essentially, fundamentally, downright; [in a complete degree] entirely, completely, totally, wholly; abundantly, fully, amply, widely; [in a great or high degree] greatly, much, indeed, very, very much, most, pretty, pretty well, enough, in a great measure, to a large extent; richly, on a large scale, ever so much; mightily, powerfully; extremely, exceedingly, intensely, exquisitely, consummately, acutely, indefinitely, immeasurably, beyond compare, beyond measure, beyond all bounds, incalculably, infinitely; [in a supreme degree] pre-eminently, superlatively, supremely, incomparably; [in a too great degree] immoderately, inordinately, exorbitantly, excessively, enormously, preposterously, monstrously, out of all proportion, with a vengeance; [in a marked degree] particularly, remarkably, singularly, curiously, uncommonly, unusually, peculiarly, notably, signally, strikingly, pointedly, mainly, chiefly, famously, egregiously, prominently, glaringly, emphatically, strangely, wonderfully, amazingly, surprisingly, astonishingly, incredibly, marvelously, stupendously; [in a violent degree] violently, furiously, severely, desperately, tremendously, extravagantly; [in a painful degree] painfully, sadly, sorely, bitterly, piteously, grievously, miserably, cruelly, woefully, lamentably, shockingly, frightfully, fearfully, dreadfully, terribly, horribly.

32 smallness *n* littleness, tininess, diminutiveness; slenderness, thinness, paltriness, slightness; paucity, fewness, sparseness, scarcity; unimportance, triviality, inconsequentiality, pettiness, insignificance; meanness, sordidness, selfishness, narrow-mindedness; small quantity, modicum, atom, particle, molecule, point, speck, dot, dab, mote, jot, iota; minutiae, details, *soupçon*, scintilla, granule; drop, droplet, drizzle, sprinkling, dash, smack, tinge; dole, scrap, shred, splinter; mite, bit, morsel, crumb, seed; snippet, snatch, slip; chip, sliver; nutshell thimbleful, spoonful, handful, mouthful; fragment, fraction, drop in the ocean; trifle.

v be small.

adj small, little, tiny, diminutive, petite, miniature, minuscule, minute, microscopic, infinitesimal, fine; unimportant, trivial, minor, secondary, trifling, inconsequential, petty, paltry, insignificant; slender, thin, slight, scanty, scant, meager, insufficient; few, sparse, scarce; low, so-so, middling, tolerable, inconsiderable, inappreciable; mean, sordid, selfish, narrow, narrow-minded, illiberal, ungenerous; feeble, weak, faint.

adv [in a small degree] to a small extent; a wee bit; slightly, imperceptibly, faintly; miserably, wretchedly; insufficiently, imperfectly; passably, pretty well, well enough; [in a certain or limited degree] partially, in part, to a certain degree; some, rather, to some degree; simply, only, purely, merely, at the least; ever so little; almost, nearly, well nigh, short of, not quite, all but, near the mark; scarcely, hardly, barely, only just, no more than; [in an uncertain degree] about, thereabouts, somewhere about; [in no degree] noway, nowise, not at all, not in the least, not a bit, not a jot, not a whit, in no respect, by no means, on no account.

33 superiority *n* supremacy, pre-eminence, ascendancy, transcendence; excellence, greatness, nobility, eminence, worthiness, preponderance, predominance, prevalence, advantage; majority; quality, high caliber.

v be superior, exceed, excel, transcend, outdo, outweigh, outrival, outrank; pass, surpass; top, cap, outstrip, eclipse, predominate, prevail; take precedence, come first.

adj superior, greater, major, higher, exceeding; supreme, greatest, utmost, paramount, pre-eminent, foremost, crowning; first-rate, important, excellent, unrivaled, matchless, priceless, unparalleled, unequaled, unsurpassed, inimitable, incomparable, superlative, beyond, compare, transcendent.

adv beyond, more, over, over and above, at its height; [in a superior or supreme degree] eminently, pre-eminently, prominently, surpassingly, superlatively, supremely, above all, to crown all, *par excellence;* principally, especially, particularly, peculiarly.

34 inferiority *n* low quality, deficiency, imperfection, shortcoming, inadequacy; mediocrity, commonalty, commonness, poorness, meanness; minority, subordination, subjection.

v be inferior, fall short of, come short of, not come up to, not pass muster; want, lack.

adj inferior, minor, less, lesser, deficient; poor, indifferent, mean, base, bad, shabby, paltry, humble, imperfect, mediocre, common, commonplace, second-rate; poorer; secondary, minor, subordinate, lower; diminished, reduced, unimportant.

adv less, subpar; short of, under

35 increase *n* growth, augmentation, enlargement, extension, expansion, addition, increment, accretion, aggrandizement; development, rise, ascent.

v increase, grow, dilate, enlarge, expand, multiply; augment, add to, enlarge, greaten; extend, spread out, prolong; advance, rise, sprout, ascend; raise, exalt, deepen, heighten, intensify, magnify, redouble; aggrandize.

adj increasing, growing; additional, incremental; developmental.

36 decrease *n* diminution, abatement, decline, reduction, wane, falling-off, contraction, dwindling, shrinking, lessening, ebb, ebbing; subtraction, abridgment, shortening; depreciation, deterioration.

v decrease, lessen, abate, fall off, decline, contract, shrink, dwindle, wane, ebb, subside; diminish, deteriorate, depreciate, languish, decay; abridge, shorten, subtract.

adj decreased, decreasing, on the wane.

37 addition *n* increment, increase, enlargement, aggrandizement, accession; supplement, adjunct, attachment, addendum; annexation, interposition, insertion; uniting, joining.

v add, annex, affix, subjoin, tack on, append, attach, join, supplement, increase, augment, make an addition to; accrue, accumulate, pile up; total, sum, add up; reinforce.

adj additional, supplemental, supplementary; extra, accessory, auxiliary.

adv in addition, more, plus; and, also, likewise, too, further, furthermore, besides, to boot, etc., and so on, and so forth; over and above, moreover; with, as well as, together with, along with, in conjunction with.

38 deduction *n* subtraction, retrenchment, withdrawal, removal; mutilation, amputation, curtailment; shortening, abbreviation; decrease, cutback.

v deduct, subtract, retrench, withdraw, remove; take from, take away; shorten, abbreviate, cut back, pare down, reduce, decrease, diminish, curtail, eliminate, deprive of; mutilate, amputate, cut off, cut away, excise; pare, thin, thin out, prune, scrape, file.

adj subtracted, subtracting; removable, reducible; deductible.

adv less, short of; minus, without, excepting, except, with the exception of, save, exclusive of.

39 [thing added] **adjunct** *n* addition, affix, suffix, appendage, annex, augmentation, increment, reinforcement, accessory, accompaniment, sequel; addendum, complement, supplement, appendix, attachment; rider, offshoot, episode, corollary.

adj additional.

40 [thing remaining] **remainder** *n* residue, remains, remnant, leftover, excess, superfluity, balance, surplus, rest, relic; leavings, odds and ends, residuum,

dregs, refuse, crumbs, stubble, ruins, skeleton, stump.

v remain, survive, be left; be left over.

adj remaining, left, left over, residual; over, odd, spare, unused; superfluous; surviving.

40a [thing deducted] **decrement** *n* discount, defect, loss, deduction.

41 mixture *n* admixture, mix, combination, mingling, amalgamation, junction; infusion, suffusion, transfusion; infiltration, interlarding, interpolation; adulteration, thing mixed: tinge, tincture, touch, dash, sprinkling, spice, seasoning, infusion, compounds: alloy, amalgam, mélange, pastiche, miscellany, medley, patchwork, hotchpotch, gallimaufry, conglomeration, jumble, potpourri, farrago; cross, hybrid, mongrel.

v mix, join; combine, blend, mingle, commingle, confuse, jumble, unite, compound, amalgamate, adulterate; interlard, interlace, intertwine, interweave, interpolate; conjoin, associate, consort; instill, imbue, infuse, suffuse, transfuse, infiltrate, dash, tinge, tincture, season, blend, cross.

adj mixed, composite, half-and-half, hybrid, cross, mongrel, heterogeneous; motley, variegated, miscellaneous, promiscuous, indiscriminate.

adv among, amongst, amid, amidst, with; in the midst of.

42 [freedom from mixture] **simpleness** *n* purity, homogeneity; elimination, sifting, purification.

v simplify; sift, winnow, eliminate, strain, clean, purify; disentangle.

adj simple, uniform, homogeneous, single, pure, clear; unmixed, unadulterated, elemental, elementary, basic.

43 junction *n* joining, union; connection, conjunction, annexation, attachment; coupling, marriage, wedlock; confluence, communication, concatenation; meeting, assemblage, assembly, reunion; joint, joining, juncture, pivot, hinge, articulation; seam, stitch, linkage, link.

v join, unite, connect, link up, link; associate; put together, piece together, bind together; attach, fix, affix, fasten, bind, secure, clinch, twist, tie, string, strap, sew, lace, stitch, hem, knit, button, buckle, hitch, lash, splice gird, tether, picket, moor, harness, leash; chain; fetter, lock, hook, couple, link, yoke, bracket; marry, wed, bridge over, span; pin, bolt, clasp, clamp, screw, rivet; solder, weld, fuse; entwine, interlace, intertwine, interweave; entangle.

adj joined, joint; corporate, compact; firm, fast, close, tight, taut, secure, set, inseparable, indissoluble.

adv jointly, in conjunction with; fast, firmly; intimately.

44 disjunction *n* disconnection, disunion, disengagement, dissociation, discontinuity; isolation, insularity, insulation, separateness; dispersion; separation, parting; detachment, segregation; divorce; division, subdivision, break, fracture, rupture; dismemberment, dislocation, severance; fissure, breach, rent, split, rift, crack, cut, slit, incision.

v disjoin, disconnect, disengage, disunite, dissociate, divorce, part, detach, separate, disentangle, cut off, rescind, discontinue; segregate, set apart, keep apart, isolate, insulate; cut adrift, loose, set free, liberate; divide, subdivide, sever, dissever, cut, saw, snip, chop, ax, cleave, rive, rend, slit, split, splinter, chip, crack, snap, break, tear, burst, rend; wrench, rupture, shatter; hack, hew, slash, slice, cut up, carve, dissect, tear to pieces; disband, disperse, dislocate, break up, apportion, divide; part, part company, separate, leave.

adj disjoined, discontinuous, disjunctive; isolated, insular; separate, apart, asunder, loose, adrift, free; unattached, unconnected.

adv separately, one by one, severally, apart, adrift, asunder.

45 link *n* connective, connection, vinculum, copula, tie, bond, bridge; junction; bracket.

v link, bond, join, connect, conjoin, fasten, pin, bind, tie; bridge, span.

46 coherence *n* cohesion, cohesiveness, adherence, adhesion, adhesiveness; connection, union, conglomeration, aggregation, consolidation; stickiness, inseparability.

v cohere, adhere, stick, cling, cleave, hold, take hold, clasp, hug; hang together, stay together; glue, cement,

paste, solder, weld; consolidate, solidify, agglomerate.

adj cohesive, adhesive, adhering, sticky; tenacious, tough; united, unified, inseparable, inextricable, *(informal)* together, *(informal)* tight.

47 incoherence *n* looseness, laxity, relaxation, nonadhesion; loosening, disjunction, disconnection; disagreement, inconsistency, incongruity.

v loosen, make loose, slacken, relax; detach, disjoin.

adj nonadhesive, noncohesive, detached, loose, slack, lax, relaxed, segregated, unconsolidated; inconsistent, incongruous, illogical, absurd, rambling.

48 combination *n* mixture; junction; union, unification, synthesis, incorporation, amalgamation, coalescence, fusion, blend, blending, mix, centralization; compound, alloy, amalgam, composition, composite.

v combine, unite, incorporate, amalgamate, absorb, blend, mix, merge, fuse, marry, consolidate, coalesce, centralize, cement, harden, solidify.

adj combined, unified.

49 decomposition *n* analysis, dissection, dissolution, breaking down; disjunction; corruption, decay, rot, putrefaction.

v decompose, analyze, dissolve; resolve into its elements, dissect, disperse, crumble; decay, rot, turn.

adj decomposed.

50 [principal part] **whole** *n* totality, entirety, total, sum, aggregate; unity, completeness, integrity, indivisibility; bulk, mass, lump; body, trunk.

v form a whole, integrate, embody, amass, aggregate, assemble; amount to, come to, add up to.

adj whole, total, full, entire, undiminished, undivided, integral, complete, unimpaired, unbroken, faultless, sound, intact; indivisible, indissoluble.

adv wholly, altogether; totally, completely, entirely, all, all in all, wholesale, in a body, collectively, in the main, on the whole.

51 part *n* division, portion, piece, fragment, fraction, lump, bit, component, constituent, ingredient, element, section, segment, subdivision; member, limb, branch, bough, off-shoot, ramification; compartment, department, class.

v part, divide, break, disjoin; partition, apportion, allot.

adj fractional, fragmentary, sectional; divided, split up.

adv partly, in part, partially; piecemeal, bit by bit, by installments, in dribs and drabs, in drips and snatches; in detail.

52 completeness *n* wholeness, entirety, totality, solidarity, fullness, intactness, unity, perfection; thoroughness.

v complete, accomplish, fulfill, finish; fill, charge, load, replenish; fill up, fill in; saturate.

adj complete, entire, whole, full, intact, undivided, one, perfect, fulfilled; full, good, absolute, thorough, solid; exhaustive, radical, sweeping, thoroughgoing; consummate, unmitigated, sheer, unqualified, unconditional; brimming, brimful, chock-full, saturated, crammed, replete, fraught.

adv completely, altogether, outright, wholly, totally quite, utterly, fully, thoroughly, in all aspects, in every respect, out and out, to all intents and purposes; throughout, from first to last, from beginning to end, from top to bottom, from head to foot, every whit, every inch.

53 incompleteness *n* deficiency, shortcoming, insufficiency, imperfection; immaturity; noncompletion.

[part wanting] defect, deficit, omission, interval, break; discontinuity, missing link.

v be incomplete, fall short of; lack; neglect.

adj incomplete, imperfect, unfinished, uncompleted; defective, deficient, wanting, lacking, failing, short, short of; meager, lame, limp, perfunctory, sketchy, crude, immature; in progress, in preparation, going on, ongoing, proceeding.

adv incompletely.

54 composition *n* constitution, make-up, form; combination, compilation, incorporation, inclusion, synthesis.

v be composed of, be made up of, consist of; include, contain, hold, comprehend, take in, admit, embrace, embody; compose, constitute, form, make.

adj constituting.

55 exclusion *n* omission, exception, rejection, repudiation; exile, seclusion, segregation, separation, elimination, prohibition; restraint, keeping out.

v exclude, bar, leave out, shut out, keep out; reject, repudiate, blackball, throw out; lay aside, put aside, set aside; relegate, segregate, separate, seclude, banish, exile; pass over, omit, eliminate, weed out, winnow.

adj exclusive, not included in; inadmissible.

56 component *n* component part, integral part, element, constituent, ingredient; contents, feature, member, part; personnel.

v enter into, be part of, form part of; merge in, share in, participate; belong to, appertain to; form, make, constitute.

adj inclusive, comprehensive.

57 extraneousness *n* extrinsicality, externality; superfluousness; foreign body, foreign substance; intrusion.

v be extraneous, be unnecessary.

adj extraneous, foreign, alien, extrinsic, external; not germane, nonessential, superfluous; excluded.

IV. Order

58 order *n* regularity, uniformity, arrangement, harmony, symmetry; course, routine, method, methodology; disposition, array, arrangement, system, economy, discipline, orderliness; gradation, progression, series, sequence, continuity; rank, place, grade, class, degree.

v order, regulate, manage, adjust, arrange, systematize, standardize, rank.

adj orderly, regular, systematic, methodical; in order, neat, tidy, well-regulated, well-organized, organized, uniform, symmetrical, businesslike, shipshape.

adv in order, methodically, in turn, in its turn; step by step, at regular intervals, systematically.

59 disorder *n* derangement, disarray, untidiness, irregularity, anomaly; anarchy, anarchism, disunion, discord; confusion, jumble, mess, muddle, hash, hodgepodge, chaos; perplexity, labyrinth, wilderness, jungle; raveling, entanglement, complication, convolution; turmoil, ferment, agitation, trouble, row, disturbance, convulsion, tumult, uproar, riot, rumpus, ruckus, scramble, fracas, melee, pandemonium.

v disorder, put out of order, derange, ruffle, rumble; confuse, jumble, mess up.

adj disorderly, out of order, out of place, irregular, desultory; anomalous, disorganized, straggling, unsystematic, untidy, slovenly, messy; indiscriminate, chaotic, confused, deranged; anarchic, inverted, convoluted, topsy-turvy; complex, complicated, perplexed, involved, raveled, entangled, knotted, tangled; troublesome, problematical; riotous, violent, turbulent, tumultuous.

adv irregularly, helter skelter; at cross purposes, *(informal)*, after the flood.

60 [reduction to order] **arrangement** *n* plan, method, organization; preparation, groundwork, planning; sorting, disposal, disposition, distribution, assortment, allotment, apportionment, graduation, groupings; analysis, classification, division, ordering, systematization.

v arrange, dispose, place, form; set out, marshal, range, array, rank, group, parcel out, allot, apportion, assign, dole out, distribute; sort, sift, put into shape; plan, prepare, organize, lay the groundwork; classify, divide, file, register, catalog, record, tabulate, index, graduate, rank; regulate, systematize, coordinate, organize, settle, fix; unravel, disentangle, straighten out.

adj arranged, ordered; methodical, orderly, regular, systematic.

61 [subversion of order] **derangement** *n* disorder, mess, disarray, disorganization; discomposure, disturbance, dislocation, perturbation, interruption.

v derange, disarrange, discompose, displace, misplace; mislay, disorder, disorganize; embroil, disconcert, convulse, unsettle, disturb, confuse, trouble, perturb, jumble, muddle, fumble; unhinge, dislocate, throw out of gear, throw out of whack; invert, turn upside down, turn

topsy-turvy; complicate, confound, tangle, entangle; litter, scatter, mix.

62 precedence *n* coming before, the lead, superiority; precursor, antecedence; importance, consequence; priority, preference.

v precede, come before, forerun, come first; head, lead the way, usher in, introduce; set the fashion, influence, establish; have precedence, take precedence; place before, prefix, preface.

adj preceding, precedent, antecedent, anterior, prior, before; former, foregoing; preliminary, prefatory, introductory; preparatory.

adv before; in advance.

63 sequence *n* coming after, following, succession, order, series; posteriority; continuation; order of succession; outcome, consequence, result, sequel.

v succeed, come after, follow, ensure; replace.

adj succeeding, following; consequent, subsequent; proximate, next; sequential, consecutive.

adv after, subsequently; behind.

64 precursor *n* antecedent, precedent, predecessor, forerunner, pioneer, leader, bellwether; herald, harbinger; prelude, preamble, preface, prolog, proem, prefix, foreword, introduction; heading, frontispiece, groundwork; preparation.

adj prefatory, introductory, preliminary, precursory.

65 sequel *n* continuation, extension, supplement, outgrowth, offshoot, result, consequence, inference, deduction; result, consequence, aftermath, outcome, effect; conclusion, end, culmination, dé-´nouement, finale, finish; appendage, suffix, epilog, postscript, tag, train, trail, wake; afterthought, afterpiece, second thoughts.

66 beginning *n* commencement, opening outset, start, initiation, inauguration; introduction, prelude; outbreak, onset, brunt; initiative, first move; origin, cause, source, bud, germ, genesis, birth, nativity, cradle; starting point, first step, square one; title page, head, heading; rudiments, basics, elements.

v begin, commence, open, start, initiate, inaugurate; conceive; set out, embark, depart; usher in, lead the way, take the lead, take the initiative, head, stand at the head, launch, set in motion, get going, take the first step, break ground; burst forth, break out; begin at the beginning, start again, start over, make a fresh start; originate, conceive, think up.

adj initial, introductory, inaugural; incipient; embryonic, rudimental, primal, essential, natal, nascent; first, foremost, leading; maiden, virgin.

adv first, in the first place, first and foremost; in the bud, in its infancy; from the beginning.

67 end *n* close, termination, conclusion, finale, finish, last word; consummation, climax, apex, dénouement; goal, destination; expiration, death, finality; limit, extreme, extremity; breakup, last stage, final stage, turning point, death blow.

v end, close, finish, terminate, conclude; expire, die, come to a close, draw to a close, run its course, run out, pass away; bring to an end, put an end to, make an end of, wrap up; get through, complete, consummate; stop, desist, call it quits.

adj final, terminal, concluding; conclusive, crowning, definitive, last, ultimate, consummate; ended, settled, decided, over, concluded, played out.

adv finally, at last, once and for all, over and done with.

68 middle *n* center, midpoint, midst; mean, midcourse, middle ground, compromise; core, kernel, heart, nucleus, nub; equidistance, bisection; equator, diaphragm, midriff.

adj middle, medial, mean, mid, median, midmost; intermediate, equidistant, central, halfway.

adv midway, halfway, in the middle.

69 [uninterrupted sequence **continuity** *n* continuousness, consecutiveness, progression, constant flow, succession, train, series, chain, string, scale, gradation; round, suite; procession, column, retinue; pedigree, genealogy, lineage; rank, file, line, row, range, tier.

v follow in a line; arrange in a series, string together, file, thread, graduate, tabulate.

adj continuous, progressive, successive, serial, consecutive, unbroken, un-

interrupted, gradual; linear, in a line; perennial, constant.

adv continuously, in succession, consecutively; gradually, step by step, in a column.

70 [interrupted sequence] **discontinuity** *n* disjunction, disconnectedness; interruption, break, fracture, fault, flaw, crack, cut; gap, interval, caesura, pause, *(informal)* breather, rest, intermission, parenthesis, episode.

v alternate; discontinue, break, interrupt, intervene; pause, rest, take a breather, stop; break in upon, interpose; disconnect.

adj discontinuous, disconnected, unconnected, broken, interrupted; fitful, spasmodic, desultory, intermittent, irregular; alternate, recurrent, periodic.

adv at intervals, in snatches, by fits and starts.

71 term *n* rank, station, stage, step, phase; scale, grade, degree, status, position, place, point, mark, period, limit; stand, standing, footing.

72 assemblage *n* collection, levee, gathering, ingathering, muster; concourse, conflux, congregation; meeting, reunion; assembly, congress, convention, conclave, council; miscellany, compilation, menagerie; crowd, throng, mob, flood, rush, rash, deluge, press, crush, horde, body, tribe, crew, gang, squad, band, party, swarm, flock, bevy; company, troop, regiment, squadron, army; host, multitude, populace, clan, brotherhood, sisterhood, association; group, cluster, clump, batch, pack, assortment; accumulation, heap, lump, pile, mass, conglomeration, conglomerate, aggregation, aggregate; quantity.

v assemble, come together, collect, gather, muster; meet, unite, join, rejoin; cluster, flock, swarm, surge, stream, herd, crowd, throng, associate; congregate, concentrate, huddle; bring together, draw together, place together, lump together; convene, invoke; compile, group, assemble, unite; amass, accumulate, store.

adj assembled; closely packed, dense, crowded, teeming, swarming, populous.

73 dispersion *n* divergence, spreading, radiation, dissemination, diffusion, dissipation, distribution, apportionment, division.

v disperse, scatter, sow, disseminate, diffuse, shed, spread, dispense, disband, distribute, apportion, divide; break up, dispel, cast forth, strew, cast, sprinkle; issue, deal out, dole out.

adj dispersed, spread, scattered, strewn, diffuse, diffusive; sparse, widespread, broadcast; adrift, stray, disheveled.

74 [place of meeting] **focus** *n* center, gathering place, haunt, rendezvous, rallying point, headquarters, club, retreat.

v focus, bring to a point, bring to a focus; center on, bring out, clarify, elucidate.

75 class *n* division, subdivision, category, heading, order, section; department, province, domain; type, kind, sort, genus, species, variety, family, race, tribe, cast, clan, breed, sect.

76 inclusion *n* admission, acceptance into, incorporation, comprehension, reception.

v include, comprise, comprehend, contain, admit, embrace, receive, accept; inclose, circumscribe, encircle, encompass, embody, incorporate; number among, count among, fall under.

adj inclusive, comprehensive, extensive, all-embracing, compendious, sweeping; including, incorporating.

77 exclusion *n* (see 55).

78 generality *n* universality, catholicity, miscellany, miscellaneousness; generalization, simplification, oversimplification; prevalence, common run.

v be general, be universal, prevail, be true for everyone; render general, generalize, universalize; make a generalization, abstract, simplify.

adj general, universal, catholic, common, ecumenical, egalitarian, worldwide; prevalent, prevailing, rife, current; generic, collective, all-encompassing, comprehensive, all-inclusive, broad, widespread.

79 specialty *n* speciality, skill, ability, talent; individuality, singularity, distinctive feature, particularity, personality, characteristic, mannerism, idiosyncrasy,

nonconformity; particulars, details, items; special feature.

v specify, particularize, individualize, specialize; designate, determine, single out, isolate, differentiate; be specific, come to the point, detail, get down to particulars.

adj special, particular, especial, individual, specific, proper, personal, original, private, respective, definite, certain, endemic, peculiar, characteristic, marked, appropriate, exclusive, singular, exceptional, idiomatic, unique.

adv specially, especially, in particular; each, apiece, severally, respectively, each to each, each to his own; in detail.

80 regulation *n* regularity, uniformity, constancy, clockwork, precision, exactness; routine, custom, formula, rule, form, procedure; standard, model, precedent, prototype; conformity, convention; nature, law, principle; normal state, ordinary condition, normalcy; hard and fast law.

adj regular, uniform, constant, steady; customary, conventional, formal, formulaic, procedural.

81 multiformity *n* variety, diversity.

adj multifold, multifarious, manifold, many-sided; heterogeneous, motley, mosaic; indiscriminate, irregular, diversified, diverse; of every description, all manner of kinds.

82 conformity *n* observance, compliance, assent; conventionality, customariness, agreement; example, instance, specimen, sample, illustration, exemplification, case in point.

v conform to, accommodate oneself to, adapt to; be regular, conform, follow the rules, obey the rules, go by the rules, comply, assent, agree, yield, give in, accept, harmonize; illustrate, stand as an example, embody.

adj conformable to rule, adaptable, agreeable, compliant, malleable; conventional, customary, standard, ordinary, common, habitual, usual, natural, normal, typical; formal, orthodox, strict, rigid, uncompromising; exemplary, illustrative.

adv by rule, in conformity with, in accordance with, in keeping with, consistent with; for the sake of conformity, as a matter of course, for form's sake; invariably, uniformly.

83 unconformity n nonconformity, unconventionality, nonobservance, informality; anomaly, variation, inconsistency, irregularity, incongruity, oddity, eccentricity, peculiarity, aberration, abnormality, exception; violation of custom, infraction, infringement; individuality, originality, mannerism, idiosyncrasy, quirk.

v be unconformable.

adj unconformable, unconventional; unnatural, odd, eccentric, peculiar, aberrant, abnormal, exceptional; anomalous, inconsistent, irregular, incongruous, arbitrary, whimsical, wanton; unusual, uncustomary, uncommon, rare, singular, unique, extraordinary; queer, quaint, strange; original, fantastic, newfangled, bizarre, outlandish, exotic, esoteric.

adv unless, except, save, beside.

V. Number

84 number n numeral, symbol, figure, cipher, digit, integer, round number, whole number, fraction; sum, total, product.

adj numeral; prime, fractional, decimal; positive, negative.

85 numeration n numbering; tallying, enumeration, reckoning, computation, calculation; arithmetic, calculus, algebra; statistics, poll, census, roll call; arithmetic operations.

v number, count, tell, tally, enumerate, add up, sum, reckon, compute, calculate, take account; muster, poll, recite; add, subtract, multiply, divide.

adj numeral, numerical; arithmetical, analytic, algebraic, statistical, numerable, computable, calculable.

86 list n catalog, index, listing, inventory, schedule, register, record, ledger, tally, file, table, calendar; directory, gazette, atlas, dictionary, thesaurus; roll, checklist.

87 unity n oneness, singleness, singularity, individuality; unification, unison, uniformity.

v unite, join, combine; isolate, insulate, seclude.

adj one, sole, single, solitary, lone; individual, apart, alone; unaccompanied, unattended, singlehanded, solo; singular, odd, unique; isolated, insular.

adv singly.

88 accompaniment n association, partnership, company; accessory, adjunct, concomitant, attachment, complement, attendant, fellow, associate, coexistence.

v accompany, join, escort, convoy, wait on; coexist with, consort with; associate with, couple with.

adj accompanying, fellow, twin, joint; associated with, coupled with; accessory, concomitant, attendant.

adv with, together with, along with, in company with, hand in hand, side by side; therewith, herewith.

89 duality n dualism, doubleness, polarity, biformity, duplexity; two, deuce, couple, brace, pair, twins.

v pair, mate, couple, bracket, pair off, yoke.

adj two, twain; dual, twin, two-sided, binary, binomial, duplex; coupled, both.

90 duplication n doubling, reduplication; iteration, repetition; renewal.

duplicate, double, copy, carbon, facsimile.

v double; redouble, reduplicate; repeat, renew; duplicate.

adj double; doubled, duplicated; twin, duplicate, second.

adv twice, once more, over again.

91 bisection n halving, bifurcation, twofold division, forking, dichotomy, (informal) fifty-fifty split.

v bisect, divide in two, halve, divide, split, cut in two, cleave, fork, bifurcate; split down the middle, (informal) go halves.

adj bisected, cloven, cleft, halved; bipartite; bifurcated; semi-, demi-, hemi-.

92 triality n trinity; three, triad, triplet, trio.

adj three, threefold, triform, tertiary.

93 triplication n tripling; triplicity.

v triple, treble, cube.

adj triple, treble; threefold, triplicate; third.

adv three times, thrice; in the third place, thirdly; triply, trebly.

94 trisection *n* tripartition, threefold division, third, third part.
v trisect, divide into three parts.

95 quaternity *n* four, tetrad, quartet, quarter.
v square, reduce to a square.
adj four, fourfold, quadrilateral.

96 quadruplication *n* quadrupling, multiplying by four.
v multiply by four, quadruplicate.
adj four, fourfold, quadruple; fourth.
adv four times, in the fourth place, fourthly.

97 quadrisection *n* quartering, quadripartition, fourfold division; fourth part, quarter.
v quarter, divide into four parts.
adj quartered, quadripartite.

98 five, etc. *n* five; six, half a dozen; seven; eight; nine; ten, decade; eleven; twelve, dozen; thirteen, baker's dozen, long dozen; twenty, score; twenty-five, quarter of a hundred; fifty, half a hundred; hundred, century, centenary; thousand.

99 quinquesection *n* fivefold division
adj quinquepartite.

100 [more than one] **plurality** *n* two or more, couple, few, several; majority, multitude.
adj plural, more than one, upwards of, some, several, many, numerous.

100a [less than one] **fraction** *n* fractional part, segment, subdivision, part, portion.

101 zero *n* nothing, naught, *(informal)* zip; none, shutout; nobody.

102 multitude *n* multitudinous, multiplicity, profusion, mass, quantity, volume, abundance, amplitude, enormity; numbers, array, scores, droves, host, throng, collection; mob, crowd, assemblage.
v be numerous, swarm with, teem with, crowd, swarm, outnumber, multiply; people, populate.
adj multitudinous, manifold, profuse, multiple, teeming, populous, crowded, thick; many, several, sundry, various, numerous; endless, infinite.

103 fewness *n* paucity, scarcity, sparseness, scantiness; small number, small quantity; infrequency.
diminution of number: reduction, weeding, elimination.
v render few, reduce, diminish, weed, thin, eliminate, eradicate.
adj few, not many, scanty, scarce, sparse, rare, few and far between, limited, meager; sporadic, occasional, infrequent; reduced, diminished, pared back.

104 repetition *n* iteration, reiteration, recapitulation, restatement; sameness, monotony, harping, recurrence, tautology; redundance; rhythm, beat, echo, reverberation; reappearance, reproduction, duplication.
v repeat, iterate, reiterate, recapitulate, restate, rehash, go over again, harp on, hammer; reproduce, duplicate, echo; recur, revert, return, reappear; resume, return to, go back to; rehearse, go over the same ground.
adj repeated, repetitious, recurrent, recurring, frequent, incessant, never-ending, unceasing; repetitive, redundant, tautological; rhythmic, reverberant, reverberating; monotonous, harping, iterative; habitual.
adv repeatedly, often, again, anew, afresh, over again, once more; over and over, again and again, year after year; ditto, encore.

105 infinity *n* infinitude, infiniteness, perpetuity, endlessness, boundlessness, inexhaustibility, immeasurability, limitlessness, vastness, expanse.
v be infinite, have no limits, know no bounds, go on forever.
adj infinite, countless, numberless, limitless, boundless, measureless, unlimited, interminable, inexhaustible, incalculable; immense, vast, endless, perpetual; incomprehensible; eternal, perfect, omnipotent, absolute.
adv infinitely, *ad infinitum.*

VI. Time

106 time *n* duration, extent; period, interval, spell, term, space, span, season, stage; course; interim, interlude; interregnum, intermission; respite, break, timeout; era, epoch, season, age, year, date.

v time, measure, pace; continue, last, endure, go on, remain, persist, stand; pass time, spend time, while away the time, waste time, kill time, fill up the time.

adj permanent, lasting, durable; timely.

adv while, whilst, during, in the course of, for the time being, in due time; meantime, meanwhile, in the meantime, in the interim; till, until, up to, yet; the whole time, all the time, throughout, for good *(informal)* for keeps.

107 absence of time *n* no time; outside time.

adv never, at no time; on no occasion, nevermore.

108 [definite duration or period of time] **period** *n* interval, age, era, eon, epoch, term, time; year, decade, century, millennium; lifetime, generation.

109 [indefinite duration] **course** *n* march of time, course of time, flux, passing time.

v elapse, lapse, flow, run, proceed, advance, pass, flit, fly, slip, slide, drag, creep, crawl; run its course; expire, go by, pass by.

adv in due time, in due course, in due season, in time.

110 [long duration] **durability** *n* permanence, persistence, continuance, lastingness, standing, stability; survival, longevity; protraction, prolongation.

v last, remain, stand, endure, abide, continue, persist; tarry, drag on, drag out, prolong, protract, eke out, draw out, lengthen; outlive, outlast, survive.

adj permanent, durable, lasting, long-standing, stable, immutable, invariable, constant; enduring, abiding, perpetual; lingering, protracted, prolonged, spun-out.

adv long, for a long time, ever so long; long ago; all day long, all the live-long day.

111 [short duration] **transience** *n* impermanence, evanescence, ephemerality, transitoriness, mortality; suddenness,

swiftness, changeableness, vicissitude, uncertainty.

v be transient, flit, pass away, fly, gallop, vanish, fade, evaporate, melt.

adj transient, transitory, evanescent, ephemeral, fleeting, flitting, flying, passing; impermanent, temporal, temporary, provisional, short-lived; perishable, precarious, vulnerable, mortal; brief, quick, brisk; sudden, momentary, instantaneous.

adv temporarily, for the moment, for a time; awhile, soon; briefly.

112 [endless duration] **perpetuity** *n* eternity, timelessness, everlastingness, endlessness, infinity; constancy, endurance, durability, ceaselessness.

v last forever, endure, go on forever; perpetuate, immortalize, eternalize.

adj perpetual, eternal, timeless, everlasting, endless; unceasing, ceaseless, interminable, neverending, continuous, incessant, uninterrupted; unfading, imperishable, unvulnerable, immortal.

adv perpetually, always, ever, evermore, forever; constantly, continuously.

113 [point of time] **instantaneousness** *n* suddenness, abruptness; moment, instant, second, twinkling, trice, flash, crack, burst.

v be instantaneous, twinkle, flash.

adj instantaneous, momentary, sudden, instant, abrupt.

adv instantaneously, in no time, *(informal)* in two shakes (of a lamb's tail), presto, suddenly, like a shot, in a moment, all of a sudden, in a jiffy; immediately, on the spur of the moment, on a moment's notice.

114 [estimation, measurement and record of time] **chronometry** *n* chronology, timetable; almanac, calendar, register, chronicle, log, annal(s), journal, diary; clock, watch, stopwatch, timepiece, chronometer.

v fix the time, mark the time; date, register, chronicle; measure time, mark time, beat time.

adj chronological.

115 [false estimate of time] **anachronism** *n* misdate, misplacement, chronological error; disregard of time.

v misdate, antedate, postdate, anticipate; take no note of time.

adj misdated; undated, overdue; anachronistic, out of place, misplaced.

116 antecedence *n* priority, anteriority, precedence, pre-existence; antecedent, predecessor, precursor, forerunner.

v precede, antedate, come before; go before, lead, forerun; dawn, presage, herald, break the ground.

adj antecedent, prior, previous, anterior, preceding, pre-existent; former, foregoing, aforementioned; precursory, introductory.

adv before, prior to; earlier, previously, ere, already, yet, beforehand.

117 posteriority *n* succession, sequence; subsequence, following, continuance; successor, sequel, follower; future, futurity.

v follow after, come after, go after, succeed, be subsequent to.

adj posterior, subsequent, following, after, later, succeeding, successive, ensuing, resulting; posthumous.

adv subsequently, after, afterwards, since, later; next, close upon, thereafter, thereupon; ultimately.

118 present time *n* the present juncture, the present day; the times, the time being, right now.

adj present, actual, instant, current, existing.

adv at this time, at this moment; at the present time, now, at present, nowadays.

119 different time *n* other time; another time.

adv at that time, at that instant; then, on that occasion; when, whenever, whensoever; at some other time, at a different time, at some time or other.

120 contemporaneousness *n* simultaneousness, synchronism, simultaneity, coincidence, concurrence, coexistence, concomitance.

v coexist, concur, accompany, go side by side, keep pace with; synchronize.

adj simultaneous, coincident, concurrent, concomitant, coexisting; contemporary, contemporaneous, coeval.

adv simultaneously, concurrently, together, at the same time.

121 the future *n* futurity, hereafter, time to come, tomorrow, morrow; millen-

nium, doomsday, day of judgment, crack of doom, flood; advent, eventuality; destiny, fate; heritage, heirs, posterity; prospect, expectation, anticipation.

v look forward, anticipate, expect, foresee; approach, await, threaten, impend, come near, draw near, come on.

adj future, to come; coming, impending, near, close at hand, in prospect; eventual, ulterior.

adv prospectively, hereafter, in future, in course of time, tomorrow; eventually, ultimately, sooner or later; henceforth, from this time; soon, early, on the eve of, on the point of, on the brink of.

122 the past *n* past time, days of old, days of yore, days gone by, yesterday, yesteryear, former times, ancient times; retrospection, memory; antiquity, history, time immemorial, remote past; ancestry, lineage, forbears; heritage.

v run its course, pass away, pass, lapse, blow over.

adj past, gone, gone by, passed away, bygone, elapsed, lapsed, expired, extinct, forgotten, irrecoverable, obsolete; former, pristine, late; foregoing, last, latter, recent; looking back, retrospective; retroactive.

adv formerly, of old, of yore, ago, over; long ago, years ago, a long while back, some time ago; lately, of late; retrospectively, ere now, before now, hitherto, heretofore; already, yet, up to this time.

123 newness *n* novelty, recentness, freshness; immaturity, greenness, youth, juvenility, innovation, uniqueness, originality; renovation, restoration; modernity, modernism, stylishness, fashionableness, newfangledness, fashion, faddishness, the latest thing, futurism, trendiness.

v renew, renovate, restore; modernize.

adj new, novel, recent, fresh; green, immature, unripe, young, youthful, untried, untested, virgin, virginal; modern, late, new, newfangled, stylish, fashionable, faddish, trendy, brand-new, up-to-date; renovated restored, spick and span.

adv newly, afresh, anew, lately, just now, of late.

124 oldness *n* age, antiquity; maturity, ripeness; decline, decay, old age, senility, superannuation; archaism, antiquarianism, relic, thing of the past; tradition, custom, common law.

v be old, have had its day, have seen its day; become old, age, fade.

adj old, ancient, antique; time-honored, venerable, traditional, vintage, of long standing; elderly, aged, hoary, decayed, senile, decrepit; primeval, primitive, aboriginal, primordial, antediluvian, prehistoric, archaic; traditional, prescriptive, customary, immemorial, inveterate, rooted; antiquated, outdated, outmoded, of other times; out of date, obsolete, out-of-fashion, out-of-style, gone by, stale, old-fashioned, timeworn, crumbling, ramshackle, run-down, wasted.

125 morning. noon *n* morning, morn, dawn, daybreak, sunrise, sunup, forenoon, break of day, peep of day, prime of day, morningtide, matins, cockcrow, first blush, antemeridian, A.M.

noon, midday, noonday, noontide, meridian, prime, height, noontime.

spring, springtime; summer, summertime, midsummer.

126 evening. midnight *n* evening, eve, eventide, dusk, vespers, nightfall, sundown, sunset, twilight, curfew, bedtime; afternoon, post meridian, P.M.

midnight, end of the day, close of the day, witching hour, dead of night.

autumn, fall, harvest time; winter.

127 youth *n* juvenility, infancy childhood, boyhood, girlhood; minority, tender years, young years, formative years, never generation, tender age; cradle, nursery; puberty.

adj young, youthful, juvenile, green, callow, budding, immature, developing, underage, formative; younger, junior.

128 age *n* old age, advanced age, senility, years, gray hairs, declining years, golden years, mature years, decrepitude, anility, superannuation, longevity, ripe age, ripe old age; maturity, seniority, eldership.

adj aged, old, advanced, gray, elderly; senile, decline, failing, waning, ripe, overripe, mellow, venerable, wrinkled, wizened; older, elder, eldest.

129 infant *n* baby, babe, babe in arms, nursling, little one, tot, toddler, chick, kid, lamb, cherub; youth, youngster, child, minor; girl, lass, maiden, miss, schoolgirl; boy, lad, stripling, master, schoolboy.

adj infantile, infantlike, puerile, girlish, boyish, childish, babyish; newborn, young.

130 veteran *n* old man, old woman, patriarch, matriarch, grandmother, grandfather, grandsire, seer, graybeard, forefather, elder.

adj aged, old.

131 adolescence *n* majority, adulthood, manhood, womanhood, maturity, ripeness, fullness, puberty, pubescence; teenage years, prepubescence.

v come of age, grow up, attain majority.

adj adolescent, teenage, pubescent, of age, grown up, full grown, adult, womanly, manly, marriageable, nubile.

132 earliness *n* punctuality, promptitude, speediness, readiness, expedition, alacrity, quickness, haste; suddenness; prematurity, precocity, precipitation, anticipation.

v be early, be beforehand; anticipate, forestall, steal a march on, get a head start; bespeak, secure, engage, pre-engage; accelerate, expedite, quicken, hasten, make haste, make time, hurry.

adj early, timely, punctual, on time, prompt; premature, precipitate, precocious, anticipatory; sudden, instantaneous, immediate, expeditious; unexpected.

adv early, soon, anon, betimes, before long; punctually, to the minute, on time, on the dot; beforehand, prematurely, precipitately, too soon, hastily, in anticipation, unexpectedly; suddenly, instantaneously, at short notice, on the spur of the moment; at once, on the spot, on the instant, at sight, straight, offhand, straightway; forthwith, summarily, immediately, shortly, quickly, speedily; presently, by and by, directly.

133 lateness *n* tardiness, slowness, sloth, tarrying, dilly-dallying, loitering; delay, procrastination, postponement, adjournment, retardation, protraction, prolongation; respite, reprieve, suspension, moratorium, stop, stay.

v be late, tarry, wait, stay, bide, take time, linger, loiter, dawdle, shilly-shally, dilly-dally; put off, defer, delay, lay over, suspend; retard, postpone, adjourn; procrastinate, prolong, protract, drag out, draw out, lengthen, table, shelve, stall.

adj late, tardy, slow, dilatory, backward, unpunctual; delayed, overdue, belated.

adv late; backward, at the eleventh hour, at length, at last; ultimately, behind time; too late; slowly, leisurely, deliberately, at one's leisure, on one's own time.

134 opportuneness *n* timeliness, opportunity, occasion, suitable time, proper time, suitability, high time; crisis, turn, juncture; turning point, given time; nick of time, golden opportunity; clear stage, open field.

v be opportune, be suitable; seize the opportunity, seize the time, seize the day, *carpe diem,* use the occasion; suit the occasion, be expeditious, strike while the iron is hot.

adj opportune, timely, well-timed, seasonable, suitable, appropriate; providential, lucky, fortunate, happy, favorable, fortuitous, propitious, auspicious.

adv opportunely, in due time, in the nick of time, just in time, now or never; by the way, by the by, speaking of, while on the subject; on the spot, on the spur of the moment, since the occasion presents itself.

135 inopportuneness *n* untimeliness, unseasonableness, improper time, unsuitable time; *(informal)* bad timing; intrusion; anachronism.

v be ill timed, mistime, intrude, break in upon, *(informal)* butt in; lose an opportunity, waste an occasion, *(informal)* blow one's chance, let the opportunity slip by; waste time.

adj inopportune, untimely, unpropitious, unseasonable, unsuitable, inauspicious, unfavorable, unfortunate, unsuited, untoward, unlucky; ill-timed, mistimed, poorly timed; unpunctual, premature.

136 frequency *n* repetition, recurrence, iteration, reinteration.

v recur, repeat, reiterate; keep on, continue; attend regularly, visit often, patronize.

adj frequent, oft-repeated, recurring, incessant, constant, continual, perpetual; habitual, customary.

adv often, oft, oftentimes, frequently, repeatedly, day after day; daily, hourly, every day; perpetually, continually, constantly, incessantly, at all times; commonly, habitually, customarily; sometimes, occasionally, at times, now and then, every once in a while, from time to time.

137 infrequency *n* rarity, rare occurrence; long shot, surprise, *(informal)* mindblower.

v be rare, be infrequent.

adj infrequent, occasional, sporadic, rare, uncommon, unusual, unheard of, unprecedented; few, scant, scarce.

adv infrequently, rarely, seldom, scarcely, hardly; not often, hardly ever.

138 regularity [of recurrence] *n* periodicity, intermittence; beat, pulse, pulsation, rhythm; alternation, oscillation, vibration; bout, round, turn, revolution, rotation, rpm; cycle, period, routine; punctuality, regularity, steadiness.

v recur, revolve, return, come in its turn, come round again; beat, pulsate, alternate.

adj regular, periodic, periodical; serial, recurrent, cyclical, cyclic, recurring, rhythmical, rhythmic; intermittent, alternate, every other; regular, steady, punctual, continual, constant, regular as clockwork.

adv regularly, periodically, serially, cyclically; intermittently, alternately; by turns, in turn, in rotation, off and on, round and round.

139 irregularity [of recurrence] *n* uncertainty, unpredictability, haphazardness, fitfulness, capriciousness.

v be irregular, be haphazard.

adj irregular, uncertain, unpredictable, haphazard, fitful, capricious, flickering; spasmodic, sporadic.

adv irregularly, fitfully, capriciously, by fits and starts.

VII. Change

140 change n alteration, modulation, modification, variation, mutation, permutation, qualification, deviation, turn, shift, innovation; diversion, break; transformation, transfiguration, transmutation, metamorphosis; conversion, revolution, inversion, reversal; displacement, transference, transposition; changeableness.

v change, alter, vary, modulate, qualify, diversify, tamper with, play with, experiment with; turn, shift, veer, tack, swerve, warp, deviate, turn aside; turn, take a turn, *(informal)* hang a turn; modify, revamp, transform, transfigure, transmute, metamorphose, convert; innovate, restructure, give a new turn to, recast, redesign, remodel.

adj changed, newfangled; changeable, variable, transformable; innovative.

141 permanence n stability, invariability, unalterability, immutability, constancy; endurance, durability, persistence; maintenance, preservation, conservation; obstinacy, immovability, inflexibility, immobility, rigidity.

v endure, bide, abide, stay, remain, last, persist, stand, stand fast; maintain, keep, keep up, preserve; subsist, live, outlive, survive.

adj permanent, lasting, unchanged, unchanging, fixed, stable, invariable, constant; enduring, durable, abiding, everlasting; intact, inviolate; persistent.

adv permanently, for good, for good and all.

142 cessation n discontinuation, discontinuance, halt, stoppage, termination, suspension, interruption, stopping; pause, rest, lull, respite, truce, break; interregnum, abeyance; completion, end, finish; stop, death.

v cease, discontinue, terminate, desist, stay; break off, leave off, hold, stop, pull up, stop short, halt, pause, rest; suspend, interrupt, delay, cut short, arrest, bring to a standstill; complete, end, finish, close up shop; wear away, go out, die out, pass away, die.

143 continuance [in action] n continuation, continuity, protraction, prolongation, maintenance, perpetuation; persistence, perseverance, repetition.

v continue, persist, go on, keep on, hold on; abide, keep, pursue, stick to; maintain course, carry on, keep up; sustain, uphold, hold up, keep going, maintain, preserve, perpetuate, prolong.

adj continuing, uninterrupted, unvarying; continuous, persistent, perpetual.

144 conversion n transformation, transmutation, reduction, change, changeover, resolution, assimilation; passage, transit, transition, shifting, flux; growth, progress, development; chemistry, alchemy.

v be converted into, become, turn into, lapse, shift; pass into, grow into, ripen into, merge into; melt, grow, ripen, mature, mellow; convert into, resolve into; make, render; mold, form, model, remodel, remake, do over, reform, reorganize; assimilate, bring into, reduce to.

adj convertible, transmutable, changeable.

145 reversion n return, revulsion, reverting, returning; alternation, rotation; inversion; recoil, reaction, reflex, repercussion, rebound, boomerang, ricochet, backlash, repulse; retrospection, retrogression, retrogradation, falling back; restoration, going back; turning point, turn of the tide.

v revert, return, turn back, reverse; relapse, regress, fall back; recoil, rebound; retreat; restore; undo, unmake; turn the tide.

146 [sudden or violent change] **revolution** n revolt, rebellion, overthrow, overturn, coup, *coup d'état*, rising, uprising, mutiny, counterrevolution; breakup, destruction, subversion, clean sweep; spasm, convulsion, throe, revulsion.

v revolt, rebel, rise, rise up; revolutionize, remodel, recast, change.

adj revolutionary, rebellious; new.

147 substitution n replacement, supplanting, commutation, exchange, change, shift.

substitute, expedient, makeshift, stopgap, equivalent, double, alternative, representative.

v substitute, put in the place of, change, exchange, interchange; replace, supplant, supersede, take the place of, stand for, represent, pinch hit, substitute for, sub; redeem, commute, alternate.

adv instead, in place of, in lieu of.

148 [double or mutual change] **interchange** *n* exchange, commutation, permutation, transposition; reciprocation, reciprocity, intercourse; barter, swap, trade; interchangeability; retaliation, reprisal, requital, retort, crossfire.

v interchange, exchange, barter, trade, swap, bandy, transpose, commute, reciprocate; give and take, battle with words; retort, requite, retaliate.

adj interchangeable, all-purpose, multi-purpose; reciprocal; mutual.

adv in exchange, vice versa, turn and turn about.

149 changeableness *n* mutability, inconstancy, volatility, instability; malleability, adaptability, versatility, mobility; vacillation, irresolution, indecision, capriciousness, oscillation, alternation, fluctuation, vicissitude; restlessness, fidgetiness, disquiet, disquietude; unrest, agitation.

v fluctuate, oscillate, vary, waver, flounder, shuffle, hem and haw, vacillate, tremble, alternate.

adj changeable, mutable, variable, malleable, adaptable, adjustable, versatile, mobile, transformable, convertible; inconstant, unsteady, unstable, unreliable, vacillating, oscillating, fluctuating; volatile, fitful, fickle, capricious, mercurial, indecisive, irresolute, flighty, impulsive, fanciful, erratic, wayward, wanton; restless, fidgety, tremulous, agitated; unfixed, unsettled.

150 stability *n* immutability, unchangeableness, constancy; firmness, fixity, solidity, steadiness, soundness, balance, stabilization, equilibrium, quiescence; immobility, immovability, fixedness; steadfastness, reliability, resolution, determination, obstinacy, stubbornness, pertinacity, tenacity, doggedness, will, pluck, resoluteness; permanence, endurance, perseverance, durability; continuity, uniformity changelessness.

v be firm, stick fast, stand firm; settle, establish, fix, set, stabilize; retain, keep hold; make sure, fasten, make solid.

adj stable, fixed, rigid, firm, steady, established, strong, sturdy, immovable, invariable, unvarying, permanent, unchangeable, unchanging, unalterable, immutable; enduring, constant, durable, lasting, abiding, secure, fast, perpetual; unwavering, steadfast, staunch, reliable, steady, solid, sound, balanced; resolute, obstinate, dogged, willful, stubborn, pertinacious, tenacious.

151 present events *n* event, occurrence, incident, affair, eventuality, happening, proceeding, transaction, fact; phenomenon; circumstance, situation, particular; adventure, episode, thrill; crisis, pass, emergency, contingency, impasse; things, doings, affairs, matters, issues; the world, life, the times.

v happen, occur, take place, come to pass, take place, come about, come round; fall out, turn out, befall, chance, prove, eventuate; turn up, crop up, arise, arrive, issue, ensue, start, hold; take its course, pass off; experience, meet with, meet up with, fall to, be one's lot, be one's fortune, find, encounter, undergo, go through, live through, endure, put up with.

adj happening, going on, doing, current; eventful, stirring, bustling, busy, full of incident.

adv eventually, finally; as things go, in the course of things, as it happens.

152 future events *n* destiny, luck, lot, chance, fortune, karma, doom, end; future, futurity, next world, hereafter; prospects, expectations, tomorrow.

v impend, hang over, hover, threaten, loom, await, come on, approach; foreordain, preordain; destine, predestine, doom, have in store for.

adj impending, destined; coming, in store, to come, at hand, near, close by, imminent, brewing, forthcoming; in the wind, in the cards, in prospect, looming, on the horizon.

adv in time, in the long run, in good time, in its own sweet time, eventually.

VIII. Causation

153 cause *n* origin, source, principle, element; prime mover, first cause; author, producer, creator; mainspring, agent, catalyst; groundwork, foundation, support; spring, fountain, well, fount, font; genesis, descent, remote cause, influence; pivot, hinge, axis, turning point; egg, germ, embryo, root, nucleus, seed; causality, causation, origination, production.

v cause, originate, give rise to, occasion, sow the seeds of, kindle, bring to pass, bring about; produce, create, set up, develop; found, broach, institute; induce, evoke, elicit, draw, provoke; determine, decide; conduce to, contribute, have a hand in, influence, effect.

adj causal, generative, productive, formative, creative; primal, primary, original, embryonic.

adv because.

154 effect *n* consequence, issue, derivation, upshot, outgrowth, development, fruit, crop, harvest, product, outcome, end, conclusion; offspring, offshoot; complications, concomitants, side effects.

v be the effect of, be due to, be owing to; originate in, originate from, rise from, spring from, proceed from, emanate from, come from, grow from, issue from, flow from, result from; depend upon, hinge upon.

adj owing to, resulting from, due to, derivable from, caused by; derived from, evolved from; derivative, hereditary.

adv consequently, as a consequence, necessarily.

155 [assignment of cause] **attribution** *n* theory, ascription, assignment, rationale, reference to, accounting for; imputation, derivation; explanation, interpretation, reason why.

v attribute to, ascribe to, impute to, refer to, point to, trace to, assign to; account for, derive from; theorize, speculate.

adj attributed, attributable, referable, due to, owing to.

adv hence, thence, therefore, *ergo*, for, since, on account of, because; why? wherefore? whence? how come? how so?

156 [absence of assignable cause] **chance** *n* fortune, fate, accident, hap, hazard, luck, fluke, *(informal)* freak; gamble, lottery, tossup, fifty-fifty chance, throw of the dice, heads or tails; probability, possibility, contigency, odds; speculation, gaming, gambling.

v chance, hap, turn up; fall to one's lot; stumble on, light on; take one's chances.

adj chancy, causal, fortuitous, accidental, *(informal)* iffy, adventitious, haphazard, random, indeterminate, flukey, *(informal)* freaky.

adv by chance, by accident; at random; perchance, as chance will have it.

157 power *n* potency, strength, puissance, might, force, energy, vigor; control, command, dominion, authority, rule, sway, ascendancy, sovereignty, omnipotence; ability, capability, capacity, facility, competence, competency, efficacy; validity, cogency.

v be powerful, control, command, rule; confer power, empower, invest, endow; arm, strengthen, authorize; compel, force.

adj powerful, potent, strong, mighty, energetic; able, capable, competent, efficacious, equal to, up to, effective, efficient, adequate; omnipotent, almighty; influential, forceful.

adv powerfully.

prep by virtue of, by dint of.

158 impotence *n* inability, incapability, incapacity, infirmity, debility, disability; inefficacy, inefficiency, incompetence, ineptitude, feebleness, weakness, frailty, powerlessness; helplessness, prostration, paralysis, collapse, exhaustion; decrepitude, senility; sexual failure, barrenness.

v be impotent; collapse, faint, swoon, drop; render powerless, disable, disarm, incapacitate, disqualify, invalidate; cramp, tie the hands, paralyze, muzzle, cripple, maim, lame, hamstring, throttle, strangle, tie up in knots; unman, unnerve, enervate; shatter, exhaust, weaken; emasculate.

adj impotent, powerless, incapable, unable, incompetent, ineffective, inefficient, ineffectual, inept, unfit, unfitted, unqualified; disabled, incapacitated, crippled, paralyzed, paralytic; decrepit, senile, exhausted, worn out, used up, limp, spent; weak, frail, infirm, feeble, helpless; harmless; sterile, barren, frigid; emasculated, inadequate, inoperative; futile, fruitless, bootless, vain.

159 strength *n* power, force, might, vigor, health, stoutness, hardiness, lustihood, stamina, energy, potency, capacity; spring, bounce, tone, elasticity, tension; virility, vitality, nerve, verve; strengthening, invigoration, refreshment.

v strengthen, invigorate, brace, nerve, fortify, sustain, harden, steel; vivify, revivify, refresh, reinforce, restore.

adj strong, mighty, vigorous, forceful, hard, stout, robust, sturdy, hardy, powerful, potent, puissant; irresistible, invincible, indomitable, unconquerable, impregnable, inextinguishable, incontestable; able-bodied, athletic, muscular, sinewy, strapping, gigantic, Herculean.

adv strongly, by force.

160 weakness *n* debility, relaxation, languor, enervation; impotence, infirmity, fragility, flaccidity; frailty, delicacy, softness; senility, decrepitude.

v be weak, drop, crumble, give way, teeter, totter, tremble, shake, halt, limp, fade, languish, decline, flag, fail; weaken, enfeeble, cramp, debilitate, shake, enervate, unnerve; relax; dilute, water down.

adj weak, feeble, infirm, sickly; languid, faint, dull, slack, spent; limp, flaccid, powerless, impotent; relaxed, unstrung, unnerved; frail, fragile, delicate, flimsy; rickety, drooping, teetering, tottering, withered, shaky, shattered; palsied, decrepit, lame; decayed, rotten, worn, seedy, wasted, laid low.

161 production *n* creation, formation, fabrication, construction, manufacture; building, architecture, erection; organization, establishment; workmanship, craftsmanship, performance; achievement, product, end result; flowering, fructification, fruition, fulfillment; gestation, evolution, development, growth; gensis, generation, procreation; authorship, publication, works, *oeuvre*.

v produce, perform, operate, do, make, form, construct, fabricate, frame, contrive, manufacture; build, raise, rear, erect, put up; set up, establish, consti-

tute, compose, organize, institute; achieve, accomplish, fulfill; bud, flower, blossom, bloom, bear fruit, bring forth; propagate, beget, generate, procreate, engender; breed, hatch, develop, bring up; induce, cause.

adj productive, constructive, formative, creative; generative; prolific, blooming.

162 [nonproduction] destruction *n* waste, dissolution, breaking up, disruption; consumption; fall, downfall, ruin, perdition; breakdown, wreck, wrack, havoc, mess, chaos, cataclysm; desolation, extinction, annihilation; demolition; overthrow, subversion, suppression; dilapidation, devastation, road to ruin.

v perish, fall, tumble, topple, fall to pieces, break up, crumble, go to the dogs, go to wrack and ruin; destroy, do away with, demolish, tear up, overturn, overthrow, wipe out, *(informal)* waste; upset, subvert, undo; waste, squander, dissipate, dispel, dissolve; smash, squash, squelch, shatter, crumble, batter, crush, pull to pieces; fell, sink, scuttle, wreck, swamp, ruin, raze, level, expunge, erase, sweep away; lay waste, ravage, gut; disorganize, dismantle, take apart; devour, devastate, desolate, sap, exterminate, extinguish, stamp out, trample out, crush out, eradicate.

adj destructive, subversive, ruinous, incendiary, deadly, lethal, fatal; destroyed, wiped out, extinct.

163 reproduction *n* renovation, restoration, renewal, revival, regeneration, revivification, resuscitation, reanimation, resurrection; reappearance; generation, childbirth.

v reproduce, renovate, restore, renew, revive, regenerate, revivify, resuscitate, breathe new life into, reanimate, refashion, resurrect, bring back to life; give birth to, multiply, people the world.

adj reproductive; regenerative, restorative; renascent, reappearing, resurgent.

164 producer *n* originator, inventor, author, founder, generator, mover, creator maker, architect; backer, angel.

165 destroyer *n* spoiler, waster, ravager, wrecker, killer, assassin, executioner;

cankerworm, bane; iconoclast, rebel, pessimist, cynic, nihilist, misanthrope.

166 parentage n family, ancestry, lineage, genealogy; procreator, progenitor.

paternity: fatherhood, fathership; father, dad, pop, sire, papa, *(informal)* old man; grandfather, grandsire.

maternity: motherhood; mother, mom, ma, mamma, mummy, mum, *(informal)* old lady; grandmother.

adj parental, familial, ancestral, lineal, paternal, maternal; patriarchal, matriarchal.

167 posterity n progeny, breed, issue, offspring, brood, litter, family, children, grandchildren, heirs; child, son, daughter; descendant, heir, scion, *(informal)* chip off the old block; heredity.

adj filial.

168 productiveness n fecundity, fertility, fruitfulness, productivity; multiplication, propagation, procreation; creativity, inventiveness, originality.

v make productive, fructify, fulfill; procreate, generate, conceive, impregnate, fertilize; teem, multiply, produce, reproduce.

adj productive, prolific, fruitful, copious; teeming, fertile, fecund; procreative, generative, life-giving.

169 unproductiveness n infertility, sterility, barrenness, unfruitfulness, impotence; unprofitableness, wastefulness.

v be unproductive, do nothing, produce nothing, come to nothing.

adj unproductive, unfruitful, infertile, barren, sterile, arid; unprofitable, useless.

170 agency n operation, force, working, function, office, maintenance, exercise, work, play; causation, instigation, instrumentality, influence.

v operate, work, do; act, perform, play, support, sustain, maintain, take effect, quicken, strike; come into play, have free play; bring to bear upon, influence.

adj operative, efficient, efficacious, effectual, practical; at work, on foot, in operation, in force, in play, in action.

adv through the agency of, by means of.

171 energy n force, power, strength, intensity, vigor, zeal, dynamism, pep, fire, spirit, ebullience, life; activity, agitation, exertion, effervescence, ferment, fermentation, ebullition, bustle.

v give energy, energize, stimulate kindle, excite, inflame, exert; strengthen, invigorate; sharpen, intensify.

adj energetic, strong, forcible, potent, forceful, active, powerful, intense, vigorous, zealous, dynamic, ebullient, spirited, animated, keen, vivid, sharp, acute, incisive trenchant, biting; invigorating, rousing, stimulating; energized.

172 inertness n inertia, inactivity, torpor, languor, dullness, immobility, passivity, passiveness, lifelessness; quiescence, latency; inexcitability, sloth, indolence, irresolution, indecisiveness, cowardice, spinelessness.

v be inert, be inactive.

adj inert, inactive, immobile, unmoving, motionless, lifeless, passive, dead; sluggish, dull, heavy, flat, slack, tame, slow, blunt, torpid, languid; latent, dormant, sleeping, smoldering, quiescent.

adv in suspense, in abeyance.

173 violence n vehemence, fury, ferocity, impetuosity, boisterousness, turbulence, ebullition, effervescence, intensity, severity, acuteness; energy, force, might; fit, paroxysm, orgasm, spasm, convulsion, throe; exacerbation, exasperation, hysterics, excitability, passion; outbreak, outburst, uproar, riot, explosion, blow-up, blast, eruption; turmoil, disorder, ferment, agitation, storm, tempest; destruction, brutality, fighting, combat, warfare, hostilities; injury, wrong, outrage, injustice.

v be violent, ferment, effervesce; romp, rampage, run wild, run riot, rush, tear, run headlong, run amuck, go wild, kick up a row, *(informal)* flip out, go beserk; bluster, rage, roar, riot, storm, boil, boil over, fume, foam; explode, go off, detonate, thunder, blow up, flare, burst; render violent, sharpen, stir up, quicken, excite, incite, urge, lash, whip up, stimulate; irritate, inflame, kindle, accelerate, aggravate, exasperate, exacerbate, convulse, infuriate, madden, fan the fire, whip into a frenzy.

adj violent, vehement, acute, sharp; rough, rude, bluff, boisterous, brusque, abrupt, wild, impetuous, rampant; disorderly, turbulent, blustering, raging, riotous, tumultuous, obstreperous; raving, frenzied, *(informal)* freaked, mad, unhinged, insane; desperate, furious, frantic, hysterical; savage, fierce, ferocious, physical, brutal, combative; uncontrollable, ungovernable, irrepressible, excited; spasmodic, convulsive, orgasmic; explosive, volcanic, stormy.

adv violently; by storm, by force.

174 moderation *n* temperateness, temperance, reasonableness, judiciousness, deliberateness, fairness; gentleness, mildness, calmness, peacefulness; quiet, calm, composure; lenity, lenience; relaxation, assuagement, tranquilization, pacification, mitigation; measure, middle ground, middle of the road.

v moderate, ally, meliorate, calm, pacify, assuage, lull, smooth, compose, still, calm, quiet, hush, sober, mitigate, soften, mollify, temper, qualify, alleviate, appease, lessen, abate, diminish; slake, curb, tame; arbitrate, referee, umpire, regulate.

adj moderate, temperate, reasonable, judicious, deliberate, fair, gentle, mild, calm, cool, sober, measured, unruffled, quiet, tranquil, still, peaceful, pacific; unexciting, even, smooth, bland, palliative; lenient, relaxed, easy going.

adv moderately, in moderation, within reason.

175 influence *n* importance, weight, pressure, preponderance, prevalence, sway; predominance, ascendancy; dominance, reign, rule, authority, power, control, capability; input, *(informal)* say, persuasion, play, leverage, vantage ground; patronage, protection, auspices.

v be influential, have a say, have input, carry weight, affect, sway, impress, bias, direct, control; move, activate, incite, impel, rouse, arouse, induce, persuade; dominate, predominate, outweigh, override, prevail.

adj influential, important, weighty; prevalent, rife, rampant, dominant, predominant; potent, powerful, effective, authoritative.

175a absence of influence *n* impotence, powerlessness; unimportance, irrelevancy.

adj uninfluential, unpersuasive, weak, impotent, *(informal)* wishywashy.

176 tendency *n* aptness, aptitude, disposition, predisposition, proclivity, proneness, propensity, susceptibility, inclination, leaning, bias, drift, trend, bent, turn; quality, nature, temperament; idiosyncrasy, cast, vein, mood, humor.

v tend, contribute, conduce, lead, dispose, incline, verge, bend to, gravitate toward, lean, drift, tend, affect; promote, influence.

adj tending, leaning; conducive, working toward, in a fair way to; liable, likely; influential, instrumental, useful, subsidiary, subservient.

177 liability *n* susceptibility, penchant, vulnerability, predilection, propensity, tendency; drawback, hindrance, obstacle, difficulty, impediment; responsibility, obligation, debt, debit, indebtedness, pledge.

v be liable, incur, lay oneself open to, run the risk of, stand a chance, expose oneself to.

adj liable, subject, exposed, likely, open, in danger of; obliged, responsible, accountable, answerable; contingent, incidental, possible.

178 concurrence *n* accordance, accord, agreement, consent, assent; cooperation, collaboration, partnership, alliance, concert, union.

v concur, conduce, conspire, contribute; agree, unite, combine, hang together, pull together, cooperate, collaborate; keep pace with, run parallel, go hand in hand with.

adj concurrent, cooperative, collaborative, joint, allied with, of one mind, at one with, in concert with.

179 counteraction *n* opposition, antagonism, contrariety, polarity; clashing, collision, interference, resistance, friction; reaction, response, counterblast, counter maneuver; neutralization, check, curb, hindrance; repression, restraint.

v counteract, run counter to, clash, cross, interfere with, conflict with; jostle, run up against, oppose, antagonize, withstand, resist, hinder, impede, check, curb, repress, restrain; recoil, react; neutralize, nullify, cancel out, undercut, undermine, undo; counterpoise, offset, balance out, compensate.

adj counteracting, antagonistic, conflicting, contrary, reactionary.

adv although.

prep in spite of, against.

Class II
Words Relating to Space

I. Space in General

180 [indefinite space] **space** *n* extension, extent, expanse, span, stretch, scope, range, latitude, spread, proportions, sweep, capacity, play, swing, expansion; elbowroom, room, breathing space, leeway; open space(s), free space, waste, desert, wild, wilderness; unlimited space, wide world, heavens, universe, solar system, outer space, abyss, the void, infinity.

adj spacious, roomy, extensive, expansive, capacious, ample; widespread, vast, worldwide, boundless, limitless, unlimited, infinite.

adv extensively, far and wide, right and left, from the four corners of the world, all over, from pole to pole, under the sun, on the face of the earth, from all points of the compass, to the four winds.

180a inextension *n* nonextension, point, atom.

181 [definite space] **region** *n* sphere, ground, soil, area, realm, quarter, orb, hemisphere, circuit, circle; domain, tract, territory, country, county, province; clime, climate, zone, meridian, latitude.

adj regional, provincial, territorial.

182 [limited space] **place** *n* spot, point; niche, nook, hole, pigeonhole; locality; locale, situation.

adv somewhere, in some place, here and there, in various places.

183 situation *n* position, locality, locale, latitude and longitude, location; footing, standing, standpoint; aspect, attitude, posture, perspective, pose; place, site, station, post, predicament, whereabouts; bearings, direction; topography, geography; map, chart.

v be situated, be located, lie, have its seat in; situate, locate.

adj situated, located; local, topical, topographical.

adv here and there, hereabouts, thereabouts, in such and such a place.

184 location *n* place, situation; establishment, settlement, installation; anchorage, mooring, encampment.

v locate, place, situate, put, lay, set, make a place for, seat; station, lodge, quarter, house, post, install; establish, fix, settle, root; graft, plant; inhabit, domesticate, colonize, take root, establish roots, come to rest, settle down, take up quarters, locate oneself, relocate; squat, perch, bivouac, burrow, get a footing, encamp.

adj located, placed, ensconced, rooted, settled, moored.

185 displacement *n* dislocation, misplacement, derangement, transposition; ejection, expulsion, banishment, removal, exile.

v displace, dislodge, disestablish; misplace, disturb, disorder, unsettle, derange, confuse; transpose, set aside, transfer, remove, unload, empty, eject, expel, banish, exile; vacate, depart, leave.

adj displaced; unplaced, unhoused, unsettled, unestablished; homeless, out of place, misplaced, out of its element.

186 presence *n* attendance, company; occupancy, occupation; ubiquity, omnipresence, permeation, pervasion, pervasiveness, diffusion, dispersion; nearness, vicinity, proximity, closeness.

v be present; look on, attend, stand by, remain, find oneself; occupy, inhabit, dwell, stay, sojourn, live, abide, lodge, nestle, roost, perch, tenant; fill, pervade, permeate, run through.

adj present, attending; occupying, inhabiting, resident, moored; ubiquitous, omnipresent, pervasive, diffused; near, close, in proximity.

adv here, there, and everywhere; in presence of.

187 absence *n* nonappearance, nonattendance, absenteeism, nonresidence; emptiness, void, vacuum, vacancy, vacuity.

v be absent; keep away, play truant, absent oneself, stay away.

adj absent, not present, away, out, not here, not in, not present, off; wanting, lacking, missing, nonexistent; vacant, empty, void, vacuous, devoid.

adv without, minus, nowhere, *sans;* elsewhere.

188 inhabitant *n* resident, dweller, occupant; tenant, inmate, boarder, lodger; native, townsman, villager, citizen; population, community, society, state, people, race, nation.

v inhabit, live, reside, dwell.

adj indigenous, native, domestic.

189 habitation *n* abode, residence, domicile, lodging, dwelling, address, habitation, housing, quarters; home, homestead, motherland, fatherland, country; nest, lair, den, cave, hole, hiding place, cell, hive, haunt, habitat, perch, roost, retreat, *(informal)* pad, *(informal)* crashpad.

v inhabit, take up one's abode.

190 [things contained] **contents** *n* stuffing, cargo, lading, freight, shipment, haul, load, bale, burden.

v load, lade, ship, haul, charge, fill, stuff.

191 receptacle *n* container, holder, repository, vessel, receiver, depository, reservoir; storage areas; bulk containers; liquid containers; wrapping.

II. Dimensions

192 size *n* proportions, dimensions, magnitude, bulk, volume; largeness, greatness; expanse, amplitude, mass; capacity, tonnage; corpulence, obesity, plumpness; hugeness, enormousness, immensity; monstrosity, enormity; giant, monster, mammoth, behemoth, leviathan, elephant; lump, bulk, block, mass, clod, thumper, whopper, strapper, *(informal)* mother, mountain, mound, heap.

v be large; become large, expand.

adj sizable, large, big, great, considerable, bulky, voluminous, ample, massive, massy; capacious, comprehensive, spacious; mighty, towering, magnificent; corpulent; stout, fat, plump, obese, portly; full-grown, stalwart, brawny; hulky, unwieldy, bulky, lumpish, whopping, thundering, thumping; overgrown; huge, immense, enormous, mighty, vast, amplitudinous, stupendous; monstrous, gigantic, colossal.

193 littleness *n* smallness, diminutiveness, tininess; epitome; microcosm; vanishing point.

v be little; become little, decrease.

adj little, small, minute, diminutive, microscopic, submicroscopic; tiny, puny, wee, miniature, pigmy, dwarf, undersized, underdeveloped, dwarfish, stunted, dumpy, squat; imperceptible, invisible, infinitesimal.

194 expansion *n* increase, enlargement, extension, growth, development; augmentation, aggrandizement, increment, amplification; spreading, swelling, distention, puffiness, dropsy.

v expand, wide, enlarge, extend, grow, increase, swell, fill out; dilate, stretch, spread; bud, sprout, shoot, germinate, open, burst forth; outgrow, overrun; spread, extend, aggrandize; distend, develop, amplify, spread out, magnify; inflate, puff up, blow up, stuff, pad, cram, fatten; exaggerate.

adj expanded, larger; swollen, expansive, widespread, overgrown, exaggerated, bloated, fat, turgid, tumid, dropsical; pot-bellied, chubby, corpulent, obese, heavy; full-blown, full-grown.

195 contraction *n* reduction, diminution; decrease, lessening, shrinking; collapse, emancipation, attenuation, atrophy; condensation, compression, compactness, compendium, squeezing.

v contract, become small, lessen, decrease, dwindle, shrink, narrow, shrivel, collapse, wither, wizen, fall away, waste, wane, ebb, decay, deteriorate; diminish, contract, draw in, constrict, condense, compress, squeeze, crush, crumple up, pinch, squash, cramp; pare, reduce, attenuate, scrape, file, grind, chip, shave, shear, cut down; circumscribe, limit, restrain, confine.

adj contracting, astringent; shrunk, shrunken, contracted; wizened, stunted, waning; compact.

196 distance *n* remoteness, farness, background, offing, far cry to, horizon, elongation; interval, remove, gap, span, reach, range; outpost, outskirts, foreign parts.

v be distant; extend to, stretch to, reach to, spread to; range.

adj distant, far off, far away, remote, far, afar, outlying, removed, at a distance, away, younder, yon; inaccessible, out of the way, unapproachable.

adv far off, far away, afar, away, a long way off.

197 nearness *n* closeness, propinquity, proximity, proximation; vicinity, neighborhood, contiguity; short distance, earshot, close quarters, stone's throw, gunshot, hair's breadth; approach, access.

v be near, adjoin, neighbor, border upon, touch, stand next to; approximate, come close to, resemble; converge, crowd.

adj near, high, close, neighboring, adjoining, adjacent, bordering; proximate, approximate; at hand, handy; intimate.

adv near, nigh, hard by, close to, close upon, within reach, at one's fingertips.

198 interval *n* separation, space, break, gap, caesura, interspace, interstice, distance, hiatus, skip, division, opening; pause, recess, interim, respite, interlude, interregnum, interruption, term, spell, period; cleft, crevice, chink, cranny, crack, slit, fissure, rift, flaw, breach, rent, gash, cut, leak; ditch, dike, gorge, ravine, abyss, gulf.

v gape, open; intervene, interrupt.

199 continuity *n* contact, contiguousness, proximity, apposition, juxtaposition, touching, abutment, meeting.

v be contiguous, join, adjoin, abut on, border, touch, meet, graze, adhere; coincide, coexist.

adj contiguous, touching, in contact, end to end; close, near.

200 length *n* distance, extent, longitude, span, reach, range; lengthiness, elonga-tion, size; duration, continuance, term, period.

v be long, stretch out, sprawl; extend to, reach to, stretch to; lengthen, stretch, elongate, extend; prolong, protract, draw out, spin out.

adj long, lengthy, extended, outstretched; lengthened, interminable; linear, lineal, longitudinal; tall, stringy, protracted, lanky.

adv lengthwise, at length, longitudinally.

201 shortness *n* brevity, littleness; shortening, abridgment, abbreviation, conciseness, condensation; retrenchment, curtailment, reduction.

v be short; shorten, abridge, abbreviate, condense, compact, compress, epitomize; retrench, cut short, reduce, pare down, clip back, cut back, prune, shear, shave, crop, chop up, hack up, truncate.

adj short, brief, curt; compendious, compact, compressed, condensed; stubby, stunted, stumpy, squat, dumpy; concise, pointed; curtailed, cut back, reduced, shortened, abbreviated, abridged.

202 breadth. thickness *n* breadth, width, latitude, amplitude, extent, diameter.

thickness, density, denseness, heaviness, bulk, body.

v be broad; expand, widen, be thick; thicken.

adj broad, wide, ample, extended, expansive, large; outspread, outstretched.

thick, dense, heavy, bulky, solid, compact; dumpy, squat, thickset.

203 narrowness. thinness *n* narrowness, slenderness, exiguity, closeness, straitness, scantiness, slightness, slimness.

thinness, slenderness, slimness, leanness, lankness, meagerness, skinniness.

v be narrow; narrow, taper, be thin; thin, slenderize, slim; dilute, water down.

adj narrow, close, slender, thin, fine, threadlike, slim, delicate; restricted, confined, limited; thin, emaciated, lean, skinny, meager, gaunt, spindly, lanky, scrawny, haggard, pinched, skeletal, wasted; frail, unsound, fragile; weak, shrill, faint, feeble; watery, waterish, diluted, unsubstantial.

204 layer *n* stratum, substratum, bed, zone, floor, stage, story, tier, slab, tablet, board, sheet, platter; scale, coat, peel, membrane, film, leaf, slice.

v slice, shave, pare, peel; plate, coat, veneer; cover; layer

adj layered, stratified, tiered; scaly, filmy, membranous, flaky.

205 filament *n* thread, fiber, strand, hair, cilia, tendril, gossamer, wire, strand, vein.

adj fibrous, threadlike, wiry, stringy, ropy; capillary.

206 height *n* altitude, stature, elevation, tallness; prominence, eminence, preeminence, loftiness, sublimity; top, peak, pinnacle, acme, summit, zenith; culmination.

v tower, soar, hover, cap, command; mount, bestride, surmount, overhang; heighten, elevate, raise up, rise up.

adj high, tall, elevated, towering, skyscraping, gigantic, huge, colossal; distinguished, prominent, eminent, preeminent, exalted, lofty, sublime; overhanging, overlying.

207 lowness *n* depression, debasement, prostration; flatness, proneness; lowlands, flatlands.

v be low; lie low, lie flat, crouch, slouch, wallow, grovel; underlie; lower, depress.

adj low, flat, level, low-lying; crouched, squat, prone, supine, prostrate, depressed; groveling, abject, sordid, mean, base, lowly, degraded, debased, ignoble, vile.

adv under, beneath, underneath, below, down, downward; underfoot, underground; downstairs, belowstairs.

208 depth *n* deepness, profundity, obscurity; depression, bottom, unfathomable space; pit, hollow, shaft, well, crater, chasm, abyss, bottomless pit; central part, midst, middle, bosom, womb, base, heart, core; soundings, draft, submersion, dive.

v deepen, hollow, plunge, sink, dig, excavate; sound, have the lead, take soundings.

adj deep, deep-seated, profound, mysterious, obscure, unfathomable; sunk, buried, submerged; bottomless, soundless, fathomless, unfathomed, abysmal, yawning, gaping.

adv beyond one's depth, out of one's depth, over one's head.

209 shallowness *n* superficiality, banality, triviality, frivolity, flimsiness, emptiness, vacancy; shallow, shoal, sand bar.

adj shallow, superficial, slight, cursory, trivial, banal, trashy, flimsy, substanceless, empty, vacuous, vacant; skin-deep, ankle-deep, knee-deep.

210 summit *n* top, peak, apex, pinnacle, vertex, acme, culmination, zenith; height, pitch, maximum, climax; crowning point, turning point, watershed.

v culminate, climax, crown, top.

adj highest, top, topmost, uppermost, tiptop; capital, head, polar; supreme, supernal.

211 base *n* bottom, stand, rest, pedestal, dado, understructure, substructure, foot, basis, foundation, ground, groundwork; principle, touchstone, fundamental part, element, ingredient; bottom, nadir, foot, sole, heel.

adj bottom, undermost, nethermost; fundamental, basic, elemental; based on, founded on, grounded on, built on; base, vile, venal.

212 verticality *n* perpendicularity, erectness; wall, precipice, cliff.

v be vertical, stand up straight, stand upright, stand erect, stand straight and tall.

adj vertical, upright, erect, perpendicular, straight, bolt upright, plumb.

adv vertically, on end, endwise.

213 horizontality *n* flatness; level, plane, stratum; horizon; recumbency, lying down, reclination, proneness, supination, prostration.

v be horizontal, lie, recline, lie down, lie flat, sprawl; render horizontal, flatten, level, prostrate, knock down, floor, fell.

adj horizontal, level, even, plane, flat, smooth; prone, supine, prostrate.

adv horizontally, on one's back.

214 suspension *n* hanging down, free swinging; pendant, tail, train, flap, pendulum.

v suspend, hang, swing, dangle; flap, trail, flow; depend.

adj suspended, pendent, hanging,

swinging, dangling, pendulous; dependent.

215 support *n* foundation, base, basis, ground, footing, hold; supporter, prop, brace, stay, rib, truss, stalk, stilts, splint; bar, rod, boom, outrigger; staff, stick, crutch; bracket, ledge, shelf, trestle, buttress.

v support, bear, carry, hold, sustain, shoulder, bolster; shore up, hold up, prop up, brace; help, aid, maintain, sustain; base, found, ground.

adj supporting, supported; fundamental.

216 parallelism *n* coextension; comparison, affinity, correspondence, semblance, likeness, resemblance, analogy, equation.

v parallel, compare, relate, associate, connect, correspond to, equate.

adj parallel, coextensive, collateral, aligned, equal; like, similar, allied, corresponding, correlative, analogous, equivalent.

217 obliquity *n* incline, inclination, slope, slant, leaning, tilt, list, bend, curve; acclivity, rise, ascent, grade, rising ground, hill, bank; declivity, decline, downhill, dip, fall; steepness.

v be oblique, slope, slant, lean, incline, stoop, decline, descend; bend, careen, slouch, sidle; render oblique, sway, bias, slat, warp, incline, bend, crook, tilt, distort.

adj oblique, inclined; sloping, tilted; askew, asquint, awry, crooked; uphill, rising, ascending; downhill, falling, descending; declining, declivitous; steep, abrupt, sharp, precipitous; diagonal, transverse.

adv obliquely, on one side; askew, askance, edgewise, at an angle; sidelong, sideways, slantwise.

218 inversion *n* subversion, reversion, contraposition, transposition, transposal, conversion; contrariety, contradiction, opposition, polarity, antithesis; reversal, overturn, somersault, turn of the tide, revulsion, revolution.

v be inverted, turn about, wheel about, go about, turn over, go over, tilt over; invert, subvert, reverse, overturn, upturn, upset, turn topsy-turvy; transpose.

adj inverted, inside out, wrong side out, upside down, topsy-turvy; inverse, reverse, obverse, opposite.

adv inversely.

219 crossing *n* intersection, grade crossing, crossroad, interchange; network, reticulation; net, netting, network, web, mesh, wicker, lace; mat, matting, plait, trellis, lattice, grating, grille, gridiron, tracery, fretwork, filigree; knot, entanglement.

v cross, intersect, interlace, intertwine, interweave, interlink, crisscross, twine, intwine, weave, twist, wreathe; dovetail, splice, link, link up; mat, plait, plat, braid; tangle, entangle, ravel; net, knot, twist.

adj crossing; crossed, matted, transverse; weaved, woven, intertwined, interlaced.

220 exteriority *n* outside, exterior; surface, superficies; covering, skin, face, appearance, façade, aspect, facet.

v be exterior, lie around, encircle.

adj exterior, external, outer, outside, outward, superficial; outlying, extraneous, foreign, extrinsic.

adv externally, out, over, outwards.

221 interiority *n* interior, inside, inner part, center, interspace; subsoil, substratum, contents, substance, pith, marrow, backbone, heart, bowels, belly, guts, lap, womb; recesses, innermost recesses, hollows, nook, niche, cave.

v be interior, be inside; inclose, circumscribe; intern; embed, insert.

adj interior, internal, inside, inner, inward, inmost, innermost; deepseated, inlaid, embedded, ingrained, innate, inherent, intrinsic, inborn; private, secret, intimate, confidential; home, domestic.

adv internally; inward, within, indoors, withindoors.

222 centrality *n* center, middle, midst; core, kernel, nucleus, heart, pole, axis, pivot, navel, nub, hub; centralization; center of gravity.

v be central; centralize, concentrate; focus on, bring into focus, get to the heart of.

adj central, middle, pivotal, focal, concentric; middlemost.

adv centrally; middle, midst.

223 covering n cover; canopy, awning, tent, marquee; umbrella, parasol, sunshade; shade, screen, shield; roof, ceiling, thatch, shed; top, lid; bandage, wrappings; coverlet, blanket, sheet, quilt, tarpaulin; skin, fleece, fur, hide; clothing, mask; peel, crust, bark, rind; veneer, coating, facing, varnish.

ν cover, superimpose, overlay, overspread; wrap, encase, face, case, veneer, paper; conceal, cover over.

adj covered, clothed, wrapped; protected.

224 lining n inner coating, coating; filling, stuffing, padding, wadding.

ν line, stuff, wad, pad, fill; coat, incrust, face, cover.

adj lined.

225 dress n clothing, covering, raiment, drapery, costume, attire, garb, apparel, wardrobe, outfit, clothes; equipment, livery, gear, rigging, trappings, togs, accouterments; uniforms, regimentals, suit.

ν dress, clothe, drape, robe, array, fit out, deck out, garb, rig out, apparel; equip, harness, outfit, uniform; cover, wrap, wrap up, sheathe, swathe, swaddle.

adj dressed, clothed, clad, invested.

226 undress n nudity, nakedness, bareness, dishabille.

ν undress, uncover, divest, expose, disrobe, strip, bare, doff, peel, take off, put off, lay open.

adj undressed, nude, naked, bare, stark-naked, exposed, in the buff, *au naturel*, in the altogether, in one's birthday suit; undressed, unclad, undraped, disrobed.

227 environment n environs, surroundings, outskirts, suburbs, purlieus, precincts, neighborhood.

ν environ, surround, encompass, compass, inclose, enclose, circle, encircle, gird, twine round, hem in.

adj surrounding, circumjacent.

adv around, about; without; on every side, on all sides, right and left, every which way.

228 interspersion n interjacence, interlocation, interpenetration, permeation; interjection, interpolation, interlineation,

intercalation; intervention, interference, interposition, intrusion; insinuation; insertion.

ν intervene, come between, get between, interpenetrate; intersperse, permeate, introduce, throw in, work in, interpose, interject, interpolate, insert; interfere, intrude, obtrude.

adj intervening, interjacent; parenthetical, episodic; intrusive.

adv between, betwixt, among, amid, amongst; in the thick of, betwixt and between; parenthetically.

229 circumscription n limitation, enclosure; confinement, restraint.

ν circumscribe, limit, bound, confine, inclose; surround, hedge in, fence in, wall in; imprison, restrain; enfold, bury, incase.

adj circumscribed, confined, restrained, imprisoned; buried in, immersed in, embosomed, embedded.

230 outline n circumference, perimeter, periphery; circuit, lines, contour, profile, silhouette.

ν outline, draw, sketch, trace, profile.

231 edge n frame, fringe, trimming, trim, edging, skirting, hem; verge, brink, brim, lip, margin, border, skirt, rim, mouth; threshold, door, porch, portal; coast, shore.

ν edge, skirt, border; trim, hem.

232 enclosure n envelope, case, wrapper; girdle; pen, fence, fold, cote, corral, stockyard, paddock, yard, pound, compound; fence, pale, paling, balustrade, rail, railing; hedge; wall, barrier, barricade; gate, gateway, door, doorway; boundary, border.

ν enclose, circumscribe.

233 limit n boundary, bounds, extent, confine, term, pale, verge; termination, terminus; frontier, marches, outer edges, unknown; boundary line, border, edge; turning point, flood gate.

ν limit, restrain, restrict, confine, check, hinder, bound, circumscribe, define.

adj limited, definite; terminal.

adv thus far, only so far, thus far and no further.

234 front n forefront, foreground, lead; face, frontage, façade, frontispiece, pro-

scenium; vanguard, front rank, first
rank, head of the column, advanced
guard.

ν front, face, confront; be in front,
stand in front; come to the front.

adj fore, foremost; front, frontal, anterior, forward.

adv before, in front, in advance;
ahead, right ahead, in the foreground; in
the lead.

235 rear *n* back, background, rearguard,
rear rank; distance, hinterland; rump,
buttocks, posterior, rear, backside, hindquarters; wake, train; reverse, other side
of the coin, *(informal)* flipside.

ν be behind, bring up the rear; rear,
bring up, nurture, raise; elevate, lift,
loft, lift up, hold up; build, put up, erect.

adj rear, back, hindmost; posterior.

adv behind, in the rear, in the background, at the heels; after, aft, rearward.

236 side *n* laterality, flank, quarter, lee,
hand; cheek, jowl, shoulder; profile, lee
side, broadside.

ν be on the side; be side by side, be
cheek to cheek; flank, skirt, outflank,
sidle.

adj sidelong, lateral; flanking, skirting; flanked.

adv sideways, sidelong; broadside, on
one side, abreast, alongside, beside, side
by side, cheek by jowl; laterally.

237 opposition *n* opposite, contraposition, opposite side, opposite poles,
polarity, antithesis, reverse, inverse;
counterpart, companion piece, complement.

ν be opposite; stand as opposites, oppose.

adj opposite, reverse, inverse, converse; antipodal, antithetical, countering, opposing; fronting, facing, diametrically opposite; complementary.

adv over, over the way, over against;
poles apart; face to face.

238 right *n* right hand, right side; offside,
starboard.

adj right-handed, dextral.

239 left *n* left had, left side; near side,
port.

adj left-handed, sinistral.

III. Form

240 form *n* shape, outline, mold, appearance, cast, cut, configuration; make, formation, frame, construction, cut, set,
build, trim; mold, model, pattern; posture, attitude, convention, rule, formality, formula, ceremony, conformity.

ν form, shape, figure, fashion, carve,
cut, chisel, hew, cast; shape, model,
mold, fashion, cast, construct, build;
stamp, cast, type.

adj formal, ceremonial, ceremonious, conventional; regular, set, fixed,
stiff, rigid.

241 formlessness *n* shapelessness, amorphism, asymmetry; disorder, chaos;
misproportion, deformity, disfigurement, defacement, mutilation, truncation.

ν deface, disfigure, deform, mutilate,
truncate.

adj formless, shapeless, amorphous,
asymmetrical, unformed, unshaped, unfashioned, unshapely, misshapen, out of
proportion, disordered, chaotic; rough,
rude, coarse, barbarous, rugged.

242 [regularity of form] symmetry *n*
shapeliness, finish, comeliness, gracefulness, grace, beauty; proportion, uniformity, parallelism; regularity, evenness, balance, order, harmony, agreement.

adj symmetrical, shapely, well set,
finished; beautiful, lovely; classic, classical, formal, chaste, severe; regular,
uniform, balanced, harmonious, ordered; even, parallel, equal.

243 [irregularity of form] distortion *n*
contortion, warp, buckle, screw, twist,
crookedness, obliquity; deformity, malformation, misproportion, disfigurement, monstrosity, ugliness; asymmetry.

ν distort, contort, warp, buckle,
screw, twist, wrest; writhe, grimace,
make faces; deform, disfigure, misshape.

adj distorted, out of shape, irregular,
unsymmetrical, awry, askew, crooked;
not true, not straight, uneven; misshapen, ill-made, ill-fashioned, ill-
proportioned, malformed, deformed.

244 angularity *n* bifurcation, bend, fork,
crook, notch, angle; elbow, knee, knuc-

kle, crotch; right angle, acute angle, obtuse angle; corner, nook, niche, recess.

v angle, tilt, bend, fork, bifurcate.

adj angular, bent, crooked, jagged, serrated; forked, bifurcate, cornered, V-shaped, hooked; akimbo.

245 curvature *n* curve, incurvature, bend; flexure, bending, crook, hook; deflection, turn, deviation, detour, sweep, curl, winding; curve, arc, arch, arcade, vault, bow, crescent, half-moon, horseshoe, loop; parabola, hyperbola.

v be curved, sweep, sag; deviate, turn; render curved, bend, curve, deflect, inflect, crook; turn, round, arch, arch over, bow, curl, coil, recurve.

adj curved, bowed, vaulted, hooked, arched, arced; circular, nonlinear, semicircular, rounded, crescent, crescent-shaped, lunar, demi-lune.

246 straightness *n* directness; inflexibility, stiffness; straight line, direct line, bee line.

v be straight, go straight; render straight, straighten, rectify, correct, right; put right, put straight, unbend, unfold, uncurl, unravel.

adj straight, even true, unbent, direct, rectilinear, linear, not curved, uncurved; square, erect, perpendicular, vertical, upright; candid, forthright, definite, reliable, plain, blunt, frank, sure, positive, irrefutable, certain, unequivocal, inescapable; honest, honorable, fair, just, equitable, impartial, aboveboard, reputable, scrupulous, worthy, lawful, licit, conscientious, decent, ethical; correct, sound, sane, accurate, true; sober, conventional, provincial, *(informal)* unhip, *(informal)* square, *(informal)* not with it.

247 [simple circularity] **circularity** *n* roundness, rotundity; circle, ring, hoop, areola; bracelet, armlet; eye, loop, wheel, cycle, orb, orbit; zone, belt, cord, band, sash, girdle, circuit; wreath, garland, crown, corona, coronet; necklace, collar; ellipse, oval.

v round; go around, encircle, circle.

adj round, rounded, circular, oval, elliptic, elliptical, egg-shaped.

248 [complex circularity] **convolution** *n* involution, winding, wave, undulation, sinuosity, meandering, twist, twirl; coil,

roll, curl, buckle, spiral, corkscrew, worm, tendril; serpent, snake, eel; maze, labyrinth.

v wind, twine, entwine, twirl, wave, undulate, meander, turn; twist, coil, roll; wrinkle, curl, frizz, frizzle; wring, contort.

adj convoluted, winding, twisted; wavy, undulating, circling, snaky, serpentine; involved, intricate, complex, complicated, labyrinthine, tortuous, mazy; spiral, coiled.

adv in and out, round and round.

249 rotundity *n* roundness, cylindricality, sphericity, globularity; cylinder, barrel, drum; roll, roller, rolling pin; sphere, globe, ball, spheroid, globule; bulb, pellet, pill, marble, pea, knob, pommel.

v sphere, form into a sphere, roll into a ball, round.

adj rotund, round, circular, ballshaped; cylindrical, spherical, globular; egg-shaped, pear-shaped, ovoid.

250 convexity *n* prominence, projection, swelling, bulge, protuberance, protrusion; hump, hunch, bunch; knob, node, nodule, bump, clump; pimple, pustule, pock, growth, polyp, blister, boil; nipple, teat, pap, breast; nose, beak, snout, nozzle; peg, button, stud, ridge; cupola, dome, arch; relief, high relief, low relief; hill, mountain, cape, ness, promontory, headland; jetty, ledge, spur.

v project, bulge, protrude, jut out, stand out, stick out, stick up, start up, shoot up, swell up; raise; emboss.

adj convex, prominent, protuberant; bossed, nodular, bunchy, hummocky, bulbous, swollen, swelling, bloated, bowed, arched, bellied; salient, in relief, raised.

251 flatness *n* smoothness, evenness; plane, level; plate, platter, table, tablet, slab.

v flatten, level, even off.

adj flat, plane, even, smooth; level, smooth, horizontal; flat as a pancake.

252 concavity *n* depression, dip, hollow, indentation, dent, cavity, dint, dimple; excavation, pit, trough; cup, basin, crater; valley, vale, dale, dell, glade, grove, glen, cave, cavern.

v render concave, depress, hollow,

scoop, scoop out, gouge; dig, delve, excavate, mine, stave in, tunnel.

adj concave, hollow, hollowed out; indented, dented, sunken, cupped; cavernous, rounded inward, incurved.

253 sharpness *n* acuteness, pointedness; point, spike, spine, needle, pin, prick, prickle, spur, barb, thorn; knife edge, cutting edge, razor edge.

v be sharp, taper to a point; sharpen, point, whet, barb, strop, grind, whittle.

adj sharp, keen, acute, trenchant; pointed, peaked, conical, spiked, spiky, tapering; studded, prickly, barbed, spiny, thorny, bristling, thistly; craggy, snaggy; cutting, sharp edged, razor sharp.

254 bluntness *n* dullness; obtuseness, roughness.

v be blunt; render blunt, dull, take off the point, round the edge.

adj blunt, dull, obtuse, dimwitted; rough, gruff; rounded, round, unsharpened, unpointed.

255 smoothness *n* polish, gloss; lubrication, lubricity.

v smooth, plane, file, scrape, shave, sand, sandpaper; level, press, flatten, roll; iron, steam press; polish, burnish, rub, wax, sleek, buff, glaze; lubricate, oil, grease.

adj smooth, polished, glossy, shiny, sleek, silken, silky; even, level, sanded; soft, downy, velvety; slippery, glassy, oily.

256 roughness *n* asperity, irregularity, corrugation, nodulation; grain, texture, pile, nap.

v roughen, rough up, crinkle, ruffle, rumple, crumple.

adj rough, uneven, irregular, rugged, scabrous, knotted, craggy, gnarled; shaggy, coarse, hairy, bristly, hirsute; scraggly, prickly, bushy; unpolished, unsmooth, rough-hewn, textured; downy, velvety, fluffy, woolly.

adv against the grain.

257 notch *n* dent, nick, cut, scratch, indentation; saw, tooth, scallop.

v notch, nick, cut, scratch, indent, jag, scarify, scallop.

adj notched, toothed, serrated.

258 fold *n* plait, ply, crease, pleat, tuck; wrinkle, ripple, rimple, pucker, ruffle.

v fold, double, plait, crumple, crease, pleat, wrinkle, crinkle, ripple, curl, rumple, frizzle, rimple, ruffle, pucker, corrugate; tuck, hem, gather.

adj folded.

259 furrow *n* groove, rut, scratch, streak, cut, crack, score, incision, slit; channel, gutter, trench, gulley, ditch, dike, moat, trough; ravine, valley.

v furrow, dig, plow; channel, flute, groove, incise, cut, engrave, etch, seam, cleave, score; wrinkle, knit, pucker

adj furrowed, ribbed, striated, fluted.

260 opening *n* hole, gap, aperture, orifice, perforation, pinhole, peephole, keyhole; slot, slit, rift, breach, cleft, chasm, fissure, rent; outlet, inlet, vent; portal, porch, gate, hatch, door, doorway, gateway; way, path, channel, passage.

v open, ope, gape, yawn; perforate, pierce, tap, bore, drill; mine, tunnel, dig to daylight; impale, spike, spear, gore, spit, stab, puncture, lance, stick, prick, riddle; uncover, unclose, lay bare, expose, bare, reveal; lay open, cut open, rip open, throw open.

adj open, unclosed, uncovered, exposed; ajar, wide-open, gaping, yawning; perforated, porous, reticulated, permeable; accessible, available, public.

261 closure *n* blockade, shutting up, obstruction, stoppage, clogging, sealing, plugging; contraction; constipation; culmination; cessation, completion, termination, windup; lid, top, cap, stopper, plug, barrier.

v close, plug, block up, stop up, fill up, cork up, cork, button up, stuff up, shut up, dam up; blockade, obstruct, hinder; bar, bolt, stop, seal, choke, throttle, shut.

adj closed, shut, unopened; unpierced, impervious, impermeable; impenetrable, impassable, pathless; tight, snug, airtight, unventilated, watertight, hermetically sealed.

262 perforator *n* piercer, borer, auger, drill, awl, scoop, corkscrew, probe, lancet, scalpel, needle, pin, stiletto, puncher, hole puncher, gouge; knife, spear, bayonet.

263 stopper *n* lid, cap, cover; cork, spike, stopcock, pin, plug, tap, faucet, valve, spigot, rammer, ramrod; wadding, stuffing, padding, stopping, bandage, tourniquet.

IV. Motion

264 motion *n* movement, action, activity, move, going; progress, locomotion; mobilization, mobility, movableness, motive power; unrest, restlessness; stream, flow, flux, run, course, stir; rate, pace, step, tread, stride, gait; velocity, speed.

v move, go, hie, budge, stir, pass, flit; hover around, hover about; shift, slide, glide, roll, roll on, flow, drift, stream, run, sweep along; wander, meander, browse, stroll, walk, perambulate; dodge, keep on one's toes, keep moving, hit the road, *(informal)* truck; move, impel, propel; mobilize.

adj moving, in motion, traveling, on the road; transitional, shifting, mobile, movable; mercurial, restless, unquiet, nomadic, transient.

adv under way; on the move, on the go, on the march.

265 rest *n* quiescence, stillness, quietude, calm, calmness, tranquillity, repose, serenity, peace, silence; pause, lull, cessation; stagnation, immobility, fixity.

v rest, be still, stand still, lie still, stand immobile, keep quiet, repose; remain, stay, pause, wait, mark time, hold, halt, stop short, cease, desist, discontinue, stop; stagnate, be inactive, immobilize; dwell, settle, settle down, establish roots; alight, arrive; stand fast, stand firm, stick fast; quell, becalm, hush, stay, lull, lull to sleep, tranquilize.

adj restful, quiescent, still, calm, tranquil, peaceful, undisturbed, unruffled, serene, silent; motionless, fixed, stationary; unmoved, stable, at rest, at a standstill, stock-still, sleeping, dormant, inactive, stagnant.

266 [locomotion by land] **journey** *n* traveling, travel, excursion, tour, trip, expedition, jaunt, pilgrimage; wayfaring, roving, gadding about, *(informal)* bumming around, nomadism, vagabondism; migration, immigration, moving; walk, promenade, constitutional, stroll, pere-grination, perambulation, march, stroll, saunter, jaunt outing, hike, airing; horsemanship, horseback riding; drive, driving, motoring, ride, spin; cycling, biking; procession, cavalcade, caravan, file, cortege, column.

v journey, travel, tour, take a trip; flit, take wing, *(informal)* hit the road, rove, ramble, roam, prowl, *(informal)* bum, *(informal)* bum around, range, traverse, scour the country, wander, meander, saunter, gad about; move, migrate, immigrate.

adj journeying, traveling, on the road; itinerant, peripatetic, rambling, roving, gadding, flitting, vagrant, nomadic, migratory, wayfaring.

267 [locomotion by water or air] **navigation** *n* voyage, sail, cruise, passage, boat ride; aquatics, boating, yachting, sailing, shipping.

flight, air travel, flying, gliding; aeronautics, aviation.

v navigate; sail, put to sea, embark, shove off, spread the sails, make sail, take oar; go boating, cruise, float, drift, coast; row, paddle, pull, scull, punt, steam; ride the waves.

fly, take off, take wing, take to the skies; aviate, soar, glide, fly over, plane, jet.

adj sailing, nautical, naval, maritime, seagoing, seafaring, ocean-going; afloat; navigable.

flying, jetting; aloft, in flight; aviational, aeronautical, aerial.

268 traveler *n* wayfarer, journeyer, rover, rambler, wanderer, free spirit, nomad, vagabond, bohemian, gypsy, itinerant, vagrant, tramp, hobo, straggler, waif; pilgrim, palmer, seeker, quester; voyager, passenger, tourist, sightseer, excursionist, vacationer, globe-trotter, jet-setter; immigrant, emigrant, refugee, fugitive; pedestrian, walker, cyclist, biker, rider, horsewoman, horseman, equestrian, driver.

269 mariner, flier *n* mariner, sailor, seaman, seafaring man, sea dog; pilot, skipper, captain, commander, helmsman, steersman; crew, hands, mates; navigator, flier, airman, aviator, aviatrix, pilot, skipper; astronaut, cosmonaut, spaceman.

270 transference *n* transfer, move, shift, transit, transition, passage, transmission, transport, transplantation, transposition; removal, relegation, deportation, extradition.

v transfer, transmit, transport, convey, carry, bear, pass; move, shift, conduct, convey, bring, fetch, reach; send, delegate, consign, turn over, hand over, deliver; transpose, transplant, displace, remove, relegate, deport, extradite; shovel, ladle.

adj transferable, transmittable, transmissible, transportable, movable, portable.

271 carrier *n* porter, bearer, messenger, runner, courier; postman, letter carrier; conductor, conveyor, transporter; freighter, ship, barge; train, locomotive; truck, vehicle, carriage; beast of burden.

272 vehicle *n* conveyance, carriage, transportation, rig; car, motorcar, automobile, *(informal)* wheels, truck; wagon, cart, coach, chaise, buggy; bicycle, bike, motorcycle, motorscooter; train, sleeping car, cattle car, boxcar.

273 ship *n* vessel, boat, liner, freighter, steamer, schooner, sailboat, motorboat, merchant ship, barge, tugboat, tanker, trawler, yacht, cruiser, yawl, ketch, brig, brigantine, square-rigger, sloop, cutter, launch; navy, fleet.

airplane, plane, jet, jumbo jet, aircraft, glider, helicopter, dirigible, blimp, balloon, spaceship, capsule, module, space station.

274 velocity *n* rapidity, quickness, swiftness, celerity, speed, alacrity; acceleration, pickup; spurt, rush, dash, race, flying, flight.

v move quickly, speed, hie, hasten, post, scamper, run, race, shoot, tear, whisk, sweep, rush, dash, dash off; bolt, bound, spring, dart, flit; hurry, hasten, haste, accelerate, *(informal)* turn on the juice, quicken, speed up, take off like a shot.

adj fast, speedy, swift, rapid, quick, brisk, fleet; nimble, agile, expeditious, light-footed, fast as a bullet, quick as lightning.

adv swiftly, apace, at full speed, at full gallop, posthaste.

275 slowness *n* languor, sluggishness, slackness, sloth, indolence; deliberateness, moderation, leisureliness; tardiness.

v move slowly, creep, crawl, lag, drawl, linger, loiter, saunter, trail, drag, dawdle; plod, trudge, lumber; grovel, sneak, steal, worm one's way, inch; waddle, wobble, shuffle, hobble, limp, shamble, amble, traipse, slouch, mince, mince steps, halt; flag, totter, teeter, stagger; retard, hinder, impede, obstruct; slacken, check, relax, moderate; brake, curb, slow, put on the brakes.

adj slow, slack, late, tardy; gentle, easy, unhurried, deliberate, gradual, moderate, leisurely; languid, sluggish, indolent, lazy; tedious, humdrum, dull, boring; dense, stupid.

adv slowly, leisurely; at half speed, at a snail's pace; gradually, little by little, step by step, inch by inch, bit by bit, one step at a time.

276 impulse *n* impetus, implosion, push, thrust, shove; propulsion; sudden impulse, yearning, craving; reaction, response, reflex; collision, clash, encounter, shock, bump, crash; impact; blow, stroke, knock, rap, tap, slap, smack, pat, dab; hit, whack, thwack, slam, punch, belt, kick, thump, cut, thrust, lunge.

v impel, push, urge, thrust, shove, heave, prod, shoulder, jostle, hustle, hurtle, jog, jolt; start, give a start to, set going, get going, drive; run against, bump against, butt against; collide with, run into, bang into, butt; strike, knock, bang, hit, thump, beat, slam, dash, punch, thwack, whack; batter, pelt, buffet, butt; hit, rap, slap, tap, pat, dab.

277 recoil *n* reflex, rebound, ricochet, boomerang, backfire, backlash; snap, elasticity; reverberation, resonance; reaction, response, rebuff, repulse, revulsion.

v recoil, rebound, richochet, boomerang, snap back, spring back, fly back; react, respond; reverberate, echo, quiver.

adj reactionary; elastic, backfiring.

278 direction *n* bearing, course, set, drift, tenor, trend, tendency, inclination;

tack, aim, determination, intention; points of the compass, cardinal points; line, path, road, range, line of march; alignment.

v direct, point, aim; tend toward, point toward, conduct to, go to; bend, tend, verge, incline, determine; steer for, make for, aim at, level at, set one's sights on, take aim, hold a course for, be bound for.

adj direct, straight; bound for; undeviating, unswerving.

adv toward, on the road to; hither, thither, whither; directly, straight, straightforward, point-blank, on a line with.

279 deviation *n* diversion, digression, departure from, aberration; divergence, zigzag, detour, circuit; warp, refraction; swerving.

v deviate, alter one's course, turn, bend, curve, swerve, heel, bear off; divert, deflect, shift, shunt, draw aside, crook, warp; stray, straggle, digress, ramble, rove, drift, go astray, go adrift; wander, wind, twist, meander; veer, turn aside, change direction, steer clear of, dodge.

adj deviating, errant, aberrant; discursive, desultory, loose, rambling, digressive, stray, erratic, undirected; circuitous, indirect, zigzag, roundabout, crooked.

adv astray, roundabout, wide of the mark; circuitously.

280 [going before] **precedence** *n* priority; leading, heading, the lead, van, vanguard; precursor, coming beforehand.

v precede, go before, forerun; usher in, introduce, herald; head, take the lead, lead the way; take precedence, have priority, come first, come before.

adv in advance, before, ahead, in the vanguard, in front.

281 [going after] **sequence** *n* coming after, following, sequel; shadow, dangler, train.

v follow, come in sequence, go after; attend, be attendant on, follow in the steps of, follow in the wake of, trail, shadow; pursue; lag, fall behind.

adj following; sequential.

adv behind, after; in the rear.

282 [motion forward] **progression** *n* progress, improvement proceeding, advance, advancement, headway; growth, rise, increase, development.

v proceed, advance, progress, get on, get along, gain ground, press onward, forge ahead, make headway, make progress, make strides, stride forward; grow, develop, increase, improve.

adj advancing; progressive, advanced.

adv forward, onward; forth, on, ahead.

283 [motion backward] **regression** *n* retrogression, retreat, recession, retirement, withdrawal; reflux, backwater, return, recoil; backsliding; deterioration, decrease, fall.

v regress, recede, return, revert, retreat, back out, back down, turn back, fall back, drop out, retire, withdraw; lose ground, drop off, fall behind; ebb, shrink, shy.

adj retrograde, retrogressive; regressive, refluent, reflex.

adv backwards; aboutface.

284 propulsion *n* propulsive force, impulse, push, projection, thrust, drive, impulsion, impetus; throw, fling, toss, shot, discharge.

v propel, project, throw, fling, cast, pitch, chuck, toss, heave, hurl; drive, sling, push, shove; send off, fire off, discharge, shoot, launch, let fly; put in motion, set in motion, start, get going, impel; expel.

adj propulsive.

285 traction *n* drawing, hauling, pulling, towing, towage; yank, tug, drag, jerk.

v draw, pull, haul, lug, drag, tug, tow, trail, train, take in tow; wrench, jerk, yank.

adj tractile; in tow.

286 [motion towards] **approach** *n* access, advent, advance; nearness, approximation.

v approach, near, draw near, move towards, get close to; gain on, get closer to; pursue, trail.

adj approaching; approximate; impending, imminent.

287 [motion from] **recession** *n* retirement, withdrawal; flight, removal, retreat; regression, return, falling back, regress; reaction, reversal, recoil; departure, leave-taking.

v recede, move back, go back, move away from, retire, withdraw; drift, abate, fade, wane, ebb, subside, drift away, fall back, shrink; react, revert, relapse, recoil, regress; run away, fly, avoid.

288 attraction *n* attractiveness, inclination, affinity; pull, magnetism, gravity.

v attract, draw, drag, pull, magnetize, exert force; interest, invite, engage, fascinate, lure, allure, charm, decoy, bait.

adj attractive, attracting, enticing, seductive, alluring; have pull, magnetic, gravitational.

289 repulsion *n* aversion, antipathy, dislike; repulse, rebuff.

v repel, push, back, drive away, chase away, rebuff, beat back; repulse, revolt, offend, sicken, disgust, displease, irritate.

adj repulsive, repellent, averse, repelling.

290 convergence *n* confluence, conflux, concurrence, concourse, congress, coming together, meeting, joining.

v converge, concur, come together, meet, join, unite; gather together, concentrate, center.

adj convergent, confluent, concurrent.

291 divergence *n* division, radiation, spread, severance, separation, refraction, deflection; ramification, furcation, branching, forking, detachment; deviation, aberration, disparity, difference, variance, heterogeneity.

v diverge, ramify, radiate, branch off, fork, spread, swerve, scatter, disperse; divide, separate, part, sever; vary, deviate, dissent, disagree.

adj divergent, radial, radiant, centrifugal.

292 arrival *n* advent, coming; reaching, attainment, landing, debarkation, disembarkation; reception, welcome, welcoming.

v arrive, get to, come to, reach a point, attain, complete; light, alight, dismount; land, disembark, debark, deplane, detrain.

293 departure *n* embarkation; outset, start, starting point, place of departure, point of departure; removal, exit; exodus, flight; leave-taking, valediction, *adieu,* farewell, goodbye.

v depart, go away, take one's leave, start, set out, leave, retire, quit, withdraw, absent, go, *(informal)* split, take off, *(informal)* cut out, move off, move out, ship out, pack it up; vacate, evacuate, abandon; sally, set forth, set forward, go forth; embark, set sail, put out to sea, shove off, get under way, enplane, entrain.

294 [motion into] **ingress** *n* entrance, entry; influx, intrusion, inroad, incursion, invasion, irruption, penetration, infiltration; insinuation, insertion.

v enter, come in, pour in, flow in; burst in, break in, invade, intrude; penetrate, infiltrate, insinuate oneself.

adj incoming, inbound.

295 [motion out of] **egress** *n* exit, issue; emergence, emanation; outbreak, outburst, eruption; evacuation, leakage, percolation, oozing, drainage, drain; outpouring, gush, effluence, effusion, discharge.

v emerge, emanate, issue; pass out of, come out of, pour out of, flow out of; exude, leak, ooze, drain, drip, trickle, dribble; gush, gush out, pour out, spout, flow out, discharge; escape, find vent.

adj outgoing, outward, outbound.

296 [motion into, actively] **reception** *n* admission, admittance, entry, entrée; importation, introduction, initiation, induction, absorption; ingestion, eating, drinking; suction, sucking; insertion, injection.

v give entrance to, admit, introduce, usher, initiate, induct; receive, import, bring in, ingest, absorb, imbibe.

297 [motion out of, actively] **ejection** *n* rejection, expulsion, eviction, dislodgment, banishment, exile; emission, effusion, discharge, evacuation, regurgitation, elimination.

v reject, eject, expel, evict, dislodge, banish, exile; push aside, push away, turn away, brush aside; empty, drain, clear out, clean out, purge, void, evacuate; vomit, spew, regurgitate, throw up, *(informal)* puke, retch, *(informal)* barf, belch out, burp out; discharge, eliminate, discard, get rid of, do away with, cast off, cut adrift, turn out, throw out, oust.

298 eating *n* dining, supping, taking nourishment; ingestion, chewing, mastication; imbibition, drinking, food, nourishment, nutrition, nutriment, sustenance, subsistence, provender, provisions, rations, keep, board, fare; drink, beverage, potion, draught.

v eat, feed, breakfast, lunch, dine, sup, break bread; taste, devour, wolf, swallow, gulp, bolt, gulp down, fall to, dig in; chew, masticate, bite, bite into, chomp, munch, crunch, gnaw, nibble, peck at; live on, live off, fatten, feast on.

drink, drink up, drink one's fill, quaff, *(informal)* down, chug, empty, sip.

adj eatable, edible, digestible; drinkable, potable; nutritious, nutritive.

299 excretion *n* discharge, emanation, exhalation, secretion, effusion, perspiration, sweat; evacuation, elimination, urination; hemorrhage, bleeding.

v excrete; emanate, exhale; secrete, perspire, seat; eliminate, evacuate; urinate.

300 [forcible ingress] **insertion** *n* implantation, injection, inoculation, infusion, importation, insinuation, interpolation; immersion, submersion, dip, plunge.

v insert, introduce, put in; inject, infuse, instill, inoculate, impregnate, imbue; graft, ingraft, implant, plant, bud; thrust in, stick in, shove in, ram in, stuff in, tuck in, press in, drive in; immerse, merge; dip, plunge.

301 [egress] **extraction** *n* removal, elimination, extrication, eradication, extirpation, extermination, ejection; wrench, squeezing, pulling.

v extract, draw, draw out, take out, pull out, tear out, rip out, pluck out; wring from, wrench, pull; root out, weed out, rake out, eradicate, uproot, pull up, extirpate; evolve, elicit, draw forth; extricate, remove, eliminate; squeeze out.

302 [motion through] **passage** *n* transmission; permeation, penetration, infiltration; ingress, egress; voyage, trip, tour, excursion, journey; way, route, channel,

avenue, road, path, way, thoroughfare, conduit.

v pass, pass through; penetrate, permeate, thread, go through, cut across; ford, traverse, cross; go, move, proceed; leave, go away, depart.

303 [motion beyond] **infringement** *n* transgression, trespass, encroachment, infraction.

v infringe, transgress, trespass, encroach; surpass, go beyond, shoot ahead of, overrun; overstep, overreach, overshoot; outstrip, outrun, outride, outdo; exceed, surmount, transcend, soar.

adv beyond the mark, ahead.

304 [motion short of] **shortcoming** *n* failure, falling short; default, defalcation; incompleteness, imperfection, deficiency, insufficiency, noncompletion.

v fall short, come up short, come short of, not reach; want, lack; fail, break down, collapse, come to nothing; fall through, cave in.

adj deficient, lacking, insufficient; incomplete, imperfect.

305 ascent *n* ascension; rising, rise, upgrowth; leap, jump; acclivity, hill, grade.

v ascend, rise, mount, climb upward, climb, arise; clamber, mount, scale, go up, get up; tower, soar, hover, surmount, scale the heights.

adj ascendant; rising, acclivitous.

306 descent *n* declension, inclination, declination, slope, declivity, grade, decline, drop, cliff, precipice, dip, hill; fall, falling, descending, sinking; downfall, tumble, slip, tilt, trip, lurch.

v descend, go down, drop down, come down, drop, fall, gravitate, slip, slide, settle; decline, set, sink, droop, wilt, slump; dismount, alight, get down; swoop down, stoop; tumble, trip, stumble, lurch, pitch, topple, tilt, sprawl.

adj declivitous, sloping, precipitous, steep; descending.

307 elevation *n* raising; erection, lift; upheaval; sublimation, exaltation; prominence, height.

v elevate, heighten, raise, lift, lift up, erect; set up, tilt up, rear, hoist, heave; uplift, upraise, uprear; exalt, enhance, advance; take up, drag up, fish up, drag, dredge.

adj elevated, stilted, rampant.

308 depression *n* lowering; dip, concavity; upset, overturn, overthrow; prostration, abasement, debasement, degradation; bow, curtsy, genuflection, kowtow, obeisance.

v depress, lower, let down, take down, cast down, let drop, let fall; sink, debase, bring low, abase, degrade, reduce; overthrow, overturn, upset, prostrate, level, fell; bow, curtsy, genuflect, kowtow, kneel, bend over, make obeisance.

adj depressed; at a low ebb; prostrate, horizontal.

309 leap *n* jump, hop, spring, bound, vault; dance, caper, frisk, buck.

v leap, jump, hop, spring, bound, vault, hurtle, hurdle; dance, caper, trip, skip, frisk, bob, flounce, start; trip the light fantastic toe, dance all night.

adj leaping; frisky, lively, springy.

310 plunge *n* dip, dash, rush, dive, leap; ducking, dunking, submersion, immersion.

v plunge, immerse, submerge, douse, souse, dunk, dip; dash, rush, hasten, hurry; dive, leap, jump; descend, drop, fall, hurtle over.

311 circular motion *n* circulation, circularity; turn, excursion; circumvention, circumnavigation, circling; turning; coil, corkscrew, spiral; full circle, full turn, turn, circuit, lap.

v turn, bend, wheel, turn a circle, turn around, make a U-turn, put about, make a complete circle; circle, go around, circuit, circumnavigate; whisk, twirl, twist.

adj circuitous, roundabout; circular.

312 rotation *n* revolution, gyration, circulation, roll; spinning, pirouette, convolution; whir, whirl, eddy, vortex, whirlpool, maelstrom; cyclone, tornado.

v rotate, turn, spin, revolve, wheel, whirl, twirl, spin around; pivot, swivel, circle around.

adj rotating, rotary, gyratory, revolving.

313 evolution *n* evolvement, unfolding, development.

v evolve, unfold, unfurl, unroll, unwind, develop.

adj evolutionary, evolutional.

314 [motion to and fro] **oscillation** *n* vibration, pulsation, undulation; pulse, beat, *(informal)* vibes, ripple, wave; alternation, coming and going, ebb and flow, ups and downs, flux and reflux; fluctuation, vacillation, irresolution.

v oscillate, vibrate, vacillate, swing, fluctuate, vary; undulate, wave; pulsate, beat, throb, ripple; reel, quake, quiver, quaver, shake; roll, toss, pitch; flounder, stagger, totter.

adj oscillating; undulatory; pulsating.

adv to and fro, up and down, back and forth, seesaw, zigzag, in and out, from side to side.

315 [irregular motion] **agitation** *n* stir, ripple, tremor, shake, jog, jolt, jar, jerk, shock, quiver, quaver, twitter, flicker, flutter; disquiet, perturbation, commotion, turbulence, turmoil, tumult; hubbub, bustle, fuss, ado, racket, fits; spasm, throe, throb, palpitation, convulsion, fit; disturbance, disorder, restlessness, hypertension; ferment, fermentation, ebullition, effervescence, hurly-burly; tempest, storm, groundswell, whirlpool, vortex; whirlwind, tornado, cyclone, twister.

v be agitated, shake, tremble, quiver, quaver, quake, shiver, twitter, writhe, toss, shuffle, tumble, stagger, bob, reel, sway; waggle, wriggle, dance, prance, stumble, shamble, flounder, totter, teeter, flounce, flop; throb, pulsate, beat, palpitate, go pit-a-pat; flutter, flicker, bicker, bustle; ferment, effervesce, foam, boil, bubble, simmer; agitate, shake, convulse, toss, tumble, bandy, flap, whisk, jerk, hitch, jolt, joggle, jostle, buffet, hustle, disturb, stir, shake up, churn, jounce, wallop, whip.

adj agitated, shaking, pulsating, tremulous, convulsive, jerky, shaky, throbbing.

adv by fits and starts; in convulsions, in fits.

Class III
Words Relating to Matter

I. Matter in General

316 materiality n corporeality, substantiality, flesh and blood, physicality; matter, body, substance, brute matter, physical elements, material; object, article, thing, materials.

science of matter; physics, natural philosophy, physical science, materialism.
materialist, physicist.

v materialize, embody, body in.

adj material, bodily, corporeal, physical, somatic; sensible, tangible palpable, touchable, substantial, unspiritual, materialistic.

317 immateriality n incorporeality, insubstantiality, spirituality, ineffability.

adj immaterial, incorporeal, unsubstantial, intangible, ineffable, untouchable, bodiless, unreal, unearthly, spiritual, psychical, otherworldly.

318 world n creation, nature, universe, solar system, galaxy, globe, earth, wide world, sphere, macrocosm; heavens, firmament, vault, celestial spaces, space, sky; heavenly bodies, planets, asteroids, comets, meteors, constellations.

adj worldly, mundane, terrestrial, earthly, sublunary; cosmic, celestial, heavenly, astral, solar, lunar.

adv in all creation, on the face of the earth, under the sun, here below.

319 gravity n gravitation, weight, heaviness, pull, pressure, load, burden.

v gravitate, weigh, pull, press, encumber, load, be heavy.

adj weighty, heavy, heavy as lead, ponderous, lumpish, cumbersome, burdensome, cumbrous, massive, unwieldy, like a ton of bricks.

320 levity n lightness, buoyancy, volatility; ferment, leaven, yeast.

v be light, float, swim, waft; lighten, leaven.

adj light, subtle, airy, weightless, ethereal, volatile, buoyant, feathery.

II. Inorganic Matter

321 density n solidity, solidness, impenetrability, impermeability; condensation, solidification, consolidation, concretion, coagulation, petrification, hardening, crystallization, thickening; solid body, mass, block, knot, lump, conglomerate.

v be dense; solidify, condense, consolidate, coagulate, congeal, set, cohere, crystallize, petrify, harden; condense, compress, thicken.

adj dense, solid, compact, close, thick, substantial, massive; impenetrable, impermeable, coherent, cohesive, indivisible, indissoluble, insoluble.

322 thinness n rarity, tenuity; rarefaction, expansion, dilation, inflation.

v thin, rarefy, expand, dilate, inflate.

adj thin, rare, fine, tenuous, compressible, flimsy, slight, light; unsubstantial.

323 hardness n rigidity, firmness, inflexibility, temper; induration, petrification, ossification, crystallization.

v harden, stiffen, cement, petrify, temper, ossify.

adj hard, solid, firm, inflexible, rigid, resistant, adamantine, impenetrable, strong, hard as a rock, hard as nails, tough.

324 softness n pliability, flexibility, pliancy, malleability, ductility, tractility, plasticity, flaccidity, elasticity; mollification, softening.

v soften, mollify, mash, knead, temper, bend, yield, give, relent, relax.

adj soft, tender, supple, pliant, pliable, flexible, limber, plastic, ductile, tractile, tractable, plastic, malleable, moldable, impressible, elastic; flabby, limp, flimsy, flaccid, doughy, mushy, squishy, waxy, soft as butter.

325 elasticity n springiness, spring, resilience, resiliency, give.

v be elastic, spring, give, bend, stretch; spring back, recoil,

adj elastic, tensile, springy, resilient, buoyant, rubbery.

326 inelasticity n want of elasticity, flaccidity, limpness, softness, mushiness.

adj inelastic, flaccid, limp.

327 tenacity n toughness, strength, cohesiveness, cohesion; stubbornness, obstinacy, grit.
adj tenacious, cohesive, tough, strong, resistant, gristly, stringy, gummy, adhesive, sticky, viscous, glutinous; stubborn, obstinate.

328 brittleness n fragility, frailty, breakability.
v be brittle; break, crack, snap, split, shiver, splinter, crumble, burst, fly, fly to pieces, shatter, give way.
adj brittle, fragile, breakable, frangible, delicate, frail, splintery, crisp.

329 structure n organization, constitution, anatomy, frame, framework, mold, form, architecture, construction, texture: tissue, grain, web, surface; coarseness; fineness.
adj structural, organizational, anatomical, anatomic, architectural textural: fine, delicate, subtle, gossamery, filmy; coarse, homespun, rough, woolly.

330 granularity n pulverulence, sandiness, graininess, friability; powder, dust, sand, grit, grain, particle, crumb, fine powder.
reduction to powder; pulverization, granulation, disintegration, abrasion, attenuation, filing.
tools for pulverization: mill, grater, rasp, file, mortar and pestle, grinder, grindstone.
v grind, pulverize, granulate, grate, scrape, file, abrade, rasp, pound, beat, crush, crumble, disintegrate.
adj granular, powdery, mealy, floury, branny, dusty, sandy, arenose, gritty, crumbly.

331 friction n attrition, rubbing, abrasion, elbow-grease.
v rub, scratch, scrape, scrub, fray, rasp, curry, scour, polish, rub out, erase, grind.

332 [absence or prevention of friction] **lubrication** n anointment, oiling, greasing, coating, lathering.
v lubricate, oil, grease, lather; anoint.

333 fluidity n liquidity, liquefaction, solubility, fluency.
v be fluid, flow, run, pour, stream; liquefy.
adj fluid, liquid, watery, serous, sappy, juicy, soluble; fluent, unstable.

334 gaseity n gaseousness, vaporousness, volatility.
adj gaseous, vaporous, airy, etheric, voluble, evaporable; flatulent, windy.

335 liquefaction n liquefying, deliquescence, melting, thawing, solubleness, dissolution.
v liquefy, melt, thaw, dissolve.
adj deliquescent, soluble, dissolvable, solvent.

336 vaporization n atomization, steaming, boiling, distillation, gasification, evaporation.
v vaporize, atomize, distill, evaporate, gasify, boil, steam.
adj vapory, vaporous, volatile, evaporable, gaseous.

337 water n liquid, serum, lymph, fluid, aqua.
v add water, water, wet, moisten, dip, immerse, submerge, plunge, douse, dunk, drown, soak, steep, wash, sprinkle, splash, souse, drench; dilute; deluge, inundate.
adj watery, aqueous, liquid, fluid, wet, moist, humid, soggy, sodden, rheumy, hydrous, juicy, lush, succulent; waterish, adulterated, transparent, thin, weak, tasteless, insipid, vapid, flat, feeble, dull.

338 air n atmosphere, stratosphere, the open, open air, blue sky, sky; weather, climate, clime; ventilation, current, breath of air, wind, breeze.
v air, ventilate, fan, aerate, freshen, refresh, cool.
adj airy, open, exposed, breezy, windy; flatulent; effervescent; atmospheric, aerial, ethereal, aeriform.
adv in the open air, out in the open, out of doors, in the wide open spaces, under the stars.

339 moisture n dampness, humidity, dankness, dew, wetness, condensation; perspiration.
v moisten, sponge, damp, bedew, wet, soak, saturate, sodden, sop, drench; perspire.
adj moist, damp, watery, humid, dank, dewy, muggy, juicy, wet; soggy, mushy, marshy, muddy.

340 dryness *n* drought, aridity; dessication, drainage, evaporation.

v dry, dry up, soak up, sponge, swab, wipe; drain, parch, evaporate.

adj dry, arid, parched, juiceless, sapless, dry as a bone.

341 ocean *n* sea, main, deep, brine, salt water, waters, high seas, waves, billows, great waters, tides.

adj oceanic, marine, maritime, seagoing, oceanographic.

342 land *n* earth, ground, dry land, mother earth, *terra firma;* continent, inlands, interior, shore, coast, terrain, dirt, soil, rock, chalk; real estate, lands, grounds, acres, acreage.

v land, alight, arrive, disembark, come ashore, go ashore, tie up, set foot on dry land.

adj earthy, terrestrial, earthly, alluvial, landed, territorial, continental.

adv ashore, on land, on dry land.

343 gulf, lake *n* gulf, bay, inlet, estuary, bayou, arm, fjord, firth, lagoon, cove, mouth, natural harbor, sound, straits.

lake, loch, lough, mere, tarn, basin, reservoir, lagoon, pond, pool.

344 plain *n* plateau, champaign, grassland, pasture, pasturage, meadow, flat, moor, heath, tundra, prairie, lowland, steppe, field, desert, basin, fields, grounds.

345 marsh *n* swamp, morass, moss, fen, bog, quagmire, slough, wash, mud.

adj marshy, swampy, boggy, quaggy, soft, muddy, sloppy, squashy.

346 island *n* isle, islet, atoll, reef, ait, key, bar, holm, ridge, eyot, archipelago.

adj insular, sea-girt.

347 [fluid in motion] **stream** *n* stream, etc. (of water) **348;** (of air) **249.** *v* flow, etc., **348;** blow, etc., **349.**

348 [water in motion] **river** *n* running water, jet, spurt, squirt, spout, splash, rush, gush, torrent; fall, cascade, inundation, deluge; rain, rainfall, storm; trickle, drizzle, shower; stream, course, flux, flow, flowing, current, tide, race; spring, rill, rivulet, stream, river, tributary; rapids, flood, whirlpool, maelstrom, vortex, eddy; wave, billow, surge, swell, ripple, surf, breaker, white caps,

rough seas, rolling seas, choppy seas; irrigation, pump, hose.

v flow, run, gush, pour, spout, roll, jet, well issue; drop, drip, dribble, drizzle, trickle, stream, overflow, inundate, deluge, flow over, splash, swash; gurgle, murmur, babble, bubble, sputter, spurt, regurgitate; ooze, flow out, squeeze; rain, rain hard, rain cats and dogs, rain in torrents, rain in buckets; flow into, open into, drain into; pour, pour out, shower down, irrigate, drench, spill.

adj fluent, tidal, streamy, showery, rainy, trickly, drizzly, bubbly.

349 [air in motion] **wind** *n* draft, air, breath of air, puff, whiff, zephyr, drift, blow; fresh wind, stiff breeze, keen blast, trade wind, gust, blast, breeze, squall, gale, storm, tempest, hurricane, whirlwind, tornado, twister, cyclone, monsoon.

v blow, waft, blow hard, blow great guns, stream, gust, blast, storm; respire, breathe, pant, puff, gasp, wheeze, cough; fan, ventilate, inflate, pump, blow up.

adj windy, drafty, breezy, stormy, tempestuous, cyclonic.

350 [channel for the passage of water] **conduit** *n* channel, duct, aqueduct, canal, trough, gutter, dike, main, gully, moat, ditch, drain, sewer, culvert, sough, siphon, pipe, tube, hose, funnel, tunnel, artery, spout, floodgate, watergate, sluice, lock, valve.

351 [channel for the passage of air] **airpipe** *n* tube, shaft, flue, chimney, funnel, vent, hole, windpipe, duct.

352 semiliquidity *n* viscosity, adhesiveness, stickiness, glutinosity, pastiness.

v thicken, mash, squash, churn, beat up, blend.

adj semiliquid, semifluid; milky, muddy, creamy, slushy, starchy, gummy, gluey, sticky, slimy, oozy, thick, succulent, viscous, viscid, glutinous, adhesive, clammy.

353 [mixture of air and water] **bubble. cloud** *n* bubble, foam, froth, head, lather, suds, spray, surf, yeast; effervescence, fermentation, bubbling, boiling, gurgling, foaming.

cloud, vapor, fog, mist, haze, steam;

nebula, nebulosity, cloudiness, opacity, dimness.

v bubble, boil, foam, froth, gurgle, lather, effervesce, ferment, fizzle.

cloud, fog, mist, steam, shadow, darken, cast over, steam up.

adj bubbly, foamy, frothy; effervescent.

cloudy, foggy, misty, hazy, steamy.

354 pulpiness *n* pulp, paste, dough, curd; fleshiness, fattiness, sponginess.

v pulp, mash, squeeze, juice, squash.

adj pulpy, pasty, doughy, fleshy, meaty, fatty.

355 unctuousness *n* unctuosity, oiliness, greasiness, lubricity; lubrication, ointment, grease, oil, anointment.

v oil, grease, lubricate.

adj unctuous, oily, greasy, oleaginous, slippery, slimy, slick.

356 oil *n* fat, butter, cream, grease, tallow, suet, lard, dripping, blubber; soap, wax; petroleum, gasoline, kerosene, propane, naphtha; vegetable oil, salad oil, olive oil, linseed oil; ointment, unguent, liniment, salve, balm.

356a resin *n* rosin, gum, wax, amber, ambergris, bitumen, pitch, tar, asphalt; varnish, lacquer, shellac, mastic, sealing wax, putty.

v resin, rosin; varnish, shellac, lacquer, overlay.

adj resinous, gummy, waxy.

III. Organic Matter

357 animate matter *n* nature, natural world, animated nature, living beings, organisms, organic remains, animal life, plant life, fauna, flora; protoplasm, cell.

science of living beings: biology, natural history, zoology, botany, anatomy, physiology, organic chemistry.

naturalist, biologist, zoologist, botanist.

adj animate, organic.

358 inanimate matter *n* mineral world, mineral kingdom, inorganic matter, brute matter.

science of the mineral kingdom: mineralogy, geology, metallurgy.

adj inanimate, inorganic, mineral.

359 life *n* existence, being; animation, vigor, vivacity, vitality, energy, vital spark, vital flame, lifeblood, spirit, soul; respiration, breath, breath of life; nourishment, nutriment, staff of life.

v be alive, live, breathe, respire, exist, subsist; be born, come into the world, see the light; quicken, revive, come to; give birth to, bring to life, vitalize; vivify, reanimate; keep alive, *(informal)* keep going, *(informal)* hang in there.

adj alive, live, vigorous, vivacious, vital, energetic, lively, alive and kicking, active.

360 death *n* decease, demise, expiration, passing, dissolution, departure, release, rest, quietus, fall; end, cessation, loss of life, extinction, dying, mortality, doom, finale, stop; last breath, final gasp, death rattle, death agonies, hand of death, dying day, *rigor mortis;* decay, fatality, natural causes, death blow.

v die, decease, pass away, pass on, perish, expire, depart, dissolve; cease, end, vanish, disappear; fail, subside, fade, sink, fall, decline, wither, decay; be taken, yield, give in, breathe one's last, end one's days, depart this life, be no more, drop off, pop off, drop dead, drop down dead, break one's neck, give up the ghost, shuffle off the mortal coil, go the way of all flesh, turn to dust, *(informal)* kick the bucket, *(informal)* go out like a light, *(informal)* croak.

adj dead, lifeless, extinct, defunct, late, gone, no more, dead and gone, dead as a door nail; deadly, fatal, lethal.

361 [destruction of life; violent death] **killing** *n* murder, homicide, assassination, slaughter, bloodshed, carnage, butchery, massacre, holocaust; suffocation, strangulation, garrote, hanging, electrocution, gassing, drawing and quartering; suicide, regicide, parricide, matricide, fratricide, infanticide; death blow, finishing stroke, *coup de grace,* execution; suicide; slaughtering, hunting, coursing, shooting, fishing; butcher, slayer, murderer, executioner, assassin, cutthroat, thug, guerilla, saboteur, garroter.

v kill, put to death, murder, slaughter, butcher, massacre, execute, behead, decapitate, guillotine, dispatch, *(informal)* waste; *(informal)* wipe out, strangle, garrote, hang, throttle, choke, stifle, suffocate, smother, asphyxiate, drown, gas, electrocute, stab, bayonet, cut, cut to pieces, cut to ribbons, mutilate, run through, put to the sword, shoot, gun down, do away with, *(informal)* blow away; hunt, spear; cut off, nip in the bud, cut down, give no quarter, decimate; commit suicide, destroy oneself, blow one's brains out, put an end to oneself.

adj murderous, homicidal, bloodthirsty, bloody, gory; mortal, fatal, lethal, deadly, deathly; suicidal.

362 corpse *n* body, remains, carcass, corse, cadaver, empty vessel, bones, skeleton, relics, mortal remains, mortal coil, clay, dust, ashes, earth, carrion, fodder, food for worms, shade, ghost.

adj corpselike, cadaverous.

363 interment *n* burial, sepulture, entombment, inhumation; cremation; funeral, funeral rites, obsequies, wake; knell, death bell, dirge, elegy; shroud, winding sheet, grave clothes; coffin, shell, sarcophagous, urn, pall, bier, catafalque, hearse; grave, pit, sepulchre, tomb, vault, crypt, catacomb, mausoleum, cemetery, burial ground, mortuary, graveyard, charnel house, morgue; monument, gravestone, tombstone, headstone, *memento mori;* exhumation, disinterment, autopsy, post mortem examination.

v inter, bury, lay in the grave, lay to rest, lay in the ground, consign to the grave, entomb; lay out, mummify, embalm; cremate; exhume, disinter, unearth.

adj burial, funeral, funeral, mortuary, sepulchral, cinerary.

364 animality *n* corporality, animal life, living being, flesh, flesh and blood; physique, strength, vigor, vitality.

adj animalistic, bodily, corporeal, fleshly.

365 vegetation *n* vegetable life, growth, plant life.

adj vegetative; rank, dense, lush, fecund.

366 animal *n* animal kingdom, brute creation, fauna; beast, brute, creature, living thing, creeping thing, dumb animal; mammal, quadruped, bird, reptile, fish, crustacean, shellfish, mollusk,

worm, insect; flocks and herds, wild animals, domestic animals, livestock, game, beasts of the field, fowls of the air.

adj animal, animalistic, zoological.

367 vegetable *n* vegetable kingdom, flora, plant life, flowerage, herbage, shrubbery, foliage, leafage, leaves, foliation, verdure, greens; tree, shrub, bush, creeper, herb, fruit, grass.

v vegetate, germinate, shoot, sprout, shoot up, grow, swell, spring up, develop, increase, flourish, blossom, bloom.

adj vegetable, vegetal, vegetative, leguminous, herbal, herbaceous, botanic, verdant.

368 [science of animals] **zoology** *n* morphology, zoography, embryology, anatomy; comparative anatomy, animal physiology, comparative physiology, anthropology, ornithology, icthyology, paleontology, entomology.

adj zoological.

369 [science of plants] **botany** *n* phytology, vegetable physiology, dendrology; flora, botanic garden.

adj botanical, herbal, horticultural.

370 [management of animals] **ranching** *n* breeding, raising; taming, domestication; veterinary science.

v ranch, raise, breed; tame, domesticate, train, housebreak; cage, bridle, restrain.

adj bred; tame, domestic, domesticated, housebroken.

371 [management of plants] **agriculture** *n* farming, cultivation, husbandry, tillage; agronomy, agrobiology, agrology, agronomics; gardening, horticulture, floriculture, landscaping, arboriculture; forestry.

v cultivate, till, till the soil, work the land, farm, garden, sow, seed, plant; reap, mow, cut; plow, plough, harrow, rake, weed, hoe, lop; garden, landscape.

adj agricultural, agrarian; arable, fertile.

372 mankind *n* human race, man, woman, humankind, human species, humanity, mortality, people, human being, person, personage, individual, creature, fellow creature, fellow man, mortal, body, soul, somebody, someone, one, party, head, hand, heart.

people, persons, folk, public, society, community, group, general public, society of men, civilization, commonwealth, commonweal, body politic, human community, population, millions, multitudes.

adj human, mortal, personal, individual; social, national, civic, public; cosmopolitan, humanitarian.

373 man *n* make, manhood, masculinity, he, him; gentleman, sir, mister, Mr., master, swain, fellow, chap, boy.

male animal: cock, drake, gander, dog, boar, stag, hart, buck, stallion, tomcat, billygoat, ram, bull, ox; gelding, steer.

adj male, masculine, manly.

374 woman *n* female; womanhood, femininity, she, her; lady, gentlewoman, madam, madame, miss, *(informal)* ma'am, Ms., Mrs., matron, girl.

female animal: hen, bitch, sow, doe, roe, mare, nannygoat, ewe, cow.

adj female, feminine, womanly.

375 sensibility *n* sensation, sensitiveness, feeling, responsiveness, impressibility; sensation, impression, touch; consciousness.

v be sensible, be sensitive to, feel, touch, perceive; render sensible, sharpen, cultivate, stir, excite, sensitize; cause sensation, impress, excite an impression, stir.

adj sensitive, sensible, sensuous; perceptive, sentient, responsive, susceptible, conscious, aware, alive, acute, sharp, keen, vivid, lively.

adv to the quick.

376 insensibility *n* lack of feeling, obtuseness, paralysis, numbness, anesthesia; insusceptibility, unresponsiveness, unconsciousness.

v be insensible; render insensible, blunt, pall, numb, benumb, paralyze, deaden, freeze, anesthetize; cloy, stuff, satiate, drown; stupefy, stun.

adj insensible, senseless, unsusceptible, unresponsive, insensitive, numb, hard, dead; dull, dense, thick, obtuse, unperceptive; anesthetic, paralytic.

377 pleasure *n* bodily pleasure, sensuality, sensuousness, physical gratification, sex, sexuality, sensual delight, ecstasy, orgasm, climax; titillation, teasing; comfort, ease, relish, delight, joy, luxury, luxuriousness, pleasure, lap of luxury.

v feel pleasure, receive pleasure, enjoy, relish, revel in, bask in, swim in, luxuriate, feast on, wallow in, gloat over, *(informal)* dig, *(informal)* get off on, *(informal)* be turned on, *(informal)* get into; give pleasure, *(informal)* turn on, thrill, excite.

adj pleasurable, sensual, sensuous, sexual, voluptuous, luxurious, ecstatic, orgasmic, climactic; agreeable, comfortable, cordial, delightful, joyful; palatable, sweet, tasty; fragrant; melodious, lovely.

adv in comfort, in ecstasy, on a bed of roses.

378 pain *n* suffering, dolor, ache, aching, smart, shoot, shooting, twinge, twitch, gripe, grip, hurt, cut, sore, soreness, tenderness, discomfort, malaise, disease; spasm, cramp, crick, stitch, convulsion, throe, throb, pang; torment, torture, rack, anguish, agony.

v feel pain, suffer, undergo pain, ache, smart, bleed, tingle, shoot, twinge, twitch, writhe, wince, hurt; inflict pain, hurt, chafe, sting, bite, gnaw, gripe, pinch, tweak, grate, gall, fret, prick, pierce, wring, convulse; torment, torture, wrack, agonize.

adj painful, dolorous, sore, tender, raw, uncomfortable; convulsive, torturous.

379 touch *n* contact, feeling, tactility, palpability, impact, feel, sensation; manipulation, handling, rubbing, massaging, fondling, fingering, kneading, stroking, brushing, grazing over.

v touch, feel, handle, finger, fondle, thumb, paw, grab, rub, massage, knead, stroke, brush, manipulate, run the fingers over, graze over.

adj tactual, tactile, palpable.

380 sensations of touch *n* itching, tickling, titillation, scratching, pricking, stinging.

v itch, tingle, creep, thrill, prick, scratch, sting.

adj itching; ticklish, scratchy, itchy.

381 numbness *n* physical insensibility, lack of feeling, deadness.

v benumb, anesthetize, deaden, dull, drug.

adj numb, dull, benumbed, insensible, unfeeling, frozen, drugged, dead, deadened, dulled.

382 heat *n* warmth, caloricity, caloric, temperature; glow, flush, warmth, intensity, ardor, passion, fever, fervor, zeal; fire, spark, flame, blaze.

v be hot, glow, flush, sweat, swelter, smoke, stew, simmer, seethe, boil, burn, broil, blaze, flame; smolder, parch, fume, pant; heat, warm, thaw, defrost; stimulate, stir, animate, arouse.

adj hot, warm, mild, genial, tepid, lukewarm, unfrozen; heated, torrid, sultry, burning, fiery; sunny, tropical, suffocating, stifling, sweltering, oppressive, reeking, baking; fiery, incandescent, ebullient, glowing, smoking, blazing, on fire, afire, in flames, aflame, ablaze; ardent, fervent, fervid, angry, furious, vehement, intense, excited, excitable, irascible, animated, violent, passionate.

383 cold *n* coldness, iciness, frigidity, chilliness, coolness.

v be cold, shiver, quake, shake, tremble, shudder, quiver; chill, freeze, refrigerate.

adj cold, chilly, chill, cool, frigid, gelid, frozen, freezing, bitter, bitter cold, numbing, nipping, cutting, shivering, bleak, raw, frost-bitten, icy, glacial, frosty, wintry, hibernal, arctic, polar; impassionate, unemotional, apathetic, unresponsive, unsympathetic, stoical, unfeeling, indifferent, coldblooded, heartless, imperturbable; polite, formal, reserved, hostile; deliberate, depressing, dispiriting, disheartening.

adj coldly, bitterly.

384 calefaction *n* heating, melting, fusion, liquefaction, combustion; cauterization; calcination; incineration, cremation; carbonization.

v heat, warm, chafe; fire, set fire to, set on fire, kindle, light, ignite, rekindle; melt, thaw, fuse, liquefy; burn, inflame, roast, broil, toast, cook, fry, grill, singe, parch, bake, scorch; brand,

cauterize, sear, burn in; boil, digest, stew, sauté, cook, scald, parboil, simmer; take fire, catch fire.

adj heated, warmed, fired, burnt, scorched; molten; flammable, combustible, volcanic.

385 refrigeration *n* cooling, congelation, glaciation, icing; solidification, hardening.

v refrigerate, keep cold, chill, ice, congeal, freeze; cool, fan, refresh; benumb, starve, pinch, nip, cut, pierce, bite; quench, put out, stamp out, extinguish.

adj cooled, frozen, chilled; incombustible, inflammable, fireproof.

386 furnace *n* oven, stove, range; hearth, heater, kiln, oil burner, space heater, blast furnace, forge, fire place, fiery furnace.

387 refrigerator *n* ice box, fridge, ice chest, frigidaire, cold storage, freezer, ice house.

388 fuel *n* firing, combustible; coal, hard coal, anthracite, bituminous coal, soft coal, carbon, coke, charcoal; wood, firewood, kindling, brushwood, log, cinder, ember, ash; turf, peat, fuel, oil, fossil fuel, petroleum, gasoline, kerosene; gas, natural gas, propane; electricity; unclear power; solar energy; waterpower, windpower.

v fuel, feed, stoke, fire; power.

adj carbonaceous; combustible, flammable, burnable.

389 thermometer *n* thermometograph, thermoscope, thermostat, telethermometer, pyrometer, calorimeter, glass, mercury.

390 taste *n* flavor, savor, sensation, gusto, relish; smack, smatch, tang, aftertaste; morsel, bit, sip.

v taste, flavor, savor, smatch, smack; tickle the palate, tickle the tastebuds; smack the lips.

adj tasty, savory, flavory, flavorful, flavored; palatable, digestible, *(informal)* edible.

391 tastelessness *n* insipidity; blandness, flatness, unsavoriness.

v be tasteless.

adj tasteless, insipid, bland, flat,

weak, mild, vapid, wishy-washy, *(informal)* plastic, pasty.

392 pungency *n* piquancy, poignancy, tang, bite, nip, sharpness, acridity, bitterness, hotness, sourness, unsavoriness.

v be pungent; make pungent, season, spice, salt, pepper, pickle, brine, devil, smoke, curry.

adj pungent, strong, full-flavored, seasoned, highly seasoned, spiced; sharp, biting, nippy, acrid, bitter, sour, stinging, spicy, salty, peppery, piquant, hot; unsavory.

393 condiment *n* seasoning, flavoring, sauce, spice, relish; salt, pepper.

v season.

394 savoriness *n* flavor, flavorfulness, taste, tastiness, relish, piquancy, zest, tang, delectability, palatability.

v be savory, tickle the palate, taste good, taste great; savor, enjoy, appreciate, relish, like, taste.

adj savory, good, tasty, palatable, nice, dainty, delectable, flavorful, appetizing, delicate, delicious, exquisite, rich, luscious, full-flavored, pungent, ambrosial.

395 unsavoriness *n* tastelessness, flavorlessness, blandness; acridness, sourness.

v be unsavory, be unpalatable, taste bad, sicken, disgust, pall, nauseate, turn the stomach, make one sick.

adj unsavory, tasteless, flavorless, bland, flat; bad tasting, ill-flavored, acrid, bitter, sour, unpalatable, inedible, offensive, repulsive, nasty, vile, sickening, nauseous, loathsome, unpleasant, awful.

396 sweetness *n* sugariness, saccharinity, syrupiness, stickiness.

v sweeten, sugar, candy.

adj sweet, sugary, syrupy, honeyed, saccharine, candied, sticky gooey, luscious, lush, cloying; sweetened.

397 sourness *n* acridity, tartness, sharpness, vinegariness, acerbity, acidity.

v sour, acidify, acerbate, curdle, acidulate, ferment, spoil.

adj sour, acid, bitter, tart, sharp, vinegary, acidulous, astringent, acerbic, acrid; fermented, rancid, bad, spoiled, turned, curdled, gone bad; styptic, hard, rough.

398 odor *n* smell, scent; effluvium; exhalation, emanation; fume, essence, redolence.

v have an odor, smell, smell of, give out a smell; smell, scent, sniff, snuff, inhale.

adj odorous, odoriferous, smelly, strong smelling, redolent, pungent.

399 inodorousness *n* absence of smell, odorlessness.

v be inodorous, not smell, have no odor, be odorless.

adj odorless, scentless, unsmelling.

400 fragrance *n* aroma, redolence, perfume, sweet smell, sweet scent, smell.

v be fragrant, smell sweet, have a perfume, scent, perfume.

adj fragrant, aromatic, redolent, spicy, scented, perfumed, sweet scented, sweet smelling, odoriferous, odorific.

401 fetor *n* bad smell, bad odor, foul smell, offensive smell, stink, stench, fume, foulness, fetidness, rancidity, rankness, fustiness, mustiness.

v have a bad smell, smell bad, smell rotten, smell, stink, reek.

adj fetid, strong smelling, bad, strong, fulsome, offensive, rank, rancid, noisome, mephitic, miasmic, musty, fusty, foul, rotten, putrid, reeking, stinking, stinky, suffocating, nauseating, nauseous, *(informal)* gross.

402 sound *n* noise, tone, pitch, sound vibrations, strain, sonority, sonorousness, twang, intonation, cadence; audibility, resonance, voice.

science of sound: acoustics, phonology, phonetics, electronic sound, reproduction.

v sound, make a noise; give out sound, emit sound; resound, echo.

adj sounding, sonorous, resonant, audible, distinct.

403 silence *n* stillness, quiet, peace, hush, lull, quiescence, dead silence; muteness, speechlessness, taciturnity.

v silence, still, hush, stifle, muffle, stop, muzzle, gag; be silent, hold one's tongue, shut up, keep quiet, be still.

adj silent, quiet, still calm, noiseless, soundless, hushed, quiescent; mute, speechless, taciturn; solemn, soft, deathlike, awful, silent as the grave.

adv silently.

404 loudness *n* loud noise, power, resonance, thunderousness, roaring, vociferousness, clamorousness; din, clang, clangor, clamor, noise, roar, uproar, hubbub, boom, racket, outcry; blast, peal, swell, flourish of trumpets, boom; thunder, explosion.

v be loud, peal, swell, clang, boom, thunder, fulminate, roar, resound, bellow, scream, holler, shout; ring in the ears, pierce the ears, split the eardrums, stun, deafen; shake, awake.

adj loud, noisy, vociferous, resounding, clamorous, deafening, stentorian, boisterous, tumultuous, sonorous, deep, full, powerful, thundering, ear-splitting, piercing, uproarious, obstreperous, shrill, sharp.

adv loudly, noisily, at the top of one's voice, at the top of one's lungs, aloud.

405 faintness *n* faint sound, whisper, breath, undertone, murmur, hum; inaudibility; hoarseness.

v whisper, breathe, murmur, hum, mutter, speak softly, speak in low tones.

adj faint, whispered, indistinct, dim, inaudible, barely audible, low, stifled, muffled, murmured, muted; gentle, soft, languid, floating, flowing; hoarse, husky.

406 [sudden and violent sounds] **snap** *n* rap, thud, burst, explosion, detonation, discharge, firing, salvo, pop, bang, blast.

v rap, snap, tap, knock, click, clash, crack, crackle, crash, beat.

407 [repeated and protracted sounds] **roll** *n* drumming, tapping, rumbling, grumbling; dingdong, whirring, droning; ratatat, rubadub, pitapat; quaver, quiver, clutter, racket; peal of bells; reverberation.

v roll, drum, rumble, grumble, rattle, clatter, patter, clack; hum, trill, shake; chime, peal, toll; tick, beat.

408 resonance *n* ring, ringing, chime, clang, clangor, boom, roll, roar, rumble, thunder, vibrato, timbre, twang, vibration, reverberation, tintinnabulation, booming, quaver, ding-dong, echoing, sonorousness.

v resound, reverberate, re-echo; ring, jingle, chink, clink; gurgle, echo, ring in the ear.

adj resonant, resounding, reverberant, reverberating; deep-toned, deep-sounding.

408a nonresonance *n* dead sound, thud, thump, muffled, drums, cracked bell; damper, mute, muffler.

v sound dead, thud, thump; muffle, dampen, mute.

adj nonresonant, dampened, muted, muffled, deadened; dead.

409 [hissing sounds] **sibilation** *n* hissing, wheezing, buzzing, zipping, whooshing; high note.

v hiss, buzz, whiz, wheeze, whoosh, zip, rustle, whistle, fizzle; squash, sneeze.

adj sibilant; hissing, wheezy.

410 [harsh sounds] **stridency** *n* discord, dissonance, harshness, raucousness, atonality, clashing, grinding, grating, rasping, sharpness, creaking, shrillness.

v creak, grate, jar, jangle, clank, clink, grid, grate; scream, yelp.

adj strident, sharp, high, acute, shrill, atonal, unharmonious, unmusical, dissonant, discordant, cacophonous; piercing, ear-piercing, cracked; creaking, harsh, coarse, hoarse, rough, gruff, grating, jarring, guttural, squawking, acute, scratching, croaking, rasping, sour, clashing.

411 cry *n* shout, scream, yell, shriek, roar, howl, wail; exclamation, outcry, clamor, vociferation; hubbub, hullabaloo, chorus, hue and cry; entreaty, appeal, solicitation, plea, plaint, prayer, crying, weeping, wailing, sobbing, lament, whimper, whimpering, tears, moaning.

v cry, roar, shout, bawl, brawl, hoop, whoop, yell, bellow, howl, scream, screech, shriek, squeak, squeal, whine, whimper, wail, weep, sob, moan, lament; cheer, hoot; grumble, groan, complain; vociferate, raise one's voice, sing out, cry out, yell out, exclaim, holler, shout at the top of one's lungs.

adj crying, clamorous; vociferous; solicitous; stentorian.

412 [animal sounds] **ululation** *n* howling, crying, belling, screeching, singing, growling, purring.

v cry, roar, bellow, bark, yelp, yap, growl, snarl, howl, bay, grunt, snort, neigh, bray, mew, purr, caterwaul, bleat, low, moo, squeak, oink, baa, crow, croak, screech, caw, coo, gobble, quack, cackle, gaggle, chuck, cluck, clack, chirp, chirrup, twitter, cuckoo, hum, buzz, hiss, blatter.

413 melody. concord *n* melodiousness, tunefulness, sweet sounds, mellifluence, musicalness, euphony; timbre, tone color, pitch; tune song, aria, theme, measure, plainsong, canticle, strain, lay.

harmony, harmoniousness; rhythm, meter; symphony, euphony, consonance, attunement, modulation, syncopation; counterpoint, polyphony; concordance, pleasing combination.

v harmonize, chime, symphonize, blend; tune, accord.

adj melodious, musical, tuneful, melodic, lyrical, euphonious, singing, ringing, sweet-sounding, euphonic, mellifluous, dulcet, mellow, clear, sweet, rich, soft, silvery, agreeable, pleasing.

concordant, harmonious, agreeing, symphonious, suiting, congenial, blending, synchronized, consistent, in rapport, in unison, confluent, conjoined, symmetrical, proportionate, consonant, compatible.

414 discord *n* dissonance, atonality; harshness; racket, noise, inharmoniousness.

v be discordant; jar, grate.

adj discordant, dissonant, atonal, harsh; out of tune, tuneless, unmelodious, inharmonious, unmusical; jarring, grating, cacophonous, screeching.

415 music *n* sweet sounds, pleasing sounds, harmonious sounds, melody, song, tune, strain, air, harmony; classical music, popular music, folk music, jazz, electronic music; orchestral music, instrumental music, symphonic music, chamber music; ragtime, reggae, swing, bebop, bop, barrelhouse, rock; pop music, vocal music, choral music, solo, duet, duo, sonata, trio, quartet, quintet, sextet, septet, octet.

v make music, perform; compose.

adj musical, lyrical; instrumental, orchestral, symphonic, vocal, choral, operatic.

416 musician [performance of music] *n* artist, performer, concert artist, player, soloist, instrumentalist, vocalist, accompanist, singer, minstrel; symphony orchestra, orchestra, chamber orchestra, band, rock and roll band, group, combo, ensemble, chamber group, quartet, trio; chorus, choir, vocal group.

v make music, play, perform, strike up, concertize, execute, accompany, present the music, solo, improvise, play the notes; sing, croon, warble, vocalize, spin a melody.

adj musical, instrumental, vocal, choral, operatic; lyrical, harmonious, brilliant, sharp, incisive.

417 musical instruments *n* orchestra, band, brass band, marching band, military band, ensemble, group; strings, plucked instruments, bowed instruments, hammered instruments; woodwinds, winds, tubed instruments, reed instruments, brass instruments; percussion; synthesizer.

418 hearing *n* audition, auscultation, listening, perception, audibility, ear; regarding, attending, heeding.

hearer, auditor, listener; eavesdropper.

v hear, listen, attend, lend an ear, bend an ear, *(informal)* tune in, give a hearing to, give audience to, prick up one's ears, be all ears; overhear, eavesdrop; heed, regard.

adj hearing, auditory, auricular.

419 deafness *n* hardness of hearing, inaudibility.

v be deaf, not hear; turn a deaf ear to, plug up one's ears; deafen, stun, split the eardrums.

adj deaf, stone-deaf, hard of hearing; deafened, stunned; unheeding, inattentive.

420 light *n* ray, beam, stream, gleam, streak; sunbeam, moonbeam, aurora, dawn, sunrise, day-break, day, daylight, light of day, sunshine, broad daylight, glow, glint, glimmering; sun, moon; flush, halo, glory, aureole; spark, scintilla, scintillation, flash, blaze, coruscation; flame, lightening, flare; luster, sheen, shimmer, reflection, refraction; brightness, brilliancy, splendor, effulgence, radiance, illumination, radiation, luminosity, lucidity.

science of light: optics, photography, radioactivity.

v shine, glow, glitter, glisten, gleam, beam, flare, flare up, glare, flash, glimmer, shimmer, flicker, sparkle, scintillate, coruscate, flash, blaze; light, reflect, dazzle, bedazzle, daze, radiate; lighten, enlighten, light, irradiate, shed light upon, cast light upon, illuminate, illumine, kindle, fire.

adj luminous, lucent; light, bright, vivid, splendid, resplendent, lustrous, shiny, radiant; sheeny, glossy, glassy, sunny, burnished; cloudless, clear, unclouded; effulgent, blazing, ablaze, phosphorescent, aglow; iridescent.

421 darkness *n* blackness; obscurity, doom, murkiness, murk; duskiness, dusk, dimness; night, midnight, dead of night; shade, shadow, umbra, penumbra; obscuration, adumbration, extinction, eclipse, total eclipse.

v be dark; darken, obscure, shade, dim, shadow, overcast, cloud, becloud; extinguish, put out, blow out, snuff out.

adj dark, obscure, black, pitch black, nocturnal, overcast, cloudy, darkened; dingy, lurid, murky, gloomy, oppressive; shadowy, shady, umbrageous.

422 dimness *n* duskiness, shadowiness, gloominess, cloudiness, mist, mistiness, haze, haziness, fogginess, paleness, shade, nebulosity, gray, grayness.

v be dim, grow dim, darken, obscure, adumbrate, becloud, cloud, shadow, shade, eclipse, cloud over; blur, dull, fade, pale; glimmer, twinkle, flutter, flicker, waver.

adj dim, dull, dingy, lackluster, darkish, darkened, gray, dark, faint, pale, cloudy, misty, murky, overcast, nebulous, shadowy, umbrageous, blurry, hazy, opaque, foggy, bleary, gloomy, lurid, leaden.

423 [source of light] **luminary** *n* natural light, sun, moon, stars, flame, fire, spark, phosphorescence; artificial light, lamp, gas lamp, oil lamp, kerosene lamp, electric light, lantern, torch, candle, taper, light bulb.

v light, illuminate.

adj self-luminous; phosphorescent, radiant.

424 shade *n* cover, awning, umbrella, parasol, sunshade; screen, curtain, shutter, blind, gauze, veil, mantle, mask, sunglasses, *(informal)* shades; cloud, mist, fog, shadow.

v shade, veil, cover, screen, curtain, veil, draw a curtain, pull the shade, cast a shadow.

adj shady, shadowy, cloudy.

425 transparency *n* transparence, translucence, diaphanousness, clearness, lucidity, limpidity, thinness, sheerness, gauziness, flimsiness.

v be transparent, transmit light.

adj transparent, pellucid, lucid, diaphanous, translucent limpid, clear, crystalline, see-through, sheer, gauzy, flimsy.

426 opacity *n* opaqueness, darkness, cloudiness, filminess, haziness, mistiness, nontransparency.

v be opaque, obstruct the passage of light.

adj opaque, impervious to light, impenetrable to light, dim, filmy, thick, smoky, misty, smoggy, shady, murky, cloudy, hazy, obscure, clouded, foggy, unclear, frosted, nontransparent, nontranslucent.

427 semitransparency *n* opalescence, milkiness, pearliness; film, mist.

v let in partial light.

adj semitransparent, semipellucid, semiopaque, opalescent, pearly, nacreous, milky.

428 color *n* hue, tint, tinge, dye, complexion, shade, tincture, cast, coloration, tone, key; primary color, secondary color, complementary color; coloring; spectrum, prism, spectroscope; pigment, paint, dye, wash, stain.

v color, dye, tinge, stain, tint, paint, wash; illuminate, emblazon.

adj colored, dyed, tinted; prismatic, chromatic; bright, vivid, intense, deep, rich, gorgeous; fresh, unfaded; gaudy, florid, garish, showy, flashy, glaring; mellow, harmonious, pearly, sweet, delicate, tender, refined; dull, gray.

429 [absence of color] **colorlessness** *n* neutral tint, black and white, chiaroscuro, monochrome; etiolation, pallor, paleness, discoloration.

v lose color, fade, turn pale, become colorless, pale; deprive of color, bleach, wash out, blanch, tarnish, etiolate, tone down, whiten.

adj uncolored, colorless, hueless, pale, pallid, faint, dull, dun, wan, sallow, dingy, ashy, gray, ashen, lackluster; discolored; light-colored, fair, blond, white.

430 whiteness *n* milkiness, frostiness, silveriness, pearliness; etiolation, albification, decoloration, colorlessness; albinism.

v whiten, bleach, blanch, etiolate, whitewash.

adj white, snowy, frosted, snow-white, milk-white, milky, chalky, pearly, ivory, silver, silvery, opaline, whitish, albinistic, etiolated, bleached, blanched, fair, light, wan, pallid, pale, lackluster, colorless, anemic, sallow, faint.

431 blackness *n* darkness, swarthiness, lividness; ink, ebony, coal, charcoal, pitch; obscurity.

v black, blacken, darken; blot, smutch, smut, smirch.

adj black, sable, somber, livid, dark, inky, ebony, pitchy, swarthy, sooty, dingy, dusky, murky; jet-black, pitch-black, black as coal, coal-black, kohl-black, black as night.

432 gray *n* grayness, neutral tint, silver, salt and pepper, dove color.

adj gray, iron-gray, silver, silvery, silverish, grayish, dun, drab, ashy, ashen, dove-colored, dapple-gray; grizzly, grizzled, hoary.

433 brown *n* brownness, beige, khaki.

adj brown, bay, dapple, auburn, nut-brown, chocolate, chestnut, cinnamon, russet, tawny, tan, brunette, mahogany, khaki, beige, ochre, sepia, hazel, brownish, coffee, cocoa, rust, roan, sorrel.

434 red *n* redness; blush, color.

v redden, blush, flush, get red in the face, turn color.

adj red, reddish, scarlet, crimson, blood red, bloody, cherry-colored, vermilion, carmine, maroon, pink, hot-pink, rosy, ruby, salmon, wine-colored; red-faced, blushing, embarrassed, red as beet, red as a lobster, flushed, burning, fuming, flaming, inflamed; ruddy, glowing, blooming, warm, hot.

435 green *n* greenness, verdure, blue and yellow.

adj green, greenish, verdant, olive, pea-green, emerald, apple, Kelly green, blue-green, aquamarine, sea-green; grassy, verdurous; fresh, new, recent, young, innocent, naive, raw, unseasoned, immature, inexperienced, ignorant; sickly, wan, pale, livid; jealous, envious.

436 yellow *n* yellowness, jaundice.

v yellow, age, turn color, dry up.

adj yellow, yellowish, gold, golden, ocher, lemon, citrine, saffron, aureate, creamy, straw-colored, flaxen, blond, tawny, sallow; sordid, cheap; cowardly, *(informal)* chicken, craven, lily-livered, contemptible, despicable, mean, cringing, groveling; jaundiced.

437 purple *n* blue and red.

adj purple, purplish, lavender, lilac, magenta, orchid, violet, plum-colored, mauve.

438 blue *n* blueness.

adj blue, bluish, azure, marine blue, navy, aquamarine, greenish blue, sapphire, turquoise, cobalt, baby blue; depressed, down in the dumps, *(informal)* in the pits, *(informal)* down, low.

439 orange *n* red and yellow; flame.

adj orange, orangy, orangish, brass, copper, apricot, tangerine, gold, flame-colored.

440 variegation *n* striation, spottiness, streakiness, iridescence, play of colors.

v variegate, diversify, streak, stripe, checker, speckle, bespeckle, fleck, dapple; dot, striate, tattoo, inlay; embroider, quilt.

adj variegated, multi-colored, many-colored, kaleidoscopic; iridescent, prismatic, opaline, nacreous, pearly; pied, piebald, mottled; dappled, salt ad pepper, marbled, flecked, speckled, spotty, studded, freckled, flecky, spotted, diversified; striped, veined, lined, striated, streaked, brindled, banded, checked, checkered, plaid, mosaic, inlaid.

441 vision *n* sight, optics, eyesight; view, look, glance, ken, glimpse, peep, peek, gaze, stare, leer; contemplation, regard, survey; point of view, outlook, viewpoint, perspective, standpoint; perspicacity, discernment, perception, penetration.

v see, behold, discern, perceive, have in sight, descry, sight, make out, discover, distinguish, recognize spy, espy, catch a glimpse of, command a view of, witness; envision, contemplate; look, view, eye, survey, scan, inspect, run the eye over, glance around; observe, watch, watch for, peep, peer, peek, pry, take a peep, leer, ogle, glare.

adj visual, ocular, optic; clearsighted, eagle-eyed, discerning; visionary, farsighted.

adv on sight, at first sight, at a glance.

442 blindness *n* sightlessness; cataract; ignorance.

v be blind, not see; grope in the dark; blind, hoodwink, dazzle; screen, hide, mask.

adj blind, eyeless, sightless, unseeing, dark, purblind, stone-blind; dimsighted, undiscerning, ignorant.

adv blindly, blindfold, darkly.

443 [imperfect vision] **dimsightedness** *n* nearsightedness, farsightedness, purblindness, prebyopia, myopia, astigmatism, color blindness, cataract, ophthalmia; squint, cross-eye, strabismus, lazy eye, cockeye, swivel eye, goggle eyes.

fallacies of vision: refraction, distortion, illusion, mirage, phantasm, vision, specter, apparition, ghost; mirror, lens.

v be dimsighted, see double, wink, blink, squint, look askance, screw up the eyes.

adj dimsighted, purblind, myopic, astigmatic, nearsighted, farsighted, colorblind; blear-eyed, goggle-eyed, cockeyed, crosseyed.

444 spectator *n* beholder, observer, looker-on, onlooker, witness, eyewitness, bystander, passerby; sightseer, audience, crowd; spy, sentinel.

v witness, behold, look on.

445 optical instruments *n* lens, magnifying glass, microscope; spectacles, monocle, eyeglasses, glasses, contact lens, goggles, pince-nez; telescope, lorgnette, binoculars, spyglass, opera glasses; mirror, looking glass, reflector; prism, kaleidoscope, stereoscope.

446 visibility *n* perceptibility, discernibleness, distinctness, clearness, clarity, perceivability, conspicuousness, definition, sharp outline; appearance, manifestation.

v be visible, appear, open to the view, present itself, show itself, reveal itself, peep up, show up, turn up, start up, pop up, crop up; glimmer, loom; burst forth, burst upon the view, come into sight, come into view, come forth, come forward, attract attention.

adj visible, perceptible, discernible, perceivable, apparent, obvious, manifest, plain, clear, distinct, definite, well-defined, outlined, well-marked; recognizable, palpable, glaring, conspicuous, in full view, in full sight, in front of one's nose, under one's nose, before one's eyes.

447 invisibility *n* indistinctness, imperceptibility, invisibleness, indefiniteness; mystery, obscurity, delitescence, haziness, cloudiness; concealment; latency.

v be invisible; be hidden; escape notice; render invisible, conceal, hide.

adj invisible, imperceptible; not in sight, out of sight, out of view, unseen; inconspicuous, covert; dim, faint, mysterious, dark, obscure, confused, indistinct, indistinguishable, shadowy, indefinite, undefined, unmarked, blurry, blurred, unfocused, out of focus, misty, veiled; concealed, hidden.

448 appearance *n* phenomenon, sight, show, scene, view; prospect, vista, perspective, lookout, outlook, bird's-eye view, scenery, landscape, picture, tableau; display, exposure; pageant, spectacle; aspect, phase, seeming, shape, form, manifestation, guise, look, complexion, color, image, mien, air, cast, carriage, comportment, demeanor; presence; feature, trait, lines, outline, contour, face, countenance, physiognomy, visage, profile, outsides.

v appear, be visible, seem, look, show,

present; figure, cut a figure; present to the view.

adj apparent, seeming, ostensible.

adv apparently, to all appearance, ostensibly, seemingly, on the face of it, at first sight, to the eye.

449 disappearance *n* evanescence, eclipse; departure, exit; loss.

v disappear, vanish, dissolve, melt, melt away, fade, pass, pass out, go, depart, leave no trace, be gone.

adj disappearing, evanescent; departed, left; missing, lost, vanished.

Class IV
Intellectual Faculties

I. Formation of Ideas

450 intellect *n* rationality, mind, understanding, reason, faculties, judgment, sense, common sense, wits, brains, *(informal)* smarts; brain, head, pate, *(informal)* noodle, skull, *(informal)* upstairs.

v intellectualize, reason, understand, realize, ruminate; note, notice, mark, be aware of, take cognizance of.

adj intellectual, mental, cerebral, rational, sensical, commonsensical.

450a absence of intellect *n* want of intellect; inanity, imbecility, brutishness, brute instinct.

adj unintellectual, unintelligent, unrational, nonrational, empty-headed.

451 thought *n* abstraction, concept, conception, opinion, judgment, belief, idea, notion, tenet, conviction, speculation, consideration, contemplation; meditation, pondering, reflection, musing, cogitation, thinking; intention, design, purpose, intent; anticipation, expectation; consideration, attention, care, regard; trifle, mote.

v think, cogitate, meditate, reflect, muse, ponder, ruminate, contemplate; consider, regard, suppose, look upon, judge, esteem, deem, count, account; bear in mind, recollect, recall, remember; intend, mean, design, purpose; believe, suppose; anticipate, expect.

adj thoughtful, contemplative, meditative, reflective, pensive, deliberate; lost in thought, absorbed, engrossed in; careful, heedful, mindful, regardful, considerate, attentive; discreet, prudent, wary, cautious, circumspect.

452 absence of thought *n* incogitancy, vacancy of mind, thoughtlessness, fatuity, vacuity, emptiness; inattention.

v not think, make the mind a blank, *(informal)* turn off the brain, *(informal)* tune out.

adj vacant, unoccupied, empty; unthinking; inattentive, absent, *(informal)* turned off, *(informal)* tuned out; thoughtless, inconsiderate, unmindful, unheedful, imprudent; unreflective.

453 idea *n* thought, conception, theory, notion; observation, impression, apprehension, perception, brainstorm, brainchild, fancy, *(informal)* flash; opinion, view, belief, sentiment, judgment, supposition; plan, object, objective, aim.

adj ideational.

454 topic *n* subject, theme, thesis, subject-matter, food for thought; business, affair, argument.

adj topical, thematic.

adv under consideration, in question.

455 curiosity *n* interest, inquisitiveness, inquiring mind, thirst for knowledge; spying, prying, meddlesomeness.

spy, eavesdropper, gossip.

v be curious, take an interest in, stare, gape, spy, pry.

adj curious, inquisitive, inquiring, prying, spying, peeping, meddlesome, interested.

456 incuriosity *n* lack of interest, incuriousness, indifference, unconcern.

v have no curiosity, take no interest in.

adj incurious, uninquisitive, uninquiring, uninterested, indifferent, impassive, bored, apathetic.

457 attention *n* attending to, attentiveness, intentiveness, care, consideration, observation, heed, regard, mindfulness, notice, watchfulness, alertness; study, scrutiny; civility, courtesy, respect, politeness.

v be attentive, attend, observe, look, see, notice, remark, regard, pay attention, heed; examine, study, scrutinize.

adj attentive, observant, mindful, heedful, thoughtful, alive, alert, awake, on the watch, wary, circumspectful, watchful, careful; polite, courteous, respectful, deferential.

458 inattention *n* inattentiveness, inconsideration, heedlessness, unmindfulness, disregard, unconcern.

v be inattentive, overlook, disregard, pay no attention to, gloss over.

adj inattentive, unobservant, unmindful, unheeding, thoughtless, blind to, deaf to, napping, asleep, lost.

459 care *n* heed, caution, prudence, pains, anxiety, regard, attention, vigilance, carefulness, solicitude, circumspection, alertness, watchfulness, wakefulness; accuracy, exactness.

v be careful, take care.

adj careful, cautious, circumspect, watchful, vigilant, guarded, wary, prudent, tactful; painstaking, meticulous, discerning, exact, thorough, concerned, scrupulous, particular, finical, conscientious, attentive, heedful, thoughtful.

460 neglect *n* disregard, dereliction, negligence, remissness, carelessness, failure, omission, default, inattention, heedlessness, recklessness.

v neglect, disregard, ignore, slight, overlook, omit, be remiss, be negligent.

adj neglectful, disregardful, remiss, careless, negligent, unmindful, inattentive, indifferent, heedless, inconsiderate, thoughtless, imprudent; unwary, unguarded; neglecting, neglected, unheeded, uncared for, unobserved, unnoticed, unattended to.

461 inquiry *n* investigation, examination, study, scrutiny, exploration, research, search, pursuit; inquiring, questioning, interrogation; query, question.

inquirer, investigator, inquisitor, inspector.

v inquire, ask, question, interrogate, query, investigate, examine, seek, search, look for, study, consider.

adj inquiring, inquisitive, curious, scrutinizing, questioning, exploring; inquisitorial, exploratory, interrogative.

462 answer *n* reply, response, retort, rejoinder; discovery, solution; rationale.

v answer, reply, respond, rebut, retort, rejoin; explain, interpret, discover, solve; satisfy, set at rest, atone for.

adj responsive; answerable, discoverable, soluble.

463 experiment *n* test, trial, examination, proof, assay, procedure; experimentation, research, investigation, analysis.

experimenter, analyzer, adventurer.

v experiment, try, test, examine, analyze, prove, assay, essay.

adj experimental, probative, analytic.

464 comparison *n* collation, association, relating, likening, correlation, comparative relation, setting side by side, juxtaposition.

v compare, collate, confront, place side by side, pit one against another, juxtapose, relate, correlate.

adj comparative, metaphorical, compared with; comparable.

465 discrimination *n* distinction, differentiation, diagnosis; appreciation, estimation, discernment, critique, judgment; nicety, refinement, taste.

v discriminate, distinguish, set apart, differentiate.

adj discriminating, critical, distinguishing, discriminative, discriminatory, choosy, picky; discerning, perceptive; tasteful, refined.

465a indiscrimination *n* indistinction, indistinctness, lack of discernment.

v be indiscriminate, not discriminate, confound, confuse.

adj indiscriminate, miscellaneous, undiscriminating.

466 measurement *n* survey, valuation, appraisement, assessment, estimate, estimation, reckoning, gauging; measure, standard, rule, gauge, scale.

v measure, survey, assess, rate, value, appraise, estimate.

adj measurable.

467 [on one side] **evidence** *n* facts, indication, sign, signal; ground, grounds, proof, testimony; information, deposition, affidavit, exhibit, citation, reference, confirmation, corroboration.

v be evident, evince, show, tell, cite, signal, indicate, imply, argue, bespeak; give evidence, testify, depose, witness.

adj evident, evidential, indicative, inferential, referential, corroborative, confirmatory.

468 counter-evidence *n* disproof, refutation, rebuttal, conflicting evidence, negation.

v rebut, refute, check, weaken, contravene, contradict, deny.

adj countervailing, contradictory, conflicting, unsupportive, uncorroborative.

469 qualification *n* modification, limitation, mitigation, narrowing, restriction, coloring, allowance, consideration, extenuation, extenuating, circumstances, condition, proviso, exception.

v qualify, modify, limit, mitigate, restrain, narrow, restrict, color, allow, allow for, make allowance for, consider, extenuate, except, make an exception, take into account, take into consideration.

adj qualified, qualifying, provided, conditional, extenuating, mitigating, admitting, supposing, with the proviso, provided that.

470 possibility *n* feasibility, practicality, likelihood, potentiality; contingency, chance.

v be possible, stand a chance, admit of, *(informal)* could be.

adj possible, imaginable, conceivable, credible, feasible, practical, performable, achievable, within reach, within the bounds of possibility, potential.

adv possibly, perhaps, perchance, peradventure, maybe.

471 impossibility *n* impracticality, unfeasibility, hopelessness.

v be impossible, have no chance.

adj impossible, not possible, inconceivable, incredible, unimaginable, unreasonable, unfeasible, impractical, unobtainable, unperformable, unachievable, beyond the bounds of reason, absurd, *(informal)* fat chance, *(informal)* no way.

472 probability *n* likelihood, likeliness, plausibility, tendency, prospect, good chance, reasonable, chance, expectation.

v be probable, point to, tend, imply, bid fair.

adj probable, likely, plausible, reasonable, presumable, well-founded, hopeful.

adv probably, in all probability, in all likelihood, most likely, presumably.

473 improbability *n* unlikelihood, bare possibility, implausibility, doubtfulness, questionableness.

v be improbable, not have much of a chance.

adj improbable, unlikely, implausible, doubtful, questionable, beyond all reasonable expectation.

474 certainty *n* fact, truth; infallibility, reliability, unquestionableness, inevitability, certitude, assurance, confidence, conviction.

v be certain, stand to reason, render certain, clinch, make sure; know.

adj certain, confident, sure, assured, convinced, satisfied, indubitable, indisputable, unquestionable, undeniable, incontestable, unimpeachable, irrefutable, unquestioned, incontrovertible, absolute, positive, plain, patent, obvious, clear; sure, inevitable, infallible, unfailing; fixed, agreed upon, settled, prescribed, determined, determinate, constant, stated, given; definite, particular, special, especial; reliable, trustworthy, dependable, trusty.

adv certainly, for certain, no doubt, doubtless, undoubtedly, *(informal)* sure enough.

475 uncertainty *n* insecurity, instability, unreliability, fallibility, danger; incertitude, doubt, doubtfulness, ambiguity, vagueness, questionableness, dubiousness; haziness, fogginess, obscurity; undependability, changeableness, variability, capriciousness, irregularity, fitfulness, chanciness.

v be uncertain, hesitate, flounder, waver; render uncertain, pose, puzzle, perplex, confuse, confound, bewilder; doubt, question.

adj uncertain, insecure, precarious, unsure, doubtful, unpredictable, problematical, unstable, unreliable, unsafe, fallible, perilous, dangerous; unassured, undecided, indeterminate, undetermined, unfixed, unsettled, indefinite, ambiguous, questionable, dubious; doubtful, vague, indistinct; undependable, changeable, variable, capricious, unsteady, irregular, fitful, desultory, chance, *(informal)* chancy.

476 reasoning *n* ratiocination, rationalism, dialectics; discussion, comment, argumentation, debate, disputation.

logic, induction, deduction, chain of thought, analysis, synthesis, syllogistic reasoning.

argument, case, proposition, terms, premises, postulate, data; inference, *argumentum ad hominem, paralipsis, a priori, a posteriori, reductio ad absurdum,* enthymeme, dilemma, on the horns of a dilemma.

reasoner, logician, dialectician, disputant, wrangler, arguer, debater, polemicist, casuist, rationalist.

arguments, reasons, pros and cons.

v to reason, discuss, argue, debate, dispute, wrangle; deduce, induce, infer, analyze, synthesize, postulate, propose, contend, demonstrate.

adj reasoning, rationalistic, dialectical, dialectic, argumentative, disputatious; logical, inductive, deductive, analytical, synthetic, syllogistic, inferential; demonstrable.

477 [the absence of reasoning] **intuition.** [false reasoning] **sophistry** *n* intuition, instinct, hunch, presentiment; insight, discernment, inspiration.

casuistry, jesuitry, perversion, equivocation, evasion, chicanery, quiddity, speciousness, *(informal)* bull, *(informal)* malarkey, bunk; false statement; fallacy, sophism.

sophist.

v intuit; reason falsely, pervert, quibble, equivocate, evade, mislead, gloss over, cavil, refine, subtilize, misrepresent, fence, beg the question.

adj intuitive, instinctive, instinctual. sophistical, equivocal, evasive, specious, fallacious, illogical, unsound, false, incorrect, untenable; inconsequential, weak, feeble, poor, flimsy, vague, nonsensical, absurd, foolish; frivolous, pettifogging, trifling, quibbling, nit-picking, subtle, over-refined.

adv intuitively, by intuition; illogically.

478 demonstration *n* proof, conclusiveness, example, verification, explanation.

v demonstrate, prove, establish, verify; evince, show, explain.

adj demonstrative, demonstrable, probative, conclusive, convincing; demonstrated, proven, proved, shown.

479 confutation *n* refutation, answer, disproof, invalidation, exposure.

v confute, refute, disprove, expose the error, overturn, invalidate.

adj confutable, refutable.

480 judgment *n* verdict, decree, decision, determination, conclusion, result, upshot, deduction, inference, assessment, opinion, estimate, criticism, critique; understanding, discrimination, discernment, perspicacity, sagacity, wisdom, intelligence, prudence, brains, taste, penetration, discretion, common sense.

judge, assessor, reviewer, critic, commentator; connoisseur.

v judge, estimate, consider, regard, esteem, appreciate, appraise, reckon, value; decide, determine, conclude, form an opinion, pass judgment; criticize, rate, rank; try, pass sentence upon, rule.

adj judicious, judicial, judgmental, determinate, conclusive; critical, discriminating, penetrating, perspicacious.

480a discovery *n* detection, determination, disclosure, trove, find.

v discover, learn of, ascertain, unearth, uncover, determine, ferret out, flush out, dig up; find out, detect, espy, descry, discern, see, notice, hit upon, stumble onto.

481 misjudgment *n* miscalculation, miscomputation, misconception, misinterpretation, misapprehension.

v misjudge, misconjecture, misconceive, misunderstand, misconstrue, misinterpret; overestimate, underestimate.

adj misjudging, ill-judging, wrongheaded, *(informal)* off base, wrong, in error.

482 overestimation *n* exaggeration, overvaluation, optimism; miscalculation.

v overestimate, overrate, overprize, overpraise, exaggerate, magnify, attach too much importance to, set too high a value on; miscalculate.

adj overestimated, overrated, inflated, pompous, pretentious.

483 underestimation *n* undervaluation, depreciation, detraction; modesty, self-depreciation; pessimism.

v underestimate, undervalue, underrate, depreciate, disparage, detract, slight, minimize, make light of, make little of, disregard.

adj underestimating, depreciating, depreciative, deprecatory; underestimated, depreciated, unvalued, unprized; modest, pessimistic.

484 belief *n* opinion, view, tenet, doctrine, dogma, creed; certainty, conviction, assurance, confidence, persuasion, believing, trust, reliance; credence, credit, acceptance, faith, assent.

v believe, credit, give credence to, accept. have faith in, give assent, accept; know, see, realize, assume, presume; thick, opine, hold, conceive. consider; rely on, put one's trust on, have confidence in.

adj certain, sure, assured, positive, cocksure, satisfied, confident, convinced, secure; believing, trusting, confiding, credulous; believed, accredited, trusted, accepted; believable, credible, trustworthy.

485 disbelief, doubt *n* disbelief, incredulity; dissent, change of mind, retraction.

uncertainty, irresolution, hesitation, hesitancy, vacillation, misgiving, suspense; scruple, qualm, mistrust, distrust, suspicion, skepticism.

unbeliever, nonbeliever; skeptic.

v disbelieve, discredit, dissent, doubt, distrust, mistrust, suspect, have qualms; hesitate, waver, demur.

adj unbelieving, incredulous, doubtful, disputable, questionable, suspicious; uncertain, unsure; doubting, hesitating, hesitant, wavering, irresolute, dubious, skeptical.

486 credulity *n* credulousness, gullibility, infatuation, superstition, self-deception, self-delusion.

gull, dupe, *(informal)* sucker.

v be credulous, swallow.

adj credulous, believing, trusting, unsuspecting, gullible; simple, silly, childish, stupid; infatuated, superstitious.

487 incredulity *n* incredulousness, caution, wariness, suspicion, doubt, skepticism, disbelief.

nonbeliever, skeptic, heretic.

v be incredulous, distrust, doubt, suspect.

adj incredulous, cautious, wary; suspicious, dubious, doubtful, skeptical, unbelieving.

488 assent *n* acknowledgment, agreement, concurrence, acquiescence, consent, allowance, approval, concord, accord, approbation.

v assent, acquiesce, accede, concur, agree, fall in, acknowledge, admit, yield, allow; own, avow, confess.

adj assenting, agreeing, concurring, consenting, of one accord, of the same mind; agreed, acquiescent.

489 dissent *n* difference, discordance, dissension, disagreement, dissatisfaction; opposition, protest; nonconformity, separation.

dissenter, protester, rebel, radical, dissident, nonconformist.

v dissent, differ, disagree, protest, contradict; repudiate.

adj dissenting, negative; dissident, contradictory, disagreeing, opposing; nonconformist.

490 knowledge *n* enlightenment, erudition, wisdom, science, letters, information, learning, scholarship, lore; understanding, discernment, perception, apprehension, comprehension, judgment.

v know, be aware of; understand, discern, perceive, realize, fathom, apprehend, comprehend, *(informal)* dig; *(informal)* be hip; learn, discover.

adj knowing, aware of, cognizant of, acquainted with, privy to; discerning, perceptive, *(informal)* sharp, shrewd; knowledgeable, educated, enlightened, erudite, wise, instructed, learned, well-educated, bookish, well-read; known, recognized, received.

491 ignorance *n* illiteracy, unenlightenment, unawareness, unlearnedness, unacquaintance, unconsciousness, inexperience, darkness, blindness, incomprehension, simplicity, stupidity.

v be ignorant, know nothing, have no idea, be blind to.

adj ignorant, illiterate, unlettered, uneducated, uninstructed, untaught, untutored, uninformed, unenlightened, nescient; shallow, superficial; stupid, dumb, thick, dull.

492 scholar *n* savant, wise man, sage, academician, thinker, intellectual, bibliomaniac, bookworm, pedant; student, pupil, disciple, learner.

493 ignoramus *n* illiterate, know-nothing, blockhead, numskull, dullard, simpleton, dunce, ass, fool, bonehead, duffer, dolt, turkey, twerp, idiot, imbecile, cretin, moron, dimwit, *(informal)* jerk.

494 truth *n* fact, reality, verity, veracity; accuracy, precision, exactness.

v be true, be the case, have a true ring.

adj true, factual, actual, real, authentic, genuine, veracious, truthful, veritable; pure, natural; accurate, exact, faithful, correct, precise; agreeing; right, proper; legitimate, rightful; to the point, *(informal)* right on, *(informal)* where it's at, *(informal)* on target.

495 error *n* fallacy, misconception, misapprehension, misunderstanding, misinterpretation, misjudgment; aberration, inexactness, laxity; mistake, fault, blunder, slip, oversight, flaw, stumble, bungle; delusion, false, impression.

v err, be in error, mistake, blunder, slip, go astray, trip up; misconceive, misapprehend, misunderstand, misinterpret, miscalculate, misjudge.

adj erroneous, in error, fallacious, mistaken, incorrect, inaccurate, false, wrong, untrue, *(informal)* off base, *(informal)* off the mark.

496 maxim *n* proverb, aphorism, dictum, saying, adage, apothegm, motto, epigram, *mot juste,* truism, words of wisdom, axiom.

adj proverbial, aphoristic, axiomatic, truistic, *(informal)* corny, trite.

adv as they say, as the saying goes.

497 absurdity *n* nonsense, imbecility, foolishness, silliness, inanity, stupidity; farce, rhapsody, farrago, blunder, bathos; inconsistency, paradox, *non sequitur,* jargon, extravagance, exaggeration.

v be absurd, talk nonsense, play, the fool.

adj absurd, nonsensical, ridiculous, silly, preposterous, foolish, inane, asinine, stupid, senseless, unreasonable, ir-

rational, incongruous, self-contradictory, paradoxical, farcical, rhapsodic, bathetic, extravagant, exaggerated, bombastic, fantastic, meaningless.

498 intelligence. wisdom *n* intelligence, intellect, mind, capacity, understanding, discernment, reason, acumen, aptitude, penetration, brains, *(informal),* smarts; knowledge, news, information, tidings.

discretion, reasonableness, judgment, discernment, insight, sense, common sense, sagacity, insight, understanding, prudence; knowledge, information, learning, sapience, erudition, enlightenment.

v be intelligent; understand, discern, reason; be wise, discriminate.

adj intelligent, understanding, intellectual, quick, bright; astute, clever, sharp, alert, bright, apt, discerning, canny, shrewd, nimble, penetrating, piercing, on the ball.

wise, discerning, judicious, sage, sapient, sensible, sound, penetrating, sagacious, intelligent, perspicacious, profound, rational, prudent, cautious, politic, reasonable, thoughtful, reflective; learned, educated, erudite, schooled.

499 imbecility. folly *n* imbecility, want of intelligence, incompetence, incapacity, vacancy, dull understanding, meanness, simplicity, shallowness, stolidity, hebetude, puerility, fatuity, silliness, foolishness, driveling, stupidity, idiocy.

frivolity, irrationality, trifling, ineptitude, silliness, eccentricity, extravagance; rashness.

v be imbecilic.

be foolish, trifle, drivel, dote, ramble.

adj imbecile, imbecilic, idiotic, fatuous, driveling; vacant, mindless, witless, brainless, weak-headed, addle-brained, muddle-headed, dull-witted, feeble-minded, half-witted, dull, shallow, stolid, dim-witted, thick-skulled; shallow, weak, wanting, soft, sappy, stupid, obtuse, blunt, stolid, doltish, thick as a brick, asinine; childish, childlike, infantile, puerile, simple.

foolish, silly, senseless, irrational, insensate, nonsensical, inept, frivolous, trifling; eccentric, crazed, rash, thoughtless, giddy, obstinate, bigoted, narrow-minded; foolish, unwise, injudicious, improper, unreasonable, ridiculous, stupid, asinine; ill-conceived, ill-advised, ill-judged, inexpedient, extravagant, frivolous, trivial, useless.

500 sage *n* wise man, master mind, thinker, philosopher, oracle, luminary, man of learning, expert, authority.

501 fool *n* simpleton, dolt, dunce, blockhead, nincompoop, ninny, numskull, ignoramus, booby, sap, dunderhead, dunderpate, idiot, natural, oaf, lout, loon, dullard; jester, buffoon, droll, zany, harlequin, clown; imbecile, moron, idiot, cretin.

502 sanity *n* soundness, mental balance, rationality, reason, sense, clearheadedness, lucidity, coherence, normality, sobriety, *(informal)* good head.
　v be sane, *(informal)* have one's act together.
　adj sane, rational, reasonable, sensible, clearheaded, level-headed, logical, sober, lucid, self-possessed, *(informal)* together.

503 insanity *n* disorder, imbalance, derangement, dementia, lunacy, madness, craziness, aberration; frenzy, raving, incoherence, delirium, delusion; *(informal)* oddity, eccentricity, twist, mania.
　v be insane, become insane, lose one's senses, go mad, rave, rant, *(informal)* lose it.
　adj insane, deranged, demented, lunatic, crazed, crazy, maniacal, mad, touched, cracked, unhinged, unsettled, daft, frenzied, possessed, delirious, far gone, wild, flighty, distracted, frantic, mad as a hatter, *(informal)* crackers, *(informal)* zonkers, *(informal)* nuts, *(informal)* zonko, *(informal)* weird, *(informal)* bananas, *(informal)* kaput.

504 madman *n* lunatic, maniac, bedlamite, raver, *(informal)* nut, *(informal)* weirdo, *(informal)* crazy; dreamer, romantic, rhapsodist, enthusiast, visionary, seer, fanatic.

505 memory *n* retention, retentiveness, remembrance, recollection, reminiscence, retrospect; recognition; reminder, hint, suggestion, keepsake, souvenir, memento, token, memorial.
　v remember, recall, recollect, call up,

call to mind, bring to mind, think back upon, haunt one's thoughts, *(informal)* flash on; remind, suggest, hint, prompt, summon up, reminisce; retain, keep in mind, bear in mind, memorize, engrave in the mind, learn by heart; keep the memory alive.
　adj reminiscent (of), mindful (of); fresh, alive, vivid; unforgotten, enduring, indelible, memorable, never to be forgotten, unforgettable, stirring, eventful.

506 oblivion *n* forgetfulness, short memory, slippery memory, untrustworthy memory, obliteration of the past, amnesia.
　v forget, be forgetful, have a short memory, lose sight of, sink into oblivion; unlearn, efface from the memory, think no more of, consign into oblivion, banish from one's thoughts.
　adj oblivious, forgetful, heedless, deaf to the past, insensible; out of mind, unremembered, forgotten, past recollection, buried, sunk into oblivion.

507 expectation *n* expectancy, anticipation, prospect, reckoning, calculation; suspense, waiting; hope, trust, assurance, confidence, reliance, presumption.
　v expect, look for, look out for, look forward to, anticipate, await, hope for, wait for, foresee, prepare for, count on, rely on; predict, prognosticate, forecast.
　adj expectant, watchful, vigilant, open-eyed, on tenterhooks, on one's toes, ready, in readiness, prepared, *(informal)* all set for; foreseen, long expected, prospective, in view, in sight, on the horizon, impending.
　adv expectantly, on the watch, on edge, with bated breath.

508 nonexpectation *n* unforeseen occurrence, surprise, shock, blow, wonder, bolt out of the blue, astonishment; miscalculation, false expectation.
　v not expect, be taken by surprise, catch unawares; burst upon, come out of nowhere, drop from the clouds; surprise, startle, stun, stagger, throw off one's guard, astonish.
　adj nonexpectant, surprised, unwarned, unaware, off one's guard; unanticipated, unexpected, unlooked for,

unforeseen; unheard of, startling; sudden.

adv unexpectedly, abruptly, suddenly, without warning.

509 [failure of expectation] **disappointment** *n* failure, defeat, frustration, unfulfillment, blighted hope, vain expectation, disillusion, *(informal)* comedown.

v be disappointed; disappoint, dash one's hopes, dash one's expectations, balk, jilt, tantalize; dumfound, disillusion, let down.

adj disappointed; disgruntled, disconcerted, aghast.

510 foresight *n* prudence, forethought, prevision, anticipation. precaution; forecast; prescience, fore-knowledge, prospect.

v foresee; look forward to, look ahead, look beyond; look into the future; see one's future, catch the lay of the land; anticipate, expect, assume, surmise, predict, forewarn.

adj anticipatory, prescient; farsighted, prudent, provident; prospective, expectant.

511 prediction *n* prophecy, forecast, augury, prognostication, foretoken, portent, divination, soothsaying, presage.

v predict, foretell, prophesy, foresee, forecast, presage, augur, prognosticate, foretoken, portend, divine.

adj prophetic, oracular, portentous, premonitory.

512 omen *n* portent, foreboding, augury, sign, harbinger; sign of the times, symbol, warning.

513 oracle *n* prophet, prophetess, seer, soothsayer, augur, fortune-teller, witch, sibyl, necromancer, sorcerer, clairvoyant, interpreter.

514 supposition *n* assumption, presumption, condition, hypothesis, theory, postulate, proposition, thesis, theorem; conjecture, suggestion, guess, guesswork, suspicion, inkling, speculation.

v suppose, conjecture, surmise, suspect, guess, divine; theorize, speculate, presume, presuppose, assume, predicate; believe, take for granted; propound, put forth, propose, advance, hazard a suggestion, suggest.

adj assumed, given; conjectural, hypothetical, presumptive, theoretical, speculative, suggestive.

515 imagination *n* imaginativeness, fancy, invention, inspiration, creativity, originality, fiction, vision, fantasy, illusion, ideality, castles in the air, dreaming, dream, golden dreams; mental image, conception, idea, notion, thought, conceit, fancy, whim, figment, romance, vision, dream, chimera, shadow, illusion, phantasm, supposition, delusion; verve, vivacity, liveliness, animation.

v imagine, fancy, conceive, dream, idealize; create, originate, think up, devise, invent, coin, fabricate.

adj imaginative, fanciful, original, inventive, creative, visionary, ideal, unreal, illusory, unsubstantial, dreamy, dreamlike, romantic, fantastic, fabulous, chimerical, fantastical; vivacious, lively, animated; imaginable, conceivable, possible, believable; imagined.

II. Communication of Ideas

516 [idea to be conveyed] **meaning** *n* tenor, spirit, gist, trend, idea, purport, significance, signification, sense, import, denotation, conotation, interpretation; intent, intention, aim, object, purpose, design.

thing signified: matter, subject matter, substance, gist, argument.

v mean, signify, denote, conote, express, import, purport; convey, imply, indicate, point to, allude to, touch on, drive at, involve; declare, affirm, state; intend, aim, design, purpose.

adj meaning; meaningful, pointed, poignant, significant, expressive.

517 meaninglessness *n* unmeaningness, absence of meaning, senselessness, emptiness, empty words, rhetoric, platitude, nonsense, jargon, gibberish, jabber, rant, bombast, *(informal)* hot air; inanity, rigmarole, absurdity, ambiguity.

v mean nothing, jabber, rant, say nothing.

adj meaningless, senseless, nonsensical, inexpressive, vague, trivial, insignificant.

518 intelligibility *n* comprehensibility, clarity, clearness, lucidity, coherence, explicitness, persicuity, precision, plain-speaking.

v be intelligible; render, intelligible, clear up, simplify, elucidate, explain; understand, comprehend, take in, catch on, grasp, follow, master.

adj intelligible, understandable, comprehensible, clear, clear as day, lucid, luminous, transparent; plain, distinct, pointed, clear-cut, obvious, explicit, precise; graphic, illustrative, expressive.

519 unintelligibility *n* incomprehensibility, vagueness, obscurity, ambiguity, uncertainty, confusion.

v be unintelligible; render, unintelligible, conceal, darken, confuse, perplex, mystify, bewilder.

adj unintelligible, incomprehensible, indecipherable, unfathomable, inexplicable, inscrutable, insoluble, impenetrable; puzzling, enigmatic, obscure, muddy, dim, nebulous, mysterious, *(informal)* strange, *(informal)* weird; inexpressible, incommunicable, ineffable, unutterable.

520 equivocalness *n* ambiguity, uncertainty, questionableness, dubiousness, indeterminateness; double-meaning, word-play, double entendre, pun, play on words, conundrum, riddle, quibble; equivocation, duplicity, prevarication, white lie.

v be equivocal; have two meanings; equivocate, prevaricate.

adj equivocal, ambiguous, uncertain, doubtful, questionable, dubious, indeterminate; duplicitous, enigmatic, double-edged, deceptive, misleading.

521 figure of speech *n* phrase, expression, euphemism, manner of speaking, colloquialism, idiom, image; metaphor, simile, imagery, poetic device, poetics, figures of beauty.

v employ figures of speech; image, speak prettily.

adj figurative, idiomatic, colloquial, colorful, imagistic, poetic, expressive, allusive.

522 interpretation *n* definition, explanation, explication, elucidation, translation; exegesis, exposition, comment, commentary, gloss; solution, answer, meaning.

v interpret, define, explain, explicate,

elucidate, translate, shed light on, cast light on, decipher, decode, unravel, disentangle, gloss, annotate, expound, comment upon; construe, understand.

adj explanatory, expository, exegetical, interpretative, interpretive; interpretable, explicable, intelligible.

adv in explanation, that is to say, namely.

523 misinterpretation *n* misapprehension, misconception, misunderstanding, misreading, misconstruction, mistake; misrepresentation, perversion, exaggeration, false coloration, falsification, travesty.

v misinterpret, misapprehend, misconceive, misunderstand, misread, misconstrue, misapply, mistake; misrepresent, pervert, misstate, garble, falsify, distort, travesty, stretch the meaning, twist the meaning.

524 interpreter *n* translator, explainer, expounder, expositor, commentator, annotator, guide, critic; spokesman, speaker, representative.

525 manifestation *n* indication, expression, exposition, demonstration, showing, display, exhibition, declaration; materialization; openness, candor.

v make manifest, show, display, reveal, disclose, open, exhibit, evince, evidence, demonstrate, declare, express, make known; appear, be plain, come to light, materialize; indicate, point out.

adj manifest, evident, obvious, apparent, plain, clear, distinct, patent, open, palpable, visible, unmistakable, conspicuous, explicit; unreserved, downright, frank, plain spoken; barefaced, bold; manifested.

adv manifestly, openly, plainly, above board, in broad daylight, in plain sight.

526 latency *n* dormancy, latentness, quiescence, obscurity, darkness, hidden meaning, obscure meaning, undercurrent, suggestion, concealment; potentiality.

v be latent, lurk, smolder, underlie.

adj latent, dormant; lurking, secret, cryptic, veiled, hidden; potential; implied, implicit; allusive.

527 information *n* enlightenment, knowledge, news, data, facts, circumstances, situations, intelligence, advice; communication, notification, announcement, record; hint, suggestion, innuendo, inkling, whisper, insinuation.

informant, authority, intelligencer, reporter; informer, eavesdropper, detective, newsmonger; messenger.

guide, guidebook, handbook, manual, map, chart.

v inform, tell, acquaint with, impart to, make acquainted with, apprize, advise, enlighten; communicate, make known, express, mention, let fall, intimate, hint, insinuate, allude to, suggest; announce, report, give an account, disclose; know, learn, find out, get the scent of.

adj informed, communicated, reported, advised, apprized of, acquainted with, enlightened, published, *(informal)* filled in; declarative, expository, communicative.

528 concealment *n* hiding, secretion, ensconcing, sheltering, covering, burying, screening; keeping secret, secrecy, hiding, disguising, veiling, camouflaging, obscuring, dissembling, obfuscation, evasiveness; reticence, reserve, reservation, suppression, silence, secretiveness.

v conceal, hide, secrete, cover, put away, ensconce, bury, screen, shelter, keep out of sight, stow away; keep secret, hide, disguise, veil, cloak, mask, camouflage, obscure, obfuscate, dissemble, be evasive.

adj concealed, hidden, secret, private, privy, confidential, in secret, close, undercover, in hiding, in disguise, covert, mysterious; furtive, stealthy, surreptitious, secretive, evasive, clandestine; reserved, reticent, suppressed, uncommunicative.

adv secretly, in secret, in private, behind closed doors, on the sly; confidentially; stealthily.

529 disclosure *n* revelation, divulgence, exposition, exposure; exposé, uncovering, muckraking; acknowledgment, avowal, confession.

v disclose, discover, uncover, lay open, expose, bring to light, unmask; reveal, make known, divulge, show, tell, unveil, unmask, communicate; let slip, let drop, betray, blurt out; acknowledge,

allow, concede, grant, admit, own up, confess.

adj disclosed, revealed.

530 [means of concealment] **ambush** *n* ambuscade, lurking place, trap, snare, pitfall; hiding place, secret place, recess, hole, cubbyhole; screen, cover, shade, blinker, veil, curtain, cloak, cloud; mask, visor, disguise, masquerade.

v ambush, lie in wait for, set a trap for.

531 publication *n* issuance, distribution; announcement, proclamation, promulgation, propagation, pronouncement, declaration, disclosure, divulgence, advertisement, publicity; edition.

v publish, issue, distribute, print; make public, make known, announce, proclaim, promulgate, propagate, circulate, spread, disseminate, declare, disclose, divulge, advertise, publicize, get into print.

adj published; current, public, in circulation, in print, in black and white.

532 news *n* information, intelligence, tidings, report, rumor, scuttlebutt, hearsay, gossip, *(informal)* the word; newsstory, headlines, copy.

reporter, newsmonger, talebearer, gossip, tattler, informer.

v transpire, make news, make headlines; be rumored.

adj in the news, in the headlines, current, in circulation, in print.

533 secret *n* mystery; problem, question, difficulty, a confidence; unintelligibility.

adj secret, hidden, concealed, unrevealed, unknown, mysterious; reticent, secretive; private.

534 messenger *n* envoy, emissary, representative, intermediary, go-between, delegate, courier, runner, errand boy; intelligencer, reporter, newsmonger, spokesman, informant; forerunner, harbinger, herald, precursor.

535 affirmation *n* statement, profession, pronouncement, deposition, assertion, declaration; confirmation, ratification, endorsement; swearing, oath, affidavit; emphasis, dogmatism.

v affirm, state, assert, aver, avow, maintain, declare, swear, asseverate, depose, testify, say, pronounce; establish, confirm, ratify, approve, endorse, assent, acknowledge; swear, emphasize.

adj affirmative, declaratory, declarative, positive, assertive, emphatic, dogmatic; confirmative, corroborative, affirming, acquiescent.

536 negation. denial *n* nullification, invalidation.

disputation, confutation, contradiction, qualification; repudiation, rejection, abjuration, disavowal, disclaimer, recantation, retraction, rebuttal.

v negate, nullify, cancel, invalidate.

deny, dispute, controvert, contravene, oppose, gainsay, contradict, rebut; reject, renounce, abjure, disclaim, disavow; recant, revoke; refuse, repudiate, disown.

adj contradictory, negative.

537 teaching *n* instruction, education, pedagogy, pedagogics, edification, tutelage, tutorship; guidance, direction, preparation, schooling, learning, discipline; lesson, lecture, disquisition, discourse, explanation, harangue, homily, sermon, lore; doctrine, dogma, tenet, principle, rule, maxim, article of faith, creed, credo, belief, opinion.

v teach, instruct, edify, educate, inform, enlighten, prepare, discipline, train, drill, tutor, prime, coach, guide, direct, school, indoctrinate, inculcate, infuse, instill, imbue; expound, interpret, lecture, discourse, hold forth, sermonize, moralize.

adj educational, scholastic, academic, pedagogic, pedagogical, didactic; edifying, instructive.

538 misteaching *n* misinformation, misdirection, misguidance, perversion, sophistry, error.

v misteach, misinform, misinstruct, misdirect, misguide, pervert, mislead, misrepresent, confuse, bewilder, lie.

539 learning *n* acquisition of knowledge, acquirements, attainment, mental cultivation, scholarship, erudition, study, inquiry, questioning, search, pursuit of knowledge.

apprenticeship, tutelage, matriculation.

v learn, acquire, gain knowledge, memorize, master, study, grind, cram, *(informal)* book, read, peruse, pore

over, wade through, ingest, burn the midnight oil, *(informal)* pull an all-nighter.

adj studious, industrious; scholarly, scholastic, well-read, learned, erudite.

540 teacher *n* instructor, tutor, lecturer, professor, don, master, schoolmaster, guide, counselor, adviser, mentor; preacher, missionary, propagandist.

541 learner *n* scholar, student, pupil, apprentice, novice, neophyte, beginner; disciple, acolyte, follower.

542 school *n* academy, educational institution, college, university, institute, seminary, place of learning.

schoolbook, textbook, text, primer, grammar, reader, workbook.

adj scholastic, academic, collegiate.

543 veracity *n* truthfulness, frankness, truth, sincerity, candor, honesty, probity, fidelity, accuracy.

v speak the truth, *(informal)* level with, *(informal)* be straight with.

adj veracious, true, truthful, sincere, honest, honorable, candid, frank, open, straightforward, honest, scrupulous, punctilious, trustworthy.

544 falsehood *n* falsification, lie, fib, untruth, distortion, deception, misrepresentation, fabrication, fiction, sham; untruthfulness, lying, prevarication, duplicity, double dealing, deceitfulness, equivocation, dissembling, cunning, guile, insincerity, dishonesty, inaccuracy.

v lie, fib, falsify, prevaricate, misrepresent, deceive, *(informal)* come on to, doctor, feign, pretend, play false, dissemble, counterfeit, fabricate.

adj false, untrue, wrong, mistaken, incorrect, erroneous; untruthful, lying, mendacious, dishonest, deceitful, treacherous, faithless, insincere, hypocritical, disingenuous, unfaithful, cunning, perfidious, two-faced, recreant; deceptive, misleading, fallacious, spurious, fraudulent, bogus, phony, sham, counterfeit.

545 deception *n* deceiving, guiling, falseness, untruthfulness; artifice, sham, cheat, imposture, deceit, treachery, subterfuge, stratagem, ruse, hoax, fraud, trick, wile, snare, trap, illusion, delusion.

v deceive, mislead, lead astray, take

in, delude, cheat, cozen, dupe, gull, fool, bamboozle, hoodwink, *(informal)* con, trick, double-cross, defraud, outwit; entrap, ensnare, betray.

adj deceptive, misleading, delusive, illusory, fallacious, specious, untrue, false, deceitful; tricky, cunning, insidious.

546 untruth *n* falsehood, fib, lie, fiction, story, tale, tall tale, fabrication, fable, forgery, invention.

v make believe, pretend, feign, sham, fib, lie.

adj untrue, false, trumped up, unfounded, invented, fictitious, fabulous.

547 dupe *n* gull, pigeon, laughingstock, greenhorn, fool, sucker, puppet, *(informal)* nebbish.

v be deceived, be the dupe of, fall into a trap, go for the bait, bite, swallow.

adj credulous, gullible, unsuspecting, trusting.

548 deceiver *n* dissembler, hypocrite, sophist, liar, *(informal)* fast talker, storyteller, *(informal)* faker, *(informal)* phony, fraud, *(informal)* four-flusher, *(informal)*, shyster, confidence man, con man, cheat, swindler, imposter, pretender, humbug, adventurer, adventuress, serpent, snake in the grass.

549 exaggeration *n* overstatement, hyperbole, extravagance, coloring, coloration, embroidery; yarn, tale, *(informal)* shaggy dog story, *(informal)* fish story; tempest in a teacup, much ado about nothing, puffery, rant.

v exaggerate, magnify, amplify, expand, overestimate, overstate; heighten, color, embroider, puff up, fill out.

adj exaggerated, overwrought, bombastic, magniloquent, hyperbolic fabulous, extravagant, preposterous.

550 [means of communication] **indication** *n* symbolism, semiology; sign, symbol, index, indicator, pointer, note, token, symptom; type, mark, figure, emblem, insigne, cipher, device, representation; signal, beacon, alarm; feature, trait, characteristic, peculiarity, quality, earmark, cast; gesture, gesticulation, motion, cue, hint, clue, scent.

v indicate, denote, betoken, designate, signify, represent, stand for, typify, symbolize; note, mark, stamp; label, ticket; make a sign, signalize, signal, gesture, gesticulate; sign, seal, attest, underline, underscore, call attention to.

adj indicative, indicatory; connotative, denotative, typical, representative, symbolic, symbolical, characteristic, significant, emblematic.

551 record *n* trace, vestige, relic, remains; monument, achievement; account, chronicles, annals, history, note, register, memorandum, document, diary, log, journal, ledger.

v record, set down, place in the record, chronicle, enter, register, enter, list, enroll; commemorate, celebrate.

552 [suppression of sign] **obliteration** *n* erasure, cancelation, deletion, blot, effacement, extinction.

v obliterate, efface, expunge, erase, cancel, delete, blot out, rub out, strike out, wipe out, leave no trace.

adj obliterated, erased, blotted out; unrecorded.

553 recorder *n* notary, clerk, registrar, register, secretary, scribe, bookkeeper; annalist, historian, historiographer, chronicler, biographer, journalist, antiquarian, memorialist.

554 representation *n* depiction, imitation, illustration, delineation, expression, imagery, portraiture, figuration.

v represent, delineate, depict, portray, picture, figure, describe, trace, copy, illustrate, symbolize; personate, personify, play, mimic.

adj representative, imitiative, illustrative, figurative, symbolic, descriptive.

555 misrepresentation *n* distortion, exaggeration, misfiguration, falsification, bad likeness, caricature.

v misrepresent, distort, overdraw, exaggerate, falsify, caricature, daub.

556 painting *n* fine art, picture, depiction, representation, pictorialization, delineation, design, drawing, likeness, copy, imitation, fake, image.

art gallery, picture gallery, studio.

v paint, design, limn, draw, sketch, pencil, color; depict, represent.

adj pictorial, picturesque.

557 sculpture *n* carving, modeling, statuary; ceramics, potting.
statue, statuette, bust; cast, mold.
v sculpt, fashion, cast, mold, model, chisel, carve, cut, shape, form, figure, hew.

558 engraving *n* etching, chiseling, incising, plate engraving, photoengraving.
v engrave, grave, carve, incise, chisel, hatch, etch, stipple, print.

559 artist *n* painter, drawer, sketcher, designer, draftsman, cartoonist, caricaturist, sculptor, engraver.

560 language *n* speech, phraseology, style, expression, diction, jargon, dialect, terminology, vernacular, lingo, tongue.
literature, letters, belles, lettres humanities, classics, dead language.
linguist.
v express, say, express by words.
adj lingual, linguistic; dialect, vernacular, current, colloquial, slangy, polyglot, literary.

561 letter *n* character, hieroglyph, symbol, alphabet, consonant, vowel.
syllable, monosyllable, dissyllable, polysyllable.
spelling, orthography; phonetics; cipher, code; monogram, anagram.
v spell.
adj literal; alphabetical; syllabic; phonetic.

562 word *n* term, symbol, name, part of speech.
dictionary, vocabulary, lexicon, index, thesaurus, glossary.
etymology, derivation, philology, terminology, lexicography.
adj literal, verbal.

563 neology *n* neologism, new-fangled expression, *(informal)* hip expression, barbarism, corruption.
neologist, word coiner.
v coin words.
adj neologic, neological; colloquial, slang, *(informal)* hip, cant, barbarous.

564 nomenclature *n* naming; name, appellation, designation, epithet, nickname, *(informal)* moniker, *(informal)* handle, label, title, head, heading; style, proper name, surname, namesake.

v name, call, term, designate, denominate, style, entitle, dub, christen, baptize, nickname, characterize, specify, label.
adj titular, nominal.

565 misnomer *n* misnaming, malapropism; sobriquet, nickname, assumed name, alias, pen name, stage name, pseudonym, nom de plume, nom de guerre.
v misname, miscall, misterm; take an assumed name.
adj misnamed; soi-disant, self-styled; so-called.

566 phrase *n* expression, set phrase, turn of speech, idiom, tag phrase, figure of speech, euphemism, motto; phraseology.
v phrase, express, put into words, find the right words, arrange in words, voice, vocalize.

567 grammar *n* rules of language, usage, forms, style, formal features, constructions, parts of speech; accidence, syntax, inflection, case, declension, conjugation; grammar book, primer, rulebook.
grammarian.
adj grammatical, syntactic, syntactical.

568 solecism *n* ungrammatical, usage, bad grammar, faulty grammar, error, slip, inconsistency, impropriety.
v solecize.
adj ungrammatical, incorrect, inaccurate, faulty, inconsistent, improper.

569 style *n* diction, phraseology, wording; composition, mode of expression, choice of words, command of language, mode, manner, method, approach; kind, form, appearance, character, touch, characteristic, mark, signature, imprint, *(informal)* name.
v style, compose, express by words; write.
adj stylistic; characteristic; expressive.

570 perspicuity *n* clearness, clarity, lucidity, plainness, plain-speaking, distinctness, explicitness, exactness, intelligibility.
adj perspicuous, pellucid, clear, lucid, intelligible, plain, distinct, explicit, exact, definite, unequivocal.

571 obscurity *n* unintelligibility, involution, confusion, indistinctness, indefiniteness, ambiguity, vagueness, inexactness, impenetrability.

adj obscure, involved, confused, unintelligible, impenetrable, indefinite, vague, inexact, hidden, dark.

572 conciseness *n* brevity, summary, abridgment, terseness, pithiness, compression, tightness.

v be concise, condense, abridge, abstract, compress, tighten; come to the point.

adj concise, brief, compendious, short, terse, laconic, pithy, trenchant, succinct, compact, tight.

adv concisely, briefly, summarily, in short.

573 diffuseness *n* long-windedness, verbosity, wordiness, verbiage, looseness, exuberance, redundancy, profuseness, richness.

v be diffuse, enlarge, amplify, expand, inflate; meander, digress, ramble, run on and on.

adj diffuse, profuse, wordy, verbose, copious, exuberant; lengthy, long-winded, protracted, prolix, diffusive, roundabout; digressive, discursive, loose.

574 vigor *n* power, force, boldness, spirit, verve, heart, ardor, enthusiasm, raciness, glow, fire, warmth; loftiness, elevation, gravity, sublimity; eloquence, strong language.

adj vigorous, nervous, powerful, forcible, forceful, trenchant, biting, incisive, impressive; spirited, lively, glowing, sparkling, racy, bold, pungent, pithy; lofty, elevated, sublime, grand, weighty; eloquent, vehement, impassioned, passionate.

575 feebleness *n* weakness, enervation, frailty, faintness.

adj feeble, tame, weak, meager, vapid, insipid; trashy, poor, dull, dry, languid; prosy, prosaic, slight; careless, loose, slip-shod, wishy-washy, sloppy, slovenly; puerile, childish.

576 plainness *n* simplicity, homeliness, restraint, severity.

v speak plainly, speak directly, come straight to the point, be straightforward, not beat around the bush.

adj plain, simple, homely, homey, unadorned, unvarnished, neat, homespun; severe, chaste, pure.

adv in plain terms, in plain English; point-blank.

577 ornament *n* floridness, ornateness, elegance, grandiloquence, magniloquence, rhetorical flourish, declamation, rhetoric, flourish, fancy talk, *(informal)* big words; pretention, inflation, bombast, fustian, rant, fine writing, fine speaking.

v ornament, overcharge, talk big, talk fancy.

adj ornate, ornamented, beautified, florid, rich, flowery, fancy; euphuistic, euphemistic; sonorous, high sounding, inflated, swelling, turgid, pompous, pedantic, stilted, high-flown, sententious, rhetorical, declamatory, grandiose, grandiloquent, magniloquent, bombastic, flashy.

578 elegance *n* taste, good taste, propriety, correctness; lucidity, purity, grace, ease; gracefulness, euphony, gentility, cultivation, polish, refinement.

purist, classicist.

adj elegant, polished, classic, classical, fine, tasteful, proper, correct; chaste, pure, graceful, easy, readable, fluent, flowing, unaffected, natural, mellifluous, euphonious, felicitous, neat, well put.

579 inelegance *n* tastelessness, vulgarity, impropriety; bad diction, awkwardness, stiffness, turgidity, abruptness; barbarism, solecism, slang, mannerism, affectation, formality.

adj inelegant, graceless, ungraceful, harsh, abrupt, dry, stiff, cramped, formal, forced, labored, awkward, ponderous, turgid; artificial, mannered, affected, euphuistic; tasteless, barbarous, uncouth, rude, crude, vulgar.

580 voice *n* vocality, intonation, articulation, enunciation, distinctness, clearness, delivery; accent, accentuation, emphasis, stress; utterance, vocalization.

v voice, speak, utter; articulate, enunciate, vocalize, intone, pronounce, accent, accentuate, deliver.

adj vocal, oral; articulate, distinct, euphonious, melodious.

581 muteness *n* dumbness, silence, speechlessness; aphasia.

v be mute, be silent, be dumb; silence, muzzle, muffle, suppress, smother, gag, strike dumb, dumfound.

adj mute, silent, dumb, mum, tonguetied; voiceless, speechless.

582 speech *n* talk, parlance, locution, conversation, parley, communication, prattle; talk, oration, address, discourse, lecture, recitation, sermon, harangue, tirade; oratory, eloquence, rhetoric, declamation.

speaker, spokesman, mouthpiece, orator, rhetorician.

v speak, utter, talk, voice, converse, communicate, pronounce, say, articulate; declaim, harangue, stump, spout, rant, lecture, sermonize, discourse, expatiate, soliloquize, address.

adj oral; talkative, conversational; declamatory.

583 [imperfect speech] **inarticulateness** *n* stammering, hesitation, muttering, mumbling, stuttering; reticence, taciturnity; speech impediment, aphasia.

v be inarticulate, stammer, hesitate, mutter, mumble, slur one's words, garble, sputter, hem and haw, whisper, croak, crack.

adj inarticulate, tongue-tied, speechless, voiceless, hesitant, reticent, taciturn.

584 loquacity *n* loquaciousness, volubility, talkativeness, verbosity, garulity, volubility; chatter, jabber, prattle, twaddle.

talker, chatterer, chatterbox, babbler, ranter.

v be loquacious, talk a mile a minute, pour forth, prate, chatter, babble, gab, run off at the mouth, jabber, jaw, gush.

adj loquacious, voluble, talkative, verbose, wordy, garrulous, chatty, chattering, glib, fluent, effusive.

585 taciturnity *n* silence, muteness, reserve, reticence, uncommunicativeness.

v be silent, keep silence, keep quiet, hold one's tongue, say nothing.

adj taciturn, silent, mute, mum, reserved, reticent, guarded, uncommunicative, close-mouthed, quiet.

586 public address *n* allocution, speech, formal speech, address, invocation.

v speak to, address; invoke, hail, salute; lecture, pronounce.

587 response *n*. See **answer 462.**

588 conversation *n* interlocution, colloquy, confabulation, talk, *(informal)* rap, discourse, verbal interchange, dialog, oral communication; chat, chit, chit-chat, small talk, table talk, idle talk, prattle, gossip; conference, parley, interview, audience, *tête-à-tête,* council, congress; palaver, debate, discussion.

v converse, confabulate, talk together, hold a conversation, carry on a conversation, engage in a discussion; bandy words, chat, chit-chat, gossip, tattle, prate; discourse with, confer with; talk it over, *(informal)* rap, *(informal)* chew the fat.

adj conversational, conversable; chatty, gossipy.

589 soliloquy *n* monolog, apostrophe, aside.

v soliloquize, talk to oneself, think out loud, apostrophize.

590 writing *n* chirography, penmanship, calligraphy, hand, script, longhand, shorthand, stenography; handwriting, signature, mark, hand; manuscript, MS., document, script, writ, author's copy, copy, original; composition, authorship, work, opus, book, volume, tome, publication, article, poetry, verse, literature.

writer, author, scribe, scrivener, clerk, copyist, secretary.

v write, pen, copy, transcribe; print, scribble, scrawl, scratch; compose, draw out, write down, set down, put pen to paper, take up the pen, take pen in hand.

adj written, in writing, in black and white.

591 printing *n* lettering, typography; type; composition, print, letterpress, text, matter; copy, impression, proof.

printer, compositor, reader, proofreader, copyeditor.

v print, compose; go to press, publish, bring out, issue.

adj typographical, printed.

592 correspondence *n* letter, epistle, missive, note, post card; communication, dispatch, bulletin, circular.

v correspond, communicate, write to, send a letter.

adj epistolary; in touch with, in communication with.

593 book *n* booklet; writing, work, volume, tome, opus, tract, treatise, brochure, handbook; novel, story; script, libretto; publication.

writer, author, essayist, editor; bookseller, publisher; librarian, bibliophile, bookworm.

594 description *n* narration, account, recounting, telling, recital, relation, statement, report, record; delineation, portrayal, characterization, representation, depiction, sketch, vignette.

v describe, set forth, narrate, account, recount, recite, rehearse, tell, relate, detail; picture, delineate, portray, characterize, limn, represent, depict.

595 dissertation *n* treatise, essay, thesis, theme, tract, discourse, disquisition, investigation, study, discussion, exposition; commentary, critique, criticism, review, article. commentator, critic, essayist, reviewer.

v discuss a subject, treat, examine, comment, criticize, explain.

596 compendium *n* abstract, précis, epitome, analysis, digest, compendium, brief, abridgment, abbreviation, condensation, summary; draft, note, synopsis, outline, syllabus, contents, prospectus; compilation, collection, album, anthology; extracts, cuttings, fragments, pieces; list, inventory, survey.

v abridge, abstract, précis, epitomize, summarize; abbreviate, shorten, condense, compress; compile, collect, note; list, inventory, survey.

adj compendious, synoptic, analytic, analytical.

597 poetry *n* poetics; verse, poesy, versification, rhyming, rhymes, making verses, metrics; doggerel.

poet, laureate, bard, troubadour, minstrel, versifier, rhymer, sonneteer, rhapsodist, poetaster.

v poeticize, sing, versify, rhyme, make verses, compose.

adj poetic, poetical, rhythmic, metrical, lyrical, tuneful, musical; beautiful, lovely, tender, sensitive.

598 prose *n* writing, fiction, imaginative writing, narrative prose.

v write prose.

adj prosy, unpoetic, rhymeless; prosaic, dull, flat, matter-of-fact, unimaginative, commonplace, humdrum, pedestrian, trite, hackneyed, mediocre, stock, ordinary; fictional.

599 the drama *n* the stage, the theater; theatricals, dramaturgy, playwriting; play, drama, stage-play, opera.

performance, acting, representation, impersonation, stage business, actor, actress, player, performer, thespian.

theater, playhouse, operahouse, amphitheater.

dramatist, playwriter, playwright.

v dramatize, act, play, perform, personate, act a part, put on the stage, enact.

adj dramatic, theatrical, histrionic, stagy.

Class V

Voluntary Powers

I. Individual Volition

600 will *n* volition, free will, freedom; choice, wish, desire, pleasure, disposition, inclination; intent, purpose, option; determination, resolution, resoluteness, decision, forcefulness; force of will, will power, self-control.

v will, see fit, think fit, decide, decree, determine, direct, command, bid.

adj willful, voluntary, volitional, intentional; free, optional, discretionary; autocratic, obdurate, adamant.

adv willfully, voluntarily, at will; of one's own accord, intentionally, deliberately.

601 necessity *n* obligation, compulsion, subjection; fate, destiny, fatality; inevitability, inevitableness, unavoidability, unavoidableness, irresistibility; requirement, requisite, demand; instinct, impulse.

v be obligated, be obliged, be fated; necessitate, compel, subject; require.

adj necessary, essential, requisite, needful; inevitable, unavoidable, ineluctable, irresistible, inexorable; compulsory; involuntary, instinctive, automatic, blind, mechanical.

adv necessarily, of necessity, willy nilly.

602 willingness *n* disposition, inclination, leaning, propensity, frame of mind, liking, humor, mood, vein, bent, penchant, aptitude; geniality, cordiality, good will; alacrity, readiness, eagerness, enthusiasm; assent, compliance, agreement.

v be willing, incline, lean to, mind, hold to, cling to; desire, acquiesce, assent, comply; find one's way to, give it a shot, *(informal)* take a swing at, *(informal)* lay into.

adj willing, fain, favorable, content, well disposed; ready, earnest, eager, desirous; genial, cordial.

adv willingly, freely, with pleasure, with all one's heart, graciously.

603 unwillingness *n* indisposition, disinclination, reluctance, dislike; aversion, indifference, slowness, lack of readiness, obstinacy; scrupulousness, hesitation, qualm, shrinking, holding back, recoil; averseness, dissent, refusal.

v be unwilling, dislike; demur, hesitate, shrink from, swerve, recoil; dissent, refuse.

adj unwilling, loath, reluctant, averse; laggard, backward, slow, slack, indifferent; scrupulous, hesitant.

adv unwillingly, grudgingly, against one's will, under protest.

604 resolution *n* determination, will, decision, strength of mind, resolve, firmness, energy, manliness, vigor, resoluteness; pluck, zeal, devotion; self-control, self-command, self-possession, self-reliance, self-restraint, self-denial; tenacity, perseverance, obstinacy, *(informal)* gumption.

v be resolute, resolve, will, determine, decide, make a resolution, conclude, fix, bring to a crisis, take a decisive step; stand firm, insist upon, make a point of, not give an inch.

adj resolute, firm, steadfast, resolved, purposeful, fixed, inflexible, bold, game, indomitable, relentless, tenacious, gritty, stern, irrevocable, obstinate.

adv resolutely, in earnest, earnestly, manfully.

604a perseverance *n* persistence, tenacity, resolution, doggedness, determination, steadfastness, indefatigability, pluck, stamina, backbone.

v persevere, persist, continue, keep on, last, stick it out, hang in there.

adj persevering, constant, steady, steadfast, persistent, tenacious, resolute, dogged, indefatigable, indomitable, staunch, true, game, *(informal)* tough.

605 irresolution *n* indecision, indetermination, instability, uncertainty; hesitation, hesitancy, vacillation, oscillation, changeableness, fluctuation, fickleness, weakness, frailty, timidity, cowardice.

v be irresolute, dawdle, dilly-dally, shilly-shally, hesitate, falter, waver, vacillate, change, fluctuate, blow hot and cold.

adj irresolute, indecisive, indeterminate, unstable, uncertain; hesitant, changeable, capricious, fickle, frail, feeble, weak, timid, *(informal)* soft, cowardly.

606 obstinacy *n* doggedness, persistence, pertinacity, resolution, intractability, firmness, immovability, inflexibility, obduracy, willfulness, perversity, stubbornness, mulishness; uncontrollability, wildness.

fixed idea, *idée fixe*, fanaticism, zealotry, infatuation, monomania; bigotry, intolerance, dogmatism.

bigot, dogmatist, zealot, fanatic.

v be obstinate, persist, die hard, fight, stick to an idea.

adj obstinate, dogged, persistent, pertinacious, resolute, intractable, firm, refractory, headstrong, willful, inflexible, immovable, perverse, stubborn, mulish, pig-headed; wayward, unruly, incorrigible, uncontrollable, wild; fanatic, zealous, monomaniacal; intolerant, dogmatic, arbitrary.

607 recantation *n* tergiversation, renunciation, abjuration, retraction, defection, apostasy, disavowal, revocation, reversal.

turncoat, apostate, renegade, deserter.

v recant, change one's mind, abjure, retract, renounce, disavow, revoke, defect, change sides.

adj changeful, irresolute, slippery, timeserving.

608 caprice n fancy, humor, whim, quirk, freak, fad, vagary, prank.

v be capricious.

adj capricious, erratic, eccentric, fitful, inconsistent, fanciful, whimsical, crotchety, freakish, wayward, wanton; contrary, captious, unreasonable, arbitrary, fickle; frivolous.

609 choice n selection, decision, pick, choosing, election, option, alternative, preference, predilection, desire.

v choose, select, elect, make a choice, prefer, pick cull, decide.

adj optional, discretional, preferential.

609a neutrality. absence of choice n neutrality, indifference; indecision, irresolution.

no choice, first come first served.

v be neutral, have no preference, waive, abstain.

take what's offered.

adj neutral, indifferent; indecisive, irresolute.

610 rejection n refusal, repudiation, renunciation; exclusion, elimination.

v reject, refuse, repudiate, decline, deny, rebuff, repel, renounce; discard, throw away, exclude, eliminate; jettison.

611 predetermination n premeditation, predeliberation, foregone conclusion; resolve, intention; fate, predestination, destiny.

v predetermine, predestine, premeditate, resolve beforehand, calculate.

adj aforethought; foregone.

adv advisedly, deliberately, intentionally.

612 impulse n sudden thought, flash, spurt, inspiration, improvisation.

v improvise, extemporize, flash on, hit on, come up with, pull out of a hat, pull out of the air; say what comes to mind.

adj impulsive, impromptu, spontaneous; extemporaneous.

adv extempore, extemporaneously; impromptu, offhand, impulsively.

613 habit n addiction, disposition, tendency, bent, wont; custom, prescription, practice, way, usage, wont, manner; prevalence, observance; conventionalism, conventionality, mode, fashion, vogue, conformity; rule, precedent, routine, rut, groove.

v habituate, inure, harden, season; accustom, familiarize; acclimate, accommodate; cling to, adhere to, acquire a habit, fall into a rut; be habitual, come into use, become a habit, take root.

adj habitual, customary, prescriptive, usual, general, ordinary, common, frequent, everyday, familiar, trite, commonplace, conventional, regular, set, stock, fixed, permanent; prevalent, current, fashionable; addictive.

adv habitually, as usual, as things go, as the world goes; as a rule, for the most part, generally.

614 disuse n desuetude, disusage, lack of practice.

v be unaccustomed, break a habit; disuse.

adj unaccustomed; unusual, original.

615 motive n reason, ground, principle, mainspring, purpose, cause, occasion, influence, impulse, instigation, spur, stimulus, incitement, incentive, inducement, consideration, temptation, motivation; intention, ulterior motive.

v motivate, induce, move, inspire, put up to, prompt, stimulate, spur, excite, arouse, rouse, incite, instigate; influence, sway, incline, dispose, lead, persuade, prevail upon, enlist, engage, invite, court, tempt, charm.

adj suasive, persuasive, seductive, attractive, provocative.

615a absence of motive n caprice, chance, absence of design.

v have no motive.

adj capricious, without rhyme or reason.

adv capriciously.

616 dissuasion n expostulation, remonstrance, deprecation, discouragement, damper, restraint, curb, check.

v dissuade, cry out against, remonstrate, expostulate, warn, disincline, indispose, shake, discourage, dishearten, disenchant; deter, hold back, restrain, repel, turn aside, wean from, damp, cool, chill, blunt.

adj dissuasive.

617 [ostensible motive, ground, or reason] **plea** n pretext, allegation, excuse; pretense, shallow excuse, lame excuse, makeshift.

v plead, allege, excuse, make a pretext of, pretend.

adj ostensible, alleged.

adv ostensibly, under the pretense of.

618 good *n* benefit, interest, service, behalf, advantage, improvement, gain, boot, profit, harvest; boon, blessing, good luck, prize, good fortune, windfall, godsend; prosperity, happiness, goodness.

v benefit, serve, profit, advantage.

adj commendable; useful, good, beneficial, advantageous.

619 evil *n* ill, harm, hurt, mischief, nuisance; damage, loss; disadvantage, drawback; disaster, accident, casualty, mishap, misfortune; calamity, catastrophe, tragedy, ruin, destruction, adversity; mental suffering, pain, anguish; outrage, wrong, injury, foul, play.

v be in trouble; harm, hurt, injure, ruin, destroy, torture.

adj evil, hurtful, injurious, harmful; disastrous, catastrophic, cataclysmic, tragic, ruinous.

620 intention *n* intent, purpose, project, undertaking, design, ambition, contemplation, view, proposal, meaning; object, aim, end, destination, mark, point, goal, target, prey, quarry, game; decision, determination, resolve, resolution, settled purpose.

v intend, mean, design, purpose, propose, contemplate, plan, expect, mediate, calculate, project, aim for, aim at, aspire at.

adj intentional, advised, express, determinate, bound for, bent upon, in view, in prospect.

adv intentionally, advisedly, wittingly, knowingly, purposely, on purpose, by design, pointedly; deliberately.

621 [absence of design] **chance** *n* destiny, lot, fate, luck, good luck, turn, *(informal)* break, *(informal)* jinx, fortune; speculation, venture, stake, shot in the dark, fluke; wager, gambling, betting.

gambler, gamester, adventurer.

v chance, chance it, tempt fate, speculate, risk, venture, hazard, stake, wager, bet, place a bet, gamble, play for.

adj unintentional, accidental, random; fortuitous, lucky; speculative, venturesome.

adv unintentionally, unwittingly.

622 pursuit *n* pursuance, enterprise, undertaking, business, adventure, essay, quest, search.

v pursue, prosecute, follow, do, engage in, undertake, endeavor, seek, aim at, fish for, press on, go after, chase.

adj in quest of, in pursuit of.

623 avoidance *n* evasion, flight, escape, retreat, recoil, departure; abstention, abstinence, forbearance, inaction.

avoider, shirker, quitter, truant; fugitive, refugee, runaway, deserter.

v avoid, shun, steer clear of, keep clear of, evade, elude, shirk, fly from, turn away from; abstain, refrain, eschew, leave alone, not get involved; shrink, hold back, retire, recoil, flinch, blink, shy, dodge, beat a retreat, turn tail, run for one's life, head for the hills, take flight, beat it out; desert, sneak off, shuffle off, slink away, steal away, slip, sneak, bolt, abscond.

adj elusive, evasive, escapist, fugitive.

624 relinquishment *n* surrender, resignation, yielding, waiver, waiving, abdication, leaving, desertion, withdrawal, secession, abandonment, renunciation.

v relinquish, surrender, give up, resign, yield, cede, waive, forswear, forgo, abdicate, leave, forsake, desert, renounce, quit, abandon, let go, resign, *(informal)* throw in the towel, call it quits, *(informal)* hang it up.

625 business *n* occupation, trade, craft, profession, calling, employment, vocation, pursuit; affair, matter, concern, transaction, undertaking; function, duty, office, position, part, role, capacity.

v employ oneself, undertake, turn one's hand to; be at work on, be engaged in, be occupied with.

adj businesslike; workaday, professional, official, functional; busy.

626 plan *n* scheme, plot, stratagem, policy, procedure, project, formula, method, system, organization, design, contrivance, device; drawing, sketch, draft, map, chart, diagram, representation; intrigue, cabal, conspiracy.

planner, designer, organizer, schemer, strategist, intriguer.

v plan, arrange, frame, scheme, plot, design, devise, contrive, invent, concoct, hatch; project, forecast; systematize, organize, cast, recast, lay groundwork.

adj procedural, formulaic, methodological, systematic, organizational; conspiratorial; strategic.

627 [path] **method** *n* road, procedure, way, means, manner, fashion, technique, process, course, route, track, beat, tack; door, gateway, channel, passage, avenue, means of access, approach.

adv how, in what way, in what manner; by what mode; one way or another, after this fashion.

628 mid-course *n* middle way, middle course, mean, golden mean; compromise, *(informal)* six of one and half a dozen of another, half measures, neutrality.

v steer a middle course, go straight; compromise, go half way, make a compromise.

adj moderate, midway; neutral, impartial.

629 circuit *n* roundabout way, digression, detour, loop, winding.

v go round about, make a circuit, detour, wind around, circle around; deviate, digress.

adj circuitous, indirect, roundabout; zigzag.

adv in a roundabout way, by an indirect course, indirectly.

630 requirement *n* requisite, requisition, need, necessity, wants, claim, demand, prerequisite; mandate, order, command, directive, injunction, charge, claim, precept.

v require, need, call for, have occasion for, necessitate, obligate; demand, request, need, order, enjoin, direct, ask.

adj requisite, necessary, essential, indispensable, needful; urgent, exigent, instant, crying.

adv of necessity.

631 instrumentality *n* mediation, intervention, medium, intermedium, vehicle, hand; aid; subservience.

go-between, intermediary, minister.

v mediate, minister, intervene; be instrumental, aid.

adj instrumental, useful, serviceable; intermediary, intermediate.

adv through, by, whereby, thereby, by the agency of, by dint of, by means of.

632 means *n* resources, wherewithal, way, ways and means, know how, ability; agency, method, approach; capital, provisions.

v have the means, find the means, possess the means.

adj instrumental.

adv by means of; herewith, therewith; wherewithal.

633 instrument *n* tool, implement, utensil, machinery, equipment.

adj instrumental; mechanical.

634 substitute *n* deputy, alternate, understudy, stand-in, proxy, *(informal)* sub, replacement.

v to substitute for, sub.

635 materials *n* raw materials, resources, stuff, stock, staples, supplies.

636 store *n* stock, fund, mine, supply, reserve, reservoir, *(informal)* stash; accumulation, hoard, storing, storage.

v store, put aside, lay away; store up, put up, hoard away, accumulate, amass, garner; reserve, husband, *(informal)* stash, hold back.

adj in store, in reserve, spare.

637 provision *n* supply, grist, resources, store, provender, stock, food; catering, providing, purveying, purveyance, supplying.

v make provision, provide, lay in, lay in a stock, lay in a store; supply, furnish, purvey, provision, cater, stock, store, replenish.

638 waste *n* consumption, expenditure, dissipation, diminution, decline, emaciation, exhaustion, loss, destruction, decay, impairment; misuse, prodigality, wasting; ruin, devastation, spoilation, desolation.

v waste, consume, spend, throw out, expend, squander, misuse, misspend, dissipate; destroy, wear away, erode, eat away, reduce, wear down, exhaust, enfeeble, wear out.

adj wasteful, prodigal, spendthrift; destructive; wasted, gone to waste.

639 sufficiency *n* adequacy, enough, competence.

v be sufficient, suffice, do, just do, satisfy; have enough.

adj sufficient, enough, adequate, ample, up to the mark, competent, commensurate, satisfactory.

adv sufficiently, amply.

640 insufficiency *n* inadequacy, incompetence, incompleteness, deficiency, imperfection, shortcoming; paucity, scarcity, dearth; dole, pittance; emptiness, poorness, depletion, flaccidity.

v be insufficient, not suffice, not do, fall short of, *(informal)* not cut it; want, lack, need, require, be in want.

adj insufficient, inadequate, too little, not enough, incomplete, deficient, imperfect, wanting, short, scarce, meager, poor, thin, sparse, scant; incompetent, perfunctory.

641 redundance *n* superfluity, superabundance, too much, too many, exuberance, profuseness, profusion, plenty, repletion, plethora, congestion, surfeit, overdose, overflow; excess, surplus; repetition, verbosity.

v superabound, overabound, swarm, overflow, run over, run riot, overrun, overdose, overload, overdo, overwhelm; supersaturate, gorge, glut, load, drench, inundate, deluge, flood; choke, cloy, suffocate, pile on, lay on thick, lavish.

adj redundant, exuberant, inordinate, superabundant, excessive, overmuch, replete, profuse, lavish; exorbitant, extravagant, overweening, *(informal)* much; superfluous, unnecessary, needless, over and above, spare, duplicate; repetitious, verbose.

adv over and above, over much, out of proportion, beyond bounds, over one's head.

642 importance *n* consequence, substance, weight, moment, prominence, consideration, significance, import, concern, emphasis, interest, momentousness, weightiness; gravity, seriousness, solemnity; pressure, urgency, stress.

v be important, deserve consideration, be worthy of notice, merit attention; attach importance, ascribe importance,

value, care for, set store by; import, signify, matter, boot, carry weight; accentuate, emphasize, lay stress on; mark, underline, underscore.

adj important, consequential, weighty, momentous, prominent, considerable, significant, notable, salient; grave, serious, earnest, grand, solemn, impressive, commanding, imposing; urgent, pressing, critical, crucial, paramount, essential, vital, prime, primary, principal, all-important, capital, foremost, of vital importance; superior, considerable; significant, telling, trenchant, emphatic.

643 unimportance *n* insignificance, immateriality, triviality, paltriness, indifference, nothing, trifling; trumpery, trash, rubbish, frippery, chaff, bauble, trifle.

v be unimportant, not matter, matter little, signify little; make light of.

adj unimportant, of little account, of small importance, immaterial, unessential, nonessential, inconsequential, insignificant, inconsiderable, so-so; commonplace, ordinary, uneventful, mere, common; trifling, trivial, slight, slender, light, flimsy, shallow; frivolous, petty, niggling, piddling; poor, paltry, pitiful, sorry, mean, meager, shabby, beggarly, worthless, cheap, tawdry, trashy, gimmicky; unworthy of consideration, unworthy of notice; useless, of no account.

644 utility *n* usefulness, efficacy, helpfulness, service, use, stead, avail, help, aid; applicability, value, worth, productiveness.

v be useful, avail, serve, perform, help, aid, benefit; act a part, discharge a function, stand one in good stead.

adj useful, serviceable, functional, advantageous, valuable, productive, profitable, helpful, effectual, effective, efficacious, beneficial, salutary; applicable, available, practical, practicable, workable.

645 inutility *n* uselessness, inefficacy, ineptitude, inaptitude, inadequacy, inefficiency, unfruitfulness, futility, worthlessness, hopelessness.

v be useless, be of no help.

adj useless, unavailing, futile, inutile, fruitless, vain, ineffectual, profitless, bootless, valueless, worthless, hopeless; unserviceable, unusable, inoperative.

646 expedience *n* expediency, fitness, utility, suitability, profitability, advisability, propriety, appropriateness, desirability; opportunism, pragmatism, realism.

v bc expedient, suit, befit, suit the occasion.

adj expedient, advantageous, opportune, fit, suitable, convenient, profitable, worthwhile, advisable, meet, proper, becoming, appropriate, desirable.

647 inexpedience *n* inexpediency, impropriety, unfitness, unsuitability, inappropriateness, undesirability; inconvenience, impracticality.

v be inexpedient, be inconvenient, hinder.

adj inexpedient, inopportune, unfit, unsuitable, disadvantageous, discommodious, unadvisable, unseemly, improper, unworkable, impractical, inconvenient, unprofitable, useless, worthless.

648 [good qualities] **goodness** *n* virtue, excellence, merit, value, worth; perfection, eminence, superiority, masterpiece, *chef d'oeuvre*, prime, flower, cream, elite, pick, pick of the litter, salt of the earth, *(informal)* A-1, *(informal)* tops, second to none; gem, jewel, treasure, one in a million; beneficence.

v be good, excel, transcend, stand the test, pass muster, challenge comparison, vie, emulate, rival, *(informal)* dwarf the competition; be beneficial, do good, profit, benefit, improve, be the making of, do a world of good, produce a good effect, do a good turn.

adj good, excellent, better, superior, above par, fine, genuine, true; best, choice, select, rare, invaluable, priceless, inestimable, superlative, perfect, inimitable, first-rate, first-class, very best, crack, prime, tip-top, capital, *(informal)* tops; beneficial, valuable, advantageous, profitable, edifying, salutary, serviceable; favorable, propitious.

649 [bad qualities] **badness** *n* harmfulness, hurtfulness, virulence, painfulness, abomination, pestilence, guilt, depravity, vice, evil, malignity, malevolence; bane, plague, evil star, ill wind, bad omen, *(informal)* jinx, *(informal)*

whammy; snake in the grass, skeleton in the closet, *(informal)* ghosts, *(informal)* demons; ill-treatment, annoyance, molestation, abuse, oppression, persecution, outrage, misusage, injury, damage.

v hurt, harm, injure, damage, pain; wrong, aggrieve, oppress, persecute, trample upon, tread upon, walk over, overburden; weigh down, run down; victimize, maltreat, molest, abuse, ill-use, bruise, scratch, maul, smite, do violence, do harm, stab, pierce.

adj hurtful, harmful, baleful, injurious, deleterious, detrimental, noxious, pernicious, mischievous; oppressive, burdensome, onerous, malign, malevolent; virulent, venomous, corrosive, poisonous, deadly, destructive; bad, ill, dreadful, horrid, horrible, dire, rank, foul, rotten, as low as one can go, *(informal)* the pits; evil, wrong, reprehensible, hateful, abominable, detestable, execrable, damnable, infernal, diabolical; vile, base, villainous, cruel, mean, low; deplorable, wretched, sad, grievous, lamentable, pitiable, pitiful, woeful, painful.

650 perfection *n* ideal, summit, paragon, model, standard, pattern, mirror; impeccability, faultlessness, excellence; masterpiece, master stroke; transcendence, superiority.

v perfect, bring to perfection, ripen, mature, complete, finish; be perfect, transcend.

adj perfect, faultless, immaculate, spotless, unblemished, impeccable, exquisite, consummate; in perfect condition, sound, intact; best, model, standard, inimitable, beyond all praise.

651 imperfection *n* deficiency, inadequacy, insufficiency, immaturity; fault, defect, weak point, weak spot, flaw, taint, blemish, weakness, shortcoming, drawback.

v be imperfect, have a defect, not pass muster, fall short.

adj imperfect, deficient, inadequate, insufficient, immature, defective, faulty, unsound, out of order, out of tune, warped, lame, frail, weak, crude, incomplete, below par, found wanting; indifferent, middling, ordinary, mediocre, average, so-so, tolerable, fair, passable, decent, not bad, bearable, better than nothing; inferior, secondary, second-rate, poor substitute.

652 cleanness n purity, purification, purgation, cleanliness; ablution, lavation; neatness, tidiness, orderliness; cathartic, purgative, laxative; detergent, disinfectant.

v clean, cleanse, purify, purge, expurgate, clarify, refine; wash, launder, scour, scrub, disinfect, fumigate, deodorize, ventilate; rout out, clear out, sweep out, make a clean sweep of, start fresh; neaten, tidy up, order, put things in order.

adj clean, pure, immaculate, spotless, stainless, unsullied, sweet; neat, spruce, tidy, trim, kempt.

653 uncleanness n impurity, defilement, contamination, taint; decay, putrefaction, corruption, mold, mildew, rot, dry rot; squalor, slovenliness, filth, dirt, smut, grime, mud, mire, muck, quagmire, slime.

v be unclean, rot, putrefy, fester, rankle, reek, stink, mold, go bad; dirty, soil, tarnish, spot, smear, blot, blur, smudge, smirch; besmear, befoul, splash, stain, sully, pollute, defile, debase, contaminate, taint, corrupt.

adj unclean, dirty, filthy, grimy, soiled; dusty, smutty, sooty, slimy; slovenly, untidy, sluttish, dowdy, unkempt, unscoured, squalid; nasty, coarse, foul, impure, offensive, abominable, beastly, reeky, fetid; moldy, musty, moth-eaten, bad, gone bad, rancid, rotten, corrupt, putrid, carious, fecal; gory, bloody; gross.

654 health n soundness, well-being, vigor, good health, bloom, color, vitality, robust health.

v be in health, be healthy, bloom, flourish, feel fine, feel good.

adj healthy, healthful, in health, well, sound, hearty, hale, strong, hardy, robust, vigorous, fit as a fiddle, in top shape, chipper, (informal) all together.

655 disease n illness, sickness, ill health, ailment, infirmity, indisposition, complaint, disorder, malady; delicacy, delicate, condition, decline, deterioration, decay.

v ail, suffer, be affected with, droop, flag, languish, sicken, pine, gasp, waste away, fail; take sick, take ill, come down with, contract a disease, catch a bug.

adj ill, sick, indisposed, not well, unwell, in poor health, in bad health, ailing, poorly, laid up, bed-ridden, out of sorts, under the weather, (informal) in bad shape; sickly, infirm, unsound, unhealthy, (informal) falling apart, weak, lame, decrepit; diseased, morbid, mangy, corrupt, contaminated, leprous.

656 salubrity n healthiness, healthfulness, wholesomeness.

v be salubrious, be good for, agree with.

adj salubrious, healthy, healthful, salutary, wholesome, sanitary, bracing, invigorating, benign, nutritious, tonic, hygienic.

657 insalubrity n unhealthiness, unsoundness.

v be unhealthy, not be good for, disagree with.

adj insalubrious, unhealthy, unwholesome, noxious, noisome, deleterious, pestilential, bad, harmful, virulent, venomous, poisonous, septic, toxic, deadly.

658 improvement n amelioration, amendment, emendation, correction, revision, reformation, restoration, repair, betterment, gain, advancement, elevation, increase, refinement, elaboration; acculturation, cultivation, civilization.

reformer, radical.

v improve, mend, amend, get better; ameliorate, better, amend, emend, correct, right, rectify, revise, reform, restore, repair; advance, progress, ascend, increase, fructify, ripen, mature; refine, enrich, elaborate; promote, cultivate, foster, enhance.

adj better, better off, all for the better; emendatory, corrective, reformative, restorative, improving, progressive, improved.

659 deterioration n debasement, recession, retrogradation, degeneracy, degeneration, degradation, deprivation, depravity, retrogression; detriment, damage, loss, injury, impairment, contamination, spoilage, corruption, adulteration; decline, declension, senility, decrepitude; decadence, decay, dilapidation, falling off, wear and tear, erosion, corrosion, rottenness, blight, atrophy, collapse.

v deteriorate, degenerate, fall off, wane, ebb, decline, droop, go down, go downhill, sink, go to seed, go to waste, lapse, break down, crack, shrivel, fade, wither, molder, rot, rankle, decay, go bad, rust, crumble, shake, totter, perish, die; taint, infect, contaminate, poison, canker, corrupt, pollute, vitiate, debase, degrade, adulterate; injure, impair, damage, harm, hurt, spoil, mar, despoil, dilapidate, waste, ravage; wound, maim, cripple, scotch, mangle, mutilate, disfigure, blemish, deface, warp; blight, rot, corrode, erode, wear away, wear out, sap, mine, undermine, shake the foundations of, break up, destroy, decimate.

adj deteriorated, unimproved, injured, degenerate, imperfect; battered, weathered, weather-beaten, all the worse for wear, stale, dilapidated, faded, shabby, threadbare, worn, far gone, *(informal)* had it; decayed, moth-eaten, worm-eaten, mildewed, rusty, moldy, seedy, time-worn, wasted, crumbling, moldering, rotten, blighted, tainted; decrepit, broken down, wornout, used up, out of commission, in a bad way, past cure, past hope, *(informal)* long gone.

660 restoration *n* reestablishment, replacement, reinstatement, renewal, rehabilitation, reconstruction, reproduction, rebuilding, renovation, revival; refreshment, resuscitation, revivification; renaissance, renascence, new birth, regeneration, reconversion; redress, retrieval, reclamation, recovery, resumption; repair, reparation, restitution, relief, deliverance, rectification, cure, healing; redemption.

v restore, recover, rally, revive, come round, pull through, get well, get over; reestablish, replace, rehabilitate, reinstate; reconstruct, rebuild, reproduce, reorganize, reconstitute, renew, renovate; redeem, reclaim, recover, retrieve, rescue, deliver; redress, recure; cure, heal, remedy, doctor, bring round; resuscitate, revive, reanimate, revivify, reinvigorate, refresh; recoup, make good, square, set to rights, correct, put in order; repair, retouch, patch up, fix.

adj restorative, recuperative, curative, remedial; restorable, remediable,

retrievable, curable; restored, convalescent, renascent, reborn.

661 relapse *n* lapse, falling back, retrogradation, deterioration, backsliding.

v relapse, lapse, fall back, slip back, sink back, suffer a relapse, fall again.

adj retrograde.

662 remedy *n* help, redress, solution, answer, panacea; cure, relief, medicine, treatment, restorative, specific, medication, ointment, balm; antidote, corrective, antitoxin, counteractive.

doctor, physician, surgeon.

v remedy, cure, heal, set right, put right, doctor, nurse, restore, recondition, repair, redress; counteract, remove, correct, right, solve.

adj remedial, restorative, corrective, palliative; medicinal, therapeutic, curative; soluble.

663 bane *n* curse, evil, plague, scourge, pain, nuisance, thorn in the side, pain in the neck; poison, virus, venom; fungus, mildew, dry rot, canker, cancer; sting, fang, thorn, bramble, briar, nettle.

adj baneful, bad, sinister, pernicious, evil, baleful, poisonous, venomous, ruinous, unwholesome, harmful, deadly.

664 safety *n* security, surety, impregnability, invulnerability; safeguard, safety valve, precaution, custody, safe keeping, preservation, protection.

protector, guardian, warden, preserver, custodian, watchdog, sentinel, scout.

v be safe; protect, take care of, care for, preserve, cover, screen, shelter, shroud, guard, defend, secure, house, garrison; watch, patrol, look out, take precautions.

adj safe, secure, snug, warm, sure, sound, on the safe side, out of danger; dependable, trustworthy, sure, reliable; cautious, wary, careful; defensible, tenable, invulnerable, impregnable, unassailable, safe and sound.

665 danger *n* hazard, insecurity, instability, precariousness, slipperiness, risk, peril, jeopardy, liability, exposure; injury, evil; warning, alarm, apprehension.

v be in danger, run into trouble, lay oneself open to, hang by a thread, totter;

endanger, expose to danger, imperil, jeopardize, adventure, venture, risk, hazard, threaten.

adj dangerous, hazardous, risky, perilous, precarious, unsafe, insecure, unstable, untrustworthy, unsteady, shaky, slippery, ominous, fearful, explosive, fraught with danger; defenseless, vulnerable, open, liable.

666 refuge *n* sanctuary, retreat, asylum, hiding place, stronghold, fortress, shelter, cover; anchor, mainstay, support, check, last resort, safeguard.

v seek refuge, take refuge, find refuge, take shelter, find safety.

667 pitfall *n* snare, trap, snag, ambush, snake in the grass, wolf in sheep's clothing, menace, complication, danger; slippery ground, weak foundation, rocks, reefs, sunken rocks, sand, quicksand, breakers, shoals, shallows, precipice, maelstrom.

668 warning *n* caution, notice, premonition, prediction, admonition, advice, lesson; alarm, omen, sign, signal, augury, portent, presage.

sentinel, sentry, watch, watchman, watchdog, patrol, scout, spy.

v warn, caution, admonish, forewarn; give notice, notify, appraise, inform; menace, threaten, portend.

adj premonitory, cautionary, advisory; ominous, portentous.

669 [indication of danger] **alarm** *n* alarum, alarm bell, tocsin, distress signal, siren, danger signal, hue and cry, SOS, cry, scream.

v alarm, sound the alarm, warn, cry out.

670 preservation *n* safekeeping, conservation; guarding, safeguard, shelter, protection, defense; maintenance, support, sustenance, continuance, retention, salvation.

v preserve, keep, conserve; guard, safeguard, shelter, shield, protect, defend, rescue; keep up, maintain, continue, support, uphold, sustain; retain; store, husband; cure, pickle, bottle, can.

adj preserved, unimpaired, uninjured, unhurt, safe, sound, intact; conservative, preservative.

671 escape *n* flight, evasion, loophole, retreat; reprieve, release, liberation; narrow escape, close call, near miss.

v escape, flee, abscond, fly, steal away, run away, *(informal)* take off, *(informal)* split; shun, fly, elude, evade, avoid.

adj stolen away, fled, *(informal)* cut out.

672 deliverance *n* extrication, disentanglement, rescue, reprieve, respite; liberation, release, emancipation, freedom; redemption, salvation.

v deliver, extricate, disentangle, rescue, reprieve, save, redeem; set free, liberate, release, emancipate, free; come to the rescue.

673 preparation *n* provision, plan, arrangement, anticipation, precaution, forecast, rehearsal; groundwork, homework, foundation, scaffolding; training, education, dissemination; readiness, ripeness, maturity.

v prepare, get ready, make ready, prime, arrange, make preparations, plan, devise, anticipate, lay the foundations, provide, order; mature, ripen, mellow, season, nurture; equip, arm, fit out, furnish; train, teach, prepare for, rehearse, make provision for, take steps, provide against.

adj prepatory, precautionary, provident, preparative, preparatory; provisional, preliminary; prepared, ready, available, all ready, handy; ripe, mature, mellow.

674 nonpreparation *n* unpreparedness, unreadiness; improvidence.

v be unprepared; extemporize, improvise.

adj unprepared, incomplete, premature, rudimental, embryonic, immature, unripe, raw, green, coarse, crude, rough, unhewn, untaught, fallow, unready; out of order, nonfunctional, *(informal)* on the fritz, in disrepair, *(informal)* out of whack; shiftless, improvident, thoughtless, careless, slack, remiss, happy-go-lucky.

675 essay *n* trial endeavor, effort, attempt, struggle, venture, adventure, speculation, experiment.

v essay, try, experiment; endeavor, strive, tempt, attempt, venture, adventure, speculate, tempt fortune, *(informal)* give it a go, *(informal)* take a shot at.

adj experimental, tentative, probationary; venturesome, adventurous, speculative.

adv experimentally, on trial.

676 undertaking *n* task, job, venture, engagement, compact, contract, enterprise; pilgrimage, quest.

v undertake, engage in, embark on, launch into, plunge into, volunteer; engage, promise, contract, take upon oneself, devote oneself to, determine, take up, take in hand; tackle, set about, fall to, begin, broach.

677 use *n* employ, exercise, application, appliance; disposal; consumption; agency, usefulness; benefit, recourse, resort, avail; utilization, utility, service, wear; usage.

v use, make use of, employ, put to use, put into operation, apply, set in motion, set to work; ply, work, wield, handle, manipulate; exert, exercise, practice, avail oneself of, profit by; resort to, have recourse to, recur to, take up, try; utilize, bring into play, press into service; use up, consume, expend, tax, task, wear.

adj useful, instrumental, utilitarian, subservient, employable, applicable, beneficial.

678 disuse *n* forbearance, abstinence; relinquishment, abandonment; desuetude.

v not use, do without, dispense with, let alone, forebear, abstain, spare, waive, neglect; keep back, reserve; disuse, lay up, shelve, set aside, put aside, leave off, have done with; supersede, discard, throw aside, relinquish, dismantle.

adj not in use, unemployed, unapplied; disused, unused, done with.

679 misuse *n* misusage, misemployment, misapplication, misappropriation; abuse, profanation, prostitution, desecration; waste.

v misuse, misemploy, misapply, misappropriate; abuse, profane, prostitute, desecrate; waste, squander, destroy; overwork, overtask, overtax.

680 action *n* movement, work, labor, performance, moving, working, performing, operation; deed, act, feat, exploit; conduct, behavior, procedure, execution; energetic activity, exercise, exertion, energy, effort; affair, encounter, meeting, engagement, conflict, combat, fight, battle.

actor, doer, worker.

v act, do, perform, execute, achieve, transact, enact; commit, perpetrate, inflict; exercise, prosecute, carry on, work, function, labor, operate, exert energy, be active; behave, conduct oneself, comport oneself; play, feign, fake, imitate.

adj in action, in operation, operative.

681 inaction *n* passivity, inactivity, idleness, solthfulness; waiting, mulling around, killing time; rest, repose,

v not act, not do, be inactive, abstain from doing, do nothing, let alone, let things take their course; stand aloof, refrain, pause, wait, bide one's time, cool one's heels, waste time, lie idle.

adj inactive, passive, idle, slothful; out of work.

682 activity *n* movement, hustle, bustle, stir, fuss, flurry, action, business; industry, assiduity, assiduousness, laboriousness, drudgery; diligence, perseverance, vigilance, wakefulness, restlessness, fidgetiness; briskness, liveliness, animation, life, vivacity, spirit, dash, energy; eagerness, zeal, ardor, vigor, abandon, exertion; earnestness, intentness, devotion.

v be active, busy oneself in, stir about, rouse oneself, speed, hasten, bustle, fuss, *(informal)* raise a ruckus; push, push ahead, *(informal)* step on it, *(informal)* move it, make progress; toil, plod, persist, persevere, hustle, *(informal)* hustle it, *(informal)* push; look sharp, keep moving, seize the opportunity, *carpe diem,* lose no time, dash off, make haste; have a hand in, trouble oneself about.

adj active, brisk, lively, busy as a bee, vivacious, alive, frisky; quick, prompt, ready, alert, spry, sharp, smart, awake, wide awake, eager, zealous; industrious, assiduous, diligent, vigilant; businesslike; restless, fussy, fidgety, busy.

683 inactivity *n* inaction, inertness, lull, quiescence; idleness, remissness, sloth, indolence, dawdling, laziness; dullness, languor, sluggishness, torpor, stupor, lethargy, procrastination.

idler, drone, dawdler, moper, lounger, loafer, sluggard, laggard, slumberer.

v be inactive, do nothing, dawdle, lag, hang back, slouch, loll, lounge, loaf, loiter, take it easy; fritter away time, idle, piddle, putter, dabble, dally, dilly-dally; languish, flag, relax; kill time, waste time.

adj inactive, motionless; indolent, lazy, slothful, idle, remiss, slack, inert, torpid, sluggish, languid, supine, heavy, dull, listless; laggard, slow, rusty, lackadaisical, irresolute; drowsy, lethargic, soporific, dreamy, dreamy-eyed.

684 haste *n* urgency, need, hurry, flurry, bustle, spurt, rush, dash, scramble, bustle, ado, precipitancy, precipitation; swiftness, celerity, alacrity, quickness, rapidity, dispatch, speed, expedition, promptitude, timeliness, promptness.

v haste, hasten, make haste, hurry, dash, push on, press on, press forward, scurry, bustle, scramble, rush, accelerate, urge, expedite, quicken, speed, precipitate, dispatch.

adj hasty, speedy, quick, hurried, swift, rapid, fast, fleet, brisk; precipitate, rash, foolhardy, reckless, indiscreet, thoughtless, headlong; testy, touchy, irascible, petulant, waspish, fretful, fiery, excitable, irritable, peevish.

685 leisure *n* spare time, free time, convenience, liberty, pause, stay, halt, lull, breather, *(informal)* letup, breathing spell, break, *(informal)* time out; interlude, vacation, holiday.

v have leisure, take one's time; rest, relax, repose.

adj leisure, spare, free; leisurely, slow, deliberate, quiet, calm, restful, peaceful, languid, easy, gradual.

686 exertion *n* effort, action, activity, endeavor, struggle, attempt, strain, trial, stress; labor, work, toil, travail; trouble, pain; energy.

v exert, exert oneself, labor, work, toil, sweat, drudge, strive, strain; work hard, rough it, buckle to, take pains, concentrate, spare no effort.

adj laborious, wearisome, burdensome, *(informal)* tough, *(informal)*

rough, strenuous, herculean, Sisyphean.

687 repose *n* rest, sleep, slumber; relaxation, breathing spell; halt, pause, respite, cessation; day of rest, Sabbath; holiday, vacation, recess.

v repose, rest; relax, unbend, slacken, catch one's breath, get one's wind, take a breather, pause; recline, lie down, go to bed, take a nap, go to sleep; take a holiday, go on vacation, shut up shop.

adj reposing, resting.

adv at rest.

688 fatigue *n* weariness, lassitude, tiredness, exhaustion, faintness; ennui, boredom, tedium, languor, yawning, drowsiness.

v be fatigued, yawn, droop, sink, flag, *(informal)* give out; gasp, pant, puff, blow, drop, swoon, faint; fatigue, tire, weary, exhaust, wear out; tax, task, strain; bore, tire, irritate, annoy.

adj fatigued, weary, drowsy, haggard, faint, exhausted, spent, tired, tired to death, worn out, *(informal)* gone; breathless.

689 refreshment *n* recovery of strength, restoration, revival, repair, relief.

v refresh, brace, strengthen, reinvigorate, revive, stimulate, freshen, cheer, enliven, reanimate; restore, repair, renew.

adj refreshing, restoring.

690 agent *n* doer, actor, performer, perpetrator, operator; practitioner, executioner, executor, executrix, minister, representative, deputy, servant, worker; participant, party to.

691 workshop *n* laboratory, factory, mill, mint, forge, studio; hive, beehive, seat of activity.

692 conduct *n* behavior, demeanor, action, actions, deportment, bearing, carriage, mien, manners; process, ways, practice, procedure, method; policy, tactics, strategy, plan; direction, management, execution, guidance, leadership, administration.

v conduct, behave, deport, act, bear; transact, execute, dispatch, discharge, proceed with, enact; direct, manage, carry on, supervise, regulate, administer, guide, lead.

adj procedural, practical, methodical, tactical, strategical, businesslike; directive, managerial, administrative, executive.

693 direction *n* guidance, advice, regulation, conduct, management, disposition, supervision, auspices, steerage, stewardship, ministration, administration, control, leadership, government, rule, command; order, command, instruction.

v direct, guide, advise, regulate, conduct, manage, control, dispose, supervise, overlook, steer, steward, pilot, minister, administer, legislate, lead, rule, govern, have charge of, command; order, instruct, prescribe.

adj directing, guiding, supervisory, managing, administering.

694 director *n* manager, governor, controller, superintendent, supervisor, overseer, inspector, foreman, surveyor, taskmaster, master, leader, boss; adviser, guide, pilot, captain, helmsman, driver; head, chief, principal, president, minister, official, functionary.

695 advice *n* counsel, opinion, recommendation, guidance, suggestion, persuasion, urging, exhortation; instruction, charge, injunction; admonition, warning, caution.

adviser, council, counselor, mentor.

v advise, give counsel to, suggest, recommend, prescribe, advocate, exhort, persuade; enjoin, enforce, charge, instruct; admonish, caution, warn; take counsel, confer, deliberate, discuss, consult, refer to; give counsel, offer counsel.

adj advisory, suggestive, persuasive, suasive; admonitory.

696 council *n* committee, court, chamber, cabinet, board, board of directors, advisory board, staff, syndicate, chapter; assembly, caucus, conclave, meeting, conference, session.

697 precept *n* direction, instruction, charge, prescript, prescription; golden rule, maxim, canon, law, code, act, statute, regulation, formula, form, technicality, rubric; order, command.

698 skill *n* skillfulness, dexterity, adroitness, expertness, proficiency, competence, facility, knack, mastery; accomplishment, acquirement, attainment, ability, craft; knowledge, wisdom, *savoir faire,* tact, wit, sagacity, discretion, finesse, craftiness, cunning, management; cleverness, ingenuity, capacity, talent, talents, faculty, endowment, *forte,* turn, gift, genius; intelligence, sharpness, readiness, invention, inventiveness, aptness, aptitude, proclivity, capacity for, genius for, felicity, capability, qualification.

v be skillful, excel in, be master of, have a knack for; take advantage of.

adj skillful, dextrous, adroit, adept, expert, apt, handy, quick, deft, proficient, masterly, crack, first-rate, conversant; skilled, experienced, practiced, competent, efficient, qualified, capable, fit, fit for, trained, prepared, finished; clever, able, ingenious, felicitous, inventive; shrewd, sharp, smart, intelligent, cunning, tactful, discreet, wise, knowledgeable.

adv skillfully, artistically, with consummate skill.

699 unskillfulness *n* want of skill, incompetence, inability, inexpertness, maladroitness, ineptitude, clumsiness, awkwardness, carelessness, bumbling, bungling; indiscretion.

v be unskillful, blunder, bungle, boggle, fumble, botch, stumble.

adj unskillful, unskilled, inexpert, incompetent, unable, inapt, bungling, inept, maladroit, awkward, clumsy, gawky; unfit, ill-qualified, unhandy, not conversant; raw, rusty, out of practice.

700 expert *n* specialist, authority, mater, professional, connoisseur, veteran, old hand, old soldier; genius, mastermind, wizard, prodigy, *(informal)* pro.

701 bungler *n* blunderer, blunderhead, fumbler, duffer, clown, *(informal)* turkey, butter-fingers, greenhorn, amateur, rookie, novice, *(informal)* Sunday driver, *(informal)* armchair quarterback.

702 cunning *n* craftiness, skillfulness, shrewdness, artfulness, wiliness, subtlety, finesse, artifice, device, stratagem, intrigue, craft, guile, chicanery, duplicity, subterfuge, deceit, deceitfulness, slyness, deception; ability, skill, adroitness, expertness.

v be cunning, maneuver, contrive, manipulate, intrigue, finesse, surprise.

adj crafty, shrewd, artful, wily, subtle, tricky, foxy, politic, insidious, stealthy, Machiavellian, deceitful, duplicitous, sly, deceptive; canny, astute; ingenious, clever, skillful, sharp.

703 artlessness *n* simplicity, innocence, naivete, unworldliness, inexperience, inexposure, plainness, plain speaking, sincerity, honesty, openness, candor, matter of factness, bluntness.

v be artless, speak one's mind, come to the point, pull no punches.

adj artless, natural, simple, innocent, naive, childlike, unsuspicious, unworldly, unartificial, plain; sincere, frank, open, candid, honest, ingenuous, guileless, straightforward, aboveboard, point-blank, plain spoken, outspoken, blunt, direct, matter of fact.

adv in plain English, in simple words, without mincing words.

704 difficulty *n* dilemma, predicament, quandary, fix, exigency, emergency, crisis, trouble, problem, scrape, entanglement, strait, pass, pinch; reluctance, unwillingness, obstinacy, stubbornness; demur, objection, obstacle; labor, task, hard task, herculean task.

v be difficult, pose, perplex, bother, nonplus, hinder; encumber, embarrass, entangle.

adj difficult, hard, arduous, troublesome, irksome, laborious, formidable; awkward, unwieldy, unmanageable; fastidious, particular, stubborn, intractable, perverse; obscure, complex, intricate, delicate, uncertain, ticklish, critical; unfeasible, impractical, impossible, hopeless; austere, rigid.

705 facility *n* ease, easiness, capability, feasibility, practicability; flexibility, pliancy, smoothness, child's play.

v be easy, run smoothly, work well; facilitate, smooth, ease, lighten, free, clear, disencumber, disentangle, extricate, unravel.

adj easy, facile; feasible, practicable, within reach, accessible; manageable, tractable, pliant, smooth.

adv easily, readily, smoothly.

706 hindrance *n* impediment, deterrent, hitch, encumbrance, obstruction, check, stricture, restraint, hobble, obstacle, stumbling block; interuption, interfer-

ence; impeding, stopping, stoppage, preventing.

v hinder, interrupt, check, impede, retard, encumber, delay, hamper, obstruct, trammel, cramp, handicap; block, thwart, frustrate, disconcert, prevent.

adj obstructive, intrusive; onerous, burdensome, cumbersome, obtrusive.

707 aid *n* help, support, succor, assistance, service, furtherance; relief, rescue, charity; assistant, helper, supporter, servant; patronage, championship, advocacy, favor, interest.

v aid, support, help, succor, assist, serve, abet, back, second; spell, relieve, rescue; sustain, uphold, prop, hold up, bolster; promote, facilitate, ease, advocate; be of help, give help, give assistance, oblige, accommodate, humor, encourage.

adj aiding, auxiliary, helpful, supportive; charitable; friendly, amicable, well-disposed, neighborly.

708 opposition *n* antagonism, hostility, resistance, counteraction; competition, enemy, foe, adversary, antagonist; opposing, resisting, combating.

v oppose, resist, combat, withstand, thwart, confront, contravene, interfere; hinder, obstruct, prevent, check; contradict, gainsay, deny, refuse, dissent.

adj adverse, antagonistic, contrary, at variance, at odds, anti, at issue, in opposition; unfavorable, unfriendly, hostile, inimical, resistant.

adv against, versus, counter to, in conflict with, at cross purposes; in spite, in defiance.

709 cooperation *n* concert, concurrence, agreement, concord, togetherness, harmony, unanimity; complicity, collusion, participation, combination, union, team-work; association, partnership, alliance, pool, coalition, confederation, fusion, fellowship, fraternity; unanimity, partisanship, spirit, party spirit, *esprit de corps*.

v cooperate, concur, combine, unite, pool, share, band together, pull together; act in concert, join forces, fraternize; conspire, be in league with; side with, go along with, join hands with, throw in one's lot with, rally round; participate, have a hand in.

adj cooperating, cooperative, participatory; in league, party to.

adv cooperatively, unanimously, shoulder to shoulder.

710 opponent *n* adversary, antagonist, competitor, rival, opposition; enemy, foe.

711 auxiliary *n* helper, aid, ally, assistant, confederate, collaborator, colleague, associate, partner, mate, friend.

712 party *n* group, gathering, assembly, assemblage, company, crew, band; clan, family, fellowship, community; body, faction, side, circle, clique, set, gang, claque, coterie, combination, ring, league, alliance, association.

v unite, join, band together, cooperate, assemble.

adj clannish, cliquish, communal, familial, fraternal.

713 discord *n* dissidence, dissonance, disagreement, clash, shock; variance, difference, dissension, misunderstanding, cross-purposes, odds, division, split, rupture, disruption, breach, schism, feud, conflict, struggle, argument, contention, quarrel, dispute, tiff, squabble, altercation, words; strife, outbreak.

v be discordant, disagree, clash, jar, conflict, differ, dissent, fall out, quarrel, dispute, squabble, wrangle, bicker, have words with; split, break, disunite, feud.

adj discordant, dissident, dissonant; divisive, disruptive; contentious, argumentative, quarrelsome, disputatious, fractious; at variance, at cross purposes.

714 concord *n* accord, harmony, sympathy, agreement, union, unison, unity, peace; amity, friendship, alliance, *detente,* understanding, togetherness, conciliation.

v agree, accord, harmonize with, fraternize, understand one another, concur, pull together; side with, sympathize with.

adj concordant, congenial, in accord; harmonious, sympathetic, friendly, fraternal, conciliatory.

adv with one voice, unanimously, in concert with.

715 defiance *n* daring, courage, courageousness, bravery, boldness; assertiveness, aggressiveness; antagonism, insubordination, recalcitrance, rebelliousness, insolence, resistance.

v defy, challenge, resist, dare, brave, flout, scorn, despise.

adj defiant, daring, courageous, brave, bold; resistant, insolent, rebellious, recalcitrant, contumacious, insubordinate, antagonistic.

adv in the face of, under one's very nose.

716 attack *n* onslaught, assault, offense, battery, onset, charge, encounter, aggression, incursion, invasion, sally, sortie, raid, foray; criticism, blame, censure, abuse.

assailant, aggressor, invader, attacker.

v assail, assault, molest, threaten, storm, charge, set upon, invade, bombard, beset, besiege, lay siege, storm; criticize, impugn, blame, censure, abuse; declare war, begin hostilities.

adj aggressive, offensive; critical, abusive.

adv on the offensive.

717 defense *n* guard, garrison, fortification, shield, shelter, screen, preservation, protection, guardianship, safeguard, security; justification, pleading, vindication.

v defend, guard, fortify, shield, shelter, screen, preserve, protect, keep safe, guard against, watch over, safeguard, secure; parry, repel, put to flight; uphold, maintain, justify, vindicate.

adj defensive, protective.

718 retaliation *n* reprisal, requital, retort, counterstroke, counterattack, retribution, reciprocation, reciprocity, recrimination, revenge, vengeance, reaction.

v retaliate, requite, retort, counterattack, revenge, repay, return, avenge.

adj retaliatory, vengeful, revengeful, retributive, reciprocal, reactive.

adv in retaliation.

719 resistance *n* opposition, withstanding, front, stand, oppugnance, reluctance, repulsion; interference, friction; insurrection, insurgence, rebellion.

v resist, withstand, stand up, stand;

confront, oppose, grapple with, rise up, revolt, rebel, repel, repulse.

adj resistant, refractory, recalcitrant, repulsive, repellent; stubborn, indomitable, obstinate.

720 contention *n* struggling, struggle, strife, discord, dissention, quarrel, disagreement, squabble, feud; rupture, break, falling out; opposition, belligerency, combat, conflict, competition, rivalry, contest; disagreement, dissension, debate, wrangle, altercation, dispute, argument, controversy.

v contend, struggle, strive, fight, battle, combat, vie, compete, rival; debate, dispute, argue, wrangle; assert, maintain, claim.

adj contentious, combative, belligerent, bellicose, warlike, quarrelsome, pugnacious; competitive.

721 peace *n* treaty, truce, accord, amity, harmony, concord; calm, quiet, tranquility, peacefulness, calmness; order, security.

v be at peace; keep the peace; make peace.

adj peaceful, tranquil, placid, serene, calm, complacent; mellow, halcyon, pacific; peaceable, amicable, friendly, amiable, mild, gentle.

722 warfare *n* fighting, hostilities, war, combat, battle, ordeal; tactics, strategy, generalship.

v war, make war, wage war, fight, give fight, battle, do battle, combat, contend, cross swords.

adj warlike, contentious, belligerent, combative, bellicose, martial, military, militant.

adv to arms.

723 pacification *n* conciliation, reconciliation, accommodation, arrangement, adjustment, compromise; amnesty, peace offering, truce, armistice, suspension of hostilities.

v pacify, reconcile, propitiate, placate, conciliate, accommodate, appease, make peace; quiet, calm, tranquilize, assuage, still, smooth, moderate, ameliorate, mollify, meliorate, soothe, bury the hatchet.

adj pacific, conciliatory.

724 mediation *n* negotiation, arbitration, parley; intervention, intercession, interposition.

mediator, arbiter, arbitrator, peacemaker, go-between, negotiator, moderator, diplomat.

v mediate, intercede, intervene, interpose, interfere; step in, negotiate, arbitrate.

adj mediatory.

725 submission *n* nonresistance, obedience, compliance, acquiescence, yielding, submissiveness, pliancy; surrender, cessation, capitulation; resignation, passivity, docility.

v succumb, submit, yield, bend, acquiesce, resign, agree, obey, comply, bow, surrender, capitulate.

adj submissive, obedient, compliant, acquiescent, passive, docile, tame, humble.

726 combatant *n* fighter, contestant, disputant, battler, litigant, contender, competitor, militarist, soldier, warrior, polemic, candidate; antagonist, foe, enemy, opponent, rival, adversary, assailant, opposition, assailer, assailant, assaulter, opposer, opponent.

727 arms *n* weapons, weaponry, armaments, armor, ammunition, munitions, deadly weapons.

v arm, outfit, ready for battle, prepare for battle.

728 arena *n* battleground, battlefield, field of battle, theater, ring, lists; playhouse, amphitheater, stage, boards; Colosseum, gymnasium, playing field.

729 completion *n* culmination, finish, conclusion, close, termination, end, finale; upshot, result; final touch, crowning touch; consummation, accomplishment, achievement, fulfillment; performance, execution; perfection, thoroughness.

v complete, finish, end, conclude, close, terminate, finalize; consummate, perfect, accomplish, do, fulfill, achieve, effect, execute, enact, dispatch, discharge.

adj whole, entire, full, intact, unbroken, one, perfect; done, consummate, perfect, thorough, through-and-through.

adv completely, thoroughly; perfectly.

730 noncompletion *n* incompleteness, nonfulfilment, nonperformance; neglect, shortcoming.

v not complete, leave unfinished, leave undone; neglect, leg alone, let slip; fall short of.

adj incomplete, unfinished, sketchy.

731 success *n* progress, advance; hit, stroke, trump card; good fortune, good luck, luck, break; prosperity, achievement, fulfillment, accomplishment; ascendancy, mastery, conquest, victory, triumph; proficiency, skill, mastery.

v succeed, attain an end, secure an objective; progress, advance; accomplish, achieve, effect, complete; prosper, find fulfillment, fulfill oneself; master, conquer, triumph, surmount, overcome.

adj successful, prosperous, well-to-do; victorious, triumphant; masterful, proficient.

adv successfully, with flying colors, in triumph.

732 failure *n* unsuccessfulness, miscarriage, abortion, failing; neglect, omission, dereliction, non-performance; deficiency, insufficiency, defectiveness; blunder, mistake, fault, slip, mishap, scrape, mess, fiasco, breakdown; decline, decay, deterioration, loss; bankruptcy, insolvency, bust, dud.

v fail, come short, fall short, disappoint, miss the mark, miscarry, abort, blunder, botch, make a mess of, *(informal)* blow it, founder, flounder, sink, go amiss, go wrong, go hard with; fall off, dwindle, decline, fade, weaken, wane, give out, cease; desert, forsake.

adj unsuccessful, abortive, stillborn, fruitless, bootless, ineffectual, inefficient, insufficient, useless; lost, undone, bankrupt; wide of the mark, erroneous, frustrated, thwarted, foiled, defeated; defective, faulty.

adv unsuccessfully, in vain, to little purpose.

733 trophy *n* medal, prize, palm, laurel, honor, accolade, decoration, reward, recognition, triumph, celebration.

734 prosperity *n* well-being, success, fortune, wealth, affluence.

v prosper, thrive, flourish, rise, make one's way, flower, grow, blossom, bloom, fructify, succeed, *(informal)* make it.

adj prosperous, successful, wealthy, rich, well-to-do, well-off; favorable, propitious, fortunate, lucky, auspicious, golden, bright.

735 adversity *n* calamity, distress, catastrophe, crisis, disaster, failure; bad luck, hard times, misfortune, *(informal)* downers, *(informal)* bummers, trouble, hardship, pressure, affliction, wretchedness.

v go downhill, go to the dogs, decay, sink, decline, come to grief, *(informal)* hit the pits, fall on evil days.

adj adverse, unfavorable, unlucky, unfortunate; calamitous, disastrous, critical, dire, catastrophic; unprosperous, hapless, in a bad way, under a cloud, in adverse circumstances, down in the mouth.

adv adversely; if worst comes to worst.

736 mediocrity *n* average capacity, ordinariness, commonplaceness, insignificance, passableness, tolerableness, indifference, inferiority, paltriness, triviality; moderation, golden mean.

v jog on, get along.

adj mediocre, average, normal, ordinary, commonplace, run-of-the-mill, insignificant, tolerable, unimportant, indifferent, inferior, poor, slight, paltry; moderate, reasonable, temperate, respectable.

II. Intersocial Volition

737 authority *n* control, influence, jurisdiction, command, rule, sway, power, dominion, supremacy; expert, adjudicator, arbiter, judge, sovereign, ruler; warrant, justification, permit, permission, sanction, liberty, authorization.

v authorize, empower, commission, allow, permit, sanction, approve; warrant, justify, legalize, support, back; rule, sway, control, administer, govern.

adj authoritative, peremptory, magisterial, imperative, dogmatic, masterful; executive, administrative, sovereign, regnant, supreme, dominant, paramount, predominant, preponderant, influential, official, decisive, valid, absolute.

738 [absence of authority] **laxity** *n* laxness, looseness, slackness, lenience, toleration, relaxation, loosening, licence, freedom.

v be lax, tolerate, relax, give a free rein.

adj lax, loose, slack, remiss, lenient, negligent, careless, weak.

739 severity *n* seriousness, gravity, sternness, harshness, austerity, rigidity, rigorousness, strictness, stringency, relentlessness, abruptness, curtness; arbitrariness, absolutism, despotism, dictatorship, autocracy, tyranny, oppression; strength, force, brute force, coercion.

tyrant, disciplinarian, despot, taskmaster, oppressor, inquisitor.

v be severe, tyrannize, domineer, dominate, bully, inflict, wreak, be hard on, ill-treat, maltreat, oppress, trample on, crush, coerce.

adj severe, serious, grave, stern, harsh, austere, rigid, stiff, dour, rigorous, strict, strait-laced, stringent, relentless, hard, inexorable, abrupt, peremptory, curt, short; arbitrary, absolute, despotic, dictatorial, autocratic, tyrannical, oppressive, coercive, inquisitorial, ruthless, cruel, malevolent, arrogant.

adv severely, with a high hand, with a heavy hand.

740 lenience *n* leniency, tolerance, toleration, moderation, mildness, gentleness, favor, indulgence, forbearance, quarter, compassion, clemency, mercy.

v be lenient, tolerate, bear with, favor, indulge, allow.

adj lenient, tolerant, mild, easy, easygoing, gentle, tender, indulgent, compassionate, sympathetic, merciful.

741 command *n* order, ordinance, direction, bidding, injunction, charge, mandate, behest, ukase, commandment, requisition, requirement, instruction, dictum, act, fiat; demand, exaction, claim, request; control, mastery, disposal, rule, sway, power, domination.

v command, order, direct, bid, demand, charge, instruct, enjoin, require, impose; degree, enact, ordain, dictate, prescribe, appoint; claim, lay claim to.

adj commanding, authoritative.

742 disobedience *n* noncompliance, nonobservance, insubordination, contumancy, infraction, infringement, defiance, unruliness, rebelliousness, obstinacy, stubbornness, resistance, mutinousness, mutiny, rebellion.

insurgent, mutineer, rebel, revolutionary, rioter, traitor, *(informal)* radical.

v disobey, transgress, violate, disregard, defy, infringe, shirk, resist, mutiny, rebel, revolt.

adj disobedient, insubordinate, contumacious, defiant, refractory, unruly, fractious, rebellious, mutinous, obstinate, stubborn, unsubmissive, uncompliant, recalcitrant, insurgent, riotous.

743 obedience *n* observance, compliance, docility, tractability, deference, respect, duty, subservience, submissiveness, obsequiousness; allegiance, loyalty, fealty, homage, devotion.

v obey, comply, submit, follow, attend to, serve.

adj obedient, submissive, compliant, tractable, docile, deferential, respectful, dutiful, loyal, subservient.

adv obediently, in compliance with, in obedience to.

744 compulsion *n* coercion, constraint, duress, enforcement, conscription, force; impulse, necessity.

v compel, force, make, drive, coerce, constrain, enforce, impel, require, necessitate, oblige, motivate; subdue, subject, bend, bow, overpower.

adj compelling, compulsory, coercive, forcible, constraining; obligatory, necessary, unavoidable, inescapable, ineluctable, irresistible, inexorable.

adv by force, forcibly, on compulsion.

745 master *n* lord, commander, commandant, chief, head, leader, director, ruler, boss, authority.

746 servant *n* subject, retainer, follower, henchman, domestic, menial, help, helper, employee, worker, laborer.

v serve, function, answer, assist, help, aid, provide, cater, satisfy; wait on, attend.

747 [insignia of authority] **scepter** *n* regalia, staff, symbol, emblem, flag, badge; title.

748 freedom *n* liberty, independence, autonomy, noninterference; immunity, franchisement, franchise, privilege, latitude, scope; ease, facility; frankness, openness; familiarity, license, looseness, laxity.

  v be free, have scope, do as one likes, do what one wants; free, liberate, permit, allow, set free.

  adj free, independent, at large, loose, scot free; unconstrained, unconfined, unchecked, unhindered, unobstructed, unbound, uncontrolled, ungoverned, unchained, unfettered, unshackled, uncurbed, unbridled, unmuzzled; unrestricted, unlimited, unconditional; absolute; discretionary; wanton, rampant, irrepressible, unvanquished; immune, exempt, freed; autonomous.

  adv freely.

749 subjection *n* dependence, subordination, thrall, thralldom, subjugation, bondage, serfdom, slavery, servitude, enslavement; service, employ, tutelage, constraint, yoke, submission, obedience.

  v be subject, be at the mercy of, depend upon, fall prey to, play second fiddle to, serve, submit; subject, subjugate, master, tame, tread down, weigh down, enslave, enthral, rule.

  adj subject, dependent, subordinate; under control, in harness.

750 liberation *n* disengagement, release, enlargement, emancipation, enfranchisement, deliverance, extrication, discharge, dismissal, acquittal, absolution.

  v liberate, set free, free, disengage, release, emancipate, enfranchise, deliver, extricate, discharge, dismiss, unfetter, disenthrall, set loose, loose, let out, acquit, absolve.

  adj liberated, freed.

751 restraint *n* restriction, circumscription, limitation, control, confinement, curb, check, suppression, constraint, repression.

  v restrain, check, keep down, repress, curb, bridle, suppress, compel, hold, keep, constrain; restrict, circumscribe, confine, hinder.

  adj restrained, constrained, restrictive, suppressive, repressive; imprisoned, pent up, under restraint.

752 prison *n* jail, gaol, cage, coop, pen, penitentiary, jailhouse, cell, block, dungeon, lock-up, stir, irons, *(informal)* calaboose; *(informal)* hoosegow, *(informal)* the joint, *(informal)* the big house.

753 keeper *n* custodian, guard *(informal)* screw, jailer, gaoler, warder, escort, body-guard; protector, guardian, governor, governess, teacher, tutor, nurse.

754 prisoner *n* captive, convict, con, jailbird.

  v be imprisoned, stand convicted.

  adj in prison, in custody, in chains, under wraps, in stir.

755 [vicarious authority] **commission** *n* delegation, consignment, assignment, deputation, legation, mission, embassy, agency, special committee; errand, charge, permit; appointment, nomination, charter.

  v commission, delegate, consign, assign, charge, entrust, authorize; appoint, name, nominate, ordain; install, induct, invest, employ, empower.

756 abrogation *n* abolition, cancelation, annulment, repeal, retraction, revocation, remission, recision, nullification, invalidation.

  v abrogate, abolish, cancel, annul, repeal, retract, revoke, rescind, nullify, void, invalidate.

  adj null and void.

757 resignation *n* abjuration, renunciation, abdication, abandonment, desertion, relinquishment, retirement.

  v resign, quit, give up, abjure, renounce, forgo, disclaim, abrogate, abandon, desert, relinquish, retire.

758 consignee *n* trustee, nominee, committee, delegation, delegate, commission; functionary, agent, representative, messenger.

759 deputy *n* substitute, proxy, delegate, representative, surrogate, alternate, second, assistant.

  v stand for, represent, answer for.

760 permission *n* authorization, warrant, sanction, liberty, license, enfranchisement, franchise, leave, permit, liberty, freedom, allowance, consent, concession, tolerance, sufferance, indulgence, favor.

v permit, allow, let, tolerate, bear with, agree to, suffer, concede, accord, favor, humor, indulge; grant, empower, franchise, charter, confer, license, authorize, warrant, sanction.

adj permitted, permissive, indulgent, libertarian, tolerant; permissible, allowable, legal, legalized, lawful, legitimate.

761 prohibition *n* interdiction, injunction, prevention, embargo, ban, restriction, disallowance.

v prohibit, forbid, interdict, veto, disallow, bar, restrict, limit; prevent, hinder, preclude, obstruct.

adv prohibitive, proscriptive, restrictive; preventive.

762 consent *n* assent, acquiescence, acceptance, acknowledgment, permission, compliance, concurrence, agreement, approval; accord, concord, consensus, settlement, ratification, confirmation.

v consent, assent, agree, concur, permit, allow, let, yield, grant, comply, accede, acquiescence.

adj compliant, agreeable, amendable.

763 offer *n* proposal, proposition, overture, tender, bid; offering, gift.

v offer, present, proffer, tender; propose, give, move, put forward advance, invite, hold out, make a motion; hawk, merchandise, offer for sale.

adj for sale, in the open market.

764 refusal *n* rejection, spurning, denial, rebuff, repulse, repudiation; abnegation, protest, renunciation, disclaimer.

v refuse, decline, reject, spurn, turn down, deny, rebuff, repulse, repudiate; resist, repel, repudiate, renounce, disclaim, rescind, revoke.

adj noncompliant, dissident, recalcitrant, reluctant.

765 request *n* claim, demand, application, appeal, solicitation, petition, suit, entreaty, supplication, prayer.

v request, ask, ask for, beg, sue, petition, entreat, supplicate, solicit, beseech, plead, implore, require, demand, importune, clamor for.

adj importunate, clamorous, solicitous.

766 [negative request] **deprecation** *n* expostulation, intercession, mediation, protest, disapproval, remonstrance.

v deprecate, protest, expostulate, enter a protest, disapprove, remonstrate.

adj deprecatory, expostulatory, remonstrative; unsought.

767 petitioner *n* claimant, aspirant, postulant, seeker, solicitor, suitor, applicant, suppliant, supplicant; competitor, bidder; beggar, mendicant, panhandler, *(informal)* bum, *(informal)* streetwalker.

768 promise *n* undertaking, word, covenant, commitment, pledge, assurance, profession, vow, oath, guarantee, warranty, obligation, contract.

v promise, undertake, engage, enter into, bind oneself, commit oneself, pledge, agree, assure, warrant, guarantee, covenant, swear, give one's word; secure, give security, underwrite.

adj promissory, upon one's oath, on one's honor; promised, pledged, committed, bound, sworn.

769 compact *n* covenant, pact, contract, treaty, agreement, negotiation, bargain, arrangement, *(informal)* deal.

v contract, negotiate, bargain, stipulate, make terms; agree, engage, promise; complete, settle, confirm, subscribe, endorse.

adj compactual, contractual, promissory.

770 conditions *n* terms, articles, clauses, provisions, provisos, stipulations, promises, obligations, covenants.

v condition, stipulate, insist upon, contract, provide, bind, tie, oblige.

adj conditional, provisional.

adv conditionally, provisionally, on condition.

771 security *n* guarantee, warranty, bond, tie, pledge, promise, contract; mortgage, lien, pawn; stake, deposit, collateral, *(informal)* IOU, *(informal)* mark, promissory note; deed, bill of sale, receipt, certificate, title; sponsorship, surety, bail.

v give security, post bail, pawn, mortgage; guarantee, warrant, assure, promise; accept, endorse, underwrite, sponsor, stand for.

772 observance *n* performance, compliance, obedience, execution, discharge, acquittance, fulfillment, satisfaction, adhesion, acknowledgment, fidelity, faithfulness.

v observe, comply with, respect, abide by, acknowledge, adhere to, be faithful to, obey, act up to; meet, fulfill; carry out, execute, perform, satisfy, discharge.

adj observant, compliant, faithful, obedient, true, honorable; punctilious, scrupulous, as good as one's word.

adv faithfully.

773 nonobservance *n* evasion, failure, omission, noncompliance, neglect, negligence, laxity, laxness, carelessness, irresponsibility, disobedience; infringement, infraction, violation, transgression.

v fail, neglect, evade, omit, elude, ignore, disregard, discard, set at naught; infringe, transgress, violate, break.

adj nonobservant, lax, loose, disdainful, evasive, elusive, negligent, irresponsible, disobedient.

774 compromise *n* adjustment, negotiation, concession; compensation.

v compromise, bend, give and take, split the differences, come to an agreement, opt for the mean, adjust, arrange, settle.

775 acquisition *n* procurement, appropriation, gain, attainment, purchase, gift, find; profit, earnings, wages, winnings, income, proceeds, produce, crop, harvest, benefit.

v acquire, appropriate, gain, win, earn, attain, gather, collect; take over, take possession of, procure, secure, obtain, get, come into, receive, get hold of; profit, turn to profit.

adj profitable, advantageous, gainful, remunerative.

776 loss *n* damage, injury, privation, lapse, forfeiture, deprivation.

v lose, incur a loss, miss, mislay, let slip, forfeit; waste, get rid of.

adj lost, bereft, minus, deprived of, cut off, rid of; long lost, irretrievable.

777 possession *n* ownership, occupancy, holding, proprietorship, tenure, tenancy, control, custody; belonging.

v possess, own, have, hold, occupy, control, command, have to oneself, have in hand, belong to.

adj possessing, possessed of, in possession of, master of, in hand, at one's disposal; possessive, custodial.

777a exemption *n* exception, immunity, impunity, release.

v exempt, excuse, release; not have, be without.

adj exempt from, immune from, devoid of, without.

778 [joint possession] **participation** *n* partnership, co-ownership, joint tenancy, common holding, communion, community of possessions; communism, socialism, collectivism; cooperation.

participant, sharer, partner, co-partner, shareholder; communist, socialist.

v participate, partake, share, share in, go halves, split up, divide, have in common, own in common.

adj participatory, joint, common, collective, communal, communist, communistic, socialist, socialistic.

779 possessor *n* holder, occupant, tenant, lessee; proprietor, proprietress, master, mistress, owner.

780 property *n* possession, possessions, goods, effects, chattels, estate, belongings, assets, means, resources land, real estate, acreage; ownership, right; attribute, quality, characteristic, feature.

781 retention *n* keeping, holding, detention, custody, preservation, maintenance.

v retain, keep, hold, hold fast, secure, withhold, preserve, detain, reserve, maintain.

adj retentive.

782 relinquishment *n* renunciation, surrender, resignation, yielding, waiver, abdication, desertion, abandonment, quitting.

v relinquish, renounce, surrender, give up, resign, yield, cede, waive, forswear, forgo, abdicate, leave, forsake, desert, quit, abandon, let go, discard, cast off, dismiss, divest oneself.

adj cast off, done away with, left, forsworn, given up, left behind.

783 transfer *n* sale, lease, release, exchange, interchange; transference, transmission, changing hands.

v transfer, convey, assign, grant, consign, make over, hand over, pass, transmit, change, exchange, interchange, change hands; devolve, succeed.

adj transferable, conveyable, transmissive, exchangeable.

784 giving *n* bestowal, presentation, concession, delivery, consignment, dispensation, endowment, investiture, award; charity, almsgiving, liberality, generosity, philanthropy; gift, donation, present, boon, favor, grant, offering; allowance, contribution, donation, bequest, legacy; alms, largesse, bounty, help, gratuity; bribe, bait.

giver, granter, donor.

v give, bestow, confer, grant, accord, award, assign, entrust, consign; invest, allow, settle upon, donate, bequeath, leave; furnish, supply, help; afford, spare, favor with, lavish; deliver, hand, pass, turn over, present, give away, dispense, dispose of, give out, deal out, dole out, mete out, fork out; pay, render, impart.

adj charitable, beneficent, tributary, liberal, generous, philanthropic.

785 receiving *n* acquisition, reception, acceptance, admission, recipient, receiver, legatee, grantee, donee, beneficiary, pensioner.

v receive, take, acquire, admit, take in, accept; come into, fall to one, accrue.

adj receiving; received.

786 apportionment *n* allotment, consignment, assignment, allocation, distribution, dispensation, division, partition; portion, lot, share, measure, dose, dole, ration, ratio, proportion, quota, allowance.

v apportion, divide, distribute, dispense, allot, share, mete, portion out, parcel out, dole out, deal, carve, administer; partition, assign, appropriate, appoint.

adj distributive; respective.

787 lending *n* loan, advance, accommodation, mortgage, investment.

v lend, loan, advance, accommodate, lend on security, pawn; let, lease.

788 borrowing *n* pledging, pawning; appropriating, stealing, theft.

v borrow, pledge, pawn, borrow money; hire, rent, lease; appropriate, use, steal from, imitate.

789 taking *n* appropriation, capture, apprehension, seizure, abduction, dispossession, deprivation, expropriation, divestment, confiscation, eviction; extortion, theft; reprisal, recovery.

v take, catch, hook, nab, bag, pocket, receive, accept; reap, cull, pluck, gather; appropriate, assume, possess oneself of, help oneself to, commandeer, make free with; take away, abduct, steal, seize, snatch, snap up, capture, get hold of, take from, take away from, dispossess, expropriate, oust, eject, divest, confiscate, usurp, strip, fleece; retake, resume, recover.

adj predatory, rapacious, parasitic, greedy, ravenous.

790 restitution *n* return, restoration, reinvestment, rehabilitation, reparation, atonement, compensation, recovery.

v return, restore, give back, render, give up, let go; recoup, reimburse, compensate, reinvest, remit, rehabilitate, repair, make good, settle up; recover, get back, redeem, take back again.

adj compensatory, redemptive, recouperative.

791 stealing *n* theft, thievery, robbery, swindling, fraud, appropriation.

v steal, take, thieve, rob, pilfer, purloin, *(informal)* swipe, filch, embezzle, swindle, appropriate, fleece, defraud, *(informal)* rip off, *(informal)* screw.

adj thievish, light-fingered, piratical, predatory.

792 thief *n* robber, pilferer, filcher, rifler, crook, *(informal)* rip-off artist, cheat; burglar, house-breaker, second-story man, safecracker.

793 booty *n* spoils, plunder; prize, loot, catch, pickings, stolen goods, *(informal)* haul.

794 barter *n* exchange, trade, traffic, commerce, business, bargain; dealing, transaction, negotiation.

v barter, trade, exchange, traffic, bargain, swap, buy and sell, give and take, deal, haggle, negotiate, drive a bargain, transact.

adj commercial, mercantile; interchangeable, in trade, for sale, marketable.

795 purchase *n* buying, purchasing, acquisition; bargain, buy.

buyer, purchaser, shopper, customer, client, patron, clientele.

v purchase, buy, acquire, get, obtain, procure; shop, market, go shopping.

796 sale *n* selling, vendition, commerce, mercantilism, transaction, exchange, auction, trade.

seller, vendor, merchant.

v sell, trade, barter, vend, exchange, deal in, dispose, merchandise, hawk.

adj salable, marketable, vendible, for sale.

797 merchant *n* trader, dealer, seller, salesman, saleswoman, tradesman, shopkeeper, retailer, hawker, huckster, peddler, broker.

798 merchandise *n* goods, wares, commodity, articles, stock, produce, product, staple commodity, store, cargo.

v merchandise, sell.

799 market *n* mart, marketplace, fair, bazaar, business district, mall, shopping center, store, department store, establishment, place of business, office.

800 money *n* finance, accounts, funds, assets, wealth, supplies, ways and means, wherewithal, capital, almighty dollar, cash, currency, hard cash, *(informal)* bucks, change, small change, *(informal)* green, greenbacks; sum, amount, balance.

adj monetary, pecuniary, financial, fiscal.

801 treasurer *n* bursar, banker, purser, receiver, steward, trustee, accountant, paymaster, cashier, teller, financier.

802 treasury *n* bank, exchequer, strongbox, stronghold, coffer, chest, depository, purse, moneybag, safe, vault, cash box, cash register, till; securities, stocks, bonds, notes.

803 wealth *n* riches, fortune, opulence, affluence, easy circumstance, *(informal)* silver spoon, independence, competence, sufficiency, solvency; provision, livelihood, maintenance, means, resources, substance; income, capital, money.

v be wealthy, be rich.

adj wealthy, rich, affluent, well-off, well-to-do, comfortable.

804 poverty *n* indigence, penury, pauperism, destitution, want, need, neediness, lack, privation, distress, difficulties, straits, bad straits.

v be poor, want, lack, starve, live from hand to mouth, go to the dogs.

adj poor, indigent, destitute, poverty-stricken, needy, penniless, broke, *(informal)* bust, hard up, insolvent, seedy, beggarly.

805 credit *n* trust, score, tally, account, *(informal)* tab, bill.

creditor, lender, usurer.

v credit, accredit, entrust, keep an account with.

806 debt *n* obligation, liability, debit, score, duty, due.

debtor, borrower.

adj liable, answerable for, in debt; unpaid, in arrear.

807 payment *n* discharge, settlement, clearance, liquidation, satisfaction, reckoning, arrangement; acknowledgment, release, receipt, voucher; installment, remittance.

v pay, settle, liquidate, discharge, quit, acquit oneself of, reckon up, satisfy, compensate, reimburse, remunerate, recompense, make payment, square accounts, balance accounts, pay in full.

adj out of debt, solvent; straight, clear.

808 nonpayment *n* default, protest, repudiation; insolvency, bankruptcy, failure.

v not pay, default, fail, stop payment; run up bills.

adj in debt.

809 expenditure *n* outlay, expenses, disbursement, payment, costs, fees.

v expend, spend, pay out, disburse, *(informal)* fork out, lay out.

810 receipt *n* value received, acknowledgment of payment.

v receive, take, get, bring in.

adj profitable, remunerative.

811 accounts *n* money matters, finance, budget, bill, score, reckoning, account; statement, ledger, inventory, register, book, books, sheet; balance.

accountant, auditor, bookkeeper, financier.

v keep accounts, enter, post, book, credit, debit, balance.

812 price *n* amount, cost, expense, charge, figure, demand, damage, fare, hire, wages; worth, rate, value, valuation, appraisal; market price, quotation; bill, invoice.

v price, set a price, fix a price, appraise, assess, charge, demand, ask, require, exact; fetch, sell for, bring in, yield, accord.

813 discount *n* abatement, reduction, depreciation, allowance, qualification, rebate, sale.

v discount, put on sale, reduce, take off, allow, deduct, abate, rebate.

814 dearness *n* expensiveness, costliness, high price; overcharge, extravagance, exorbitance.

v be expensive, cost a lot; overcharge, bleed, fleece, extort.

adj dear, expensive, costly, precious; extravagant, exorbitant, unreasonable; priceless.

815 cheapness *n* low price, depreciation, bargain, value, *(informal)* steal, *(informal)* great buy.

v be cheap, cost little.

adj cheap, moderate, reasonable, inexpensive, dirt cheap.

816 liberality *n* generosity, munificence, bounty, bounteousness, hospitality, charity.

v be liberal, spend freely, give, spare no expense.

adj liberal, free, generous, bountiful, hospitable, munificent, beneficient, princely, charitable.

817 economy *n* frugality, thrift, thriftiness, saving, care, husbandry, retrenchment, parsimony.

v economize, save, retrench, husband.

adj economical, frugal, careful, thrifty, chary, parsimonious.

818 prodigality *n* unthriftiness, waste, wastefulness, profusion, profuseness, extravagance, profligacy, lavishness, squandering.

prodigal, spendthrift, squanderer.

v be prodigal, squander, lavish, misspend, waste, dissipate, fritter one's money.

adj prodigal, profuse, unthrifty, improvident, wasteful, profligate, extravagant, lavish.

819 parsimony *n* stinginess, illiberality, avarice, rapidity, rapacity, venality, cupidity, selfishness.

miser, niggard, churl, skinflint, codger, scrimp, *(informal)* tightwad, usurer, Scrooge.

v be parsimonious, grudge, begrudge, stint, pinch, hold back, withhold, starve, famish.

adj parsimonious, penurious, stingy, cheap, miserly, mean, pennywise, niggardly, tight, ungenerous, churlish, mercenary, venal, covetous, usurious, avaricious, greedy, rapacious, selfish.

Class VI

Words Relating to the Sentient and Moral Powers

I. Affections in General

820 affections *n* character, qualities, disposition, nature, spirit, temper, temperament, idiosyncracy, habit, bent, bias, predisposition, proclivity, propensity, humor, mood, sympathy; soul, heart, inner man, essence; passion, driving spirit, ruling passion.

adj affected, characterized, formed, cast, molded, tempered, predisposed, prone, inclined, imbued; inborn, ingrained, deep-rooted.

adv at heart.

821 feeling *n* consciousness, impression; emotion, passion, sentiment, sensibility; sympathy, empathy; fervor, ardor, zeal, warmth, tenderness, sensitivity, sentimentality, susceptibility, pity; sentiment, opinion.

v feel, receive an impression, respond to.

adj feeling, emotional, sensitive, tender; sympathetic; emotional, impassioned, passionate, fervent, tender, sensitive; heart-felt, thrilling, rapturous, soul-stirring; moved, touched, affected.

adj heart and soul, from the bottom of one's heart.

822 sensibility *n* responsiveness, sensitiveness, awareness, susceptibility, impressibility, tenderness, sentimentality, sentimentalism; excitability; appreciation, understanding, moral sensibility.

v be sensitive, have a soft spot in one's heart.

adj sensitive, impressionable, susceptible, tender, warm-hearted, sentimental; excitable; aware, understanding, appreciative.

823 insensibility *n* insensitiveness, impassivity, apathy, coldness, callousness; imperturbable; dullness, boorishness.

v be insensitive, not care, be unaffected, have no interest in.

adj insensitive, unconscious, unaware; inattentive, indifferent, lukewarm; apathetic, impassive, unimpressionable; cold-blooded, cold-hearted, unmoved, unaffected, callous, thick-skinned, uncaring.

adv in cold blood.

824 excitation *n* excitation of feeling; mental excitation; galvanism, stimulation, provocation, inspiration, infection; animation, agitation, perturbation; fascination, intoxication, ravishment; irritation, anger, passion, thrill.

v excite, affect, touch, move, impress, interest, animate, inspire, infect, awake; evoke, provoke; stir up, wake up, light up; rouse, arouse, stir, fire, kindle, inflame; stimulate, quicken, sharpen, whet, wet the appetite, fan the fire, raise to a fervor; absorb, rivet, intoxicate, fascinate, enrapture; agitate, perturb, ruffle, fluster, disturb, startle, shock, stagger, astound, electrify, galvanize; irritate.

adj excited, excitable, wrought up, overwrought, upset, hysterical, hot, red-hot, flushed, feverish, boiling, ebullient, seething, fuming, raging, raving, frantic, mad, distracted, beside oneself; exciting, warm, glowing, fervid, soul-stirring, thrilling, overwhelming, overpowering, sensational.

825 [excess of sensitiveness] **excitability** *n* impetuosity, vehemence, boisterousness, impatience, intolerance, irritability, restlessness, agitation; passion, excitement, fever, tumult, ebullition, tempest, fit, paroxysm, explosion, outburst, agony; violence, rage, fury, furor, desperation, madness, distraction, delirium, frenzy, hysterics.

v be impatient, lose patience, fuss, fidget; lose one's temper, flare up, burn, boil over, foam, fume, rage, rant, run wild, go mad, go into hysterics.

adj excitable, high-strung, nervous, irritable, impatient, intolerant; feverish, hysterical, delirious, mad; hurried, restless, fidgety, fussy; vehement, violent, wild, furious, fierce, fiery, hotheaded; overzealous, enthusiastic, impassioned, fanatical; rabid, clamorous, turbulent, tumultuous, boisterous; impulsive, impetuous, passionate, uncontrolled, uncontrollable, ungovernable, irrepressible, volcanic.

826 inexcitability *n* imperturbability, even temper, dispassion, patience, impassivity; coolness, calmness, composure, placidity, serenity, quietude; self-possession, self-restraint, stoicism; resignation, submission, sufferance, endurance, forbearance, fortitude, moderation, restraint.

v bear, endure, tolerate, suffer, put up with, reconcile oneself to, resign oneself to, brook, swallow, make the best of, stomach; compose, appease, propitiate, repress, calm down, cool down.

adj inexcitable, imperturbable, unsusceptible, dispassionate, enduring, stoical, staid, sober, sedate; easygoing, peaceful, placid, calm, cool; composed, collected, unruffled, content, resigned, subdued.

II. Personal Affections

827 pleasure *n* happiness, gladness, delectation, enjoyment, delight, joy, glee, cheer, cheerfulness, well-being, satisfaction, gratification, comfort, ease; felicity, bliss, enchantment, transport, rapture, ravishment, ecstasy, luxury, sensuality, voluptuousness.

v be pleased, joy, enjoy oneself, have one's head in the clouds, fall into raptures; be pleased with, derive pleasure from, take pleasure in, *(informal)* get into, delight in, rejoice in, indulge in, luxuriate in, relish, love, enjoy, like, *(informal)* dig, take a fancy to, take a shine to.

adj happy, blissful, joyful, gladsome, cheerful; comfortable, at ease, content; ecstatic.

adv happily, with pleasure.

828 pain *n* suffering, distress, torture, misery, dolor, anguish, agony, torment, throe, pang, ache, smart, twinge, stitch; displeasure, dissatisfaction, discomfort, discomposure, disquiet, malaise, inquietude, uneasiness, vexation, discontent, dejection, weariness; annoyance, irritation, worry, affliction, bore, bother, mortification, plague; care, solicitude, trouble, trial, ordeal, burden, load, fret; prostration, desolation, despair.

v suffer, afflict, torture, torment, distress, despair; hurt, harm, injure, trouble, grieve, disquiet, discomfort, discompose, worry, irritate, vex, mortify, plague.

adj uncomfortable, uneasy, weary; unhappy, infelicitous, poor, wretched, miserable, woebegone, careworn, cheerless, sorry, sorrowful, stricken, in tears, in despair.

829 pleasurableness *n* pleasantness, agreeableness, delectability, delight, congeniality; sprightliness, cheer, cheerfulness, liveliness; attraction, attractiveness, charm, fascination enchantment, witchery, seduction, winning ways, amenity, amiability; loveliness, beauty, brightness; goodness.

v be pleasurable, afford pleasure, offer pleasure, please, charm, delight, gladden, cheer; attract, invite, allure, stimulate, interest, captivate, fascinate, enchant, entrance, enrapture, bewitch,

ravish, enravish, transport; agree with, satisfy, gratify; slake, satiate, quence; regale, refresh, treat, amuse.

adj pleasurable, pleasant, agreeable, enjoyable, delightful, congenial, amiable; comfortable, cordial, genial, gladsome, sweet, delectable, nice, dainty, delicate, delicious, luscious, luxurious, voluptuous, sensual; attractive, lovely, beautiful, seductive, rapturous, ecstatic, beatific, heavenly; fair, sunny, bright; gay, sprightly, merry, cheery, cheerful, lively, vivacious.

830 painfulness *n* trouble, care, trial, affliction, blow, burden, curse, mishap, misfortune, adversity; annoyance, nuisance, grievance, bore, bother, vexation, mortification; wound, sore, sore subject, thorn in the side, skeleton in the closet; sorry sight, heavy news, bad news; affront, insult, offense.

v pain, hurt, wound, sadden, displease, annoy, trouble, disturb, cross, perplex, irk, vex, mortify, worry, plague, bother, pester, harass, badger, bait, heckle, irritate, anger, persecute, provoke; harrow, torment, torture; affront, insult, give offense, offend, maltreat, mistreat; sicken, disgust, revolt, nauseate, repel, shock, horrify, appal.

adj painful, hurtful, dolorous; unpleasant, disagreeable, unpalatable, bitter, distasteful; unwelcome, undesirable, obnoxious; dismal, dreary, melancholy, grievous, piteous, woeful, rueful, mournful, deplorable, pitiable, lamentable, pathetic; invidious, vexatious, troublesome, irksome, wearisome, worrisome; intolerable, insufferable, unsupportable, unbearable, unendurable, grim, dreadful, fearful, frightful, dire, odious, hateful, repulsive, repellant, abhorrent, horrid, horrible, offensive, nauseous, loathsome, vile, hideous; sore, severe, grave, hard, harsh, cruel; ruinous, disastrous, calamitous, tragic; burdensome, onerous, oppressive, cumbersome.

adv painfully.

831 content *n* contentment, complacency, satisfaction, ease, serenity, comfort; conciliation, resignation.

v gratify, satisfy, set at ease, comfort, appease, conciliate, reconcile.

adj contented, complacent, satisfied,

sanguine, comfortable; assenting, acceding, resigned, willing, agreeable.

adv to one's heart's content.

832 discontent *n* discontentment, dissatisfaction, uneasiness, disquietude, restlessness, displeasure.

v be discontented, repine, regret, fret, chafe, grumble; dissatisfy, disappoint, disconcert.

adj discontented, dissatisfied, displeased, uneasy, restless, dejected, malcontent, regretful, down in the dumps.

833 regret *n* sorrow, lamentation, grief; remorse, penitence, contrition, repentance.

v regret, deplore, lament, feel sorry about, grieve at, bemoan, bewail, rue, mourn for, repent.

adj regretful, sorry, lamentable, rueful; penitent, contrite.

834 relief *n* deliverance, alleviation, ease, assuagement, mitigation, comfort, solace, consolation; help, assistance, aid.

v relieve, ease, alleviate, assuage, mitigate, allay, comfort, soothe, lessen, abate, diminish; cheer, comfort, console; aid, help, assist, succor, refresh, remedy, support.

adj soothing, consoling, assuaging, comforting, palliative, curative.

835 aggravation *n* worsening, heightening, intensification, exaggeration; *(informal)* annoyance, irritation, vexation.

v aggravate, worsen, intensify, heighten, increase, make serious, make grave.

adj worse, intensified, irritated.

adv from bad to worse, out of the frying pan and into the fire.

836 cheerfulness *n* geniality, high spirits, liveliness, vivacity, joviality, jocularity, mirth, merriment, exhilaration.

v cheer, gladden, enliven, inspirit, delight, rejoice, exhilarate, animate, encourage; shout, applaud, acclaim, salute.

adj cheery, gay, blithe, happy, lively, spirited, sprightly, joyful, joyous, mirthful, buoyant, sparkling, vivacious, gleeful, sunny, jolly; pleasant, bright, gay, winsome, gladdening, cheery, cheering, inspiring, animating, hearty, robust.

adv cheerfully.

837 dejection *n* depression, heaviness, heavy heart, melancholy, sadness, dumps, doldrums, despondency, gloom, weariness, disgust, despair, hopelessness.

v be dejected, lose heart, frown, mope, droop, despond, brood over, sink, despair.

adj unhappy, depressed, dispirited, disheartened, discouraged, despondent, *(informal)* down, downhearted, sad, melancholy, lugubrious, heartsick, dismal, gloomy, miserable, desolate; pessimistic, cynical.

adv with a long face, with tears in one's eyes.

838 rejoicing *n* exaltation, triumph, jubilation, reveling, merrymaking, celebration, paean; smile, smirk, grin, giggle, titter, laughter, guffaw, shout, peal of laughter.

v rejoice, congratulate oneself, clap one's hands, dance, skip, sing, hurrah, cry for joy, leap with joy, exalt, triumph; smile, smirk, grin, giggle, titter, chuckle, cackle, laugh, crow, burst out, shout, split, roar, shake one's sides, split one's sides.

adj jubilant, exultant, triumphant, flushed, *(informal)* high, elated, laughing, convulsed with laughter.

839 lamentation *n* lament, howl, wail, wailing, complaint, moan, moaning, groan, sob, sigh; dirge, elegy, monody, threnody.

v lament, bewail, bemoan, deplore, grieve, scream, sob, cry, weep, mourn over, sorrow over.

adj lamenting, in mourning, sorrowful, mournful, lamentable, tearful, plaintive.

840 amusement *n* enjoyment, entertainment, recreation, diversion, relaxation, pastime, pleasure, playing, festivity.

v amuse, entertain, cheer, divert, enliven, interest; amuse oneself, play, sport, make merry.

adj amusing, entertaining, diverting, relaxing, pleasant, witty, jovial, jolly, playful.

841 weariness *n* ennui, lassitude, fatigue, exhaustion, boredom; tedium, monotony, dullness.

v weary, tire, fatigue, bore, exhaust.

adj wearisome, tiresome, boring, tedious, irksome, monotonous, humdrum, dull, prosaic, trying; weary, drowsy, exhausted, tired, wearied, fatigued; uninterested, impatient, dissatisfied.

842 wit *n* drollery, facetiousness, pleasantry, repartee, cleverness, humor, fun; understanding, intelligence, sagacity, wisdom, intellect, mind, sense.
v joke, jest, banter, pun.
adj witty, quick, quick-witted, nimble, sharp, clever, facetious, whimsical, pleasant, humorous, playful, sparkling, scintillating; intelligent, sagacious, wise, perceptive, insightful.

843 dullness *n* heaviness, flatness, stupidity, obtuseness, lack of originality, banality.
v be dull, blunt, deaden, benumb.
adj dull, uninteresting, unimaginative, dry, prosaic, matter-of-fact, commonplace, boring, tedious, dreary, vapid; stupid, stolid, slow, flat.

844 humorist *n* wit, wag, comedian, comedienne, joker, jester, wisecracker, epigrammatist, punster, buffoon, clown, fool, satirist, lampooner, cutup, funnyman.

845 beauty *n* loveliness, pulchritude, elegance, grace, gracefulness, comeliness, seemliness, fairness, attractiveness, brilliance, radiance, splendor, gorgeousness, magnificence, sublimity.
v beautify.
adj beautiful, handsome, comely, seemly, attractive, lovely, pretty, fair, fine, elegant, beauteous, graceful, pulchritudinous, brilliant, radiant, gorgeous, magnificent; artistic, aesthetic, picturesque.

846 ugliness *n* homeliness, inelegance, unsightliness, distortion, disfigurement, deformity, frightfulness.
v deface, disfigure, distort.
adj ugly, displeasing, hard-featured, unlovely, unsightly, unseemly, homely; hideous, gruesome, repulsive, offensive, revolting, terrible, base, vile, squalid, gross, monstrous, heinous; disagreeable, unpleasant, objectionable.

847 ornament *n* ornamentation, adornment, decoration, embellishment, frills, finery.

v ornament, embellish, adorn, decorate, beautify.
adj ornamental, decorative; ornamented, ornate, embellished, beautified.

848 blemish *n* disfigurement, deformity, defect, flaw, fault, taint, blot, spot, speck.
v stain, sully, spot, taint, tarnish, injur, mar, damage, deface, impair.
adj disfigured, injured, imperfect, discolored, freckled, pitted.

849 simplicity *n* plainness, homeliness; clarity, chasteness, restraint, severity, lack of adornment, lack of affectation.
v simplify, uncomplicate, clarify, strip to essentials, get back to basics.
adj simple, plain, homely, natural, unadorned, unaffected, unembellished, neat, unassuming, unpretentious; chaste, severe; clear, straightforward, lucid.

850 [good taste] taste *n* good taste, delicacy, refinement, polish, elegance, grace, discrimination, culture, cultivation.
v show taste, appreciate, judge, criticize, discriminate.
adj tasteful, in good taste, decorous, attractive, cultivated, cultured, refined, discriminative, polished, felicitous, appropriate, suitable, apt, becoming, pleasing.
adj tastefully, elegantly.

851 [bad taste] vulgarity *n* bad taste, barbarism, coarseness, lack of decorum, ill-breeding, boorishness; gaudiness, tawdriness, finery, frippery, tinsel.
v be vulgar; vulgarize.
adj vulgar, in bad taste, unrefined, boorish, common, coarse, ill-bred, ill-mannered, ignoble, mean, plebeian, crude, rude, shabby; gaudy, tawdry, flashy, garish, crass, showy, *(informal)* tacky.

852 fashion *n* custom, style, vogue, mode, rage, craze; conventionality, conformity; society, polite society, beau monde; manners, breeding, air, demeanor, *savoir-faire,* gentility, decorum, propriety, etiquette.
v be fashionable, be the rage; fashion, adapt, suit, fit, adjust; make, shape, frame, form, mold.

adj fashionable, in vogue, à la mode, all the rage; modish, stylish, conventional, customary; well-bred, well-mannered, civil, polite, courteous, polished, refined, genteel, decorous.

853 ridiculousness *n* outrageousness, silliness, absurdity.

v be ridiculous, make a fool of oneself, play the fool.

adj absurd, preposterous, extravagant, asinine, laughable, nonsensical, silly, funny, ludicrous, droll, comical, farcical, outlandish, outrageous, fantastic.

854 fop *n* fine gentleman, dandy, *(informal)* dude, coxcomb, beau, man about town, prig, jackanapes.

855 affectation *n* affectedness, pretense, pretention, airs, mannerisms, unnaturalness, display, show, sham, feigning, simulation, foppery.

v affect, act a part, put on airs, pretend, assume, feign, counterfeit, simulate, pose, attitudinize.

adj affected, pretentious, ostentatious, feigned, artificial, stilted, mannered, stagey, theatrical, modish, unnatural.

856 ridicule *n* derision, scoffing, mockery, gibes, jeers, taunts, raillery; satire, burlesque, sneer, banter, wit, irony.

v ridicule, deride, banter, chaff, twit, mock, taunt, make fun of, sneer at, burlesque, satirize, rail at, lampoon jeer at, scoff at *(informal)* put down.

adj derisory, derisive, sarcastic, ironic, ironical, burlesque, mocking.

857 [object and cause of ridicule] **laughing-stock** *n* butt, game, fair game, fool, dupe, original, oddity, queer fish, square, straight, buffoon.

858 hope *n* confidence, trust, reliance, faith, assurance; expectation, expectancy, anticipation, aspiration, longing, desire, dream, wish.

v hope, trust, rely on, lean on, have faith in; hope for, expect, presume, anticipate; long for, desire.

adj hopeful, expectant, sanguine, optimistic, confident; probable, promising, propitious, reassuring, encouraging, cheering, inspiriting.

859 hopelessness *n* despair, desperation, despondency, dejection, pessimism.

v despair, give up hope, despond.

adj hopeless, despairing, desperate, despondent, forlorn, disconsolate; irremediable, remediless, unremedial, incurable.

860 fear *n* apprehension, consternation, dismay, alarm, trepidation, dread, terror, fright, horror, panic; anxiety, solicitude, suspicion, misgiving, concern; awe, reverence, veneration.

v fear, be afraid of, apprehend, distrust, dread; revere, venerate, reverence.

adj fearful, afraid, apprehensive, dismayed, alarmed, frightened, terrified, horrified, aghast, terror-stricken, horror-stricken, panic-stricken; anxious, concerned, solicitous, suspicious; fearful, awesome, awe-inspiring; awful, dreadful, terrible.

861 courage *n* fearlessness, dauntlessness, intrepidity, guts, fortitude, pluck, spirit, nerve, heroism, daring, audacity, bravery, mettle, valor, hardihood, bravado, gallantry.

v dare, venture, look danger in the face, take heart, take the bull by the horns.

adj courageous, fearless, dauntless, intrepid, *(informal)* gutsy, spirited, stout-hearted, resolute, bold, heroic, daring, audacious, brave, valorous, enterprising, adventurous, gallant.

862 cowardice *n* fear, poltroonery, dastardliness, faint-heartedness, yellow streak, dread, timidity, baseness, abject fear.

coward, poltroon, craven, sneak, lily-liver, *(informal)* chicken.

v be cowardly, cower, skulk, quail, hide.

adj cowardly, fearful, craven, dastardly, pusillanimous, recreant, timid, timorous, faint-hearted, lily-livered, chicken-hearted, fearful, afraid, scared, spineless, *(informal)* chicken.

863 rashness *n* haste, impetuosity, recklessness, impulsiveness, heedlessness, thoughtlessness, imprudence, indiscretion, audacity, carelessness, foolhardiness.

v be rash, plunge.

adj rash, hasty, impetuous, reckless,

headlong, precipitate, impulsive, thoughtless, heedless, imprudent, indiscreet, careless, unwary, foolhardy, presumptuous, audacious.

864 caution *n* prudence, discretion, circumspection, heed, care, wariness, heedfulness, vigilance, forethought; warning, admonition, advice, injunction, counsel.

v be cautious, take care; warn, admonish, advise, counsel.

adj cautious, prudent, heedful, careful, watchful, discreet, wary, vigilant, alert, provident chary, circumspect, guarded.

865 desire *n* longing, fancy, craving, yearning, wish, want, need, hunger, appetite, thirst; request, wish, ambition, aspiration; love, passion, lust.

v desire, wish for, long for, crave, want, wish, covet, fancy; ask, request, solicit; lust for.

adj desirous, desiring, craving, wishful, hungry, thirsty, covetous, fervent, ardent, lustful.

866 indifference *n* unconcern, listlessness, apathy, insensibility, coolness, insensitiveness, inattention.

v be indifferent, take no interest in, have no heart for, spurn, disdain.

adj indifferent, unconcerned, listless, apathetic, cool, cold, lukewarm, insensitive, inattentive.

867 dislike *n* disinclination, disrelish, distaste, disgust, repugnance, antipathy, antagonism, aversion, hatred, horror, loathing.

v dislike, disrelish, be averse to, be disinclined, be reluctant, have no taste for; disgust, repel, nauseate, hate, loathe.

adj disliking, disinclined, averse, loath; dislikable, distasteful, disagreeable, offensive, repulsive, repugnant, repellent, abhorrent, nauseating, disgusting, loathsome.

868 fastidiousness *n* nicety; hypercriticism; discernment, discrimination, judiciousness, keenness, perspicacity.

v be fastidious, split hairs.

adj fastidious, nice, dainty, delicate; hard to please, finicky, hypercritical, fussy, querulous, meticulous, exacting,

scrupulous, proper, priggish, prim; discerning, discriminative, judicious, keen, sharp, perspicacious, sagacious.

869 satiety *n* repletion, saturation, glut, surfeit; disgust, weariness.

v sate, satiate, saturate, cloy, glut, stuff, gorge, surfeit; gall, disgust, bore, tire, weary.

adj satiated, glutted, stuffed, gorged, surfeited; disgusted, bored, tired, weary.

870 wonder *n* surprise, marvel, astonishment, stupefaction, amazement, awe, admiration, bewilderment, puzzlement.

v wonder, think, speculate, conjecture, meditate, ponder, question; marvel, admire, be surprised, start, stare, startle, astonish, amaze, astound, stagger, stupefy, bewilder, dumfound.

adj marvelous, wonderful, extraordinary, remarkable, awesome, startling, wondrous, miraculous, astonishing, amazing, astounding, unique, curious, strange, odd, peculiar; astonished, surprised, aghast, agog, startled, breathless, awe-struck, spell-bound, lost in wonder, amazed, fascinated, bewildered.

871 expectance *n* expectancy, expectation.

v expect, foresee, assume, not be surprised, make nothing of.

adj expecting, expectant, relied on, expected, figured on, foreseen.

872 prodigy *n* phenomenon, wonder, marvel, miracle; freak, monstrosity, spectacle, curiosity; genius, intellectual giant, wizard, mastermind, expert, sage, child genius, wunderkind.

873 repute *n* estimation, reputation, account, regard, report; name, standing, distinction, credit, respect, respectability, dignity, greatness, eminence, honor, renown.

v consider, esteem, account, hold, regard, deem, reckon; be held in high repute, be distinguished.

adj reputed, regarded, accounted; reputable, respected, respectable, esteemed, celebrated, distinguished, dignified, honored, renowned, eminent.

874 disrepute *n* disgrace, dishonor, disfavor, discredit, ill repute, low repute, bad name, shame, degradation, obloquy, debasement, ignominy, infamy, stain, spot, blot, tarnish, taint.

v disgrace oneself, have a bad name, shame, disgrace, dishonor, tarnish, stain, taint, blot.

adj disreputable, base, low, unsavory, shady, unworthy, disgraced, vile, ignominious, dishonorable, opprobrious, shameful, disgraceful, infamous, tainted, tarnished.

875 nobility *n* distinction, eminence, stateliness, majesty, grandeur, dignity, loftiness, profundity, highmindedness; rank, condition, high birth, gentility, quality, royalty, aristocracy, lord, lady.

v be noble; ennoble.

adj noble, exalted, honorable, dignified, imposing, stately; titled, aristocratic, patrician, high-born.

876 commonalty *n* the common people, the lower classes, commoners, multitude, proletariat, populace, rank and file, bourgeoisie, general public, citizenry, peasantry, crowd, herd, rabble.

adj common, mean, low, base, ignoble, vulgar, homely, plebeian, proletarian, low-born, obscure, rustic, boorish, uncivilized.

877 title *n* honor, name, designation, decoration.

adj titled.

878 pride *n* self-respect, self-assurance, self-esteem, conceit, vanity, egotism, arrogance, vainglory, self-importance; insolence, haughtiness, superciliousness, presumption.

v be proud, presume, swagger, give oneself airs.

adj proud, high-minded, dignified, stately, noble, imposing, honorable, creditable; self-assured, self-satisfied, contented, egotistical, vain, conceited, arrogant, haughty, smug, overbearing, over-confident, snobbish, supercilious, presumptuous.

879 humility *n* modesty, humbleness, meekness, lowliness, submissiveness.

v lower, abase, debase, degrade, humiliate, mortify, shame, subdue, crush, break.

adj humble, low, lowly, unassuming, plain, common, poor, meek, modest,

submissive, unpretentious; respectful, polite, courteous.

adj with downcast eyes, on bended knee.

880 vanity *n* pride, conceit, self-esteem, self-complacency, egotism, self-admiration, self-love, self-glorification; hollowness, emptiness, sham, triviality.

v be vain, have too high an opinion of oneself, inflate, puff up.

adj vain, conceited, egotistical, self-complacent, proud, vainglorious, arrogant, overweening, inflated; useless, hollow, trifling, trivial.

881 modesty *n* humility, diffidence, timidity, bashfulness; moderation, decency, propriety, simplicity, chastity, prudery, prudishness.

v be modest, retire, give way to, stay in the background.

adj modest, humble, diffident, timid, timorous, bashful, sheepish, shy; moderate, humble, unpretentious, decent, becoming, proper, inextravagant, unostentatious, retiring, unassuming, unobtrusive; demure, prudish, chaste, pure, virtuous.

adv modestly, humbly, quietly, privately, without ceremony.

882 ostentation *n* pretention, pretentiousness, semblance, show, showiness, pretense, display, pageantry, pomp, pompousness, flourish, splendor.

v show off, parade, display, exhibit, blazon forth, emblazon, flaunt.

adj ostentatious, pretentious, showy, flashy, grand, pompous, garish, gaudy, flaunting, high-sounding, sumptuous, theatrical, dramatic, solemn, majestic, ceremonious, punctilious, over-blown.

adv with a flourish.

883 celebration *n* ceremony, ceremonial, commemoration, solemnization, observance, memorialization, festival, festivity.

v celebrate, commemorate, observe, keep; proclaim, announce; praise, extol, laud, glorify, honor, applaud, commend; solemnize, ritualize.

adj celebrational, commemorative, honorific, commendatory; celebrated, famous, renowned, illustrious, eminent, famed.

adv in honor of, in commemoration of, in celebration of.

884 boasting *n* bragging, swaggering, braggadocio, bravado.

boaster, braggart, blusterer, *(informal)* windbag.

v exaggerate, brag, vaunt, swagger, crow, strut, talk big.

adj boasting, boastful, pretentious, vainglorious, elated, exultant, jubilant, triumphant.

885 [undue assumption of superiority] **insolence** *n* boldness, rudeness, disrespect, impertinence, impudence, haughtiness, arrogance, audacity, abusiveness, contemptuousness.

v be insolent, swagger, assume, presume, take liberties, ride roughshod over.

adj insolent, bold, rude, disrespectful, impertinent, impudent, brazen, brassy, haughty, arrogant, audacious, presumptuous, overbearing, abusive, contemptuous, insulting.

886 servility *n* submissiveness, obsequiousness, abasement, slavishness, cringing, fawning, meanness, baseness, groveling, sycophancy, slavery.

toady, sycophant, boot-licker, *(informal)* apple-polisher, *(informal)* brown-noser.

v be servile, cringe, bow, stoop, kneel, toady, fawn, lick the boots of; sneak, crawl, crouch, cower.

adj servile, obsequious, slavish, cringing, fawning, sycophantic, groveling, sniveling, mealy-mouthed, abject, base, mean.

887 blusterer *n* swaggerer, braggart, boaster, windbag, bully, ruffian, rowdy, redneck.

III. Sympathetic Affections

888 friendship *n* amity, friendliness, harmony, concord, fellow-feeling, sympathy, good will, affection; companionship, comradeship, fellowship, fraternity, intimacy.

v be friendly, have an acquaintance with, keep company with, know, sympathize with, befriend, make friends with.

adj friendly, kind, kindly, amiable neighborly, brotherly, cordial, genial, well-disposed, benevolent, kind-hearted, affectionate; helpful, advantageous, propitious; acquainted, familiar, intimate.

adv amicably, with open arms.

889 enmity *n* unfriendliness, dislike, discord, ill will, antagonism, animosity, hostility, malevolence, hatred.

v be at odds with.

adj inimical, unfriendly, alienated, estranged, hostile.

890 friend *n* companion, acquaintance, crony, chum, pal, mate, fellow, bosom buddy, intimate, confidant; well-wisher, patron, supporter, backer, advocate, partisan, defender, sympathizer; ally, associate.

891 enemy *n* foe, adversary, opponent, antagonist, attacker.

892 sociality *n* sociableness, gregariousness, social interaction, social intercourse, comradeship, camaraderie, companionship, cordiality, good fellowship, conviviality.

v be sociable, consort with, fraternize, welcome.

adj sociable, gregarious, social, warm, genial, cordial, friendly, convivial, amicable, clubbish, chummy, neighborly, hospitable.

893 seclusion. exclusion *n* privacy, retirement, withdrawal, solitude, sequestration, retreat, isolation, hiding, secrecy. elimination, prohibition, exception, omission, preclusion, rejection, ejection, expulsion, banishment, ostracism, exile.

recluse, hermit, cenobite, outcast, castaway, pariah, wastrel, foundling.

v seclude oneself, retire, withdraw, retreat, sequester, isolate, hide. exclude, eliminate, prohibit, reject, eject, expel.

adj secluded, retired, withdrawn, sequestered, private, isolated, solitary, excluded, eliminated, prohibited, omitted, precluded, rejected, ejected, repulsed, banished, ostracized, exiled.

894 courtesy *n* civility, sociability, politeness, good manners, good behavior, affability, gentility, graciousness, courtliness, respect.

v be courteous, behave well.

adj courteous, civil, polite, well-mannered, well-bred, gentlemanly, gallant, urbane, debonair, affable, gracious, courtly, respectful, obliging.

895 discourtesy *n* disrespect, ill-breeding, bad manners, tactlessness, rudeness, impudence, vulgarity.

v be discourteous.

adj discourteous, ill-bred, ill-mannered, ill-behaved, ungentlemanly, uncivil, impolite, ungracious, vulgar, crude, disrespectful, rude.

896 congratulations *n* felicitation, compliment, salute, salutation.

v congratulate, offer congratulations, salute.

adj congratulatory; complimentary.

897 love *n* affection, liking, regard, friendliness, kindness, kindliness, tenderness, fondness, devotion, warmth, attachment, yearning, passion, rapture, adoration, idolatry.

lover, admirer, suitor, adorer, wooer; beau, sweetheart, flame, love, truelove, paramour, boyfriend, girlfriend, ladylove, idol, darling, angel, beloved.

v love, like, be fond of, have affection for, be enamored of, be in love with, cherish, adore, revere, adulate, idolize.

adj loving, smitten, affectionate, tender, fond, attached, enamored, devoted, amorous, passionate, adoring; lovable, adorable, winning, enchanting, bewitching.

898 hate *n* dislike, aversion, animosity, hatred, antipathy, detestation, loathing, abhorrence, odium, horror, repugnance.

v hate, dislike, detest, abhor, loathe, despise, execrate, abominate.

adj hateful, detestable, odious, abominable, loathsome, abhorrent, repugnant, invidious, obnoxious, offensive, disgusting, nauseating, revolting, vile, repulsive; hating, averse from, set against, bitter, spiteful, malicious.

899 favorite *n* pet, minion, idol, jewel, spoiled child, apple of one's eye, man after one's own heart; love, dear, darling, honey, sweetheart.

900 resentment *n* displeasure, pique, umbrage, animosity, bitterness, envy, jealousy, anger, wrath, indignation.

v resent, take offense, bristle over, chafe, fume, frown, pout, snarl, gnash,

growl, scowl, glower, grouch, bear a grudge.

adj resentful, offended, bitter, worked up, angry, wrathful, irate, indignant; envious, jealous.

901 irascibility *n* irritability, excitability, sensitivity.

v be irascible, quick to fly off the handle, have a temper.

adj irascible, testy, short-tempered, hot-tempered, quick-tempered, touchy, temperamental, irritable, snappish, petulant, overly sensitivie, choleric.

901a sullenness *n* moodiness, moroseness, churlishness, sluggishness.

v be sullen, frown, scowl, sulk, pout.

adj silent, reserved, sulky, morose, moody, ill-humored, sour, vexatious, bad-tempered, surly, cross, grumpy, peevish, perverse; gloomy, dismal, cheerless, overcast, somber, mournful, dark; slow, sluggish, dull stagnant.

902 [expression of affection or love] **endearment** *n* embrace, caress, hug, kiss, blandishment, dalliance, love token.

v endear, embrace, caress, blandish, flirt, dally.

adj endearing.

903 marriage *n* wedding, nuptials, matrimony, wedlock; union, alliance, association, confederation.

married man, married woman, husband, wife, spouse, mate, partner, consort, better half, *(informal)* old man, *(informal)* old lady.

v marry, tie the knot, take to the altar, wive, couple.

adj married, wed, united.

904 celibacy *n* sexual abstinence; bachelorhood.

celibate, unmarried man, bachelor, unmarried woman, spinster, old maid, virgin, maiden; priest.

adj celibate, unmarried.

905 divorce *n* marital separation, legal separation; separation, disunion, isolation.

v divorce, *(informal)* split up, separate, isolate.

adj divorced, separated, *(informal)* split up.

906 benevolence *n* kindness, kindliness, humanity, tenderness, kindheartedness, unselfishness, generosity, liberality, charity, philanthropy, altruism.

good Samaritan, sympathizer, altruist.

v wish well, take an interest in, treat well, comfort, benefit, assist, aid.

adj benevolent, kind, kindly, well-disposed, kind-hearted, humane, tender, tender-hearted, unselfish, generous,, liberal, benevolent, obliging, charitable, philanthropic, altruistic.

907 malevolence *n* ill will, enmity, rancor, resentment, malice, maliciousness, spite, spitefulness, grudge, hate, hatred, venom.

v bear ill will.

adj malevolent, malicious, resentful, spiteful, begrudging, hateful, venomous, vicious, hostile, ill-natured, evil-minded, rancorous.

908 malediction *n* curse, swear, imprecation, denunciation, cursing, damning, damnation, execration; slander.

v curse, swear, imprecate, denounce, damn, execrate; slander.

909 threat *n* menace, danger, indication, portent, foreboding, prognostication; intimidation.

v threaten, menace, endanger, indicate, presage, impend, portend, augur, forebode, foreshadow, prognosticate; frighten, denounce, intimidate, cow, badger.

adj threatening, menacing, endangering, impending, arguring, foreshadowing, foreboding, ominous, inauspicious, sinister, frightening, intimidating.

910 philanthropy *n* humaneness, compassion, humanitarianism, benevolence, helpfulness, munificence, public spirit, charity.

philanthropist, humanitarian, patriot.

adj philanthropic, humanitarian, benevolent, munificent, altruistic, public spirited, civic minded, charitable.

911 misanthropy *n* hatred of mankind, incivism.

misanthrope, man-hater; misogynist, woman-hater.

adj misanthropic, antisocial, uncivil.

912 benefactor *n* succorer, patron, supporter, contributor, friend.

913 evildoer *n* wrongdoer, troublemaker, subversive, oppressor, destroyer.

914 pity *n* sympathy, compassion, commiseration, condolence, mercy.

v pity, commiserate, feel sorry for, be sorry for, sympathize with, feel for.

adj pitying, compassionate, sympathetic, touched, moved, affected, feeling.

914a pitilessness *n* cruelty, meanness, ruthlessness, hard-heartedness.

v have no pity for.

adj pitiless, merciless, cruel, mean, unmerciful, ruthless, implacable, relentless, inexorable, hard-hearted, stony.

915 condolence *n* lamentation, sympathy, consolation.

v condole with, console, sympathize, lament.

916 gratitude *n* thanks, thankfulness, appreciation, indebtedness.

v be grateful, thank, appreciate.

adj grateful, appreciative, thankful, obliged, beholding, indebted, in one's debt.

917 ingratitude *n* thanklessness, unthankfulness.

ingrate.

v be ungrateful.

adj ungrateful, unthankful, unmindful, thankless.

918 forgiveness *n* pardon, excuse, indulgence, remission, reprieve, amnesty, grace, absolution.

v forgive, pardon, excuse, absolve reprieve, acquit.

adj forgiving.

919 revenge *n* vengeance, retaliation, requital, reprisal, retribution, vindictiveness, vengefulness.

avenger, vindicator, nemesis.

v revenge, avenge, retaliate, requite, vindicate.

adj revengeful, vengeful, vindictive, spiteful, malevolent, resentful, malicious, malignant, unforgiving, implacable.

920 jealousy *n* envy, resentment; suspicion; watchfulness, vigilance.

v be jealous.

adj jealous, envious, resentful; suspicious; solicitous, watchful, vigilant.

921 envy *n* jealousy, enviousness, grudge, covetousness.

v envy, covet, begrudge, resent.

adj envious, covetous, jealous, begrudging.

IV. Moral Affections

922 right *n* virtue, justice, fairness, integrity, equity, equitableness, uprightness, rectitude, morality, morals, goodness, honor, lawfulness; accuracy, truth.

v be right; do right.

adj right, just, good, equitable, moral, fair, upright, honest, lawful; correct, proper, suitable, fit; correct, true, accurate; genuine, legitimate, rightful.

adv righteously, rightfully, lawfully, rightly, justly, fairly, equitably.

923 wrong *n* evil, wickedness, misdeed, sin, vice, immorality, iniquity, inequity, injustice, unlawfulness.

adj wrong, injure, harm, maltreat, abuse, oppress, cheat, defraud, dishonor.

adj wrong, bad, evil, wicked, sinful, immoral, iniquitous, reprehensible, unjust, crooked, dishonest; erroneous, inaccurate, incorrect, false, untrue, mistaken; improper, unappropriate, unfit; awry, amiss, out of order.

adv wrongly, wickedly, sinfully.

924 claim *n* due, right, privilege, prerogative, prescription, demand, sanction, warrant, license.

claimant, appellant.

v claim, deserve, have the right, be entitled.

adj claiming, having a right to, privileged, prescribed, sanctioned allowed, licensed, authorized, due.

925 [absence of right] **unrightfulness** *n* impropriety, illegitimacy, presumption.

usurper, pretender.

v be unentitled.

adj unrightful, having no right to unentitled, unauthorized, unwarranted, illegitimate, not licensed.

926 duty *n* obligation, function, responsibility, onus, burden, business; conscience, moral imperative, sense of duty; homage, respect, reverence.

v do one's duty, behoove, become, be-

fit, beseem; observe, perform, fulfill, discharge.

adj obligatory, binding, imperative, incumbent, under obligation, obliged, bound, tied, duty bound; dutiful, respectful, docile, submissive, deferential, reverential, obedient.

927 dereliction of duty *n* nonobservance, nonperformance, neglect, failure, carelessness, fault, infraction, violation, transgression.

v neglect, slight, fail, violate.

adj undutiful, negligent, careless, at fault, failing, in violation.

927a exemption *n* immunity, impunity, privilege, freedom, exception, excuse, dispensation.

v exempt, excuse, release, acquit, discharge, free.

adj exempt, immune, privileged, freed, excepted, excused, unbound.

928 respect *n* esteem, deference, regard, consideration, estimation, veneration, reverence, homage, honor, admiration, approbation, approval, affection, feeling; respects, regards, duty; regard, consideration, attention, devotion.

v honor, revere, reverence, esteem, venerate, regard, consider, defer to, admire, adulate, adore, love; regard, heed, attend, notice, consider.

adj respectful, courteous, polite, well-mannered, well-bred, civil, deferential; respected, estimable, venerable, admirable; respecting, heeding, considering, regarding, attending.

929 disrespect *n* discourtesy, impoliteness, rudeness, crudeness, incivility, impudence, impertinence, irreverence, derision.

v hold in disrespect, be disrespectful, insult, deride, scoff, mock, sneer, jeer, deride, ridicule, scorn.

adj disrespectful, discourteous, impolite, rude, crude, uncivil, impudent, impertinent, irreverent insulting, derisive, scornful.

930 contempt *n* scorn, disdain, derision, contumely; dishonor, disgrace, shame.

v feel contempt for, contemn, scorn, disdain, deride, despise.

adj contemptible, despicable, mean, low, miserable, abject, base, vile; contemptuous, scornful, disdainful, derisive; dishonorable, disgraceful, shameful.

931 approbation *n* approval, sanction, esteem, admiration, commendation.

v approbate, approve, esteem, value, honor, admire, appreciate, sanction, endorse, commend, praise.

adj commendatory, complimentary, laudatory; approved, praised, in high esteem, in favour; praiseworthy, commendable, good, meritorious, estimable, creditable.

932 disapprobation *n* disapproval, dislike, disesteem, odium, disparagement, deprecation, denunciation, censure.

v disapprove, dislike, object to, frown upon, censure, blame, reproach, reprove, admonish, berate.

adj disapproving, disparaging, reproachful, defamatory, denunciatory, condemnatory.

933 flattery *n* adulation, charming, lip-service, *(informal)* brown-nosing, fawning, flunkeyism, sycophancy.

v flatter, curry favor, slobber over, *(informal)* lay it on thick, wheedle, fawn, court, *(informal)* brown-nose, pander to, overpraise.

adj flattering, adulatory, honey-mouthed, smooth-tongued, servile, sycophantic.

934 detraction *n* detracting, disparagement, belittling, defamation, vilification, calumny, abuse, slander, aspersion, deprecation.

v detract, run down, criticize, decry, disparage, blacken, belittle, depreciate, cast aspersions, defame, malign, abuse, slander, vilify.

adj detracting, disparaging, belittling, derogatory, depreciating, calumnious, abusive, slanderous, vilifying, scurrilous.

935 flatterer *n* adulator, toady, flunkey, *(informal)* apple-polisher, fawner, sycophant, *(informal)* brown-noser, bootlicker, opportunist, courtier.

936 detractor *n* reprover, critic, carper, slanderer, *(informal)* hatchet man, backbiter, defamer, castigator, satirist, cynic, reviler.

937 vindication *n* exoneration, exculpation, acquittal; justification, warrant, support, defense.

apologist, vindicator, defender.

v vindicate, exonerate, acquit, clear; uphold, justify, maintain, defend, support.

adj vindicating, vindicated, exonerated, exonerating, exculpatory, acquitted; justified, warranted, supported.

938 accusation *n* arraignment, indictment, charge, incrimination, impeachment; accusal, blaming, inculpation, charging, imputation.

accuser, prosecutor, plaintiff; relator, informer; appellant.

v charge; arraign, indict, charge, incriminate, impeach; blame, inculpate, charge, involve, point to, impute.

adj accused, accusing, accusatory, accusative, incriminatory, imputative.

939 probity *n* honesty, uprightness, virtue, rectitude, integrity.

v be honorable.

adj honest, honorable, virtuous, upright, scrupulous, high-principled.

940 improbity *n* dishonesty, wickedness, immorality, evil.

v be dishonest, play false.

adj dishonest, dishonorable, unscrupulous, immoral, wicked, evil.

941 knave *n* rogue, rascal, blackguard, sneak, villain, scoundrel.

942 disinterestedness *n* impartiality, fairness, lack of bias, unselfishness, generosity, liberality.

v be disinterested.

adj disinterested, unbiased, unprejudiced, unselfish, impartial, fair, generous, liberal.

943 selfishness *n* self-interest, self-seeking, self-love, egoism, egotism, solipsism, illiberality, parsimony, stinginess, meanness.

v be selfish, cultivate one's own garden, look after oneself, feather one's own nest.

adj selfish, self-centered, self-indulgent, self-interested, self-seeking, egotistical, solipsistic, illiberal, parsimonious, stingy, cheap, mean.

944 virtue *n* virtuousness, goodness, uprightness, morality, ethics, probity, rectitude, integrity; excellence, merit, quality, asset; innocence, chastity, purity.

v be virtuous, have the virtue of.

adj virtuous, right, upright, moral, righteous, good, chaste, pure.

945 vice *n* fault, sin, depravity, iniquity, immorality, wickedness; blemish, blot, imperfection, defect.

v sin, err, transgress, trespass.

adj vicious, immoral, depraved, profligate, wicked, sinful, sinning, corrupt, bad, iniquitous, reprehensible, blameworthy, censurable, wrong, improper; spiteful, malignant, malicious, malevolent; faulty, defective; ill-tempered, bad-tempered, refractory.

946 innocence *n* purity, virtue, virtuousness, faultlessness, spotlessness; guiltlessness, blamelessness; uprightness, honesty; naïveté, simplicity, artlessness, guilelessness, ingenuousness.

v be innocent.

adj innocent, pure, untainted, sinless, virtuous, virginal, blameless, faultless, impeccable, spotless, immaculate; guiltless, blameless; upright, honest, forthright; naïve, simple, unsophisticated, artless, guileless, ingenuous.

947 guilt *n* guiltiness, culpability, criminality; sinfulness.

v be guilty.

adj guilty, culpable, to blame, in fault.

948 good man *n* model, paragon, hero, soldier, saint, salt of the earth, *(informal)* ace.

949 bad man *n* wrong-doer, evil-doer, sinner, scoundrel, miscreant, villain, wretch, monster, devil, demon, scum of the earth.

950 penitence *n* contrition, atonement, compunction, repentance, remorse, regret.

penitent, prodigal son.

v be penitent, repent, rue, regret.

adj penitent, sorry, contrite, repenting; repentant, atoning, amending, remorseful, regretful; penitential.

951 impenitence *n* irrepentance, obduracy, hardness of heart.

v be impenitent, show no remorse.

adj impenitent, uncontrite, not sorry, obdurate, unrepentant, remorseless; unrepenting, unrepented, unatoned; irreclaimable.

952 atonement *n* satisfaction, reparation, compensation, amends, quittance; redemption, expiation, reclamation, conciliation, propitiation.

v atone, atone for; give satisfaction, satisfy, make amends; expiate, propitiate, reclaim, redeem, repair, absolve, purge, shrive, do penance, repent.

adj atoning, propitiating, propitiatory, redemptive, expiating, expiatory.

953 temperance *n* moderation, self-restraint, self-control, continence; sobriety, even-temperednes, calmness, coolness, detachment, dispassion.

vegetarian; teetotaler; abstainer.

v be temperate, abstain, forbear, restrain.

adj temperate, moderate, self-controlled, self-restrained, frugal, sparing; sober, calm, cool, detached, dispassionate.

954 intemperance *n* excess, exorbitance, inordinateness, extravagance; indulgence, high living, self-indulgence, epicurism, epicureanism, sybaritism; inabstinence, alcoholism.

v be intemperate, indulge, wallow in.

adj intemperate, excessive, exorbitant, inordinate, extravagant; indulgent, self-indulgent, epicurean.

954a sensualist *n* sybarite, voluptuary, pleasure-seeker, epicure, epicurean, libertine, hedonist.

955 asceticism *n* puritanism, austerity, abstemiousness, self-abnegation, self-denial, total abstinence, self-motification.

ascetic, anchorite, puritan, martyr; hermit, recluse.

v abstain, deny oneself, fast, starve.

adj ascetic, puritanical, austere, abstemious, rigorous, rigid, stern, severe, harsh, strict, self-denying, self-mortifying.

956 fasting *n* day of fasting; going hungry, starving oneself, starvation.

v fast, starve, famish.

adj fasting, starving, unfed; starved, half-starved, hungry.

957 gluttony *n* greed, greediness, voracity; epicurism, gormandizing, gulosity, crapulence, over-eating, *(informal)* piggishness.

glutton, epicure, cormorant, hog, *(informal)* pig.

v be gluttonous, hog; overeat, gorge, stuff oneself, make a pig of oneself, guzzle, bolt, devour, engorge, gobble up.

adj gluttonous, greedy, voracious; epicurean, gormandizing, crapulent, swinish, *(informal)* piggish.

958 sobriety *n* abstinence, teetotalism.

teetotaler, abstainer.

v be sober, abstain, take the pledge.

adj sober, unintoxicated, on the wagon, *(informal)* straight, *(informal)* dry, dry as a bone.

959 drunkenness *n* intemperance, drinking, inebriety, insobriety, intoxication, alcoholism.

drunkard, sot, tippler, drinker, inebriate, dipsomaniac, alcoholic, *(informal)* boozer, *(informal)* lush, *(informal)* juicer.

v be drunk, drink, imbibe, booze, guzzle, swill, soak, sot, lush, drink like a fish, hit the bottle.

adj drunk, drunken, sotted, intoxicated, inebriated, tipsy, tight, *(informal)* potted, *(informal)* stewed, *(informal)* stewed to the gills, dead drunk, *(informal)* plowed, *(informal)* plastered, *(informal)* tanked, *(informal)* wasted, *(informal)* juiced, *(informal)* blown away, *(informal)* high, *(informal)* flying, *(informal)* feeling no pain.

960 purity *n* cleanness; decency, decorum, delicacy; continence, chastity, innocence, modesty, virtue, virginity; simplicity, genuineness, faultlessness, perfection; guiltlessness, honesty, uprightness.

virgin, vestal virgin.

v be pure.

adj pure, decent, delicate; innocent, continent, chaste, virginal, modest, virtuous, undefiled, unsullied, unstained, untainted, uncorrupted, clean, spotless, immaculate; simple, genuine, faultless, perfect; honest, upright; unmixed, unadulterated, uncontaminated.

961 impurity *n* indecency, indelicacy; incontinence, immodesty, lewdness, concupiscence, prurience, lechery; grossness, obscenity, ribaldry, smut, bawdry; uncleanness, adulteration, contamination, defilement; fault, flaw, imperfection; guilt, sin, sinfulness.

v be impure.

adj impure, indecent, indelicate; incontinent, immodest, unchaste, concupiscent, lewd, prurient, lecherous; gross, obscene, ribald, dirty, smutty, bawdy; unclean, sullied, defiled, contaminated, adulterated, tainted, stained, corrupted, jaded; faulty, flawed, imperfect; guilty, sinning, sinful, wicked.

962 libertine *n* rake, roué, debauchee, lecher, sensualist, voluptuary, profligate, seducer, deceiver, courtesan, prostitute, strumpet, harlot, whore, street-walker, trollop, hussy, bitch, slut, minx.

963 legality *n* legitimacy, legitimateness, lawfulness; duty, obligation.

law, code, constitution, charter, statute, regulation, decree, order.

v legalize; legislate, enact, ordain, decree, codify, formulate, pass a law.

adj legal, legitimate, authorized, licit, lawful, legalized, legislated; constitutional.

964 illegality *n* illegitimacy, unlawfulness, illicitness, lawlessness.

v be illegal, offend against the law, violate the law.

adj illegal, unlawful, illegitimate, illicit, contraband, unconstitutional, unchartered, unwarranted, unauthorized, unlicensed, proscribed, prohibited, outlawed, criminal; lawless, arbitrary, despotic, unanswerable, unaccountable.

965 [executive] **jurisdiction** *n* judicature, authority, power, right, control; territory, range, magistracy.

v judge, sit in judgment; administer.

adj jurisdictive, judicial, administrative; inquisitorial.

966 tribunal *n* court, courtroom, board, bench, court of law, court of justice, bar of justice, judgment seat, dock, forum, witness-chair.

967 judge *n* justice, judiciary, magistrate, judicator, adjudicator, jurist, juror; moderator, arbiter, arbitrator, umpire, referee.

v judge, adjudge, determine, hear a cause, try a case, pass sentence.

adj judicial, judicious, juridical, legal, juristic, judicatory, jurisdictive.

968 lawyer *n* attorney, attorney-at-law, counselor, barrister, solicitor, pleader, counsel, advocate, counselor-at-law, legal adviser; prosecutor, prosecuting attorney, district attorney, public prosecutor, attorney general.

bar, legal profession.

v practice law, be called to the bar, plead, read the law.

adj learned in the law.

969 lawsuit *n* suit, action, cause, dispute, contention; case, debate, litigation, legal proceedings, legal action, legal process, trial, debate, pleadings, argument, argumentation, disputation, prosecution; writ, summons, subpoena, affidavit, suitor, party to a suit, litigant, verdict, decision; precedent.

v go to the law, sue, file a claim, bring to trial, put on trial, serve, serve with a writ, cite, arraign, prosecute, bring an action against, indict, impeach, attach, summon.

adj litigious.

970 acquittal *n* clearance, exculpation, exoneration, absolution, discharge, pardon; impunity, immunity.

v acquit, exculpate, exonerate, clear, absolve, pardon; discharge, release, liberate, set free.

adj acquitted, cleared, exculpated, exonerated; discharged, released, set free.

971 condemnation *n* conviction, guilty verdict, proscription.

v condemn, convict, find guilty, damn, doom, proscribe; stand condemned.

adj condemned, condemnatory, convicted.

972 punishment *n* sentence, judgment, penalty, retribution, discipline, chastisement, castigation, reproof, correction.

v punish, inflict punishment, correct, discipline, penalize, reprove, castigate, chasten, administer correction. scold, berate, jail, incarcerate, execute, torture, banish, flog, whip, lash, scourge.

adj punishing, punitive, castigatory,

penalized, penalizing; punished, castigated.

973 reward *n* recompense, prizes, desert, compensation, pay, remuneration, requital, merit; bounty, premium, bonus; reparation, redress; retribution, reckoning, amends.

v reward, recompense, requite, compensate, pay, remunerate.

adj rewarding, remunerative, compensatory, retributive, reparatory; rewarded.

974 penalty *n* punishment, retribution, pain, pains, penance; fine, forfeit, damages, sequestration, incarceration, confiscation.

v penalize, punish; fine, confiscate, sequester; penalized, punished.

975 scourge *n* punishment, flogging; affliction, calamity, plague, bane, pest, nuisance; whip, lash, strap, throng, rod, cane, stick; prison, house of correction.

gaoler, jailer, executioner, hangman.

976 deity *n* divinity, god, godhead, omnipotence, providence, lord, the almighty, supreme being, first cause, prime mover, author, creator, the infinite, the eternal, the all-powerful, the all-merciful, omnipresence.

adj divine, godly, almighty, holy, hallowed, sacred, heavenly, celestial, sacrosanct; superhuman, supernatural, spiritual, ghostly, unearthly.

977 angel *n* glorified spirit, beneficent spirit, ministering spirit, heavenly spirit, winged being, seraph, cherub, archangel, helper, spirit, guardian; *(informal)* friend, patron, protector, guardian angel, love.

adj angelic, seraphic, cherubic, spiritual, ethereal; pure, good righteous, ideal, beautiful; *(informal)* adorable, entrancing, transporting, rapturous, lovely, enrapturing.

978 devil *n* Satan, Lucifer, Beelzebub; tempter, evil one, evil spirit, serpent, prince of darkness, demon, evil incarnate.

diabolism, satanism.

adj devilish, satanic, diabolic, infernal, hellish.

979 fabulous spirit n god, goddess, fairy, fay, sylph, faun, nymph, nereid, dryad, sea-maid, oread, naiad, mermaid, kelpie, nixie, sprite, pixie, elf.

adj fabulous, mythological, imaginary, sylphic.

980 demon n demonology; devil, fiend, evil spirit, incubus, monster, succubus, succuba, fury, harpy, ghoul, vampire, ogre, gnome, imp, kobold, dwarf, urchin, troll, sprite, bad fairy, leprechaun; ghost, specter, apparition, spirit, shade, shadow, vision, hobgoblin, wraith, spook, banshee, siren, satyr.

adj demonic, supernatural, weird, uncanny, unearthly, spectral, ghostly, ghostlike, elfin, fiendish, impish, haunted.

981 heaven n kingdom of heaven, kingdom of god, heavenly kingdom, paradise, nirvana; celestial bliss, glory.

adj heavenly, celestial, supernal, unearthly, paradisaic, paradisical, beatific, elysian, blissful, beautiful, divine, blessed, beautified, glorified.

982 hell n Gehenna, inferno, Hades, Erebus, pandemonium, abyss, limbo; [*informal*] torment, torture, pain, agony, suffering.

adj hellish, infernal, stygian, satanic, diabolic, devilish; [*informal*] painful, agonizing, excruciating, horrifying, unendurable.

983 theology n theosophy, divinity, hagiography, theologics, theism, monotheism, religion, religious persuasion, dogma, creed, credo, doctrine, tenent, articles of faith.

theologian, theologue, divine.

adj theological, religious, theosophical, hagiological.

983a orthodoxy n soundness; strictness, faithfulness, adherence, observance; truth, true faith, religious truth.

adj orthodox, sound, strict, faithful, catholic, doctrinal, authoritative, official, traditional; scriptural, divine, Christian; conventional, established, approved, prescriptive, prevailing, customary.

984 heterodoxy n unorthodoxy, nonconformity, iconoclasm, doubt, skepticism, recusancy, dissent, misbelief, error, heresy, schism, apostasy.

pagan, heathen, dissenter, nonconformist, skeptic, heretic, atheist.

adj heterodox, nonconformist, nonconforming, iconoclastic, doubting, skeptical, unscriptural, unorthodox, uncanonical, recusant, dissenting, misbelieving, heretical, schismatic.

985 revelation n disclosure, discovery, expression, declaration, expression, utterance, publication, admission, convession, acknowledgment; enlightenment, proclamation, announcement; Christian Revelation. Scriptures, Word of God.

adj revelatory; instructive; confessional.

986 religious writings n Scriptures, *Bible,* Old Testament, New Testament, The Vedas, Upanishads, Bhagavad Gita, Koran, Alcoran, Avesta.

987 piety n godliness, devoutness, devotion, humility, veneration, sanctity, grace, holiness; reverence, regard, respect.

believer, devotee, pietist, righteous man.

v be pious, have faith; believe, revere, venerate, sanctify, consecrate.

adj pious, devout, godly, reverent, religious, holy, sacred, pietistic, saintly; devoted, humble, reverential.

988 impiety n irreverence, irreligion, scoffing, profaneness, profanity, blasphemy, desecration, sacrilege, sin, sinfulness; hypocrisy, cant, sanctimony, sanctimoniousness.

sinner, scoffer, blasphemer, sacrilegist, hypocrite.

v be impious, scoff, swear, profane, blaspheme, desecrate, revile, commit sacrilege.

989 irreligion n ungodliness, laxity, impiety, indifference, apathy, skepticism, doubt, disbelief, incredulity, agnosticism, freethinking, atheism, infidelity.

skeptic, doubter, nonbeliever, agnostic, cynic, freethinker, atheist, infidel, heathen.

v be irreligious, doubt, disbelieve, lack faith, question.

adj irreligious, godless, ungodly, unholy, unhallowed, undevout; skeptical, doubting, unbelieving, indifferent, apathetic, incredulous, freethinking, agnostic, atheistic, faithless; worldly, earthly, unspiritual.

990 worship *n* reverence, homage, adoration, honor; regard, idolizing, idolatry, deification; prayer, supplication, petition; service, celebration, rites.

worshiper, congregation, suppliant, communicant, celebrant.

v worship, adore, adulate, idolize, deify, love, like; pray, kneel, bow, fall on one's knees; invoke, supplicate, offer prayers, petition; praise, bless, laud, glorify, magnify, sing praises.

adj worshiping, revering, adoring, honoring; worshipful, reverential, honorific, celebrational.

991 idolatry *n* idolism, idolatrousness, idolization, fetishism, idol-worship, deification, demonology; blind adoration, extravagant love, fervor, ardency, enchantment, hero worship.

idol, image, icon, symbol, statue, false god, pagan deity.

v idolize, worship idols, idolatrize, worship, glorify, put on a pedestal, canonize, deify, apotheosize; dote upon, treasure, prize.

adj idolatrous, idol-worshiping, pagan, fetishistic; adoring, impassioned, lovesick.

992 sorcery *n* occultism, magic, witchery, enchantment, witchcraft, spell, necromancy, divination, charm, conjuration, bewitchery, spiritualism.

v practice sorcery, conjure, charm, enchant, bewitch, divine, entrance, mesmerize, cast a spell, call up spirits, raise spirits.

adj magic, magical, bewitching, enchanting, charming, incantory, weird, cabalistic, talismanic; charmed, bewitched, enchanted.

993 spell *n* charm, incantation, exorcism, voodoo, trance, rapture, suggestion, jinx, hocus-pocus, mumbo-jumbo, abracadabra.

994 sorcerer *n* magician, conjuror, necromancer, wizard, witch, exorcist, charmer, medicine man, shaman, medium, clairvoyant, mesmerist, soothsayer, guru.

995 churchdom *n* church, ministry, priesthood, sisterhood, prelacy, hierarchy.

v call, ordain, consecrate, bestow, elect.

adj ecclesiastical, clerical, priestly, pastoral, ministerial, hierarchical.

996 clergy *n* clerical, ministry, priesthood, the cloth, clergyman, divine, ecclesiastic, churchman, pastor, shepherd, minister, preacher, parson, father, reverend, priest, rabbi.

v receive the call, take orders.

adj clerical; ordained.

997 laity *n* fold, flock, congregation, assembly, brethren, people; layman, parishioner.

v secularize.

adj lay, laical, secular, civil, temporal.

998 rite *n* ceremony, observance, function, service, procedure, form, usage.

v perform a rite.

adj ritualistic, ceremonial.

999 canonicals *n* religious garments, vestments, robe, gown, surplice.

1000 temple *n* place of worship, house of god, cathedral, church, chapel, meetinghouse, synagogue, tabernacle, mosque, shrine, pantheon; monastery, priory, abbey, friary, convent, nunnery, cloister; parsonage, rectory, vicarage.

adj churchly, cloistered, monastic.

Index

abstraction *n* 451
absurd *adj* 47, 471, 477, 497, 853
absurdity *n* 497
absurdity *n* 517, 853
abundance *n* 31, 102
abundant *adj* 31
abundantly *adv* 31
abuse *n* 694, 697, 716, 934; *v* 649, 679, 716, 923, 934
abusive *adj* 716, 885, 934
abusiveness *n* 885
abutment *n* 199
abut on *v* 199
abysmal *adj* 208
abyss *n* 180, 198, 208, 982
academic *adj* 537, 542
academician *n* 492
academy *n* 542
accede *v* 488, 762
acceding *adj* 831
accelerate *v* 132, 173, 274, 684
acceleration *n* 274
accent *n* 580; *v* 580
accentuate *v* 580, 642
accentuation *n* 580
accept *v* 76, 82, 484, 771, 785, 789
acceptance *n* 484, 762, 785
acceptance into *n* 76
accepted *adj* 484
access *n* 197, 286
accessible *adj* 260, 705
accession *n* 37
accessory *n* 39, 88; *adj* 37, 88
accidence *n* 567
accident *n* 156, 619
accidental *adj* 6, 156, 621
acclaim *v* 836
acclimate *v* 613
acclivitous *adj* 305

acclivity *n* 217, 305
accolade *n* 733
accommodate *v* 23, 613, 707, 723, 787
accommodate oneself to *v* 82
accommodation *n* 723, 787
accompaniment *n* 88
accompaniment *n* 39
accompanist *n* 416
accompany *v* 88, 120, 416
accompanying *adj* 88
accomplish *v* 52, 161, 729, 731
accomplishment *n* 698, 729, 731
accord *n* 23, 178, 488, 714, 721, 762; *v* 23, 413, 714, 760, 784, 812
accordance *n* 16, 23, 178
accordant *adj* 23
accordingly *adv* 8
accord with *v* 16
account *n* 551, 594, 805, 811, 873; *v* 451, 594, 873
accountable *adj* 177
accountant *n* 801, 811
accounted *adj* 873
account for *v* 155
accounting for *n* 155
accounts *n* 811
accounts *n* 800
accouterments *n* 225
accredit *v* 805
accredited *adj* 484
accretion *n* 35
accrue *v* 37, 785
acculturation *n* 658
accumulate *v* 37, 72, 636
accumulation *n* 72, 636
accuracy *n* 459, 494, 543, 922

accurate *adj* 246, 494, 922
accusal *n* 938
accusation *n* 938
accusative *adj* 938
accusatory *adj* 938
accused *adj* 938
accuser *n* 938
accusing *adj* 938
accustom *v* 613
ace *n* 948
acerbate *v* 397
acerbic *adj* 397
acerbity *n* 397
ache *n* 378, 828; *v* 378
achievable *adj* 470
achieve *v* 161, 680, 729, 731
achievement *n* 161, 551, 729, 731
aching *n* 378
acid *adj* 397
acidify *v* 397
acidity *n* 397
acidulate *v* 397
acidulous *adj* 397
acknowledge *v* 488, 529, 535, 772
acknowledgment *n* 488, 529, 762, 772, 807, 985
acknowledgment of payment *n* 810
acme *n* 206, 210
acolyte *n* 541
acoustics *n* 402
acquaintance *n* 890
acquainted *adj* 888
acquainted with *adj* 490, 527
acquaint with *v* 527
acquiesce *v* 488, 602, 725, 762
acquiescence *n* 488, 725, 762
acquiescent *adj* 488, 535, 725

acquire ν 539, 775, 785, 795
acquire a habit ν 613
acquirement n 698
acquirements n 539
acquisition n 775
acquisition n 785, 795
acquisition of knowledge n 539
acquit ν 750, 918, 927a, 937, 970
acquit oneself of ν 807
acquittal n 970
acquittal n 750, 937
acquittance n 772
acquitted adj 937, 970
acreage n 342, 780
acres n 342
acrid adj 392, 395, 397
acridity n 392, 397
acridness n 395
act n 680, 697, 741; ν 170, 599, 680, 692
act a part ν 599, 644, 855
act in concert ν 709
acting n 599
action n 680
action n 264, 682, 686, 692, 969
actions n 692
activate ν 175
active adj 171, 359, 682
activity n 682
activity n 171, 264, 686
actor n 599, 680, 690
actress n 599
actual adj 1, 118, 494
actuality n 1
actually adv 1
act up to ν 772
acumen n 498
acute adj 171, 173, 253, 375, 410, 410
acute angle n 244
acutely adv 31
acuteness n 173, 253

adage n 496
adamant adj 600
adamantine adj 323
adapt ν 23, 852
adaptability n 149
adaptable adj 82, 149
adapt to ν 82
add ν 37, 85
addendum n 37, 39
addiction n 613
addictive adj 613
addition n 37
addition n 35, 39
additional adj 35, 37, 39
addle-brained adj 499
address n 189, 582, 586; ν 582, 586
add to ν 35
add up ν 37, 85
add up to ν 50
add water ν 337
adept adj 698
adequacy n 639
adequate adj 157, 639
adhere ν 46, 199
adherence n 46, 983a
adhere to ν 613, 772
adhering adj 46
adhesion n 46, 772
adhesive adj 46, 327, 352
adhesiveness n 46, 352
adieu n 293
ad infinitum adv 104
adjacent adj 197
adjoin ν 197, 199
adjoining adj 197
adjourn ν 133
adjournment n 133
adjudge ν 967
adjudicator n 737, 967
adjunct n 39
adjunct n 37, 88
adjust ν 23, 27, 58, 774, 852
adjustable adj 149
adjustment n 723, 774

administer n 965; ν 692, 693, 737, 786, 965
administer correction ν 972
administering adj 693
administration n 692, 693
administrative adj 692, 737, 965
admirable adj 928
admiration n 870, 928, 931
admire ν 870, 928, 931
admirer n 897
admission n 76, 296, 785, 985
admit ν 54, 76, 296, 488, 529, 785
admit of ν 470
admittance n 296
admitting adj 469
admixture n 41
admonish ν 668, 695, 864, 932
admonition ν 668, 695, 864
admonitory adj 695
ado n 315, 684
adolescence n 131
adolescent adj 131
adorable adj 897, 977
adoration n 897, 990
adore ν 897, 928, 990
adorer n 897
adoring adj 897, 990, 991
adorn ν 847
adornment n 847
adrift adj 10, 44, 73; adv 44
adroit adj 698
adroitness n 698, 702
adulate ν 897, 928, 990
adulation n 933
adulator n 935
adulatory adj 933
adult adj 131

adulterate *v* 41, 659
adulterated *adj* 337, 961
adulteration *n* 41, 659, 961
adulthood *n* 131
adumbrate *v* 422
adumbration *n* 421
advance *n* 282, 286, 731, 787; *v* 35, 109, 282, 307, 514, 658, 731, 763, 787
advanced *adj* 128, 282
advanced age *n* 128
advanced guard *n* 234
advancement *n* 282, 658
advancing *adj* 282
advantage *n* 33, 618; *v* 618
advantageous *adj* 618, 644, 646, 648, 775, 888
advent *n* 121, 286, 292
adventitious *adj* 6, 8, 156
adventure *n* 151, 622, 675; *v* 665, 675
adventurer *n* 463, 548, 621
adventuress *n* 548
adventurous *adj* 675, 861
adversary *n* 708, 710, 726, 891
adverse *adj* 708, 735
adversely *adv* 735
adversity *n* 735
adversity *n* 619, 830
advertise *v* 531
advertisement *n* 531
advice *n* 695
advice *n* 527, 668, 693, 864
advisability *n* 646
advisable *adj* 646
advise *v* 527, 693, 695, 864
advised *adj* 527, 620

advisedly *adv* 611, 620
adviser *n* 540, 694, 695
advisory *adj* 668, 695
advisory board *n* 696
advocacy *n* 707
advocate *n* 890, 968; *v* 695, 707
aerate *v* 338
aerial *adj* 267, 338
aeriform *adj* 338
aeronautical *n* 267
aeronautics *n* 267
aesthetic *adj* 845
afar *adj* 196; *adv* 196
affability *n* 894
affable *adj* 894
affair *n* 151, 454, 625, 680
affairs *n* 151
affect *v* 9, 175, 176, 824, 855
affectation *n* 855
affectation *n* 579
affected *adj* 579, 820, 821, 855, 914
affectedness *n* 855
affection *n* 888, 897, 928
affectionate *adj* 888, 897
affections *n* 820
affidavit *n* 467, 535, 969
affiliated *adj* 9, 11
affiliation *n* 11
affinity *n* 9, 17, 216, 288
affirm *v* 516, 535
affirmation *n* 535
affirmative *adj* 535
affirming *adj* 535
affix *n* 39; *v* 37, 43
afflict *v* 828
affliction *n* 735, 828, 830, 975
affluence *n* 734, 803
affluent *adj* 803
afford *v* 784

afford pleasure *v* 829
affront *n* 830; *v* 830
afire *adj* 382
aflame *adj* 382
afloat *adj* 1, 267
aforementioned *adj* 116
aforethought *adj* 611
afraid *adj* 860, 862
afresh *adv* 104, 123
aft *adv* 235
after *adj* 117; *adv* 63, 117, 235, 281
aftermath *n* 65
afternoon *n* 126
afterpiece *n* 65
aftertaste *n* 390
after the flood *adv* 59
after this fashion *adv* 627
afterthought *n* 65
afterwards *adv* 117
again *adv* 104
again and again *adv* 104
against *adv* 708; *prep* 179
against one's will *adv* 603
against the grain *adv* 256
age *n* 128
age *n* 106, 108, 124; *v* 124, 435
aged *adj* 124, 128, 130
agency *n* 170
agency *n* 632, 677, 755
agent *n* 690
agent *n* 153, 758
agglomerate *n* 46
aggrandize *v* 35, 194
aggrandizement *n* 35, 37, 194
aggravate *n* 173, 835
aggravation *n* 835
aggregate *n* 50, 72; *v* 50
aggregation *n* 46, 72
aggression *n* 716
aggressive *adj* 716

aggressiveness *n* 715
aggressor *n* 716
aggrieve *v* 649
aghast *adj* 509, 860, 870
agile *adj* 274
agitate *v* 315, 824
agitated *adj* 149, 315
agitation *n* 315
agitation *n* 59, 149, 171, 173, 824, 825
aglow *adj* 420
agnostic *adj* 989
agnosticism *n* 989
ago *adv* 122
agog *adj* 870
agonize *v* 378
agonizing *adj* 982
agony *n* 378, 825, 828, 982
agrarian *adj* 371
agree *v* 23, 82, 178, 488, 714, 725, 762, 768, 769
agreeable *adj* 23, 82, 377, 413, 762, 829, 831
agreeableness *n* 829
agreed *adj* 488
agreed upon *adj* 474
agreeing *adj* 23, 413, 488, 494
agreement *n* 23
agreement *n* 16, 17, 82, 178, 242, 488, 602, 709, 714, 762, 769
agree to *v* 760
agree with *v* 656, 829
agricultural *adj* 371
agriculture *n* 371
agrobiology *n* 371
agrology *n* 371
agronomics *n* 371
agronomy *n* 371
ahead *adv* 234, 280, 282, 303
aid *n* 707
aid *n* 631, 644, 711,

834; *v* 215, 631, 644, 707, 746, 834, 906
aiding *adj* 707
ail *v* 655
ailing *adj* 655
ailment *n* 655
aim *n* 278, 453, 516, 620; *v* 278, 516
aim at *v* 278, 620, 622
aim for *v* 620
air *n* 338
air *n* 349, 415, 448, 852; *v* 338
aircraft *n* 273
airing *n* 266
airman *n* 269
air-pipe *n* 351
airplane *n* 273
airs *n* 855
airtight *adj* 261
air travel *n* 267
airy *adj* 4, 320, 334, 338
ait *n* 346
ajar *adj* 260
akimbo *adj* 244
akin *adj* 11
akin to *adj* 17
alacrity *n* 132, 274, 602, 684
à la mode *adj* 852
alarm *n* 669
alarm *n* 550, 665, 668, 860; *v* 669
alarm bell *n* 669
alarmed *adj* 860
alarum *n* 669
albeit *adv* 30
albification *n* 430
albinism *n* 430
albinistic *adj* 430
album *n* 596
alchemy *n* 144
alcoholic *n* 959
alcoholism *n* 954, 959
Alcoran *n* 986
alert *adj* 457, 498, 682, 864

alertness *n* 457, 459
algebra *n* 85
algebraic *adj* 85
alias *n* 565
alien *adj* 10, 57
alienated *adj* 889
alight *v* 265, 292, 306, 342
aligned *adj* 216
alignment *n* 278
alike *adj* 17
alive *adj* 359, 375, 457, 505, 682
alive and kicking *adj* 359
all *adv* 50
allay *v* 834
all but *adv* 32
all day long *adv* 110
allegation *n* 617
allege *v* 617
alleged *adj* 617
allegiance *n* 743
all-embracing *adj* 76
all-encompassing *adj* 78
alleviate *v* 174, 834
alleviation *n* 834
all for the better *adj* 658
alliance *n* 9, 11, 178, 709, 712, 714, 903
allied *adj* 9, 11, 216
allied to *adj* 17
allied with *adj* 178
all-important *adj* 642
all in all *adv* 50
all-inclusive *adj* 78
all manner of kinds *adj* 81
allocation *n* 786
allocution *n* 586
all of a sudden *adv* 113
all one *adj* 27
allot *v* 51, 60, 786
allotment *n* 60, 786
all over *adv* 180
allow *v* 469, 488, 529,

737, 740, 748, 760,
762, 784, 813
allowable *adj* 760
allowance *n* 469, 488,
760, 784, 786, 813
allowed *adj* 924
allow for *v* 469
alloy *n* 41, 48
all-purpose *adj* 148
all ready *adj* 673
all set for *adj* 507
all the livelong day *adv*
110
all the rage *adj* 852
all the time *adv* 106
all the worse for wear
adj 659
allude to *v* 516, 527
allure *v* 288, 829
alluring *adj* 288
allusive *adj* 521, 526
alluvial *adj* 342
ally *n* 711, 890; *v* 174
almanac *n* 114
almighty *adj* 157, 976
almighty dollar *n* 800
almost *adv* 32
alms *n* 784
almsgiving *n* 784
aloft *n* 267
alone *adj* 87
alongside *adv* 236
a long way off *adv* 196
a long while back *adv*
122
along with *adv* 37, 88
aloud *adv* 404
alphabet *n* 561
alphabetical *adj* 561
already *adv* 116, 122
also *adv* 37
alter *v* 15, 140
alteration *n* 20a, 140
altercation *n* 713, 720
altered *adj* 15, 20a
alter ego *n* 17
alternate *n* 534, 759; *v*
12, 20a, 70, 138,

147, 149 *adj* 12, 70,
138
alternately *adv* 138
alternation *n* 138, 145,
149, 314
alternative *n* 147, 609
alter one's course *v* 279
although *adv* 30, 179
altitude *n* 206
altogether *adv* 50, 52
altruism *n* 906
altruist *n* 906
altruistic *adj* 906, 910
always *adv* 16, 112
amalgam *n* 41, 48
amalgamate *v* 41, 48
amalgamation *n* 41, 48
amass *v* 50, 72, 636
amateur *n* 701
amaze *v* 870
amazed *adj* 870
amazement *n* 870
amazing *adj* 870
amazingly *adv* 31
amber *n* 356a
ambergris *n* 356a
ambiguity *n* 475, 517,
519, 520, 571
ambiguous *adj* 475,
520
ambition *n* 620, 865
amble *v* 275
ambrosial *adj* 394
ambuscade *n* 530
ambush *n* 530
ambush *n* 667; *v* 530
ameliorate *v* 658, 723
amelioration *n* 658
amenable *adj* 762
amend *v* 658
amending *adj* 950
amendment *n* 658
amends *n* 30, 952, 973
amenity *n* 829
amiability *n* 829
amiable *adj* 721, 829,
888

amicable *adj* 707, 721,
892
amicably *adv* 888
amid *adv* 41, 228
amidst *adv* 41
amiss *adj* 923
amity *n* 714, 721, 888
ammunition *n* 727
amnesia *n* 506
amnesty *n* 723, 918
among *adv* 41, 228
amongst *adv* 41, 228
amorous *adj* 897
amorphism *n* 241
amorphous *adj* 241
amount *n* 25, 26, 800,
812
amount to *v* 50
amphitheater *n* 599,
728
ample *adj* 31, 180, 192,
202, 639
amplification *n* 194
amplify *v* 194, 549, 573
amplitude *n* 102, 192,
202
amplitudinous *adj* 192
amply *adv* 31, 639
amputate *v* 38
amputation *n* 38
amuse *v* 829, 840
amusement *n* 840
amuse oneself *v* 840
amusing *adj* 840
anachronism *n* 115
anachronism *n* 135
anachronistic *adj* 115
anagram *n* 561
analogous *adj* 12, 17,
216
analogy *n* 9, 17, 216
analysis *n* 49, 60, 463,
476, 596
analytic *adj* 85, 463,
596
analytical *adj* 476, 596
analyze *v* 49, 463, 476
analyzer *n* 463

anarchic *adj* 59
anarchism *n* 59
anarchy *n* 59
anatomic *adj* 329
anatomical *adj* 329
anatomy *n* 329, 357, 368
ancestral *adj* 166
ancestry *n* 122, 166
anchor *n* 666
anchorage *n* 184
anchorite *n* 955
ancient *adj* 124
ancient times *n* 122
and *adv* 37
and everywhere *adv* 186
and so forth *adv* 37
anemic *adj* 430
anesthesia *n* 376
anesthetic *adj* 376
anesthetize *v* 376, 381
anew *adv* 104, 123
angel *n* 977
angel *n* 164, 897
angelic *adj* 977
anger *n* 824, 900; *v* 830
angle *n* 244; *v* 244
angry *adj* 382, 900
anguish *n* 378, 619, 828
angular *adj* 244
angularity *n* 244
anility *n* 128
animal *n* 366
animal *adj* 366
animalistic *adj* 364, 366
animality *n* 364
animal kingdom *n* 366
animal life *n* 357, 364
animal physiology *n* 368
animate *v* 382, 824, 836; *adj* 357
animated *adj* 171, 382, 515
animated nature *n* 357
animate matter *n* 357
animating *adj* 836

animation *n* 359, 515, 682, 824
animosity *n* 889, 898, 900
ankle-deep *adj* 209
annalist *n* 553
annal(s) *n* 114
annals *n* 551
annex *n* 39; *v* 37
annexation *n* 37, 43
annihilate *v* 2
annihilation *n* 2, 162
annotate *v* 522
annotator *n* 524
announce *v* 527, 531, 883
announcement *n* 527, 531, 985
annoy *v* 688, 830
annoyance *n* 649, 828, 830, 835
annul *v* 756
annulment *n* 756
anoint *v* 332
anointment *n* 332, 355
anomalous *adj* 59, 83
anomaly *n* 59, 83
anon *adv* 132
another *adj* 15
another time *n* 119
answer *n* 462
answer *n* 479, 522, 662; *v* 462, 746
answerable *adj* 177, 462
answerable for *adj* 806
answer for *v* 759
antagonism *n* 14, 24, 179, 708, 715, 867, 889
antagonist *n* 708, 710, 726, 891
antagonistic *adj* 14, 24, 179, 708, 715
antagonize *v* 14, 179
antecedence *n* 116
antecedence *n* 62

antecedent *n* 64, 116; *adj* 62, 116
antedate *v* 115, 116
antediluvian *adj* 124
antemeridian *n* 125
anterior *adj* 62, 116, 234
anteriority *n* 116
anthology *n* 596
anthracite *n* 388
anthropology *n* 368
anti *adj* 708
anticipate *v* 115, 121, 132, 451, 507, 510, 673, 858
anticipation *n* 121, 132, 451, 507, 510, 673, 858
anticipatory *adj* 132, 510
antidote *n* 662
antipathy *n* 14, 289, 867, 898
antipodal *adj* 237
antipodean *adj* 14
antipodes *n* 14
antiquarian *n* 553
antiquarianism *n* 124
antiquated *adj* 124
antique *adj* 124
antiquity *n* 122, 124
antisocial *adj* 911
antithesis *n* 14, 218, 237
antithetical *adj* 14, 237
antitoxin *n* 662
anxiety *n* 459, 860
anxious *adj* 860
any *adj* 25
apace *adv* 274
apart *adj* 44, 87; *adv* 44
apathetic *adj* 383, 456, 823, 866, 989
apathy *n* 823, 866, 989
ape *v* 19
aperture *n* 260
apex *n* 8, 67, 210

aphasia *n* 581, 583
aphorism *n* 496
aphoristic *adj* 496
apiece *adv* 79
aping *n* 19
apologist *n* 937
apostasy *n* 607, 984
apostate *n* 607
a posteriori n 476
apostrophe *n* 589
apostrophize *v* 589
apothegm *n* 496
apotheosize *v* 991
appal *v* 830
apparel *n* 225; *v* 225
apparent *adj* 446, 448, 525
apparently *adv* 448
apparition *n* 4, 443, 980
appeal *n* 411, 765
appear *v* 446, 448, 525
appearance *n* 448
appearance *n* 220, 240, 446, 569
appease *v* 174, 723, 826, 831
appellant *n* 924, 938
appellation *n* 564
append *v* 37
appendage *n* 39, 65
appendix *n* 39
appertain to *v* 9, 56
appetite *n* 865
appetizing *adj* 394
applaud *v* 836, 883
apple *adj* 435
apple of one's eye *n* 899
apple-polisher *n* 886, 935
appliance *n* 677
applicability *n* 644
applicable *adj* 644, 677
applicant *n* 767
application *n* 677, 765
apply *v* 677
appoint *v* 741, 755, 786
appointment *n* 755

apportion *v* 44, 51, 60, 73, 786
apportionment *n* 786
apportionment *n* 60, 73
apposite *adj* 23
apposition *n* 23, 199
appraisal *n* 812
appraise *v* 466, 480, 668, 812
appraisement *n* 466
appreciate *v* 394, 480, 850, 916, 931
appreciation *n* 465, 822, 916
appreciative *adj* 822, 916
apprehend *v* 490, 860
apprehension *n* 453, 490, 665, 789, 860
apprehensive *adj* 860
apprentice *n* 541
apprenticeship *n* 539
apprize *v* 527
apprized of *adj* 527
approach *n* 286
approach *n* 197, 569, 627, 632; *v* 121, 152, 286
approaching *adj* 286
approbate *v* 931
approbation *n* 931
approbation *n* 488, 928
appropriate *v* 775, 786, 788, 789, 791; *adj* 79, 134, 646, 850
appropriateness *n* 646
appropriating *n* 788
appropriation *n* 775, 789, 791
approval *n* 488, 762, 928, 931
approve *v* 535, 737, 931
approved *adj* 931, 983a
approximate *v* 17, 197; *adj* 17, 197, 286
approximation *n* 9, 17, 19, 286
apricot *adj* 439

a priori n 476
apt *adj* 23, 498, 698, 850
aptitude *n* 176, 498, 602, 698
aptness *n* 176, 698
aqua *n* 337
aquamarine *v* 435, 438
aquatics *n* 267
aqueduct *n* 350
aqueous *adj* 337
arable *adj* 371
arbiter *n* 724, 737, 967
arbitrariness *n* 739
arbitrary *adj* 83, 606, 608, 739, 964
arbitrate *v* 174, 724
arbitration *n* 724
arbitrator *n* 724, 967
arc *n* 245
arcade *n* 245
arced *adj* 245
arch *n* 245, 250; *v* 245; *adj* 31
archaic *adj* 124
archaism *n* 124
archangel *n* 977
arched *adj* 245, 250
archetype *n* 22
archipelago *n* 346
architect *n* 164
architecture *n* 161, 329
arch over *v* 245
arctic *adj* 383
ardency *n* 991
ardent *adj* 382, 865
ardor *n* 382, 574, 682, 821
arduous *adj* 704
area *n* 181
arena *n* 728
arenose *adj* 330
areola *n* 247
argue *v* 24, 467, 476, 720
arguer *n* 476
argument *n* 454, 476, 516, 713, 720, 969

argumentation *n* 476, 969

argumentative *adj* 476, 713

arguments *n* 476

argumentum ad hominem n 476

aria *n* 413

arid *adj* 169, 340

aridity *n* 340

arise *v* 151, 305

aristocracy *n* 875

aristocratic *adj* 875

arithmetic *n* 85

arithmetical *adj* 85

arithmetic operations *n* 85

arm *n* 343; *v* 157, 673, 727

armaments *n* 727

armistice *n* 723

armlet *n* 247

armor *n* 727

arms *n* 727

army *n* 72

aroma *n* 400

aromatic *adj* 400

around *adv* 227

arouse *v* 175, 382, 615, 824

arraign *v* 938, 969

arraignment *n* 938

arrange *v* 58, 60, 626, 673, 774

arranged *adj* 60

arrange in a series *v* 69

arrange in words *v* 566

arrangement *n* 60

arrangement *n* 58, 673, 723, 769

arrangement *n* 807

array *n* 58, 102; *v* 60, 225

arrest *v* 142

arrival *n* 292

arrive *v* 151, 265, 292, 342

arrogance *n* 878, 885

arrogant *adj* 739, 878, 885, 880

artery *n* 350

artful *adj* 702

artfulness *n* 702

art gallery *n* 556

article *n* 3, 316, 590, 595

article of faith *n* 537

articles *n* 770, 798

articles of faith *n* 983

articulate *v* 580, 582; *adj* 580

articulation *n* 43, 580

artifice *n* 545, 702

artificial *adj* 579, 855

artificial light *n* 423

artist *n* 559

artist *n* 416

artistic *adj* 845

artistically *adv* 698

artless *adj* 703, 946

artlessness *n* 703

artlessless *n* 946

as a consequence *adv* 154

as a matter of course *adv* 82

as a rule *adv* 613

ascend *v* 35, 305, 658

ascendancy *n* 33, 157, 175, 731

ascendant *adj* 305

ascending *adj* 217

ascension *n* 305

ascent *n* 305

ascent *n* 35, 217

ascertain *v* 480a

ascetic *n* 955; *adj* 955

asceticism *n* 955

as chance will have it *adv* 156

ascribe importance *v* 642

ascribe to *v* 155

ascription *n* 155

as good as one's word *adj* 772

ash *n* 388

ashen *adj* 429, 432

ashes *n* 362

ashore *adv* 342

ashy *adj* 429, 432

aside *n* 589

as if *adv* 17

as if it were *adv* 17

asinine *adj* 497, 499, 853

as it happens *adv* 151

as it were *adv* 17

ask *v* 461, 630, 765, 812, 865

askance *adv* 217

askew *adj* 217, 243; *adv* 217

ask for *v* 765

asleep *adj* 458

as low as one can go *adj* 649

as matters stand *adv* 8

aspect *n* 183, 220, 448

aspects *n* 5

asperity *n* 256

aspersion *n* 934

asphalt *n* 356a

asphyxiate *v* 361

aspirant *n* 767

aspiration *n* 858, 865

aspire at *v* 620

asquint *adj* 217

as regards *adv* 9

ass *n* 493

assail *v* 716

assailant *n* 716, 726

assailer *n* 726

assassin *n* 165, 361

assassination *n* 361

assault *n* 716; *v* 716

assaulter *n* 726

assay *n* 463; *v* 463

assemblage *n* 72

assemblage *n* 43, 102, 712

assemble *v* 50, 72, 72, 712

assembled *adj* 72

assembly n 43, 72, 696, 712, 997

assent n 488

assent n 23, 82, 178, 484, 602, 762; v 82, 488, 535, 602, 762

assenting adj 488, 831

assert v 535, 720

assertion n 535

assertive adj 535

assertiveness n 715

assess v 466, 812

assessment n 466, 480

assessor n 480

asset n 944

assets n 780, 800

asseverate v 535

assiduity n 682

assiduous adj 682

assiduousness n 682

assign v 60, 755, 783, 784, 786

assignment n 155, 755, 786

assign to v 155

assimilate v 16, 144

assimilation n 144

assist v 707, 746, 834, 906

assistance n 707, 834

assistant n 707, 711, 759

associate n 88, 711, 890; v 9, 41, 43, 72, 216

associated adj 9

associated with adj 88

associate with v 88

association n 9, 72, 88, 464, 709, 712, 903

assortment n 60, 72

assuage v 174, 723, 834

assuagement n 174, 834

assuaging adj 834

assume v 484, 510, 514, 789, 855, 871, 885

assumed adj 514

assumed name n 565

assumption n 514

assurance n 474, 484, 507, 768, 858

assure v 768, 771

assured adj 474, 484

asteroids n 318

as the saying goes adv 496

as the world goes adv 613

as they say adv 496

as things go adv 151, 613

astigmatic adj 443

astigmatism n 443

astonish v 508, 870

astonished adj 870

astonishing adj 870

astonishingly adv 31

astonishment n 508, 870

astound v 824, 870

astounding adj 870

astral adj 318

astray adv 279

astringent adj 195, 397

astronaut n 269

astute adj 498, 702

asunder adj 44; adv 44

as usual adv 613

as well as adv 37

asylum n 666

asymmetrical adj 241

asymmetry n 241, 243

at a different time adv 119

at a distance adj 196

at a glance adv 441

at all events adv 30

at all times adv 136

at a low ebb adj 308

at an angle adv 217

at any rate adv 30

at a snail's pace adv 275

at a standstill adj 265

at bottom adv 5

at cross purposes adj 713; adv 59, 708

at ease adj 827

at fault adj 927

at first sight adv 441, 448

at full gallop adv 274

at full speed adv 274

at half speed adv 275

at hand adj 152, 197

at heart adv 82

atheism n 989

atheist n 984, 989

atheistic adj 989

athletic adj 159

at intervals adv 70

at issue adj 708

at its height adv 33

at large adj 748

atlas n 86

at last adv 67, 133

at length adv 133, 200

atmosphere n 338

atmospheric adj 338

at no time adv 107

at odds adj 708

atoll n 346

atom n 32, 180a

atomization n 336

atomize v 336

atonal adj 410, 414

atonality n 410, 414

at once adv 132

atone v 30, 952

atone for v 462, 952

atonement n 952

atonement n 790, 950

at one's disposal adj 777

at one's fingertips adv 197

at one's leisure adv 133

at one with adj 178

atoning adj 950, 952

at present adv 118

at random adv 156

at regular intervals adv 58

at rest adj 265; adv 687

atrophy n 195, 659

at short notice *adv* 132
at sight *adv* 132
at some other time *adv* 119
at some time or other *adv* 119
attach *v* 37, 43, 969
attached *adj* 897
attach importance *v* 642
attachment *n* 37, 39, 43, 88, 897
attach too much importance to *v* 482
attack *n* 716
attacker *n* 716, 891
attain *v* 292, 775
attain an end *v* 731
attain majority *v* 131
attainment *n* 292, 539, 698, 775
attempt *n* 675, 686; *v* 675
attend *v* 186, 281, 418, 457, 746, 928
attendance *n* 186
attendant *n* 88; *adj* 88
attending *n* 418; *adj* 186, 928
attending to *n* 457
attend regularly *v* 136
attend to *v* 743
attention *n* 457
attention *n* 451, 459, 928
attentive *adj* 451, 457, 459
attentiveness *n* 457
attenuate *v* 195
attenuation *n* 195, 330
attest *v* 550
at that instant *adv* 119
at that time *adv* 119
at the eleventh hour *adv* 133
at the heels *adv* 235
at the least *adv* 32
at the present time *adv* 118

at the same time *adv* 30, 120
at the top of one's lungs *adv* 404
at the top of one's voice *adv* 404
at this moment *adv* 118
at this time *adv* 118
at times *adv* 136
attire *n* 225
attitude *n* 8, 183, 240
attitudinize *v* 855
attorney *n* 968
attorney-at-law *n* 968
attorney general *n* 968
attract *v* 288, 829
attract attention *v* 446
attracting *adj* 288
attraction *n* 288
attraction *n* 829
attractive *adj* 288, 615, 829, 845, 850
attractiveness *n* 288, 829, 845
attributable *adj* 155
attribute *n* 780
attributed *adj* 155
attribute to *v* 155
attribution *n* 155
attrition *n* 331
attunement *n* 413
at variance *adj* 24, 708, 713
at will *adv* 600
at work *adj* 170
auburn *adj* 433
auction *n* 796
audacious *adj* 861, 863, 885
audacity *n* 861, 863, 885
audibility *n* 402, 418
audible *adj* 402
audience *n* 444, 588
audition *n* 418
auditor *n* 418, 811
auditory *adj* 418
auger *n* 262

augment *v* 35, 37
augmentation *n* 35, 39, 194
augur *n* 513; *v* 511, 909
auguring *adj* 909
augury *n* 511, 512, 668
au naturel *adj* 226
aureate *adj* 435
aureole *n* 420
auricular *adj* 418
aurora *n* 420
auscultation *n* 418
auspices *n* 175, 693
auspicious *adj* 134, 734
austere *adj* 704, 739, 955
austerity *n* 739, 955
authentic *adj* 494
author *n* 153, 164, 590, 593, 976
authoritative *adj* 175, 737, 741, 983a
authority *n* 737
authority *n* 157, 175, 500, 527, 700, 745, 965
authorization *n* 737, 760
authorize *v* 157, 737, 755, 760
authorized *adj* 924, 963
author's copy *n* 590
authorship *n* 161, 590
autocracy *n* 739
autocratic *adj* 600, 739
automatic *adj* 601
automobile *n* 272
autonomous *adj* 748
autonomy *n* 748
autopsy *n* 363
autumn *n* 126
auxiliary *n* 711
auxiliary *adj* 37, 707
avail *n* 644, 677; *v* 644
available *adj* 260, 644, 673
avail oneself of *v* 677
avarice *n* 819

avaricious *adj* 819
avenge *v* 718, 919
avenger *n* 919
avenue *n* 302, 627
aver *v* 535
average *n* 29; *adj* 29,
  651, 736
average capacity *n* 736
averse *adj* 289, 603,
  867
averse from *adj* 898
averseness *n* 603
aversion *n* 289, 603,
  867, 898
Avesta *n* 986
aviate *v* 267
aviation *n* 267
aviational *adj* 267
aviator *n* 269
aviatrix *n* 269
avoid *v* 287, 623, 671
avoidance *n* 623
avoider *n* 623
avow *v* 488, 535
avowal *n* 529
await *v* 121, 152, 507
awake *v* 404, 824; *adj*
  457, 682
award *n* 784; *v* 784
aware *adj* 375, 822
awareness *n* 822
aware of *adj* 490
away *adj* 187, 196; *adv*
  196
awe *n* 860, 870
a wee bit *adv* 32
awe-inspiring *adj* 860
awesome *adj* 860, 870
awe-struck *adj* 870
awful *adj* 395, 403, 860
awhile *adv* 111
awkward *adj* 579, 699,
  704
awkwardness *n* 579,
  699
awl *n* 262
awning *n* 223, 424
awry *adj* 217, 243, 923

ax *v* 44
axiom *n* 496
axiomatic *adj* 496
axis *n* 153, 222

B

baa *v* 412
babble *v* 348, 584
babbler *n* 584
babe *n* 129
babe in arms *n* 129
baby *n* 129
baby blue *adj* 438
babyish *adj* 129
bachelor *n* 904
bachelorhood *n* 904
back *n* 235; *v* 707, 737;
  adj 235
back and forth *adv* 314
backbiter *n* 936
backbone *n* 5, 221,
  604a
back down *v* 283
backer *n* 164, 890
backfire *n* 277
backfiring *adj* 277
background *n* 196, 235
backlash *n* 145, 277
back out *v* 283
backside *n* 235
backsliding *n* 283, 661
backward *adj* 133, 603;
  adv 133
backwards *adv* 283
backwater *n* 283
bad *adj* 34, 397, 401,
  649, 653, 657, 663,
  923, 945
bad diction *n* 579
bad fairy *n* 980
badge *n* 747
badger *v* 830, 909
bad grammar *n* 568
bad likeness *n* 555
bad luck *n* 735
bad man *n* 949
bad manners *n* 895
bad name *n* 874

badness *n* 649
bad news *n* 830
bad odor *n* 401
bad omen *n* 649
bad smell *n* 401
bad straits *n* 804
bad taste *n* 851
bad tasting *adj* 395
bad-tempered *adj*
  901a, 945
bad timing *n* 135
bag *v* 789
bail *n* 771
bait *n* 784; *v* 288, 830
bake *v* 384
baker's dozen *n* 98
baking *adj* 382
balance *n* 27, 29, 40,
  150, 242, 800, 811; *v*
  27, 30, 811
balance accounts *v* 807
balanced *adj* 27, 150,
  242
balance out *v* 30, 179
bale *n* 190
baleful *adj* 649, 663
balk *v* 509
ball *n* 249
ballast *n* 30
balloon *n* 273
ball-shaped *adj* 249
balm *n* 356, 662
balustrade *n* 232
bamboozle *v* 545
ban *n* 761
banal *adj* 209
banality *n* 209, 843
bananas *adj* 503
band *n* 72, 247, 416,
  417, 712
bandage *n* 223, 263
banded *adj* 440
band together *v* 709,
  712
bandy *v* 148, 315
bandy words *v* 588
bane *n* 663
bane *n* 165, 649, 975

baneful *adj* 663
bang *n* 406; *v* 276
bang into *v* 276
banish *v* 55, 185, 297, 972
banished *adj* 893
banish from one's thoughts *v* 506
banishment *n* 185, 297, 893
bank *n* 217, 802
banker *n* 801
bankrupt *adj* 732
bankruptcy *v* 732, 808
banshee *n* 980
banter *n* 856; *v* 842, 856
baptize *v* 564
bar *n* 215, 346, 968; *v* 55, 261, 761
barb *n* 253; *v* 253
barbarism *n* 563, 579, 851
barbarous *adj* 241, 563, 579
barbed *adj* 253
bard *n* 597
bare *v* 226, 260; *adj* 226
barefaced *adj* 525
barely *adv* 32
barely audible *adj* 405
bareness *n* 226
bare possibility *n* 473
barf *v* 297
bargain *n* 769, 794, 795, 815; *v* 769, 794
barge *n* 271, 273
bark *n* 223; *v* 412
bar of justice *n* 966
barrel *n* 249
barrelhouse *n* 415
barren *adj* 158, 169
barrenness *n* 158, 169
barricade *n* 232
barrier *n* 232, 261
barrister *n* 968
barter *n* 794

barter *n* 148; *v* 148, 794, 796
base *n* 211
base *n* 208, 215; *v* 215; *adj* 34, 207, 211, 649, 846, 874, 876, 886, 930
based on *adj* 19, 211
baseless *adj* 2, 4
baseness *n* 862, 886
bashful *adj* 881
bashfulness *n* 881
basic *adj* 5, 42, 211
basics *n* 66
basin *n* 252, 343, 344
basis *n* 211, 215
bask in *v* 377
batch *n* 25, 72
bathetic *adj* 497
bathos *n* 497
batter *v* 162, 276
battered *adj* 659
battery *n* 716
battle *n* 680, 722; *v* 720, 722
battlefield *n* 728
battleground *n* 728
battler *n* 726
battle with words *v* 148
bauble *n* 643
bawdry *n* 961
bawdy *adj* 961
bawl *v* 411
bay *n* 343; *v* 412; *adj* 433
bayonet *n* 262; *v* 361
bayou *n* 343
bazaar *n* 799
be *v* 1
be absent *v* 187
be absurd *v* 497
beacon *n* 550
be active *v* 680, 682
be affected with *v* 655
be afraid of *v* 860
be agitated *v* 315
beak *n* 250
be alive *v* 359

be all ears *v* 418
beam *n* 420; *v* 420
be an example *v* 22
bear *v* 215, 270, 692, 826
bearable *adj* 651
bear a grudge *v* 900
bear a resemblance *v* 17
bearer *n* 271
bear fruit *v* 161
bear ill will *v* 907
bearing *n* 9, 278, 692
bearings *n* 183
bear in mind *v* 451, 505
bear no resemblance *v* 18
bear off *v* 279
be artless *v* 703
bear upon *v* 9
bear with *v* 740, 760
beast *n* 366
beastly *adj* 653
beast of burden *n* 271
beasts of the field *n* 366
beat *n* 104, 138, 314, 627; *v* 138, 276, 314, 315, 330, 406, 407
beat a retreat *v* 623
beat back *v* 289
beatific *adj* 829, 981
beatified *adj* 981
beat it out *v* 623
be at odds with *v* 889
be at peace *v* 721
be attendant on *v* 281
be attentive *v* 457
be at the mercy of *v* 749
beat time *v* 114
beat up *v* 352
be at work on *v* 625
beau *n* 897, 854
beau monde *n* 852
beauteous *adj* 845
beautified *adj* 577, 847
beautiful *adj* 242, 597, 829, 845, 977, 981
beautify *v* 845, 847
beauty *n* 845

beauty *n* 242, 829
be averse to *v* 867
be aware of *v* 450, 490
be beforehand *v* 132
be behind *v* 235
be beneficial *v* 648
be blind *v* 442
be blind to *v* 491
be blunt *v* 254
bebop *n* 415
be born *v* 359
be bound for *v* 278
be brittle *v* 328
be broad *v* 202
be called to the bar *v* 968
becalm *v* 265
be capricious *v* 608
be careful *v* 459
because *adv* 153, 155
be cautious *v* 864
be central *v* 222
be certain *v* 474
be cheap *v* 815
be cheek to cheek *v* 236
becloud *v* 421, 422
be cold *v* 383
become *v* 144, 926
become a habit *v* 613
become colorless *v* 429
become insane *v* 503
become large *v* 192
become little *v* 193
become old *v* 124
become small *v* 195
becoming *adj* 646, 850, 881
be composed of *v* 54
be concise *v* 572
be contiguous *v* 199
be contrary *v* 14
be converted into *v* 144
be courteous *v* 894
be cowardly *v* 862
be credulous *v* 486
be cunning *v* 702
be curious *v* 455
be curved *v* 245

bed *n* 204
be dark *v* 421
bedazzle *v* 420
be deaf *v* 419
be deceived *v* 547
be dejected *v* 837
be dense *v* 321
bedew *v* 339
be difficult *v* 704
be diffuse *v* 573
be dim *v* 422
be dimsighted *v* 443
be disappointed *v* 509
be discontented *v* 832
be discordant *v* 414, 713
be discourteous *v* 895
be dishonest *v* 940
be disinclined *v* 867
be disinterested *v* 942
be disrespectful *v* 929
be distant *v* 196
be distinguished *v* 873
bedlamite *n* 504
bed-ridden *adj* 655
be drunk *v* 959
bedtime *n* 126
be due to *v* 154
be dull *v* 843
be dumb *v* 581
be early *v* 132
be easy *v* 705
beehive *n* 691
be elastic *v* 325
bee line *n* 246
Beelzebub *n* 978
be enamored of *v* 897
be engaged in *v* 625
be entitled *v* 924
be equivocal *v* 520
be evasive *v* 528
be evident *v* 467
be expedient *v* 646
be expeditious *v* 134
be expensive *v* 814
be exterior *v* 220
be extraneous *v* 57
be faithful to *v* 772

befall *v* 151
be fashionable *v* 852
be fastidious *v* 868
be fated *v* 601
be fatigued *v* 688
be firm *v* 150
befit *v* 23, 646, 926
be fluid *v* 333
be fond of *v* 897
be foolish *v* 499
before *adj* 62; *adv* 62, 116, 234, 280
beforehand *adv* 116, 132
before long *adv* 132
before now *adv* 122
before one's eyes *adj* 446
be forgetful *v* 506
befoul *v* 653
be fragrant *v* 400
be free *v* 748
befriend *v* 888
be friendly *v* 888
beg *v* 765
be general *v* 78
beget *v* 161
beggar *n* 767
beggarly *adj* 643, 804
begin *v* 66, 676
begin at the beginning *v* 66
begin hostilities *v* 716
beginner *n* 541
beginning *n* 66
be gluttonous *v* 957
be gone *v* 449
be good *v* 648
be good for *v* 656
be grateful *v* 916
be great *v* 31
begrudge *v* 819, 921
begrudging *adj* 907, 921
beg the question *v* 277, 477
be guilty *v* 947
be habitual *v* 613

behalf *n* 618
be haphazard *v* 139
be hard on *v* 739
behave *v* 680, 692
behave well *v* 894
behavior *n* 680, 692
behead *v* 361
be healthy *v* 654
be heavy *v* 319
be held in high repute *v* 873
behemoth *n* 192
behest *n* 741
be hidden *v* 447
behind *adv* 63, 235, 281
behind closed doors *adv* 528
behind time *adv* 133
be hip *v* 490
behold *v* 441, 444
beholder *n* 444
beholding *adj* 916
be honorable *v* 939
behoove *v* 926
be horizontal *v* 213
be hot *v* 382
be identical *v* 13
beige *n* 433; *adj* 433
be ignorant *v* 491
be illegal *v* 964
be ill timed *v* 135
be imbecilic *v* 499
be impatient *v* 825
be impenitent *v* 951
be imperfect *v* 651
be impious *v* 988
be important *v* 642
be impossible *v* 471
be impotent *v* 158
be imprisoned *v* 754
be improbable *v* 473
be impure *v* 961
be inactive *v* 172, 265, 681, 683
be inarticulate *v* 583
be in a state *v* 7
be inattentive *v* 458

be incomplete *v* 53
be inconvenient *v* 647
be incredulous *v* 487
be in danger *v* 665
be indifferent *v* 866
be indiscriminate *v* 465a
be in error *v* 495
be inert *v* 172
be inexpedient *v* 647
be inferior *v* 34
be infinite *v* 104
be influential *v* 175
be infrequent *v* 137
be in front *v* 234
being *n* 1, 3, 359
be in health *v* 654
be inherent *v* 5
be in league with *v* 709
be in love with *v* 897
be innocent *v* 946
be inodorous *v* 399
be insane *v* 503
be insensible *v* 376
be insensitive *v* 823
be inside *v* 221
be insolent *v* 885
be instantaneous *v* 113
be instrumental *v* 631
be insufficient *v* 640
be intelligent *v* 498
be intelligible *v* 518
be intemperate *v* 954
be interior *v* 221
be intrinsic *v* 5
be in trouble *v* 619
be inverted *v* 218
be invisible *v* 447
be in want *v* 640
be irascible *v* 901
be irregular *v* 139
be irreligious *v* 989
be irresolute *v* 605
be jealous *v* 920
be large *v* 192
be late *v* 133
belated *adj* 133
be latent *v* 526

be lax *v* 738
belch out *v* 297
be left *v* 40
be left over *v* 40
be lenient *v* 740
be liable *v* 177
be liberal *v* 816
belief *n* 484
belief *n* 451, 453, 537
believable *adj* 484, 515
believe *v* 451, 484, 514, 987
believed *adj* 484
believer *n* 987
believing *n* 484; *adj* 484, 486
be light *v* 320
be little *v* 193, 934
belittling *n* 934; *adj* 934
belles lettres *n* 560
bellicose *adj* 720, 722
bellied *adj* 250
belligerency *n* 720
belligerent *adj* 720, 722
belling *n* 412
bellow *v* 404, 411, 412
bellwether *n* 64
belly *n* 221
be located *v* 183
be long *v* 200
belonging *n* 777
belongings *n* 780
belonging to *adj* 9
belong to *v* 9, 56, 777
be loquacious *v* 584
be loud *v* 404
beloved *n* 897
be low *v* 207; *adv* 207
below par *adj* 651
belowstairs *adv* 207
belt *n* 247, 276
be made up of *v* 54
be master of *v* 698
bemoan *v* 833, 839
be modest *v* 881
be mute *v* 581
be narrow *v* 203

bench *n* 966
bend *n* 217, 244, 245; *v*
 217, 244, 245, 278,
 279, 311, 324, 325,
 725, 744, 774
bend an ear *v* 418
bending *n* 245
bend over *v* 308
bend to *v* 176
be near *v* 197
beneath *adv* 207
benefactor *n* 912
beneficence *n* 648
beneficent *adj* 784
beneficent spirit *n* 977
beneficial *adj* 618, 644,
 648, 677
beneficiary *n* 785
beneficient *adj* 816
benefit *n* 618, 677, 775;
 v 618, 644, 648, 906
be negligent *v* 460
be neutral *v* 609a
benevolence *n* 906
benevolence *n* 910
benevolent *adj* 888,
 906, 906, 910
benign *adj* 656
be noble *v* 875
be no more *v* 360
bent *n* 176, 602, 613,
 820; *adj* 244
bents *n* 5
bent upon *adj* 620
benumb *v* 376, 381,
 385, 843
benumbed *adj* 381
be numerous *v* 102
be obligated *v* 601
be obliged *v* 601
be oblique *v* 217
be obstinate *v* 606
be occupied with *v* 625
be odorless *v* 399
be of help *v* 707
be of no help *v* 645
be old *v* 124
be one's fortune *v* 151

be one's lot *v* 151
be on the side *v* 236
be opaque *v* 426
be opportune *v* 134
be opposite *v* 237
be owing to *v* 154
be parsimonious *v* 819
be part of *v* 56
be penitent *v* 950
be perfect *v* 650
be pious *v* 987
be plain *v* 525
be pleased *v* 827
be pleased with *v* 827
be pleasurable *v* 829
be poor *v* 804
be possible *v* 470
be powerful *v* 157
be present *v* 186
be probable *v* 472
be prodigal *v* 818
be proud *v* 878
be pungent *v* 392
be pure *v* 960
bequeath *v* 784
bequest *n* 784
be rare *v* 137
be rash *v* 863
berate *v* 932, 972
bereft *adj* 776
be regular *v* 82
be related to *v* 11
be reluctant *v* 867
be remiss *v* 460
be resolute *v* 604
be rich *v* 803
be ridiculous *v* 853
be right *v* 922
be rumored *v* 532
be safe *v* 664
be salubrious *v* 656
be sane *v* 502
be savory *v* 394
beseech *v* 765
beseem *v* 926
be selfish *v* 943
be sensible *v* 375
be sensitive *v* 822

be sensitive to *v* 375
be servile *v* 886
beset *v* 716
be severe *v* 739
be sharp *v* 253
be short *v* 201
beside *adv* 83, 236
be side by side *v* 236
beside oneself *adj* 824
besides *adv* 37
beside the mark *adj* 10
besiege *v* 716
be silent *v* 403, 581, 585
be similar *v* 17
be situated *v* 183
be skillful *v* 698
be small *v* 32
besmear *v* 653
be sober *v* 958
be sociable *v* 892
be sorry for *v* 914
bespeak *v* 132, 467
be specific *v* 79
bespeckle *v* 440
best *adj* 648, 650
be still *v* 265, 403
bestow *v* 784, 995
bestowal *n* 784
be straight *v* 246
be straightforward *v* 576
be straight with *v* 543
bestride *v* 206
be subject *v* 749
be subsequent to *v* 117
be sufficient *v* 639
be suitable *v* 134
be sullen *v* 901a
be superior *v* 33
be surprised *v* 870
bet *v* 621
be taken *v* 360
be taken by surprise *v*
 508
be tasteless *v* 391
be temperate *v* 953
be that as may *adv* 30
be the case *v* 494
be the dupe of *v* 547

be the effect of *v* 154
be the making of *v* 648
be the rage *v* 852
be thick *v* 202
be thin *v* 203
betimes *adv* 132
betoken *v* 550
be transient *v* 111
be transparent *v* 425
betray *v* 529, 545
be true *v* 494
be true for everyone *v* 78
better *v* 658; *adj* 648, 658
better half *n* 903
betterment *n* 658
better off *adj* 658
better than nothing *adj* 651
betting *n* 621
between *adv* 228
betwixt *adv* 228
betwixt and between *adv* 228
be unaccustomed *v* 614
be unaffected *v* 823
be uncertain *v* 475
be unclean *v* 653
be uncomfortable *v* 83
be unentitled *v* 925
be unequal *v* 28
be ungrateful *v* 917
be unhealthy *v* 657
be uniform *v* 16
be unimportant *v* 643
be unintelligible *v* 519
be universal *v* 78
be unlike *v* 18
be unnecessary *v* 57
be unpalatable *v* 395
be unprepared *v* 674
be unproductive *v* 169
be unsavory *v* 395
be unskillful *v* 699
be unwilling *v* 603
be useful *v* 644
be useless *v* 645
be vain *v* 880

beverage *n* 298
be vertical *v* 212
be violent *v* 173
be virtuous *v* 944
be visible *v* 446, 448
be vulgar *v* 851
bevy *n* 72
bewail *v* 833, 839
be weak *v* 160
be wealthy *v* 803
bewilder *v* 475, 519, 538, 870
bewildered *adj* 870
bewilderment *n* 870
be willing *v* 602
be wise *v* 498
bewitch *v* 829, 992
bewitched *adj* 992
bewitchery *n* 992
bewitching *adj* 897, 992
be without *v* 777a
be worthy of notice *v* 642
beyond *adv* 33
beyond all bounds *adv* 31
beyond all praise *adj* 650
beyond all reasonable expectation *adj* 473
beyond bounds *adv* 641
beyond compare *adj* 33; *adv* 31
beyond measure *adv* 31
beyond one's depth *adv* 208
beyond the bounds of reason *adj* 471
beyond the mark *adv* 303
Bhagavad Gita *n* 986
bias *n* 176, 820; *v* 175, 217
Bible n 986
bibliomaniac *n* 492
bibliophile *n* 593
bicker *v* 315, 713

bicycle *n* 272
bid *n* 763; *v* 600, 741
bidder *n* 767
bidding *n* 741
bide *v* 133, 141
bide one's time *v* 681
bid fair *v* 472
bier *n* 363
biformity *n* 89
bifurcate *v* 91, 244; *adj* 244
bifurcated *adj* 91
bifurcation *n* 91, 244
big *adj* 31, 192
bigot *n* 606
bigoted *n* 499
bigotry *n* 606
big words *n* 577
bike *n* 272
biker *n* 268
biking *n* 266
bill *n* 805, 811, 812
bill of sale *n* 771
billow *n* 348
billows *n* 341
billygoat *n* 373
binary *adj* 89
bind *v* 9, 43, 45, 770
binding *adj* 926
bind oneself *v* 768
bind together *v* 43
binoculars *n* 445
binomial *adj* 89
biographer *n* 553
biologist *n* 357
biology *n* 357
bipartite *adj* 91
bird *n* 366
bird's-eye view *n* 448
birds of a feather *n* 17
birth *n* 66
bisect *v* 91
bisected *adj* 91
bisection *n* 91
bisection *n* 68
bit *n* 32, 51, 390
bit by bit *adv* 26, 51, 275

bitch *n* 374, 962
bite *n* 392; *v* 298, 378, 385, 547
bite into *v* 298
biting *adj* 171, 392, 574
bitter *adj* 383, 392, 395, 397, 830, 898, 900
bitter cold *adj* 383
bitterly *adv* 31, 383
bitterness *n* 392, 900
bitumen *n* 356a
bituminous coal *n* 388
bivouac *v* 184
bizarre *adj* 83
black *v* 431; *adj* 421, 431
black and white *n* 429
black as coal *adj* 431
black as night *adj* 431
blackball *v* 55
blacken *v* 431, 934
blackguard *n* 941
blackness *n* 431
blackness *n* 421
blame *n* 716; *v* 716, 932, 938
blameless *adj* 946
blamelessness *n* 946
blameworthy *adj* 945
blaming *n* 938
blanch *v* 429, 430
blanched *adj* 430
bland *adj* 174, 391, 395
blandish *v* 902
blandishment *n* 902
blandness *n* 391, 395
blank *n* 2, 4; *adj* 2, 4
blanket *n* 223
blaspheme *v* 988
blasphemer *n* 988
blasphemy *n* 988
blast *n* 173, 349, 404, 406; *v* 349
blast furnace *n* 386
blatter *v* 412
blaze *n* 382, 420; *v* 382, 420

blazing *adj* 382, 420
blazon forth *v* 882
bleach *v* 429, 430
bleached *adj* 430
bleak *adj* 383
blear-eyed *adj* 443
bleary *adj* 422
bleat *v* 412
bleed *v* 378, 814
bleeding *n* 299
blemish *n* 848
blemish *n* 651, 945; *v* 659
blend *n* 48; *v* 41, 41, 48, 352, 413
blending *n* 48, 413
bless *v* 990
blessed *adj* 981
blessing *n* 618
blight *n* 659; *v* 659
blighted *adj* 659
blighted hope *n* 509
blimp *n* 273
blind *n* 424; *v* 442; *adj* 442, 601
blind adoration *n* 991
blindfold *adv* 442
blindly *adv* 442
blindness *n* 442
blindness *n* 491
blind to *adj* 458
blink *v* 443, 623
blinker *n* 530
bliss *n* 827
blissful *adj* 827, 981
blister *n* 250
blithe *adj* 836
bloated *adj* 194, 250
block *n* 192, 321, 752; *v* 706
blockade *n* 261; *v* 261
blockhead *n* 493, 501
block up *v* 261
blond *adj* 429, 435
blood *n* 11
blood red *adj* 434
blood relation *n* 11
bloodshed *n* 361

bloodthirsty *adj* 361
bloody *adj* 361, 434, 653
bloom *n* 654; *v* 161, 367, 654, 734
blooming *adj* 161, 434
blossom *v* 161, 367, 734
blot *n* 552, 848, 874, 945; *v* 431, 653, 874
blot out *v* 552
blotted out *adj* 552
blow *n* 276, 349, 508, 830; *v* 347, 349, 688
blow great guns *v* 349
blow hard *v* 349
blow hot and cold *v* 605
blown away *adj* 959
blow one's brains out *v* 361
blow one's chance *v* 135
blow out *v* 421
blow over *v* 122
blow-up *n* 173; *v* 173, 194, 349
blubber *n* 356
blue *n* 438
blue *adj* 438
blue and red *n* 437
blue and yellow *n* 435
blue-green *adj* 435
blueness *n* 438
blue sky *n* 338
bluff *adj* 173
bluish *adj* 438
blunder *n* 495, 497, 732; *v* 495, 699, 732
blunderer *n* 701
blunderhead *n* 701
blunt *v* 376, 616, 843; *adj* 172, 246, 254, 499, 703
bluntness *n* 254
bluntness *n* 703
blur *v* 422, 653
blurred *adj* 447
blurry *adj* 422, 447
blurt out *v* 529
blush *n* 434; *v* 434

blushing *adj* 434
bluster *v* 173
blusterer *n* 887
blusterer *n* 884
blustering *adj* 173
boar *n* 373
board *n* 204, 298, 696, 966
boarder *n* 188
board of directors *n* 696
boards *n* 728
boaster *n* 884, 887
boastful *adj* 884
boasting *n* 884
boasting *adj* 884
boat *n* 273
boating *n* 267
boat ride *n* 267
bob *v* 309, 315
bodiless *adj* 4, 317
bodiliness *n* 3
bodily *adj* 3, 316, 364
bodily pleasure *n* 377
body *n* 3, 50, 72, 202, 316, 362, 372, 712
body-guard *n* 753
body in *v* 316
body politic *n* 372
bog *n* 345
boggle *v* 699
boggy *adj* 345
bogus *adj* 544
bohemian *n* 268
boil *n* 250; *v* 173, 315, 336, 353, 382, 384
boiling *n* 336, 353; *adj* 824
boil over *v* 173, 825
boisterous *adj* 173, 404, 825
boisterousness *n* 173, 825
bold *adj* 525, 574, 604, 715, 861, 885
boldness *n* 574, 715, 885
bolster *v* 215, 707

bolt *v* 43, 261, 274, 298, 623, 957
bolt out of the blue *n* 508
bolt upright *adj* 212
bombard *v* 716
bombast *n* 517, 577
bombastic *adj* 497, 549, 577
bond *n* 9, 45, 771; *v* 45
bondage *n* 749
bonds *n* 802
bonehead *n* 493
bones *n* 362
bonus *n* 973
booby *n* 501
book *n* 593
book *n* 590, 811; *v* 539, 811
bookish *adj* 490
bookkeeper *n* 553, 811
booklet *n* 593
books *n* 811
bookseller *n* 593
bookworm *n* 492, 593
boom *n* 215, 404, 408; *v* 404
boomerang *n* 145, 277; *v* 277
booming *n* 408
boon *n* 618, 784
boorish *adj* 851, 876
boorishness *n* 823, 851
boot *n* 618; *v* 642
bootless *adj* 158, 645, 732
bootlicker *n* 886, 935
booty *n* 793
booze *v* 959
boozer *n* 959
bop *n* 415
border *n* 231, 232, 233; *v* 199, 231
bordering *adj* 197
border upon *v* 197
bore *n* 828, 830; *v* 260, 688, 841, 869
bored *adj* 456, 869
boredom *n* 688, 841

borer *n* 262
boring *adj* 275, 841, 843
borrow *v* 788
borrower *n* 806
borrowing *n* 788
borrow money *v* 788
bosom *n* 208
bosom buddy *n* 890
boss *n* 694, 745
bossed *adj* 250
botanic *adj* 367
botanical *adj* 369
botanic garden *n* 369
botanist *n* 357
botany *n* 369
botany *n* 357
botch *v* 699, 732
both *adj* 89
bother *n* 828, 830; *v* 704, 830
bottle *v* 670
bottom *n* 208, 211; *adj* 211
bottomless *adj* 208
bottomless pit *n* 208
bough *n* 51
bounce *n* 159
bound *n* 309; *v* 229, 233, 274, 309; *adj* 768, 926
boundary *n* 232, 233
boundary line *n* 233
bound for *adj* 278, 620
boundless *adj* 104, 180
boundlessness *n* 105
bounds *n* 233
bounteousness *n* 816
bountiful *adj* 816
bounty *n* 784, 816, 973
bourgeois *adj* 29
bourgeoisie *n* 876
bout *n* 138
bow *n* 245, 308; *v* 245, 308, 725, 744, 886, 990
bowed *adj* 245, 250

bowed instruments *n* 417

bowels *n* 221

boxcar *n* 272

boy *n* 129, 373

boyfriend *n* 897

boyhood *n* 127

boyish *adj* 129

brace *n* 89, 215; *v* 159, 215, 689

bracelet *n* 247

bracing *adj* 656

bracket *n* 45, 215; *v* 43, 89

brag *v* 884

braggadocio *n* 884

braggart *n* 884, 887

bragging *n* 884

braid *v* 219

brain *n* 450

brainchild *n* 453

brainless *adj* 499

brains *n* 450, 480, 498

brainstorm *n* 453

brake *v* 275

bramble *n* 663

branch *n* 51

branching *n* 291

branch off *v* 291

brand *v* 384

brand-new *adj* 123

branny *adj* 330

brass *adj* 439

brass band *n* 417

brass instruments *n* 417

brassy *adj* 885

bravado *n* 861, 884

brave *v* 715; *adj* 715, 861

bravery *n* 715, 861

brawl *v* 411

brawny *adj* 192

bray *v* 412

brazen *adj* 885

breach *n* 44, 198, 260, 713

breadth *n* 202

breadth *n* 202

break *n* 44, 53, 70, 106, 140, 142, 198, 621, 685, 720, 731; *v* 44, 51, 70, 328, 713, 773, 879

breakability *n* 328

breakable *adj* 328

break a habit *v* 614

break bread *v* 298

breakdown *n* 162, 732; *v* 304, 659

breaker *n* 348

breakers *n* 667

breakfast *v* 298

break ground *v* 66

break in *v* 294

breaking down *n* 49

breaking up *n* 162

break in upon *v* 70, 135

break of day *n* 125

break off *v* 142

break one's neck *v* 360

break out *v* 66

break the ground *v* 116

breakup *n* 67, 146; *v* 44, 73, 162, 659

breast *n* 250

breath *n* 359, 405

breathe *v* 1, 349, 359, 405

breathe new life into *v* 163

breathe one's last *v* 360

breather *n* 70; *n* 685

breathing space *n* 180

breathing spell *n* 685, 687

breathless *adj* 688, 870

breath of air *n* 338, 349

breath of life *n* 359

bred *adj* 370

breed *n* 75, 167; *v* 161, 370

breeding *n* 370, 852

breeze *n* 338, 349

breezy *adj* 338, 349

brethren *n* 997

brevity *n* 201, 572

brewing *adj* 152

briar *n* 663

bribe *n* 784

bridge *n* 45; *v* 45

bridge over *v* 43

bridle *v* 370, 751

brief *n* 596; *adj* 111, 201, 572

briefly *adv* 111, 572

brig *n* 273

brigantine *n* 273

bright *adj* 420, 428, 498, 734, 829, 836

brightness *n* 420, 829

brilliance *n* 845

brilliancy *n* 420

brilliant *adj* 416, 845

brim *n* 231

brimful *adj* 52

brimming *adj* 52

brindled *adj* 440

brine *n* 341; *v* 392

bring *v* 270

bring about *v* 153

bring an action against *v* 969

bring back to life *v* 163

bring forth *v* 161

bring in *v* 296, 810, 812

bring into *v* 144

bring into focus *v* 222

bring into play *v* 677

bring into relation with *v* 9

bring low *v* 308

bring out *v* 74, 591

bring round *v* 660

bring to a crisis *v* 604

bring to a focus *v* 74

bring to an end *v* 67

bring to a point *v* 74

bring to a standstill *v* 142

bring to bear upon *v* 170

bring together *v* 72

bring to life *v* 359

bring to light *v* 529

bring to mind *v* 505

bring to pass *v* 153
bring to perfection *v* 650
bring to trial *v* 969
bring up *v* 161, 235
bring up the rear *v* 235
brink *v* 231
brisk *adj* 111, 274, 682, 684
briskness *n* 682
bristle over *v* 900
bristling *adj* 253
bristly *adj* 256
brittle *adj* 328
brittleness *n* 328
broach *v* 153, 676
broach *adj* 78, 202
broadcast *adj* 73
broad daylight *n* 420
broadside *n* 236; *adv* 236
brochure *n* 593
broil *v* 382, 384
broke *adj* 804
broken *adj* 70
broken down *adj* 659
broker *n* 797
brood *n* 167
brood over *v* 837
brook *v* 826
brother *n* 27
brotherhood *n* 11, 17, 72
brotherly *adj* 888
brown *n* 433
brown *adj* 433
brownish *adj* 433
brownness *n* 433
brown-nose *v* 933
brown-noser *n* 886, 935
brown-nosing *n* 933
browse *v* 264
bruise *v* 649
brunette *adj* 433
brunt *n* 66
brush *v* 379
brush aside *v* 297
brushing *n* 379

brushwood *n* 388
brusque *adj* 173
brutal *adj* 173
brutality *n* 173
brute *n* 366
brute creation *n* 366
brute force *n* 739
brute instinct *n* 450a
brute matter *n* 316, 358
brutishness *n* 450a
bubble *n* 353
bubble *n* 353; *v* 315, 348, 353
bubbling *n* 353
bubbly *adj* 348, 353
buck *n* 309, 373
buckle *n* 243, 248; *v* 43, 243
buckle to *v* 686
bud *n* 66; *v* 161, 194, 300
budding *adj* 127
budge *v* 264
budget *n* 811
buff *v* 255
buffet *v* 276, 315
buffoon *n* 501, 844, 857
buggy *n* 272
build *n* 240; *v* 161, 235, 240
building *n* 161
built on *adj* 211
bulb *n* 249
bulbous *adj* 250
bulge *n* 250; *v* 250
bulk *n* 31, 50, 202
bulk containers *n* 191
bulky *adj* 192, 202
bull *n* 373, 477
bulletin *n* 592
bully *n* 887; *v* 739
bum *v* 266
bum around *v* 266
bumbling *n* 699
bumming around *n* 266
bump *n* 250, 276
bump against *v* 276
bunch *n* 250

bunchy *adj* 250
bungle *n* 495; *v* 699
bungler *n* 701
bungling *n* 699; *adj* 699
bunk *n* 477
buoyancy *n* 320
buoyant *adj* 320, 325, 836
burden *n* 190, 319, 828, 830, 926
burdensome *adj* 319, 649, 686, 706, 830
burglar *n* 792
burial *n* 363; *adj* 363
burial ground *n* 363
buried *adj* 208, 506
buried in *adj* 229
burlesque *n* 21, 856; *v* 856; *adj* 856
burn *v* 382, 384, 825
burnable *adj* 388
burn in *v* 384
burning *adj* 382, 434
burnish *v* 255
burnished *adj* 420
burnt *adj* 384
burn the midnight oil *v* 539
burp out *v* 297
burrow *v* 184
bursar *n* 801
burst *n* 113, 406; *v* 44, 173, 328
burst forth *v* 66, 194, 446
burst in *v* 294
burst out *v* 838
burst upon *v* 508
burst upon the view *v* 446
bury *v* 229, 363, 528
burying *n* 528
bury the hatchet *v* 723
bush *n* 367
bushy *adj* 256
business *n* 625
business *n* 454, 622, 682, 794, 926

business district *n* 799
businesslike *adj* 58,
 625, 682, 692
bust *n* 557, 732
bustle *n* 171, 315, 682,
 684; *v* 315, 682, 684
bustling *adj* 151
busy *adj* 151, 625, 682
busy as a bee *adj* 682
busy oneself in *v* 682
but *adv* 30
butcher *n* 361; *v* 361
butchery *n* 361
butt *n* 857; *v* 276
butt against *v* 276
butter *n* 356
butter-fingers *n* 701
butt in *v* 135
buttocks *n* 235
button *n* 250; *v* 43
button up *v* 261
buttress *n* 215
buy *n* 795; *v* 795
buy and sell *v* 794
buyer *n* 795
buying *n* 795
buzz *v* 409, 412
buzzing *n* 409
by *adv* 631
by accident *adv* 156
by and by *adv* 132
by an indirect course
 adv 629
by chance *adv* 156
by degrees *adv* 26
by design *adv* 620
by dint of *adv* 631;
 prep 157
by fits and starts *adv*
 70, 139, 315
by force *adv* 159, 173,
 744
bygone *adj* 122
by installments *adv* 51
by intuition *adv* 477
by means of *adv* 170,
 631, 632
by no means *adv* 32

by rule *adv* 82
bystander *n* 444
by storm *adv* 173
by the agency of *adv*
 631
by the by *adv* 10, 134
by the way *adv* 10, 134
by turns *adv* 138
by virtue of *prep* 157

C

cabal *n* 626
cabalistic *adj* 992
cabinet *n* 696
cackle *v* 412, 838
cacophonous *adj* 410,
 414
cadaver *n* 362
cadaverous *adj* 362
cadence *n* 402
caesura *n* 70, 198
cage *n* 752; *v* 370
calamitous *adj* 735, 830
calamity *n* 619, 735,
 975
calcination *n* 384
calculable *adj* 85
calculate *v* 85, 611, 620
calculation *n* 85, 507
calculus *n* 85
calefaction *n* 384
calendar *n* 86, 114
caliber *n* 26
call *v* 564, 995
call attention to *v* 550
call for *v* 630
calligraphy *n* 590
calling *n* 625
call it quits *v* 67, 624
callous *adj* 823
callousness *n* 823
callow *adj* 127
call to mind *v* 505
call up *v* 505
call up spirits *v* 992
calm *n* 174, 265, 721;
 v 174, 723; *adj*
 174, 265, 403, 685,

721, 826, 953
calm down *v* 826
calmness *n* 174, 265,
 721, 826, 953
caloric *n* 382
caloricity *n* 382
calorimeter *n* 389
calumnious *adj* 934
calumny *n* 934
camaraderie *n* 892
camouflage *v* 528
camouflaging *n* 528
can *v* 670
canal *n* 350
cancel *v* 536, 552, 756
cancelation *n* 552, 756
cancel out *v* 179
cancer *n* 663
candid *adj* 246, 543,
 703
candidate *n* 726
candied *adj* 396
candle *n* 423
candor *n* 525, 543, 703
candy *v* 396
cane *n* 975
canker *n* 663; *v* 659
cankerworm *n* 165
canny *adj* 498, 702
canon *n* 697
canonicals *n* 999
canonize *v* 991
canopy *n* 223
cant *n* 988; *adj* 563
canticle *n* 413
cap *n* 261, 263; *v* 33,
 206
capability *n* 157, 175,
 698, 705
capable *adj* 157, 698
capacious *adj* 180, 192
capacity *n* 157, 159,
 180, 192, 498, 625,
 698
capacity for *n* 698
cape *n* 250
caper *n* 309; *v* 309
capillary *adj* 205

capital *n* 632, 800, 803;
　adj 210, 642, 648
capitulate *v* 725
capitulation *n* 725
caprice *n* 608
caprice *n* 615a
capricious *adj* 139,
　149, 475, 605, 608,
　615a
capriciously *adv* 139,
　615a
capriciousness *n* 139,
　149, 475
capsule *n* 273
captain *n* 269, 694
captious *adj* 608
captivate *v* 829
captive *n* 754
capture *n* 789; *v* 789
car *n* 272
caravan *n* 266
carbon *n* 21, 90, 388
carbonaceous *adj* 388
carbonization *n* 384
carcass *n* 362
cardinal points *n* 278
care *n* 459
care *n* 451, 457, 817,
　828, 830, 864
careen *v* 217
care for *v* 642, 664
careful *adj* 451, 457,
　459, 664, 817, 864
carefulness *n* 459
careless *adj* 460, 575,
　674, 738, 863, 927
carelessness *n* 460, 699,
　773, 863, 927
caress *n* 902; *v* 902
careworn *adj* 828
cargo *n* 190, 798
caricature *n* 21, 555; *v*
　19, 555
caricaturist *n* 559
carious *adj* 653
carmine *adj* 434
carnage *n* 361
carpe diem *v* 134, 682

carper *n* 936
carriage *n* 271, 272,
　448, 692
carrier *n* 271
carrion *n* 362
carry *v* 215, 270
carry on *v* 143, 680, 692
carry on a conversation
　v 588
carry out *v* 772
carry weight *v* 175, 642
cart *n* 272
cartoonist *n* 559
carve *v* 44, 240, 557,
　558, 786
carving *n* 557
cascade *n* 348
case *n* 7, 232, 476, 567,
　969; *v* 223
case in point *n* 82
cash *n* 800
cash box *n* 802
cashier *n* 801
cash register *n* 802
cast *n* 21, 75, 176, 240,
　428, 448, 550, 557; *v*
　73, 240, 284, 557,
　626; *adj* 820
cast a shadow *v* 424
cast a spell *v* 992
cast aspersions *v* 934
castaway *n* 893
cast down *v* 308
cast forth *v* 73
castigate *v* 972
castigated *adj* 972
castigation *n* 972
castigator *n* 936
castigatory *adj* 972
castles in the air *n* 515
cast light on *v* 522
cast light upon *v* 420
cast off *v* 297, 782; *adj*
　782
cast over *v* 353
casualty *n* 619
casuist *n* 476
casuistry *n* 477

cataclysm *n* 162
cataclysmic *adj* 619
catacomb *n* 363
catafalque *n* 363
catalog *n* 86; *v* 60
catalyst *n* 153
cataract *n* 442, 443
catastrophe *n* 619, 735
catastrophic *adj* 619,
　735
catch *n* 793; *v* 789
catch a bug *v* 655
catch a glimpse of *v* 441
catch fire *v* 384
catch on *v* 518
catch one's breath *v* 687
catch the lay of the land
　v 510
catch unawares *v* 508
category *n* 75
cater *v* 637, 746
catering *n* 637
caterwaul *v* 412
cathartic *n* 652
cathedral *n* 1000
catholic *adj* 78, 983a
catholicity *n* 78
cattle car *n* 272
caucus *n* 696
causal *adj* 153, 156
causality *n* 153
causation *n* 153, 170
cause *n* 153
cause *n* 66, 615, 969; *v*
　153, 161
caused by *adj* 154
cause sensation *v* 375
cauterization *n* 384
cauterize *v* 384
caution *n* 864
caution *n* 459, 487,
　668, 695; *v* 668, 695
cautionary *adj* 668
cautious *adj* 451, 459,
　487, 498, 664, 864
cavalcade *n* 266
cave *n* 189, 221, 252
cave in *n* 304

cavern n 252

cavernous adj 252

cavil v 477

cavity n 252

caw v 412

cease v 142, 265, 360, 732

ceaseless adj 112

ceaselessness n 112

cede v 624, 782

ceiling n 223

celebrant n 990

celebrate v 551, 883

celebrated adj 873, 883

celebration n 883

celebration n 733, 838, 990

celebrational adj 883, 990

celerity n 274, 684

celestial adj 318, 976, 981

celestial bliss n 981

celestial spaces n 318

celibacy n 904

celibate n 904; adj 904

cell n 189, 357, 752

cement v 46, 48, 323

cemetery n 363

cenobite n 893

censurable adj 945

censure n 716, 932; v 716, 932

census n 85

centenary n 98

center n 29, 68, 74, 221, 222; v 290

center of gravity n 222

center on v 74

central adj 68, 222

centrality n 222

centralization n 48, 222

centralize v 48, 222

centrally adv 222

central part n 208

centrifugal adj 291

century n 98, 108

ceramics n 557

cerebral adj 450

ceremonial n 883; adj 240, 998

ceremonious adj 240, 882

ceremony n 240, 883, 998

certain adj 79, 246, 474, 484

certainly adv 474

certainty n 474

certainty n 484

certificate n 771

certitude n 474

cessation n 142

cessation n 261, 265, 360, 687, 725

chafe v 378, 384, 832, 900

chaff n 643; v 856

chain n 69; v 43

chain of thought n 476

chaise n 272

chalk n 342

chalky adj 430

challenge v 715

challenge comparison v 648

chamber n 696

chamber group n 416

chamber music n 415

chamber orchestra n 416

champaign n 344

championship n 707

chance n 156, 621

chance n 152, 470, 615a; v 151, 156, 621; adj 475

chance it v 621

chanciness n 475

chancy adj 156, 475

change n 140

change n 20a, 144, 147, 800; v 15, 20a, 140, 146, 147, 605, 783

changeable adj 140, 144, 149, 475, 605

changeableness n 149

changeableness n 111, 140, 475, 605

changed adj 15, 20a, 140

change direction v 279

changeful adj 607

change hands v 783

changelessness n 150

change of mind n 485

change one's mind v 607

changeover n 144

change sides v 607

changing hands n 783

channel n 260, 302, 350, 627; v 259

chaos n 59, 162, 241

chaotic adj 59, 241

chap n 373

chapel n 1000

chapter n 696

character n 5, 7, 561, 569, 820

characteristic n 79, 550, 569, 780; adj 5, 15, 79, 550, 569

characterization n 594

characterize v 564, 594

characterized adj 820

charcoal n 388, 431

charge n 630, 695, 697, 716, 741, 755, 812, 938; v 52, 190, 695, 716, 741, 755, 812, 938, 938, 938

charging n 938

charitable adj 707, 784, 816, 906, 910

charity n 707, 784, 816, 906, 910

charm n 829, 992, 993; v 288, 615, 829, 992

charmed adj 992

charmer n 994

charming n 933; adj 992

charnel house n 363

chart n 183, 527, 626

charter *n* 755, 963; *v*
 760
chary *adj* 817, 864
chase *v* 622
chase away *v* 289
chasm *n* 208, 260
chaste *adj* 242, 576,
 578, 849, 881, 944,
 960
chasten *v* 972
chasteness *n* 849
chastisement *n* 972
chastity *n* 881, 944, 960
chat *n* 588; *v* 588
chattels *n* 780
chatter *n* 584; *v* 584
chatterbox *n* 584
chatterer *n* 584
chattering *adj* 584
chatty *adj* 584, 588
cheap *adj* 435, 643,
 815, 819, 943
cheapness *n* 815
cheat *n* 545, 548, 792; *v*
 545, 923
check *n* 179, 616, 666,
 706, 751; *v* 179, 233,
 275, 468, 706, 708,
 751
checked *adj* 440
checker *v* 440
checkered *adj* 440
checklist *n* 86
cheek *n* 236
cheek by jowl *adv* 236
cheer *n* 827, 829; *v*
 411, 689, 829, 834,
 836, 840
cheerful *adj* 827, 829
cheerfully *adv* 836
cheerfulness *n* 836
cheerfulness *n* 827, 829
cheering *adj* 836, 858
cheerless *adj* 828, 901a
cheery *adj* 829, 836,
 836
chemistry *n* 144
cherish *v* 897

cherry-colored *adj* 434
cherub *n* 129, 977
cherubic *adj* 977
chest *n* 802
chestnut *adj* 433
chew *v* 298
chewing *n* 298
chew the fat *v* 588
chiaroscuro *n* 429
chicanery *n* 477, 702
chick *n* 129
chicken *n* 862; *adj* 862
chicken-hearted *adj*
 862
chief *n* 694, 745
chiefly *adv* 31
child *n* 129, 167
childbirth *n* 163
child genius *n* 872
childhood *n* 127
childish *adj* 129, 486,
 499, 575
childlike *adj* 499, 703
children *n* 167
child's play *n* 705
chill *v* 383, 385, 616;
 adj 383
chilled *adj* 385
chilliness *n* 383
chilly *adj* 383
chime *n* 408; *v* 407, 413
chimera *n* 515
chimerical *adj* 515
chimney *n* 351
chink *n* 198; *v* 408
chip *n* 32; *v* 44, 195
chip off the old block *n*
 17, 167
chipper *adj* 654
chirography *n* 590
chirp *v* 412
chirrup *v* 412
chisel *v* 240, 557, 558
chiseling *n* 558
chit *n* 588
chit-chat *n* 588; *v* 588
chock-full *adj* 52
chocolate *adj* 433

choice *n* 609
choice *n* 600; *adj* 648
choice of words *n* 569
choir *n* 416
choke *v* 261, 361, 641
choleric *adj* 901
chomp *v* 298
choose *v* 609
choosing *n* 609
choosy *adj* 465
chop *v* 44
choppy seas *n* 348
chop up *v* 201
choral *adj* 415, 416
choral music *n* 415
chorus *n* 411, 416
christen *v* 564
Christian *adj* 983a
Christian Revelation *n*
 985
chromatic *adj* 428
chronicle *n* 114; *v* 114,
 551
chronicler *n* 553
chronicles *n* 551
chronological *adj* 114
chronological error *n*
 115
chronology *n* 114
chronometer *n* 114
chronometry *n* 114
chubby *adj* 194
chuck *v* 284, 412
chuckle *v* 838
chug *v* 298
chum *n* 890
chummy *adj* 892
church *n* 995, 1000
churchdom *n* 995
churchman *n* 996
churl *n* 819
churlish *adj* 819
churlishness *n* 901a
churn *v* 315, 352
cilia *n* 205
cinder *n* 388
cinerary *adj* 363
cinnamon *adj* 433

cipher *n* 84, 550, 561
circle *n* 181, 247, 712;
  v 227, 247, 311
circle around *v* 312, 629
circling *n* 311; *adj* 248
circuit *n* 629
circuit *n* 181, 230, 247,
  279, 311; *v* 311
circuitous *adj* 279, 311,
  629
circuitously *adv* 279
circular *n* 592; *adj* 245,
  247, 249, 311
circularity *n* 247
circularity *n* 311
circular motion *n* 311
circulate *v* 531
circulation *n* 311, 312
circumference *n* 230
circumjacent *adj* 227
circumnavigate *v* 311
circumnavigation *n* 311
circumscribe *v* 76, 195,
  221, 229, 232, 233,
  751
circumscribed *adj* 229
circumscription *n* 229
circumscription *n* 751
circumspect *adj* 451,
  459, 864
circumspectful *adj* 457
circumspection *n* 459,
  864
circumstance *n* 8
circumstance *n* 151
circumstances *n* 7, 527
circumstantial *adj* 8
circumvention *n* 311
citation *n* 467
cite *v* 467, 969
citizen *n* 188
citizenry *n* 876
citrine *adj* 435
civic *adj* 372
civic minded *adj* 910
civil *adj* 852, 894, 928,
  997
civility *n* 457, 894

civilization *n* 372, 658
clack *v* 407, 412
clad *adj* 225
claim *n* 924
claim *n* 630, 741, 765;
  v 720, 741, 924
claimant *n* 767, 924
claiming *adj* 924
claim relationship with *v*
  11
clairvoyant *n* 513, 994
clamber *v* 305
clammy *adj* 352
clamor *n* 404, 411
clamor for *v* 765
clamorous *adj* 404,
  411, 765, 825
clamorousness *n* 404
clamp *v* 43
clan *n* 72, 75, 712
clandestine *adj* 528
clang *n* 404, 408; *v* 404
clangor *n* 404, 408
clank *v* 410
clannish *adj* 712
clap one's hands *v* 838
claque *n* 712
clarify *v* 74, 652, 849
clarity *n* 446, 518, 570,
  849
clash *n* 276, 713; *v* 24,
  179, 406, 713
clashing *n* 179, 410;
  adj 24, 410
clasp *v* 43, 46
class *n* 75
class *n* 51, 58
classic *adj* 242, 578
classical *adj* 242, 578
classical music *n* 415
classicist *n* 578
classics *n* 560
classification *n* 60
classify *v* 60
clatter *v* 407
clauses *n* 770
clay *n* 362

clean *v* 42, 652; *adj*
  652, 960
cleanliness *n* 652
cleanness *n* 652
cleanness *n* 960
clean out *v* 297
cleanse *v* 652
clean sweep *n* 146
clear *v* 705, 937, 970;
  adj 42, 413, 420,
  425, 446, 474, 518,
  525, 570, 807, 849
clearance *n* 807, 970
clear as day *adj* 518
clear-cut *adj* 518
cleared *adj* 970
clearheaded *adj* 502
clearheadedness *n* 502
clearness *n* 425, 446,
  518, 570, 580
clear out *v* 297, 652
clear-sighted *adj* 441
clear stage *n* 134
clear up *v* 518
cleave *v* 44, 46, 91, 259
cleft *n* 198, 260; *adj* 91
clemency *n* 740
clergy *n* 996
clergyman *n* 996
clerical *n* 996; *adj* 995,
  996
clerk *n* 553, 590
clever *adj* 498, 698,
  702, 842
cleverness *n* 698, 842
click *v* 406
client *n* 795
clientele *n* 795
cliff *n* 212, 306
climactic *adj* 8, 377
climate *n* 181, 338
climax *n* 8, 67, 210,
  377; *v* 210
climb *v* 305
climb upward *v* 305
clime *n* 181, 338
clinch *v* 43, 474
cling *v* 46

cling to v 602, 613
clink v 408, 410
clip back v 201
clique n 712
cliquish adj 712
cloak n 530; v 528
clock n 114
clockwork n 80
clod n 192
clogging n 261
close n 67, 729; v 67,
   261, 729; adj 17, 43,
   186, 197, 199, 203,
   321, 528
close at hand adj 121
close by adj 152
close call n 671
closed adj 261
closely packed adj 72
close-mouthed adj 585
closeness n 186, 197,
   203
close of the day n 126
close quarters n 197
close to adv 197
close upon adv 117,
   197
close up shop v 142
closure n 261
clothe v 225
clothed adj 223, 225
clothes n 225
clothing n 223, 225
cloud n 353
cloud n 353, 424, 530;
   v 353, 421, 422
clouded adj 426
cloudiness n 353, 422,
   426, 447
cloudless adj 420
cloud over v 422
cloudy adj 353, 421,
   422, 424, 426
cloven adj 91
clown n 501, 701, 844
cloy v 376, 641, 869
cloying adj 396
club n 74

clubbish adj 892
cluck v 412
clue n 550
clump n 72, 250
clumsiness n 699
clumsy adj 699
cluster n 72; v 72
clutter n 407
coach n 272; v 537
coagulate v 321
coagulation n 321
coal n 388, 431
coal-black adj 431
coalesce v 13, 48
coalescence n 48
coalescent adj 13
coalition n 709
coarse adj 241, 256,
   329, 410, 653, 674,
   851
coarseness n 329, 851
coast n 231, 342; v 267
coat n 204; v 204, 224
coating n 223, 224, 332
cobalt adj 438
cock n 373
cockcrow n 125
cockeye n 443
cockeyed adj 443
cocksure adj 484
cocoa adj 433
code n 561, 697, 963
codger n 819
codify v 963
coequal adj 27
coerce v 739, 744
coercion n 739, 744
coercive adj 739, 744
coeval adj 120
coexist v 120, 199
coexistence n 88, 120
coexisting adj 120
coexist with v 88
coextension n 216
coextensive adj 216
coffee adj 433
coffer n 802
coffin n 363

cogency n 157
cogitate v 451
cogitation n 451
cognizant of adj 490
cohere v 46, 321
coherence n 46
coherence n 502, 518
coherent adj 321
cohesion n 46, 327
cohesive adj 46, 321,
   327
cohesiveness n 46, 327
coil n 248, 311; v 245,
   248
coiled adj 248
coin v 515
coincide v 13, 199
coincidence n 120
coincident adj 13, 120
coinciding adj 13
coin words v 563
coke n 388
cold n 383
cold adj 383, 866
cold-blooded adj 383,
   823
cold-hearted adj 823
coldly adv 383
coldness n 383, 823
cold storage n 387
collaborate v 178
collaboration n 178
collaborative adj 178
collaborator n 711
collapse n 158, 195,
   659; v 158, 195, 304
collar n 247
collate v 464
collateral n 771; adj 6,
   216
collation n 464
colleague n 711
collect v 72, 596, 775
collected adj 826
collection n 72, 102,
   596
collective adj 78, 778
collectively adv 50

collectivism *n* 778
college *n* 542
collegiate *adj* 542
collide with *v* 276
collision *n* 179, 276
colloquial *adj* 521, 560, 563
colloquialism *n* 521
colloquy *n* 588
collusion *n* 709
colonize *v* 184
color *n* 428
color *n* 434, 448, 654; *v* 428, 469, 549, 556
coloration *n* 428, 549
colorblind *adj* 443
color blindness *n* 443
colored *adj* 428
colorful *adj* 521
coloring *n* 428, 469, 549
colorless *adj* 429, 430
colorlessness *n* 429
colorlessness *n* 430
colossal *adj* 192, 206
Colosseum *n* 728
column *n* 69, 266
combat *n* 173, 680, 720, 722; *v* 708, 720, 722
combatant *n* 726
combating *n* 708
combative *adj* 173, 720, 722
combination *n* 48
combination *n* 41, 54, 709, 712
combine *v* 41, 48, 87, 178, 709
combined *adj* 48
combo *n* 416
combustible *n* 388; *adj* 384, 388
combustion *n* 384
come about *v* 151
come after *v* 63, 117
come ashore *v* 342

come before *v* 62, 116, 280
come between *v* 228
come close to *v* 197
comedian *n* 844
comedienne *n* 844
come-down *n* 509; *v* 306
come down with *v* 655
come first *v* 33, 62, 280
come forth *v* 446
come forward *v* 446
come from *v* 154
come in *v* 294
come in its turn *v* 138
come in sequence *v* 281
come into *v* 775, 785
come into play *v* 170
come into sight *v* 446
come into the world *v* 359
come into use *v* 613
come into view *v* 446
comeliness *n* 242, 845
comely *adj* 845
come near *v* 121
come of age *v* 131
come on *v* 121, 152
come on to *v* 544
come out of *v* 295
come out of nowhere *v* 508
come round *v* 151, 660
come round again *v* 138
come short *v* 732
come short of *v* 34, 304
come straight to the point *v* 576
come to *v* 50, 292, 359
come to a close *v* 67
come to an agreement *v* 774
come together *v* 72, 290
come to grief *v* 735
come to light *v* 525
come to nothing *v* 169, 304
come to pass *v* 151

come to rest *v* 184
come to the front *v* 234
come to the point *v* 79, 572, 703
come to the rescue *v* 672
comets *n* 318
come up short *v* 304
come up to *v* 27
come up with *v* 612
comfort *n* 377, 827, 831, 834; *v* 831, 834, 834, 906
comfortable *adj* 23, 377, 803, 827, 829, 831
comforting *adj* 834
comical *adj* 853
coming *n* 292; *adj* 121, 152
coming after *n* 63, 281
coming and going *n* 314
coming before *n* 62
coming beforehand *n* 280
coming together *n* 290
command *n* 741
command *n* 157, 630, 693, 697, 737; *v* 157, 206, 600, 693, 741, 777
commandant *n* 745
command a view of *v* 441
commandeer *v* 789
commander *n* 269, 745
commanding *adj* 642, 741
commandment *n* 741
command of language *n* 569
commemorate *v* 551, 883
commemoration *n* 883
commemorative *adj* 883
commence *v* 66
commencement *n* 66
commend *v* 883, 931

commend ν 883, 931

commendable adj 618, 931

commendation n 931

commendatory adj 883, 931

commensurate adj 23, 639

comment n 476, 522; ν 595

commentary n 522, 595

commentator n 480, 524, 595

comment upon ν 522

commerce n 794, 796

commercial adj 794

commingle ν 41

commiserate ν 914

commiseration n 914

commission n 755

commission n 758; ν 737, 755

commit ν 680

commitment n 768

commit oneself ν 768

commit sacrilege ν 988

commit suicide ν 361

committed adj 768

committee n 696, 758

commodity n 798

common adj 34, 78, 82, 613, 643, 778, 851, 876, 879

commonalty n 876

commonalty n 34

commoners n 876

common holding n 778

common law n 124

commonly adv 136

commonness n 34

commonplace adj 29, 34, 598, 613, 643, 736, 843

commonplaceness n 736

common run n 78

common sense n 450, 480, 498

commonsensical adj 450

commonweal n 372

commonwealth n 372

commotion n 315

communal adj 712, 778

communicant n 990

communicate ν 527, 529, 582, 592

communicated adj 527

communication n 43, 527, 582, 592

communicative adj 527

communion n 778

communism n 778

communist n 778; adj 778

communistic adj 778

community n 188, 372, 712

community of possessions n 778

commutation n 147, 148

commute ν 147, 148

compact n 769

compact n 202, 676; ν 201; adj 43, 195, 201, 202, 321, 572

compactness n 195

compactual adj 769

companion n 890

companion piece n 237

companionship n 888, 892

company n 72, 88, 186, 712

comparable adj 464

comparative adj 26, 464

comparative anatomy n 368

comparative physiology n 368

comparative relation n 464

compare ν 216, 464

compared with adj 464

comparison n 464

comparison n 9, 216

compartment n 51

compass n 26; ν 227

compassion n 740, 910, 914

compassionate adj 740, 914

compatible adj 23, 413

compel ν 157, 601, 744, 751

compelling adj 744

compendious adj 76, 201, 572, 596

compendium n 596

compendium n 195, 596

compensate ν 30, 179, 790, 807, 973

compensating adj 30

compensation n 30

compensation n 774, 790, 952, 973

compensatory adj 30, 790, 973

compete ν 720

competence n 157, 639, 698, 803

competency n 157

competent adj 157, 639, 698

competition n 708, 720

competitive adj 720

competitor n 710, 726, 767

compilation n 54, 72, 596

compile ν 72, 596

complacency n 831

complacent adj 721, 831

complain ν 411

complaint n 655, 839

complement n 39, 88, 237

complementary adj 12, 237

complementary color n 428

complete ν 52, 67, 142,

292, 650, 729, 731,
769; adj 31, 50, 52
completely adv 31, 50,
52, 729
completeness n 52
completeness n 50
completion n 729
completion n 142, 261
complex adj 59, 482,
704
complexion n 7, 428,
448
compliance n 82, 602,
725, 743, 762, 772
compliant adj 82, 725,
743, 762, 772
complicate v 61
complicated adj 59, 248
complication n 59, 667
complications n 154
complicity n 709
compliment n 896
complimentary adj
896, 931
comply v 82, 602, 725,
743, 762
comply with n 772
component n 56
component n 51
component part n 56
comportment n 448
comport oneself v 680
compose v 54, 161,
174, 415, 569, 590,
591, 597, 826
composed adj 826
composite n 48; adj 41
composition n 54
composition n 48, 569,
590, 591
compositor n 591
composure n 174, 826
compound n 48, 232; v
41
comprehend v 54, 76,
490, 518
comprehensibility n 518
comprehensible adj 518

comprehension n 76,
490
comprehensive adj 56,
76, 78, 192
compress v 195, 201,
321, 572, 596
compressed adj 201
compressible adj 322
compression n 195, 572
comprise v 76
compromise n 774
compromise n 29, 30,
68, 628, 723; v 628,
774
compulsion n 744
compulsion n 601
compulsory adj 601,
744
compunction n 950
computable adj 85
computation n 85
compute v 85
comradeship n 888, 892
con n 754; v 545
concatenation n 43
concave adj 252
concavity n 252
concavity n 308
conceal v 223, 447,
519, 528
concealed adj 447, 528,
533
concealment n 528
concealment n 447, 526
concede v 529, 760
conceit n 515, 878, 880
conceited adj 878, 880
conceivable adj 470,
515
conceive v 66, 168, 484,
515
concentrate v 72, 222,
290, 686
concentric adj 222
concept n 451
conception n 451, 453,
515
conceptual adj 2

concern n 9, 625, 642,
860; v 9
concerned adj 459, 860
concerning adv 9
concert n 178, 709
concert artist n 416
concertize v 416
concession n 760, 774,
784
conciliatory adj 723
conciliate v 723, 831
conciliation n 714, 723,
831, 952
conciliatory adj 714
concise adj 201, 572
concisely adv 572
conciseness n 572
conciseness n 201
conclave n 72, 696
conclude v 67, 480,
604, 729
concluded adj 67
concluding adj 67
conclusion n 65, 67,
154, 480, 729
conclusive adj 67, 478,
480
conclusiveness n 478
concoct v 626
concomitance n 120
concomitant n 88; adj
88, 120
concomitants n 154
concord n 413, 714
concord n 23, 413, 488,
709, 721, 762, 888
concordance n 413
concordant adj 413,
714
concourse n 72, 290
concrete adj 3
concretion n 321
concupiscence n 961
concupiscent adj 961
concur v 120, 178, 290,
488, 709, 714, 762
concurrence n 178

concurrence *n* 23, 120, 290, 488, 709, 762
concurrent *adj* 120, 178, 290
concurrently *adv* 120
concurring *adj* 488
condemn *v* 971
condemnation *n* 971
condemnatory *adj* 932, 971
condemned *adj* 971
condensation *n* 195, 201, 321, 339, 596
condense *v* 195, 201, 321, 572, 596
condensed *adj* 201
condiment *n* 393
condition *n* 7, 8, 469, 514, 875; *v* 770
conditional *adj* 8, 469, 770
conditionally *adv* 8, 770
conditions *n* 770
condolence *n* 915
condolence *n* 914
condole with *v* 915
conduce *v* 176, 178
conduce to *v* 153
conducive *adj* 176
conduct *n* 692
conduct *n* 680, 693; *v* 270, 692, 693
conduct oneself *v* 680
conductor *n* 271
conduct to *v* 278
conduit *n* 350
conduit *n* 302
confabulate *v* 588
confabulation *n* 588
confederate *n* 711
confederation *n* 709, 903
confer *v* 695, 760, 784
conference *n* 588, 696
confer power *v* 157
confer with *v* 588
confess *v* 488, 529

confession *n* 529, 985
confessional *adj* 985
confidant *n* 890
confidence *n* 474, 484, 507, 533, 858
confidence man *n* 548
confident *adj* 474, 484, 858
confidential *adj* 221, 528
confidentially *adv* 528
confiding *adj* 484
configuration *n* 240
confine *n* 233; *v* 195, 229, 233, 751
confined *adj* 203, 229
confinement *n* 229, 751
confirm *v* 535, 769
confirmation *n* 467, 535, 762
confirmative *adj* 535
confirmatory *adj* 467
confiscate *v* 789, 974
confiscation *n* 789, 974
conflict *n* 24, 680, 713, 720; *v* 713
conflicting *adj* 14, 24, 179, 468
conflicting evidence *n* 468
conflict with *v* 179
confluence *n* 43, 290
confluent *adj* 290, 413
conflux *n* 72, 290
conform *v* 82
conformable to rule *adj* 82
conformity *n* 82
conformity *n* 16, 23, 80, 240, 613, 852
conform to *v* 16, 82
confound *v* 61, 465a, 475
confront *v* 234, 464, 708, 719
confuse *v* 41, 59, 61, 185, 465a, 475, 519, 538

confused *adj* 59, 447, 571
confusion *n* 59, 519, 571
confutable *adj* 479
confutation *n* 479
confutation *n* 536
confute *v* 479
congeal *v* 321, 385
congelation *n* 385
congenial *adj* 23, 413, 714, 829
congeniality *n* 829
congenital *adj* 5
congestion *n* 641
conglomerate *n* 72, 321
conglomeration *n* 41, 46, 72
congratulate *v* 896
congratulate oneself *v* 838
congratulations *n* 896
congratulatory *adj* 896
congregate *v* 72
congregation *n* 72, 990, 997
congress *n* 72, 290, 588
congruity *n* 23
congruous *adj* 23
conical *adj* 253
conjectural *adj* 514
conjecture *n* 514; *v* 514, 870
conjoin *v* 41, 45
conjoined *adj* 413
conjugation *n* 567
conjunction *n* 8, 43
conjuration *n* 992
conjure *v* 992
conjuror *n* 994
con man *n* 548
connect *v* 9, 43, 45, 216
connected *adj* 9, 11
connection *n* 9, 11, 43, 45, 46
connective *n* 45
connoisseur *n* 480, 700
connotation *adj* 516

connotative *n* 550

connote *v* 516

conquer *v* 731

conquest *n* 731

consanguineous *adj* 11

consanguinity *n* 11

conscience *n* 926

conscientious *adj* 246, 459

conscious *adj* 375

consciousness *v* 375, 821

conscription *n* 744

consecrate *v* 987, 995

consecutive *adj* 63, 69

consecutively *adv* 69

consecutiveness *n* 69

consensus *n* 762

consent *n* 762

consent *n* 23, 178, 488, 760; *v* 762

consenting *adj* 488

consequence *n* 62, 63, 65, 154, 642

consequent *adj* 63

consequential *adj* 642

consequently *adv* 154

conservation *n* 141, 670

conservative *adj* 670

conserve *v* 670

consider *v* 451, 461, 469, 480, 484, 873, 928

considerable *adj* 31, 192, 642

considerate *adj* 451

consideration *n* 451, 457, 469, 615, 642, 928

considering *adj* 928

consign *v* 270, 755, 783, 784

consignee *n* 758

consignment *n* 755, 784, 786

consign to oblivion *n* 506

consign to the grave *v* 363

consistency *n* 16, 23

consistent *adj* 16, 23, 413

consistent with *adv* 82

consist in *v* 1

consist of *v* 54

consolation *n* 834, 915

console *v* 834, 915

consolidate *n* 46, 48, 321

consolidation *n* 46, 321

consoling *adj* 834

consonance *n* 413

consonant *n* 561; *adj* 23, 413

consort *n* 903; *v* 41

consort with *v* 88, 892

conspicuous *adj* 446, 525

conspicuousness *n* 446

conspiracy *n* 626

conspiratorial *adj* 626

conspire *v* 178, 709

constancy *n* 16, 80, 112, 141, 150

constant *adj* 16, 69, 80, 110, 136, 138, 141, 150, 474, 604a

constant flow *n* 69

constantly *adv* 112, 136

constellations *n* 318

consternation *n* 860

constipation *n* 261

constituent *n* 51, 56

constitute *v* 54, 56, 161

constituting *adj* 54

constitution *n* 5, 7, 54, 329, 963

constitutional *n* 266; *adj* 963

constrain *v* 744, 751

constrained *adj* 751

constraining *adj* 744

constraint *n* 744, 749, 751

constrict *v* 195

construct *v* 161, 240

construction *n* 5, 161, 240, 329

constructions *n* 567

constructive *adj* 161

construe *v* 522

consult *v* 695

consume *v* 638, 677

consummate *v* 67, 729; *adj* 31, 52, 67, 650, 729

consummately *adv* 31

consummation *n* 67, 729

consumption *n* 162, 638, 677

contact *n* 199, 379

contact lens *n* 445

contain *v* 54, 76

container *n* 191

contaminate *v* 653, 659

contaminated *adj* 655, 961

contamination *n* 653, 659, 961

contemn *v* 930

contemplate *v* 441, 451, 620

contemplation *n* 441, 451, 620

contemplative *adj* 451

contemporaneous *adj* 120

contemporaneousness *n* 120

contemporary *adj* 120

contempt *n* 930

contemptible *adj* 435, 930

contemptuous *adj* 885, 930

contemptuousness *n* 885

contend *v* 476, 720, 722

contender *n* 726

content *n* 831

content *adj* 602, 826, 827

contented *adj* 831, 878
contention *n* 720
contention *n* 713, 969
contentious *adj* 713, 720, 722
contentment *n* 831
contents *n* 190
contents *n* 56, 221, 596
contest *n* 720
contestant *n* 726
contiguity *n* 199
contiguity *n* 197
contiguous *adj* 199
contiguousness *n* 199
continence *n* 953, 960
continent *n* 342; *adj* 960
continental *adj* 342
contingency *n* 151, 156, 470
contingent *adj* 8, 177
continual *adj* 136, 138
continually *adv* 136
continuance *n* 143
continuance *n* 110, 117, 200, 670
continuation *n* 63, 65, 143
continue *v* 1, 106, 110, 136, 143, 604a, 670
continuing *adj* 143
continuity *n* 69
continuity *n* 16, 58, 143, 150
continuous *adj* 69, 112, 143
continuously *adv* 69, 112
continuousness *n* 69
contort *v* 243, 248
contortion *n* 243
contour *n* 230, 448
contraband *adj* 964
contract *n* 676, 768, 769, 771; *v* 36, 195, 676, 769, 770
contract a disease *v* 655
contracted *adj* 195

contracting *adj* 195
contraction *n* 195
contraction *n* 36, 261
contractual *adj* 769
contradict *v* 14, 468, 489, 536, 708
contradiction *n* 14, 218, 536
contradictory *adj* 14, 468, 489, 536
contraposition *n* 218, 237
contrariety *n* 14
contrariety *n* 15, 179, 218
contrary *adj* 14, 179, 608, 708
contrast *n* 14, 15; *v* 15
contrasted *adj* 14
contrast with *v* 14
contravene *v* 14, 468, 536, 708
contribute *v* 153, 176, 178
contribution *n* 784
contributor *n* 912
contrite *adj* 833, 950
contrition *n* 833, 950
contrivance *n* 626
contrive *v* 161, 626, 702
control *n* 157, 175, 693, 737, 741, 751, 777, 965; *v* 157, 175, 693, 737, 777
controller *n* 694
controversy *n* 720
controvert *v* 536
contumacious *adj* 715, 742
contumancy *n* 742
contumely *n* 930
conundrum *n* 520
convalescent *adj* 660
convene *v* 72
convenience *n* 685
convenient *adj* 646
convention *n* 72, 80, 240

conventional *adj* 80, 82, 240, 246, 613, 852, 983a
conventionalism *n* 613
conventionality *n* 82, 613, 852
converge *v* 197, 290
convergence *n* 290
convergent *adj* 290
conversable *adj* 588
conversant *adj* 698
conversation *n* 588
conversation *n* 582
conversational *adj* 582, 588
converse *v* 582, 588; *adj* 14, 237
conversion *n* 144
conversion *n* 140, 218
convert *v* 140
convertibility *n* 13
convertible *adj* 144, 149
convert into *v* 144
convex *adj* 250
convexity *n* 250
convey *v* 270, 516, 783
conveyable *adj* 783
conveyance *n* 272
conveyor *n* 271
convict *n* 754; *v* 971
convicted *adj* 971
conviction *n* 451, 474, 484, 971
convinced *adj* 474, 484
convincing *adj* 478
convivial *adj* 892
conviviality *n* 892
convoluted *adj* 59, 248
convolution *n* 248
convolution *n* 59, 312
convoy *v* 88
convulse *v* 61, 173, 315, 378
convulsed with laughter *adj* 838
convulsion *n* 59, 146, 173, 315, 378

convulsive *adj* 173,
315, 378
coo *v* 412
cook *v* 384, 384
cool *v* 338, 385, 616;
adj 174, 383, 826,
866, 953
cool down *v* 826
cooled *adj* 385
cooling *n* 385
coolness *n* 383, 826,
866, 953
cool one's heels *v* 681
coop *n* 752
cooperate *v* 178, 709,
712
cooperating *adj* 709
cooperation *n* 709
cooperation *n* 23, 178,
778
cooperative *adj* 178,
709
cooperatively *adv* 709
coordinate *v* 60
co-ownership *n* 778
co-partner *n* 778
copious *adj* 168, 573
copper *adj* 439
copula *n* 45
copy *n* 21
copy *n* 13, 19, 22, 90,
532, 556, 590, 591; *v*
19, 554, 590
copyeditor *n* 591
copying *n* 19
copyist *n* 590
cord *n* 247
cordial *adj* 377, 602,
829, 888, 892
cordiality *n* 602, 892
core *n* 5, 68, 208, 222
cork *n* 263; *v* 261
corkscrew *n* 248, 262,
311
cork up *v* 261
cormorant *n* 957
corner *n* 244
cornered *adj* 244

corny *adj* 496
corollary *n* 39
corona *n* 247
coronet *n* 247
corporal *adj* 3
corporality *n* 3, 364
corporate *adj* 43
corporeal *adj* 3, 316,
364
corporeality *n* 316
corpse *n* 362
corpselike *adj* 362
corpulence *n* 192
corpulent *adj* 192, 194
corral *n* 232
correct *v* 246, 658, 660,
662, 972; *adj* 246,
494, 578, 922, 922
correction *n* 658, 972
corrective *n* 662; *adj*
658, 662
correctness *n* 578
correlate *v* 12, 464
correlation *n* 12
correlation *n* 9, 464
correlative *adj* 12, 216
correspond *v* 12, 23,
592
correspondence *n* 592
correspondence *n* 12,
13, 17, 23, 216
correspondent *adj* 23
corresponding *adj* 12,
17, 216
correspond to *v* 216
corroboration *n* 467
corroborative *adj* 467,
535
corrode *v* 659
corrosion *n* 659
corrosive *adj* 649
corrugate *v* 258
corrugation *n* 256
corrupt *v* 653, 659; *adj*
653, 655, 945
corrupted *adj* 961
corruption *n* 49, 563,
653, 659

corse *n* 362
cortege *n* 266
coruscate *v* 420
coruscation *n* 420
cosmic *adj* 318
cosmonaut *n* 269
cosmopolitan *adj* 372
cost *n* 812
cost a lot *v* 814
costliness *n* 814
cost little *v* 815
costly *adj* 814
costs *n* 809
costume *n* 225
cote *n* 232
coterie *n* 712
cough *v* 349
could be *v* 470
council *n* 696
council *n* 72, 588, 695
counsel *n* 695, 864,
968; *v* 864
counselor *n* 540, 695,
968
counselor-at-law *n* 968
count *v* 85, 451
count among *v* 76
countenance *n* 448
counter *adj* 14
counteract *v* 30, 179,
662
counteracting *adj* 179
counteraction *n* 179
counteraction *n* 708
counteractive *n* 662
counterattack *n* 718; *v*
718
counterbalance *n* 27; *v*
30
counterblast *n* 179
counter-evidence *n* 468
counterfeit *n* 21; *v* 19,
544, 855; *adj* 19, 544
countering *adj* 237
counter maneuver *n* 179
counterpart *n* 17, 21,
237
counterpoint *n* 413

counterpoise *n* 30; *v* 30, 179

counterrevolution *n* 146

counterstroke *n* 718

counter to *adv* 708

countervail *v* 30

countervailing *adj* 468

countless *adv* 104

count on *v* 507

country *n* 181, 189

county *n* 181

coup *n* 146

coup de grace n 361

coup d'état n 146

couple *n* 89, 100; *v* 43, 89, 903

coupled *adj* 89

coupled with *adj* 88

couple with *v* 88

coupling *n* 43

courage *n* 861

courage *n* 715

courageous *adj* 715, 861

courageousness *n* 715

courier *n* 271, 534

course *n* 109

course *n* 58, 106, 264, 278, 348, 627

course of time *n* 109

coursing *n* 361

court *n* 696, 966; *v* 615, 933

courteous *adj* 457, 852, 879, 894, 928

courtesan *n* 962

courtesy *n* 894

courtesy *n* 457

courtier *n* 935

courtliness *n* 894

courtly *adj* 894

court of justice *n* 966

court of law *n* 966

courtroom *n* 966

cove *n* 343

covenant *n* 768, 769; *v* 768

covenants *n* 770

cover *n* 223, 263, 424, 530, 666; *v* 30, 204, 223, 224, 225, 424, 528, 664

covered *adj* 223

covering *n* 223

covering *n* 220, 225, 528

coverlet *n* 223

cover over *v* 223

covert *adj* 447, 528

covet *v* 865, 921

covetous *adj* 819, 865, 921

covetousness *n* 921

cow *n* 374; *v* 909

coward *n* 862

cowardice *n* 862

cowardice *n* 172, 605

cowardly *adj* 435, 605, 862

cower *v* 862, 886

coxcomb *n* 854

cozen *v* 545

crack *n* 44, 70, 113, 198, 259; *v* 44, 328, 406, 583, 659; *adj* 648, 698

cracked *adj* 410, 503

cracked bell *n* 408a

crackers *adj* 503

crackle *v* 406

crack of doom *n* 121

cradle *n* 66, 127

craft *n* 625, 698, 702

craftiness *n* 698, 702

craftsmanship *n* 161

crafty *adj* 702

craggy *adj* 253, 256

cram *v* 194, 539

crammed *adj* 52

cramp *n* 378; *v* 158, 160, 195, 706

cramped *adj* 579

cranny *n* 198

crapulence *n* 957

crapulent *adj* 957

crash *n* 276; *v* 406

crashpad *n* 189

crass *adj* 851

crater *n* 208, 252

crave *v* 865

craven *n* 862; *adj* 435, 862

craving *n* 276, 865; *adj* 865

crawl *v* 109, 275, 886

craze *n* 852

crazed *adj* 499, 503

craziness *n* 503

crazy *n* 504; *adj* 503

creak *v* 410

creaking *n* 410; *adj* 410

cream *n* 356, 648

creamy *adj* 352, 435

crease *n* 258; *v* 258

create *v* 153, 515

creation *n* 161, 318

creative *adj* 153, 161, 515

creativity *n* 168, 515

creator *n* 153, 164, 976

creature *n* 3, 366, 372

credence *n* 484

credible *adj* 470, 484

credit *n* 805

credit *n* 484, 873; *v* 484, 805, 811

creditable *adj* 878, 931

credo *n* 537, 983

credulity *n* 486

credulous *adj* 484, 486, 547

credulousness *n* 486

creed *n* 484, 537, 983

creep *v* 109, 275, 380

creeper *n* 367

creeping thing *n* 366

cremate *v* 363

cremation *n* 363, 384

crescent *n* 245; *adj* 245

crescent-shaped *adj* 245

cretin *n* 493, 501

crevice *n* 198

crew _n_ 72, 269, 712
crick _n_ 378
criminal _adj_ 964
criminality _n_ 947
crimson _adj_ 434
cringe _v_ 886
cringing _n_ 886; _adj_ 435, 886
crinkle _v_ 256, 258
cripple _v_ 158, 659
crippled _adj_ 158
crisis _n_ 8, 134, 151, 704, 735
crisp _adj_ 328
criss-cross _v_ 219
critic _n_ 480, 524, 595, 936
critical _adj_ 8, 465, 480, 642, 704, 716, 735
criticism _n_ 480, 595, 716
criticize _v_ 480, 595, 716, 850, 934
critique _n_ 465, 480, 595
croak _v_ 412, 583
croaking _adj_ 410
crony _n_ 890
crook _n_ 244, 245, 792; _v_ 217, 245, 279
crooked _adj_ 217, 243, 244, 279, 923
crookedness _n_ 243
croon _v_ 416
crop _n_ 154, 775; _v_ 201
crop up _v_ 151, 446
cross _n_ 41; _v_ 41, 179, 219, 302, 830; _adj_ 41, 901a
crossed _adj_ 219
cross-eye _n_ 443
crosseyed _adj_ 443
cross-fire _n_ 148
crossing _n_ 219
crossing _adj_ 219
cross-purposes _n_ 713
crossroad _n_ 219
cross swords _v_ 722
crotch _n_ 244

crotchety _adj_ 608
crouch _v_ 207, 886
crouched _adj_ 207
crow _v_ 412, 838, 884
crowd _n_ 72, 102, 444, 876; _v_ 72, 102, 197
crowded _adj_ 72, 102
crown _n_ 247; _v_ 210
crowning _adj_ 33, 67
crowning point _n_ 210
crowning touch _n_ 729
crucial _adj_ 642
crude _adj_ 53, 579, 651, 674, 851, 895, 929
crudeness _n_ 929
cruel _adj_ 649, 739, 830, 914a
cruelly _adv_ 31
cruelty _n_ 914a
cruise _n_ 267; _v_ 267
cruiser _n_ 273
crumb _n_ 32, 330
crumble _v_ 49, 160, 162, 328, 330, 659
crumbling _adj_ 124, 659
crumbly _adj_ 330
crumbs _n_ 40
crumple _v_ 256, 258
crumple up _v_ 195
crunch _v_ 298
crush _n_ 72; _v_ 162, 195, 330, 739, 879
crush out _v_ 162
crust _n_ 223
crustacean _n_ 366
crutch _n_ 215
cry _n_ 411
cry _n_ 669; _v_ 411, 412, 839
cry for joy _v_ 838
crying _n_ 411, 412; _adj_ 411, 630
cry out _v_ 411, 669
cry out against _v_ 616
crypt _n_ 363
cryptic _adj_ 526
crystalline _adj_ 425

crystallization _n_ 321, 323
crystallize _v_ 321
cubbyhole _n_ 530
cube _v_ 93
cuckoo _v_ 412
cue _n_ 550
cull _v_ 609, 789
culminate _v_ 210
culmination _n_ 65, 206, 210, 261, 729
culpability _n_ 947
culpable _adj_ 947
cultivate _v_ 371, 375, 658
cultivated _adj_ 850
cultivate one's own garden _v_ 943
cultivation _n_ 371, 578, 658, 850
culture _n_ 850
cultured _adj_ 850
culvert _n_ 350
cumbersome _adj_ 319, 706, 830
cumbrous _adj_ 319
cunning _n_ 702
cunning _n_ 544, 698; _adj_ 544, 545, 698
cup _n_ 252
cupidity _n_ 819
cupola _n_ 250
cupped _adj_ 252
curable _adj_ 660
curative _adj_ 660, 662, 834
curb _n_ 179, 616, 751; _v_ 174, 179, 275, 751
curd _n_ 354
curdle _v_ 397
curdled _adj_ 397
cure _n_ 660, 662; _v_ 660, 662, 670
curfew _n_ 126
curiosity _n_ 455
curiosity _n_ 872
curious _adj_ 455, 461, 870

curiously *adv* 31
curl *n* 245, 248; *v* 245, 248, 258
currency *n* 800
current *n* 338, 348; *adj* 1, 78, 118, 151, 531, 532, 560, 613
curry *v* 331, 392
curry favor *v* 933
curse *n* 663, 830, 908; *v* 908
cursing *n* 908
cursory *adj* 209
curt *adj* 201, 739
curtail *v* 38
curtailed *adj* 201
curtailment *n* 38, 201
curtain *n* 424, 530; *v* 424
curtness *n* 739
curtsy *n* 308; *v* 308
curvature *n* 245
curve *n* 217, 245, 245; *v* 245, 279
curved *adj* 245
custodial *adj* 777
custodian *n* 664, 753
custody *n* 664, 777, 781
custom *n* 80, 124, 613, 852
customarily *adv* 136
customariness *n* 82
customary *adj* 80, 82, 124, 136, 613, 852, 983a
customer *n* 795
cut *n* 44, 70, 198, 240, 257, 259, 276, 378; *v* 44, 240, 257, 259, 361, 371, 385, 557
cut across *v* 302
cut adrift *v* 44, 297
cut a figure *v* 448
cut away *v* 38
cutback *n* 38; *v* 38, 201; *adj* 201
cut down *v* 195, 361
cut in two *v* 91

cut off *v* 38, 44, 361; *adj* 776
cut open *v* 260
cut out *v* 293
cut short *v* 142, 201
cutter *n* 273
cutthroat *n* 361
cutting *adj* 253, 383
cutting edge *n* 253
cuttings *n* 596
cut to pieces *v* 361
cut to ribbons *v* 361
cutup *n* 844; *v* 44
cycle *n* 138, 247
cyclic *adj* 138
cyclical *adj* 138
cyclically *adv* 138
cycling *n* 266
cyclist *n* 268
cyclone *n* 312, 315, 349
cyclonic *adj* 349
cylinder *n* 249
cylindrical *adj* 249
cylindricality *n* 249
cynic *n* 165, 936, 989

D

dab *n* 32, 276; *v* 276
dabble *v* 683
dad *n* 166
dado *n* 211
daft *adj* 503
daily *adv* 136
dainty *adj* 394, 829, 868
dale *n* 252
dalliance *n* 902
dally *v* 683, 902
damage *n* 619, 649, 659, 776, 812; *v* 649, 659, 848
damages *n* 974
damn *v* 908, 971
damnable *adj* 649
damnation *n* 908
damning *n* 908
damp *v* 339, 616; *adj* 339

dampen *v* 408a
dampened *adj* 408a
damper *n* 408a, 616
dampness *n* 339
dam up *v* 261
dance *n* 309; *v* 309, 315, 838
dance all night *v* 309
dandy *n* 854
danger *n* 665
danger *n* 475, 667, 909
dangerous *adj* 475, 665
danger signal *n* 669
dangle *v* 214
dangler *n* 281
dangling *adj* 214
dank *adj* 339
dankness *n* 339
dapple *v* 440; *adj* 433
dappled *adj* 440
dapple-gray *adj* 432
dare *v* 715, 861
daring *n* 715, 861; *adj* 715, 861
dark *adj* 421, 422, 431, 442, 447, 571, 901a
darken *v* 353, 421, 422, 431, 519
darkened *adj* 421, 422
darkish *adj* 422
darkly *adv* 442
darkness *n* 421
darkness *n* 426, 431, 491, 526
darling *n* 897, 899
dart *v* 274
dash *n* 32, 41, 274, 310, 682, 684; *v* 41, 274, 276, 310, 684
dash off *v* 274, 682
dash one's expectations *v* 509
dash one's hopes *v* 509
dastardliness *n* 862
dastardly *adj* 862
data *n* 476, 527
date *n* 106; *v* 114
daub *v* 555

daughter _n_ 167
dauntless _adj_ 861
dauntlessness _n_ 861
dawdle _v_ 133, 275, 605, 683
dawdler _n_ 683
dawdling _n_ 683
dawn _n_ 125, 420; _v_ 116
day _n_ 420
day after day _adv_ 136
daybreak _n_ 125, 420
daylight _n_ 420
day of fasting _n_ 956
day of judgment _n_ 121
day of rest _n_ 687
days gone by _n_ 122
days of old _n_ 122
days of yore _n_ 122
daze _v_ 420
dazzle _v_ 420, 442
de _n_ 220, 234
dead _adj_ 172, 360, 376, 381, 408a
dead and gone _adj_ 360
dead as a door nail _adj_ 360
dead drunk _adj_ 959
deaden _v_ 376, 381, 843
deadened _adj_ 381, 408a
dead heat _n_ 27
dead language _n_ 560
deadly _adj_ 162, 360, 361, 649, 657, 663
deadly weapons _n_ 727
deadness _n_ 381
dead of night _n_ 126, 421
dead silence _n_ 403
dead sound _n_ 408a
deaf _adj_ 419
deafen _v_ 404, 419
deafened _adj_ 419
deafening _adj_ 404
deafness _n_ 419
deaf to _adj_ 458
deaf to the past _adj_ 506
deal _v_ 786, 794
dealer _n_ 797
deal in _v_ 796

dealing _n_ 794
deal out _v_ 73, 784
dear _n_ 899; _adj_ 814
dearness _n_ 814
dearth _n_ 640
death _n_ 360
death _n_ 67, 142
death agonies _n_ 360
death bell _n_ 363
death blow _n_ 67, 360, 361
deathlike _adj_ 403
deathly _adj_ 361
death rattle _n_ 360
debark _v_ 292
debarkation _n_ 292
debase _v_ 308, 653, 659, 879
debased _adj_ 207
debasement _n_ 207, 308, 659, 874
debate _n_ 476, 588, 720, 969; _v_ 476, 720
debater _n_ 476
debauchee _n_ 962
debilitate _v_ 160
debility _n_ 158, 160
debit _n_ 177, 806; _v_ 811
debonair _adj_ 894
debt _n_ 806
debt _n_ 177
debtor _n_ 806
decade _n_ 98, 108
decadence _n_ 659
decapitate _v_ 361
decay _n_ 49, 124, 360, 638, 653, 655, 659, 732; _v_ 36, 49, 195, 360, 659, 735
decayed _adj_ 124, 160, 659
decease _n_ 360; _v_ 360
deceit _n_ 545, 702
deceitful _adj_ 544, 545, 702
deceitfulness _n_ 544, 702
deceive _v_ 544, 545

deceiver _n_ 548
deceiver _n_ 962
deceiving _n_ 545
decency _n_ 881, 960
decent _adj_ 246, 651, 881, 960
deception _n_ 545
deception _n_ 21, 544, 702
deceptive _adj_ 520, 544, 545, 702
decide _v_ 153, 480, 600, 604, 609
decided _adj_ 31, 67
decidedly _adv_ 31
decimal _adj_ 84
decimate _v_ 361, 659
decipher _v_ 522
decision _n_ 480, 600, 604, 609, 620, 969
decisive _adj_ 737
deck out _v_ 225
declaim _v_ 582
declamation _n_ 577, 582
declamatory _adj_ 577, 582
declaration _n_ 525, 531, 535, 985
declarative _adj_ 527, 535
declaratory _adj_ 535
declare _v_ 516, 525, 531, 535
declare war _v_ 716
declension _n_ 306, 567, 659
declination _n_ 306
decline _n_ 36, 124, 217, 306, 638, 655, 659, 732; _v_ 36, 160, 217, 306, 360, 610, 659, 732, 735, 764; _adj_ 128
declining _adj_ 217
declining years _n_ 128
declivitous _adj_ 217, 306
declivity _n_ 217, 306

decode *v* 522
decoloration *n* 430
decompose *v* 49
decomposed *adj* 49
decomposition *n* 49
decorate *v* 847
decoration *n* 733, 847, 877
decorative *adj* 847
decorous *adj* 850, 852
decorum *n* 852, 960
decoy *v* 288
decrease *n* 36
decrease *n* 38, 195, 283; *v* 36, 38, 193, 195
decreased *adj* 36
decreasing *adj* 36
decree *n* 480, 963; *v* 600, 741, 963
decrement *n* 40a
decrepit *adj* 124, 158, 160, 655, 659
decrepitude *n* 128, 158, 160, 659
decry *v* 934
deduce *v* 476
deduct *v* 38, 813
deductible *adj* 38
deduction *n* 38
deduction *n* 40a, 65, 476, 480
deductive *adj* 476
deed *n* 680, 771
deem *v* 451, 873
deep *n* 341; *adj* 208, 404, 428
deepen *v* 35, 208
deepness *n* 208
deep-rooted *adj* 820
deep-seated *adj* 208, 221
deep-sounding *adj* 408
deep-toned *adj* 408
deface *v* 241, 659, 846, 848
defacement *n* 241
defalcation *n* 304

defamation *n* 934
defamatory *adj* 932
defame *v* 934
defamer *n* 936
default *n* 304, 460, 808; *v* 808
defeat *n* 509
defeated *adj* 732
defect *n* 40a, 53, 651, 848, 945; *v* 607
defection *n* 607
defective *adj* 53, 651, 732, 945
defectiveness *n* 732
defend *v* 664, 670, 717, 937
defender *n* 890, 937
defense *n* 717
defense *n* 670, 937
defenseless *adj* 665
defensible *adj* 664
defensive *adj* 717
defer *v* 133
deference *n* 743, 928
deferential *adj* 457, 743, 926, 928
defer to *v* 928
defiance *n* 715
defiance *n* 742
defiant *adj* 715, 742
deficiency *n* 28, 34, 53, 304, 640, 651, 732
deficient *adj* 28, 34, 53, 304, 640, 651
deficit *n* 53
defile *v* 653
defiled *adj* 961
defilement *n* 653, 961
define *v* 233, 522
definite *adj* 79, 233, 246, 446, 474, 570
definition *n* 446, 522
definitive *adj* 67
deflect *v* 245, 279
deflection *n* 245, 291
deform *v* 241, 243
deformed *adj* 243

deformity *n* 241, 243, 846, 848
defraud *v* 545, 791, 923
defrost *v* 382
deft *adj* 698
defunct *adj* 2, 360
defy *v* 715, 742
degeneracy *n* 659
degenerate *v* 659; *adj* 659
degeneration *n* 659
degradation *n* 308, 659, 874
degrade *v* 308, 659, 879
degraded *adj* 207
degree *n* 26
degree *n* 58, 71
deification *n* 990, 991
deify *v* 990, 991
deity *n* 976
dejected *adj* 832
dejection *n* 837
dejection *n* 828, 859
delay *n* 133; *v* 133, 142, 706
delayed *adj* 133
delectability *n* 394, 829
delectable *adj* 394, 829
delectation *n* 827
delegate *n* 534, 758, 759; *v* 270, 755
delegation *n* 755, 758
delete *v* 552
deleterious *adj* 649, 657
deletion *n* 552
deliberate *v* 695; *adj* 174, 275, 383, 451, 685
deliberately *adv* 133, 600, 611, 620
deliberateness *n* 174, 275
delicacy *n* 160, 655, 850, 960
delicate *adj* 160, 203, 328, 329, 394, 428, 704, 829, 868, 960

delicate condition *n* 655

delicious *adj* 394, 829

delight *n* 377, 827, 829; *v* 829, 836

delightful *adj* 377, 829

delight in *v* 827

delineate *v* 554, 594

delineation *n* 554, 556, 594

deliquescence *n* 335

deliquescent *adj* 335

delirious *adj* 503, 825

delirium *n* 503, 825

delitescence *n* 447

deliver *v* 270, 580, 660, 672, 750, 784

deliverance *n* 672

deliverance *n* 660, 750, 834

delivery *n* 580, 784

dell *n* 252

delude *v* 545

deluge *n* 72, 348; *v* 337, 348, 641

delusion *n* 495, 503, 515, 545

delusive *adj* 545

delve *v* 252

demand *n* 601, 630, 741, 765, 812, 924; *v* 630, 741, 765, 812

demeanor *n* 448, 692, 852

demented *adj* 503

dementia *n* 503

demi- *adj* 91

demi-lune *adj* 245

demise *n* 360

demolish *v* 162

demolition *n* 162

demon *n* 980

demon *n* 949, 978

demonic *adj* 980

demonology *n* 980, 991

demonstrable *adj* 476, 478

demonstrate *v* 476, 478, 525

demonstrated *adj* 478

demonstration *n* 478

demonstration *n* 525

demonstrative *adj* 478

demur *n* 704; *v* 485, 603

demure *adj* 881

den *n* 189

dendrology *n* 369

denial *n* 536

denial *n* 764

denominate *v* 564

denotation *n* 516

denotative *adj* 550

denote *v* 516, 550

denounce *v* 908, 909

dénouement *n* 65, 67

dense *adj* 72, 202, 275, 321, 365, 376

denseness *n* 202

density *n* 321

density *n* 202

dent *v* 252, 257

dented *adj* 252

denunciation *n* 908, 932

denunciatory *adj* 932

deny *v* 468, 536, 610, 708, 764

deny oneself *v* 955

deodorize *v* 652

depart *v* 66, 185, 293, 302, 360, 449

departed *adj* 2, 449

department *n* 51, 75

department store *n* 799

depart this life *v* 360

departure *n* 293

departure *n* 287, 360, 449, 623

departure from *n* 279

depend *v* 214

dependable *adj* 474, 664

dependence *n* 749

dependent *adj* 214, 749

depend upon *v* 154, 749

depict *v* 554, 556, 594

depiction *n* 554, 556, 594

deplane *v* 292

depletion *n* 640

deplorable *adj* 649, 830

deplore *v* 833, 839

deport *v* 270, 692

deportation *n* 270

deportment *n* 692

depose *v* 467, 535

deposit *n* 771

deposition *n* 467, 535

depository *n* 191, 802

depraved *adj* 945

depravity *n* 649, 659, 945

deprecate *v* 766

deprecation *n* 766

deprecation *n* 616, 932, 934

deprecatory *adj* 483, 766

depreciate *v* 36, 483, 934

depreciated *adj* 483

depreciating *adj* 483, 934

depreciation *n* 36, 483, 813, 815

depreciative *adj* 483

depress *v* 207, 252, 308

depressed *adj* 207, 308, 438, 837

depressing *adj* 383

depression *n* 308

depression *n* 207, 208, 252, 837

deprivation *n* 659, 776, 789

deprived of *adj* 776

deprive of *v* 38

deprive of color *v* 429

depth *n* 208

deputation *n* 755

deputy *n* 759

deputy *n* 634, 690

derange *v* 59, 61, 185

deranged *adj* 59, 503

derangement n 61
derangement n 59, 185, 503
dereliction n 460, 732
dereliction of duty n 927
deride v 856, 929, 930
derision n 856, 929, 930
derisive adj 856, 929, 930
derisory adj 856
derivable from adj 154
derivation n 154, 155, 562
derivative adj 154
derived from adj 154
derive from v 155
derive pleasure from v 827
derogatory adj 934
descend v 217, 306, 310
descendant n 167
descending n 306; adj 217, 306
descent n 306
descent n 153
describe v 554, 594
description n 594
descriptive adj 554
descry v 441, 480a
desecrate v 679, 988
desecration n 679, 988
desert n 180, 344, 973; v 623, 624, 732, 757, 782
deserter n 607, 623
desertion n 624, 757, 782
deserve v 924
deserve consideration v 642
design n 22, 451, 516, 556, 620, 626; v 451, 516, 556, 620, 626
designate v 79, 550, 564
designation n 564, 877
designer n 559; 626
desirability n 646

desirable adj 646
desire n 865
desire n 600, 609, 858; v 602, 858, 865
desiring adj 865
desirous adj 602, 865
desist v 67, 142, 265
desolate v 162; adj 837
desolation n 162, 638, 828
despair n 828, 837, 859; v 828, 837, 859
despairing adj 859
desperate adj 173, 859
desperately adv 31
desperation n 825, 859
despicable adj 435, 930
despise v 715, 898, 930
despoil v 659
despond v 837, 859
despondency n 837, 859
despondent adj 837, 859
despot n 739
despotic adj 739, 964
despotism n 739
dessication n 340
destination n 67, 620
destine v 152
destined adj 152
destiny n 121, 152, 601, 611, 621
destitute adj 804
destitution n 804
destroy v 2, 162, 619, 638, 659, 679
destroyed adj 162
destroyer n 165
destroyer n 913
destroy oneself v 361
destruction n 162
destruction n 146, 173, 619, 638
destructive adj 162, 638, 649
desuetude n 614, 678

desultory adj 59, 70, 279, 475
detach v 44, 47
detached adj 10, 47, 953
detachment n 44, 291, 953
detail v 79, 594
details n 32, 79
detain v 781
detect v 480a
detection n 480a
detective n 527
detention n 781
deter v 616
detergent n 652
deteriorate v 36, 195, 659
deteriorated adj 659
deterioration n 659
deterioration n 36, 283, 655, 661, 732
determinate adj 474, 480, 620
determination n 150, 278, 480, 600, 604, 620, 480a, 604a
determine v 79, 153, 278, 480, 600, 604, 676, 967, 480a
determined adj 474
deterrent n 706
detest v 898
detestable adj 649, 898
detestation n 898
detonate v 173
detonation n 406
detour n 245, 279, 629; v 629
detract v 483, 934
detracting n 934; adj 934
detraction n 934
detraction n 483
detractor n 936
detrain v 292
detriment n 659
detrimental adj 649

deuce *n* 89
devastate *v* 162
devastation *n* 162, 638
develop *v* 153, 161,
194, 282, 313, 367
developing *adj* 127
development *n* 35, 144,
154, 161, 194, 282,
313
developmental *adj* 35
deviant *adj* 15
deviate *v* 20a, 140, 245,
279, 291, 629
deviating *adj* 15, 279
deviation *n* 279
deviation *n* 20a, 140,
245, 291
device *n* 550, 626, 702
devil *n* 978
devil *n* 949, 980; *v* 392
devilish *adj* 978, 982
devise *v* 515, 626, 673
devoid *adj* 187
devoid of *adj* 777a
devolve *v* 783
devoted *adj* 897, 987
devotee *n* 987
devote oneself to *v* 676
devotion *n* 604, 682,
743, 897, 928, 987
devour *v* 162, 298, 957
devout *adj* 987
devoutness *n* 987
dew *n* 339
dewy *adj* 339
dexterity *n* 698
dextral *adj* 238
dextrous *adj* 698
diabolic *adj* 978, 982
diabolical *adj* 649
diabolism *n* 978
diagnosis *n* 465
diagonal *adj* 217
diagram *n* 626
dialect *n* 560
dialectic *adj* 476, 560
dialectical *adj* 476
dialectician *n* 476

dialects *n* 476
dialog *n* 588
diameter *n* 202
diametrically opposite
adj 237
diaphanous *adj* 425
diaphanousness *n* 425
diaphragm *n* 68
diary *n* 114, 551
dichotomy *n* 91
dictate *v* 741
dictatorial *adj* 739
dictatorship *n* 739
diction *n* 560, 569
dictionary *n* 86
dictum *n* 496, 741
didactic *adj* 537
die *n* 22; *v* 2, 67, 142,
360, 659
die hard *v* 606
die out *v* 2, 142
differ *v* 15, 489, 713
difference *n* 15
difference *n* 18, 24, 28,
291, 489, 713
different *adj* 15, 18
differentiate *v* 18, 79,
465
differentiation *n* 465
different time *n* 119
differ from *v* 14, 18
difficult *adj* 704
difficulties *n* 804
difficulty *n* 704
difficulty *n* 177, 533
diffidence *n* 881
diffident *adj* 881
diffuse *v* 73; *adj* 73,
573
diffused *adj* 186
diffuseness *n* 573
diffusion *n* 73, 186
diffusive *adj* 73, 573
dig *v* 208, 252, 259,
490, 827
digest *n* 596; *v* 384
digestible *adj* 299, 390
dig in *v* 298

digit *n* 84
dignified *adj* 873, 875,
878
dignity *n* 873, 875
digress *v* 279, 573, 629
digression *n* 279, 629
digressive *adj* 279, 573
dig to daylight *v* 260
dig up *v* 480a
dike *n* 198, 259, 350
dilapidate *v* 659
dilapidated *adj* 659
dilapidation *n* 162, 659
dilate *v* 35, 194, 322
dilation *n* 322
dilatory *adj* 133
dilemma *n* 476, 704
diligence *n* 682
diligent *adj* 682
dilly-dally *v* 133, 605,
683
dilly-dallying *n* 133
dilute *v* 160, 203, 337
diluted *adj* 203
dim *v* 421; *adj* 405,
422, 426, 447, 519
dimensions *n* 31, 192
diminish *v* 36, 38, 103,
174, 195, 834
diminished *adj* 34, 103
diminution *n* 36, 195,
638
diminution of number *n*
103
diminutive *adj* 32, 193
diminutiveness *n* 32,
193
dimness *n* 422
dimness *n* 343, 421
dimple *n* 252
dim-sighted *adj* 442,
443
dimsightedness *n* 443
dimwit *n* 493
dimwitted *adj* 254, 499
din *n* 404
dine *v* 298
dingdong *n* 407, 408

dingy *adj* 421, 422, 429, 431

dining *n* 298

dint *n* 252

dip *n* 217, 252, 300, 306, 308, 310; *v* 300, 310, 337

diplomat *n* 724

dipsomaniac *n* 959

dire *adj* 649, 735, 830

direct *v* 175, 278, 537, 600, 630, 692, 693, 741; *adj* 246, 278, 703

directing *adj* 693

direction *n* 278, 693

direction *n* 183, 537, 692, 697, 741

directive *n* 630; *adj* 692

direct line *n* 246

directly *adv* 132, 278

directness *n* 246

director *n* 694

director *n* 745

directory *n* 86

dirge *n* 363, 839

dirigible *n* 273

dirt *n* 342, 653

dirt cheap *adj* 815

dirty *v* 653; *adj* 653, 961

disability *n* 158

disable *v* 158

disabled *adj* 158

disadvantage *n* 619

disadvantageous *adj* 647

disagree *v* 24, 291, 489, 713

disagreeable *adj* 24, 830, 846, 867

disagreeing *adj* 24, 489

disagreement *n* 24

disagreement *n* 10, 15, 47, 489, 713, 720

disagree with *v* 657

disallow *v* 761

disallowance *n* 761

disappear *v* 2, 4, 360, 449

disappearance *n* 449

disappearing *adj* 449

disappoint *v* 509, 732, 832

disappointed *adj* 509

dissapointment *n* 509

disapprobation *n* 932

disapproval *n* 766, 932

disapprove *v* 766, 932

disapproving *adj* 932

disarm *v* 158

disarrange *v* 61

disarray *n* 59, 61

disaster *n* 619, 735

disastrous *adj* 619, 735, 830

disavow *n* 536; *v* 607

disavowal *n* 536, 607

disband *v* 44, 73

disbelief *n* 485

disbelief *n* 485, 487, 989

disbelieve *v* 485, 989

disburse *v* 809

disbursement *n* 809

discard *v* 297, 610, 678, 773, 782

discern *v* 441, 480a, 490, 498

discernible *adj* 446

discernibleness *n* 446

discerning *adj* 441, 459, 465, 490, 498, 868

discernment *n* 441, 465, 477, 480, 490, 498, 868

discharge *n* 284, 295, 297, 299, 406, 750, 772, 807, 970; *v* 284, 295, 297, 692, 729, 750, 772, 807, 926, 927a, 970

discharge a function *v* 644

discharged *adj* 970

disciple *n* 492, 541

disciplinarian *n* 739

discipline *n* 58, 537, 972; *v* 537, 972

disclaim *n* 536; *v* 757, 764

disclaimer *n* 536, 764

disclose *v* 525, 527, 529, 531

disclosed *adj* 529

disclosure *n* 529

disclosure *n* 480a, 531, 985

discoloration *n* 429

discolored *adj* 429, 848

discomfort *n* 378, 828; *v* 828

discommodious *adj* 647

discompose *v* 61, 828

discomposure *n* 61, 828

disconcert *v* 61, 706, 832

disconcerted *adj* 509

disconnect *v* 44, 70

disconnected *adj* 10, 70

disconnectedness *n* 70

disconnection *n* 10, 44, 47

disconsolate *adj* 859

discontent *n* 832

discontent *n* 828

discontented *adj* 832

discontentment *n* 832

discontinuance *n* 142

discontinuation *n* 142

discontinue *v* 44, 70, 142, 265

discontinuity *n* 70

discontinuity *n* 44, 53

discontinuous *adj* 44, 70

discord *n* 414, 713

discord *n* 24, 59, 410, 720, 889

discordance *n* 489

discordant *adj* 24, 410, 414, 713

discount *n* 813
discount *n* 40a; *v* 813
discourage *v* 616
discouraged *adj* 837
discouragement *n* 616
discourse *n* 537, 582, 588, 595; *v* 537, 582
discourse with *v* 588
discourteous *adj* 895, 929
discourtesy *n* 895
discourtesy *n* 929
discover *v* 441, 462, 480a, 490, 529
discoverable *adj* 462
discovery *n* 480a
discovery *n* 462, 985
discredit *n* 874; *v* 485
discreet *adj* 451, 698, 864
discrepancy *n* 15, 24
discretion *n* 480, 498, 698, 864
discretional *adj* 609
discretionary *adj* 600, 748
discriminate *v* 15, 465, 498, 850
discriminating *adj* 465, 480
discrimination *n* 465
discrimination *n* 15, 480, 850, 868
discriminative *adj* 15, 465, 850, 868
discriminatory *adj* 465
discursive *adj* 279, 573
discuss *v* 476, 695
discuss a subject *v* 595
discussion *n* 476, 588, 595
disdain *n* 930; *v* 866, 930
disdainful *adj* 773, 930
disease *n* 655
disease *n* 378
diseased *adj* 655
disembark *v* 292, 342

disembarkation *n* 292
disenchant *v* 616
disencumber *v* 705
disengage *v* 44, 750
disengagement *n* 44, 750
disentangle *v* 42, 44, 60, 522, 672, 705
disentanglement *n* 672
disenthrall *v* 750
disestablish *v* 185
disesteem *n* 932
disfavor *n* 874
disfigure *v* 241, 243, 659, 846
disfigured *adj* 848
disfigurement *n* 241, 243, 846, 848
disgrace *n* 874, 930; *v* 874
disgraced *adj* 874
disgraceful *adj* 874, 930
disgrace oneself *v* 874
disgruntled *adj* 509
disguise *n* 530; *v* 528
disguising *n* 528
disgust *n* 837, 867, 869; *v* 289, 395, 830, 867, 869
disgusted *adj* 869
disgusting *adj* 867, 898
dishabille *n* 226
dishearten *v* 616
disheartened *adj* 837
disheartening *adj* 383
disheveled *adj* 73
dishonest *adj* 544, 923, 940
dishonesty *n* 544, 940
dishonor *n* 874, 930; *v* 874, 923
dishonorable *adj* 874, 930, 940
disillusion *n* 509; *v* 509
disinclination *n* 603, 867
disincline *v* 616

disinclined *adj* 867
disinfect *v* 652
disinfectant *n* 652
disingenuous *adj* 544
disintegrate *v* 330
disintegration *n* 330
disinter *v* 363
disinterested *adj* 942
disinterestedness *n* 942
disinterment *n* 363
disjoin *v* 44, 47, 51
disjoined *adj* 44
disjunction *n* 44
disjunction *n* 10, 47, 49, 70
disjunctive *adj* 44
dislikable *adj* 867
dislike *n* 867
dislike *n* 289, 603, 889, 898, 932; *v* 603, 867, 898, 932
disliking *adj* 867
dislocate *v* 44, 61
dislocation *n* 44, 61, 185
dislodge *v* 185, 297
dislodgment *n* 297
dismal *adj* 830, 837, 901a
dismantle *v* 162, 678
dismay *n* 860
dismayed *adj* 860
dismemberment *n* 44
dismiss *v* 750, 782
dismissal *n* 750
dismount *v* 292, 306
disobedience *n* 742
disobedience *n* 773
disobedient *adj* 742, 773
disobey *v* 742
disorder *n* 59
disorder *n* 61, 173, 241, 315, 503, 655; *v* 59, 61, 185
disordered *adj* 241
disorderly *adj* 59, 173

disorganization *n* 61
disorganize *v* 61, 162
disorganized *adj* 59
disown *n* 536
disparage *v* 483, 934
disparagement *n* 932, 934
disparaging *adj* 932, 934
disparate *adj* 18, 24, 28
disparity *n* 15, 18, 24, 28, 291
dispassion *n* 826, 953
dispassionate *adj* 826, 953
dispatch *n* 592, 684; *v* 361, 684, 692, 729
dispel *v* 73, 162
dispensation *n* 784, 786, 927a
dispense *v* 73, 784, 786
dispense with *v* 678
disperse *v* 44, 49, 73, 291
dispersed *adj* 73
dispersion *n* 73
dispersion *n* 44, 186
dispirited *adj* 837
dispiriting *adj* 383
displace *v* 61, 185, 270
displaced *adj* 185
displacement *n* 185
displacement *n* 140
display *n* 448, 525, 855, 882; *v* 525, 882
displease *v* 289, 830
displeased *adj* 832
displeasing *adj* 846
displeasure *n* 828, 832, 900
disposal *n* 60, 677, 741
dispose *v* 60, 176, 615, 693, 796
dispose of *v* 784
disposition *n* 58, 60, 176, 600, 602, 613, 693, 820
dispossess *v* 789

dispossession *n* 789
disproof *n* 468, 479
disproportion *n* 24
disproportionate *adj* 24
disprove *v* 479
disputable *adj* 485
disputant *n* 476, 726
disputation *n* 476, 536, 969
disputatious *adj* 476, 713
dispute *n* 536, 713, 720, 969; *v* 24, 476, 713, 720
disputing *adj* 24
disqualify *v* 158
disquiet *n* 149, 315, 828; *v* 828
disquietude *n* 149, 832
disquisition *n* 537, 595
disregard *n* 458, 460; *v* 458, 460, 483, 742, 773
disregardful *adj* 460
disregard of time *n* 115
disrelish *n* 867; *v* 867
disreputable *adj* 874
disrepute *n* 874
disrespect *n* 929
disrespect *n* 885, 895
disrespectful *adj* 885, 895, 929
disrobe *v* 226
disrobed *adj* 226
disruption *n* 162, 713
disruptive *adj* 713
dissatisfaction *n* 489, 828, 832
dissatisfied *adj* 832, 841
dissatisfy *v* 832
dissect *v* 44, 49
dissection *n* 49
dissemble *v* 528, 544
dissembler *n* 548
dissembling *n* 528, 544
disseminate *v* 73, 531
dissemination *n* 73, 673

dissension *n* 24, 489, 713, 720
dissent *n* 489
dissent *n* 485, 603, 984; *v* 291, 485, 489, 603, 708, 713
dissenter *n* 489, 984
dissenting *adj* 24, 489, 984
dissention *n* 720
dissertation *n* 595
dissever *v* 44
dissidence *n* 24, 713
dissident *n* 489; *adj* 489, 713, 764
dissimilar *adj* 18
dissimilarity *n* 18
dissimilarity *n* 15, 28
dissimilitude *n* 18
dissipate *v* 162, 638, 818
dissipation *n* 73, 638
dissociate *v* 44
dissociation *n* 10, 44
dissolution *n* 49, 162, 335, 360
dissolvable *adj* 335
dissolve *v* 2, 4, 49, 162, 335, 360, 449
dissonance *n* 24, 410, 414, 713
dissonant *adj* 24, 410, 414, 713
dissuade *v* 616
dissuasion *n* 616
dissuasive *adj* 616
dissyllable *n* 561
distance *n* 196
distance *n* 198, 200, 235
distanced *adj* 10
distant *adj* 196
distaste *n* 867
distasteful *adj* 830, 867
distend *v* 194
distention *n* 194
distill *v* 336
distillation *n* 336

distinct *adj* 402, 446, 518, 525, 570, 580

distinction *n* 15, 31, 465, 873, 875

distinctive *adj* 15

distinctive feature *n* 79

distinctness *n* 446, 570, 580

distinguish *v* 15, 441, 465

distinguished *adj* 206, 873

distinguishing *adj* 465

distort *v* 217, 243, 523, 555, 846

distorted *adj* 243

distortion *v* 243

distortion *n* 443, 544, 555, 846

distracted *adj* 503, 824

distraction *n* 825

distress *n* 735, 804, 828; *v* 828

distress signal *n* 669

distribute *v* 60, 73, 531, 786

distribution *n* 60, 73, 531, 786

distributive *adj* 786

district attorney *n* 968

distrust *n* 485; *v* 485, 487, 860

disturb *v* 61, 185, 315, 824, 830

disturbance *n* 59, 61, 315

disunion *n* 24, 44, 59, 905

disunite *v* 44, 713

disusage *n* 614

disuse *n* 614, 678

disuse *v* 614, 678

disused *adj* 678

ditch *n* 198, 259, 350

ditto *n* 21; *adv* 104

dive *n* 208, 310; *v* 310

diverge *v* 20a, 291

divergence *n* 291

divergence *n* 15, 18, 24, 73, 279

divergency *n* 20a

divergent *adj* 15, 24, 291

divers *adj* 15

diverse *adj* 15, 81

diversified *adj* 15, 16a, 18, 20a, 81, 440

diversify *v* 15, 18, 140, 440

diversion *n* 140, 279, 840

diversity *n* 15, 16a, 18, 81

divert *v* 279, 840

diverting *adj* 840

divest *v* 226, 789

divestment *n* 789

divest oneself *v* 782

divide *v* 44, 44, 51, 60, 73, 85, 91, 291, 778, 786

divided *adj* 51

divide into four parts *v* 97

divide into three parts *v* 94

divide in two *v* 91

divination *n* 511, 992

divine *n* 996; *v* 511, 514, 992; *adj* 976, 981, 983a

divinity *n* 976, 983

division *n* 44, 51, 60, 73, 75, 198, 291, 713, 786

divisive *adj* 713

divorce *n* 905

divorce *n* 44; *v* 44, 905

divorced *adj* 905

divulge *v* 529, 531

divulgence *n* 529, 531

do *v* 161, 170, 622, 639, 680, 729

do a good turn *v* 648

do as one likes *v* 748

do away with *v* 162, 297, 361

do a world of good *v* 648

do battle *v* 722

docile *adj* 725, 743, 926

docility *n* 725, 743

dock *n* 966

doctor *n* 662; *v* 544, 660, 662

doctrinal *adj* 983a

doctrine *n* 484, 537, 983

document *n* 551

dodge *v* 264, 279, 623

doe *n* 374

doer *n* 680, 690

doff *v* 226

dog *n* 373

dogged *adj* 150, 640a, 606

doggedness *n* 150, 604a, 606

doggerel *n* 597

dogma *n* 484, 537, 983

dogmatic *adj* 535, 606, 737

dogmatism *n* 535, 606

dogmatist *n* 606

do good *v* 648

do harm *v* 649

doing *adj* 151

doings *n* 151

doldrums *n* 837

dole *n* 32, 640, 786

dole out *v* 60, 73, 784, 786

dolor *n* 378, 828

dolorous *adj* 378, 830

dolt *n* 493, 501

doltish *adj* 499

domain *n* 75, 181

dome *n* 250

domestic *n* 746; *adj* 188, 221, 370

domestic animals *n* 366

domesticate *v* 184, 370

domesticated *adj* 370

domestication *n* 370
domicile *n* 189
dominance *n* 175
dominant *adj* 175, 737
dominate *v* 175, 739
domination *n* 741
domineer *v* 739
dominion *n* 157, 737
don *n* 540
donate *v* 784
donation *n* 784
done *adj* 729
done away with *adj* 782
donee *n* 785
done with *adj* 678
donor *n* 784
do nothing *v* 169, 681, 683
doom *n* 152, 360, 421; *v* 152, 971
doomsday *n* 121
do one's duty *v* 926
door *n* 231, 232, 260, 627
doorway *n* 232, 260
do over *v* 144
do penance *v* 952
do right *v* 922
dormancy *n* 526
dormant *adj* 172, 265, 526
dose *n* 25, 786
dot *n* 32; *v* 440
dote *v* 499
dote upon *v* 991
double *n* 17, 90, 147; *v* 90, 258; *adj* 90, 147
double-cross *v* 545
doubled *adj* 90
double dealing *n* 544
double-edged *adj* 520
double entendre *n* 520
double-meaning *n* 520
doubleness *n* 89
doubling *n* 90
doubt *n* 485
doubt *n* 475, 487, 984,

989; *v* 475, 485, 487, 989
doubter *n* 989
doubtful *adj* 473, 475, 485, 487, 520
doubtfulness *n* 473, 475
doubting *adj* 485, 984, 989
doubtless *adv* 474
dough *n* 354
doughy *adj* 324, 354
dour *adj* 739
douse *v* 310, 337
dove color *n* 432
dove-colored *adj* 432
dovetail *v* 23, 219
do violence *v* 649
dowdy *adj* 653
do what one wants *v* 748
do without *v* 678
down *v* 298; *adj* 837; *adv* 207
downfall *n* 162, 306
downhearted *adj* 837
downhill *n* 217; *adj* 217
down in the dumps *adj* 438, 832
down in the mouth *adj* 735
downright *adj* 525; *adv* 31
downstairs *adv* 207
downward *adv* 207
downy *adj* 255, 256
dozen *n* 98
drab *adj* 432
draft *n* 208, 349, 596, 626
draftsman *n* 559
drafty *adj* 349
drag *n* 285; *v* 109, 275, 285, 288, 307
drag on *v* 110
drag out *v* 110, 133
drag up *v* 307
drain *n* 295, 350; *v* 295, 297, 340

drainage *n* 295, 340
drain into *v* 348
drake *n* 373
drama *n* 599
dramatic *adj* 599, 882
dramatist *n* 599
dramatize *v* 599
dramaturgy *n* 599
drape *v* 225
drapery *n* 225
draught *n* 298
draw *n* 27; *v* 153, 230, 285, 288, 301, 556
draw a curtain *v* 424
draw aside *v* 279
drawback *n* 177, 619, 651
drawer *n* 559
draw forth *v* 301
draw in *v* 195
drawing *n* 285, 556, 626
drawing and quartering *n* 361
drawl *v* 275
drawn *adj* 27
draw near *v* 121, 286
drawn game *n* 27
draw out *v* 110, 133, 200, 301, 590
draw to a close *v* 67
draw together *v* 72
dread *n* 860, 862; *v* 860
dreadful *adj* 649, 830, 860
dreadfully *adv* 31
dream *n* 4, 515, 515, 858; *v* 515
dreamer *n* 504
dreaming *n* 515
dreamlike *adj* 515
dreamy *adj* 4, 515, 683
dreamy-eyed *adj* 683
dreary *adj* 16, 830, 843
dredge *v* 307
dregs *n* 40
drench *v* 337, 339, 348, 641

dress *n* 225
dress *v* 225
dressed *adj* 225
dribble *v* 295, 348
drift *n* 176, 278, 349; *v* 176, 264, 267, 279, 287
drift away *v* 287
drill *n* 262; *v* 260, 537
drink *n* 298; *v* 298, 959
drinkable *adj* 299
drinker *n* 959
drinking *n* 296, 298, 959
drink like a fish *v* 959
drink one's fill *v* 298
drink up *v* 298
drip *v* 295, 348
dripping *n* 356
drive *n* 266, 284; *v* 276, 284, 744
drive a bargain *v* 794
drive at *v* 516
drive away *v* 289
drive in *v* 300
drivel *n* 499
driveling *n* 499; *adj* 499
driver *n* 268, 694
driving *n* 266
driving spirit *n* 820
drizzle *n* 32, 348; *v* 348
drizzly *adj* 348
droll *n* 501; *adj* 853
drollery *n* 842
drone *n* 683
droning *n* 407
droop *v* 306, 655, 659, 688, 837
drooping *adj* 160
drop *n* 32, 306; *v* 158, 160, 306, 310, 348, 688
drop by drop *adv* 26
drop dead *v* 360
drop down *v* 306
drop down dead *v* 360

drop from the clouds *v* 508
drop in the ocean *n* 32
droplet *n* 32
drop off *v* 283, 360
drop out *v* 283
dropsical *adj* 194
dropsy *n* 194
drought *n* 340
droves *n* 102
drown *v* 337, 361, 376
drowsiness *n* 688
drowsy *adj* 683, 688, 841
drudge *v* 686
drudgery *n* 682
drug *v* 381
drugged *adj* 381
drum *n* 249; *v* 407
drumming *n* 407
drunk *adj* 959
drunkard *n* 959
drunken *adj* 959
drunkenness *n* 959
dry *v* 340; *adj* 340, 575, 579, 843, 958
dryad *n* 979
dry as a bone *adj* 340, 958
dry land *n* 342
dryness *n* 340
dry rot *n* 653, 663
dry up *v* 340, 435
dual *adj* 89
dualism *n* 89
duality *n* 89
dub *v* 564
dubious *adj* 475, 485, 487, 520
dubiousness *n* 475, 520
ducking *n* 310
duct *n* 350, 351
ductile *adj* 324
ductility *n* 324
dud *n* 732
dude *n* 854
due *n* 806, 924; *adj* 924
duet *n* 415

due to *adj* 154, 155
duffer *n* 493, 701
dulcet *adj* 413
dull *v* 254, 381, 422; *adj* 160, 172, 254, 275, 337, 376, 381, 422, 428, 429, 491, 499, 575, 598, 683, 841, 843, 901a
dullard *n* 493, 501
dulled *adj* 381
dullness *n* 843
dullness *n* 172, 254, 683, 823, 841
dull understanding *n* 499
dull-witted *adj* 499
dumb *adj* 491, 581
dumb animal *n* 366
dumbness *n* 581
dumfound *v* 509, 581, 870
dumps *n* 837
dumpy *adj* 193, 201, 202
dun *adj* 429, 432
dunce *n* 493, 501
dunderhead *n* 501
dunderpate *n* 501
dungeon *n* 752
dunk *v* 310, 337
dunking *n* 310
duo *n* 415
dupe *n* 547
dupe *n* 486, 857; *v* 545
duplex *adj* 89
duplexity *n* 89
duplicate *n* 13, 21, 90; *v* 19, 90, 104; *adj* 19, 90, 641
duplicated *adj* 90
duplication *n* 90
duplication *n* 19, 104
duplicitous *adj* 520, 702
duplicity *n* 520, 544, 702
durability *n* 110

durability n 112, 141,
150
durable adj 106, 110,
141, 150
duration n 106, 200
duress n 744
during adv 106
dusk n 126, 421
duskiness n 421, 422
dusky adj 431
dust n 330, 362
dusty adj 330, 653
dutiful adj 743, 926
duty n 926
duty n 625, 743, 806,
928, 963
duty bound adj 926
dwarf n 980; adj 193
dwarfish adj 193
dwell v 186, 188, 265
dweller n 188
dwelling n 189
dwindle v 36, 195, 732
dwindling n 36
dye n 428; v 428
dyed adj 428
dying n 360
dying day n 360
dynamic adj 171

E

each adv 79
each to each adv 79
each to his own adv 79
eager adj 602, 682
eagerness n 602, 682
eagle-eyed adj 441
ear n 418
earlier adv 116
earliness n 132
early adj 132; adv
121, 132
earmark n 550
earn v 775
earnest adj 602, 642
earnestly adv 604
earnestness n 682
earnings n 775

ear-piercing adj 410
earshot n 197
ear-splitting adj 404
earth n 318, 342, 362
earthly adj 318, 342,
989
earthy adj 342
ease n 377, 578, 705,
748, 827, 831, 834; v
705, 707, 834
easily adv 705
easiness n 705
easy adj 275, 578, 685,
705, 740
easy circumstance n 803
easy going adj 174,
740, 826
eat v 298
eatable adj 299
eat away v 638
eating n 298
eating n 296
eavesdrop v 418
eavesdropper n 418,
455, 527
ebb n 36; v 36, 195,
283, 287, 659
ebb and flow n 314
ebbing n 36
ebon adj 431
ebony n 431
ebullience n 171
ebullient adj 171, 382,
824
ebullition n 171, 173,
315, 825
eccentric adj 83, 499,
608
eccentricity n 83, 499,
503
ecclesiastic n 996
ecclesiastical adj 995
echo n 21, 104; v 104,
277, 402, 408
echoing n 408
eclipse n 421, 449; v
33, 422
economical adj 817

economize v 817
economy n 817
economy n 58
ecstasy n 377, 827
ecstatic adj 377, 827,
829
ecumenical adj 78
eddy n 312, 348
edge n 231
edge n 233; v 231
edgewise adv 217
edging n 231
edible adj 299
edification n 537
edify v 537
edifying adj 537, 648
edition n 531
editor n 593, 805
educate v 537
educated adj 490, 498
education n 537, 673
educational adj 537
educational institution n
542
eel n 248
efface v 552
efface from the memory
v 506
effacement n 552
effect n 154
effect n 65; v 153, 729,
731
effective adj 157, 175,
644
effects n 780
effectual adj 170, 644
effervesce v 173, 315,
353
effervescence n 171,
173, 315, 353
effervescent adj 338,
353
efficacious adj 157,
170, 644
efficacy n 157, 644
efficient adj 157, 170,
698
effigy n 21

effluence *n* 295
effluvium *n* 398
effort *n* 675, 680, 686
effulgence *n* 420
effulgent *adj* 420
effusion *n* 295, 297, 299
effusive *adj* 584
egalitarian *adj* 29, 78
egg *n* 153
egg-shaped *adj* 247, 249
ego *n* 5
egoism *n* 943
egotism *n* 878, 880, 943
egotistical *adj* 878, 880, 943
egregiously *adv* 31
egress *n* 295
egress *n* 302
eight *n* 98
eject *v* 185, 297, 789, 893
ejected *adj* 893
ejection *n* 297
ejection *n* 185, 301, 893
eke out *v* 110
elaborate *v* 658
elaboration *n* 658
elapse *v* 109
elapsed *adj* 122
elastic *adj* 277, 324, 325
elasticity *n* 325
elasticity *n* 159, 277, 324
elated *adj* 838, 884
elbow *n* 244
elbow-grease *n* 331
elbowroom *n* 180
elder *n* 130; *adj* 128
elderly *adj* 124, 128
eldership *n* 128
eldest *adj* 128
elect *v* 609, 995
election *n* 609
electricity *n* 388
electric light *n* 423
electrify *v* 824

electrocute *v* 361
electrocution *n* 361
electronic music *n* 415
electronic sound reproduction *n* 402
elegance *n* 578
elegance *n* 577, 845, 850
elegant *adj* 578, 845
elegantly *adv* 850
elegy *n* 363, 839
element *n* 51, 56, 153, 211
elemental *adj* 42, 211
elementary *adj* 42
elements *n* 66
elephant *n* 192
elevate *v* 206, 235, 307
elevated *adj* 206, 307, 574
elevation *n* 307
elevation *n* 206, 574, 658
eleven *n* 98
elf *n* 979
elfin *adj* 980
elicit *v* 153, 301
eliminate *v* 38, 42, 55, 103, 297, 299, 301, 610, 893
eliminated *adj* 893
elimination *n* 42, 55, 103, 297, 299, 301, 610, 893
elite *n* 648
ellipse *n* 247
elliptic *adj* 247
elliptical *adj* 247
elongate *v* 200
elongation *n* 196, 200
eloquence *n* 574, 582
eloquent *adj* 574
elsewhere *adv* 187
elucidate *v* 74, 518, 522
elucidation *n* 522
elude *v* 623, 671, 773
elusive *adj* 623, 773
elysian *adj* 981

emaciated *adj* 203
emaciation *n* 638
emanate *v* 295, 299
emanate from *v* 154
emanation *n* 295, 299, 398
emancipate *v* 672, 750
emancipation *n* 195, 672, 750
emasculate *v* 158
emasculated *adj* 158
embalm *v* 363
embargo *n* 761
embark *v* 66, 267, 293
embarkation *n* 293
embark on *v* 676
embarrass *v* 704
embarrassed *adj* 434
embassy *n* 755
embed *v* 221
embedded *adj* 221, 229
embellish *v* 847
embellished *adj* 847
embellishment *n* 847
ember *n* 388
embezzle *v* 791
emblazon *v* 428, 882
emblem *n* 550, 747
emblematic *adj* 550
embody *v* 50, 54, 76, 82, 316
embosomed *adj* 229
emboss *v* 250
embrace *n* 902; *v* 54, 76, 902
embroider *v* 440, 549
embroidery *n* 549
embroil *v* 61
embryo *n* 153
embryology *n* 368
embryonic *adj* 66, 153, 674
emend *v* 658
emendation *n* 658
emendatory *adj* 658
emerald *adj* 435
emerge *v* 295
emergence *n* 295

emergency *n* 8, 151, 704

emigrant *n* 268

eminence *n* 31, 33, 206, 648, 873, 875

eminent *adj* 206, 873, 883

eminently *adv* 33

emissary *n* 534

emission *n* 297

emit sound *v* 402

emotion *n* 821

emotional *adj* 821

empathy *n* 821

emphasis *n* 535, 580, 642

emphasize *v* 535, 642

emphatic *adj* 535, 642

emphatically *adv* 31

employ *n* 677, 749; *v* 677, 755

employable *adj* 677

employee *n* 746

employ figures of speech *v* 521

employment *n* 625

employ oneself *v* 625

empower *v* 157, 737, 755, 760

emptiness *n* 2, 187, 209, 452, 517, 640, 880

empty *v* 185, 297; *adj* 2, 4, 187, 209, 298, 452

empty-headed *adj* 450a

empty vessel *n* 362

empty words *n* 517

emulate *v* 19, 648

enact *v* 599, 680, 692, 729, 741, 963

enamored *adj* 897

encamp *v* 184

encampment *n* 184

encase *v* 223

enchant *v* 829, 992

enchanted *adj* 992

enchanting *adj* 897, 992

enchantment *n* 827, 829, 991, 992

encircle *v* 76, 220, 227, 247

enclose *v* 227, 232

enclosure *n* 232

enclosure *n* 229

encompass *v* 76, 227

encore *adv* 104

encounter *n* 276, 680, 716; *v* 151

encourage *v* 707, 836

encouraging *adj* 858

encroach *v* 303

encroachment *n* 303

encumber *v* 319, 704, 706

encumbrance *n* 706

end *n* 67

end *n* 65, 142, 152, 154, 360, 620, 729; *v* 67, 142, 360, 729

endanger *v* 665, 909

endangering *adj* 909

endear *v* 902

endearing *adj* 902

endearment *n* 902

endeavor *n* 675, 686; *v* 622, 675

ended *adj* 67

endemic *adj* 79

endless *adj* 102, 104, 112

endlessness *n* 105, 112

end of the day *n* 126

end one's days *v* 360

endorse *v* 535, 769, 771, 931

endorsement *n* 535

endow *v* 157

endowment *n* 698, 784

end result *n* 161

end to end *adj* 199

endurance *n* 112, 141, 150, 826

endure *v* 1, 106, 110, 112, 141, 151, 826

enduring *adj* 110, 141, 150, 505, 826

endwise *adv* 212

enemy *n* 891

enemy *n* 708, 710, 726

energetic *adj* 157, 171, 359

energetic activity *n* 680

energize *v* 171

energized *adj* 171

energy *n* 171

energy *n* 157, 159, 173, 359, 604, 680, 682, 686

enervate *v* 158, 160

enervation *n* 575

enfeeble *v* 160, 638

enfold *v* 229

enforce *v* 695, 744

enforcement *n* 744

enfranchise *v* 750

enfranchisement *n* 750, 760

engage *v* 132, 288, 615, 676, 768, 769

engage in *v* 622, 676

engage in a discussion *v* 588

engagement *n* 676, 680

engender *v* 161

engorge *v* 957

engrave *v* 259, 558

engrave in the mind *v* 505

engraver *n* 559

engraving *n* 558

engrossed in *adj* 451

enhance *v* 307, 658

enigmatic *adj* 519, 520

enjoin *v* 630, 695, 741

enjoy *v* 377, 394, 827

enjoyable *adj* 829

enjoyment *n* 827, 840

enjoy oneself *v* 827

enlarge *v* 31, 35, 35, 194, 573

enlargement *n* 35, 37, 194, 750
enlighten *v* 420, 527, 537
enlightened *adj* 490, 527
enlightenment *n* 490, 498, 527, 985
enlist *v* 615
enliven *v* 689, 836, 840
enmity *n* 889
enmity *n* 907
ennervation *n* 160
ennoble *v* 875
ennui *n* 688, 841
enormity *n* 102, 192
enormous *adj* 31, 192
enormously *adv* 31
enormousness *n* 31, 192
enough *n* 639; *adj* 639; *adv* 31
enplane *v* 293
enrapture *v* 824, 829
enrapturing *adj* 977
enravish *v* 829
enrich *v* 658
enroll *v* 551
ensconce *v* 528
ensconced *adj* 184
ensconcing *n* 528
ensemble *n* 416, 417
enslave *v* 749
enslavement *n* 749
ensnare *v* 545
ensue *v* 63, 151
ensuing *adj* 117
entangle *v* 43, 61, 219, 704
entangled *adj* 59
entanglement *n* 59, 219, 704
enter *v* 294, 551, 811
enter a protest *v* 766
enter into *v* 56, 768
enterprise *n* 622, 676
enterprising *adj* 861
entertain *v* 840
entertaining *adj* 840

entertainment *n* 840
enthral *v* 749
enthusiasm *n* 574, 602
enthusiast *n* 504
enthusiastic *adj* 825
enthymeme *n* 476
enticing *adj* 288
entire *adj* 50, 52, 729
entirely *adv* 31, 50
entirety *n* 50, 52
entitle *v* 564
entity *n* 1
entomb *v* 363
entombment *n* 363
entomology *n* 368
entrain *v* 293
entrance *n* 294; *v* 829, 992
entrancing *adj* 977
entrap *v* 545
entreat *v* 765
entreaty *n* 411, 765
entrée *n* 296
entrust *v* 755, 784, 805
entry *n* 294, 296
entwine *v* 43, 248
enumerate *v* 85
enumeration *n* 85
enunciate *v* 580
enunication *n* 580
envelope *n* 232
envious *adj* 435, 900, 920, 921
enviousness *n* 921
environ *v* 227
environment *n* 227
environs *n* 227
envision *v* 441
envoy *n* 534
envy *n* 921
envy *n* 900, 920; *v* 921
eon *n* 108
ephemeral *adj* 111
ephemerality *n* 111
epicure *n* 945a 957
epicurean *n* 945a; *adj* 954, 957
epicureanism *n* 954

epicurism *n* 954, 957
epigram *n* 496
epigrammatist *n* 844
epilog *n* 65
episode *n* 39, 70, 151
episodic *adj* 228
epistle *n* 592
epistolary *adj* 592
epithet *n* 564
epitome *n* 193, 596
epitomize *v* 201, 596
epoch *n* 106, 108
equal *n* 27; *v* 27; *adj* 13, 27, 30 216, 242
equality *n* 27
equality *n* 13
equalization *n* 30
equalize *v* 27, 30
equally *adv* 27
equal to *adj* 157
equate *v* 216
equation *n* 30, 216
equator *n* 68
equestrian *n* 268
equidistance *n* 68
equidistant *adj* 68
equilibrium *n* 27, 150
equip *v* 225, 673
equipment *n* 225, 633
equipose *n* 27
equitable *adj* 246, 922
equitableness *n* 922
equitably *adv* 922
equity *n* 922
equivalance *n* 27
equivalent *n* 27, 30, 147; *adj* 12, 13, 27, 30, 216
equivocal *adj* 477, 520
equivocalness *n* 520
equivocate *v* 477, 520
equivocation *n* 477, 520, 544
era *n* 106, 108
eradicate *v* 103, 162, 301
eradication *n* 301
erase *v* 162, 331, 552

every once in a while
adv 136
every other adj 138
every which way adv
227
every whit adv 52
evict v 297
eviction n 297, 789
evidence n 467
evidence v 525
evident adj 467, 525
evidential adj 467
evil n 619
evil n 649, 663, 665,
923, 940; adj 619,
649, 663, 923, 940
evildoer n 913
evil-doer n 949
evil incarnate n 978
evil-minded adj 907
evil one n 978
evil spirit n 978, 980
evil star n 649
evince v 467, 478, 525
evoke v 153, 824
evolution n 313
evolution n 161
evolutional adj 313
evolutionary adj 313
evolve v 301, 313
evolved from adj 154
evolvement n 313
ewe n 374
exacerbate v 173
exacerbation n 173
exact v 812; adj 17, 21,
459, 494, 570
exacting adj 868
exaction n 741
exactness n 13, 80, 459,
494, 570
exaggerate v 194, 482,
549, 555, 884
exaggerated adj 194,
497, 549
exaggeration n 549
exaggeration n 482,
497, 523, 555, 835

exalt v 35, 307, 838
exaltation n 307, 838
exalted adj 206, 875
examination n 461, 463
examine v 457, 461,
463, 595
example n 22, 82, 478
exasperate v 173
exasperation n 173
excavate v 208, 252
excavation n 252
exceed v 33, 303
exceeding adj 33
exceedingly adv 31
excel v 33, 648
excel in v 698
excellence n 33, 648,
650, 944
excellent adj 33, 648
except v 469; adv 38,
83
excepted adj 927a
excepting adv 38
exception n 55, 83, 469,
777a, 893, 927a
exceptional adj 20, 79,
83
excess n 40, 641, 954
excessive adj 31, 641,
954
excessively adv 31
exchange n 12, 147,
148, 783, 794, 796; v
12, 147, 148, 783,
794, 796
exchangeable adj 783
exchequer n 802
excise v 38
excitability n 825
excitability n 173, 822,
901
excitable adj 382, 684,
822, 824, 825
excitation n 824
excitation of feeling n
824
excite v 171, 173, 375,
377, 615, 824

excite an impression v
375
excited adj 173, 382,
824
excitement n 825
exciting adj 824
exclaim v 411
exclamation n 411
exclude v 55, 610, 893
excluded adj 57, 893
exclusion n 5, 77, 893
exclusion n 610
exclusive adj 55, 79
exclusive of adv 38
excrete v 299
excretion n 299
excruciating adj 982
exculpate v 970
exculpated adj 970
exculpation n 937, 970
exculpatory adj 937
excursion n 226, 302,
311
excursionist n 268
excuse n 617, 918,
927a; v 617, 777a,
918, 927a
excused adj 927a
execrable adj 649
execrate v 898, 908
execration n 908
execute v 361, 416,
680, 692, 729, 772,
972
execution n 361, 680,
692, 729, 772
executioner n 165, 361,
690; 975
executive adj 692, 737
executor n 690
executrix n 690
exegesis n 522
exegetical adj 522
exemplar n 22
exemplary adj 82
exemplification n 82
exempt v 777a, 927a;
adj 748, 927a

expose the error *v* 479
expose to danger *v* 665
exposition *n* 522, 525, 529, 595
expositor *n* 524
expository *adj* 522, 527
expostulate *v* 616, 766
expostulation *n* 616, 766
expostulatory *adj* 766
exposure *n* 448, 479, 529, 665
expound *v* 522, 537
expounder *n* 524
express *v* 516, 525, 527, 560, 566; *adj* 620
express by words *v* 560, 569
expression *n* 521, 525, 554, 560, 566, 985, 985
expressive *adj* 516, 518, 521, 569
expropriate *v* 789
expropriation *n* 789
expulsion *n* 185, 297, 893
expunge *v* 162, 552
expurgate *v* 652
exquisite *adj* 394, 650
exquisitely *adv* 31
extant *adj* 1
extemporaneous *adj* 612
extemporaneously *adv* 612
extempore *adv* 612
extemporize *v* 612, 674
extend *v* 35, 194, 200
extended *adj* 200, 202
extend to *v* 196, 200
extension *n* 35, 65, 180, 194
extensive *adj* 31, 76, 180
extensively *adv* 180
extent *n* 26, 106, 180, 200, 202, 233
extenuate *v* 469

extenuating *adj* 469
extenuating circumstances *n* 469
extenuation *n* 469
exterior *n* 220; *adj* 220
exteriority *n* 220
exterminate *v* 162
extermination *n* 301
external *adj* 6, 57, 220
externality *n* 57
externally *adv* 220
externals *n* 6
extinct *adj* 2, 122, 162, 360
extinction *n* 2, 162, 360, 421, 552
extinguish *v* 162, 385, 421
extirpate *v* 301
extirpation *n* 301
extol *v* 883
extort *v* 814
extortion *n* 789
extra *adj* 37
extract *v* 301
extraction *n* 301
extracts *n* 596
extradite *v* 270
extradition *n* 270
extraneous *adj* 6, 10, 57, 220
extraneousness *n* 57
extraneousness *n* 6
extraordinary *adj* 31, 83, 870
extravagance *n* 497, 499, 549, 814, 818, 954
extravagant *adj* 31, 497, 499, 549, 641, 814, 818, 853, 954
extravagant love *n* 991
extravagantly *adv* 31
extreme *n* 67; *adj* 31
extremely *adv* 31
extremity *n* 67
extricate *v* 301, 672, 705, 750

extrication *n* 301, 672, 750
extrinsic *adj* 6, 57, 220
extrinsicality *n* 6
extrinsicality *n* 57
extrinsically *adv* 6
exuberance *n* 573, 641
exuberant *adj* 573, 641
exude *v* 295
exultant *adj* 838, 884
eye *n* 247; *v* 441
eye for an eye *n* 30
eyeglasses *n* 445
eyeless *adj* 442
eyesight *n* 441
eyewitness *n* 444
eyot *n* 346

F

fable *n* 546
fabric *n* 7
fabricate *v* 161, 515, 544
fabrication *n* 161, 544, 546
fabulous *adj* 2, 515, 546, 549, 979
fabulous spirit *n* 979
façade *n* 220, 234
face *n* 220, 234, 448; *v* 223, 224, 234
facet *n* 220
facetious *adj* 842
facetiousness *n* 842
face to face *adv* 237
facile *adj* 705
facilitate *v* 705, 707
facility *n* 705
facility *n* 157, 698, 748
facing *n* 223; *adj* 237
facsimile *n* 13, 21, 90
fact *n* 1, 151, 474, 494
faction *n* 712
factious *adj* 24
factory *n* 691
facts *n* 467, 527
factual *adj* 494
faculties *n* 450

faculty n 698
fad n 608
faddish adj 123
faddishness n 123
fade v 4, 111, 124, 160,
  287, 360, 422, 429,
  449, 659, 732
faded adj 659
fail v 160, 304, 360,
  655, 732, 773, 808,
  927
failing n 732; adj 53,
  128, 927
failure n 732
failure n 304, 460, 509,
  735, 773, 808, 927
fain adj 602
faint v 158, 688; adj
  32, 160, 203, 405,
  422, 429, 430, 447,
  688
faint-hearted adj 862
faint-heartedness n 862
faintly adv 32
faintness n 405
faintness n 575, 688
faint sound n 405
fair n 799; adj 174,
  246, 429, 430, 651,
  829, 845, 922, 942
fair game n 857
fairly adv 922
fairness n 174, 845,
  922, 942
fairy n 979
faith n 484, 858
faithful adj 17, 21, 494,
  772, 983a
faithfully adv 772
faithfulness n 772, 983a
faithless adj 544, 989
fake n 556; v 680; adj
  19
fake god n 991
faker n 548
fall n 126, 162, 217,
  283, 306, 348, 360; v
  162, 306, 310, 360

fallacious adj 4, 477,
  495, 544, 545
fallacy n 4, 477, 495
fall again v 661
fall away v 195
fall back v 145, 283,
  287, 661
fall behind v 281, 283
fallibility n 475
fallible adj 475
fall in v 488
falling n 306; adj 217
falling back n 145, 287,
  661
falling-off n 36, 659
falling out n 720
falling short n 304
fall into a rut v 613
fall into a trap v 547
fall into raptures v 827
fall off v 36, 659, 732
fall on evil days v 735
fall on one's knees v 990
fall out v 151, 713
fallow adj 674
fall prey to v 749
fall short v 304, 651,
  732
fall short of v 28, 34,
  53, 640, 730
fall through v 304
fall to v 151, 298, 676
fall to one v 785
fall to one's lot v 156
fall to pieces v 162
fall under v 76
false adj 19, 477, 495,
  544, 545, 546, 923
false coloration n 523
false expectation n 508
false god n 991
falsehood n 544
falsehood n 546
false impression n 495
falseness n 545
false statement n 477
falsification n 523, 544,
  555

falsify v 523, 544, 555
falter v 605
famed adj 883
familial adj 11, 166,
  712
familiar adj 613, 888
familiarity n 748
familiarize v 613
family n 11, 75, 166,
  167, 712
family likeness n 17
famish v 819, 956
famous adj 883
famously adv 31
fan v 338, 349, 385
fanatic n 504, 606; adj
  606
fanatical adj 825
fanaticism n 606
fanciful adj 149, 515,
  608
fancy n 453, 515, 608,
  865; v 515, 865; adj
  577
fancy talk n 577
fang n 663
fantastic adj 83, 497,
  515, 853
fantastical adj 515
fantasy n 515
fan the fire v 173, 824
far adj 196
far and wide adv 180
far away adj 196; adv
  196
farce n 497
farcical adj 497, 853
far cry to n 196
fare n 298, 812
farewell n 293
farfetched adj 10
far gone adj 503, 659
farm v 371
farming n 371
farness n 196
far off adj 196; adv
  196
farrago n 41, 497

farsighted *adj* 441, 443, 510

farsightedness *n* 443

fascinate *v* 288, 824, 829

fascinated *adj* 870

fascination *n* 824, 829

fashion *n* 852

fashion *n* 7, 123, 613, 627; *v* 240, 557, 852

fashionable *adj* 123, 613, 852

fashionableness *n* 123

fast *v* 955, 956; *adj* 43, 150, 274, 684; *adv* 43

fast as a bullet *adj* 274

fasten *v* 43, 45, 150

fastidious *adj* 704, 868

fastidiousness *n* 868

fasting *n* 956

fasting *adj* 956

fast talker *n* 548

fat *n* 356; *adj* 192, 194

fatal *adj* 162, 360, 361

fatality *n* 360, 601

fat chance *adj* 471

fate *n* 121, 156, 601, 611, 621

father *n* 166, 996

fatherhood *n* 166

fatherland *n* 189

fathership *n* 166

fathom *v* 490

fathomless *adj* 208

fatigue *n* 688

fatigue *n* 841; *v* 688, 841

fatigued *adj* 688, 841

fatten *v* 194, 298

fattiness *n* 354

fatty *adj* 354

fatuity *n* 452, 499

fatuous *adj* 499

faucet *n* 263

fault *n* 70, 495, 651, 732, 848, 927, 945, 961

faultless *adj* 50, 650, 946, 960

faultlessness *n* 650, 946, 960

faulty *adj* 568, 651, 732, 945, 961

faulty grammar *n* 568

faun *n* 979

fauna *n* 357, 366

favor *n* 707, 740, 760, 784; *v* 740, 760

favorable *adj* 134, 602, 648, 734

favorite *n* 899

favor with *v* 784

fawn *v* 886, 933

fawner *n* 935

fawning *n* 886, 933; *adj* 886

fay *n* 979

fealty *n* 743

fear *n* 860

fear *n* 862; *v* 860

fearful *adj* 665, 830, 860, 862

fearfully *adv* 31

fearless *adj* 861

fearlessness *n* 861

feasibility *n* 470, 705

feasible *adj* 470, 705

feast on *v* 298, 377

feat *n* 680

feather one's own nest *v* 943

feathery *adj* 320

feature *n* 56, 79, 448, 550, 780

features *n* 5

fecal *adj* 653

fecund *adj* 168, 365

fecundity *n* 168

feeble *adj* 32, 158, 160, 203, 337, 477, 575, 605

feeble-minded *adj* 499

feebleness *n* 575

feebleness *n* 158

feed *v* 298, 388

feel *n* 379; *v* 375, 379, 821

feel contempt for *v* 930

feel fine *v* 654

feel for *v* 914

feel good *v* 654

feeling *n* 821

feeling *n* 375, 379, 928; *adj* 821, 914

feeling no pain *adj* 959

feel pain *v* 378

feel pleasure *v* 377

feel sorry about *v* 833

feel sorry for *v* 914

fees *n* 809

feign *v* 544, 546, 680, 855

feigned *adj* 855

feigning *n* 855

felicitation *n* 896

felicitous *adj* 23, 578, 698, 850

felicity *n* 698, 827

fell *v* 162, 213, 308

fellow *n* 17, 27, 88, 373, 890; *adj* 88

fellow creature *n* 372

fellow-feeling *n* 888

fellow man *n* 372

fellowship *n* 709, 712, 888

female *n* 374; *adj* 374

female animal *n* 374

feminine *adj* 374

femininity *n* 374

fen *n* 345

fence *n* 232; *v* 277, 477

fence in *v* 229

ferment *n* 59, 171, 173, 315, 320; *v* 173, 315, 353, 397

fermentation *n* 171, 315, 353

fermented *adj* 397

ferocious *adj* 173

ferocity *n* 173

ferret out *v* 480a

fertile *adj* 168, 371

fertility *n* 168
fertilize *v* 168
fervent *adj* 382, 821, 865
fervid *adj* 382, 824
fervor *n* 382, 821, 991
fester *v* 653
festival *n* 883
festivity *n* 840, 883
fetch *v* 270, 812
fetid *adj* 401, 653
fetidness *n* 401
fetishism *n* 991
fetishistic *adj* 991
fetor *n* 401
fetter *v* 43
feud *n* 713, 720; *v* 713
fever *n* 382, 825
feverish *adj* 824, 825
few *n* 100; *adj* 32, 103, 137
few and far between *adj* 103
fewness *n* 103
fewness *n* 32
fiasco *n* 732
fiat *n* 741
fib *n* 544, 546; *v* 544, 546
fiber *n* 205
fibrous *adj* 205
fickle *adj* 149, 605, 608
fickleness *n* 605
fiction *n* 515, 544, 546, 598
fictional *adj* 598
fictitious *adj* 546
fidelity *n* 543, 772
fidget *v* 825
fidgetiness *n* 149, 682
fidgety *adj* 149, 682, 825
field *n* 344
field of battle *n* 728
fields *n* 344
fiend *n* 980
fiendish *adj* 980
fierce *adj* 173, 825

fiery *adj* 382, 684, 825
fiery furnace *n* 386
fifty *n* 98
fifty-fifty chance *n* 156
fifty-fifty split *n* 91
fight *n* 680; *v* 606, 720, 722
fighter *n* 726
fighting *n* 173, 722
figment *n* 515
figuration *n* 554
figurative *adj* 521, 554
figure *n* 84, 550, 812; *v* 240, 448, 554, 557
figured on *adj* 871
figure of speech *n* 521
figure of speech *n* 566
figures of beauty *n* 521
filament *n* 205
filch *v* 791
filcher *n* 792
file *n* 69, 86, 266, 330; *v* 38, 60, 69, 195, 255, 330
file a claim *v* 969
filial *adj* 167
filiation *n* 11
filigree *n* 219
filing *n* 330
fill *v* 52, 186, 190, 224
filled in *adj* 527
fill in *v* 52
filling *n* 224
fill out *v* 194, 549
fill up *v* 52, 261
fill up the time *v* 106
film *n* 204, 427
filminess *n* 426
filmy *adj* 204, 329, 426
filth *n* 653
filthy *adj* 653
final *adj* 67
finale *n* 65, 67, 360, 729
final gasp *n* 360
finality *n* 67
finalize *v* 729
finally *adv* 67, 151

final stage *n* 67
final touch *n* 729
finance *n* 800, 811
financial *adj* 800
financier *n* 801, 811
find *n* 480a, 775; *v* 151
find fulfillment *v* 731
find guilty *v* 971
find oneself *v* 186
fine one's way to *v* 602
find out *v* 480a, 527
find refuge *v* 666
find safety *v* 666
find the means *v* 632
find the right words *v* 566
find vent *v* 295
fine *n* 974; *v* 974; *adj* 32, 203, 322, 329, 578, 648, 845
fine art *n* 556
fine gentleman *n* 854
fineness *n* 329
fine powder *n* 330
finery *n* 847, 851
fine speaking *n* 577
finesse *n* 698, 702; *v* 702
fine writing *n* 577
finger *v* 379
fingering *n* 379
finical *adj* 459
finicky *adj* 868
finish *n* 65, 67, 142, 242, 729; *v* 52, 67, 142, 650, 729
finished *adj* 242, 698
finishing stroke *n* 361
fire *n* 171, 382, 423, 574; *v* 384, 388, 420, 824
fired *adj* 384
fire off *v* 284
fire place *n* 386
fireproof *adj* 385
firewood *n* 388
firing *n* 388, 406

firm *adj* 43, 150, 323, 604, 606
firmament *n* 318
firmly *adv* 43
firmness *n* 150, 323, 604, 606
first *adj* 66; *adv* 66
first and foremost *adv* 66
first blush *n* 125
first cause *n* 153, 976
first-class *adj* 648
first come first served *n* 607, 609a
first move *n* 66
first rank *n* 234
first-rate *adj* 33, 648, 698
first step *n* 66
firth *n* 343
fiscal *adj* 800
fish *n* 366
fish for *v* 622
fishing *n* 361
fish story *n* 549
fish up *v* 307
fissure *n* 44, 198, 260
fit *n* 7, 173, 315, 825; *v* 23, 852; *adj* 646, 698, 922
fit as a fiddle *adj* 654
fit for *adj* 698
fitful *adj* 70, 139, 149, 475, 608
fitfully *adv* 139
fitfulness *n* 139, 475
fitness *n* 646
fit out *v* 225, 673
fits *n* 315
five, etc. *n* 98
five *n* 98
fivefold division *n* 99
fix *n* 704; *v* 43, 60, 150, 184, 604, 660
fix a price *v* 812
fixed *adj* 5, 141, 150, 240, 265, 474, 604, 613

fixed idea *n* 606
fixedness *n* 150
fixity *n* 150, 265
fix the time *v* 114
fizzle *v* 353, 409
fjord *n* 343
flabby *adj* 324
flaccid *adj* 160, 324, 326
flaccidity *n* 160, 324, 326, 640
flag *n* 747; *v* 160, 275, 655, 683, 688
flaky *adj* 204
flame *n* 382, 420, 423, 439, 897; *v* 382, 897
flame-colored *adj* 439
flaming *adj* 434
flammable *adj* 384, 388
flank *n* 236; *v* 236
flanked *adj* 236
flanking *adj* 236
flap *n* 214; *v* 214, 315
flare *n* 420; *v* 173, 420
flare up *v* 420, 825
flash *n* 113, 420, 453, 612; *v* 113, 420
flash on *v* 505; *v* 612
flashy *adj* 428, 577, 851, 882
flat *n* 344; *adj* 172, 207, 213, 251, 337, 391, 395, 598, 843
flat as a pancake *adj* 251
flatlands *n* 207
flatness *n* 251
flatness *n* 207, 213, 391, 843
flatten *v* 213, 251, 255
flatter *v* 933
flatterer *n* 935
flattering *adj* 933
flattery *n* 933
flatulent *adj* 334, 338
flaunt *v* 882
flaunting *adj* 882
flavor *n* 390, 394; *v* 390

flavored *adj* 390
flavorful *adj* 390, 394
flavorfulness *n* 394
flavoring *n* 393
flavorless *adj* 395
flavorlessness *n* 395
flavory *adj* 390
flaw *n* 70, 198, 495, 651, 848, 961
flawed *adj* 961
flaxen *adj* 435
fleck *v* 440
flecked *adj* 440
flecky *adj* 440
fled *adj* 671
flee *v* 671
fleece *n* 223; *v* 789, 791, 814
fleet *n* 273; *adj* 274, 684
fleeting *adj* 111
flesh *n* 364
flesh and blood *n* 3, 316, 364
fleshiness *n* 354
fleshly *adj* 364
fleshy *adj* 354
flexibility *n* 324, 705
flexible *adj* 324
flexure *n* 245
flicker *n* 315; *v* 315, 420, 422
flickering *adj* 139
flier *n* 269
flier *n* 269
flight *n* 267, 274, 287, 293, 623, 671
flighty *adj* 149, 503
flimsiness *n* 4, 209, 425
flimsy *adj* 160, 209, 322, 324, 425, 477, 643
flinch *v* 623
fling *n* 284; *v* 284
flip out *v* 173
flipside *n* 235
flirt *v* 902

flit *v* 109, 111, 264, 266, 274
flitting *adj* 111, 266
float *v* 267, 320
floating *adj* 405
flock *n* 72, 997; *v* 72
flocks and herds *n* 366
flog *v* 972
flogging *n* 975
flood *n* 72, 121, 348; *v* 641
flood gate *n* 233, 350
floor *n* 204; *v* 213
flop *v* 315
flora *n* 357, 367, 369
floriculture *n* 371
florid *adj* 428, 577
floridness *n* 577
flounce *v* 309, 315
flounder *v* 149, 314, 315, 475, 732
flourish *n* 577, 882; *v* 367, 654, 734
flourish of trumpets *n* 404
floury *adj* 330
flout *v* 715
flow *n* 264, 348; *v* 109, 214, 264, 333, 347, 348
flower *n* 648; *v* 161, 734
flowerage *n* 367
flowering *n* 161
flowery *adj* 577
flow from *v* 154
flow in *v* 294
flowing *n* 348; *adj* 405, 578
flow into *v* 348
flow out *v* 295, 348
flow out of *v* 295
flow over *v* 348
fluctuate *v* 149, 314, 605
fluctuating *adj* 149
fluctuation *n* 149, 314, 605

flue *n* 351
fluency *n* 333
fluent *adj* 333, 348, 578, 584
fluffy *adj* 256
fluid *n* 337; *adj* 333, 337
fluidity *n* 333
fluke *n* 156, 621
flukey *adj* 156
flunkey *n* 935
flunkeyism *n* 933
flurry *n* 682, 684
flush *n* 382, 420; *v* 382, 434
flushed *adj* 434, 824, 838
flush out *v* 480a
fluster *v* 824
flute *v* 259
fluted *adj* 259
flutter *n* 315; *v* 315, 422
flux *n* 109, 144, 264, 348
flux and reflux *n* 314
fly *v* 109, 111, 267, 287, 328, 671
fly back *v* 277
fly from *v* 623
flying *n* 274, 267; *adj* 111, 267, 959
fly over *v* 267
fly to pieces *v* 328
foam *n* 353; *v* 173, 315, 353, 825
foaming *n* 353
foamy *adj* 353
focal *adj* 222
focus *n* 74
focus *v* 74
focus on *v* 222
fodder *n* 362
foe *n* 708, 710, 726, 891
fog *n* 353, 424
fogginess *n* 422, 475
foggy *adj* 422, 426, 353

foil *n* 14
foiled *adj* 732
fold *n* 258
fold *n* 232, 997; *v* 258
folded *adj* 258
foliage *n* 367
foliation *n* 367
folk *n* 372
folk music *n* 415
follow *v* 19, 63, 281, 518, 622, 743
follow after *v* 117
follower *n* 117, 541, 746
follow in a line *v* 69
following *n* 63, 117, 281; *adj* 63, 117, 281
follow in the steps of *v* 281
follow in the wake of *v* 281
follow the rules *v* 82
folly *n* 499
fond *adj* 897
fondle *v* 379
fondling *n* 379
fondness *n* 897
font *n* 153
food *n* 298, 637
food for thought *n* 454
food for worms *n* 362
fool *n* 501
fool *n* 493, 547, 844, 857; *v* 545
foolhardiness *n* 863
foolhardy *adj* 684, 863
foolish *adj* 477, 497, 499
foolishness *n* 497, 499
foot *n* 211
footing *n* 8, 71, 183, 215
fop *n* 854
foppery *n* 855
for *adv* 155
for a long time *adv* 110
for a time *adv* 111
foray *n* 716

forbear *v* 678, 953
forbearance *n* 623, 678, 740, 826
forbears *n* 122
forbid *v* 761
force *n* 157, 159, 170, 171, 173, 574, 739, 744; *v* 157, 744
forced *adj* 10, 579
forceful *adj* 157, 159, 171, 574
forcefulness *n* 600
force of will *n* 600
for certain *adv* 474
forcible *adj* 171, 574, 744
forcibly *adv* 744
ford *v* 302
fore *adj* 234
forebode *v* 909
foreboding *n* 512, 909; *adj* 909
forecast *n* 510, 511, 673; *v* 507, 511, 626
forefather *n* 130
forefront *n* 234
foregoing *adj* 62, 116, 122
foregone *adj* 611
foregone conclusion *n* 611
foreground *n* 234
foreign *adj* 10, 57, 220
foreign body *n* 57
foreign parts *n* 196
foreign substance *n* 57
fore-knowledge *n* 510
foreman *n* 694
foremost *adj* 33, 66, 234, 642
forenoon *n* 125
foreordain *v* 152
forerun *v* 62, 116, 280
forerunner *n* 64, 116, 534
foresee *v* 121, 507, 510, 511, 871
foreseen *adj* 507, 871

foreshadow *v* 909
foreshadowing *adj* 909
foresight *n* 510
forestall *v* 132
forestry *n* 371
foretell *v* 511
forethought *n* 510, 864
foretoken *n* 511; *v* 511
forever *adv* 16, 112
forewarn *v* 510, 668
foreword *n* 64
forfeit *n* 974; *v* 776
forfeiture *n* 776
for form's sake *adv* 82
forge *n* 386, 691
forge ahead *v* 282
forgery *n* 19, 21, 546
forget *v* 506
forgetful *adj* 506
forgetfulness *n* 506
forgive *v* 918
forgiveness *n* 918
forgiving *adj* 918
forgo *v* 624, 757, 782
for good *adv* 106, 141
for good and all *adv* 141
forgotten *adj* 122, 506
fork *n* 244; *v* 91, 244, 291
forked *adj* 244
for keeps *adv* 106
forking *n* 91, 291
fork out *v* 784
forlorn *adj* 859
form *n* 240
form *n* 7, 21, 54, 80, 329, 448, 569, 697, 998; *v* 54, 56, 60, 144, 161, 240, 557, 852
formal *adj* 80, 82, 240, 242, 383, 579
formal features *n* 567
formality *n* 240, 579
formal speech *n* 586
form an opinion *v* 480
formation *n* 161, 240

formative *adj* 127, 153, 161
formative years *n* 127
form a whole *v* 50
formed *adj* 820
former *adj* 62, 116, 122
formerly *adv* 122
former times *n* 122
formidable *adj* 704
form into a sphere *v* 249
formless *adj* 241
formlessness *n* 241
form part of *v* 56
forms *n* 567
formula *n* 80, 240, 626, 697
formulaic *adj* 80, 626
formulate *v* 963
forsake *v* 624, 732, 782
for sale *adj* 763, 794, 796
forswear *v* 624, 782
forsworn *adj* 782
forte n 698
forth *adv* 282
forthcoming *adj* 152
for the moment *adv* 111
for the most part *adv* 613
for the sake of conformity *adv* 82
for the time being *adv* 106
forthright *adj* 246, 946
forthwith *adv* 132
fortification *n* 717
fortify *v* 159, 717
fortitude *n* 826, 861
fortress *n* 666
fortuitous *adj* 134, 156, 621
fortunate *adj* 134, 734
fortune *n* 152, 156, 621, 734, 803
fortune-teller *n* 513
forum *n* 966
forward *adj* 234; *adv* 282

fossil fuel *n* 388
foster *v* 658
foul *adj* 401, 649, 653
foulness *n* 401
foul play *n* 619
foul smell *n* 401
found *v* 153, 215
foundation *n* 153, 211, 215, 673
founded on *adj* 211
founder *n* 164; *v* 732
foundling *n* 893
found wanting *adj* 651
fount *n* 153
fountain *n* 153
four *n* 95; *adj* 95, 96
four-flusher *n* 548
fourfold *adj* 95, 96
fourfold division *n* 97
fourth *adj* 96
fourthly *adv* 96
fourth part *n* 97
four times *adv* 96
fowls of the air *n* 366
foxy *adj* 702
fracas *n* 59
fraction *n* 100a
fraction *n* 32, 51, 84
fractional *adj* 51, 84
fractional part *n* 100a
fractious *adj* 713, 742
fracture *n* 44, 70
fragile *adj* 160, 203, 328
fragility *n* 160, 328
fragment *n* 32, 51
fragmentary *adj* 51
fragments *n* 596
fragrance *n* 400
fragrant *adj* 377, 400
frail *adj* 158, 160, 203, 328, 605, 651
frailty *n* 158, 160, 328, 575, 605
frame *n* 7, 231, 240, 329; *v* 161, 626, 852
frame of mind *n* 602
framework *n* 329

franchise *n* 748, 760; *v* 760
franchisement *n* 748
frangible *adj* 328
frank *adj* 246, 525, 543, 703
frankness *n* 543, 748
frantic *adj* 173, 503, 824
fraternal *adj* 712, 714
fraternity *n* 11, 709, 888
fraternize *v* 709, 714, 892
fratricide *n* 361
fraud *n* 545, 548, 791
fraudulent *adj* 544
fraught *adj* 52
fraught with danger *adj* 665
fray *v* 331
freak *n* 156; *v* 608, 872
freaked *adj* 173
freakish *adj* 608
freckled *adj* 440, 848
free *v* 672, 705, 748, 750, 927a; *adj* 44, 600, 685, 748, 816
freed *adj* 748, 750, 927a
freedom *n* 748
freedom *n* 600, 672, 738, 760, 927a
freely *adv* 602, 748
free space *n* 180
free spirit *n* 268
free swinging *n* 214
freethinker *n* 989
freethinking *n* 989; *adj* 989
free time *n* 685
free will *n* 600
freeze *v* 376, 383, 385
freezer *n* 387
freezing *adj* 383
freight *n* 190
freighter *n* 271, 273
frenzied *adj* 173, 503

frenzy *n* 503, 825
frequency *n* 136
frequent *adj* 104, 136, 613
frequently *adv* 136
fresh *adj* 123, 428, 435, 505
freshen *v* 338, 689
freshness *n* 123
fresh wind *n* 349
fret *n* 828; *v* 378, 832
fretful *adj* 684
fretwork *n* 219
friability *n* 330
friction *n* 331
friction *n* 179, 719
fridge *n* 387
friend *n* 890
friend *n* 711, 912, 977
friendliness *n* 888, 897
friendly *adj* 707, 714, 721, 888, 892
friendship *n* 888
friendship *n* 714
fright *n* 860
frighten *v* 909
frightened *adj* 860
frightening *adj* 909
frightful *adj* 830
frightfully *adv* 31
frightfulness *n* 846
frigid *adj* 158, 383
frigidaire *n* 387
frigidity *n* 383
frills *n* 847
fringe *n* 231
frippery *n* 643, 851
frisk *n* 309; *v* 309
frisky *adj* 309, 682
fritter away time *v* 683
fritter one's money *v* 818
frivolity *n* 4, 209, 499
frivolous *adj* 4, 477, 499, 608, 643
frizz *v* 248
frizzle *v* 248, 258

from all points of the
  compass *adv* 180
from bad to worse *adv*
  835
from beginning to end
  adv 52
from first to last *adv* 52
from head to foot *adv*
  52
from pole to pole *adv*
  180
from side to side *adv*
  314
from the beginning *adv*
  66
from the bottom of one's
  heart *adv* 821
from the four corners of
  the world *adv* 180
from this time *adv* 121
from time to time *adv*
  136
from top to bottom *adv*
  52
front *n* 234
front *n* 719; *v* 234; *adj*
  234
frontage *n* 234
frontal *adj* 234
frontier *n* 233
fronting *adj* 237
frontispiece *n* 64, 234
front rank *n* 234
frost-bitten *adj* 383
frosted *adj* 426, 430
frostiness *n* 430
frosty *adj* 383
froth *n* 353; *v* 353
frothy *adj* 353
frown *v* 837, 900, 901a
frown upon *v* 932
frozen *adj* 381, 383,
  385
fructification *n* 161
fructify *v* 168, 658, 734
frugal *adj* 817, 953
frugality *n* 817
fruit *n* 154, 367

fruitful *adj* 168
fruitfulness *n* 168
fruition *n* 161
fruitless *adj* 158, 645,
  732
frustrate *v* 706
frustrated *adj* 732
frustration *n* 509
fry *v* 384
fuel *n* 388
fuel *v* 388
fuel oil *n* 388
fugitive *n* 268, 623; *adj*
  623
fulfill *v* 52, 161, 168,
  729, 772, 926
fulfilled *adj* 52
fulfillment *n* 161, 729,
  731, 772
fulfill oneself *v* 731
full *adj* 31, 50, 52, 52,
  404, 729
full-blown *adj* 194
full circle *n* 311
full-flavored *adj* 392,
  394
full grown *adj* 131,
  192, 194
fullness *n* 31, 52, 131
full of incident *adj* 151
full turn *n* 311
fully *adv* 31, 52
fulminate *v* 404
fulsome *adj* 401
fumble *v* 61, 699
fumbler *n* 701
fume *n* 398, 401; *v* 173,
  382, 825, 900
fumigate *v* 652
fuming *adj* 434, 824
fun *n* 842
function *n* 170, 625,
  926, 998; *v* 680, 746
functional *adj* 625, 644
functionary *n* 694, 758
fund *n* 636
fundamental *adj* 5,
  211, 215

fundamentally *adv* 31
fundamental part *n* 211
funds *n* 800
funeral *n* 363; *adj* 363
funeral rites *n* 363
funereal *adj* 363
fungus *n* 663
funish *v* 784
funnel *n* 350, 351
funny *adj* 853
funnyman *n* 844
fur *n* 223
furcation *n* 291
furious *adj* 173, 382,
  825
furiously *adv* 31
furnace *n* 386
furnish *v* 637, 673
furor *n* 825
furrow *n* 259
furrow *v* 259
furrowed *adj* 259
further *adv* 37
furtherance *n* 707
furthermore *adv* 37
furtive *adj* 528
fury *n* 173, 825, 980
fuse *v* 43, 48, 384
fusion *n* 48, 384, 709
fuss *n* 315, 682; *v* 682,
  825
fussy *adj* 682, 825, 868
fustian *n* 577
fustiness *n* 401
fusty *adj* 401
futile *adj* 158, 645
futility *n* 645
future *n* 117, 152; *adj*
  121
future events *n* 152
futurism *n* 123

G

gab *v* 584
gad about *v* 266
gadding *adj* 266
gadding about *n* 266
gag *v* 403, 581

gaggle *v* 412
gain *n* 618, 658, 775; *v* 775
gainful *adj* 775
gain ground *v* 282
gain knowledge *v* 539
gain on *v* 286
gainsay *v* 536, 708
gait *n* 264
galaxy *n* 318
gale *n* 349
gall *v* 378, 869
gallant *adj* 861, 894
gallantry *n* 861
gallimaufry *n* 41
gallop *v* 111
galvanism *n* 824
galvanize *v* 824
gamble *n* 156; *v* 621
gambler *n* 621
gambling *n* 156, 621
game *n* 366, 620, 857; *adj* 604, 604a
gamester *n* 621
gaming *n* 156
gander *n* 373
gang *n* 72, 712
gaol *n* 752
gaoler *n* 753
gap *n* 70, 196, 198, 260
gape *v* 198, 260, 455
gaping *adj* 208, 260
garb *n* 225; *v* 225
garble *v* 523, 583
garden *v* 371, 371
gardening *n* 371
garish *adj* 428, 851, 882
garland *n* 247
garner *v* 636
garrison *n* 717; *v* 664
garrote *n* 361; *v* 361
garroter *n* 361
garrulity *n* 584
garrulous *adj* 584
gas *n* 388; *v* 361
gaseity *n* 334
gaseous *adj* 334, 336

gaseousness *n* 334
gash *n* 198
gasification *n* 336
gasify *v* 336
gas lamp *n* 423
gasoline *n* 356, 388
gasp *v* 349, 655, 688
gassing *n* 361
gate *n* 232, 260
gateway *n* 232, 260, 627
gather *v* 72, 258, 775, 789
gathering *n* 72, 712
gathering place *n* 74
gather together *v* 290
gaudiness *n* 851
gaudy *adj* 428, 851, 882
gauge *n* 466
gauging *n* 466
gaunt *adj* 203
gauze *n* 424
gauziness *n* 425
gauzy *adj* 425
gawky *adj* 699
gay *adj* 829, 836
gaze *n* 441
gazette *n* 86
gear *n* 225
Gehenna *n* 982
gelding *n* 373
gelid *adj* 383
gem *n* 648
genealogy *n* 69, 166
general *adj* 78, 613
generality *n* 78
generalization *n* 78
generalize *v* 78
generally *adv* 613
general public *n* 372, 876
generalship *n* 722
generate *v* 161, 168
generation *n* 11, 108, 161, 163
generative *adj* 153, 161, 168
generator *n* 164

generic *adj* 78
generosity *n* 784, 816, 906, 942
generous *adj* 784, 816, 906, 942
genesis *n* 66, 153, 161
genial *adj* 382, 602, 829, 888, 892
geniality *n* 602, 836
genius *n* 698, 700, 872
genius for *n* 698
genteel *adj* 852
gentility *n* 578, 852, 875, 894
gentle *adj* 174, 275, 405, 721, 740
gentleman *n* 373
gentlemanly *adj* 894
gentleness *n* 174, 740
gentlewoman *n* 374
genuflect *v* 308
genuflection *n* 308
genuine *adj* 494, 648, 922, 960
genuineness *n* 960
genus *n* 75
geography *n* 183
geology *n* 358
germ *n* 66, 153
germinate *v* 194, 367
gestation *n* 161
gesticulate *v* 550
gesticulation *n* 550
gesture *n* 550; *v* 550
get *v* 775, 795, 810
get a footing *v* 184
get a head start *v* 132
get along *v* 282, 736
get back *v* 790
get back to basics *v* 849
get better *v* 658
get between *v* 228
get closer to *v* 286
get close to *v* 286
get down *v* 306
get down to particulars *v* 79
get going *v* 66, 276, 284

get hold of *v* 775, 789
get into *v* 827
get into print *v* 531
get on *v* 282
get one's wind *v* 687
get over *v* 660
get ready *v* 673
get red in the face *v* 434
get rid of *v* 297, 776
get the scent of *v* 527
get through *v* 67
get to *v* 292
get to the heart of *v* 222
get under way *v* 293
get up *v* 305
get well *v* 660
ghost *n* 362, 980; 443
ghostlike *adj* 980
ghostly *adj* 976, 980
ghoul *n* 980
giant *n* 192
gibberish *n* 517
gibes *n* 856
giddy *adj* 499
gift *n* 698, 763, 775, 784
gigantic *adj* 31, 159, 192, 206
giggle *n* 838; *v* 838
gimmicky *adj* 643
gird *v* 43, 227
girdle *n* 232, 247
girl *n* 129, 374
girlfriend *n* 897
girlhood *n* 127
girlish *adj* 129
gist *n* 5, 516
give *n* 325; *v* 324, 325, 763, 784, 816
give a free rein *v* 738
give a hearing to *v* 418
give an account *v* 527
give and take *v* 148, 774, 794
give a new turn to *v* 140
give assent *v* 484
give assistance *v* 707
give a start to *v* 276

give audience to *v* 418
give away *v* 784
give back *v* 790
give birth to *v* 163, 359
give counsel *v* 695
give counsel to *v* 695
give credence to 484
give energy *v* 171
give entrance to *v* 296
give evidence *v* 467
give fight *v* 722
give help *v* 707
give in *v* 82, 360
give it a shot *v* 602
given *adj* 474, 514
give no quarter *v* 361
give notice *v* 668
given time *n* 134
given up *adj* 782
give offense *v* 830
give oneself airs *v* 878
give one's word *v* 768
give out *v* 732, 784
give out a smell *v* 398
give out sound *v* 402
give pleasure *v* 377
giver *n* 784
give rise to *v* 153
give satisfaction *v* 952
give security *v* 768, 771
give up *v* 624, 757, 782, 790
give up hope *v* 859
give up the ghost *v* 360
give way *v* 160, 328
give way to *v* 881
giving *n* 784
glacial *adj* 383
glaciation *n* 385
gladden *v* 829, 836
gladdening *adj* 836
glade *n* 252
gladness *n* 827
gladsome *adj* 827, 829
glance *n* 441
glance around *v* 441
glare *v* 420, 441
glaring *adj* 428, 446

glaringly *adv* 31
glass *n* 389
glasses *n* 445
glassy *adj* 255, 420
glaze *v* 255
gleam *n* 420; *v* 420
glee *n* 827
gleeful *adj* 836
glen *n* 252
glib *adj* 584
glide *v* 264, 267
glider *n* 273
gliding *n* 267
glimmer *v* 420, 422, 446
glimmering *n* 420
glimpse *n* 441
glint *n* 420
glisten *v* 420
glitter *v* 420
gloat over *v* 377
globe *n* 249, 318
globe-trotter *n* 268
globular *adj* 249
globularity *n* 249
globule *n* 249
gloom *n* 837
gloominess *n* 422
gloomy *adj* 421, 422, 837, 901a
glorified *adj* 981
glorified spirit *n* 977
glorify *v* 883, 990, 991
glory *n* 420, 981
gloss *n* 255, 522; *v* 522
glossary *n* 562
gloss over *v* 458, 477
glossy *adj* 255, 420
glow *n* 382, 420, 574; *v* 382
glower *v* 900
glowing *adj* 382, 434, 574, 824
glue *v* 46
gluey *adj* 352
glut *n* 869; *v* 641, 869
glutinosity *n* 352
glutinous *adj* 327, 352

glutted *adj* 869
glutton *n* 957
gluttonous *adj* 957
gluttony *n* 957
gnarled *adj* 256
gnash *v* 900
gnaw *v* 298, 378
gnome *n* 980
go *v* 264, 293, 302, 449
go about *v* 218
go adrift *v* 279
go after *v* 117, 281, 622
goal *n* 67, 620
go along with *v* 709
go amiss *v* 732
go around *v* 247, 311
go ashore *v* 342
go astray *v* 279, 495
go away *v* 293, 302
go back *v* 287
go back to *v* 104
go bad *v* 653, 659
gobble *v* 412
gobble up *v* 957
go before *v* 116, 280
go beserk *v* 173
go-between *n* 534, 631, 724
go beyond *v* 303
go boating *v* 267
go by *v* 109
go by the rules *v* 82
god *n* 976, 979
goddess *n* 979
godhead *n* 976
godless *adj* 989
godliness *n* 987
godly *adj* 976, 987
go down *v* 306, 659
go downhill *v* 659, 735
godsend *n* 618
go forth *v* 293
go for the bait *v* 547
goggle-eyed *adj* 443
goggle eyes *n* 443
goggles *n* 445
go half way *v* 628
go halves *v* 91; *v* 778

go hand in hand with *v* 178
go hard with *v* 732
going *n* 264
going back *n* 145
going hungry *n* 956
going on *adj* 53, 151
go into hysterics *v* 825
gold *adj* 435, 439
golden *adj* 435, 734
golden dreams *n* 515
golden mean *n* 29, 628, 736
golden opportunity *n* 134
golden rule *n* 697
golden years *n* 128
go mad *v* 503, 825
gone *adj* 2, 122, 360
gone bad *adj* 397, 653
gone by *adj* 122, 124
gone to waste *adj* 638
good *n* 618
good *adj* 52, 394, 618, 648, 922, 931, 944, 977
good behavior *n* 894
goodbye *n* 293
good chance *n* 472
good fellowship *n* 892
good fortune *n* 618, 731
good head *n* 502
good health *n* 654
good luck *n* 618, 621, 731
goodly *adj* 31
good man *n* 948
good manners *n* 894
goodness *n* 648
goodness *n* 618, 829, 922, 944
goods *n* 780, 798
good samaritan *n* 906
good taste *n* 578, 850
good will *n* 602, 888
gooey *adj* 396
go off *v* 173
go on *v* 106, 143

go on forever *v* 104, 112
go on vacation *v* 687
go out *v* 142
go over *v* 218
go over again *v* 104
go over the same ground *v* 104
go pit-a-pat *v* 315
gore *v* 260
gorge *n* 198; *v* 641, 869, 957
gorged *adj* 869
gorgeous *adj* 428, 845
gorgeousness *n* 845
gormandizing *n* 957; *adj* 957
go round about *v* 629
gory *adj* 361, 653
go shopping *v* 795
go side by side *v* 120
gossamer *n* 205
gossamery *adj* 329
gossip *n* 455, 532, 588; *v* 588
gossipy *adj* 588
go straight *v* 246, 628
go the way of all flesh *v* 360
go through *v* 151, 302
go to *v* 278
go to bed *v* 687
go to press *v* 591
go to seed *v* 659
go to sleep *v* 687
go to the dogs *v* 162, 735, 804
go to the law *v* 969
go to waste *v* 659
go to wrack and ruin *v* 162
gouge *n* 262; *v* 252
go up *v* 305
govern *v* 693, 737
governess *n* 753
government *n* 693
governor *n* 694, 753
go wild *v* 173
gown *n* 999

go wrong *v* 732
grab *v* 379
grace *n* 242, 578, 845, 850, 918, 987
graceful *adj* 578, 845
gracefulness *n* 242, 578, 845
graceless *adj* 579
gracious *adj* 894
graciously *adv* 602
graciousness *n* 894
gradation *n* 26, 58, 69
grade *n* 26, 58, 71, 217, 305, 306
grade crossing *n* 219
gradual *adj* 26, 69, 275, 685
gradually *adv* 26, 69, 275
graduate *v* 60, 69
graduation *n* 60
graft *v* 184, 300
grain *n* 5, 256, 329, 330
graininess *n* 330
grammar *n* 567
grammar *n* 542
grammar book *n* 567
grammarian *n* 567
grammatical *adj* 567
grand *adj* 574, 642, 882
grandchildren *n* 167
grandeur *n* 875
grandfather *n* 130, 166
grandiloquence *n* 577
grandiloquent *adj* 577
grandiose *adj* 577
grandmother *n* 130, 166
grandsire *n* 130, 166
grant *n* 784; *v* 529, 760, 762, 783, 784
grantee *n* 785
granter *n* 784
granular *adj* 330
granularity *n* 330
granulate *v* 330
granulation *n* 330
granule *n* 32

graphic *adj* 518
grapple with *v* 719
grasp *v* 518
grass *n* 367
grassland *n* 344
grassy *adj* 435
grate *v* 330, 378, 410, 414
grateful *adj* 916
grater *n* 330
gratification *n* 827
gratify *v* 829, 831
grating *n* 219, 410; *adj* 410, 414
gratitude *n* 916
gratuity *n* 784
grave *n* 363; *v* 558; *adj* 642, 739, 830
grave clothes *n* 363
gravestone *n* 363
graveyard *n* 363
gravitate *v* 306, 319
gravitate toward *v* 176
gravitation *n* 319
gravitational *adj* 288
gravity *n* 319
gravity *n* 288, 574, 642, 739
gray *n* 432
gray *n* 422; *adj* 128, 422, 428, 429, 432
graybeard *n* 130
gray hairs *n* 128
grayish *adj* 432
grayness *n* 422, 432
graze *v* 199
graze over *v* 379
grazing over *n* 379
grease *n* 355, 356; *v* 255, 332, 355
greasiness *n* 355
greasing *n* 332
greasy *adj* 355
great *adj* 31, 192
greaten *v* 35
greater *adj* 33
greatest *adj* 33
greatly *adv* 31

greatness *n* 31
greatness *n* 33, 192, 873
great waters *n* 341
greed *n* 957
greediness *n* 957
greedy *adj* 789, 819, 957
green *n* 435
green *adj* 123, 127, 435, 674
greenbacks *n* 800
greenhorn *n* 547, 701
greenish *adj* 435
greenish blue *adj* 438
greenness *n* 123, 435
greens *n* 367
gregarious *adj* 892
gregariousness *n* 892
gridiron *n* 219
grief *n* 833
grievance *n* 830
grieve *v* 828, 839
grieve at *v* 833
grievous *adj* 649, 830
grievously *adv* 31
grill *v* 384
grille *n* 219
grim *adj* 830
grimace *v* 243
grime *n* 653
grimy *adj* 653
grin *n* 838; *v* 838
grind *v* 195, 253, 330, 331, 410, 539
grinder *n* 330
grinding *n* 410
grindstone *n* 330
grip *n* 378
gripe *n* 378; *v* 378
grist *n* 637
gristly *adj* 327
grit *n* 327, 330
gritty *adj* 330, 604
grizzled *adj* 432
grizzly *adj* 432
groan *n* 839; *v* 411

groove *n* 259, 613; *v*
 259
grope in the dark *v* 442
gross *adj* 653, 846, 961
grossness *n* 961
grouch *v* 900
ground *n* 181, 211, 215,
 342, 467, 615; *v* 215
grounded on *adj* 211
groundless *adj* 4
grounds *n* 342, 344,
 467
groundswell *n* 315
groundwork *n* 60, 64,
 153, 211, 673
group *n* 72, 372, 416,
 417, 712; *v* 60, 72
groupings *n* 60
grove *n* 252
grovel *v* 207, 275
groveling *n* 886; *adj*
 207, 435, 886
grow *v* 35, 144, 194,
 282, 367, 734
grow dim *v* 422
grow from *v* 154
growing *adj* 35
grow into *v* 144
growl *v* 412, 900
growling *n* 412
grown up *adj* 131
growth *n* 35, 144, 161,
 194, 250, 282, 365
grow up *v* 131
grudge *n* 907, 921; *v*
 819
grudgingly *adv* 603
gruesome *adj* 846
gruff *adj* 254, 410
grumble *v* 407, 411,
 832
grumbling *n* 407
grumpy *adj* 901a
grunt *v* 412
guarantee *n* 768, 771; *v*
 768, 771
guard *n* 717, 753; *v*
 664, 670, 717

guard against *v* 717
guarded *adj* 459, 585,
 864
guardian *n* 664, 753,
 977
guardian angel *n* 977
guardianship *n* 717
guarding *n* 670
guerilla *n* 361
guess *n* 514; *v* 514
guesswork *n* 514
guffaw *n* 838
guidance *n* 537, 692,
 693, 695
guide *n* 524, 527, 540,
 694; *v* 537, 692, 693
guidebook *n* 527
guiding *adj* 693
guile *n* 544, 702
guileless *adj* 703, 946
guilelessness *n* 946
guiling *n* 545
guillotine *v* 361
guilt *n* 947
guilt *n* 649, 961
guiltiness *n* 947
guiltless *adj* 946
guiltlessness *n* 946, 960
guilty *adj* 947, 961
guilty verdict *n* 971
guise *n* 448
gulf *n* 343
gulf *n* 198, 343
gull *n* 486, 547; *v* 545
gulley *n* 259
gullibility *n* 486
gullible *adj* 486, 547
gully *n* 350
gulosity *n* 957
gulp *v* 298
gulp down *v* 298
gum *n* 356a
gummy *adj* 327, 352,
 356a
gun down *v* 361
gunshot *n* 197
gurgle *v* 348, 353, 408
gurgling *n* 353

guru *n* 994
gush *n* 295, 348; *v* 295,
 348, 584
gush out *v* 295
gust *n* 349; *v* 349
gusto *n* 390
gut *v* 162
guts *n* 221, 861
gutsy *adj* 861
gutter *n* 259, 350
guttural *adj* 410
guzzle *v* 957, 959
gymnasium *n* 728
gypsy *n* 268
gyration *n* 312

H

habit *n* 613
habit *n* 5, 820
habitat *n* 189
habitation *n* 189
habitation *n* 189
habitual *adj* 82, 104,
 136, 613
habitually *adv* 136, 613
habituate *v* 613
hack *v* 44
hackneyed *adj* 598
hack up *v* 201
Hades *n* 982
haggard *adj* 203, 688
haggle *v* 794
hagiography *n* 983
hagiological *adj* 983
hail *v* 586
hair *n* 205
hair's breadth *n* 197
hairy *adj* 256
halcyon *adj* 721
hale *adj* 654
half a dozen *n* 98
half a hundred *n* 98
half and half *adj* 27, 41
half measures *n* 628
half-moon *n* 245
half-starved *adj* 956
halfway *adj* 68; *adv* 68
half-witted *adj* 499

hallowed *adj* 976

halo *n* 420

halt *n* 142, 685, 687; *v* 142, 160, 265, 275

halve *v* 91

halved *adj* 91

halving *n* 91

hammer *v* 104

hammered instruments *n* 417

hamper *v* 706

hamstring *v* 158

hand *n* 236, 372, 590, 590, 631; *v* 784

handbook *n* 527, 593

handful *n* 25, 32

handicap *v* 706

hand in hand *adv* 88

handle *n* 564; *v* 379, 677

handling *n* 379

hand of death *n* 360

hand over *v* 270, 783

hands *n* 269

handsome *adj* 845

handwriting *n* 590

handy *adj* 197, 673, 698

hang *v* 214, 361

hang a turn *v* 140

hang back *v* 683

hang by a thread *v* 665

hanging *n* 361; *adj* 214

hanging down *n* 214

hang in there *v* 604a

hang it up *v* 624

hangman *n* 975

hang over *v* 152

hang together *v* 46, 178

hap *n* 156; *v* 156

haphazard *adj* 139, 156

haphazardness *n* 139

hapless *adj* 735

happen *v* 1, 151

happening *n* 8, 151; *adj* 151

happily *adv* 827

happiness *n* 618, 827

happy *adj* 23, 134, 827, 836

happy-go-lucky *adj* 674

harangue *n* 537, 582; *v* 582

harass *v* 830

harbinger *n* 64, 512, 534

hard *adj* 159, 323, 376, 397, 704, 739, 830

hard and fast law *n* 80

hard as a rock *adj* 323

hard as nails *adj* 323

hard by *adv* 197

hard cash *n* 800

hard coal *n* 388

harden *v* 48, 159, 321, 323, 613

hardening *n* 321, 385

hard-featured *adj* 846

hard-hearted *adj* 914a

hard-heartedness *n* 914a

hardihood *n* 861

hardiness *n* 159

hardly *adv* 32, 137

hardly ever *adv* 137

hardness *n* 323

hardness of hearing *n* 419

hardness of heart *n* 951

hard of hearing *adj* 419

hardship *n* 735

hard task *n* 704

hard times *n* 735

hard to please *adj* 868

hard up *adj* 804

hardy *adj* 159, 654

harlequin *n* 501

harlot *n* 962

harm *n* 619; *v* 619, 649, 659, 828, 923

harmful *adj* 619, 649, 657, 663

harmfulness *n* 649

harmless *adj* 158

harmonious *adj* 23,

242, 413, 416, 428, 714

harmoniousness *n* 413

harmonious sounds *n* 415

harmonize *v* 23, 82, 413

harmonize with *v* 714

harmony *n* 23, 58, 242, 413, 415, 709, 714, 721, 888

harness *v* 43, 225

harping *n* 104; *adj* 104

harp on *v* 104

harpy *n* 980

harrow *v* 371, 830

harsh *adj* 410, 414, 579, 739, 830, 955

harshness *n* 410, 414, 739

hart *n* 373

harvest *n* 154, 618, 775

harvest time *n* 126

hash *n* 59

haste *n* 684

haste *n* 132, 863; *v* 274, 684

hasten *v* 132, 274, 310, 682, 684

hastily *adv* 132

hasty *adj* 684, 863

hatch *n* 260; *v* 161, 558, 626

hatchet man *n* 936

hate *n* 898

hate *n* 907; *v* 867, 898

hateful *adj* 649, 830, 898, 907

hating *adj* 898

hatred *n* 867, 889, 898, 907

hatred of mankind *n* 911

haughtiness *n* 878, 885

haughty *adj* 878, 885

haul *n* 190; *v* 190, 285

hauling *n* 285

haunt *n* 74, 189

haunted *adj* 980

haunt one's thoughts *v* 505

have *v* 777

have a bad name *v* 874

have a bad smell *v* 401

have a defect *v* 651

have affection for *v* 897

have a hand in *v* 153, 682, 709

have a knack for *v* 698

have an acquaintance with *v* 888

have an odor *v* 398

have a perfume *v* 400

have a say *v* 175

have a short memory *v* 506

have a soft spot in one's heart *v* 822

have a temper *v* 901

have a true ring *v* 494

have charge of *v* 693

have confidence in *v* 484

have done with *v* 678

have enough *v* 639

have faith *v* 987

have faith in *v* 484, 858

have free play *v* 170

have had its day *v* 124

have in common *v* 778

have in hand *v* 777

have input *v* 175

have in sight *v* 441

have in store for *v* 152

have its seat in *v* 183

have leisure *v* 685

have no bearing upon *v* 10

have no chance *v* 471

have no connection with *v* 10

have no curiosity *v* 456

have no heart for *v* 866

have no idea *v* 491

have no interest in *v* 823

have no limits *v* 104

have no motive *v* 615a

have no odor *v* 399

have no pity for *v* 914a

have no preference *v* 609a

have no relation to *v* 10

have no taste for *v* 867

have nothing to do with *v* 10

have occasion for *v* 630

have one's act together *v* 502

have one's head in the clouds *v* 827

have precedence *v* 62

have priority *v* 280

have pull *adj* 288

have qualms *v* 485

have recourse to *v* 677

have scope *v* 748

have seen its day *v* 124

have the advantage *v* 28

have the lead *v* 208

have the means *v* 632

have the right *v* 924

have the virtue of *v* 944

have to do with *v* 9

have too high an opinion of oneself *v* 889

have to oneself *v* 777

have two meanings *v* 520

have words with *v* 713

having a right to *adj* 924

having no right to *adj* 925

havoc *n* 162

hawk *v* 763, 796

hawker *n* 797

hazard *n* 156, 665; *v* 621, 665

hazard a suggestion *v* 514

hazardous *adj* 665

haze *n* 353, 422

hazel *adj* 433

haziness *n* 422, 426, 447, 475

hazy *adj* 353, 422, 426

head *n* 66, 353, 372, 450, 564, 694, 745; *v* 62, 66, 280; *adj* 210

head for the hills *v* 623

heading *n* 64, 66, 75, 280, 564

headland *n* 250

headlines *n* 532

headlong *adj* 684, 863

head of the column *n* 234

headquarters *n* 74

heads or tails *n* 156

headstone *n* 363

headstrong *adj* 606

headway *n* 282

heal *v* 660, 662

healing *n* 660

health *n* 654

health *n* 159

healthful *adj* 654, 656

healthfulness *n* 656

healthiness *n* 656

healthy *adj* 654, 656

heap *n* 31, 72, 192

hear *v* 418

hear a cause *v* 967

hearer *n* 418

hearing *n* 418

hearing *adj* 418

hearsay *n* 532

hearse *n* 363

heart *n* 5, 68, 208, 221, 222, 372, 574, 820

heart and soul *adv* 821

heart-felt *adj* 821

hearth *n* 386

heartless *adj* 383

heartsick *adj* 837

hearty *adj* 654, 836

heat *n* 382

heat *v* 382, 384

heated *adj* 382, 384

heater *n* 386

heath *n* 344

heathen *n* 984, 989

heating *n* 384

heave *v* 276, 284, 307

heaven *n* 981

heavenly *adj* 318, 829, 976, 981

heavenly bodies *n* 318

heavenly kingdom *n* 981

heavenly spirit *n* 977

heavens *n* 180, 318

heaviness *n* 202, 319, 837, 843

heavy *n* 202; *adj* 172, 194, 319, 683

heavy as lead *adj* 319

heavy heart *n* 837

heavy news *n* 830

hebetude *n* 499

heckle *v* 830

hedge *n* 232

hedge in *v* 229

hedonist *n* 954a

heed *n* 457, 459, 864; *v* 418, 457, 928

heedful *adj* 451, 457, 459, 864

heedfulness *n* 864

heeding *n* 418; *adj* 928

heedless *adj* 460, 506, 863

heedlessness *n* 458, 460, 863

heel *n* 211; *v* 279

he him *n* 373

height *n* 206

height *n* 26, 125, 210, 307

heighten *v* 35, 206, 307, 549, 835

heightening *n* 835

heinous *adj* 846

heir *n* 167

heirs *n* 121, 167

helicopter *n* 273

hell *n* 982

hellish *adj* 978, 982

helmsman *n* 269, 694

help *n* 644, 662, 707, 746, 784, 834; *v* 215, 644, 707, 746, 784, 834

helper *n* 707, 711, 746, 977

helpful *adj* 644, 707, 888

helpfulness *n* 644, 910

helpless *adj* 158

helplessness *n* 158

help oneself to *v* 789

helter skelter *adv* 59

hem *n* 231; *v* 43, 231, 258

hem and haw *v* 149, 583

hemi- *adj* 91

hem in *v* 227

hemisphere *n* 181

hemorrhage *n* 299

hen *n* 374

hence *adv* 155

henceforth *adv* 121

henchman *n* 746

her *n* 374

herald *n* 64, 534; *v* 116, 280

herb *n* 367

herbaceous *adj* 367

herbage *n* 367

herbal *adj* 367, 369

Herculean *adj* 159

herculean *adj* 686

herculean task *n* 704

herd *n* 876; *v* 72

here *adv* 186

hereabouts *adv* 183

hereafter *n* 121, 152; *adv* 121

here and there *adv* 182, 183

here below *adv* 318

hereditary *adj* 5, 154

heredity *n* 167

heresy *n* 984

heretic *n* 487, 984

heretical *adj* 984

heretofore *adv* 122

herewith *adv* 88, 632

heritage *n* 11, 121, 122

hermetically sealed *adj* 261

hermit *n* 893, 955

hero *n* 948

heroic *adj* 861

heroism *n* 861

hero worship *n* 991

hesitancy *n* 485, 605

hesitant *adj* 485, 583, 603, 605

hesitate *v* 475, 485, 583, 603, 605

hesitating *adj* 485

hesitation *n* 485, 583, 603, 605

heterodox *adj* 984

heterodoxy *n* 984

heterogeneity *n* 10, 16a, 291

heterogeneous *adj* 10, 15, 41, 81

hew *v* 44, 240, 557

hiatus *n* 198

hiburnal *adj* 383

hidden *adj* 447, 526, 528, 533, 571

hidden meaning *n* 526

hide *n* 223; *v* 442, 447, 528, 862, 893

hideous *adj* 830, 846

hiding *n* 528, 893

hiding place *n* 189, 530, 666

hie *v* 264, 274

hierarchical *adj* 995

hierarchy *n* 995

hieroglyph *n* 561

high *adj* 206, 410, 838, 959

high birth *n* 875

high-born *adj* 875

high caliber *n* 33

higher *adj* 33

highest *adj* 210

high-flown *adj* 577

high living *n* 954

highly seasoned *adj* 392

high-minded *adj* 878

highmindedness *n* 875

high note *n* 409

high price *n* 814
high-principled *adj* 939
high relief *n* 250
high seas *n* 341
high sounding *adj* 577,
882
high spirits *n* 836
high-strung *adj* 825
high time *n* 134
hike *n* 266
hill *n* 217, 250, 305,
306
hinder *v* 179, 233, 261,
275, 647, 704, 706,
708, 751, 761
hindmost *adj* 235
hindquarters *n* 235
hindrance *n* 706
hindrance *n* 177, 179
hinge *n* 43, 153
hinge upon *v* 154
hint *n* 505, 527, 550; *v*
505, 527
hinterland *n* 235
hip *adj* 563
hire *n* 812; *v* 788
hirsute *adj* 256
hiss *v* 409, 412
hissing *n* 409; *adj* 409
historian *n* 553
historiographer *n* 553
history *n* 122, 551
histrionic *adj* 599
hit *n* 276
hitch *n* 706; *v* 43, 315
hither *adv* 278
hitherto *adv* 122
hit on *v* 612
hit the bottle *v* 959
hit the road *v* 264, 266
hit upon *v* 480a
hive *n* 189, 691
hoard *n* 636
hoard away *v* 636
hoarse *adj* 405, 410
hoarseness *n* 405
hoary *adj* 124, 432
hoax *n* 545

hobble *n* 706; *v* 275
hobgoblin *n* 980
hobo *n* 268
hocus-pocus *n* 993
hodgepodge *n* 59
hoe *v* 371
hog *n* 957; *v* 957
hoist *v* 307
hold *n* 215; *v* 46, 54,
142, 151, 215, 265,
484, 751, 777, 781,
873
hold a conversation *v*
588
hold a course for *v* 278
hold back *v* 616, 623,
636, 819
holder *n* 191, 779
hold fast *v* 781
hold forth *v* 537
hold in disrespect *v* 929
holding *n* 777, 781
holding back *n* 603
hold on *v* 143
hold one's tongue *v* 403,
585
hold out *v* 763
hold to *v* 602
hold up *v* 143, 215, 235,
707
hole *n* 182, 189, 260,
351, 530
hole puncher *n* 262
holiday *n* 685, 687
holiness *n* 987
holler *v* 404, 411
hollow *n* 208, 252; *v*
208, 252; *adj* 4, 252,
880
hollowed out *adj* 252
hollowness *n* 4, 880
hollows *n* 221
holm *n* 346
holocaust *n* 361
holy *adj* 976, 987
homage *n* 743, 926,
928, 990
home *n* 189; *adj* 221

homeless *adj* 185
homeliness *n* 576, 846,
849
homely *adj* 576, 846,
849, 876
homespun *adj* 329, 576
homestead *n* 189
homework *n* 673
homey *adj* 576
homicidal *adj* 361
homicide *n* 361
homily *n* 537
homogeneity *n* 9, 16, 42
homogeneous *adj* 16,
42
honest *adj* 246, 543,
703, 922, 939, 946,
960
honesty *n* 543, 703,
939, 946, 960
honey *n* 899
honeyed *adj* 396
honey-mouthed *adj* 933
honor *n* 733, 873, 877,
922, 928, 990; *v* 883,
928, 931
honorable *adj* 246, 543,
772, 875, 878, 939
honored *adj* 873
honorific *adj* 883, 990
honoring *adj* 990
hoodwink *v* 442, 545
hook *n* 245; *v* 43, 789
hooked *adj* 244, 245
hoop *n* 247; *v* 411
hoot *v* 411
hop *n* 309; *v* 309
hope *n* 858
hope *n* 507; *v* 858
hope for *v* 507, 858
hopeful *adj* 472, 858
hopeless *adj* 645, 704,
859
hopelessness *n* 859
hopelessness *n* 471,
645, 837
horde *n* 72
horizon *n* 196, 213

horizontal *adj* 213, 251, 308
horizontality *n* 213
horizontally *adv* 213
horrible *adj* 649, 830
horribly *adv* 31
horrid *adj* 649, 830
horrified *adj* 860
horrify *v* 830
horrifying *adj* 982
horror *n* 860, 867, 898
horror-stricken *adj* 860
horseback riding *n* 266
horseman *n* 268
horsemanship *n* 266
horse-shoe *n* 245
horsewoman *n* 268
horticultural *adj* 369
horticulture *n* 371
hose *n* 348, 350
hospitable *adj* 816, 892
hospitality *n* 816
host *n* 72, 102
hostile *adj* 14, 24, 383, 708, 889, 907
hostilities *n* 173, 722
hostility *n* 708, 889
hot *adj* 382, 392, 434, 824
hot air *n* 517
hotchpotch *n* 41
hotheaded *adj* 825
hotness *n* 392
hot pink *adj* 434
hot-tempered *adj* 901
hourly *adv* 136
house *v* 184, 664
housebreak *v* 370
house-breaker *n* 792
housebroken *adj* 370
house of correction *n* 975
house of god *n* 1000
housing *n* 189
hover *v* 152, 206, 305
hover about *v* 264
hover around *v* 264
how *adv* 627

howbeit *adv* 30
however *adv* 30
howl *n* 411, 839; *v* 411, 412
howling *n* 412
hub *n* 222
hubbub *n* 315, 404, 411
huckster *n* 797
huddle *v* 72
hue *n* 428
hue and cry *n* 411, 669
hueless *adj* 429
hug *n* 902; *v* 46
huge *adj* 31, 192, 206
hugeness *n* 192
hulky *adj* 192
hullabaloo *n* 411
hum *n* 405; *v* 405, 407, 412
human *adj* 372
human being *n* 372
human community *n* 372
humane *adj* 906
humaneness *n* 910
humanitarian *n* 910; *adj* 372, 910
humanitarianism *n* 910
humanities *n* 560
humanity *n* 372, 906
humankind *n* 372
human race *n* 372
human species *n* 372
humble *adj* 34, 725, 879, 881, 987
humbleness *n* 879
humbly *adv* 881
humbug *n* 548
humdrum *adj* 275, 598, 841
humid *adj* 337, 339
humidity *n* 339
humiliate *v* 879
humility *n* 879
humility *n* 881, 987
hummocky *adj* 250
humor *n* 5, 176, 602,

608, 820, 842; *v* 707, 760
humorist *n* 844
humorous *adj* 842
hump *n* 250
hunch *n* 250, 477
hundred *n* 98
hunger *n* 865
hungry *adj* 865, 956
hunt *v* 361
hunting *n* 361
hurdle *v* 309
hurl *v* 284
hurly-burly *n* 315
hurrah *v* 838
hurricane *n* 349
hurried *adj* 684, 825
hurry *n* 684; *v* 132, 274, 310, 684
hurt *n* 378, 619; *v* 378, 619, 649, 659, 828, 830
hurtful *adj* 619, 649, 830
hurtfulness *n* 649
hurtle *v* 276, 309
hurtle over *v* 310
husband *n* 903; *v* 636, 670, 817
husbandry *n* 371, 817
hush *n* 403; *v* 174, 265, 403
hushed *adj* 403
husky *adj* 405
hussy *n* 962
hustle *n* 682; *v* 276, 315, 682
hybrid *n* 41; *adj* 41
hydrous *adj* 337
hygienic *adj* 656
hyperbola *n* 245
hyperbole *n* 549
hyperbolic *adj* 549
hypercritical *adj* 868
hypercriticism *n* 868
hypertension *n* 315
hypocrisy *n* 988
hypocrite *n* 548, 988

hypocritical *adj* 544
hypothesis *n* 514
hypothetical *adj* 514
hysterical *adj* 173, 824, 825

I

ice *v* 385
ice box *n* 387
ice chest *n* 387
ice house *n* 387
iciness *n* 383
icing *n* 385
icon *n* 991
iconoclasm *n* 984
iconoclast *n* 165
iconoclastic *adj* 984
icthyology *n* 368
icy *adj* 383
idea *n* 453
idea *n* 451, 515, 516
ideal *n* 650; *adj* 2, 515, 977
ideality *n* 515
idealize *v* 515
ideational *adj* 453
idée fixe *n* 606
identical *adj* 13, 17
identically *adv* 13
identity *n* 13
identity *n* 17, 27
idiocy *n* 499
idiom *n* 521, 566
idiomatic *adj* 79, 521
idiosyncracy *n* 820
idiosyncrasies *n* 5
idiosyncrasy *n* 79, 83, 176
idiosyncratic *adj* 5
idiot *n* 493, 501, 501
idiotic *adj* 499
idle *v* 683; *adj* 681, 683
idleness *n* 681, 683
idler *n* 683
idle talk *n* 588
idol *n* 897, 899, 991
idolatrize *v* 991
idolatrous *adj* 991

idolatrousness *n* 991
idolatry *n* 991
idolatry *n* 897, 990
idolism *n* 991
idolization *n* 991
idolize *v* 897, 990, 991
idolizing *n* 990
idol-worship *n* 991
idol-worshiping *adj* 991
if *adv* 8
iffy *adj* 156
if it so happen *adv* 8
if so *adv* 8
if worst comes to worst *adv* 735
ignite *v* 384
ignoble *adj* 207, 851, 876
ignominious *adj* 874
ignominy *n* 874
ignoramus *n* 493
ignoramus *n* 501
ignorance *n* 491
ignorance *n* 442
ignorant *adj* 435, 442, 491
ignore *v* 460, 773
ill *n* 619; *adj* 649, 655
ill-advised *adj* 499
ill-behaved *adj* 895
ill-bred *adj* 851, 895
ill-breeding *n* 851, 895
ill-conceived *adj* 499
illegal *adj* 964
illegality *n* 964
illegitimacy *n* 925, 964
illegitimate *adj* 925, 964
ill-fashioned *adj* 243
ill-flavored *adj* 395
ill health *n* 655
ill-humored *adj* 901a
illiberal *adj* 32, 943
illiberality *n* 819, 943
illicit *adj* 964
illicitness *n* 964
illiteracy *n* 491
illiterate *n* 493; *adj* 491

ill-judged *adj* 499
ill-judging *adj* 481
ill-made *adj* 243
ill-mannered *adj* 851, 895
ill-natured *adj* 907
illness *n* 655
illogical *adj* 47, 477
illogically *adv* 477
ill-proportioned *adj* 243
ill-qualified *adj* 699
ill repute *n* 874
ill-tempered *adj* 945
ill-timed *adj* 135
ill-treat *v* 739
ill-treatment *n* 649
illuminate *v* 420, 423, 428
illumination *n* 420
illumine *v* 420
ill-use *v* 649
illusion *n* 4, 443, 515, 545
illusory *adj* 4, 515, 545
illustrate *v* 82, 554
illustration *n* 82, 554
illustrative *adj* 82, 518, 554
illustrious *adj* 883
ill will *n* 889, 907
ill wind *n* 649
image *n* 17, 21, 448, 521, 556, 991; *v* 521
imagery *n* 521, 554
imaginable *adj* 470, 515
imaginary *adj* 4, 979
imagination *n* 515
imaginative *adj* 2, 515
imaginativeness *n* 515
imaginative writing *n* 598
imagine *v* 515
imagined *adj* 515
imagistic *adj* 521
imbalance *n* 15, 28, 503
imbalanced *adj* 28

imbecile *n* 493, 501;
adj 499
imbecilic *adj* 499
imbecility *n* 499
imbecility *n* 450a, 497,
499
imbibe *v* 296, 959
imbibition *n* 298
imbue *v* 41, 300, 537
imbued *adj* 820
imitate *v* 19, 680, 788
imitation *n* 19
imitation *n* 21, 554,
556; *adj* 19
imitative *adj* 17, 19,
554
immaculate *adj* 650,
652, 946, 960
immaterial *adj* 4, 317,
643
immateriality *n* 317
immateriality *n* 643
immature *adj* 53, 123,
127, 435, 651, 674
immaturity *n* 53, 123,
651
immeasurability *n* 105
immeasurably *adv* 31
immediate *adj* 132
immediately *adv* 113,
132
immemorial *adj* 124
immense *adj* 31, 104,
192
immensity *n* 31, 192
immerse *v* 300, 310,
337
immersed in *adj* 229
immersion *n* 300, 310
immigrant *n* 268
immigrate *v* 266
immigration *n* 266
imminent *adj* 152, 286
immobile *adj* 172
immobility *n* 141, 150,
172, 265
immobilize *v* 265
immoderately *adv* 31

immodest *adj* 961
immodesty *n* 961
immoral *adj* 923, 940,
945
immorality *n* 923, 940,
945
immortal *adj* 112
immortalize *v* 112
immovability *n* 141,
150, 606
immovable *adj* 150,
606
immune *adj* 748, 927a
immune from *adj* 777a
immunity *n* 748, 777a,
927a, 970
immutability *n* 141, 150
immutable *adj* 110, 150
imp *n* 980
impact *n* 276, 379
impair *v* 659, 848
impairment *n* 638, 659
impale *v* 260
impart *v* 784
impartial *adj* 246, 628,
942
impartiality *n* 942
impart to *v* 527
impassable *adj* 261
impasse *n* 151
impassionate *adj* 383
impassioned *adj* 574,
821, 825, 991
impassive *adj* 456, 823
impassivity *n* 823, 826
impatience *n* 825
impatient *adj* 825, 841
impeach *v* 938, 969
impeachment *n* 938
impeccability *n* 650
impeccable *adj* 650,
946
impede *v* 179, 275, 706
impediment *n* 177, 706
impeding *n* 706
impel *v* 175, 264, 276,
284, 744
impend *v* 121, 152, 909

impending *adj* 121,
152, 286, 507, 909
impenetrability *n* 321,
571
impenetrable *adj* 261,
321, 323, 519, 571
impenetrable to light
adj 426
impenitence *n* 951
impenitent *adj* 951
imperative *adj* 737, 926
imperceptibility *n* 447
imperceptible *adj* 193,
447
imperceptibly *adv* 32
imperfect *adj* 34,
53, 304, 640, 651,
659, 848, 961
imperfection *n* 651
imperfection *n* 28, 34,
53, 304, 640, 945,
961
imperfectly *adv* 32
imperil *v* 665
imperishable *adj* 112
impermanence *n* 111
impermanent *adj* 111
impermeability *n* 321
impermeable *adj* 261,
321
impersonate *v* 19
impersonation *n* 19, 599
impertinence *n* 885,
929
impertinent *adj* 885,
929
imperturbability *n* 826
imperturbable *n* 823;
adj 383, 826
impervious *adj* 261
impervious to light *adj*
426
impetuosity *n* 173, 825,
863
impetuous *adj* 173,
825, 863
impetus *n* 276, 284
impiety *n* 988

impiety n 989
impish adj 980
implacable adj 914a, 919
implant v 300
implantation n 300
implanted adj 5
implausibility n 473
implausible adj 473
implement n 633
implicit adj 526
implied adj 526
implore v 765
implosion n 276
imply v 467, 472, 516
impolite adj 895, 929
impoliteness n 929
import n 516, 642; v 296, 516, 642
importance n 642
importance n 31, 62, 175
important adj 31, 33, 175, 642
importation n 296, 300
importunate adj 765
importune v 765
impose v 741
imposing adj 642, 875, 878
impossibility n 471
impossible adj 471, 704
imposter n 548
imposture n 545
impotence n 158
impotence n 160, 169, 175a
impotent adj 158, 160, 175a
impractical adj 471, 647, 704
impracticality n 471, 647
imprecate v 908
imprecation n 908
impregnability n 664
impregnable adj 159, 664

impregnate v 168, 300
impress v 175, 375, 824
impressibility n 375, 822
impressible adj 324
impression n 375, 453, 591, 821
impressionable adj 822
impressive adj 574, 642
imprint n 569
imprison v 229
inprisoned adj 229, 751
improbability n 473
improbable adj 473
improbity n 940
impromptu adj 612; adv 612
improper adj 499, 568, 647, 923, 945
improper time n 135
impropriety n 568, 579, 647, 925
improve v 282, 648, 658
improved adj 658
improvement n 658
improvement n 282, 618
improvidence n 674
improvident adj 674, 818
improving adj 658
improvisation n 612
improvise v 416, 612, 674
imprudence n 863
imprudent adj 452, 460, 863
impudence n 885, 895, 929
impudent adj 885, 929
impugn v 716
impulse n 276, 612
impulse n 284, 601, 615, 744
impulsion n 284
impulsive adj 149, 612, 825, 863
impulsively adv 612

impulsiveness n 863
impunity n 777a, 927a, 970
impure adj 653, 961
impurity n 961
impurity n 653
imputation n 155, 938
imputative adj 938
impute v 938
impute to v 155
in a bad way adj 659, 735
in abeyance adv 172
inability n 158, 699
in a body adv 50
inabstinence n 954
inaccessible adj 196
in accord adj 714
in accordance with adj 23; adv 82
inaccuracy n 544
inaccurate adj 495, 568, 923
in a column adv 69
inaction n 681
inaction n 623, 683; adj 170, 680
inactive adj 172, 265, 681, 683
inactivity n 683
inactivity n 172, 681
in addition adv 37
inadequacy n 28, 34, 640, 645, 651
inadequate adj 28, 158, 640, 651
inadmissible adj 55
in advance adv 62, 234, 280
in adverse circumstances adj 735
in a fair way to adj 176
in a great measure adv 31
in a jiffy adv 113
in a line adj 69
in all aspects adv 52

in all creation *adv* 318
in all likelihood *adv* 472
in all probability *adv* 472
in a moment *adv* 113
in and out *adv* 248, 314
inane *adj* 497
inanimate *adj* 358
inanimate matter *n* 358
inanity *n* 4, 450a, 497, 517
in anticipation *adv* 132
inapplicable *adj* 10
inappreciable *adj* 32
inappropriateness *n* 647
inapt *adj* 699
inaptitude *n* 645
in a roundabout way *adv* 629
in arrear *adj* 806
inarticulate *adj* 583
inarticulateness *n* 583
inattention *n* 458
inattention *n* 452, 460, 866
inattentive *adj* 419, 452, 458, 460, 823, 866
inattentiveness *n* 458
inaudibility *n* 405, 419
inaudible *adj* 405
inaugural *adj* 66
inaugurate *v* 66
inauguration *n* 66
inauspicious *adj* 135, 909
in bad health *adj* 655
in bad taste *adj* 851
inbeing *n* 5
in black and white *adj* 531, 590
inborn *adj* 5, 221, 820
inbound *adj* 294
inbred *adj* 5
in broad daylight *adv* 525

incalculable *adj* 104
incalculably *adv* 31
incandescent *adj* 382
incantation *n* 993
incantory *adj* 992
incapability *n* 158
incapable *adj* 158
incapacitate *v* 158
incapacitated *adj* 158
incapacity *n* 158, 499
incarcerate *v* 972
incarceration *n* 974
incase *v* 229; *adv* 8
in celebration of *adv* 883
incendiary *adj* 162
incentive *n* 615
incertitude *n* 475
incessant *adj* 104, 112, 136
incessantly *adv* 136
inch *v* 275
in chains *adj* 754
inch by inch *adv* 26, 275
incident *n* 151
incidental *adj* 6, 8, 10, 177
incidentally *adv* 10
incineration *n* 384
incipient *adj* 66
in circulation *adj* 531, 532
incise *v* 259, 558
incising *n* 558
incision *n* 44, 259
incisive *adj* 171, 416, 574
incite *v* 173, 175, 615
incitement *n* 615
incivility *n* 929
incivism *n* 911
inclination *n* 176, 217, 278, 288, 306, 600, 602
incline *n* 217; *v* 176, 217, 278, 602, 615
inclined *adj* 217, 820

inclose *v* 76, 221, 227, 229
include *v* 54, 76
including *adj* 76
inclusion *n* 76
inclusion *n* 54
inclusive *adj* 56, 76
incogitancy *n* 452
incoherence *n* 47
incoherence *n* 503
in cold blood *adv* 823
incombustible *adj* 385
income *n* 775, 803
in comfort *adv* 377
incoming *adj* 294
in commemoration of *adv* 883
incommunicable *adj* 519
in communication with *adj* 592
in company with *adv* 88
incomparable *adj* 33
incomparably *adv* 31
imcompatible *adj* 24
incompetence *n* 158, 499, 640, 699
incompetent *adj* 158, 640, 699
incomplete *adj* 53, 304, 640, 651, 674, 730
incompletely *adv* 53
incompleteness *n* 53
incompleteness *n* 304, 640, 730
in compliance with *adv* 743
incomprehensibility *n* 519
incomprehensible *adj* 104, 519
incomprehension *n* 491
inconceivable *adj* 471
in concert with *adj* 178; *adv* 714
in conflict with *adv* 708
in conformity with *adv* 82

incongruity *n* 24, 47, 83

incongruous *adj* 24, 47, 83, 497

in conjunction with *adv* 37, 43

in connection with *adv* 9

inconsequence *n* 10

inconsequential *adj* 32, 477, 643

inconsequentiality *n* 32

inconsiderable *adj* 32, 643

inconsiderate *adj* 452, 460

inconsideration *n* 458

inconsistency *n* 15, 16a, 47, 83, 497, 568

inconsistent *adj* 14, 16a, 47, 83, 568, 608

inconsistent with *adj* 24

inconspicuous *adj* 447

inconstancy *n* 149

inconstant *adj* 149

in contact *adj* 199

incontestable *adj* 159, 474

incontinence *n* 961

incontinent *adj* 961

incontrovertible *adj* 474

inconvenience *n* 647

inconvenient *adj* 647

in convulsions *adv* 315

incorporate *v* 48, 76

incorporating *adj* 76

incorporation *n* 48, 54, 76

incorporeal *adj* 4, 317

incorporeality *n* 317

incorrect *adj* 477, 495, 544, 568, 923

incorrigible *adj* 606

in course of time *adv* 121

increase *n* 35

increase *n* 37, 194, 282, 658; *v* 31, 35,

37, 194, 282, 367, 658, 835

increasing *adj* 35

incredible *adj* 471

incredibly *adv* 31

incredulity *n* 487

incredulity *n* 485, 989

incredulous *adj* 485, 487, 989

incredulousness *n* 487

increment *n* 35, 37, 39, 194

incremental *adj* 35

incriminate *v* 938

incrimination *n* 938

incriminatory *adj* 938

incrust *v* 224

incubus *n* 980

inculcate *v* 537

inculpate *v* 938

inculpation *n* 938

incumbent *adj* 926

incur *v* 177

incurable *adj* 5, 859

incur a loss *v* 776

incuriosity *n* 456

incurious *adj* 456

incuriousness *n* 456

incursion *n* 294, 716

incurvature *n* 245

incurved *adj* 252

in custody *adj* 754

in danger of *adj* 177

in debt *adj* 806, 808

indebted *adj* 916

indebtedness *n* 177, 916

indecency *n* 961

indecent *adj* 961

indecipherable *adj* 519

indecision *n* 149, 605, 609a

indecisive *adj* 149, 605, 609a

indecisiveness *n* 172

indeed *adv* 31

indefatigability *n* 604a

indefatigable *adj* 604a

in defiance *adv* 708

indefinite *adj* 447, 475, 571

indefinitely *adv* 31

indefiniteness *n* 447, 571

indelible *adj* 505

indelicacy *n* 961

indelicate *adj* 961

indemnification *n* 30

indemnify *v* 30

indemnity *n* 30

indent *v* 257

indentation *n* 252, 257

indented *adj* 252

independence *n* 10, 748, 803

independent *adj* 10, 748

in despair *adj* 828

in detail *adv* 51, 79

indeterminate *adj* 156, 475, 520, 605

indeterminateness *n* 520

indetermination *n* 605

index *n* 86, 550; *v* 60, 562

indicate *v* 467, 516, 525, 550, 909

indication *n* 550

indication *n* 467, 525, 909

indicative *adj* 467, 550

indicator *n* 550

indicatory *adj* 550

indict *v* 938, 969

indictment *n* 938

indifference *n* 866

indifference *n* 456, 603, 609a, 643, 736, 989

indifferent *adj* 34, 383, 456, 460, 603, 609a, 651, 736, 823, 866, 989

indigence *n* 804

indigenous *adj* 5, 188

indigent *adj* 804

indignant *adj* 900

indignation *n* 900
indirect *adj* 279, 629
indirectly *adv* 629
indiscreet *adj* 684, 863
indiscretion *n* 699, 863
indiscriminate *adj* 41, 59, 81, 465a
indiscrimination *n* 465a
in disguise *adj* 528
indispensable *adj* 630
indispose *v* 616
indisposed *adj* 655
indisposition *n* 603, 655
indisputable *adj* 474
in disrepair *adj* 674
indissoluble *adj* 43, 50, 321
indistinct *adj* 405, 447, 475
indistinction *n* 465a
indistinctness *n* 447, 465a, 571
indistinguishable *adj* 13, 447
individual *n* 372; *adj* 79, 87, 372
individuality *n* 79, 83, 87
individualize *v* 79
indivisibility *n* 50
indivisible *adj* 50, 321
indoctrinate *v* 537
indolence *n* 172, 275, 683
indolent *adj* 275, 683
indomitable *adj* 159, 604, 604a, 719
indoors *adv* 221
in dribs and drabs *adv* 51
in drips and snatches *adv* 51
indubitable *adj* 474
induce *v* 153, 161, 175, 476, 615
inducement *n* 615
induct *v* 296, 755

induction *n* 296, 476
inductive *adj* 476
in due course *adv* 109
in due season *adv* 109
in due time *adv* 106, 109, 134
indulge *v* 740, 760, 954
indulge in *v* 827
indulgence *n* 740, 760, 918, 954
indulgent *adj* 740, 760, 954
induration *n* 323
industrious *adj* 539, 682
industry *n* 682
in earnest *adv* 604
inebriate *n* 959
inebriated *adj* 959
inebriety *n* 959
in ecstasy *adv* 377
inedible *adj* 395
ineffability *n* 317
ineffable *adj* 2, 317, 519
in effect *adv* 5
ineffective *adj* 158
ineffectual *adj* 158, 645, 732
inefficacy *n* 158, 645
inefficiency *n* 158, 645
inefficient *adj* 158, 732
inelastic *adj* 326
inelasticity *n* 326
inelegance *n* 579
inelegance *n* 846
inelegant *adj* 579
ineluctable *adj* 601, 744
inept *adj* 158, 499, 699
ineptitude *n* 158, 499, 645, 699
inequality *n* 28
inequality *n* 15, 24
inequity *n* 15, 24, 923
ineradicable *adj* 5
in error *adj* 481, 495
inert *adj* 172, 683

inertia *n* 172
inertness *n* 172
inertness *n* 683
inescapable *adj* 246, 744
inestimable *adj* 648
in every respect *adv* 52
inevitability *n* 474, 601
inevitable *adj* 474, 601
inevitableness *n* 601
inexact *adj* 571
inexactness *n* 495, 571
in exchange *adv* 148
inexcitability *n* 826
inexcitability *n* 172
inexcitable *adj* 826
inexhaustibility *n* 105
inexhaustible *adj* 104
inexistence *n* 2
inexistent *adj* 2
inexorable *adj* 601, 739, 744, 914a
inexpedience *n* 647
inexpediency *n* 647
inexpedient *adj* 499, 647
inexpensive *adj* 815
inexperience *n* 491, 703
inexperienced *adj* 435
inexpert *adj* 699
inexpertness *n* 699
in explanation *adv* 522
inexplicable *adj* 519
inexposure *n* 703
inexpressible *adj* 519
inexpressive *adj* 517
inextension *n* 180a
inextinguishable *adj* 159
inextravagant *adj* 881
inextricable *adj* 46
in fact *adv* 1
infallibility *n* 474
infallible *adj* 474
infamous *adj* 874
infamy *n* 874
infancy *n* 127
infant *n* 129

infanticide *n* 361
infantile *adj* 129, 499
infantlike *adj* 129
infatuated *adj* 486
infatuation *n* 486, 606
in fault *adj* 947
in favour *adj* 931
infect *v* 659, 824
infection *n* 824
infelicitous *adj* 828
infer *v* 476
inference *n* 65, 476, 480
inferential *adj* 467, 476
inferior *adj* 28, 34, 651, 736
inferiority *n* 34
inferiority *n* 28, 736
infernal *adj* 649, 978, 982
inferno *n* 982
infertile *adj* 169
infertility *n* 169
infidel *n* 989
infidelity *n* 989
infiltrate *v* 41, 294
infiltration *n* 41, 294, 302
infinite *adj* 31, 102, 104, 180
infinitely *adv* 31, 104
infiniteness *n* 105
infinitesimal *adj* 32, 193
infinitude *n* 105
infinity *n* 105
infinity *n* 112, 180
infirm *adj* 158, 160, 655
infirmity *n* 158, 160, 655
in fits *adv* 315
inflame *v* 171, 173, 384, 824
inflamed *adj* 434
in flames *adj* 382
inflammable *adj* 385

inflate *v* 194, 322, 349, 573, 880
inflated *adj* 482, 577, 880
inflation *n* 322, 577
inflect *v* 245
inflection *n* 567
inflexibility *n* 141, 246, 323, 606
inflexible *adj* 323, 604, 606
inflict *v* 680, 739
inflict pain *v* 378
inflict punishment *v* 972
in flight *adj* 267
influence *n* 175
influence *n* 153, 170, 615, 737; *v* 62, 153, 170, 176, 615
influential *adj* 157, 175, 176, 737
influx *n* 294
in force *adj* 170
inform *v* 527, 537, 668
informality *n* 83
informant *n* 527, 534
information *n* 527
information *n* 467, 490, 498, 532
informed *adj* 527
informer *n* 527, 532, 938
infraction *n* 83, 303, 742, 773, 927
infrequency *n* 137
infrequency *n* 103
infrequent *adj* 103, 137
infrequently *adv* 137
infringe *v* 303, 742, 773
infringement *n* 303
infringement *n* 83, 742, 773
in front *adv* 234, 280
in front of one's nose *adj* 446
in full sight *adj* 446
in full view *adj* 446
infuriate *v* 173

infuse *v* 41, 300, 537
infusion *n* 41, 300
in future *adv* 121
ingathering *n* 72
ingenious *adj* 698, 702
ingenuity *n* 698
ingenuous *adj* 703, 946
ingenuousness *n* 946
ingest *v* 296, 539
ingestion *n* 296, 298
in good taste *adj* 850
in good time *adv* 152
ingraft *v* 300
ingrained *adj* 5, 221, 820
ingrate *n* 917
ingratitude *n* 917
ingredient *n* 51, 56, 211
ingress *n* 294
ingress *n* 302
inhabit *v* 184, 186, 188, 189
inhabitant *n* 188
inhabiting *adj* 186
inhale *v* 398
in hand *adj* 777
inharmonious *adj* 24, 414
inharmoniousness *n* 414
in harmony with *adj* 23
in harness *adj* 749
in health *adj* 654
inherence *n* 5
inherent *adj* 5, 221
inherited *adj* 5
in hiding *adj* 528
in high esteem *adj* 931
in honor of *adv* 883
inhumation *n* 363
inimical *adj* 708, 889
inimitable *adj* 20, 33, 648, 650
iniquitous *adj* 923, 945
iniquity *n* 923, 945
initial *adj* 66
initiate *v* 66, 296
initiation *n* 66, 296
initiative *n* 66

in its infancy *adv* 66

in its own sweet time *adv* 152

in its turn *adv* 58

inject *v* 300

injection *n* 296, 300

injudicious *adj* 499

injunction *n* 630, 695, 741, 761, 864

injur *v* 848

injure *v* 619, 649, 659, 828, 923

injured *adj* 659, 848

injurious *adj* 619, 649

injury *n* 173, 619, 649, 659, 665, 776

injustice *n* 173, 923

ink *n* 431

in keeping with *adj* 23; *adv* 82

inkling *n* 514, 527

inky *adj* 431

inlaid *adj* 221, 440

inlands *n* 342

inlay *v* 440

in league *adj* 709

inlet *n* 260, 343

in lieu of *adv* 147

inmate *n* 188

in moderation *adv* 174

inmost *adj* 221

in motion *adj* 264

in mourning *adj* 839

innate *adj* 5, 221

inner *adj* 221

inner coating *n* 224

inner man *n* 820

innermost *adj* 221

innermost recesses *n* 221

inner part *n* 221

innocence *n* 946

innocence *n* 703, 944, 960

innocent *adj* 435, 703, 946, 960

in no respect *adv* 32

in no time *adv* 113

innovate *v* 140

innovation *n* 20a, 123, 140

innovative *adj* 140

innuendo *n* 527

in obedience to *adv* 743

inoculate *v* 300

inoculation *n* 300

inodorousness *n* 399

in one's birthday suit *adj* 226

in one's debt *adj* 916

in operation *adj* 170, 680

inoperative *adj* 158, 645

inopportune *adj* 135, 647

inopportuneness *n* 135

in opposition *adj* 708

in order *adj* 58; *adv* 58

inordinate *adj* 31, 641, 954

inordinately *adv* 31

inordinateness *n* 954

inorganic *adj* 358

inorganic matter *n* 358

in part *adv* 32, 51

in particular *adv* 79

in perfect condition *adj* 650

in place of *adv* 147

in plain English *adv* 576, 703

in plain sight *adv* 525

in plain terms *adv* 576

in play *adj* 170

in poor health *adj* 655

in possession of *adj* 777

in preparation *adj* 53

in presence of *adv* 186

in print *adj* 531, 532

in prison *adj* 754

in private *adv* 528

in progress *adj* 53

in prospect *adj* 121, 152, 620

in proximity *adj* 186

in pursuit of *adj* 622

input *n* 175

in question *adv* 454

in quest of *adj* 622

inquietude *n* 828

inquire *v* 461

inquirer *n* 461

inquiring *n* 461; *adj* 455, 461

inquiring mind *n* 455

inquiry *n* 461

inquiry *n* 539

inquisitive *adj* 455, 461

inquisitiveness *n* 455

inquisitor *n* 461, 739

inquisitorial *adj* 461, 739, 965

in rapport *adj* 413

in readiness *adj* 507

in reality *adv* 1

in relief *adj* 250

in reserve *adj* 636

in retaliation *adv* 718

inroad *n* 294

in rotation *adv* 138

insalubrious *adj* 657

insalubrity *n* 657

insane *adj* 173, 503

insanity *n* 503

inscrutable *adj* 519

in secret *adj* 528; *adv* 528

insect *n* 366

insecure *adj* 475, 665

insecurity *n* 475, 665

insensate *adj* 499

insensibility *n* 376, 823

insensibility *n* 866

insensible *adj* 376, 381, 506

insensitive *adj* 376, 823, 866

insensitiveness *n* 823, 866

inseparability *n* 46

inseparable *adj* 43, 46

insert *v* 221, 228, 300

insertion *n* 300

insertion *n* 37, 228, 294, 296
in short *adv* 572
inside *n* 221; *adj* 221
inside out *adj* 218
insidious *adj* 545, 702
insight *n* 477, 498; *adj* 507
insightful *adj* 842
insigne *n* 550
insignificance *n* 32, 643, 736
insignificant *adj* 4, 32, 517, 643, 736
in simple words *adv* 703
insincere *adj* 544
insincerity *n* 544
insinuate *v* 527
insinuate oneself *v* 294
insinuation *n* 228, 294, 300, 527
insipid *adj* 337, 391, 575
insipidity *n* 391
insist upon *v* 604, 770
in snatches *adv* 70
insobriety *n* 959
insolence *n* 885
insolence *n* 715, 878
insolent *adj* 715, 885
insoluble *adj* 321, 519
insolvency *n* 732, 808
insolvent *adj* 804
in some degree *adv* 26
in some place *adv* 182
inspect *v* 441
inspector *n* 694; 461
inspiration *n* 477, 515, 612, 824
inspire *v* 615, 824
inspiring *adj* 836
inspirit *v* 836
inspiriting *adj* 858
in spite *adv* 708
in spite of *prep* 179
instability *n* 149, 475, 605, 665

install *v* 184, 755
installation *n* 184
installment *n* 807
instance *n* 82
instant *n* 113; *adj* 113, 118, 630
instantaneous *adj* 111, 113, 132
instantaneously *adv* 113, 132
instantaneousness *n* 113
instead *adv* 147
instigate *v* 615
instigation *n* 170, 615
instill *v* 41, 300, 537
instinct *n* 477, 601
instinctive *adj* 5, 477, 601
instinctual *adj* 5, 477
in stir *adj* 754
institute *n* 542; *v* 153, 161
in store *adj* 152, 636
instruct *v* 537, 693, 695, 741
instructed *adj* 490
instruction *n* 537, 693, 695, 697, 741
instructive *adj* 537, 985
instructor *n* 540
instrument *n* 633
instrument *adj* 415
instrumental *adj* 176, 416, 631, 632, 633, 677
instrumentalist *n* 416
instrumentality *n* 631
instrumentality *n* 170
instrumental music *n* 415
insubordinate *adj* 715, 742
insubordination *n* 715, 742
insubstantiality *n* 2, 317
in succession *adv* 69

in such and such a place *adv* 183
in such wise *adv* 8
insufferable *adj* 830
insufficiency *n* 640
insufficiency *n* 53, 304, 651, 732
insufficient *adj* 28, 32, 304, 640, 651, 732
insufficiently *adv* 32
insular *adj* 10, 44, 87, 346
insularity *n* 44
insulate *v* 44, 87
insulation *n* 44
insult *n* 830; *v* 830, 929
insulting *adj* 885, 929
insurgence *n* 719
insurgent *n* 742; *adj* 742
insurrection *n* 719
insusceptibility *n* 376
in suspense *adv* 172
intact *adj* 50, 52, 141, 650, 670, 729
intactness *n* 52
intaglio *n* 22
intangible *adj* 2, 4, 317
in tears *adj* 828
integer *n* 84
integral *adj* 50
integral part *n* 56
integrate *v* 50
integrity *n* 50, 922, 939, 944
intellect *n* 450
intellect *n* 498, 842
intellectual *n* 492; *adj* 450, 498
intellectual giant *n* 872
intellectualize *v* 450
intelligence *n* 498
intelligence *n* 480, 498, 527, 532, 698, 842
intelligencer *n* 527, 534
intelligent *adj* 498, 698, 842
intelligibility *n* 518

intelligibility *n* 570
intelligible *adj* 518, 522, 570
intemperance *n* 954
intemperance *n* 959
intemperate *adj* 954
intend *v* 451, 516, 620
intense *adj* 31, 171, 382, 428
intensely *adv* 31
intensification *n* 835
intensified *adj* 835
intensify *v* 35, 171, 835
intensity *n* 26, 31, 171, 173, 382
intent *n* 451, 516, 600, 620
intention *n* 620
intention *n* 278, 451, 516, 611, 615
intentional *adj* 600, 620
intentionally *adv* 600, 611, 620
intentiveness *n* 457
intentness *n* 682
inter *v* 363
interact *v* 12
intercalation *n* 228
intercede *v* 724
intercession *n* 724, 766
interchange *n* 148
interchange *n* 12, 219, 783; *v* 12, 147, 148, 783
interchangeability *n* 148
interchangeable *adj* 12, 148, 794
intercourse *n* 148
interdepend *v* 12
interdependence *n* 12
interdict *v* 761
interdiction *n* 761
interest *n* 455, 618, 642, 707; *v* 288, 824, 829, 840
interested *adj* 455
interfere *v* 228, 708, 724

interference *n* 179, 228, 706, 719
interfere with *v* 179
interim *n* 106, 198
interior *n* 221, 342; *adj* 221
interiority *n* 221
interjacence *n* 228
interjacent *adj* 228
interject *v* 228
interjection *n* 228
interlace *v* 41, 43, 219
interlaced *adj* 219
interlard *v* 41
interlarding *n* 41
interlineation *n* 228
interlink *v* 219
interlocation *n* 228
interlocution *n* 588
interlude *n* 106, 198, 685
intermediary *n* 534, 631; *adj* 631
intermediate *adj* 29, 68, 631
intermedium *n* 631
interment *n* 363
interminable *adj* 104, 112, 200
intermission *n* 70, 106
intermittence *n* 138
intermittent *adj* 70, 138
intermittently *adv* 138
intern *v* 221
internal *adj* 5, 221
internally *adv* 221
interpenetrate *v* 228
interpenetration *n* 228
interpolate *v* 41, 228
interpolation *n* 41, 228, 300
interpose *v* 70, 228, 724
interposition *n* 37, 228, 724
interpret *v* 462, 522, 537
interpretable *adj* 522
interpretation *n* 522

interpretation *n* 155, 516
interpretative *adj* 522
interpreter *n* 524
interpreter *n* 513
interpretive *adj* 522
interregnum *n* 106, 142, 198
interrogate *v* 461
interrogation *n* 461
interrogative *adj* 461
interrupt *v* 70, 142, 198, 706
interrupted *adj* 70
interruption *n* 61, 70, 142, 198, 706
intersect *v* 219
intersection *n* 219
interspace *n* 198, 221
intersperse *v* 228
interspersion *n* 228
interstice *n* 198
intertwine *v* 41, 43, 219
intertwined *adj* 219
interval *n* 198
interval *n* 53, 70, 106, 196
intervene *v* 70, 198, 228, 631, 724
intervening *adj* 228
intervention *n* 228, 631, 724
interview *n* 588
interweave *v* 41, 43, 219
in the altogether *adj* 226
in the background *adv* 235
in the blood *adj* 5
in the bud *adv* 66
in the buff *adj* 226
in the cards *adj* 152
in the course of *adv* 106
in the course of things *adv* 151
in the event of *adv* 8
in the face of *adv* 715

in the first place *adv* 66
in the foreground *adv* 234
in the fourth place *adv* 96
in the genes *adj* 5
in the headlines *adj* 532
in the interim *adv* 106
in the lead *adv* 234
in the long run *adv* 29, 152
in the main *adv* 50
in the matter of *adv* 9
in the meantime *adv* 106
in the middle *adv* 68
in the midst of *adv* 41
in the news *adj* 532
in the nick of time *adv* 134
in the open air *adv* 338
in the open market *adj* 763
in the rear *adv* 235, 281
in the same category *adj* 9
in the thick of *adv* 228
in the third place *adv* 93
in the vanguard *adv* 280
in the wide open spaces *adv* 338
in the wind *adj* 152
intimacy *n* 888
intimate *n* 890; *v* 527; *adj* 197, 221, 888
intimately *adv* 43
in time *adv* 109, 152
intimidate *v* 909
intimidating *adj* 909
intimidation *n* 909
intolerable *adj* 830
intolerance *n* 606, 825
intolerant *adj* 606, 825
intonation *n* 402, 580
intone *v* 580
in top shape *adj* 654
in touch with *adj* 592

in tow *adj* 285
intoxicate *v* 824
intoxicated *adj* 959
intoxication *n* 824, 959
intractability *n* 606
intractable *adj* 606, 704
in trade *adj* 794
intrepid *adj* 861
intrepidity *n* 861
intricate *adj* 248, 704
intrigue *n* 626, 702; *v* 702
intriguer 626
intrinsic *adj* 5, 221
intrinsicality *n* 5
intrinsically *adv* 5
in triumph *adv* 731
introduce *v* 62, 228, 280, 296, 300
introduction *n* 64, 66, 296, 300
introductory *adj* 62, 64, 66, 116
intrude *v* 135, 228, 294
intrusion *n* 57, 135, 228, 294
intrusive *adj* 228, 706
intuit *v* 477
intuition *n* 477
intuition *n* 477
intuitive *adj* 477
intuitively *adv* 477
in turn *adv* 58, 138
intwine *v* 219
in two shakes (of a lamb's tail) *adv* 113
inundate *v* 337, 348, 641
inundation *n* 348
in unison *adj* 413
inure *v* 613
inutile *adj* 645
inutility *n* 645
invade *v* 294, 716
invader *n* 716
in vain *adv* 732
invalidate *v* 158, 479, 536, 756

invalidation *n* 479, 536, 756
invaluable *adj* 648
invariability *n* 16, 141
invariable *adj* 5, 16, 110, 141, 150
invariably *adv* 16, 82
in various places *adv* 182
invasion *n* 294, 716
invent *v* 515, 626
invented *adj* 546
invention *n* 515, 546, 698
inventive *adj* 515, 698
inventiveness *n* 168, 698
inventor *n* 164
inventory *n* 86, 596, 811; *v* 596
inverse *n* 237; *adj* 218, 237
inversely *adv* 218
inversion *n* 218
inversion *n* 14, 140, 145
invert *v* 14, 61, 218
inverted *adj* 59, 218
invest *v* 157, 755, 784
invested *adj* 225
investigate *v* 461
investigation *n* 461, 463, 595
investigator *n* 461
investiture *n* 784
investment *n* 787
inveterate *adj* 124
invidious *adj* 830, 898
in view *adj* 507, 620
invigorate *v* 159, 171
invigorating *adj* 171, 656
invigoration *n* 159
invincible *adj* 159
inviolate *adj* 141
in violation *adj* 927
invisibility *n* 447
invisible *adj* 193, 447
invisibleness *n* 447

invite v 288, 615, 763, 829
invocation n 586
in vogue adj 852
invoice n 812
invoke v 72, 586, 990
involuntary adj 601
involution n 248, 571
involve v 516, 938
involved adj 59, 248, 571
invulnerability n 664
invulnerable adj 664
inward adj 221; adv 221
in what manner adv 627
in what way adv 627
in writing adj 590
iota n 32
irascibility n 901
irascible adj 382, 684, 901
irate adj 900
iridescence n 440
iridescent adj 429, 440
irk v 830
irksome adj 704, 830, 841
iron v 255
iron-gray adj 432
ironic adj 856
ironical adj 856
irons n 752
irony n 856
irradiate v 420
irrational adj 497, 499
irrationality n 499
irreclaimable adj 951
irreconcilability n 10
irreconcilable adj 24
irrecoverable adj 122
irrefutable adj 246, 474
irregular adj 16a, 59, 70, 81, 83, 139, 243, 256, 475
irregularity n 139

irregularity n 16a, 59, 83, 256, 475
irregularly adv 59, 139
irrelation n 10
irrelevancy n 175a
irrelevant adj 10
irreligion n 989
irreligion n 988
irreligious adj 989
irremediable adj 859
irrepentance n 951
irrepressible adj 173, 748, 825
irresistibility n 601
irresistible adj 159, 601, 744
irresolute adj 149, 485, 605, 607, 609a, 683
irresolution n 605
irresolution n 149, 172, 314, 485, 609a
irrespective adj 10
irresponsibility n 773
irresponsible adj 773
irretrievable adj 776
irreverence n 929, 988
irreverent adj 929
irrevocable adj 604
irrigate v 348
irrigation n 348
irritability n 825, 901
irritable adj 684, 825, 901
irritate v 173, 289, 688, 824, 828, 830
irritated adj 835
irritation n 824, 828, 835
irruption n 294
island n 346
isle n 346
islet n 346
isolate v 44, 79, 87, 893, 905
isolated adj 10, 44, 87, 893
isolation n 44, 893, 905
issuance n 531

issue n 154, 167, 295; v 73, 151, 295, 531, 591
issue from v 154
issues n 151
itch v 380
itching n 380; adj 380
itchy adj 380
items n 79
iterate v 104
iteration n 90, 104, 136
iterative adj 104
itinerant n 268; adj 266

J

jabber n 517, 584; v 517, 584
jackanapes n 854
jaded adj 961
jag v 257
jagged adj 244
jail n 752; v 972
jailbird n 754
jailer n 753; 975
jailhouse n 752
jangle v 410
jar n 315; v 24, 410, 414, 713
jargon n 497, 517, 560
jarring adj 410, 414
jaundice n 435, 436
jaundiced adj 435
jaunt n 266
jaw v 584
jazz n 415
jealous adj 435, 900, 920, 921
jealousy n 920
jealousy n 900, 921
jeopardize v 665
jeer v 929
jeer at v 856
jeers n 856
jeopardy n 665
jerk n 285, 315, 493; v 285, 315
jerky adj 315
jest v 842

jester *n* 501, 844
jesuitry *n* 477
jet *n* 273, 348; *v* 267, 348
jet-black *adj* 431
jet-setter *n* 268
jetting *adj* 267
jettison *v* 610
jetty *n* 250
jewel *n* 648, 899
jibe *v* 23
jilt *v* 509
jingle *v* 408
jinx *n* 621; *n* 993
job *n* 676
jocularity *n* 836
jog *n* 315; *v* 276
joggle *v* 315
jog on *v* 736
join *v* 37, 41, 43, 45, 72, 87, 88, 199, 290, 712
joined *adj* 43
join forces *v* 709
join hands with *v* 709
joining *n* 37, 43, 290
joint *n* 43; *adj* 43, 88, 178, 778
jointly *adv* 43
joint tenancy *n* 778
joke *v* 842
joker *n* 844
jolly *adj* 836, 840
jolt *n* 315; *v* 276, 315
jostle *v* 179, 276, 315
jot *n* 32
jounce *v* 315
journal *n* 114, 551
journalist *n* 553
journey *n* 266
journey *n* 302; *v* 266
journeyer *n* 268
journeying *adj* 266
jovial *adj* 840
joviality *n* 836
jowl *n* 236
joy *n* 377, 827; *v* 827

joyful *adj* 377, 827, 836
joyous *adj* 836
jubilant *adj* 838, 884
jubilation *n* 838
judge *n* 967
judge *n* 480, 737, 965; *v* 451, 480, 850, 965, 967
judgment *n* 480
judgment *n* 450, 451, 453, 465, 490, 498, 972
judgmental *adj* 480
judgment seat *n* 966
judicator *n* 965, 967
judicatory *adj* 967
judicature *n* 965
judicial *adj* 480, 965, 967
judiciary *n* 967
judicious *adj* 174, 480, 498, 868, 967
judiciousness *n* 174, 868
juice *v* 354
juiced *adj* 959
juiceless *adj* 340
juicer *n* 959
juicy *adj* 333, 337, 339
jumble *n* 41, 59; *v* 41, 59, 61
jumbo jet *n* 273
jump *n* 305, 309; *v* 309, 310
junction *n* 43
junction *n* 41, 45, 48
juncture *n* 8, 43, 134
jungle *n* 59
junior *adj* 127
juridical *adj* 967
jurisdiction *n* 965
jurisdiction *n* 737
jurisdictive *adj* 965, 967
jurist *n* 967
juristic *adj* 967
juror *n* 967

just *adj* 246, 922
just as *adv* 17
just do *v* 639
justice *n* 922, 967
justification *n* 717, 737, 937
justified *adj* 937
justify *v* 717, 737, 937
just in time *adv* 134
justly *adv* 922
just now *adv* 123
jut out *v* 250
juvenile *adj* 127
juvenility *n* 123, 127
juxtapose *v* 464

K

kaleidoscope *n* 445
kaleidoscopic *adj* 440
kaput *adj* 503
karma *n* 152
keen *adj* 171, 253, 375, 868
keen blast *n* 349
keenness *n* 868
keep *n* 298; *v* 141, 143, 670, 751, 781, 883
keep accounts *v* 811
keep alive *v* 359
keep an account with *v* 805
keep apart *v* 44
keep away *v* 187
keep back *v* 678
keep clear of *v* 623
keep cold *v* 385
keep company with *v* 888
keep down *v* 751
keeper *n* 753
keep going *v* 143
keep hold *v* 150
keeping *n* 781
keeping out *n* 55
keeping secret *n* 528
keep in mind *v* 505
keep moving *v* 264, 682

keep on *v* 136, 143, 604a

keep on one's toes *v* 264

keep out *v* 55

keep out of sight *v* 528

keep pace with *v* 27, 120, 178

keep quiet *v* 265, 403, 585

keep safe *v* 717

keepsake *n* 505

keep secret *v* 528

keep silence *v* 585

keep the memory alive *v* 505

keep the peace *v* 721

keep up *v* 141, 143, 670

Kelly green *adj* 435

kelpie *n* 979

kempt *adj* 652

ken *n* 441

kernel *n* 68, 222

kerosene *n* 356, 388

kerosene lamp *n* 423

ketch *n* 273

key *n* 346, 428

keyhole *n* 260

khaki *n* 433; *adj* 433

kick *n* 276

kick up a row *v* 173

kid *n* 129

kill *v* 361

killer *n* 165

killing *n* 361

killing time *n* 681

kill time *v* 106, 683

kiln *n* 386

kind *n* 75, 569; *adj* 888, 906

kind-hearted *adj* 888, 906

kindheartedness *n* 906

kindle *v* 153, 171, 173, 384, 420, 824

kindliness *n* 897, 906

kindling *n* 388

kindly *adj* 888, 906

kindness *n* 897, 906

kindred *n* 11; *adj* 11

kinfolk *n* 11

kingdom of god *n* 981

kingdom of heaven *n* 981

kinsman *n* 11

kiss *n* 902

kith and kin *n* 11

knack *n* 698

knave *n* 941

knead *v* 324, 379

kneading *n* 379

knee *n* 244

knee-deep *adj* 209

kneel *v* 308, 886, 990

knell *n* 363

knife *n* 262

knife edge *n* 253

knit *v* 43, 259

knob *n* 249, 250

knock *n* 276; *v* 276, 406

knock down *v* 213

knot *n* 219, 321; *v* 219

knotted *adj* 59, 256

know *v* 474, 484, 490, 527, 888

know how *n* 632

knowing *adj* 490

knowingly *adv* 620

knowledge *n* 490

knowledge *n* 498, 527, 698

knowledgeable *adj* 490, 698

known *adj* 490

know no bounds *v* 104

know-nothing *n* 493; *v* 491

knuckle *n* 244

kobold *n* 980

kohl-black *adj* 431

Koran *n* 986

L

label *n* 564; *v* 550, 564

labor *n* 680, 686, 704; *v* 680, 686

laboratory *n* 691

labored *adj* 579

laborer *n* 746

laborious *adj* 686, 704

laboriousness *n* 682

labyrinth *n* 59, 248

labyrinthine *adj* 248

lace *n* 219; *v* 43

lack *n* 804; *v* 34, 53, 304, 640, 804

lackadaisical *adj* 683

lack faith *v* 989

lacking *adj* 53, 187, 304

lackluster *adj* 422, 429, 430

lack of adornment *n* 849

lack of affectation *n* 849

lack of bias *n* 942

lack of connection *n* 10

lack of decorum *n* 851

lack of discernment *n* 465a

lack of feeling *n* 376, 381

lack of interest *n* 456

lack of originality *n* 843

lack of practice *n* 614

lack of readiness *n* 603

lack of uniformity *n* 16a

laconic *adj* 572

lacquer *n* 356a; *v* 356a

lad *n* 129

lade *v* 190

lading *n* 190

ladle *v* 270

lady *n* 374, 875

ladylove *n* 897

lag *v* 275, 281, 683

laggard *n* 683; *adj* 603, 683

lagoon *n* 343

laical *adj* 997

laid low *adj* 160

laid up *adj* 655

laim *v* 158

lair *n* 189

laity *n* 997

lake *n* 343
lake *n* 343
lamb *n* 129
lame *adj* 53, 160, 651, 655
lame excuse *n* 617
lament *n* 411, 839; *v* 411, 833, 839, 915
lamentable *adj* 649, 830, 833, 839
lamentably *adv* 31
lamentation *n* 839
lamentation *n* 833, 915
lamenting *adj* 839
lamp *n* 423
lampoon *v* 856
lampooner *n* 844
lance *v* 260
lancet *n* 262
land *n* 342
land *n* 780; *v* 292, 342
landed *adj* 342
landing *n* 292
lands *n* 342
landscape *n* 448; *v* 371
landscaping *n* 371
language *n* 560
languid *adj* 160, 172, 275, 405, 575, 683, 685
languish *v* 36, 160, 655, 683
languor *n* 160, 172, 275, 683, 688
lankness *n* 203
lanky *adj* 200, 203
lantern *n* 423
lap *n* 221, 311
lap of luxury *n* 377
lapse *n* 661, 776; *v* 109, 122, 144, 659, 661
lapsed *adj* 122
lard *n* 356
large *adj* 31, 192, 202
largeness *n* 192
larger *adj* 194
largesse *n* 784

lash *n* 975; *v* 43, 173, 972
lass *n* 129
lassitude *n* 688, 841
last *v* 1, 106, 110, 141, 604a; *adj* 67, 122
last breath *n* 360
last forever *v* 112
lasting *adj* 106, 110, 141, 150
lastingness *n* 110
last resort *n* 666
last stage *n* 67
last word *n* 67
late *adj* 122, 123, 133, 275, 360; *adv* 133
lately *adv* 122, 123
latency *n* 526
latency *n* 172, 447
lateness *n* 133
latent *adj* 172, 526
latentness *n* 526
later *adj* 117; *adv* 117
lateral *adj* 236
laterality *n* 236
laterally *adv* 236
lather *n* 353; *v* 332, 353
lathering *n* 332
latitude *n* 180, 181, 202, 748
latitude and longitude *n* 183
latter *adj* 122
lattice *n* 219
laud *v* 883, 990
laudatory *adj* 931
laugh *v* 838
laughable *adj* 853
laughing *adj* 838
laughing-stock *n* 857
laughingstock *n* 547
laughter *n* 838
launch *n* 273; *v* 66, 284
launch into *v* 676
launder *v* 652
laureate *n* 597
laurel *n* 733
lavation *n* 652

lavender *adj* 437
lavish *v* 641, 784, 818; *adj* 641, 818
lavishness *n* 818
law *n* 80, 697, 963
lawful *adj* 246, 760, 922, 963
lawfully *adv* 922
lawfulness *n* 922, 963
lawless *adj* 964
lawlessness *n* 964
lawsuit *n* 969
lawyer *n* 968
lax *adj* 47, 738, 773
laxative *n* 652
laxity *n* 738
laxity *n* 47, 495, 748, 773, 989
laxness *n* 738, 773
lay *n* 413; *v* 184; *adj* 997
lay aside *v* 55
lay away *v* 636
lay bare *v* 260
lay claim to *v* 741
layer *n* 204
layer *v* 204
layered *adj* 204
lay groundwork *v* 626
lay in *v* 637
lay in a stock *v* 637
lay in a store *v* 637
lay in the grave *v* 363
lay in the ground *v* 363
lay it on thick *v* 933
layman *n* 997
lay oneself open to *v* 177, 665
lay on thick *v* 641
lay open *v* 226, 260, 529
lay out *v* 363, 809
lay over *v* 133
lay siege *v* 716
lay stress on *v* 642
lay the foundations *v* 673
lay the groundwork *v* 60
lay to rest *v* 363

let slip *v* 529, 730, 776
letter *n* 561
letter *n* 592
letter carrier *n* 271
lettering *n* 591
letterpress *n* 591
letters *n* 490, 560
let the opportunity slip by *v* 135
let things take their course *v* 681
levee *n* 72
level *n* 26, 27, 213, 251; *v* 16, 27, 162, 213, 251, 255, 308; *adj* 16, 27, 207, 213, 251, 255
level at *v* 278
level-headed *adj* 502
level with *v* 543
leverage *n* 175
leviathan *n* 192
levity *n* 320
lewd *adj* 961
lewdness *n* 961
lexicography *n* 562
lexicon *n* 562
liability *n* 177
liability *n* 665, 806
liable *adj* 176, 177, 665, 806
liar *n* 548
liberal *adj* 784, 816, 906, 942
liberality *n* 816
liberality *n* 784, 906, 942
liberate *v* 44, 672, 748, 750, 970
liberated *adj* 750
liberation *n* 750
liberation *n* 671, 672
libertarian *adj* 760
libertine *n* 962
libertine *n* 954a
liberty *n* 685, 737, 748, 760, 760
librarian *n* 593

libretto *n* 593
licence *n* 738
license *n* 748, 760, 924; *v* 760
licensed *adj* 924
licit *adj* 246, 963
lick the boots of *v* 886
lid *n* 223, 261, 263
lie *n* 544, 546; *v* 183, 213, 538, 544 546
lie around *v* 220
lie down *v* 213, 687
lie flat *v* 207, 213
lie idle *v* 681
lie in *v* 1
lie in wait for *v* 530
lie low *v* 207
lien *n* 771
lie still *v* 265
life *n* 359
life *n* 151, 171, 682
lifeblood *n* 5, 359
life-giving *adj* 168
lifeless *adj* 172, 360
lifelessness *n* 172
lifelike *adj* 17, 21
lifetime *n* 108
lift *n* 307; *v* 235, 307
lift up *v* 235, 307
light *n* 420
light *n* 7; *v* 292, 384, 420, 423; *adj* 320, 322, 420, 430, 643
light bulb *n* 423
light-colored *adj* 429
lighten *v* 320, 420, 705
lightening *n* 420
light-fingered *adj* 791
light-footed *adj* 274
lightness *n* 320
light of day *n* 420
light on *v* 156
light up *v* 824
like *v* 394, 827, 897, 990; *adj* 17, 216
like a shot *adv* 113
like a ton of bricks *adj* 319

likelihood *n* 470, 472
likeliness *n* 472
likely *adj* 176, 177, 472
likeness *n* 17, 21, 216, 556
likening *n* 464
like two peas in a pod *n* 17
likewise *adv* 37
liking *n* 602, 897
lilac *adj* 437
lily-liver *n* 862
lily-livered *adj* 435, 862
limb *n* 51
limber *adj* 324
limbo *n* 982
limit *n* 233
limit *n* 67, 71; *v* 195, 229, 233, 469, 761
limitation *n* 229, 469, 751
limited *adj* 103, 203, 233
limitless *adj* 104, 180
limitlessness *n* 105
limn *v* 556, 594
limp *v* 160, 275; *adj* 53, 158, 160, 324, 326
limpid *adj* 425
limpidity *n* 425
limpness *n* 326
line *n* 69, 278; *v* 224
lineage *n* 11, 69, 122, 166
lineal *adj* 166, 200
linear *adj* 69, 200, 246
lined *adj* 224, 440
line of march *n* 278
liner *n* 273
lines *n* 230, 448
linger *v* 133, 275
lingering *adj* 110
lingo *n* 560
lingual *adj* 560
linguist *n* 560
linguistic *adj* 560

loom *v* 152, 446
looming *adj* 152
loon *n* 501
loop *n* 245, 247, 629
loophole *n* 671
loose *v* 44, 750; *adj* 44, 47, 279, 573, 575, 738, 748, 773
loosen *v* 47
looseness *n* 47, 573, 738, 748
loosening *n* 47, 738
loot *n* 793
lop *v* 371
loquacious *adj* 584
loquaciousness *n* 584
loquacity *n* 584
lord *n* 745, 875, 976
lore *n* 490, 537
lorgnette *n* 445
lose *v* 776
lose an opportunity *v* 135
lose color *v* 429
lose ground *v* 283
lose heart *v* 837
lost it *v* 503
lose no time *v* 682
lose one's senses *v* 503
lose one's temper *v* 825
lose patience *v* 825
lose sight of *v* 506
loss *n* 776
loss *n* 40a, 449, 619, 638, 659, 732
loss of life *n* 360
lost *adj* 2, 449, 458, 732, 776
lost in thought *adj* 451
lost in wonder *adj* 870
lot *n* 25, 152, 621, 786
lottery *n* 156
loud *adj* 404
loudly *adv* 404
loudness *n* 404
loud noise *n* 404
lough *n* 343
lounge *v* 683

lounger *n* 683
lout *n* 501
lovable *adj* 897
love *n* 897
love *n* 865, 897, 899, 977; *v* 827, 928, 990
loveliness *n* 829, 845
lovely *adj* 242, 377, 597, 829, 845, 977
lover *n* 897
lovesick *adj* 991
love token *n* 902
loving *adj* 897
low *v* 412; *adj* 32, 207, 405, 438, 649, 874, 876, 879, 930
low-born *adj* 876
lower *v* 207, 308, 879; *adj* 34
lowering *n* 308
lowland *n* 344
lowlands *n* 207
lowliness *n* 879
lowly *adj* 207, 879
low-lying *adj* 207
lowness *n* 207
low price *n* 815
low quality *n* 34
low relief *n* 250
low repute *n* 874
loyal *adj* 743
loyalty *n* 743
lubricate *v* 255, 332, 355
lubrication *n* 332
lubrication *n* 255, 355
lubricity *n* 255, 355
lucent *adj* 420
lucid *adj* 425, 502, 518, 570, 849
lucidity *n* 420, 425, 502, 518, 570, 578
Lucifer *n* 978
luck *n* 152, 156, 621, 731
lucky *adj* 134, 621, 734
ludicrous *adj* 853
lug *v* 285

lugubrious *adj* 837
lukewarn *adj* 382, 823, 866
lull *n* 142, 265, 403, 683, 685; *v* 174, 265
lull to sleep *v* 265
lumber *v* 275
luminary *n* 423
luminary *n* 500
luminosity *n* 420
luminous *adj* 420, 518
lump *n* 50, 51, 72, 192, 321
lumpish *adj* 192, 319
lump together *v* 72
lunacy *n* 503
lunar *adj* 245, 318
lunatic *n* 504; *adj* 503
lunch *v* 298
lunge *n* 276
lurch *n* 306; *v* 306
lure *v* 288
lurid *adj* 421, 422
lurk *v* 526
lurking *adj* 526
lurking place *n* 530
luscious *adj* 394, 396, 829
lush *n* 959; *v* 959; *adj* 337, 365, 396
lust *n* 865
luster *n* 420
lust for *v* 865
lustful *adj* 865
lustihood *n* 159
lustrous *adj* 420
luxuriate *v* 377
luxuriate in *v* 827
luxurious *adj* 377, 829
luxuriousness *n* 377
luxury *n* 377, 827
lying *n* 544; *adj* 544
lying down *n* 213
lymph *n* 337

M

ma *n* 166
ma'am *n* 374
Machiavellian *adj* 702
machinery *n* 633
macrocosm *n* 318
mad *adj* 173, 503, 824, 825
madam *n* 374
madame *n* 374
mad as a hatter *adj* 503
madden *v* 173
madman *n* 504
madness *n* 503, 825
maelstrom *n* 312, 348, 667
magenta *adj* 437
magic *n* 992; *adj* 992
magical *adj* 992
magician *n* 994
magisterial *adj* 737
magistracy *n* 965
magistrate *n* 967
magnetic *adj* 288
magnetism *n* 288
magnetize *v* 288
magnificence *n* 845
magnificent *adj* 192, 845
magnify *v* 35, 194, 482, 549, 990
magnifying glass *n* 445
magniloquence *n* 577
magniloquent *adj* 549, 577
magnitude *n* 25, 31, 192
mahogany *adj* 433
maiden *n* 129, 904; *adj* 66
maim *v* 158, 659
main *n* 341, 350
mainly *adv* 31
mainspring *n* 153, 615
mainstay *n* 666
maintain *v* 141, 143, 170, 215, 535, 670, 717, 720, 781, 937

maintain course *v* 143
maintenance *n* 141, 143, 170, 670, 781, 803
majestic *adj* 882
majesty *n* 875
major *adj* 33
majority *n* 33, 100, 131
make *n* 240; *v* 54, 56, 144, 161, 744, 852
make a choice *v* 609
make a circuit *v* 629
make a clean sweep of *v* 652
make a complete circle *v* 311
make a compromise *v* 628
make acquainted with *v* 527
make a fool of oneself *v* 853
make a fresh start *v* 66
make a generalization *v* 78
make allowance for *v* 469
make amends *v* 30, 952
make a mess of *v* 732
make a motion *v* 763
make an addition to *v* 37
make an end of *v* 67
make an exception *v* 469
make a noise *v* 402
make a pig of oneself *v* 957
make a place for *v* 184
make a point of *v* 604
make a pretext of *v* 617
make a resolution *v* 604
make a sign *v* 550
make a U-turn *v* 311
make believe *v* 546
make faces *v* 243
make for *v* 278
make free with *v* 789
make friends with *v* 888
make fun of *v* 856

make good *v* 660, 790
make grave *v* 835
make haste *v* 132, 682, 684
make headlines *v* 532
make headway *v* 282
make known *v* 525, 527, 529, 531
make light of *v* 483, 643
make little of *v* 483
make loose *v* 47
make manifest *v* 525
make merry *v* 840
make music *v* 415, 416
make news *v* 532
make nothing of *v* 871
make obeisance *v* 308
make one sick *v* 395
make one's way *v* 734
make out *v* 441
make over *v* 783
make payment *v* 807
make peace *v* 721, 723
make preparations *v* 673
make productive *v* 168
make progress *v* 282, 682
make provision *v* 637
make provision for *v* 673
make public *v* 531
make pungent *v* 392
maker *n* 164
make ready *v* 673
make sail *v* 267
make serious *v* 835
makeshift *n* 147, 617
make solid *v* 150
make strides *v* 282
make sure *v* 150, 474
make terms *v* 769
make the best of *v* 826
make the mind a blank *v* 452
make time *v* 132
make-up *n* 54
make up for *v* 30
make use of *v* 677
make verses *v* 597

make war v 722
making verses n 597
maladroit adj 699
maladroitness n 699
malady n 655
malaise n 378, 828
malapropism n 565
malarkey n 477
malcontent adj 832
male n 373; adj 373
male animal n 373, 374
malediction n 908
malevolence n 907
malevolence n 649, 889
malevolent adj 649,
    739, 907, 919, 945
malformation n 243
malformed adj 243
malice n 907
malicious adj 898, 907,
    919, 945
maliciousness n 907
malign v 934; adj 649
malignant adj 919, 945
malignity n 649
mall n 799
malleability n 149, 324
malleable adj 82, 149,
    324
maltreat v 649, 739,
    830, 923
mamma n 166
mammal n 366
mammoth n 192; adj
    31
man n 373
man n 372
man about town n 854
man after one's own
    heart n 899
manage v 58, 692, 693
manageable adj 705
management n 692,
    693, 698
manager n 694
managerial adj 692
managing adj 693
mandate n 630, 741

maneuver v 702
manfully adv 604
mangle v 659
mangy adj 655
man-hater n 911
manhood n 131, 373
mania n 503
maniac n 504
maniacal adj 503
manifest adj 446, 525
manifestation n 525
manifestation n 446,
    448
manifested adj 525
manifestly adv 525
manifold adj 15, 81,
    102
manipulate v 379, 677,
    702
manipulation n 379
mankind n 372
mankind n 372
manliness n 604
manly adj 131, 373
manner n 569, 613, 627
mannered adj 579, 855
mannerism n 79, 83,
    579
mannerisms n 855
manner of speaking n
    521
manners n 692, 852
man of learning n 500
mantle n 424
manual n 527
manufacture n 161; v
    161
manuscript n 590
many adj 100, 102
many-colored adj 440
many-sided adj 81
map n 183, 527, 626
mar v 659, 848
marble n 249
marbled adj 440
march n 266
marches n 233
marching band n 417

march of time n 109
mare n 374
margin n 231
marine adj 341
marine blue adj 438
mariner n 269
mariner n 269
marital separation n 905
maritime adj 267, 341
mark n 26, 71, 550,
    569, 590, 620; v 450,
    550, 642
marked adj 79
market n 799
market v 795
marketable adj 794,
    796
marketplace n 799
market price n 812
mark the time v 114
mark time v 114, 265
maroon adj 434
marquee n 223
marriage n 903
marriage n 43
marriageable adj 131
married adj 903
married man n 903
married woman n 903
marrow n 5, 221
marry v 43, 48, 903
marsh n 345
marshal v 60
marshy adj 339, 345
mart n 799
martial adj 722
martyr n 955
marvel n 870, 872; v
    870
marvelous adj 31, 870
marvelously adv 31
masculine adj 373
masculinity n 373
mash v 324, 352, 354
mask n 223, 424, 530; v
    442, 528
masquerade n 530

mass *n* 25, 31, 50, 72, 102, 192, 321
massacre *n* 361; *v* 361
massage *v* 379
massaging *n* 379
massive *adj* 192, 319, 321
massy *adj* 192
master *n* 745
master *n* 129, 540, 694, 700, 779; *v* 518, 539, 731, 749
masterful *adj* 731, 737
masterly *adj* 698
master mind *n* 500, 700, 872
master of *adj* 777
masterpiece *n* 648, 650
master stroke *n* 650
mastery *n* 698, 731, 741
mastic *n* 356a
masticate *v* 298
mastication *n* 298
mat *n* 219; *v* 219
match *n* 17, 27; *v* 17, 23, 27
matchless *adj* 33
mate *n* 17, 27, 711, 890, 903; *v* 89
material *n* 316; *adj* 3, 316
material existence *n* 3
materialism *n* 316
materialist *n* 316
materialistic *adj* 3, 316
materiality *n* 316
materiality *n* 3
materialization *n* 525
materialize *v* 316, 525
materials *n* 635
materials *n* 316
maternal *adj* 166
maternity *n* 11, 166
mates *n* 269
matins *n* 125
matriarch *n* 130
matriarchal *adj* 166
matricide *n* 361

matriculation *n* 539
matrimony *n* 903
matrix *n* 22
matted *adj* 219
matter *n* 3, 316, 516, 591, 625; *v* 642
matter little *v* 643
matter of fact *n* 1; *adj* 598, 703, 843
matter of factness *n* 703
matters *n* 151
matting *n* 219
mature *v* 144, 650, 658, 673; *adj* 673
mature years *n* 128
maturity *n* 124, 128, 131, 673
maul *v* 649
mausoleum *n* 363
mauve *adj* 437
maxim *n* 496
maxim *n* 537, 697
maximum *n* 210
maybe *adv* 470
maze *n* 248
mazy *adj* 248
meadow *n* 344
meager *adj* 32, 53, 103, 203, 575, 640, 643
meagerness *n* 203
mealy *adj* 330
mealy-mouthed *adj* 886
mean *n* 29
mean *n* 68, 628; *v* 451, 516, 620; *adj* 29, 32, 34, 68, 207, 435, 643, 649, 819, 851, 876, 886, 914a, 930, 943
meander *v* 248, 264, 266, 279, 573
meandering *n* 248
meaning *n* 516
meaning *n* 522, 620; *adj* 516
meaningful *adj* 516
meaningless *adj* 497, 517

meaninglessness *n* 517
meanness *n* 32, 34, 499, 886, 914a, 943
mean nothing *v* 517
means *n* 632
means *n* 627, 780, 803
means of access *n* 627
meantime *adv* 106
meanwhile *adv* 106
measurable *adj* 466
measure *n* 25, 26, 174, 413, 466, 786; *v* 106, 466
measured *adj* 174
measure for measure *n* 30
measureless *adj* 104
measurement *n* 466
measurement *n* 25
measure time *v* 114
meaty *adj* 354
mechanical *adj* 601, 633
medal *n* 733
meddlesome *adj* 455
meddlesomeness *n* 455
medial *adj* 68
median *n* 29; *adj* 68
meditate *v* 620, 631, 724
mediation *n* 724
mediation *n* 631, 766
mediator *n* 724
mediatory *adj* 724
medication *n* 662
medicinal *adj* 662
medicine *n* 662
medicine man *n* 994
mediocre *adj* 28, 29, 34, 598, 651, 736
mediocrity *n* 736
mediocrity *n* 28, 34
meditate *v* 451, 870
meditation *n* 451
meditative *adj* 451
medium *n* 29, 631, 994
medley *n* 41
meek *adj* 879

meekness *n* 879

meet *v* 23, 72, 199, 290, 772; *adj* 646

meeting *n* 43, 72, 199, 290, 680, 696

meetinghouse *n* 1000

meet up with *v* 151

meet with *v* 151

melancholy *n* 837; *adj* 830, 837

mélange *n* 41

melee *n* 59

meliorate *v* 174, 723

mellifluence *n* 413

mellifluous *adj* 413, 578

mellow *v* 144, 673; *adj* 128, 413, 428, 673, 721

melodic *adj* 413

melodious *adj* 377, 413, 580

melodiousness *n* 413

melody *n* 413

melody *n* 415

melt *v* 111, 144, 335, 384, 449

melt away *v* 4, 449

melting *n* 335, 384

member *n* 51, 56

membrane *n* 204

membranous *adj* 204

memento *n* 505

memento mori *n* 363

memorable *adj* 505

memorandum *n* 551

memorial *n* 505

memorialist *n* 553

memorialization *n* 883

memorize *v* 505, 539

memory *n* 505

memory *n* 122

menace *n* 667, 909; *v* 668, 909

menacing *adj* 909

menagerie *n* 72

mend *v* 658

mendacious *adj* 544

mendicant *n* 767

menial *n* 746

mental *adj* 450

mental balance *n* 502

mental cultivation *n* 539

mental excitation *n* 824

mental image *n* 515

mental suffering *n* 619

mention *v* 527

mentor *n* 540, 695

mephitic *adj* 401

mercantile *adj* 794

mercantilism *n* 796

mercenary *adj* 819

merchandise *n* 798

merchandise *v* 763, 796, 798

merchant *n* 797

merchant *n* 796

merchant ship *n* 273

merciful *adj* 740

merciless *adj* 914a

mercurial *adj* 149, 264

mercury *n* 389

mercy *n* 740, 914

mere *n* 343; *adj* 643

merely *adv* 32

merge *v* 48, 300

merge in *v* 56

merge into *v* 144

meridian *n* 125, 181

merit *n* 648, 944, 973

merit attention *v* 642

meritorious *adj* 931

mermaid *n* 979

merriment *n* 836

merry *adj* 829

merrymaking *n* 838

mesh *n* 219

mesmerist *n* 994

mesmerize *v* 992

mess *n* 59, 61, 162, 732

messenger *n* 534

messenger *n* 271, 527, 758

mess up *v* 59

messy *adj* 59

metallurgy *n* 358

metamorphose *v* 140

metamorphosis *n* 140

metaphor *n* 521

metaphorical *adj* 464

mete *v* 786

meteors *n* 318

mete out *v* 784

meter *n* 413

method *n* 627

method *n* 58, 60, 569, 626, 632, 692

methodical *adj* 58, 60, 692

methodically *adv* 58

methodological *adj* 626

methodology *n* 58

meticulous *adj* 459, 868

metrical *adj* 597

metrics *n* 597

mettle *n* 861

mew *v* 412

miasmic *adj* 401

microcosm *n* 193

microscope *n* 445

microscopic *adj* 32, 193

mid *adj* 68

mid-course *n* 628

midcourse *n* 68

midday *n* 125

middle *n* 68

middle *n* 29, 208, 222; *adj* 29, 68, 222; *adv* 222

middle class *adj* 29

middle course *n* 628

middle ground *n* 68, 174

middlemost *adj* 222

middle of the road *n* 174

middle way *n* 628

middling *adj* 32, 651

midmost *adj* 68

midnight *n* 126

midnight *n* 421

mid-point *n* 29, 68

midriff *n* 68

midst n 68, 208, 222; adv 222
midsummer 125
midway adj 628; adv 68
mien n 448, 692
might n 31, 157, 159, 173
mightily adv 31
mighty adj 31, 157, 159, 192, 192
migrate v 266
migration n 266
migratory adj 266
mild adj 174, 382, 391, 721, 740
mildew n 653, 663
mildewed adj 659
mildness n 174, 740
militant adj 722
militarist n 726
military adj 722
military band n 417
milkiness n 427, 430
milk-white adj 430
milky adj 352, 427, 430
mill n 330, 691
millennium n 108, 121
millions n 372
mimic v 19, 554
mimicry n 19
mince v 275
mince steps v 275
mind n 450, 498, 842; v 602
mindblower n 137
mindful adj 451, 457
mindfulness n 457
mindful (of) adj 505
mindless adj 499
mine n 636; v 252, 260, 659
mineral adj 358
mineral kingdom n 358
mineralogy n 358
mineral world n 358
mingle v 41

mingling n 41
miniature adj 32, 193
minimize v 483
minion n 899
minister n 631, 690, 694, 996; v 631, 693
ministerial adj 995
ministering spirit n 977
ministration n 693
ministry n 995, 996
minor n 129; adj 32, 34
minority n 34, 127
minstrel n 416, 597
mint n 22, 691
minus adj 776; adv 38, 187
minuscule adj 32
minute adj 32, 193
minutiae n 32
minx n 962
miracle n 872
miraculous adj 870
mirage 443
mire n 653
mirror n 445, 650; v 19; 443
mirth n 836
mirthful adj 836
misanthrope n 165
misanthropic adj 911
misanthropy n 911
misapplication n 679
misapply v 523, 679
misapprehend v 495, 523
misapprehension n 481, 495, 523
misappropriate v 679
misappropriation n 679
misbelieve n 984
misbelieving adj 984
miscalculate v 482, 495
miscalculation n 481, 482, 508
miscall v 565
miscarriage n 732
miscarry v 732

miscellaneous adj 15, 41, 465a
miscellaneousness n 78
miscellany n 41, 72, 78
mischief n 619
mischievous adj 649
miscomputation n 481
misconceive v 481, 495, 523
misconception n 481, 495, 523
misconjecture v 481
misconstruction n 523
misconstrue v 481, 523
miscreant n 949
misdate n 115; v 115
misdated adj 115
misdeed n 923
misdirect v 538
misdirection n 538
misemploy v 679
misemployment n 679
miser n 819
miserable adj 828, 837, 930
miserably adv 31, 32
miserly adj 819
misery n 828
misfiguration n 555
misfortune n 619, 735, 830
misgiving n 485, 860
misguidance n 538
misguide v 538
mishap n 619, 732, 830
misinform v 538
misinformation n 538
misinstruct v 538
misinterpret v 481, 495, 523
misinterpretation n 523
misinterpretation n 481, 495
misjudge v 481, 495
misjudging adj 481
misjudgment n 481
misjudgment n 495

mislay *v* 61, 776
mislead *v* 477, 538, 545
misleading *adj* 520,
544, 545
mismatch *n* 24; *v* 15
mismatched *adj* 24
misname *v* 565
misnamed *adj* 565
misnaming *n* 565
misnomer *n* 565
misogynist *n* 911
misplace *v* 61, 185
misplaced *adj* 115, 185
misplacement *n* 115,
185
misproportion *n* 241,
243
misread *v* 523
misreading *n* 523
misrepresent *v* 277,
477, 523, 538, 544,
555
misrepresentation *n*
555
misrepresentation *n*
523, 544
miss *n* 129, 374; *v* 776
misshape *v* 243
misshapen *adj* 241, 243
missing *adj* 187, 449
missing link *n* 53
mission *n* 755
missionary *n* 540
missive *n* 592
misspend *v* 638, 818
misstate *v* 523
miss the mark *v* 732
mist *n* 353, 422, 424,
427; *v* 353
mistake *n* 495, 523,
732; *v* 495, 523
mistaken *adj* 495, 544,
923
misteach *v* 538
misteaching *n* 538
mister *n* 373
misterm *v* 565
mistime *v* 135

mistimed *adj* 135
mistiness *n* 422, 426
mistreat *v* 830
mistress *n* 779
mistrust *n* 485; *v* 485
misty *adj* 353, 422,
426, 447
misunderstand *v* 481,
495, 523
misunderstanding *n*
495, 523, 713
misusage *n* 649, 679
misuse *n* 679
misuse *n* 638; *v* 638,
679
mite *n* 32
mitigate *v* 174, 469, 834
mitigating *adj* 469
mitigation *n* 174, 469,
834
mix *n* 41, 48; *v* 41, 48,
61
mixed *adj* 41
mixture *n* 41
mixture *n* 48
moan *n* 839; *v* 411
moaning *n* 411, 839
moat *n* 259, 350
mob *n* 72, 102
mobile *adj* 149, 264
mobility *n* 149, 264
mobilization *n* 264
mobilize *v* 264
mock *v* 19, 856, 929;
adj 17, 19
mockery *n* 856
mocking *n* 19; *adj* 856
mode *n* 7, 569, 613,
852
model *n* 21, 22, 80,
240, 650, 948; *v* 144,
240, 557; *adj* 650
modeled after *adj* 19
modeled on *adj* 19
modeling *n* 557
model oneself on *v* 19
mode of expression *n*
569

moderate *v* 174, 275,
723; *adj* 174, 275,
628, 736, 815, 881,
953
moderately *adv* 174
moderation *n* 174
moderation *n* 275, 736,
740, 826, 881, 953
moderator *n* 724, 967
modern *adj* 123
modernism *n* 123
modernity *n* 123
modernize *v* 123
modest *adj* 483, 879,
881, 960
modestly *adv* 881
modesty *n* 881
modesty *n* 483, 879,
960
modicum *n* 32
modification *n* 20a,
140, 469
modified *adj* 15, 20a
modify *v* 15, 20a, 140,
469
modish *adj* 852, 855
modulate *v* 140
modulation *n* 140, 413
module *n* 22, 273
moist *adj* 337, 339
moisten *v* 337, 339
moisture *n* 339
mold *n* 7, 21, 22, 240,
329, 557, 653; *v* 144,
240, 557, 653, 852
moldable *adj* 324
molded *adj* 820
molder *v* 659
moldering *adj* 659
moldy *adj* 653, 659
molecule *n* 32
molest *v* 649, 716
molestation *n* 649
mollification *n* 324
mollify *v* 174, 324, 723
mollusk *n* 366
molten *adj* 384
mom *n* 166

moment *n* 113, 642
momentary *adj* 111, 113
momentous *adj* 642
momentousness *n* 642
monetary *adj* 800
money *n* 800
money *n* 803
moneybag *n* 802
money matters *n* 811
mongrel *n* 41; *adj* 41
moniker *n* 564
monochrome *n* 429
monocle *n* 445
monody *n* 839
monogram *n* 561
monolog *n* 589
monomania *n* 606
monomaniacal *adj* 606
monosyllable *n* 561
monotheism *n* 983
monotonous *adj* 16, 27, 104, 841
monotony *n* 16, 27, 104, 841
monsoon *n* 349
monster *n* 192, 949, 980
monstrosity *n* 192, 243, 872
monstrous *adj* 31, 192, 846
monstrously *adv* 31
monument *n* 363, 551
moo *v* 412
mood *n* 7, 176, 602, 820
moodiness *n* 901a
moods *n* 5
moody *adj* 901a
moon *n* 420, 423
moonbeam *n* 420
moor *n* 344; *v* 43
moored *adj* 184, 186
mooring *n* 184
mope *v* 837
moper *n* 683
moral *adj* 922, 944
moral imperative *n* 926

morality *n* 922, 944
moralize *v* 537
morals *n* 922
moral sensibility *n* 822
morass *n* 345
moratorium *n* 133
morbid *adj* 655
more *adv* 33, 37
more or less *adj* 25
moreover *adv* 37
more than one *adj* 100
morgue *n* 363
morn *n* 125
morning *n* 125
morning *n* 125
morningtide *n* 125
moron *n* 493, 501
morose *adj* 901a
moroseness *n* 901a
morphology *n* 368
morrow *n* 121
morsel *n* 32, 390
mortal *n* 372; *adj* 111, 361, 372
mortal coil *n* 362
mortality *n* 111, 360, 372
mortal remains *n* 362
mortar and pestle *n* 330
mortgage *n* 771, 787; *v* 771
mortification *n* 828, 830
mortify *v* 828, 830, 879
mortuary *n* 363; *adj* 363
mosaic *adj* 81, 440
moss *n* 345
most *adv* 31
most likely *adv* 472
mote *n* 32, 451
moth-eaten *adj* 653, 659
mother *n* 166, 192
mother earth *n* 342
motherhood *n* 166
motherland *n* 189
motion *n* 264

motion *n* 550
motionless *adj* 172, 265, 683
motivate *v* 615, 744
motivation *n* 615
motive *n* 615
motive power *n* 264
mot juste n 496
motley *adj* 16a, 41, 81
motorboat *n* 273
motorcar *n* 272
motorcycle *n* 272
motoring *n* 266
motorscooter *n* 272
mottled *adj* 440
motto *n* 496, 566
mound *n* 192
mount *v* 206, 305
mountain *n* 192, 250
mourn for *v* 833
mournful *adj* 830, 839, 901a
mourn over *v* 839
mouth *n* 231, 343
mouthful *n* 25, 32
mouthpiece *n* 582
movable *adj* 264, 270
movableness *n* 264
move *n* 264, 270; *v* 175, 264, 266, 270, 302, 615, 763, 824
move away from *v* 287
move back *v* 287
moved *adj* 821, 914
movement *n* 264, 680, 682
move off *v* 293
move out *v* 293
move quickly *v* 274
mover *n* 164
move slowly *v* 275
move to the center *v* 29
move towards *v* 286
moving *n* 266, 680; *adj* 264
mow *v* 371
Mr. *n* 373
Ms. *n* 374

much *adj* 641; *adv* 31

much ado about nothing *n* 549

much the same *adj* 17, 27

muck *n* 653

muckraking *n* 529

mud *n* 345, 653

muddle *n* 59; *v* 61

muddle-headed *adj* 499

muddy *adj* 339, 345, 352, 519

muffle *v* 403, 408a, 590

muffled *adj* 405, 408a

muffled drums *n* 408a

muffler *n* 408a

muggy *adj* 339

mulish *adj* 606

mulishness *n* 606

mulling around *n* 681

multi-colored *adj* 440

multifarious *adj* 16a, 81

multifold *adj* 81

multiformity *n* 81

multiple *adj* 102

multiplication *n* 168

multiplicity *n* 102

multiply *v* 35, 85, 102, 163, 168

multiply by four *v* 96

multiplying by four *n* 96

multi-purpose *adj* 148

multitude *n* 102

multitude *n* 31, 72, 100, 876

multitudes *n* 372

multitudinous *n* 102; *adj* 102

mum *n* 166; *adj* 581, 585

mumble *v* 583

mumbling *n* 583

mumbo-jumbo *n* 993

mummify *v* 363

mummy *n* 166

munch *v* 298

mundane *adj* 318

munificence *n* 816, 910

munificent *adj* 816, 910

munitions *n* 727

murder *n* 361; *v* 361

murderer *n* 361

murderous *adj* 361

murk *n* 421

murkiness *n* 421

murky *adj* 421, 422, 426, 431

murmur *n* 405; *v* 348, 405

murmured *adj* 405

muscular *adj* 159

muse *v* 451

mushiness *n* 326

mushy *adj* 324, 339

music *n* 415

musical *adj* 413, 415, 416, 597

musical instruments *n* 417

musicalness *n* 413

musician *n* 416

musing *n* 451

muster *n* 72; *v* 72, 85

mustiness *n* 401

musty *adj* 401, 653

mutability *n* 149

mutable *adj* 149

mutation *n* 140

mute *n* 408a; *v* 408a; *adj* 403, 581, 585

muted *adj* 405, 408a

muteness *n* 581

muteness *n* 403, 585

mutilate *v* 38, 241, 361, 659

mutilation *n* 38, 241

mutineer *n* 742

mutinous *adj* 742

mutinousness *n* 742

mutiny *n* 146, 742; *v* 742

mutter *v* 405, 583

muttering *n* 583

mutual *adj* 12, 148

mutuality *n* 12

muzzle *v* 158, 403, 581

myopia *n* 443

myopic *adj* 443

mysterious *adj* 208, 447, 519, 528, 533

mystery *n* 447, 533

mystify *v* 519

N

nab *v* 789

nacreous *adj* 427, 440

nadir *n* 211

naiad *n* 979

naive *adj* 435, 703, 946

naivete *n* 703, 946

naked *adj* 226

nakedness *n* 226

name *n* 13, 562, 564, 569, 873, 877; *v* 564, 755

namely *adv* 522

namesake *n* 564

naming *n* 564

nannygoat *n* 374

nap *n* 256

naphtha *n* 356

napping *adj* 458

narrate *v* 594

narration *n* 594

narrative prose *n* 598

narrow *v* 195, 203, 469; *adj* 32, 203

narrow escape *n* 671

narrowing *n* 469

narrow-minded *adj* 32, 499

narrow-mindedness *n* 32

narrowness *n* 203

narrowness *n* 203

nascent *adj* 66

nasty *adj* 395, 653

natal *adj* 66

nation *n* 188

national *adj* 372

native *n* 188; *adj* 188

nativity *n* 66

natural *n* 501; *adj* 82, 494, 578, 703, 849

natural causes *n* 360
natural gas *n* 388
natural harbor *n* 343
natural history *n* 357
naturalist *n* 357
natural light *n* 423
natural philosophy *n* 316
natural world *n* 357
nature *n* 5, 80, 176, 318, 357, 820
naught *n* 4, 101
nauseate *v* 395, 830, 867
nauseating *adj* 401, 867, 898
nauseous *adj* 395, 401, 830
nautical *adj* 267
naval *adj* 267
navel *n* 222
navigable *adj* 267
navigate *v* 267
navigation *n* 267
navigator *n* 269
navy *n* 273; *adj* 438
near *v* 286; *adj* 17, 121, 152, 186, 197, 199; *adv* 197
nearly *adv* 32
near miss *n* 671
nearness *n* 197
nearness *n* 9, 186, 286
near side *n* 239
nearsighted *adj* 443
nearsightedness *n* 443
near the mark *adv* 32
neat *adj* 58, 576, 578, 652, 849
neaten *v* 652
neatness *n* 652
nebbish *n* 547
nebula *n* 353
nebulosity *n* 353, 422
nebulous *adj* 422, 519
necessarily *adv* 154, 601

necessary *adj* 601, 630, 744
necessitate *v* 601, 630, 744
necessity *n* 601
necessity *n* 630, 744
neck and neck race *n* 27
necklace *n* 247
necromancer *n* 513, 994
necromancy *n* 992
need *n* 630, 684, 804, 865; *v* 630, 640
needful *adj* 601, 630
neediness *n* 804
needle *n* 253, 262
needless *adj* 641
needy *adj* 804
negate *v* 536
negation *n* 536
negation *n* 468
negative *n* 22; *adj* 14, 84, 489, 536
neglect *n* 460
neglect *n* 730, 732, 773, 927; *v* 53, 460, 678, 730, 773, 927
neglected *adj* 460
neglectful *adj* 460
neglecting *adj* 460
negligence *n* 460, 773
negligent *adj* 460, 738, 773, 927
negotiate *v* 724, 769, 794
negotiation *n* 724, 769, 774, 794
negotiator *n* 724
neigh *v* 412
neighbor *v* 197
neighborhood *n* 197, 227
neighboring *adj* 197
neighborly *adj* 707, 888, 892
nemesis *n* 919
neologic *adj* 563
neological *adj* 563

neologism *n* 563
neologist *n* 563
neology *n* 563
neophyte *n* 541
nereid *n* 979
nerve *n* 159, 861; *v* 159
nervous *adj* 574, 825
nescient *adj* 491
ness *n* 250
nest *n* 189
nestle *v* 186
net *n* 219; *v* 219
nethermost *adj* 211
netting *n* 219
nettle *n* 663
network *n* 219
neutral *adj* 29, 609a, 628
neutrality *n* 690a
neutrality *n* 29, 609a, 628
neutralization *n* 179
neutralize *v* 30, 179
neutral tint *n* 429, 432
never *adv* 107
never-ending *adj* 104, 112
nevermore *adv* 107
nevertheless *adv* 30
never to be forgotten *adj* 505
new *adj* 18, 123, 146, 435
new birth *n* 660
newborn *adj* 129
newfangled *adj* 83, 123, 140
new-fangled expression *n* 563
newfangledness *n* 123
newly *adv* 123
newness *n* 123
news *n* 532
news *n* 498, 527
newsmonger *n* 527, 532, 534
newsstory *n* 532
New Testament *n* 986

next adj 63; adv 117
next generation n 127
next world n 152
nibble v 298
nice adj 394, 829, 868
nice distinction n 15
nicety n 465, 868
niche n 182, 221, 244
nick n 257; v 257
nickname n 564, 565; v 564
nick of time n 134
niggard n 819
niggardly adj 819
niggling adj 643
nigh adj 197; adv 197
night n 421
nightfall n 126
nihilist n 165
nil n 4
nimble adj 274, 498, 842
nincompoop n 501
nine n 98
ninny n 501
nip n 392; v 385
nip in the bud v 361
nipping adj 383
nipple n 250
nippy adj 392
nirvana n 981
nit-picking adj 477
nixie n 979
nobility n 875
nobility n 33
noble adj 31, 875, 878
nobody n 101
no choice n 609a
nocturnal adj 421
node n 250
no doubt adv 474
nodular adj 250
nodulation n 256
nodule n 250
noise n 402, 404, 414
noiseless adj 403
noisily adv 404
noisome adj 401, 657

noisy adj 404
nomad n 268
nomadic adj 264, 266
nomadism n 266
nom de guerre n 565
nom de plume n 565
nomenclature n 564
nominal adj 564
nominate v 755
nomination n 755
nominee n 758
no more adj 360
no more than adv 32
nonadhesion n 47
nonadhesive adj 47
nonappearance n 187
nonattendance n 187
nonbeliever n 485, 487, 989
noncohesive adj 47
noncompletion n 730
noncompletion n 53, 304
noncompliance n 742, 773
noncompliant adj 764
nonconforming adj 984
nonconformist n 489, 984; adj 489, 984
nonconformity n 16a, 24, 79, 83, 489, 984
none n 101
nonentity n 2
nonessential adj 57, 643
nonetheless adv 30
nonexistence n 2
nonexistent adj 2, 187
nonexpectant adj 508
nonexpectation n 508
nonextension n 180a
nonfulfillment n 730
nonfunctional adj 674
nonimitation n 20
noninterference n 748
nonlinear adj 245
nonobservance n 773

nonobservance n 83, 742, 927
nonobservant adj 773
nonpayment n 808
nonperformance n 730, 732, 927
nonplus n 704
nonpreparation n 674
nonrational adj 450a
non-relation n 10
nonresidence n 187
nonresistance n 725
nonresonance n 408a
nonresonant adj 408a
nonsense n 497, 517
nonsensical adj 477, 497, 499, 517, 853
non sequitur n 497
nontranslucent adj 426
nontransparency n 426
nontransparent adj 426
noodle n 450
nook n 182, 221, 244
noon n 125
noon n 125
noonday n 125
noontide n 125
noontime n 125
normal adj 5, 29, 82, 736
normalcy n 80
normality n 502
normal state n 80
nose n 250
not a bit adv 32
notable adj 31, 642
notably adv 31
not act v 681
not a jot adv 32
notary n 553
not at all adv 32
not a whit adv 32
not bad adj 651
not beat around the bush v 576
not be good for v 657
not be surprised v 871
not care v 823

notch *n* 257
notch *n* 244; *v* 257
notched *adj* 257
not come up to *v* 28, 34
not come up to snuff *v* 28
not complete *v* 730
not conversant *adj* 699
not curved *adj* 246
not cut it *v* 640
not discriminate *v* 465a
not do *v* 640, 681
note *n* 550, 551, 592, 596; *v* 450, 550, 596
not enough *adj* 640
notes *n* 802
noteworthy *adj* 31
not exist *v* 2
not expect *v* 508
not germane *adj* 57
not get involved *v* 623
not give an inch *v* 604
not have *v* 777a
not have much of a chance *v* 473
not hear *v* 419
not here *adj* 187
nothing *n* 4, 101, 643
nothingness *n* 2, 4
notice *n* 457, 668; *v* 450, 457, 480a, 928
notification *n* 527
notify *v* 668
no time *n* 107
not in *adj* 187
not included in *adj* 55
not in sight *adj* 447
not in the least *adv* 32
not in use *adj* 678
notion *n* 451, 453, 515
not licensed *adj* 925
not many *adj* 103
not matter *v* 643
not often *adv* 137
not pass muster *v* 34, 651
not pay *v* 808
not pertinent *adj* 10

not possible *adj* 471
not present *adj* 187, 187
not quite *adv* 32
not reach *v* 304
not see *v* 442
not smell *v* 399
not sorry *adj* 951
not straight *adj* 243
not suffice *v* 640
not the same *adj* 15
not think *v* 452
not true *adj* 243
not use *v* 678
not well *adj* 655
not with it *adj* 246
notwithstanding *adv* 30
nourishment *n* 298, 359
novel *n* 593; *adj* 18, 123
novelty *n* 18, 123
novice *n* 541, 701
now *adv* 118
nowadays *adv* 118
now and then *adv* 136
no way *adj* 471
noway *adv* 32
nowhere *adv* 187
nowise *adv* 32
now or never *adv* 134
noxious *adj* 649, 657
nozzle *n* 250
nuance *n* 15
nub *n* 68, 222
nubile *adj* 131
nuclear power *n* 388
nucleus *n* 68, 153, 222
nude *adj* 226
nudity *n* 226
nuisance *n* 619, 663, 830, 975
null and void *adj* 756
nullification *n* 536, 756
nullify *v* 2, 30, 179, 536, 756
nullity *n* 4
numb *v* 376; *adj* 376, 381
number *n* 84

number *v* 85
number among *v* 76
numbering *n* 85
numberless *adj* 104
numbers *n* 102
numbing *adj* 383
numbness *n* 381
numbness *n* 376
numerable *adj* 85
numeral *n* 84; *adj* 84, 85
numeration *n* 85
numerical *adj* 85
numerous *adj* 100, 102
numskull *n* 493, 501
nuptials *n* 903
nurse *n* 753; *v* 662
nursery *n* 127
nursling *n* 129
nurture *v* 235, 673
nut *n* 504
nutbrown *adj* 433
nutriment *n* 298, 359
nutrition *n* 298
nutritious *adj* 299, 656
nutritive *adj* 299
nuts *adj* 503
nutshell *n* 32

O

oaf *n* 501
oath *n* 535, 768
obduracy *n* 606, 951
obdurate *adj* 600, 951
obedience *n* 743
obedience *n* 725, 749, 772
obedient *adj* 725, 743, 772, 926
obediently *adv* 743
obeisance *n* 308
obese *adj* 192, 194
obesity *n* 192
obey *v* 725, 743, 772
obey the rules *v* 82
obfuscate *v* 528
obfuscation *n* 528

object n 3, 316, 453, 516, 620
objection n 704
objectionable adj 846
objective n 453; adj 6
object to v 932
obligate v 630
obligation n 177, 601, 768, 806, 926, 963
obligations n 770
obligatory adj 744, 926
oblige adj 707, 744, 770
obliged adj 177, 916, 926
obliging adj 894, 906
oblique adj 217
obliquely adv 217
obliquity n 217
obliquity n 243
obliterate v 2, 552
obliterated adj 552
obliteration n 552
obliteration n 2
obliteration of the past n 506
oblivion n 506
oblivious adj 506
obloquy n 874
obnoxious adj 830, 898
obscene adj 961
obscenity n 961
obscuration n 421
obscure v 421, 422, 528; adj 208, 421, 426, 447, 519, 571, 704, 876
obscure meaning n 526
obscuring n 528
obscurity n 571
obscurity n 208, 421, 431, 447, 475, 519, 526
obsequies n 363
obsequious adj 886
obsequiousness n 743, 886
observance n 772

observance n 82, 613, 743, 883, 983a, 998
observant adj 457, 772
observation n 453, 457
observe v 441, 457, 772, 883, 926
observer n 444
obsolete adj 122, 124
obstacle n 177, 704, 706
obstinacy n 606
obstinacy n 141, 150, 327, 603, 604, 704, 742
obstinate adj 150, 327, 499, 604, 606, 719, 742
obstreperous adj 173, 404
obstruct v 261, 275, 706, 708, 761
obstruction n 261, 706
obstructive adj 706
obstruct the passage of light v 426
obtain v 775, 795
obtrude v 228
obtrusive adj 706
obtuse adj 254, 376, 499
obtuse angle n 244
obtuseness n 254, 376, 843
obverse adj 218
obvious adj 446, 474, 518, 525
occasion n 8, 134, 615; v 153
occasional adj 103, 137
occasionally adv 136
occultism n 992
occupancy n 186, 777
occupant n 188, 779
occupation n 186, 625
occupy v 186, 777
occupying adj 186
occur v 1, 151
occurrence n 151

ocean n 341
ocean-going adj 267
oceanic adj 341
oceanographic adj 341
ocher adj 435
ochre adj 433
octet n 415
ocular adj 441
odd adj 40, 83, 87, 870
oddity n 83, 503, 857
odds n 28, 156, 713
odds and ends n 40
odious adj 830, 898
odium n 898, 932
odor n 398
odoriferous adj 398, 400
odorific adj 400
odorless adj 399
odorlessness n 399
odorous adj 398
oeuvre n 161
of age adj 131
of a piece adj 16, 17
of every description adj 81
off adj 187
off and on adv 138
off base adj 10, 481, 495
offend v 289, 830
offend against the law v 964
offended adj 900
offense n 716, 830
offensive adj 395, 401, 653, 716, 830, 846, 867, 898
offensive smell n 401
offer n 763
offer v 763
offer congratulations v 896
offer counsel v 695
offer for sale v 763
offering n 763, 784
offer pleasure v 829
offer prayers v 990

offhand *adv* 132, 612

office *n* 170, 625, 799

official *n* 694; *adj* 625, 737, 983a

offing *n* 196

off one's guard *adj* 508

off-set *n* 30; *v* 30, 179

offshoot *n* 39, 51, 65, 154

offside *n* 238

offspring *n* 154, 167

off the mark *adj* 495

of late *adv* 122, 123

of little account *adj* 643

of long standing *adj* 124

of necessity *adv* 601, 630

of no account *adj* 643

of old *adv* 122

of one accord *adj* 488

of one mind *adj* 178

of one's own accord *adv* 600

of other times *adj* 124

of small importance *adj* 643

oft *adv* 136

often *adv* 104, 136

oftentimes *adv* 136

of the same mind *adj* 488

oft-repeated *adj* 136

of various kinds *adj* 16a

of vital importance *adj* 642

of yore *adv* 122

ogle *v* 441

ogre *n* 980

oil *n* 356

oil *n* 355; *v* 255, 332, 355

oil burner *n* 386

oiliness *n* 355

oiling *n* 332

oil lamp *n* 423

oily *adj* 255, 355

oink *v* 412

ointment *n* 355, 356, 662

old *adj* 124, 128, 130

old age *n* 124, 128

older *adj* 128

old-fashioned *adj* 124

old hand *n* 700

old lady *n* 166, 903

old maid *n* 904

old man *n* 130, 166, 903

oldness *n* 124

old soldier *n* 700

Old Testament *n* 986

old woman *n* 130

oleaginous *adj* 355

olive *adj* 435

olive oil *n* 356

omen *n* 512

omen *n* 668

ominous *adj* 665, 668, 909

omission *n* 53, 55, 460, 732, 773, 893

omit *v* 55, 460, 773

omitted *adj* 893

omnipotence *n* 157, 976

omnipotent *adj* 104, 157

omnipresence *n* 186, 976

omnipresent *adj* 186

on *adv* 125, 282

on a bed of roses *adv* 377

on account of *adv* 155

on a large scale *adv* 31

on a level with *adj* 27

on a line with *adv* 278

on all sides *adv* 227

on a moment's notice *adv* 113

on an equal footing with *adj* 27

on a par with *adj* 27

on bended knee *adv* 879

once and for all *adv* 67

once more *adv* 90, 104

on compulsion *adv* 744

on condition *adv* 770

on dry land *adv* 342

one *n* 372; *adj* 13, 52, 87, 729

one and the same *adj* 27

one by one *adv* 44

on edge *adv* 507

one in a million *n* 648

on end *adv* 212

oneness *n* 87

one of a kind *adj* 20

onerous *adj* 649, 706, 830

oneself *n* 13

one's own *n* 11

one's own flesh and blood *n* 11

one step at a time *adv* 275

on every side *adv* 227

one way or another *adv* 627

on fire *adj* 382

on foot *adj* 170

ongoing *adj* 53

on land *adv* 342

onlooker *n* 444

only *adv* 32

only just *adv* 32

only so far *adv* 233

on no account *adv* 32

on no occasion *adv* 107

on one's back *adv* 213

one one's honor *adj* 768

on one side *adv* 217, 236

on one's own time *adv* 133

on one's toes *adj* 507

on purpose *adv* 620

onset *n* 66, 716

on sight *adv* 441

onslaught *n* 716

on target *adj* 494

on tenterhooks *adj* 507

on that occasion *adv* 119

on the average *adv* 29
on the ball *adj* 498
on the brink of *adv* 121
on the dot *adv* 132
on the eve of *adv* 121
on the face of it *adv* 448
on the face of the earth *adv* 180, 318
on the go *adv* 264
on the horizon *adj* 152, 507
on the horns of a dilemma *n* 476
on the instant *adv* 132
on the march *adv* 264
on the move *adv* 264
on the offensive *adv* 716
on the other hand *adv* 30
on the point of *adv* 121
on the road *adj* 264, 266
on the road to *adv* 278
on the safe side *adj* 664
on the sly *adv* 528
on the spot *adv* 132, 134
on the spur of the moment *adv* 113, 132, 134
on the wagon *adj* 958
on the wane *adj* 36
on the watch *adj* 457; *adv* 507
on the whole *adv* 50
on time *adj* 132; *adv* 132
ontology *n* 1
on trial *adv* 675
onus *n* 926
onward *adv* 282
ooze *v* 295, 348
oozing *n* 295
oozy *adj* 352
opacity *n* 426
opacity *n* 353
opalescence *n* 427

opalescent *adj* 427
opaline *adj* 430, 440
opaque *adj* 422, 426
opaqueness *n* 426
ope *v* 260
open *v* 66, 194, 198, 260, 525; *adj* 177, 260, 338, 525, 543, 665, 703
open air *n* 338
open-eyed *adj* 507
open field *n* 134
opening *n* 260
opening *n* 66, 198, 260
open into *v* 348
openly *adv* 525
openness *n* 525, 703, 748
open space(s) *n* 180
open to the view *v* 446
opera *n* 599
opera glasses *n* 445
operahouse *n* 599
operate *v* 161, 170, 680
operatic *adj* 415, 416
operation *n* 170, 680
operation *adj* 170, 680
operator *n* 690
ophthalmia *n* 443
opine *v* 484
opinion *n* 451, 453, 480, 484, 537, 695, 821
opponent *n* 710
opponent *n* 726, 891
opportune *adj* 134, 646
opportunely *adv* 134
opportuneness *n* 134
opportunism *n* 646
opportunist *n* 935
opportunity *n* 134
oppose *v* 14, 179, 237, 536, 708, 719
opposed *adj* 14
opposer *n* 726
opposing *n* 708; *adj* 14, 237, 489

opposite *n* 237; *adj* 14, 218, 237
oppositeness *n* 14
opposite poles *n* 237
opposite side *n* 237
opposition *n* 237, 708
opposition *n* 14, 24, 218, 489, 710, 719, 720, 726
opposition *n* 179
oppress *v* 649, 739, 923
oppression *n* 649, 739
oppressive *adj* 382, 421, 649, 739, 830
oppressor *n* 739, 913
opprobrious *adj* 874
oppugnance *n* 719
opt for the mean *v* 774
optic *adj* 441
optical instruments *n* 445
optics *n* 420, 441
optimism *n* 482
optimistic *adj* 858
option *n* 600, 609
optional *adj* 600, 609
opulence *n* 803
opus *n* 590, 593
oracle *n* 513
oracle *n* 500
oracular *adj* 511
oral *adj* 580, 582
oral communication *n* 588
orange *n* 439
orange *adj* 439
orangish *adj* 439
orangy *adj* 439
oration *n* 582
orator *n* 582
oratory *n* 582
orb *n* 181, 247
orbit *n* 247
orchestra *n* 416, 417
orchestral *adj* 415
orchestral music *n* 415
orchid *adj* 437

ordain *v* 741, 755, 963, 995

ordained *adj* 996

ordeal *n* 722, 828

order *n* 58

order *n* 63, 75, 242, 630, 693, 697, 721, 741, 963; *v* 58, 630, 652, 673, 693, 741

ordered *adj* 60, 242

ordering *n* 60

orderliness *n* 58, 652

orderly *adj* 58, 60

order of succession *n* 63

ordinance *n* 741

ordinariness *n* 736

ordinary *adj* 82, 598, 613, 643, 651, 736

ordinary condition *n* 80

oread *n* 979

organic *adj* 357

organic chemistry *n* 357

organic remains *n* 357

organisms *n* 357

organization *n* 60, 161, 329, 626

organizational *adj* 329, 626

organize *v* 60, 161, 626

organized *adj* 58

organizer *n* 626

orgasm *n* 173, 377

orgasmic *adj* 173, 377

orifice *n* 260

origin *n* 66, 153

original *n* 22, 590, 857; *adj* 20, 79, 83, 153, 515, 614

originality *n* 18, 20, 83, 123, 168, 515

originate *v* 66, 153, 515

originate from *v* 154

originate in *v* 154

origination *n* 153

originator *n* 164

ornament *n* 577, 847

ornament *v* 577, 847

ornamental *adj* 847

ornamentation *n* 847

ornamented *adj* 577, 847

ornate *adj* 577, 847

ornateness *n* 577

ornithology *n* 368

orthodox *adj* 82, 983a

orthodoxy *n* 983a

orthography *n* 561

oscillate *v* 149, 314

oscillating *adj* 149, 314

oscillation *n* 314

oscillation *n* 138, 149, 605

ossification *n* 323

ossify *n* 323

ostensible *adj* 448, 617

ostensibly *adv* 448, 617

ostentation *n* 882

ostentatious *adj* 855, 882

ostracism *n* 893

ostracized *adj* 893

other *adj* 15

other side of the coin *n* 235

other time *n* 119

otherwordly *adj* 317

oust *v* 297, 789

out *adj* 187; *adv* 220

out and out *adv* 52

outbound *adj* 295

outbreak *n* 66, 173, 295, 713

outburst *n* 173, 295, 825

outcast *n* 893

outcome *n* 63, 65, 154

outcry *n* 404, 411

outdated *adj* 124

outdo *v* 33, 303

outer *adj* 220

outer edges *n* 233

outer space *n* 180

outfit *n* 225; *v* 225, 727

outgoing *adj* 295

outgrow *v* 194

outgrowth *n* 65, 154

outing *n* 266

out in the open *adv* 338

outlandish *adj* 10, 83, 853

outlast *v* 110

outlawed *adj* 964

outlay *n* 809

outlet *n* 260

outline *n* 230

outline *n* 240, 448, 596; *v* 230

outlined *adj* 446

outlive *v* 110, 141

outlook *n* 441, 448

outlying *adj* 196, 220

outmoded *adj* 124

outnumber *v* 102

out of all proportion *adv* 31

out of commission *adj* 659

out of danger *adj* 664

out of date *adj* 124

out of debt *adj* 807

out of doors *adv* 338

out-of-fashion *adj* 124

out of focus *adj* 447

out of its element *adj* 185

out of joint *adj* 24

out of mind *adj* 506

out of one's depth *adv* 208

out of order *adj* 59, 651, 674, 923

out of place *adj* 59, 115, 185

out of practice *adj* 699

out of proportion *adj* 241; *adv* 641

out of shape *adj* 243

out of sight *adj* 447

out of sorts *adj* 655

out of step *adj* 24

out-of-style *adj* 124

out of the frying pan and into the fire *adv* 835

out-of-the-way *adj* 10, 196
out of tune *adj* 24, 414, 651
out of view *adj* 447
out of work *adj* 681
outpost *n* 196
outpouring *n* 295
outrage *n* 173, 619, 649
outrageous *adj* 31, 853
outrageousness *n* 853
outrank *v* 33
outride *v* 303
outrigger *n* 215
outright *adv* 52
outrival *v* 33
outrun *v* 303
outset *n* 66, 293
outside *n* 220; *adj* 220
outsides *n* 448
outside time *n* 107
outskirts *n* 196, 227
outspoken *adj* 703
outspread *adj* 202
outstretched *adj* 200, 202
outstrip *v* 33, 303
outward *adj* 220, 295
outwards *adv* 220
outweigh *v* 33, 175
outwit *v* 545
oval *n* 247; *adj* 247
oven *n* 386
over *adj* 40, 67; *adv* 33, 122, 220, 237
overabound *v* 641
over again *adv* 90, 104
over against *adv* 237
over and above *adj* 641; *adv* 33, 37, 641
over and done with *adv* 67
over and over *adv* 104
overbearing *adj* 878, 885
over-blown *adj* 882
overburden *v* 649

overcast *v* 421; *adj* 421, 422, 901a
overcharge *n* 814; *v* 577, 814
overcome *v* 731
over-confident *adj* 878
overdo *v* 641
overdose *n* 641; *v* 641
overdraw *v* 555
overdue *adj* 115, 133
overeat *v* 957
over-eating *n* 957
overestimate *v* 481, 482, 549
overestimated *adj* 482
overestimation *n* 482
overflow *n* 641; *v* 348, 641
overgrown *adj* 192, 194
overhang *v* 206
overhanging *adj* 206
overhear *v* 418
overlay *v* 223, 356a
overload *v* 641
overlook *v* 458, 460, 693
overlying *adj* 206
overly sensitive *adj* 901
overmatch *v* 28
overmuch *adj* 641; *adv* 641
over one's head *adv* 208, 641
overpower *v* 744
overpowering *adj* 824
overpraise *v* 482, 933
overprize *v* 482
overrate *v* 482
overrated *adj* 482
overreach *v* 303
over-refined *adj* 477
override *v* 175
overripe *adj* 128
overrun *v* 194, 303, 641
overseer *n* 694
overshoot *v* 303
oversight *n* 495
oversimplification *n* 78

overspread *v* 223
overstate *v* 549
overstatement *n* 549
overstep *v* 303
overtask *v* 679
overtax *v* 679
over the way *adv* 237
overthrow *n* 146, 162, 308; *v* 162, 308
overture *n* 763
overturn *n* 146, 218, 308; *v* 162, 218, 308, 479
overvaluation *n* 482
overweening *adj* 641, 880
overwhelm *v* 641
overwhelming *adj* 824
overwork *v* 679
overwrought *adj* 549, 824
overzealous *adj* 825
ovoid *adj* 249
owing to *adj* 154, 155
own *v* 488, 777
owner *n* 779
ownership *n* 777, 780
own in common *v* 778
own up *v* 529

P

P.M. *n* 126
pace *n* 264; *v* 106
pacific *adj* 174, 721, 723
pacification *n* 723
pacification *n* 174
pacify *v* 174, 723
pack *n* 72
pack it up *v* 293
pact *n* 23, 769
pad *n* 189; *v* 194, 224
padding *n* 224, 263
paddle *v* 267
paddock *n* 232
paean *n* 838
pagan *n* 984; *adj* 991
pagan deity *n* 991

pageant *n* 448
pageantry *n* 882
pain *n* 378, 828
pain *n* 619, 663, 686,
 974, 982; *v* 649, 830
painful *adj* 378, 649,
 830, 982
painfully *adv* 31, 830
painfulness *n* 830
painfulness *n* 649
pain in the neck *n* 663
pains *n* 459, 974
painstaking *adj* 459
paint *n* 428; *v* 428, 556
painter *n* 559
painting *n* 556
pair *n* 17, 89; *v* 89
pair off *v* 89
pal *n* 890
palatability *n* 394
palatable *adj* 377, 390,
 394
palaver *n* 588
pale *n* 232, 233; *v* 422,
 429; *adj* 422, 429,
 430, 435
paleness *n* 422, 429
paleontology *n* 368
paling *n* 232
pall *n* 363; *v* 376, 395
palliative *adj* 174, 662,
 834
pallid *adj* 429, 430
pallor *n* 429
palm *n* 733
palmer *n* 268
palpability *n* 379
palpable *adj* 3, 316,
 379, 446, 525
palpitate *v* 315
palpitation *n* 315
palsied *adj* 160
paltriness *n* 32, 643,
 736
paltry *adj* 32, 34, 643,
 736
panacea *n* 662
pandemonium *n* 59, 982

pander to *v* 933
pang *n* 378, 828
panhandler *n* 767
panic *n* 860
panic-stricken *adj* 860
pant *v* 349, 382, 688
pap *n* 250
papa *n* 166
paper *v* 223
par *n* 27
parabola *n* 245
parade *v* 882
paradigm *n* 22
paradisaic *adj* 981
paradise *n* 981
paradisical *adj* 981
paradox *n* 497
paradoxical *adj* 497
paragon *n* 650, 948
paralipsis *n* 476
parallel *n* 17; *v* 9,17,
 19, 216; *adj* 17, 216,
 242
parallelism *n* 216
parallelism *n* 13, 17,
 23, 242
paralysis *n* 158, 376
paralytic *adj* 158, 376
paralyze *v* 158, 376
paralyzed *adj* 158
paramount *adj* 33, 642,
 737
paramour *n* 897
paraphrase *n* 19, 21
parasitic *adj* 789
parasol *n* 223, 424
parboil *v* 384
parcel out *v* 60, 786
parch *v* 340, 382, 384
parched *adj* 340
pardon *n* 918, 970; *v*
 918, 970
pare *v* 38, 195, 204
pared back *adj* 103
pare down *v* 38, 201
parentage *n* 166
parentage *n* 11
parental *adj* 166

parenthesis *n* 70
parenthetical *adj* 10,
 228
parenthetically *adv* 10,
 228
pariah *n* 893
parishioner *n* 997
parity *n* 27
parlance *n* 582
parley *n* 582, 588, 724
parody *n* 19, 21; *v* 19
paroxysm *n* 173, 825
parricide *n* 361
parry *v* 717
parsimonious *adj* 817,
 819, 943
parsimony *n* 819
parsimony *n* 817, 943
parson *n* 996
part *n* 51
part *n* 56, 100a, 625; *v*
 44, 51, 291
partake *v* 778
part company *v* 44
partial *adj* 28
partially *adv* 32, 51
participant *n* 690, 778
participate *v* 56, 709,
 778
participation *n* 778
participation *n* 709
participatory *adj* 709,
 778
particle *n* 32, 330
particular *n* 151; *adj*
 79, 459, 474, 704
particularity *n* 79
particularize *v* 79
particularly *adv* 31, 33
particulars *n* 79
parting *n* 44
partisan *n* 890
partisanship *n* 709
partition *n* 786; *v* 51,
 786
partly *adv* 51
partner *n* 711, 778, 903

partnership *n* 88, 178, 709, 778
part of speech *n* 562
parts of speech *n* 567
party *n* 712
party *n* 72, 372
party spirit *n* 709
party to *n* 690; *adj* 709
party to a suit *n* 969
pass *n* 7, 8, 151, 704; *v* 33, 109, 122, 264, 270, 302, 449, 783, 784
passable *adj* 651
passableness *n* 736
passably *adv* 32
passage *n* 302
passage *n* 144, 260, 267, 270, 627
pass a law *v* 963
pass away *v* 2, 67, 111, 122, 142, 360
pass by *v* 109
passed away *adj* 122
passenger *n* 268
passerby *n* 444
passing *n* 360; *adj* 111
passing time *n* 109
pass into *v* 144
passion *n* 173, 382, 820, 821, 824, 825, 865, 897
passionate *adj* 382, 574, 821, 825, 897
passive *adj* 172, 681, 725
passiveness *n* 172
passivity *n* 172, 681, 725
pass judgment *v* 480
pass muster *v* 648
pass off *v* 151
pass on *v* 360
pass out *v* 449
pass out of *v* 295
pass over *v* 55
pass sentence *v* 967

pass sentence upon *v* 480
pass through *v* 302
pass time *v* 106
past *adj* 122
past cure *adj* 659
paste *n* 354; *v* 46
past hope *adj* 659
pastiche *n* 41
pastime *n* 840
pastiness *n* 352
pastor *n* 996
pastoral *adj* 995
past recollection *adj* 506
past time *n* 122
pasturage *n* 344
pasture *n* 344
pasty *adj* 354, 391
pat *n* 276; *v* 276; *adj* 23
patch up *v* 660
patchwork *n* 41; *adj* 16a
pate *n* 450
patent *adj* 474, 525
paternal *adj* 166
paternity *n* 11, 166
path *n* 260, 278, 302
pathetic *adj* 830
pathless *adj* 261
patience *n* 826
patriarch *n* 130
patriarchal *adj* 166
patrician *adj* 875
patriot *n* 910
patrol *v* 664, 668
patron *n* 795, 890, 912, 977
patronage *n* 175, 707
patronize *v* 136
patter *v* 407
pattern *n* 22, 240, 650
pattern after *v* 19
paucity *n* 32, 103, 640
pauperism *n* 804
pause *n* 70, 142, 198, 265, 685, 687; *v* 70, 142, 265, 681, 687

paw *v* 379
pawn *n* 771; *v* 771, 787, 788
pawning *n* 788
pay *n* 973; *v* 784, 807, 973
pay attention *v* 457
pay in full *v* 807
paymaster *n* 801
payment *n* 807
payment *n* 809
pay no attention to *v* 458
pay out *v* 809
pea *n* 249
peace *n* 721
peace *n* 265, 403, 714
peaceable *adj* 721
peaceful *adj* 174, 265, 685, 721, 826
peacefulness *n* 174, 721
peacemaker *n* 724
peace offering *n* 723
pea-green *adj* 435
peak *n* 206, 210
peaked *adj* 253
peal *n* 404; *v* 404, 407
peal of bells *n* 407
peal of laughter *n* 838
pearliness *n* 427, 430
pearly *adj* 427, 428, 430, 440
pear-shaped *adj* 249
peasantry *n* 876
peat *n* 388
peck at *v* 298
peculiar *adj* 5, 79, 83, 870
peculiarities *n* 5
peculiarity *n* 83, 550
peculiarly *adv* 31, 33
pecuniary *adj* 800
pedagogic *adj* 537
pedagogical *adj* 537
pedagogies *n* 537
pedagogy *n* 537
pedant *n* 492
pedantic *adj* 577
peddler *n* 797

pedestal n 211
pedestrian n 268; adj 598
pedigree n 69
peek n 441; v 441
peel n 204, 223; v 204, 226
peep n 441; v 441
peephole n 260
peeping adj 455
peep of day n 125
peep up v 446
peer n 27; v 441
peevish adj 684, 901a
peg n 250
pellet n 249
pellucid adj 425, 570
pelt v 276
pen n 232, 752; v 590
penalize v 972, 974
penalized v 974; adj 972
penalizing adj 972
penalty n 974
penalty n 972
penance n 974
penchant n 177, 602
pencil v 556
pendant n 214
pendent adj 214
pendulous adj 214
pendulum n 214
penetrate v 294, 302
penetrating adj 480, 498
penetration n 294, 302, 441, 480, 498
penitence n 950
penitence n 833
penitent n 950; adj 833, 950
penitential adj 950
penitentiary n 752
penmanship n 590
pen name n 565
penniless adj 804
pennywise adj 819
pensioner n 785

pensive adj 451
pent up adj 751
penumbra n 421
penurious adj 819
penury n 804
people n 188, 372, 997; v 102
people the world v 163
pep n 171
pepper n 393; v 392
peppery adj 392
peradventure adv 470
perambulate v 264
perambulation n 266
perceivability n 446
perceivable adj 446
perceive v 375, 441, 490
perceptibility n 446
perceptible adj 446
perception n 418, 441, 453, 490
perceptive adj 375, 465, 490, 842
perch n 189; v 184, 186
perchance adv 156, 470
percolation n 295
percussion n 417
perdition n 162
peregrination n 266
peremptory adj 737, 739
perennial adj 69
perfect v 650, 729; adj 31, 52, 104, 648, 650, 729, 960
perfection n 650
perfection n 52, 648, 729, 960
perfectly adv 729
perfidious adj 544
perforate v 260
perforated adj 260
perforation n 260
perforator n 262
perform v 161, 170,

415, 416, 599, 644, 680, 772, 926
performable adj 470
performance n 161, 599, 680, 729, 772
perform a rite v 998
performer n 416, 599, 690
performing n 680
perfume n 400; v 400
perfumed adj 400
perfunctory adj 53, 640
perhaps adv 470
peril n 665
perilous adj 475, 665
perimeter n 230
period n 108
period n 71, 106, 138, 198, 200
periodic adj 70, 138
periodical adj 138
periodically adv 138
periodicity n 138
peripatetic adj 266
periphery n 230
perish v 2, 162, 360, 659
perishable adj 111
permanence n 141
permanence n 16, 110, 150
permanent adj 106, 110, 141, 150, 613
permanently adv 141
permeable adj 260
permeate v 186, 228, 302
permeation n 186, 228, 302
permissible adj 760
permission n 760
permission n 737, 762
permissive adj 760
permit n 737, 755, 760; v 737, 748, 760, 762
permitted adj 760
permutation n 140, 148
pernicious adj 649, 663

perpendicular *adj* 212, 246

perpendicularity *n* 212

perpetrate *v* 680

perpetrator *n* 690

perpetual *adj* 104, 110, 112, 136, 143, 150

perpetually *adv* 112, 136

perpetuate *v* 112, 143

perpetuation *n* 143

perpetuity *n* 112

perpetuity *n* 105

perplex *v* 475, 519, 704, 830

perplexed *adj* 59

perplexity *n* 59

persecute *v* 649, 830

persecution *n* 649

perseverance *n* 604a

perseverance *n* 143, 150, 604, 682

persevere *v* 604a, 682

persevering *adj* 604a

persicuity *n* 518

persist *v* 106, 110, 141, 143, 604a, 606, 682

persistence *n* 110, 141, 143, 604a, 606

persistent *adj* 141, 143, 604a, 606

person *n* 3, 372

personage *n* 372

personal *adj* 5, 79, 372

personality *n* 5, 13, 79

personate *v* 19, 554, 599

personify *v* 554

personnel *n* 56

persons *n* 372

perspective *n* 183, 441, 448

perspicacious *adj* 480, 498, 868

perspicacity *n* 441, 480, 868

perspicuity *n* 570

perspicuous *adj* 570

perspiration *n* 299, 339

perspire *v* 299, 339

persuade *v* 175, 615, 695

persuasion *n* 175, 484, 695

persuasive *adj* 615, 695

pertain to *v* 9

pertinacious *adj* 150, 606

pertinacity *n* 150, 606

pertinent *adj* 23

perturb *v* 61, 824

perturbation *n* 61, 315, 824

peruse *v* 539

pervade *v* 186

pervasion *n* 186

pervasive *adj* 186

pervasiveness *n* 186

perverse *adj* 606, 704, 901a

perversion *n* 477, 523, 538

perversity *n* 606

pervert *v* 477, 523, 538

pessimism *n* 483, 859

pessimist *n* 165

pessimistic *adj* 483, 837

pest *n* 975

pester *v* 830

pestilence *n* 649

pestilential *adj* 657

pet *n* 899

petite *adj* 32

petition *n* 765, 990; *v* 765, 990

petitioner *n* 767

petrification *n* 321, 323

petrify *v* 321, 323

petroleum *n* 356, 388

pettifogging *adj* 477

pettiness *n* 32

petty *adj* 32, 643

petulant *adj* 684, 901

phantasm *n* 443, 515

phantom *n* 4

phase *n* 7, 8, 71, 448

phenomenon *n* 151, 448, 872

philanthropic *adj* 784, 906, 910

philanthropist *n* 910

philanthropy *n* 910

philanthropy *n* 784, 906

philology *n* 562

philosopher *n* 500

phonetic *adj* 561

phonetics *n* 402, 561

phonology *n* 402

phony *n* 548; *adj* 19, 544

phosphorescence *n* 423

phosphorescent *adj* 420, 423

photoengraving *n* 558

photography *n* 420

phrase *n* 566

phrase *n* 521; *v* 566

phraseology *n* 560, 566, 569

physical *adj* 3, 173, 316

physical elements *n* 316

physical gratification *n* 377

physical insensibility *n* 381

physicality *n* 316

physical science *n* 316

physician *n* 662

physicist *n* 316

physics *n* 316

physiognomy *n* 448

physiology *n* 357

physique *n* 364

phytology *n* 369

pick *n* 609, 648; *v* 609

picket *v* 43

pickings *n* 793

pickle *n* 7; *v* 392, 670

pick of the litter *n* 648

pickup *n* 274

picky *adj* 465

pictorial *adj* 556

pictorialization *n* 556

picture *n* 448, 556; *v* 554, 594

picture gallery *n* 556

picturesque *adj* 556, 845

piddle *v* 683

piddling *adj* 643

piebald *adj* 440

piece *n* 51

piecemeal *adv* 51

pieces *n* 596

piece together *v* 43

pied *adj* 440

pierce *v* 260, 378, 385, 649

piercer *n* 262

pierce the ears *v* 404

piercing *adj* 404, 410, 498

pietist *n* 987

pietistic *adj* 987

piety *n* 987

pig *n* 957

pigeon *n* 547

pigeonhole *n* 182

piggish *adj* 957

piggishness *n* 957

pig-headed *adj* 606

pigment *n* 428

pigmy *adj* 193

pile *n* 72, 256

pile on *v* 641

pile up *v* 37

pilfer *v* 791

pilferer *n* 792

pilgrim *n* 268

pilgrimage *n* 266, 676

pill *n* 249

pilot *n* 269, 694; *v* 693

pimple *n* 250

pin *n* 253, 262, 263; *v* 43, 45

pince-nez *n* 445

pinch *n* 8, 704; *v* 195, 378, 385, 819

pinched *adj* 203

pinch hit *v* 147

pine *v* 655

pinhole *n* 260

pink *adj* 434

pinnacle *n* 206, 210

pioneer *n* 64

pious *adj* 987

pipe *n* 350

piquancy *n* 392, 394

piquant *adj* 392

pique *n* 900

piratical *adj* 791

pirouette *n* 312

pit *n* 208, 252, 363

pitapat *n* 407

pitch *n* 26, 210, 356a, 402, 413, 431; *v* 284, 306, 314

pitch black *adj* 421, 431

pitchy *adj* 431

piteous *adj* 830

piteously *adv* 31

pitfall *n* 667

pitfall *n* 530

pith *n* 5, 221

pithiness *n* 572

pithy *adj* 572, 574

pitiable *adj* 649, 830

pitiful *adj* 643, 649

pitiless *adj* 914a

pitilessness *n* 914a

pit one against another *v* 464

pittance *n* 640

pitted *adj* 848

pity *n* 914

pity *n* 821; *v* 914

pitying *adj* 914

pivot *n* 43, 153, 222; *v* 312

pivotal *adj* 222

pixie *n* 979

placate *v* 723

place *n* 182

place *n* 8, 58, 71, 183, 184; *v* 60, 184

place a bet *v* 621

place before *v* 62

placed *adj* 184

place in the record *v* 551

place of business *n* 799

place of departure *n* 293

place of learning *n* 542

place of worship *n* 1000

place side by side *v* 464

place together *v* 72

placid *adj* 721, 826

placidity *n* 826

plagiarism *n* 19

plaque *n* 649, 663, 828, 975; *v* 828, 830

plaid *adj* 440

plain *n* 344

plain *adj* 16, 246, 446, 474, 518, 525, 570, 576, 703, 849, 879

plainly *adv* 525

plainness *n* 576

plainness *n* 570, 703, 849

plainsong *n* 413

plain-speaking *n* 518, 570, 703

plain spoken *adj* 525, 703

plaint *n* 411

plaintiff *n* 938

plaintive *adj* 839

plait *n* 219, 258; *v* 219, 258

plan *n* 626

plan *n* 60, 453, 673, 692; *v* 60, 620, 626, 673

plane *n* 213, 251; *v* 255, 267, 273; *adj* 213, 251

planets *n* 318

planning *n* 60

plant *v* 184, 300, 371

plant life *n* 357, 365, 367

plastered *adj* 959

plastic *adj* 324

plasticity *n* 324

plat *v* 219

plate *n* 22, 251; *v* 204

plateau *n* 344

plate engraving *n* 558
platitude *n* 517
platter *n* 204, 251
plausibility *n* 472
plausible *adj* 472
play *n* 170, 175, 180, 599; *v* 170, 416, 554, 599, 680, 840
played out *adj* 67
player *n* 416, 599
play false *v* 544, 940
play for *v* 621
playful *adj* 840, 842
playhouse *n* 599, 728
playing *n* 840
playing field *n* 728
play of colors *n* 440
play on words *n* 520
play second fiddle to *v* 749
play the fool *v* 497, 853
play the notes *v* 416
play truant *v* 187
play with *v* 140
playwright *n* 599
playwriter *n* 599
playwriting *n* 599
plea *n* 617
plea *n* 411
plead *v* 617, 765, 968
pleader *n* 968
pleading *n* 717
pleadings *n* 969
pleasant *adj* 829, 836, 840, 842
pleasantness *n* 829
pleasantry *n* 842
please *v* 829
pleasing *adj* 413, 850
pleasing combination *n* 413
pleasing sounds *n* 415
pleasurable *adj* 377, 829
pleasurableness *n* 829
pleasure *n* 377
pleasure *n* 827

pleasure *n* 377, 600, 840
pleasure-seeker *n* 954a
pleat *n* 258; *v* 258
plebeian *adj* 851, 876
pledge *n* 177, 768, 771; *v* 768, 788
pledged *adj* 768
pledging *n* 788
plenty *n* 641
plethora *n* 641
pliability *n* 324
pliable *adj* 324
pliancy *n* 324, 705, 725
pliant *adj* 324, 705
plight *n* 7, 8
plod *v* 275, 682
plot *n* 626; *v* 626
plough *v* 371
plow *v* 259, 371
plowed *adj* 959
pluck *n* 150, 604, 604a, 861; *v* 789
plucked instruments *n* 417
pluck out *v* 301
plug *n* 261, 263; *v* 261
plugging *n* 261
plug up one's ears *v* 419
plumb *adj* 212
plum-colored *adj* 437
plump *adj* 192
plumpness *n* 192
plunder *n* 793
plunge *n* 310
plunge *n* 300; *v* 208, 300, 310, 337, 863
plunge into *v* 676
plural *adj* 100
plurality *n* 100
plus *adv* 37
ply *n* 258; *v* 677
pock *n* 250
pocket *v* 789
poesy *n* 597
poet *n* 597
poetaster *n* 597
poetic *adj* 521, 597

poetical *adj* 597
poetic device *n* 521
poeticize *v* 597
poetics *n* 521, 597
poetry *n* 597
poetry *n* 590
poignancy *n* 392
poignant *adj* 516
point *n* 8, 26, 32, 71, 180a, 182, 253, 620; *v* 253, 278
point-blank *adj* 703; *adv* 278, 576
pointed *adj* 201, 253, 516, 518
pointedly *adv* 31, 620
pointedness *n* 253
pointer *n* 550
point of departure *n* 293
point of view *n* 441
point out *v* 525
points of the compass *n* 278
point to *v* 155, 472, 516, 938
point toward *v* 278
poison *v* 659, 663
poisonous *adj* 649, 657, 663
polar *adj* 210, 383
polarity *n* 89, 179, 218, 237
pole *n* 222
polemic *n* 726
polemicist *n* 476
poles apart *adv* 237
policy *n* 626, 692
polish *n* 255, 578, 850; *v* 255, 331
polished *adj* 255, 578, 850, 852
polite *adj* 383, 457, 852, 879, 894, 928
politeness *n* 457, 894
polite society *n* 852
politic *adj* 498, 702
poll *n* 85; *v* 85
pollute *v* 653, 659

poltroon *n* 862
poltroonery *n* 862
polyglot *adj* 560
polyp *n* 250
polyphony *n* 413
polysyllable *n* 561
pommel *n* 249
pomp *n* 882
pompous *adj* 482, 577, 882
pompousness *n* 882
pond *n* 343
ponder *v* 451, 870
pondering *n* 451
ponderous *adj* 319, 579
pool *n* 343, 709; *v* 709
poor *adj* 34, 477, 575, 640, 643, 736, 804, 828, 879
poorer *adj* 34
poorly *adj* 655
poorly timed *adj* 135
poorness *n* 34, 640
poor substitute *adj* 651
pop *n* 166, 406
pop music *n* 415
pop off *v* 360
populace *n* 72, 876
popular music *n* 415
populate *v* 102
population *n* 188, 372
populous *adj* 72, 102
pop up *v* 446
porch *n* 231, 260
pore over *v* 539
porous *adj* 260
port *n* 239
portable *adj* 270
portal *n* 231, 260
portend *v* 511, 668, 909
portent *n* 511, 512, 668, 909
portentous *adj* 511, 668
porter *n* 271;532
portion *n* 51, 100a, 786
portion out *v* 786
portly *adj* 192
portrait *n* 21

portraiture *n* 554
portray *v* 554, 594
portrayal *n* 594
pose *n* 183; *v* 475, 704, 855
position *n* 8, 71, 183, 625
positive *adj* 1, 31, 84, 246, 474, 484, 535
possess *v* 777
possessed *adj* 503
possessed of *adj* 777
possessing *adj* 777
possession *n* 777
possession *n* 780
possessions *n* 780
possessive *adj* 777
possess oneself of *v* 789
possessor *n* 779
possess the means *v* 632
possibility *n* 470
possibility *n* 2, 156
possible *adj* 2, 177, 470, 515
possibly *adv* 470
post *n* 183; *v* 184, 274, 811
post bail *v* 771
post card *n* 592
postdate *v* 115
posterior *n* 235; *adj* 117, 235
posteriority *n* 117
posteriority *n* 63
posterity *n* 167
posterity *n* 121
posthaste *adv* 274
posthumous *adj* 117
postman *n* 271
post meridian *n* 126
post mortem examination *n* 363
postpone *v* 133
postponement *n* 133
postscript *n* 65
postulant *n* 767
postulate *n* 476, 514; *v* 476

posture *n* 8, 183, 240
potable *adj* 298
pot-bellied *adj* 194
potency *n* 157, 159
potent *adj* 157, 159, 171, 175
potential *n* 2; *adj* 2, 470, 526
potentiality *n* 470, 526
potion *n* 298
potpourri *n* 41
potted *adj* 959
potting *n* 557
pound *n* 232; *v* 330
pour *v* 333, 348
pour forth *v* 584
pour in *v* 294
pour out *v* 295, 348
pour out of *v* 295
pout *v* 900, 901a
poverty *n* 804
poverty-stricken *adj* 804
powder *n* 330
powdery *adj* 330
power *n* 157
power *n* 159, 171, 175, 404, 574, 737, 741, 965; *v* 388
powerful *adj* 157, 159, 171, 175, 404, 574
powerfully *adv* 31, 157
powerless *adj* 158, 160
powerlessness *n* 158, 175a
practicability *n* 705
practicable *adj* 644, 705
practical *adj* 170, 470, 644, 692
practicality *n* 470
practically *adv* 5
practice *n* 613, 692; *v* 677
practiced *adj* 698
practice law *v* 968
practice sorcery *v* 992
practitioner *n* 690

pragmatism *n* 646
prairie *n* 344
praise *v* 883, 931, 990
praised *adj* 931
praiseworthy *adj* 931
prance *v* 315
prank *n* 608
prate *v* 584, 588
prattle *n* 582, 584, 588
pray *n* 990
prayer *n* 411, 765, 990
preacher *n* 540, 996
preamble *n* 64
precarious *adj* 111,
    475, 665
precariousness *n* 665
precaution *n* 510, 664,
    673
precautionary *adj* 673
precede *v* 62, 116, 280
precedence *n* 62, 280
precedence *n* 116
precedent *n* 22, 64, 80,
    613, 969; *adj* 62
preceding *adj* 62, 116
precept *n* 697
precept *n* 630
precincts *n* 227
precious *adj* 31, 814
precipice *n* 212, 306,
    667
precipitancy *n* 684
precipitate *v* 684; *adj*
    132, 684, 863
precipitately *adv* 132
precipitation *n* 132, 684
precipitous *adj* 217,
    306
précis *n* 596; *v* 596
precise *adj* 494, 518
precision *n* 80, 494, 518
preclude *v* 761
precluded *adj* 893
preclusion *n* 893
precocious *adj* 132
precocity *n* 132
precursor *n* 64

precursor *n* 62, 116,
    280, 534
precursory *adj* 64, 116
predatory *adj* 789, 791
predecessor *n* 64, 116
predeliberation *n* 611
predestination *n* 611
predestine *v* 152, 611
predetermination *n*
    611
predetermine *v* 611
predicament *n* 8, 183,
    704
predicate *v* 514
predict *v* 507, 510, 511
prediction *n* 511
prediction *n* 668
predilection *n* 177, 609
predisposed *adj* 820
predisposition *n* 176,
    820
predominance *n* 33,
    175
predominant *adj* 175,
    737
predominate *v* 33, 175
pre-eminence *n* 33, 206
pre-eminent *adj* 33,
    206
pre-eminently *adv* 31,
    33
pre-engage *v* 132
pre-existence *n* 116
pre-existent *adj* 116
preface *n* 64; *v* 62
prefatory *adj* 62, 64
prefer *v* 609
preference *n* 62, 609
preferential *adj* 609
prefix *n* 64; *v* 62
prehistoric *adj* 124
prelacy *n* 995
preliminary *adj* 62, 64,
    673
prelude *n* 64, 66
premature *adj* 132,
    135, 674
prematurely *adv* 132

prematurity *n* 132
premeditate *v* 611
premeditation *n* 611
premises *n* 476
premium *n* 973
premonition *n* 668
premonitory *adj* 511,
    668
preordain *v* 152
preparation *n* 673
preparation *n* 60, 64,
    537
preparative *adj* 673
preparatory *adj* 62, 673
prepare *v* 60, 537, 673
prepared *adj* 507, 673,
    698
prepare for *v* 507, 673
prepare for battle *v* 727
prepatory *adj* 673
preponderance *n* 33,
    175
preponderant *adj* 737
preposterous *adj* 497,
    549, 853
preposterously *adv* 31
prepubescence *n* 131
prerequisite *n* 630
prerogative *n* 924
presage *n* 511, 668; *v*
    116, 511, 909
presbyopia *n* 443
prescience *n* 510
prescient *adj* 510
prescribe *v* 693, 695,
    741
prescribed *adj* 474, 924
prescript *n* 697
prescription *n* 613, 697,
    924
prescriptive *adj* 124,
    613, 983a
presence *n* 186
presence *n* 1, 448
present *n* 784; *v* 448,
    763, 784; *adj* 118,
    186
presentation *n* 784

present events n 151
presentiment n 477
present itself v 446
presently adv 132
present the music v 416
present time n 118
present to the view v 448
preservation n 670
preservation n 141,
664, 717, 781
preservative adj 670
preserve v 141, 143,
664, 670, 717, 781
preserved adj 670
preserver n 664
president n 694
press n 72; v 255, 319
press forward v 684
press in v 300
pressing adj 642
press into service v 677
press on v 622, 684
press onward v 282
pressure n 175, 319,
642, 735
presto adv 113
presumable adj 472
presumably adv 472
presume v 484, 514,
858, 878, 885
presumption n 507,
514, 878, 925
presumptive adj 514
presumptuous adj 863,
878, 885
presuppose v 514
pretend v 544, 546,
617, 855
pretender n 548, 925
pretense n 617, 855,
882
pretention n 577, 855,
882
pretentious adj 482,
855, 882, 884
pretentiousness n 882
pretext n 617
pretty adj 845; adv 31

pretty well adv 31, 32
prevail v 33, 78, 175
prevailing adj 78, 983a
prevail upon v 615
prevalence n 33, 78,
175, 613
prevalent adj 1, 78,
175, 613
prevaricate v 520, 544
prevarication n 520,
544
prevent v 706, 708, 761
preventing n 706
prevention n 761
preventive adj 761
previous adj 116
previously adv 116
prevision n 510
prey n 620
price n 812
price v 812
priceless adj 33, 648,
814
prick n 253; v 260, 378,
380
pricking n 380
prickle n 253
prickly adj 253, 256
prick up one's ears v 418
pride n 878
pride n 880
priest n 904, 996
priesthood n 995, 996
priestly adj 995
prig n 854
priggish adj 868
prim adj 868
primal adj 66, 153
primary adj 153, 642
primary color n 428
prime n 125, 648; v
537, 673; adj 84,
642, 648
prime mover n 153, 976
prime of day n 125
primer n 542, 567
primeval adj 124
primitive adj 124

primordial adj 124
princely adj 816
prince of darkness n 978
principal n 694; adj
642
principally adv 33
principle n 5, 80, 153,
211, 537, 615
print n 591; v 531, 558,
590, 591
printed adj 591
printer n 591
printing n 591
prior adj 62, 116
priority n 62, 116, 280
prior to adv 116
prism n 428, 445
prismatic adj 428, 440
prison n 752
prison n 975
prisoner n 754
pristine adj 122
privacy n 893
private adj 79, 221,
528, 533, 893
privately adv 881
privation n 776, 804
privilege n 748, 924,
927a
privileged adj 924,
927a
privy adj 528
privy to adj 490
prize n 618, 733, 793,
973; v 991
probability n 472
probability n 156
probable adj 472, 858
probably adv 472
probationary adj 675
probative adj 463, 478
probe n 262
probity n 939
probity n 543, 944
problem n 533, 704
problematical adj 59,
475

proneness *n* 176, 207, 213

pronounce *v* 535, 580, 582, 586

pronouncement *n* 531, 535

proof *n* 463, 467, 478, 591

proofreader *n* 591

prop *n* 215; *v* 707

propagandist *n* 540

propagate *v* 161, 531

propagation *n* 168, 531

propane *n* 356, 388

propel *v* 264, 284

propensity *n* 176, 177, 602, 820

proper *adj* 79, 494, 578, 646, 868, 881, 922

proper name *n* 564

proper time *n* 134

property *n* 780

prophecy *n* 511

prophesy *v* 511

prophet *n* 513

prophetess *n* 513

prophetic *adj* 511

propinquity *n* 197

propitiate *v* 723, 826, 952

propitiating *adj* 952

propitiation *n* 952

propitiatory *adj* 952

propitious *adj* 134, 648, 734, 858, 888

proportion *n* 9, 242, 786

proportionate *adj* 413

proportions *n* 180, 192

proposal *n* 620, 763

propose *v* 476, 514, 620, 763

proposition *n* 476, 514, 763

propound *v* 514

proprietor *n* 779

proprietorship *n* 777

proprietress *n* 779

propriety *n* 578, 646, 852, 881

propulsion *n* 284

propulsion *n* 276

propulsive *adj* 284

propulsive force *n* 284

prop up *v* 215

prosaic *adj* 575, 598, 841, 843

pros and cons *n* 476

proscenium *n* 234

proscribe *v* 971

proscribed *adj* 964

proscription *n* 971

proscriptive *adj* 761

prose *n* 598

prosecute *v* 622, 680, 969

prosecuting attorney *n* 968

prosecution *n* 969

prosecutor *n* 938, 968

prospect *n* 121, 448, 472, 507, 510

prospective *adj* 507, 510

prospectively *adv* 121

prospects *n* 152

prospectus *n* 596

prosper *v* 731, 734

prosperity *n* 734

prosperity *n* 618, 731

prosperous *adj* 731, 734

prostitute *n* 962; *v* 679

prostitution *n* 679

prostrate *v* 213, 308; *adj* 207, 213, 308

prostration *n* 158, 207, 213, 308, 828

prosy *adj* 575, 598

protect *v* 664, 670, 717

protected *adj* 223

protection *n* 175, 664, 670, 717

protective *adj* 717

protecter *n* 664, 753, 977

protest *n* 489, 764, 766, 808; *v* 489, 766

protestor *n* 489

protoplasm *n* 357

prototype *n* 22

prototype *n* 80

protract *v* 110, 133, 200

protracted *adj* 110, 200, 573

protraction *n* 110, 133, 143

protrude *v* 250

protrusion *n* 250

protuberance *n* 250

protuberant *adj* 250

proud *adj* 878, 880

prove *v* 151, 463, 478

proved *adj* 478

proven *adj* 478

provender *n* 298, 637

proverb *n* 496

proverbial *adj* 496

provide *v* 637, 673, 746, 770

provide against *v* 673

provided *adj* 469; *adv* 8

provided that *adj* 469

providence *n* 976

provident *adj* 510, 673, 864

providential *adj* 134

providing *n* 637

province *n* 75, 181

provincial *adj* 181, 246

provision *n* 637

provision *n* 673, 803; *v* 637

provisional *adj* 8, 111, 673, 770

provisionally *adv* 8, 770

provisions *n* 298, 632, 770

proviso *n* 469

provisos *n* 770

provocation *n* 824
provocative *adj* 615
provoke *v* 153, 824, 830
prowl *v* 266
proximate *adj* 63, 197
proximation *n* 197
proximity *n* 186, 197, 199
proxy *n* 634, 759
prudence *n* 459, 480, 498, 510, 864
prudent *adj* 451, 459, 498, 510, 864
prudery *n* 881
prudish *adj* 881
prudishness *n* 881
prune *v* 38, 201
prurience *n* 961
prurient *adj* 961
pry *v* 441, 455
prying *n* 455; *adj* 455
pseudo *adj* 17
pseudonym *n* 565
psychical *adj* 317
puberty *n* 127, 131
pubescence *n* 131
pubescent *adj* 131
public *n* 372; *adj* 260, 372, 531
public address *n* 586
publication *n* 531
publication *n* 161, 590, 593, 985
publicity *n* 531
publicize *v* 531
public prosecutor *n* 968
public spirit *n* 910
public spirited *adj* 910
publish *v* 531, 591
published *adj* 527, 531
publisher *n* 593
pucker *n* 258; *v* 258, 259
puerile *adj* 129, 499, 575
puerility *n* 499
puff *n* 349; *v* 349, 688
puffery *n* 549

puffiness *n* 194
puff up *v* 194, 549, 880
pugnacious *adj* 720
puissance *n* 157
puissant *adj* 159
puke *v* 297
pulchritude *n* 845
pulchritudinous *adj* 845
pull *n* 288, 319; *v* 267, 285, 288, 301, 319
pull an all-nighter *v* 539
pulling *n* 285, 301
pull no punches *v* 703
pull out *v* 301
pull out of a hat *v* 612
pull out of the air *v* 612
pull the shade *v* 424
pull through *v* 660
pull together *v* 178, 709, 714
pull to pieces *v* 162
pull up *v* 142, 301
pulp *n* 354; *v* 354
pulpiness *n* 354
pulpy *adj* 354
pulsate *v* 138, 314, 315
pulsating *adj* 314, 315
pulsation *n* 138, 314
pulse *n* 138, 314
pulverization *n* 330
pulverize *v* 330
pulverulence *n* 330
pump *n* 348; *v* 349
pun *n* 520; *v* 842
punch *n* 22, 276; *v* 276
puncher *n* 262
punctilious *adj* 543, 772, 882
punctual *adj* 132, 138
punctuality *n* 132, 138
punctually *adv* 132
puncture *v* 260
pungency *n* 392
pungent *adj* 392, 394, 398, 574
punish *v* 972, 974
punished *v* 974; *adj* 972

punishing *adj* 972
punishment *n* 972
punishment *n* 974, 975
punitive *adj* 972
punster *n* 844
punt *v* 267
puny *adj* 193
pupil *n* 492, 541
puppet *n* 547
purblind *adj* 442, 443
purblindness *n* 443
purchase *n* 795
purchase *n* 775; *v* 795
purchaser *n* 795
purchasing *n* 795
pure *adj* 42, 494, 576, 578, 652, 881, 944, 946, 960, 977
purely *adv* 32
purgation *n* 652
purgative *n* 652
purge *v* 297, 652, 952
purification *n* 42, 652
purify *v* 42, 652
purist *n* 578
puritan *n* 955
puritanical *adj* 955
puritanism *n* 955
purity *n* 960
purity *n* 42, 578, 652, 944, 946
purlieus *n* 227
purloin *v* 791
purple *n* 437
purple *adj* 437
purplish *adj* 437
purport *n* 516; *v* 516
purpose *n* 451, 516, 600, 615, 620; *v* 451, 516, 620
purposeful *adj* 604
purposely *adv* 620
purr *v* 412
purring *n* 412
purse *n* 802
purser *n* 801
pursuance *n* 622

pursue *v* 143, 286, 281, 622

pursuit *n* 622

pursuit *n* 461, 625

pursuit of knowledge *n* 539

purvey *v* 637

purveyance *n* 637

purveying *n* 637

push *n* 276, 284; *v* 276, 284, 682

push ahead *v* 682

push aside *v* 297

push away *v* 297

push back *v* 289

push on *v* 684

pusillanimous *adj* 862

pustule *n* 250

put *v* 184

put about *v* 311

put an end to *v* 67

put an end to oneself *v* 361

put aside *v* 55, 636, 678

put away *v* 528

put down *v* 856

put forth *v* 514

put forward *v* 763

put in *v* 300

put in motion *v* 284

put in order *v* 660

put in the place of *v* 147

put into operation *v* 677

put into shape *v* 60

put into words *v* 566

put off *v* 133, 226

put on airs *v* 855

put on a pedestal *v* 991

put one's trust on *v* 484

put on sale *v* 813

put on the brakes *v* 275

put on the stage *v* 599

put on trial *v* 969

put out *v* 385, 421

put out of order *v* 59

put out to sea *v* 293

put pen to paper *v* 590

putrefaction *n* 49, 653

putrefy *v* 653

putrid *adj* 401, 653

put right *v* 246, 662

put straight *v* 246

putter *v* 683

put things in order *v* 652

put to death *v* 361

put to flight *v* 717

put together *v* 43

put to sea *v* 267

put to the sword *v* 361

put to use *v* 677

putty *n* 356a

put up *v* 161, 235, 636

put up to *v* 615

put up with *v* 151, 826

puzzle *v* 475

puzzlement *n* 870

puzzling *adj* 519

Q

quack *v* 412

quadrilateral *adj* 95

quadripartite *adj* 97

quadripartition *n* 97

quadrisection *n* 97

quadruped *n* 366

quadruple *adj* 96

quadruplicate *v* 96

quadruplication *n* 96

quadrupling *n* 96

quaff *v* 298

quaggy *adj* 345

quagmire *n* 345, 653

quail *v* 862

quaint *adj* 83

quake *v* 314, 315, 383

qualification *n* 469

qualification *n* 140, 536, 698, 813

qualified *adj* 469, 698

qualify *v* 140, 174, 469

qualifying *adj* 469

qualities *n* 820

quality *n* 5, 33, 176, 550, 780, 875, 944

qualm *n* 485, 603

quandary *n* 704

quantitative *adj* 25

quantity *n* 25

quantity *n* 31, 72, 102

quarrel *n* 713, 720; *v* 24, 713

quarrelsome *adj* 713, 720

quarry *n* 620

quarter *n* 95, 97, 181, 236, 740; *v* 97, 184

quartered *adj* 97

quartering *n* 97

quarter of a hundred *n* 98

quarters *n* 189

quartet *n* 95, 415, 416

quasi *adv* 17

quaternity *n* 95

quaver *n* 315, 407, 408; *v* 314, 315

queer *adj* 83

queer fish *n* 857

quell *v* 265

quench *v* 385, 829

querulous *adj* 868

query *n* 461; *v* 461

quest *n* 622, 676

quester *n* 268

question *n* 461, 533; *v* 461, 475, 870, 989

questionable *adj* 473, 475, 485, 520

questionableness *n* 473, 475, 520

questioning *n* 461, 539; *adj* 461

quibble *n* 520; *v* 477

quibbling *adj* 477

quick *adj* 111, 274, 498, 682, 684, 698, 842

quick as lightning *adj* 274

quicken *v* 132, 170, 173, 274, 359, 684, 824

quickly *adv* 132

quickness *n* 132, 274, 684

quicksand *n* 667

quick-tempered *adj* 901

quick to fly off the handle *v* 901

quick-witted *adj* 842

quiddity *n* 477

quid pro quo *n* 30

quiescence *n* 150, 172, 265, 403, 526, 683

quiescent *adj* 172, 265, 403

quiet *n* 174, 403, 721; *v* 174, 723; *adj* 174, 403, 585, 685

quietly *adv* 881

quietude *n* 265, 826

quietus *n* 360

quilt *n* 223; *v* 440

quinquepartite *adj* 99

quinquesection *n* 99

quintessence *n* 5

quintet *n* 415

quirk *n* 83, 608

quit *v* 293, 624, 757, 782, 807

quite *adv* 52

quits *n* 27; *adj* 27

quittance *n* 952

quitter *n* 623

quitting *n* 782

quiver *n* 315, 407; *v* 277, 314, 315, 383

quota *n* 786

R

rabbi *n* 996

rabble *n* 876

rabid *adj* 825

race *n* 11, 75, 188, 274, 348; *v* 274

raciness *n* 574

rack *n* 378

racket *n* 315, 404, 407, 414

racy *adj* 574

radial *adj* 291

radiance *n* 420, 845

radiant *adj* 291, 420, 423, 845

radiate *v* 291, 420

radiation *n* 73, 291, 420

radical *n* 489, 658, 742; *adj* 52

radioactivity *n* 420

rage *n* 825, 852; *v* 173, 825

raging *adj* 173, 824

ragtime *n* 415

raid *n* 716

rail *n* 232

rail at *v* 856

railing *n* 232

raillery *n* 856

raiment *n* 225

rain *n* 348; *v* 348

rain cats and dogs *v* 348

rainfall *n* 348

rain hard *v* 348

rain in buckets *v* 348

rain in torrents *v* 348

rainy *adj* 348

raise *v* 35, 161, 235, 250, 307, 370

raised *adj* 250

raise one's voice *v* 411

raise spirits *v* 992

raise to a fervor *v* 824

raise up *v* 206

raising *n* 307, 370

rake *n* 962; *v* 371

rake out *v* 301

rally *v* 660

rallying point *n* 74

rally round *v* 709

ram *n* 373

ramble *v* 266, 279, 499, 573

rambler *n* 268

rambling *adj* 47, 266, 279

ramification *n* 51, 291

ramify *v* 291

ram in *v* 300

rammer *n* 263

rampage *v* 173

rampant *adj* 173, 175, 307, 748

ramrod *n* 263

ramshackle *adj* 124

ranch *v* 370

ranching *n* 370

rancid *adj* 397, 401, 653

rancidity *n* 401

rancor *n* 907

rancorous *adj* 907

random *adj* 156, 621

range *n* 26, 69, 180, 196, 200, 278, 386, 965; *v* 60, 196, 266

rank *n* 26, 58, 69, 71, 875; *v* 58, 60, 480; *adj* 365, 401, 649

rank and file *n* 876

rankle *v* 653, 659

rankness *n* 401

rant *n* 517, 549, 577; *v* 503, 517, 582, 825

ranter *n* 584

rap *n* 276, 406, 588; *v* 276, 406, 588

rapacious *adj* 789, 819

rapacity *n* 819

rapid *adj* 274, 684

rapidity *n* 274, 684, 819

rapids *n* 348

rapture *n* 827, 897, 993

rapturous *adj* 821, 829, 977

rare *adj* 20, 83, 103, 137, 322, 648

rarefaction *n* 322

rarefy *v* 322

rarely *adv* 137

rare occurrence *n* 137

rarity *n* 137, 322

rascal *n* 941

rash *n* 72; *adj* 499, 684, 863

rashness *n* 863

rashness *n* 499

rasp *n* 330; *v* 330, 331

rasping n 410; adj 410
ratatat n 407
rate n 26, 264, 812; v 466, 480
rather adv 32
ratification n 535, 762
ratify v 535
ratio n 9, 26, 786
ratiocination n 476
ration n 786
rational adj 450, 498, 502
rationale n 155, 462
rationalism n 476
rationalist n 476
rationalistic adj 476
rationality n 450, 502
rations n 298
rattle v 407
raucousness n 410
ravage v 162, 659
ravager n 165
rave v 503
ravel v 219
raveled adj 59
raveling n 59
ravenous adj 789
raver n 504
ravine n 198, 259
raving n 503; adj 173, 824
ravish v 829
ravishment n 824, 827
raw adj 378, 383, 435, 674, 699
raw materials n 635
ray n 420
raze n 162
razor edge n 253
razor sharp adj 253
reach n 26, 196, 200; v 27, 270
reach a point v 292
reaching n 292
reach to v 196, 200
react v 179, 277, 287
reaction n 145, 179, 276, 277, 287, 718

reactionary adj 179, 277
reactive adj 718
read v 539
readable adj 578
reader n 542, 591
readily adv 705
readiness n 132, 602, 673, 698
read the law v 968
ready adj 507, 602, 673, 682
ready for battle v 727
real adj 1, 494
real estate n 342, 780
realism n 646
reality n 1, 494
realize v 450, 484, 490
realm n 181
reanimate v 163, 359, 660, 689
reanimation n 163
reap v 371, 789
reappear v 104
reappearance n 104, 163
reappearing adj 163
rear n 235
rear n 235; v 161, 235, 307; adj 235
rearguard n 235
rear rank n 235
rearward adv 235
reason n 450, 498, 502, 615; v 450, 498
reasonable adj 174, 472, 498, 502, 736, 815
reasonable chance n 472
reasonableness n 174; 498
reasoner n 476
reason falsely v 477
reasoning n 476
reasoning adj 476
reasons n 476
reason why n 155
reassuring adj 858

rebate n 813; v 813
rebel n 165, 489; v 146, 719, 742
rebellion n 146, 719, 742
rebellious adj 146, 715, 742
rebelliousness n 715, 742
reborn adj 660
rebound n 145, 277; v 145, 277
rebuff n 277, 289, 764; v 289, 610, 764
rebuild v 660
rebuilding n 660
rebut v 462, 468, 536
rebuttal n 468, 536
recalcitrance n 715
recalcitrant adj 715, 719, 742, 764
recall v 451, 505
recant v 536, 607
recantation n 607
recantation n 536
recapitulate v 104
recapitulation n 104
recast v 140, 146, 626
recede v 283, 287
receipt n 810
receipt n 771, 807
receive v 76, 296, 775, 785, 789, 810
receive an impression v 821
received adj 490, 785
receive pleasure v 377
receiver n 191, 785, 801
receive the call v 996
receiving n 785
receiving adj 785
recent adj 122, 123, 435
recentness n 123
receptacle n 191
reception n 296

reception *n* 76, 292, 785

recess *n* 198, 244, 530, 687

recesses *n* 221

recession *n* 287

recession *n* 283, 659

recipient *n* 785

reciprocal *adj* 12, 148, 718

reciprocally *adv* 12

reciprocate *v* 12, 148

reciprocation *n* 12, 148, 718

reciprocity *n* 12, 148, 718

recision *n* 756

recital *n* 594

recitation *n* 582

recite *v* 85, 594

reckless *adj* 684, 863

recklessness *n* 460, 863

reckon *v* 85, 480, 873

reckoning *n* 85, 466, 507, 807, 811, 973

reckon up *v* 807

reclaim *v* 660, 952

reclamation *n* 660, 952

reclination *n* 213

recline *v* 213, 687

recluse *n* 893, 955

recognition *n* 505, 733

recognizable *adj* 446

recognize *v* 441

recognized *adj* 490

recoil *n* 277

recoil *n* 145, 283, 287, 603, 623; *v* 145, 179, 277, 287, 325, 603, 623

recollect *v* 451, 505

recollection *n* 505

recommend *v* 695

recommendation *n* 695

recompense *n* 973; *v* 30, 807, 973

reconcilable *adj* 23

reconcile *v* 723, 831

reconcile oneself to *v* 826

reconciliation *n* 723

recondition *v* 662

reconstitute *v* 660

reconstruct *v* 660

reconstruction *n* 660

reconversion *n* 660

record *n* 551

record *n* 86, 527, 594; *v* 60, 551

recorder *n* 53

recount *v* 594

recounting *n* 594

recoup *v* 660, 790

recouperative *adj* 790

recourse *n* 677

recover *v* 660, 789, 790

recovery *n* 660, 789, 790

recovery of strength *n* 689

recreant *adj* 544, 862

recreation *n* 840

recrimination *n* 718

rectification *n* 660

rectify *v* 246, 658

rectilinear *adj* 246

rectitude *n* 922, 939, 944

recumbency *n* 213

recuperative *adj* 660

recur *v* 104, 136, 138

recure *v* 660

recurrence *n* 104, 136

recurrent *adj* 70, 104, 138

recurring *adj* 104, 136, 138

recur to *v* 677

recurve *v* 245

recusancy *n* 984

recusant *adj* 984

red *n* 434

red *adj* 434

red and yellow *n* 439

red as a lobster *adj* 434

red as beet *adj* 434

redden *v* 434

reddish *adj* 434

redeem *v* 30, 147, 660, 672, 790, 952

redemption *n* 660, 672, 952

redemptive *adj* 790, 952

redesign *v* 140

red-faced *adj* 434

red-hot *adj* 824

redneck *n* 887

redness *n* 434

redolence *n* 398, 400

redolent *adj* 398, 400

redouble *v* 35, 90

redress *n* 660, 662, 973; *v* 660, 662

reduce *v* 38, 103, 195, 201, 308, 638, 813

reduced *adj* 34, 103, 201

reduce to *v* 144

reduce to a square *v* 95

reducible *adj* 38

reductio ad absurdum n 476

reduction *n* 36, 103, 144, 195, 201, 813

reduction to power *n* 330

redundance *n* 641

redundance *n* 104

redundancy *n* 573

redundant *adj* 104, 641

reduplicate *v* 90

reduplication *n* 90

re-echo *v* 408

reed instruments *n* 417

reef *n* 346

reefs *n* 667

reek *v* 401, 653

reeking *adj* 382, 401

reeky *adj* 653

reel *v* 314, 315

reestablish *v* 660

reestablishment *n* 660

refashion *v* 163

referable *adj* 155
referable to *adj* 9
referee *n* 967; *v* 174
reference *n* 9, 467
reference to *n* 155
referential *adj* 467
refer to *v* 9, 155, 695
refine *v* 477, 652, 658
refined *adj* 428, 465, 850, 852
refinement *n* 465, 578, 658, 850
reflect *v* 19, 420, 451
reflection *n* 420, 451
reflective *adj* 451, 498
reflector *n* 445
reflex *n* 145, 276, 277; *adj* 283
reflexion *n* 21
refluent *adj* 283
reflux *n* 283
reform *v* 144, 658
reformation *n* 658
reformative *adj* 658
reformer *n* 658
refraction *n* 279, 291, 420, 443
refractory *adj* 606, 719, 742, 945
refrain *v* 623, 681
refresh *v* 159, 338, 385, 660, 689, 829, 834
refreshing *adj* 689
refreshment *n* 689
refreshment *n* 159, 660
refrigerate *v* 383, 385
refrigeration *n* 385
refrigerator *n* 387
refuge *n* 666
refugee *n* 268, 623
refusal *n* 764
refusal *n* 603, 610
refuse *n* 40; *v* 536, 603, 610, 708, 764
refutable *adj* 479
refutation *n* 468, 479
refute *v* 468, 479
regale *n* 829

regalia *n* 747
regard *n* 441, 451, 457, 459, 873, 897, 928, 987, 990; *v* 9, 418, 451, 457, 480, 873, 928
regarded *adj* 873
regardful *adj* 451
regarding *n* 418; *adj* 928
regards *n* 928
regenerate *v* 163
regeneration *n* 163, 660
regenerative *adj* 163
reggae *n* 415
regicide *n* 361
regiment *n* 72
regimentals *n* 225
region *n* 181
regional *adj* 181
register *n* 86, 114, 551, 553, 811; *v* 60, 114, 551
registrar *n* 553
regnant *adj* 737
regress *n* 287; *v* 145, 283, 287
regression *n* 283
regression *n* 287
regressive *adj* 283
regret *n* 833
regret *n* 950; *v* 832, 833, 950
regretful *adj* 832, 833, 950
regular *adj* 16, 58, 60, 80, 138, 240, 242, 613
regular as clockwork *adj* 138
regularity *n* 138
regularity *n* 16, 58, 80, 138, 242
regularly *adv* 138
regulate *v* 58, 60, 174, 692, 693
regulation *n* 80

regulation *n* 693, 697, 963
regurgitate *v* 297, 348
regurgitation *n* 297
rehabilitate *v* 660, 790
rehabilitation *n* 660, 790
rehash *v* 104
rehearsal *n* 673
rehearse *v* 104, 594, 673
reign *n* 175
reimburse *v* 790, 807
reinforce *v* 37, 159
reinforcement *n* 39
reinstate *v* 660
reinstatement *n* 660
reinvest *v* 790
reinvestment *n* 790
reinvigorate *v* 660, 689
reiterate *v* 104, 136
reiteration *n* 104, 136
reject *v* 55, 297, 536, 610, 764, 893
rejected *adj* 893
rejection *n* 610
rejection *n* 55, 297, 536, 764, 893
rejoice *v* 836, 838
rejoice in *v* 827
rejoicing *n* 838
rejoin *v* 72, 462
rejoinder *n* 462
rekindle *v* 384
relapse *n* 661
relapse *v* 145, 287, 661
relate *v* 12, 216, 464, 594
related *adj* 9, 11
relate to *v* 9
relating *n* 464
relating to *adj* 9
relation *n* 9
relation *n* 11, 594
relationship *n* 9, 11
relative *n* 11; *adj* 9
relative to *adj* 9
relator *n* 938

relax v 47, 160, 275, 324, 683, 685, 687, 738

relaxation n 47, 160, 174, 687, 738, 840

relaxed adj 47, 160, 174

relaxing adj 840

release n 360, 671, 672, 750, 777a, 783, 807; v 672, 750, 777a, 927a, 970

released adj 970

relegate v 55, 270

relegation n 270

relent v 324

relentless adj 604, 739, 914a

relentlessness n 739

relevant adj 9

reliability n 150, 474

reliable adj 150, 246, 474, 664

reliance n 484, 507, 858

relic n 40, 124, 551

relics n 362

relied on adj 871

relief n 834

relief n 250, 660, 662, 689, 707

relieve v 707, 834

religion n 983

religious adj 983, 987

religious garments n 999

religious persuasion n 983

religious truth n 983a

religious writings n 986

relinquish v 624, 678, 757, 782

relinquishment n 624, 782

relinquishment n 678, 757

relish n 377, 390, 393, 394; v 377, 394, 827

relocate v 184

reluctance n 603, 704, 719

reluctant adj 603, 764

rely on v 484, 507, 858

remain v 1, 40, 106, 110, 141, 186, 265

remainder n 40

remaining adj 40

remains n 40, 362, 551

remake v 144

remark v 457

remarkable adj 31, 870

remarkably adv 31

remediable adj 660

remedial adj 660, 662

remediless adj 859

remedy n 662

remedy v 660, 662, 834

remember v 451, 505

remembrance n 505

remind v 505

reminder n 505

reminisce v 505

reminiscence n 505

reminiscent (of) adj 505

remiss adj 460, 674, 683, 738

remission n 756, 918

remissness n 460, 683

remit v 790

remittance n 807

remnant n 40

remodel v 140, 144, 146

remonstrance n 616, 766

remonstrate v 616, 766

remonstrative adj 766

remorse n 833, 950

remorseful adj 950

remorseless adj 951

remote adj 10, 196

remote cause n 153

remoteness n 196

remote past n 122

removable adj 38

removal n 38, 185, 270, 287, 293, 301

remove n 196; v 2, 38, 185, 270, 301, 662

removed adj 196

remunerate v 30, 807, 973

remuneration n 973

remunerative adj 775, 810, 973

renaissance n 660

renascence n 660

renascent adj 163, 660

rend v 44

render v 144, 784, 790

render blunt v 254

render certain v 474

render concave v 252

render curved v 245

render few v 103

render general v 78

render horizontal v 213

render insensible v 376

render intelligible v 518

render invisible v 447

render oblique v 217

render powerless v 158

render sensible v 375

render straight v 246

render uncertain v 475

render unintelligible v 519

render violent v 173

rendezvous n 74

renegade n 607

renew v 90, 123, 163, 660, 689

renewal n 90, 163, 660

renounce v 536, 607, 610, 624, 757, 764, 782

renovate v 123, 163, 660

renovated adj 123

renovation n 123, 163, 660

renown n 31, 873

renowned adj 873, 883

rent _n_ 44, 198, 260; _v_ 788

renunciation _n_ 607, 610, 624, 757, 764, 782

reorganize _v_ 144, 660

repair _n_ 658, 660, 689; _v_ 658, 660, 662, 689, 790, 952

reparation _n_ 30, 660, 790, 952, 973

reparatory _adj_ 973

repartee _n_ 842

repay _v_ 718

repeal _n_ 756; _v_ 756

repeat _v_ 90, 104, 136

repeated _adj_ 104

repeatedly _adv_ 104, 136

repel _v_ 289, 610, 616, 717, 719, 764, 830, 867

repellant _adj_ 830

repellent _adj_ 289, 719, 867

repelling _adj_ 289

repent _v_ 833, 950, 952

repentance _n_ 833, 950

repentant _adj_ 950

repenting _adj_ 950

repercussion _n_ 145

repetition _n_ 104

repetition _n_ 17, 90, 136, 143, 641

repetitious _adj_ 104, 641

repetitive _adj_ 104

repine _v_ 832

replace _v_ 63, 147, 660

replacement _n_ 147, 634, 660

replenish _v_ 52, 637

replete _adj_ 52, 641

repletion _n_ 641, 869

replica _n_ 13, 19, 21

reply _n_ 462; _v_ 462

report _n_ 532, 594, 873; _v_ 527

reported _adj_ 527

reporter _n_ 527, 532, 534

repose _n_ 687

repose _n_ 265, 681; _v_ 265, 685, 687

reposing _adj_ 687

repository _n_ 191

reprehensible _adj_ 649, 923, 945

represent _v_ 147, 550, 554, 556, 594, 759

representation _n_ 554

representation _n_ 17, 19, 21, 550, 556, 594, 599, 626

representative _n_ 147, 524, 534, 690, 758, 759; _adj_ 17, 550, 554

representing _adj_ 17

repress _v_ 179, 751, 826

repression _n_ 179, 751

repressive _adj_ 751

reprieve _n_ 133, 671, 672, 918; _v_ 672, 918

reprint _n_ 21

reprisal _n_ 148, 718, 789, 919

reproach _v_ 932

reproachful _adj_ 932

reproduce _v_ 19, 104, 163, 168, 660

reproduction _n_ 163

reproduction _n_ 13, 19, 21, 104, 660

reproductive _adj_ 163

reproof _n_ 972

reprove _v_ 932, 972

reprover _n_ 936

reptile _n_ 366

repudiate _v_ 55, 489, 536, 610, 764

repudiation _n_ 55, 536, 610, 764, 808

repugnance _n_ 867, 898

repugnant _adj_ 867, 898

repulse _n_ 145, 277, 289, 764; _v_ 289, 719, 764

repulsed _adj_ 893

repulsion _n_ 289

repulsion _n_ 719

repulsive _adj_ 289, 395, 719, 830, 846, 867, 898

reputable _adj_ 246, 873

reputation _n_ 873

repute _n_ 873

reputed _adj_ 873

request _n_ 765

request _n_ 741, 865; _v_ 630, 765, 865

require _v_ 601, 630, 640, 741, 744, 765, 812

requirement _n_ 630

requirement _n_ 601, 741

requisite _n_ 601, 630; _adj_ 601, 630

requisition _n_ 630, 741

requital _n_ 30, 148, 718, 919, 973

requite _v_ 148, 718, 919, 973

rescind _v_ 44, 756, 764

rescue _n_ 672, 707; _v_ 660, 670, 672, 707

research _n_ 461, 463

resemblance _n_ 13, 17, 216

resemble _v_ 17, 197

resembling _adj_ 17

resent _v_ 900, 921

resentful _adj_ 900, 907, 919, 920

resentment _n_ 900

resentment _n_ 907, 920

reservation _n_ 528

reserve _n_ 528, 585, 636; _v_ 636, 678, 781

reserved _adj_ 383, 528, 585, 901a

reservoir _n_ 191, 343, 636

reside _v_ 188

residence _n_ 189

resident _n_ 188; _adj_ 186

residual _adj_ 40

residue n 40
residuum n 40
resign v 624, 725, 757, 782
resignation n 757
resignation n 624, 725, 782, 826, 831
resigned adj 826, 831
resign oneself to v 826
resilience n 325
resiliency n 325
resilient adj 325
resin n 356a
resin v 356a
resinous adj 356a
resist v 179, 708, 715, 719, 742, 764
resistance n 719
resistance n 179, 708, 715, 742
resistant adj 323, 327, 708, 715, 719
resisting n 708
resolute adj 150, 604, 604a, 606, 861
resolutely adv 604
resoluteness n 150, 600, 604
resolution n 604
resolution n 144, 150, 600, 604a, 606, 620
resolve n 604, 611, 620; v 604
resolve beforehand v 611
resolved adj 604
resolve into v 144
resolve into its elements v 49
resonance n 408
resonance n 277, 402, 404
resonant adj 402, 408
resort n 677
resort to v 677
resound v 402, 404, 408
resounding adj 404, 408

resources n 632, 635, 637, 780, 803
respect n 928
respect n 457, 743, 873, 894, 926, 987; v 772
respectability n 873
respectable adj 736, 873
respected adj 873, 928
respectful adj 457, 743, 879, 894, 926, 928
respecting adj 928
respective adj 79, 786
respectively adv 79
respects n 928
respiration n 359
respire v 349, 359
respite n 106, 133, 142, 198, 672, 687
resplendent adj 420
respond v 277, 462
respond to v 821
response n 587
response n 179, 276, 277, 462
responsibility n 177, 926
responsible adj 177
responsive adj 375, 462
responsiveness n 375, 822
rest n 265
rest n 40, 70, 142, 211, 360, 681, 687; v 70, 142, 265, 685, 687
restate v 104
restatement n 104
restful adj 265, 685
resting adj 687
restitution n 790
restitution n 660
restless adj 149, 264, 682, 825, 832
restlessness n 149, 264, 315, 682, 825, 832
restorable adj 660

restoration n 660
restoration n 123, 145, 163, 658, 689, 790
restorative n 662; adj 163, 658, 660, 662
restore v 123, 145, 159, 163, 658, 660, 662, 689, 790
restored adj 123, 660
restore equilibrium v 27
restoring adj 689
restrain v 179, 195, 229, 233, 370, 469, 616, 751, 953
restrained adj 229, 751
restraint n 751
restraint n 55, 179, 229, 576, 616, 706, 826, 849
restrict v 233, 469, 751, 761
restricted adj 203
restriction n 469, 751, 761
restrictive adj 751, 761
restructure v 140
result n 63, 65, 480, 729
result from v 154
resulting adj 117
resulting from adj 154
resume v 104, 789
resumption n 660
resurgent adj 163
resurrect v 163
resurrection n 163
resuscitate v 163, 660
resuscitation n 163, 660
retailer n 797
retain v 150, 505, 670, 781
retainer n 746
retake v 789
retaliate v 148, 718, 919
retaliation n 718
retaliation n 30, 148, 919
retaliatory adj 718
retard v 133, 275, 706

retardation _n_ 133
retch _v_ 297
retention _n_ 781
retention _n_ 505, 670
retentive _adj_ 781
retentiveness _n_ 505
reticence _n_ 528, 583, 585
reticent _adj_ 528, 533, 583, 585
reticulated _adj_ 260
reticulation _n_ 219
retinue _n_ 69
retire _v_ 283, 287, 293, 623, 757, 881, 893
retired _adj_ 893
retirement _n_ 283, 287, 757, 893
retiring _adj_ 881
retort _n_ 148, 462, 718; _v_ 148, 462, 718
retouch _v_ 660
retract _v_ 607, 756
retraction _n_ 485, 536, 607, 756
retreat _n_ 74, 189, 283, 287, 623, 666, 671, 893; _v_ 145, 283, 893
retrench _v_ 38, 201, 817
retrenchment _n_ 38, 201, 817
retribution _n_ 718, 919, 972, 973, 974
retributive _adj_ 718, 973
retrievable _adj_ 660
retrieval _n_ 660
retrieve _v_ 660
retroactive _adj_ 122
retrogradation _n_ 145, 659, 661
retrograde _adj_ 283, 661
retrogression _n_ 145, 283, 659
retrogressive _adj_ 283
retrospect _n_ 505
retrospection _n_ 122, 145
retrospective _adj_ 122

retrospectively _adv_ 122
return _n_ 145, 283, 287, 790; _v_ 104, 138, 145, 283, 718, 790
returning _n_ 145
return to _v_ 104
reunion _n_ 43, 72
revamp _v_ 140
reveal _v_ 260, 525, 529
revealed _adj_ 529
reveal itself _v_ 446
revelation _n_ 985
revelation _n_ 529
revelatory _adj_ 985
revel in _v_ 377
reveling _n_ 838
revenge _n_ 919
revenge _n_ 718; _v_ 718, 919
revengeful _adj_ 718, 919
reverberant _adj_ 104, 408
reverberate _v_ 277, 408
reverberating _adj_ 104, 408
reverberation _n_ 104, 277, 407, 408
revere _v_ 860, 897, 928, 987
reverence _n_ 860, 926, 928, 987, 990; _v_ 860, 928
reverend _n_ 996
reverent _adj_ 987
reverential _adj_ 926, 987, 990
revering _adj_ 990
reversal _n_ 14, 140, 218, 287, 607
reverse _n_ 235, 237; _v_ 145, 218; _adj_ 14, 218, 237
reversion _n_ 145
reversion _n_ 218
revert _v_ 14, 104, 145, 283, 287
reverting _n_ 145
review _n_ 595

reviewer _n_ 480, 595
revile _v_ 988
reviler _n_ 936
revise _v_ 658
revision _n_ 658
revival _n_ 163, 660, 689
revive _v_ 163, 359, 660, 689
revivification _n_ 163, 660
revivify _v_ 159, 163, 660
revocation _n_ 607, 756
revoke _v_ 536, 607, 756, 764
revolt _n_ 146; _v_ 146, 289, 719, 742, 830
revolting _adj_ 846, 898
revolution _n_ 146
revolution _n_ 138, 140, 218, 312
revolutionary _adj_ 146, 742
revolutionize _v_ 146
revolve _v_ 138, 312
revolving _adj_ 312
revulsion _n_ 145, 146, 218, 277
reward _n_ 973
reward _n_ 733; _v_ 973
rewarded _adj_ 973
rewarding _adj_ 973
rhapsodic _adj_ 497
rhapsodist _n_ 504, 597
rhapsody _n_ 497
rhetoric _n_ 517, 577, 582
rhetorical _adj_ 577
rhetorical flourish _n_ 577
rhetorician _n_ 582
rheumy _adj_ 337
rhyme _v_ 597
rhymeless _adj_ 598
rhymer _n_ 597
rhymes _n_ 597
rhyme with _v_ 17
rhyming _n_ 597
rhythm _n_ 104, 138, 413
rhythm _n_ 413

rhythmic *adj* 104, 138, 597
rhythmical *adj* 138
rib *n* 215
ribald *adj* 961
ribaldry *n* 961
ribbed *adj* 259
rich *adj* 394, 413, 428, 577, 734, 803
riches *n* 803
richly *adv* 31
richness *n* 573
rickety *adj* 160
ricochet *n* 145, 277; *v* 277
riddle *n* 520; *v* 260
ride *n* 226
rider *n* 39, 268
ride roughshod over *v* 885
ride the waves *v* 267
ridge *n* 250, 346
ridicule *n* 856
ridicule *v* 856, 929
ridiculous *adj* 497, 499
ridiculousness *n* 853
rid of *adj* 776
rife *adj* 78, 175
rifler *n* 792
rift *n* 44, 198, 260
rig *n* 272
rigging *n* 225
right *n* 238, 922
right *n* 780, 924, 965; *v* 246, 658, 662; *adj* 494, 922, 944
right ahead *adv* 234
right and left *adv* 180, 227
right angle *n* 244
righteous *adj* 944, 977
righteously *adv* 922
righteous man *n* 987
rightful *adj* 494, 922
rightfully *adv* 922
right hand *n* 238
right-handed *adj* 238
rightly *adv* 922

right now *n* 118
right on *adj* 494
right side *n* 238
rigid *adj* 82, 150, 240, 323, 704, 739, 955
rigidity *n* 141, 323, 739
rigmarole *n* 517
rigor mortis *n* 360
rigorous *adj* 739, 955
rigorousness *n* 739
rig out *v* 225
rill *n* 348
rim *n* 231
rimple *n* 258; *v* 258
rind *n* 223
ring *n* 247, 408, 712, 728; *v* 408
ringing *n* 408; *adj* 413
ring in the ear *v* 408
ring in the ears *v* 404
riot *n* 59, 173; *v* 173
rioter *n* 742
riotous *adj* 59, 173, 742
ripe *adj* 128, 673
ripe age *n* 128
ripen *v* 144, 650, 658, 673
ripeness *n* 124, 131, 673
ripen into *v* 144
ripe old age *n* 128
rip open *v* 260
rip out *v* 301
ripple *n* 258, 314, 315, 348; *v* 258, 314
rise *n* 35, 217, 282, 305; *v* 35, 146, 305, 734
rise above *v* 31
rise from *v* 154
rise up *v* 146, 206, 719
rising *n* 146, 305; *adj* 217, 305
rising ground *n* 217
risk *n* 665; *v* 621, 665
risky *adj* 665
rite *n* 998
rites *n* 990

ritualistic *adj* 998
ritualize *v* 883
rival *n* 710, 726; *v* 648, 720
rivalry *n* 720
rive *v* 44
river *n* 348
river *n* 348
rivet *v* 43, 824
rivulet *n* 348
road *n* 278, 302, 627
road to ruin *n* 162
roam *v* 266
roan *adj* 433
roar *n* 404, 408, 411; *v* 173, 404, 411, 412, 838
roaring *n* 404
roast *v* 384
rob *v* 791
robber *n* 792
robbery *n* 791
robe *n* 999; *v* 225
robust *adj* 159, 654, 836
robust health *n* 654
rock *n* 342, 415
rock and roll band *n* 416
rocks *n* 667
rod *n* 215, 975
roe *n* 374
rogue *n* 941
role *n* 625
roll *n* 407
roll *n* 86, 248, 249, 312, 408; *v* 248, 255, 264, 314, 348, 407
roll call *n* 85
roller *n* 249
rolling pin *n* 249
rolling seas *n* 348
roll into a ball *v* 249
roll on *v* 264
romance *n* 515
romantic *n* 504; *adj* 515
romp *v* 173
roof *n* 223

rookie *n* 701
room *n* 180
roomy *adj* 180
roost *n* 189; *v* 186
root *n* 153; *v* 184
rooted *adj* 124, 184
root out *v* 301
ropy *adj* 205
rosin *n* 356a; *v* 356a
rosy *adj* 434
rot *n* 49, 653; *v* 49,
    653, 659
rotary *adj* 312
rotate *v* 312
rotating *adj* 312
rotation *n* 312
rotation *n* 138, 145
rotten *adj* 160, 401,
    649, 653, 659
rottenness *n* 659
rotund *adj* 249
rotundity *n* 249
rotundity *n* 247
roué *n* 962
rough *adj* 16a, 173,
    241, 254, 256, 329,
    397, 410, 674
roughen *v* 256
rough-hewn *adj* 256
rough it *v* 686
roughness *n* 256
roughness *n* 254
rough seas *n* 348
rough up *v* 256
round *n* 69, 138; *v* 245,
    247, 249; *adj* 247,
    249, 254
roundabout *adj* 279,
    311, 573, 629; *adv*
    279
roundabout way *n* 629
round and round *adv*
    138, 248
rounded *adj* 245, 247,
    254
rounded inward *adj* 252
roundness *n* 247, 249
round number *n* 84

round the edge *v* 254
rouse *v* 175, 615, 824
rouse oneself *v* 682
rousing *adj* 171
route *n* 302, 627
routine *n* 16, 58, 80,
    138, 613; *adj* 16, 138
rout out *v* 652
rove *v* 266, 279
rover *n* 268
roving *n* 266; *adj* 266
row *n* 59, 69; *v* 267
rowdy *n* 887
royalty *n* 875
rpm *n* 138
rub *v* 255, 331, 379
rubadub *n* 407
rubbery *adj* 325
rubbing *n* 331, 379
rubbish *n* 643
rub out *v* 331, 552
rubric *n* 697
ruby *adj* 434
ruckus *n* 59
ruddy *adj* 434
rude *adj* 173, 241, 579,
    851, 885, 895, 929
rudeness *n* 885, 895,
    929
rudimental *adj* 66, 674
rudiments *n* 66
rue *v* 833, 950
rueful *adj* 830, 833
ruffian *n* 887
ruffle *n* 258; *v* 59, 256,
    258, 824
rugged *adj* 241, 256
ruin *n* 162, 619, 638; *v*
    162, 619
ruinous *adj* 162, 619,
    663, 830
ruins *n* 40
rule *n* 80, 157, 175,
    240, 466, 537, 613,
    693, 737, 741; *v* 157,
    480, 693, 737, 749
rulebook *n* 567
ruler *n* 737, 745

rules of language *n* 567
ruling passion *n* 820
rumble *n* 408; *v* 59, 407
rumbling *n* 407
ruminate *v* 450, 451
rumor *n* 532
rump *n* 235
rumple *v* 256, 258
rumus *n* 59
run *n* 264; 109, 264,
    274, 333, 348
run abreast *v* 27
run against *v* 276
run amuck *v* 173
runaway *n* 623
run away *v* 287, 671
run counter to *v* 179
run down *v* 649, 934;
    adj 124
run for one's life *v* 623
run headlong *v* 173
run into *v* 276
run into trouble *v* 665
run its course *v* 67, 109,
    122
runner *n* 271, 534
running water *n* 348
run off at the mouth *v*
    584
run of the mill *adj* 29,
    736
run on and on *v* 573
run out *v* 67
run over *v* 641
run parallel *v* 178
run riot *v* 173, 641
run smoothly *v* 705
run the eye over *v* 441
run the fingers over *v*
    379
run the risk of *v* 177
run through *v* 186, 361
run up against *v* 179
run up bills *v* 808
run wild *v* 173, 825
rupture *n* 44, 713, 720;
    v 44
ruse *n* 545

rush *n* 72, 274, 310, 348, 684; *v* 173, 274, 310, 684
russet *adj* 433
rust *v* 659; *adj* 433
rustic *adj* 876
rustle *v* 409
rusty *adj* 659, 683, 699
rut *n* 259, 613
ruthless *adj* 739, 914a

S

Sabbath *n* 687
sable *adj* 431
saboteur *n* 361
saccharine *adj* 396
saccharinity *n* 396
sacred *adj* 976, 987
sacrilege *n* 988
sacrilegist *n* 988
sacrosanct *adj* 976
sad *adj* 649, 837
sadden *v* 830
sadly *adv* 31
sadness *n* 837
safe *n* 802; *adj* 664, 670
safe and sound *adj* 664
safecracker *n* 792
safeguard *n* 664, 666, 670, 717; *v* 670, 717
safekeeping *n* 664, 670
safety *n* 664
safety valve *n* 664
saffron *adj* 435
sag *v* 245
sagacious *adj* 498, 842, 868
sagacity *n* 480, 498, 698, 842
sage *n* 500
sage *n* 492, 872; *adj* 498
sail *n* 267; *v* 267
sailboat *n* 273
sailing *n* 267; *adj* 267
sailor *n* 269
saint *n* 948

saintly *adj* 987
salable *adj* 796
salad oil *n* 356
sale *n* 796
sale *n* 783, 813
salesman *n* 797
saleswoman *n* 797
salient *adj* 250, 642
sallow *adj* 429, 430, 435
sally *n* 716; *v* 293
salmon *adj* 434
salt *n* 393; *v* 392
salt and pepper *n* 432; *adj* 440
salt of the earth *n* 648, 948
salt water *n* 341
salty *adj* 392
salubrious *adj* 656
salubrity *n* 656
salutary *adj* 644, 648, 656
salutation *n* 896
salute *n* 896; *v* 586, 836, 896
salvation *n* 670, 672
salve *n* 356
salvo *n* 406
sameness *n* 13, 16, 17, 104
sample *n* 82
sanctify *v* 987
sanctimoniousness *n* 988
sanctimony *n* 988
sanction *n* 737, 760, 924, 931; *v* 737, 760, 931
sanctioned *adj* 924
sanctity *n* 987
sanctuary *n* 666
sand *n* 330, 667; *v* 255
sand bar *n* 209
sanded *adj* 255
sandiness *n* 330
sandpaper *v* 255
sandy *adj* 330

sane *adj* 246, 502
sanguine *adj* 831, 858
sanitary *adj* 656
sanity *n* 502
sans adv 187
sap *n* 5, 501; *v* 162, 659
sapience *n* 498
sapient *adj* 498
sapless *adj* 340
sapphire *adj* 438
sappy *adj* 333, 499
sarcastic *adj* 856
sarcophagous *n* 363
sash *n* 247
Satan *n* 978
satanic *adj* 978, 982
satanism *n* 978
sate *v* 869
satiate *v* 376, 829, 869
satiated *adj* 869
satiety *n* 869
satire *n* 856
satirist *n* 844, 936
satirize *v* 856
satisfaction *n* 772, 807, 827, 831, 952
satisfactory *adj* 639
satisfied *adj* 474, 484, 831
satisfy *v* 462, 639, 746, 772, 807, 829, 831, 952
saturate *v* 52, 339, 869
saturated *adj* 52
saturation *n* 869
satyr *n* 980
sauce *n* 393
saunter *n* 266; *v* 266, 275
sauté *v* 384
savage *adj* 173
savant *n* 492
save *v* 672, 817; *adv* 38, 83
saving *n* 817
savoir faire n 698, 852
savor *n* 390; *v* 390, 394

savoriness n 394
savory adj 390, 394
saw n 257; v 44
say n 175; v 535, 560, 582
saying n 496
say nothing v 517, 585
say what comes to mind v 612
scabrous adj 256
scaffolding n 673
scald v 384
scale n 69, 71, 204, 466; v 305
scale the heights v 305
scallop n 257; v 257
scalpel n 262
scaly adj 204
scamper v 274
scan v 441
scant adj 32, 137, 640
scantiness n 103, 203
scanty adj 32,103
scarce adj 32, 103, 137, 640
scarcely adv 32, 137
scarcity n 32, 103, 640
scared adj 862
scarify v 257
scarlet adj 434
scatter v 61, 73, 291
scattered adj 73
scene n 448
scenery n 448
scent n 398, 550; v 398, 400
scented adj 400
scentless adj 399
scepter n 747
schedule n 86
scheme n 626; v 626
schemer n 626
schism n 713, 984
schismatic adj 984
scholar n 492
scholar n 541
scholarly adj 539
scholarship n 490, 539

scholastic adj 537, 539, 542
school n 542
school v 537
schoolbook n 542
schoolboy n 129
schooled adj 498
schoolgirl n 129
schooling n 537
schoolmaster n 540
schooner n 273
science n 490
science of existence n 1
science of light n 420
science of living beings n 357
science of matter n 316
science of sound n 402
science of the mineral kingdom n 358
scintilla n 32, 420
scintillate v 420
scintillating adj 842
scintillation n 420
scion n 167
scoff v 929, 988
scoff at v 856
scoffer n 988
scoffing n 856, 988
scold v 972
scoop n 262; v 252
scoop out v 252
scope n 26, 180, 748
scorch v 384
scorched adj 384
score n 98, 259, 805, 806, 811; v 259
scores n 102
scorn n 930; v 715, 929, 930
scornful adj 929, 930
scotch v 659
scot free adj 748
scoundrel n 941, 949
scour v 331, 652
scourge n 975
scourge v 663, 972
scour the country v 266

scout n 664, 668
scowl v 900, 901a
scraggly adj 256
scramble n 59, 684; v 684
scrap n 32
scrape n 704, 732; v 38, 195, 255, 330, 331
scratch n 257, 259; v 257, 331, 380, 590, 649
scratching n 380; adj 410
scratchy adj 380
scrawl v 590
scrawny adj 203
scream n 411, 669; v 404, 410, 411, 839
screech v 411, 412
screeching n 412; adj 414
screen n 223, 424, 530, 717; v 424, 442, 528, 664, 717
screening n 528
screw n 243; v 43, 243
screw up the eyes v 443
scribble v 590
scribe n 553, 590
scrimp v 819
script n 590, 593
scriptural adj 983a
Scriptures n 985, 986
scrivener n 590
Scrooge n 819
scrub v 331, 652
scruple n 485
scrupulous adj 246, 459, 543, 603, 772, 868, 939
scrupulousness n 603
scrutinize v 457
scrutinizing adj 461
scrutiny n 457, 461
scull v 267
sculpt v 557
sculptor n 559
sculpture n 557

self-mortification *n* 955
self-possessed *adj* 502
self-possession *n* 604, 826
self-reliance *n* 604
self-respect *n* 878
self-restrained *adj* 953
self-restraint *n* 604, 826, 953
selfsame *adj* 13
self-satisfied *adj* 878
self-seeking *n* 943; *adj* 943
self-styled *adj* 565
sell *v* 796, 798
seller *n* 796, 797
sell for *v* 812
selling *n* 796
semblance *n* 17, 19, 21, 216, 882
semi- *adj* 91
semi-circular *adj* 245
semifluid *adj* 352
semiliquid *adj* 352
semiliquidity *n* 352
seminary *n* 542
semiology *n* 550
semiopaque *adj* 427
semipellucid *adj* 427
semitranparency *n* 427
semitransparent *adj* 427
send *v* 270
send a letter *v* 592
send off *v* 284
senile *adj* 124, 128, 158
senility *n* 124, 128, 158, 160, 659
seniority *n* 128
sensation *n* 375, 379, 390
sensational *adj* 824
sensations of touch *n* 380
sense *n* 450, 498, 502, 516, 842

senseless *adj* 376, 497, 499, 517
senselessness *n* 517
sense of duty *n* 926
sensibility *n* 375, 822
sensibility *n* 821
sensible *adj* 316, 375, 498, 502
sensical *adj* 450
sensitive *adj* 375, 597, 821, 822
sensitiveness *n* 375, 822
sensitivity *n* 821, 901
sensitize *v* 375
sensual *adj* 377, 829
sensual delight *n* 377
sensualist *n* 954a
sensualist *n* 962
sensuality *n* 377, 827
sensuous *adj* 375, 377
sensuousness *n* 377
sentence *n* 972
sententious *adj* 577
sentient *adj* 375
sentiment *n* 453, 821
sentimental *adj* 822
sentimentalism *n* 822
sentimentality *n* 821, 822
sentinel *n* 444, 664, 668
sentry *n* 668
separate *v* 44, 55, 291, 905; *adj* 44
separated *adj* 905
separately *adv* 44
separateness *n* 44
separation *n* 44, 55, 198, 291, 489, 905
sepia *adj* 433
septet *n* 415
septic *adj* 657
sepulchral *adj* 363
sepulchre *n* 363
sepulture *n* 363
sequel *n* 65
sequel *n* 39, 63, 117, 281
sequence *n* 63, 281

sequence *n* 58, 117, 281
sequential *adj* 63, 281
sequester *v* 893, 974
sequestered *adj* 893
sequestration *n* 893, 974
seraph *n* 977
seraphic *adj* 977
serene *adj* 265, 721
serenity *n* 265, 826, 831
serfdom *n* 749
serial *adj* 69, 138
serially *adv* 138
series *n* 58, 63, 69
serious *adj* 642, 739
seriousness *n* 642, 739
sermon *n* 537, 582
sermonize *v* 537, 582
serous *adj* 333
serpent *n* 248, 548, 978
serpentine *adj* 248
serrated *adj* 244, 257
serum *n* 337
servant *n* 746
servant *n* 690, 707
serve *v* 618, 644, 707, 743, 746, 749, 969
serve with a writ *n* 969
service *n* 618, 644, 677, 707, 749, 990, 998
serviceable *adj* 631, 644, 648
servile *adj* 886, 933
servility *n* 886
servitude *n* 749
session *n* 696
set *n* 7, 240, 278, 712; *v* 150, 184, 306, 321; *adj* 43, 240, 613
set about *v* 676
set against *adj* 898
set an example *v* 22
set apart *v* 44, 465
set a price *v* 812
set aside *v* 55, 185, 678
set at ease *v* 831
set at naught *v* 773

set a trap for *v* 530

set at rest *v* 462

set down *v* 551, 590

set fire to *v* 384

set foot on dry land *v* 342

set forth *v* 293, 594

set forward *v* 293

set free *v* 44, 672, 748, 750, 970; *adj* 970

set going *v* 276

set in motion *v* 66, 284, 677

set in one's ways *adj* 5

set loose *v* 750

setoff *n* 30

set one's sights on *v* 278

set on fire *v* 384

set out *v* 60, 66, 293

set phrase *n* 566

set right *v* 662

set sail *v* 293

set store by *v* 642

set the fashion *v* 62

setting side by side *n* 464

settle *v* 60, 150, 184, 265, 306, 769, 774, 807

settled *adj* 67, 184, 474

settle down *v* 184, 265

settled purpose *n* 620

settlement *n* 23, 184, 762, 807

settle up *v* 790

settle upon *v* 784

set too high a value on *v* 482

set to rights *v* 660

set to work *v* 677

set up *v* 153, 161, 307

set upon *v* 716

seven *n* 98

sever *v* 44, 291

several *n* 100; *adj* 100, 102

severally *adv* 44, 79

severance *n* 44, 291

severe *adj* 242, 576, 739, 830, 849, 955

severely *adv* 31, 739

severity *n* 739

severity *n* 173, 576, 849

sew *v* 43

sewer *n* 350

sex *n* 377

sextet *n* 415

sexual *adj* 377

sexual abstinence *n* 904

sexual failure *n* 158

sexuality *n* 377

shabby *adj* 34, 643, 659, 851

shade *n* 424

shade *n* 15, 26, 223, 362, 421, 422, 428, 530, 980; *v* 421, 422, 424

shading off *adj* 26

shadow *n* 4, 21, 281, 421, 424, 515, 980; *v* 281, 353, 421, 422

shadowiness *n* 422

shadowy *adj* 4, 421, 422, 424, 447

shady *adj* 421, 424, 426, 874

shaft *n* 208, 351

shaggy *adj* 256

shaggy dog story *n* 549

shake *n* 315; *v* 160, 314, 315, 383, 404, 407, 616, 659

shake one's sides *v* 838

shake the foundations of *v* 659

shake up *v* 315

shaking *adj* 315

shaky *adj* 160, 315, 665

shallow *n* 209; *adj* 209, 491, 499, 643

shallow excuse *n* 617

shallowness *n* 209

shallowness *n* 499

shallows *n* 667

sham *n* 544, 545, 855, 880; *v* 546; *adj* 544

shaman *n* 994

shamble *v* 275, 315

shame *n* 874, 930; *v* 874, 879

shameful *adj* 874, 930

shape *n* 448; *v* 240, 557, 852

shapeless *adj* 241

shapelessness *n* 241

shapeliness *n* 242

shapely *adj* 242

share *n* 786; *v* 709, 778, 786

shareholder *n* 778

share in *v* 56, 778

sharer *n* 778

sharp *adj* 171, 173, 217, 253, 375, 392, 397, 404, 410, 416; *adj* 490, 498, 682, 698, 702, 842, 868

sharp edged *adj* 253

sharpen *v* 171, 173, 253, 375, 824

sharpness *n* 253

sharpness *n* 392, 397, 410, 698

sharp outline *n* 446

shatter *v* 44, 158, 162, 328

shattered *adj* 160

shave *v* 195, 201, 204, 255

she *n* 374

shear *v* 195, 201

sheathe *v* 225

shed *n* 223; *v* 73

shed light on *v* 522

shed light upon *v* 420

sheen *n* 420

sheeny *adj* 420

sheepish *adj* 881

sheer *adj* 52, 425

sheerness *n* 425

sheet *n* 204, 223, 811

shelf *n* 215

shell *n* 363

shellac *n* 356a; *v* 356a

shellfish *n* 366

shelter *n* 666, 670, 717; *v* 528, 664, 670, 717

sheltering *n* 528

shelve *v* 133, 678

shepherd *n* 996

shield *n* 223, 717; *v* 670, 717

shift *n* 140, 147, 270; *v* 140, 144, 264, 270, 279

shifting *n* 144; *adj* 264

shiftless *adj* 674

shilly-shally *v* 133, 605

shimmer *n* 420; *v* 420

shine *v* 420

shiny *adj* 255, 420

ship *n* 273

ship *n* 271; *v* 190

shipment *n* 190

ship out *v* 293

shipping *n* 267

shipshape *adj* 58

shirk *v* 623, 742

shirker *n* 623

shiver *v* 315, 328, 383

shivering *adj* 383

shoal *n* 209

shoals *n* 667

shock *n* 276, 315, 508, 713; *v* 824, 830

shockingly *adv* 31

shoot *n* 378; *v* 194, 274, 284, 361, 367, 378

shoot ahead of *v* 303

shooting *n* 361, 378

shoot up *v* 250, 367

shop *v* 795

shopkeeper *n* 797

shopper *n* 795

shopping center *n* 799

shore *n* 231, 342

shore up *v* 215

short *adj* 28, 53, 201, 572, 640, 739

shortcoming *n* 304

shortcoming *n* 28, 34, 53, 640, 651, 730

short distance *n* 197

shorten *v* 36, 38, 201, 596

shortened *adj* 201

shortening *n* 36, 38, 201

shorthand *n* 590

short-lived *adj* 111

shortly *adv* 132

short memory *n* 506

shortness *n* 201

short of *adj* 53; *adv* 32, 34, 38

short-tempered *adj* 901

shot *n* 284

shot in the dark *n* 621

shoulder *n* 236; *v* 215, 276

shoulder to shoulder *adv* 709

shout *n* 411, 838; *v* 404, 411, 836, 838

shout at the top of one's lungs *v* 411

shove *n* 276; *v* 276, 284

shove in *v* 300

shovel *v* 270

shove off *v* 267, 293

show *n* 448, 855, 882; *v* 448, 467, 478, 525, 529

shower *n* 348

shower down *v* 348

showery *adj* 348

showiness *n* 882

showing *n* 525

show itself *v* 446

shown *adj* 478

show no remorse *v* 951

show off *v* 882

show taste *v* 850

show up *v* 446

showy *adj* 428, 851, 882

shred *n* 32

shrewd *adj* 490, 498, 698, 702

shrewdness *n* 702

shriek *n* 411; *v* 411

shrill *adj* 203, 404, 410

shrillness *n* 410

shrink *v* 36, 195, 283, 287, 623

shrink from *v* 603

shrinking *n* 36, 195, 603

shrive *v* 952

shrivel *v* 195, 659

shroud *n* 363; *v* 664

shrub *n* 367

shrubbery *n* 367

shrunk *adj* 195

shrunken *adj* 195

shudder *v* 383

shuffle *v* 149, 275, 315

shuffle off *v* 623

shuffle off the mortal coil *v* 360

shun *v* 623, 671

shunt *v* 279

shut *v* 261; *adj* 261

shutout *n* 101; *v* 55

shutter *n* 424

shutting up *n* 261

shut up *v* 261, 403

shut up shop *v* 687

shy *v* 283, 623; *adj* 881

shyster *n* 548

sibilant *adj* 409

sibilation *n* 409

sibyl *n* 513

sick *adj* 655

sicken *v* 289, 395, 655, 830

sickening *adj* 395

sickly *adj* 160, 435, 655

sickness *n* 655

side *n* 236

side *n* 712

side by side *adv* 88, 236

side effects *n* 154

sidelong *adj* 236; *adv* 217, 236

sketcher *n* 559
sketchy *adj* 53, 730
skill *n* 698
skill *n* 79, 702, 731
skilled *adj* 698
skillful *adj* 698, 702
skillfully *adv* 698
skillfulness *n* 698, 702
skin *n* 220, 223
skin-deep *adj* 209
skinflint *n* 819
skinniness *n* 203
skinny *adj* 203
skip *n* 198; *v* 309, 838
skipper *n* 269
skirt *n* 231; *v* 231, 236
skirting *n* 231; *adj* 236
skulk *v* 862
skull *n* 450
sky *n* 318, 338
skyscraping *adj* 206
slab *n* 204, 251
slack *adj* 47, 160, 172,
    275, 603, 674, 683,
    738
slacken *v* 47, 275, 687
slackness *n* 275, 738
slake *v* 174, 829
slam *n* 276; *v* 276
slander *n* 908, 934; *v*
    908, 934
slanderer *n* 936
slanderous *adj* 934
slang *n* 579; *adj* 563
slangy *adj* 560
slant *n* 217; *v* 217
slantwise *adv* 217
slap *n* 276; *v* 276
slash *v* 44
slaughter *n* 361; *v* 361
slaughtering *n* 361
slavery *n* 749, 886
slavish *adj* 886
slavishness *n* 886
slayer *n* 361
sleek *v* 255; *adj* 255
sleep *n* 687
sleeping *adj* 172, 265

sleeping car *n* 272
slender *adj* 32, 203,
    643
slenderize *v* 203
slenderness *n* 32, 203
slice *n* 204; *v* 44, 204
slick *adj* 355
slide *v* 109, 264, 306
slight *v* 460, 483, 927;
    adj 432, 209, 322,
    575, 643, 736
slightly *adv* 32
slightness *n* 4, 32, 203
slim *v* 203; *adj* 203
slime *n* 653
slimness *n* 203
slimy *adj* 352, 355, 653
sling *v* 284
slink away *v* 623
slip *n* 32, 306, 495,
    568, 732; *v* 109, 306,
    495, 623
slip back *v* 661
slipperiness *n* 665
slippery *adj* 255, 355,
    607, 665
slippery ground *n* 667
slippery memory *n* 506
slip-shod *adj* 575
slit *n* 44, 198, 259, 260;
    v 44
sliver *n* 32
slobber over *v* 933
sloop *n* 273
slope *n* 217, 306; *v* 217
sloping *adj* 217, 306
sloppy *adj* 345, 575
slot *n* 260
sloth *n* 133, 172, 275,
    683
slothful *adj* 681, 683
slothfulness *n* 681
slouch *v* 207, 217, 275,
    683
slough *n* 345
slovenliness *n* 653
slovenly *adj* 59, 575,
    653

slow *v* 275, 420; *adj*
    133, 172, 275, 603,
    683, 685, 843, 901a
slowly *adv* 133, 275
slowness *n* 275
slowness *n* 133, 603
sluggard *n* 683
sluggish *adj* 172, 275,
    683, 901a
sluggishness *n* 275,
    683, 901a
sluice *n* 350
slumber *n* 687
slumberer *n* 683
slump *v* 306
slur one's words *v* 583
slushy *adj* 352
slut *n* 962
sluttish *adj* 653
sly *adj* 702
slyness *n* 702
smack *n* 32, 276, 390; *v*
    390
smack the lips *v* 390
small *adj* 32, 193
small change *n* 800
smallness32
smallness *n* 193
small number *n* 103
small quantity *n* 32, 103
small talk *n* 588
smart *n* 378, 828; *v*
    378; *adj* 682, 698
smarts *n* 450, 498
smash *v* 162
smatch *n* 390; *v* 390
smear *v* 653
smell *n* 398, 400; *v*
    398, 401
smell bad *v* 401
smell of *v* 398
smell rotten *v* 401
smell sweet *v* 400
smelly *adj* 398
smile *n* 838; *v* 838
smirch *v* 431, 653
smirk *n* 838; *v* 838
smite *v* 649

smitten *adj* 897
smoggy *adj* 426
smoke *v* 382, 392
smoking *adj* 382
smoky *adj* 426
smolder *v* 382, 526
smoldering *adj* 172
smooth *v* 16, 174, 255,
 705, 723; *adj* 174,
 213, 251, 255, 705
smoothly *adv* 705
smoothness *n* 255
smoothness *n* 251, 705
smooth-tongued *adj*
 933
smother *v* 361, 581
smudge *v* 653
smug *adj* 878
smut *n* 653, 961; *v* 431
smutch *v* 431
smutty *adj* 653,961
snag *n* 667
snaggy *adj* 253
snake *n* 248
snake in the grass *n* 548,
 649, 667
snaky *adj* 248
snap *n* 406
snap *n* 277; *v* 44, 328,
 406
snap back *v* 277
snappish *adj* 901
snap up *v* 789
snare *n* 530, 545, 667
snarl *v* 412, 900
snatch *n* 32; *v* 789
sneak *n* 941; *v* 275,
 623, 862, 886
sneak off *v* 623
sneer *n* 856; *v* 929
sneer at *v* 856
sneeze *v* 409
sniff *v* 398
snip *v* 44
snippet *n* 32
sniveling *adj* 886
snobbish *adj* 878

snort *v* 412
snout *n* 250
snow-white *adj* 430
snowy *adj* 430
snuff *v* 398
snuff out *v* 421
snug *adj* 261, 664
soak *v* 337, 339, 959
soak up *v* 340
soap *n* 356
soar *v* 31, 206, 267,
 303, 305
sob *n* 839; *v* 411, 839
sobbing *n* 411
sober *v* 174; *adj* 174,
 246, 502, 826, 953,
 958
sobriety *n* 958
sobriety *n* 502, 953
sobriquet *n* 565
so-called *adj* 565
sociability *n* 894
sociable *adj* 892
sociableness *n* 892
social *adj* 372, 892
social interaction *n* 892
social intercourse *n* 892
socialism *n* 778
socialist *n* 778; *adj* 778
socialistic *adj* 778
sociality *n* 892
society *n* 188, 372, 852
society of men *n* 372
sodden *v* 339; *adj* 337
soft *adj* 255, 324, 345,
 403, 405, 413, 499
soft as butter *adj* 324
soft coal *n* 388
soften *v* 174, 324
softening *n* 324
softness *n* 324
softness *n* 160, 326
soggy *adj* 337, 339
soi-disant adj 565
soil *n* 181, 342; *v* 653
soiled *adj* 653
sojourn *v* 186

solace *n* 834
solar *adj* 318
solar energy *n* 388
solar system *n* 180, 318
solder *v* 43, 46
soldier *n* 726, 948
sole *n* 211; *adj* 87
solecism *n* 568
solecism *n* 579
solecize *v* 568
solemn *adj* 403, 642,
 882
solemnity *n* 642
solemnization *n* 883
solemnize *v* 883
solicit *v* 765, 865
solicitation *n* 411, 765
solicitor *n* 767, 968
solicitous *adj* 411, 765,
 860, 920
solicitude *n* 459, 828,
 860
solid *adj* 16, 52, 150,
 202, 321, 323
solidarity *n* 52
solid body *n* 321
solidification *n* 321, 385
solidify *v* 46, 48, 321
solidity *n* 150, 321
solidness *n* 321
soliloquize *v* 582, 589
soliloquy *n* 589
solipsism *n* 943
solipsistic *adj* 943
solitary *adj* 87, 893
solitude *n* 893
solo *n* 415; *adj* 87; *v*
 416
soloist *n* 416
solubility *n* 333
soluble *adj* 333, 335,
 462, 662
solubleness *n* 335
solution *n* 462, 522, 662
solve *v* 462, 662
solvency *n* 803
solvent *adj* 335, 807

somatic *adj* 316
somber *adj* 431, 901a
some *adj* 25, 100, *adv* 32
somebody *n* 372
someone *n* 372
somersault *n* 218
something like *adj* 17
some time ago *adv* 122
sometimes *adv* 136
somewhere *adv* 182
somewhere about *adv* 32
son *n* 167
sonata *n* 415
song *n* 413, 415
sonneteer *n* 597
sonority *n* 402
sonorous *adj* 402, 404, 577
sonorousness *n* 402, 408
soon *adv* 111, 121, 132
sooner or later *adv* 121
soothe *v* 723, 834
soothing *adj* 834
soothsayer *n* 513, 994
soothsaying *n* 511
sooty *adj* 431, 653
sop *v* 339
sophism *n* 477
sophist *n* 477, 548
sophistical *adj* 477
sophistry *n* 477
sophistry *n* 538
soporific *adj* 683
sorcerer *n* 994
sorcerer *n* 513
sorcery *n* 992
sordid *adj* 32, 207, 435
sordidness *n* 32
sore *n* 378, 830; *adj* 378, 830
sorely *adv* 31
soreness *n* 378
sore subject *n* 830
sorority *n* 11

sorrel *adj* 433
sorrow *n* 833
sorrowful *adj* 828, 839
sorrow over *v* 839
sorry *adj* 643, 828, 833, 950
sorry sight *n* 830
sort *n* 75; *v* 60
sortie *n* 716
sorting *n* 60
SOS *n* 669
so-so *adj* 32, 643, 651
sot *n* 959; *v* 959
so to speak *adv* 17
sotted *adj* 959
sough *n* 350
soul *n* 5, 359, 372, 820
soul-stirring *adj* 821, 824
sound *n* 402
sound *n* 343; *v* 208, 402; *adj* 50, 150, 246, 498, 650, 654, 664, 670, 983a
sound dead *v* 408a
sounding *adj* 402
soundings *n* 208
soundless *adj* 208, 403
soundness *n* 150, 502, 654, 983a
sound the alarm *v* 669
sound vibrations *n* 402
soupçon n 32
sour *v* 397; *adj* 392, 395, 397, 410, 901a
source *n* 66, 153
sourness *n* 397
sourness *n* 392, 395
souse *v* 310, 337
souvenir *n* 505
sovereign *n* 737; *adj* 737
sovereignty *n* 157
sow *n* 374; *v* 73, 371
sow the seeds of *v* 153
space *n* 180
space *n* 106, 198, 318

space heater *n* 386
spaceman *n* 269
spaceship *n* 273
space station *n* 273
spacious *adj* 180, 192
span *n* 106, 180, 196, 200; *v* 43, 45
spare *v* 678, 784; *adj* 40, 636, 641, 685
spare no effort *v* 686
spare no expense *v* 816
spare time *n* 685
sparing *adj* 953
spark *n* 382, 420, 423
sparkle *v* 420
sparkling *adj* 574, 836, 842
sparse *adj* 32, 73, 103, 640
sparseness *n* 32, 103
spasm *n* 146, 173, 315, 378
spasmodic *adj* 70, 139, 173
speak *v* 580, 582
speak directly *v* 576
speaker *n* 524, 582
speaking of *adv* 134
speak in low tones *v* 405
speak one's mind *v* 703
speak plainly *v* 576
speak prettily *v* 521
speak softly *v* 405
speak the truth *v* 543
speak to *v* 586
spear *n* 262; *v* 260, 361
special *n* 79; *adj* 20, 79, 474
special committee *n* 755
specialist *n* 700
speciality *n* 79
specialize *v* 79
specially *adv* 79
specialty *n* 79
species *n* 75
specific *n* 662; *adj* 79

specify *v* 79, 564
specimen *n* 82
specious *adj* 477, 545
speciousness *n* 477
speck *n* 32, 848
speckle *v* 440
speckled *adj* 440
spectacle *n* 448, 872
spectacles *n* 445
spectator *n* 444
specter *n* 980; 443
spectral *adj* 2, 4, 980
spectroscope *n* 428
spectrum *n* 428
speculate *v* 155, 514,
   621, 675, 870
speculation *n* 156, 451,
   514, 621, 675
speculative *adj* 514,
   621, 675
speech *n* 582
speech *n* 560, 586
speech impediment *n*
   583
speechless *adj* 403,
   581, 583
speechlessness *n* 403,
   590
speed *n* 264, 274, 684;
   v 274, 682, 684
speedily *adv* 132
speediness *n* 132
speed up *v* 274
speedy *adj* 274, 684
spell *n* 993
spell *n* 106, 198, 992; *v*
   561, 707
spell-bound *adj* 870
spelling *n* 561
spend *v* 638, 809
spend freely *v* 816
spendthrift *adj* 638,
   818
spend time *v* 106
spent *adj* 158, 160, 688
spew *v* 297

sphere *n* 26, 181, 249,
   318; *v* 249
spherical *adj* 249
sphericity *n* 249
spheroid *n* 249
spice *n* 41, 393; *v* 392
spiced *adj* 392
spick and span *adj* 123
spicy *adj* 392, 400
spigot *n* 263
spike *n* 253, 263; *v* 260
spiked *adj* 253
spiky *adj* 253
spill *v* 348
spin *n* 266; *v* 312
spin a melody *v* 416
spin around *v* 312
spindly *adj* 203
spine *n* 253
spineless *adj* 862
spinelessness *n* 172
spinning *n* 312
spin out *v* 200
spinster *n* 904
spiny *adj* 253
spiral *n* 248, 311; *adj*
   248
spirit *n* 5, 171, 359,
   516, 574, 682, 709,
   820, 861, 977, 980
spirited *adj* 171, 574,
   836, 861
spiritual *adj* 2, 317,
   976, 977
spiritualism *n* 992
spirituality *n* 317
spit *v* 260
spite *n* 907
spiteful *adj* 898, 907,
   919, 945
spitefulness *n* 907
splash *n* 348; *v* 337,
   348, 653
splendid *adj* 420
splendor *n* 420, 845,
   882
splice *v* 43, 219

splint *n* 215
splinter *n* 32; *v* 44, 328
splintery *adj* 328
split *n* 44, 713; *v* 44,
   91, 293, 328, 713,
   838
split down the middle *v*
   91
split hairs *v* 868
split one's sides *v* 838
split the difference *v* 29
split the differences *v*
   774
split the eardrums *v*
   404, 419
split up *v* 778, 905; *adj*
   51, 905
spoil *v* 397, 659
spoilage *n* 659
spoilation *n* 638
spoiled *adj* 397
spoiled child *n* 899
spoiler *n* 165
spoils *n* 793
spokesman *n* 524, 534,
   582
sponge *v* 339, 340
sponginess *n* 354
sponsor *v* 771
sponsorship *n* 771
spontaneous *adj* 612
spook *n* 980
spoonful *n* 25, 32
sporadic *adj* 103, 137,
   139
sport *v* 840
spot *n* 182, 848, 874; *v*
   653, 848
spotless *adj* 650, 652,
   946, 960
spotlessness *n* 946
spotted *adj* 440
spottiness *n* 440
spotty *adj* 440
spouse *n* 903
spout *n* 348, 350; *v*
   295, 348, 582

stand out *v* 250
standpoint *n* 183, 441
stand still *v* 265
stand straight and tall *v* 212
stand the test *v* 648
stand to reason *v* 474
stand up *v* 719
stand upright *v* 212
stand up straight *v* 212
staple commodity *n* 798
staples *n* 635
starboard *n* 238
starchy *adj* 352
stare *n* 441; *v* 455, 870
stark *adj* 31
stark-naked *adj* 226
stars *n* 423
start *n* 66, 293; *v* 66, 151, 276, 284, 293, 309, 870
start again *v* 66
start fresh *v* 652
starting point *n* 66, 293
startle *v* 508, 824, 870
startled *adj* 870
startling *adj* 508, 870
start over *v* 66
start up *v* 250, 446
starvation *n* 956
starve *v* 385, 804, 819, 955, 956
starved *adj* 956
starving *adj* 956
starving oneself *n* 956
stash *n* 636; *v* 636
state *n* 7
state *n* 188; *v* 516, 535
stated *adj* 474
stateliness *n* 875
stately *adj* 875, 878
statement *n* 535, 594, 811
station *n* 26, 71, 183; *v* 184
stationary *adj* 265
statistical *adj* 85

statistics *n* 85
statuary *n* 557
statue *n* 557, 963, 991
statuette *n* 557
stature *n* 206
status *n* 7, 8, 71
statute *n* 697; 963
staunch *adj* 150, 604a
stave in *v* 252
stay *n* 133, 215, 685; *v* 1, 133, 141, 142, 186, 265
stay away *v* 187
stay in the background *v* 881
stay together *v* 46
stead *n* 644
steadfast *adj* 150, 604, 604a
steadfastness *n* 150, 604a
steadiness *n* 138, 150
steady *adj* 80, 138, 150, 604a
steal *v* 275, 789, 791
steal a march on *v* 132
steal away *v* 623, 671
steal from *v* 788
stealing *n* 791
stealing *n* 788
stealthily *adv* 528
stealthy *adj* 528, 702
steam *n* 353; *v* 267, 336, 353
steamer *n* 273
steaming *n* 336
steam press *v* 255
steam up *v* 353
steamy *adj* 353
steel *v* 159
steep *v* 337; *adj* 217, 306
steepness *n* 217
steer *n* 373; *v* 693
steerage *n* 693
steer a middle course *v* 628

steer clear of *v* 279, 623
steer for *v* 278
steersman *n* 269
stench *n* 401
stencil *n* 21
stenography *n* 590
stentorian *adj* 404, 411
step *n* 71, 264
step by step *adv* 26, 58, 69, 275
step in *v* 724
steppe *n* 344
stereoscope *n* 445
sterile *adj* 158, 169
sterility *n* 169
stern *adj* 604, 739, 955
sternness *n* 739
stew *v* 382, 384
steward *n* 801; *v* 693
stewardship *n* 693
stewed *adj* 959
stewed to the gills *adj* 959
stick *n* 215, 975; *v* 46, 260
stick fast *v* 150, 265
stick in *v* 300
stickiness *n* 46, 352, 396
stick it out *v* 604a
stick out *v* 250
stick to *v* 143
stick to an idea *v* 606
stick up *v* 250
sticky *adj* 46, 327, 352, 396
stiff *adj* 240, 579, 739
stiff breeze *n* 349
stiffen *v* 323
stiffness *n* 246, 579
stifle *v* 361, 403
stifled *adj* 405
stifling *adj* 382
stiletto *n* 262
still *v* 174, 403, 723; *adj* 174, 265, 403; *adv* 30

still-born *adj* 732
stillness *n* 265, 403
stilted *adj* 307, 577, 855
stilts *n* 215
stimulate *v* 171, 173, 382, 615, 689, 824, 829
stimulating *adj* 171
stimulation *n* 824
stimulus *n* 615
sting *v* 378, 380, 663
stinginess *n* 819, 943
stinging *n* 380; *adj* 392
stingy *adj* 819, 943
stink *n* 401; *v* 401, 653
stinking *adj* 401
stinky *adj* 401
stint *v* 819
stipple *v* 558
stipulate *v* 769, 770
stipulations *n* 770
stir *n* 264, 315, 682, 752; *v* 264, 315, 375, 382, 824
stir about *v* 682
stirring *adj* 151, 505
stir up *v* 173, 824
stitch *n* 43, 378, 828; *v* 43
stock *n* 11, 25, 635, 636, 637, 798; *v* 637; *adj* 598, 613
stocks *n* 802
stock-still *adj* 265
stockyard *n* 232
stoical *adj* 383, 826
stoicism *n* 826
stoke *v* 388
stolen away *adj* 671
stolen goods *n* 793
stolid *adj* 499, 843
stolidity *n* 499
stomach *v* 826
stone-blind *adj* 442
stone-deaf *adj* 419
stone's throw *n* 197

stony *adj* 914a
stoop *v* 217, 306, 886
stop *n* 133, 142, 360; *v* 67, 70, 142, 261, 265, 403
stopcock *n* 263
stopgap *n* 147
stoppage *n* 142, 261, 706
stop payment *v* 808
stopper *n* 263
stopper *n* 261
stopping *n* 142, 263, 706
stop short *v* 142, 265
stop up *v* 261
stopwatch *n* 114
storage *n* 636
storage areas *n* 191
store *n* 636
store *n* 31, 637, 798, 799; *v* 72, 636, 637, 670
store up *v* 636
storing *n* 636
storm *n* 173, 315, 348, 349; *v* 173, 349, 716
stormy *adj* 173, 349
story *n* 204, 546, 593
storyteller *n* 548
stout *adj* 159, 192
stout-hearted *adj* 861
stoutness *n* 159
stove *n* 386
stow away *v* 528
strabismus *n* 443
straggle *v* 279
straggler *n* 268
straggling *adj* 59
straight *n* 857; *adj* 212, 246, 278, 807, 958; *adv* 132, 278
straighten *v* 246
straighten out *v* 60
straightforward *adj* 543, 703, 849; *adv* 278

straight line *n* 246
straightness *n* 246
straightway *adv* 132
strain *n* 402, 413, 415, 686; *v* 42, 686, 688
strait *n* 704
strait-laced *adj* 739
straitness *n* 203
straits *n* 343, 804
strand *n* 205, 205
strange *adj* 10, 83, 519, 870
strangely *adv* 31
strangle *v* 158, 361
strangulation *n* 361
strap *n* 975; *v* 43
strapper *n* 192
strapping *adj* 159
stratagem *n* 545, 626, 702
strategic *adj* 626
strategical *adj* 692
strategist *n* 626
strategy *n* 692, 722
stratified *adj* 204
stratosphere *n* 338
stratum *n* 204, 213
straw-colored *adj* 435
stray *v* 279; *adj* 73, 279
streak *n* 259, 420; *v* 440
streaked *adj* 440
streakiness *n* 440
stream *n* 347
stream *n* 264, 347, 348, 420; *v* 72, 264, 333, 348, 349
streamy *adj* 348
street-walker *n* 962
strength *n* 159
strength *n* 25, 26, 31, 157, 171, 327, 364, 739
strengthen *v* 157, 159, 171, 689
strengthening *n* 159
strength of mind *n* 604
strenuous *adj* 686

stress *n* 580, 642, 686
stretch *n* 180; *v* 194, 200, 325
stretch out *v* 200
stretch the meaning *v* 523
stretch to *v* 196, 200
strew *v* 73
strewn *adj* 73
striate *v* 440; *adj* 440
striated *adj* 259
striation *n* 440
stricken *adj* 828
strict *adj* 82, 739, 955, 983a
strictness *n* 739, 983a
stricture *n* 706
stride *n* 264
stride forward *v* 282
stridency *n* 410
strident *adj* 410
strife *n* 713, 720
strike *v* 170, 276
strike a balance *v* 27
strike dumb *v* 581
strike out *v* 552
strike up *v* 416
strike while the iron is hot *v* 134
strikingly *adv* 31
string *n* 69; *v* 43
stringency *n* 739
stringent *adj* 739
strings *n* 417
string together *v* 69
stringy *adj* 200, 205, 327
strip *v* 226, 789
stripe *v* 440
striped *adj* 440
stripling *n* 129
strip to essentials *v* 849
strive *v* 675, 686, 720
stroke *n* 276, 731; *v* 379
stroking *n* 379
stroll *n* 266; *v* 264
strong *adj* 31, 150, 157,

159, 171, 323, 327, 392, 401, 654
strongbox *n* 802
stronghold *n* 666, 802
strong language *n* 574
strongly *adv* 159
strong smelling *adj* 398, 401
strop *v* 253
structural *adj* 329
structure *n* 329
structure *n* 7
struggle *n* 675, 686, 713, 720; *v* 720
struggling *n* 720
strumpet *n* 962
strut *v* 884
stubble *n* 40
stubborn *adj* 150, 327, 606, 704, 719, 742
stubbornness *n* 150, 327, 606, 704, 742
stubby *adj* 201
stud *n* 250
studded *adj* 253, 440
student *n* 492, 541
studio *n* 556, 691
studious *adj* 539
study *n* 457, 461, 539, 595; *v* 457, 461, 539
stuff *n* 3, 635; *v* 190, 194, 224, 376, 869
stuffed *adj* 869
stuff in *v* 300
stuffing *n* 190, 224, 263
stuff oneself *v* 957
stuff up *v* 261
stumble *n* 495; *v* 306, 315, 699
stumble on *v* 156
stumble onto *v* 480a
stumbling block *n* 706
stump *n* 40; *v* 582
stumpy *adj* 201
stun *v* 376, 404, 419, 508
stunned *adj* 419

stunted *adj* 193, 195, 201
stupefaction *n* 870
stupefy *v* 376, 870
stupendous *adj* 31, 192
stupendously *adv* 31
stupid *adj* 275, 486, 491, 497, 499, 843
stupidity *n* 491, 497, 499, 843
stupor *n* 683
sturdy *adj* 150, 159
stuttering *n* 583
stygian *adj* 982
style *n* 569
style *n* 7, 560, 564, 567, 852; *v* 564, 569
stylish *adj* 123, 852
stylishness *n* 123
stylistic *adj* 569
styptic *adj* 397
suasive *adj* 615, 695
sub *n* 634; *v* 147, 634
subdivide *v* 44
subdivision *n* 44, 51, 75, 100a
subdue *v* 744, 879
subdued *adj* 826
subject *n* 454, 746; *v* 601, 744, 749; *adj* 177, 749
subjection *n* 749
subjection *n* 34, 601
subjective *adj* 5
subject-matter *n* 454, 516
subjoin *v* 37
subjugate *v* 749
subjugation *n* 749
sublimation *n* 307
sublime *adj* 206, 574
sublimity *n* 206, 574, 845
sublunary *adj* 318
submerge *v* 310, 337
submerged *adj* 208

submersion n 208, 300, 310

submicroscopic adj 193

submission n 725

submission n 749, 826

submissive adj 725, 743, 879, 926

submissiveness n 725, 743, 879, 886

submit v 725, 743, 749

subordinate adj 34, 749

subordination n 34, 749

subpar adv 34

subpoena n 969

subscribe v 769

subsequence n 117

subsequent adj 63, 117

subsequently adv 63, 117

subservience n 631, 743

subservient adj 176, 677, 743

subside v 36, 287, 360

subsidiary adj 176

subsist v 1, 141, 359

subsistence n 1, 298

subsoil n 221

substance n 3, 25, 221, 316, 516, 642, 803

substanceless adj 209

substantial adj 1, 3, 316, 321

substantiality n 3

substantiality n 316

substantially adv 5

substantive adj 1, 3

substitute n 634

substitute n 147, 759; v 147

substitute for v 147

substitution n 147

substratum n 204, 221

substructure n 211

subterfuge n 545, 702

subtilize v 477

subtle adj 320, 329, 477, 702

subtlety n 15, 702

subtract v 36, 38, 85

subtracted adj 38

subtracting adj 38

subtraction n 36, 38

suburbs n 227

subversion n 14, 146, 162, 218

subversive n 913; adj 162

subvert v 162, 218

succeed v 63, 117, 731, 734, 783

succeeding adj 63, 117

success n 731

success n 734

successful adj 731, 734

successfully adv 731

succession n 63, 69, 117

successive adj 69, 117

successor n 117

succinct adj 572

succor n 707; v 707, 834

succorer n 912

succuba n 980

succubus n 980

succulent adj 337, 352

succumb v 725

sucker n 486, 547

sucking n 296

suction n 296

sudden adj 111, 113, 132, 508

sudden impulse n 276

suddenly adv 113, 132, 508

suddenness n 111, 113, 132

sudden thought n 612

suds n 353

sue v 765, 969

suet n 356

suffer v 378, 655, 760, 826, 828

sufferance n 760, 826

suffer a relapse v 661

suffering n 378, 828, 982

suffice v 639

sufficiency n 639

sufficiency n 31, 803

sufficient adj 31, 639

sufficiently adv 639

suffix n 39, 65

suffocate v 361, 641

suffocating adj 382, 401

suffocation n 361

suffuse v 41

suffusion n 41

sugar v 396

sugariness n 396

sugary adj 396

suggest v 505, 514, 527, 695

suggestion n 505, 514, 526, 527, 695, 993

suggestive adj 514, 695

suicidal adj 361

suicide n 361, 361

suit n 225, 765, 969; v 23, 646, 852

suitability n 134, 646

suitable adj 134, 646, 850, 922

suitable time n 134

suite n 69

suiting adj 413

suitor n 767, 897, 969

suit the occasion v 134, 646

sulk v 901a

sulky adj 901a

sullenness n 901a

sullied adj 961

sully v 653, 848

sultry adj 382

sum n 50, 84, 800; v 37, 85

summarily adv 132, 572

summarize v 596

summary n 572, 596

survive *v* 1, 40, 110, 141
surviving *adj* 40
susceptibility *n* 176, 177, 821, 822
susceptible *adj* 375, 822
suspect *v* 485, 487, 514
suspend *v* 133, 142, 214
suspended *adj* 214
suspense *n* 485, 507
suspension *n* 214
suspension *n* 133, 142
suspension of hostilities *n* 723
suspicion *n* 485, 487, 514, 860, 920
suspicious *adj* 485, 487, 860, 920
sustain *v* 143, 159, 170, 215, 670, 707
sustenance *n* 298, 670
swab *v* 340
swaddle *v* 225
swagger *v* 878, 884, 885
swaggerer *n* 887
swaggering *n* 884
swain *n* 373
swallow *v* 298, 486, 547, 826
swamp *n* 345; *v* 162
swampy *adj* 345
swap *n* 148; *v* 148, 794
swarm *n* 72; *v* 72, 102, 641
swarming *adj* 72
swarm with *v* 102
swarthiness *n* 431
swarthy *adj* 431
swash *v* 348
swathe *v* 225
sway *n* 157, 175, 737, 741; *v* 175, 217, 315, 615, 737
swear *n* 908; *v* 535, 768, 908, 988
swearing *n* 535

sweat *n* 299; *v* 299, 382, 686
sweep *n* 180, 245; *v* 245, 274
sweep along *v* 264
sweep away *v* 162
sweeping *adj* 52, 76
sweep out *v* 652
sweet *adj* 377, 396, 413, 428, 652, 829
sweeten *v* 396
sweetened *adj* 396
sweetheart *n* 897, 899
sweetness *n* 396
sweet scent *n* 400
sweet scented *adj* 400
sweet smell *n* 400
sweet smelling *adj* 400
sweet-sounding *adj* 413
sweet sounds *n* 413, 415
swell *n* 348, 404; *v* 194, 367, 404
swelling *n* 194, 250; *adj* 250, 577
swell up *v* 250
swelter *v* 382
sweltering *adj* 382
swerve *v* 140, 279, 291, 603
swerving *n* 279
swift *adj* 274, 684
swiftly *adv* 274
swiftness *n* 111, 274, 684
swill *v* 959
swim *v* 320
swim in *v* 377
swindle *v* 791
swindler *n* 548
swindling *n* 791
swing *n* 180, 415; *v* 214, 314
swinging *adj* 214
swinish *adj* 957
swivel *v* 312
swivel eye *n* 443
swollen *adj* 194, 250

swoon *v* 158, 688
swoop down *v* 306
sworn *adj* 768
sybarite *n* 954a
sybaritism *n* 954
sycophancy *n* 886, 933
sycophant *n* 886, 935
sycophantic *adj* 886, 933
syllabic *adj* 561
syllable *n* 561
syllabus *n* 596
syllogistic *adj* 476
syllogistic reasoning *n* 476
sylph *n* 979
sylphic *adj* 979
symbol *n* 84, 512, 550, 561, 562, 747, 991
symbolic *adj* 550, 554
symbolical *adj* 550
symbolism *n* 550
symbolize *v* 550, 554
symmetrical *adj* 27, 58, 242, 413
symmetry *n* 242
symmetry *n* 27, 58
sympathetic *adj* 714, 740, 821, 914
sympathize *v* 915
sympathizer *n* 890, 906
sympathize with *v* 714, 888, 914
sympathy *n* 714, 820, 821, 888, 914, 915
symphonic *adj* 415
symphonic music *n* 415
symphonious *adj* 413
symphonize *v* 413
symphony *n* 413
symphony orchestra *n* 416
symptom *n* 550
synagogue *n* 1000
synchronism *n* 120
synchronize *v* 120
synchronized *adj* 413

take up one's abode *v* 189

take upon oneself *v* 676

take up quarters *v* 184

take up the pen *v* 590

take what's offered *v* 607

take wing *v* 266, 267

taking *n* 789

taking nourishment *n* 298

tale *n* 546, 549

talebearer *n* 532

talent *n* 79, 698

talents *n* 698

talismanic *adj* 992

talk *n* 582, 588; *v* 582

talk a mile a minute *v* 584

talkative *adj* 582, 584

talkativeness *n* 584

talk big *v* 577, 884

talker *n* 584

talk fancy *v* 577

talk it over *v* 588

talk nonsense *v* 497

talk together *v* 588

talk to oneself *v* 589

tall *adj* 200, 206

tallness *n* 206

tallow *n* 356

tall tale *n* 546

tally *n* 86, 805; *v* 23, 85

tallying *n* 85

tame *v* 174, 370, 749; *adj* 172, 370, 575, 725

taming *n* 370

tamper with *v* 140

tan *adj* 433

tang *n* 390, 392, 394

tangerine *adj* 439

tangibility *n* 3

tangible *adj* 3, 316

tangle *v* 61, 219

tangled *adj* 59

tanked *adj* 959

tanker *n* 273

tantalize *v* 509

tantamount *adj* 27

tap *n* 263, 276; *v* 260, 276, 406

taper *n* 423; *v* 203

tapering *adj* 253

taper to a point *v* 253

tapping *n* 407

tar *n* 356a

tardiness *n* 133, 275

tardy *adj* 133, 275

target *n* 620

tarn *n* 343

tarnish *n* 874; *v* 429, 653, 848, 874

tarnished *adj* 874

tarpaulin *n* 223

tarry *v* 110, 133

tarrying *n* 133

tart *adj* 397

tartness *n* 397

task *n* 676, 704; *v* 677, 688

taskmaster *n* 694, 739

taste *n* 390, 850

taste *n* 394, 465, 480, 578; *v* 298, 390, 394

taste bad *v* 395

tasteful *adj* 465, 578, 850

tastefully *adv* 850

taste good *v* 394

taste great *v* 394

tasteless *adj* 337, 391, 395, 579

tastelessness *n* 391

tastelessness *n* 395, 579

tastiness *n* 394

tasty *adj* 377, 390, 394

tattle *v* 588

tattler *n* 532

tattoo *v* 440

taunt *v* 856

taunts *n* 856

taut *adj* 43

tautological *adj* 104

tautology *n* 104

tawdriness *n* 851

tawdry *adj* 643, 851

tawny *adj* 433, 435

tax *v* 677, 688

teach *v* 537, 673

teacher *n* 540

teacher *n* 753

teaching *n* 537

team-work *n* 709

tear *v* 44, 173, 274

tearful *adj* 839

tear out *v* 301

tears *n* 411

tear to pieces *v* 44

tear up *v* 162

teasing *n* 377

teat *n* 250

technicality *n* 697

technique *n* 627

tedious *adj* 275, 841, 843

tedium *n* 688, 841

teem *v* 168

teeming *adj* 72, 102, 168

teem with *v* 102

teenage *adj* 131

teenage years *n* 131

teeter *v* 160, 275, 315

teetering *adj* 160

teetotaler *n* 953, 958

teetotalism *n* 958

telescope *n* 445

telethermometer *n* 389

tell *v* 85, 467, 527, 529, 594

teller *n* 801

telling *n* 594; *adj* 642

temper *n* 5, 7, 323, 820; *v* 174, 323, 324

temperament *n* 5, 176, 820

temperamental *adj* 901

temperance *n* 953

temperance *n* 174

temperate *adj* 174, 736, 953

temperateness *n* 174

temperature *n* 382

tempered *adj* 820

tempest *n* 173, 315, 349, 825

tempest in a teacup *n* 549

tempestuous *adj* 349

temple *n* 1000

temporal *adj* 111, 997

temporarily *adv* 111

temporary *adj* 111

tempt *v* 615, 675

temptation *n* 615

tempter *n* 978

tempt fate *v* 621

tempt fortune *v* 675

ten *n* 98

tenable *adj* 664

tenacious *adj* 46, 150, 327, 604, 604a

tenacity *n* 327

tenacity *n* 150, 604, 604a

tenancy *n* 777

tenant *n* 188, 779; *v* 186

tend *v* 176, 278, 472

tendencies *n* 5

tendency *n* 176

tendency *n* 177, 278, 472, 613

tender *n* 763; *v* 763; *adj* 324, 378, 428, 597, 740, 821, 822, 897, 906

tender age *n* 127

tender-hearted *adj* 906

tenderness *n* 378, 821, 822, 897, 906

tender years *n* 127

tending *adj* 176

tendril *n* 205, 248

tend toward *v* 278

tenet *n* 451, 484, 537, 983

tenor *n* 7, 26, 278, 516

tensile *adj* 325

tension *n* 159

tent *n* 223

tentative *adj* 675

tenuity *n* 322

tenuous *adj* 322

tenure *n* 777

tepid *adj* 382

tergiversation *n* 607

term *n* 71

term *n* 106, 108, 198, 200, 233, 562; *v* 564

terminal *adj* 67, 233

terminate *v* 67, 142, 729

termination *n* 67, 142, 233, 261, 729

terminology *n* 560, 562

terminus *n* 233

terms *n* 476, 770

terrain *n* 342

terrestrial *adj* 318, 342

terrible *adj* 846, 860

terribly *adv* 31

terrified *adj* 860

territorial *adj* 181, 342

territory *n* 181, 965

terror *n* 860

terror-stricken *adj* 860

terse *adj* 572

terseness *n* 572

tertiary *adj* 92

test *n* 463; *v* 463

testify *v* 467, 535

testimony *n* 467

testy *adj* 684, 901

tête-à-tête *n* 588

tether *v* 43

tetrad *n* 95

text *n* 22, 542, 591

textbook *n* 542

texture *n* 256, 329

textured *adj* 256

thank *v* 916

thankful *adj* 916

thankfulness *n* 916

thankless *adj* 917

thanklessness *n* 917

thanks *n* 916

that being the case *adv* 8

thatch *n* 223

that is to say *adv* 522

thaw *v* 335, 382, 384

thawing *n* 335

the all-merciful *n* 976

the all-powerful *n* 976

the almighty *n* 976

theater *n* 599, 728

theatrical *adj* 599, 855, 882

theatricals *n* 599

the cloth *n* 996

the common people *n* 876

the converse *n* 14

the drama *n* 599

the eternal *n* 976

theft *n* 788, 789, 791

the future *n* 121

the infinite *n* 976

the inverse *n* 14

theism *n* 983

the latest thing *n* 123

the lead *n* 62, 280

the like *n* 17

the lower classes *n* 876

thematic *adj* 454

theme *n* 413, 454, 595

then *adv* 119

thence *adv* 155

theologian *n* 983

theological *adj* 983

theologics *n* 983

theologue *n* 983

theology *n* 983

the open *n* 338

the opposite *n* 14

theorem *n* 514

theoretical *adj* 514

theorize *v* 155, 514

theory *n* 155, 453, 514

theosophical *adj* 983

throw in one's lot with v 709

throw in the towel v 624

throw off one's guard v 508

throw of the dice n 156

throw open v 260

throw out v 55, 297, 638

throw out of gear v 61

throw out of whack v 61

throw up v 297

thrust n 276, 284; v 276

thrust in v 300

thud n 406, 408a; v 408a

thug n 361

thumb v 379

thump n 276, 408a; v 276, 408a

thumper n 192

thumping adj 192

thunder n 404, 408; v 173, 404

thundering adj 192, 404

thunderousness n 404

thus adv 8

thus far adv 233

thus far and no further adv 233

thwack n 276; v 276

thwart v 706, 708

thwarted adj 732

tick v 407

ticket v 550

tickle the palate v 390, 394

tickle the tastebuds v 390

tickling n 380

ticklish adj 380, 704

tidal adj 348

tide n 348

tides n 341

tidiness n 652

tidings n 498, 532

tidy adj 58, 652

tidy up v 652

tie n 9, 11, 27, 45, 771; v 9, 43, 45, 770

tied adj 926

tier n 69, 204

tiered adj 204

ties of blood n 11

tie the hands v 158

tie the knot v 903

tie up v 342

tie up in knots v 158

tiff n 713

tight adj 43, 46; adj 261, 572, 819, 959

tighten v 572

tightness n 572

till n 802; v 371; adv 106

tillage n 371

till the soil v 371

tilt n 217, 306; v 217, 244, 306

tilted adj 217

tilt over v 218

tilt up v 307

timber n 413

timbre n 408

time n 106

time n 108; v 106

time-honored adj 124

time immemorial n 122

timeless adj 112

timelessness n 112

timeliness n 134, 684

timely adj 106, 132, 134

timeout n 106

timepiece n 114

timeserving adj 607

timetable n 114

time to come n 121

timeworn adj 124, 659

timid adj 605, 862, 881

timidity n 605, 862, 881

timorous adj 862, 881

tincture n 41, 428; v 41

tinge n 32, 41, 428; v 41, 428

tingle v 378, 380

tininess n 32, 193

tinsel n 851

tint n 26, 428; v 428

tinted adj 428

tintinnabulation n 408

tiny adj 32, 193

tippler n 959

tipsy adj 959

tiptop adj 210, 648

tirade n 582

tire v 688, 841, 869

tired adj 688, 841, 869

tiredness n 688

tired to death adj 688

tiresome adj 841

tissue n 329

tit for tat n 30

titillation n 377, 380

title n 877

title n 564, 747, 771

titled adj 875, 877

title page n 66

titter n 838; v 838

titular adj 564

to a certain degree adv 32

toady n 886, 935; v 886

to a large extent adv 31

to all appearance adv 448

to all intents and purposes adv 27, 52

to and fro adv 314

to arms adv 722

to a small extent adv 32

toast v 384

to blame adj 947

to boot adv 37

to come adj 121, 152

to crown all adv 33

tocsin n 669

toddler n 129

together adj 46, 502; adv 120

togetherness *n* 709, 714

together with *adv* 37, 88

togs *n* 225

toil *n* 686; *v* 682, 686

token *n* 505, 550

tolerable *adj* 32, 651, 736

tolerableness *n* 736

tolerance *n* 740, 760

tolerant *adj* 740, 760

tolerate *v* 738, 740, 760, 826

toleration *n* 738, 740

to little purpose *adv* 732

toll *v* 407

tomb *n* 363

tombstone *n* 363

tomcat *n* 373

tome *n* 590, 593

tomorrow *n* 121, 152; *adv* 121

tone *n* 7, 26, 159, 402, 428

tone color *n* 413

tone down *v* 429

tongue *n* 560

tongue-tied *adj* 581, 583

tonic *adj* 656

tonnage *n* 192

too *adv* 37

tool *n* 633

too late *adv* 133

too little *adj* 640

tools for pulverization *n* 330

too many *n* 641

too much *n* 641

to one's heart's content *adv* 831

too soon *adv* 132

tooth *n* 257

toothed *adj* 257

top *n* 206, 210, 223,

261; *v* 33, 210; *adj* 210

topic *n* 454

topical *adj* 183, 454

topmost *adj* 210

topographical *adj* 183

topography *n* 183

topple *v* 28, 162, 306

topsy-turvy *adj* 59, 218

torch *n* 423

to reason *v* 476

torment *n* 378, 828; *v* 378, 828, 830

tornado *n* 312, 315, 349

torpid *adj* 172, 683

torpor *n* 172, 683

torrent *n* 348

torrid *adj* 382

tortuous *adj* 248

torture *n* 378, 828, 982; *v* 378, 619, 828, 830, 972

torturous *adj* 378

to some degree *adv* 32

to some extent *adv* 26

toss *n* 284; *v* 284, 314, 315

tossup *n* 156

to substitute for *v* 634

tot *n* 129

total *n* 50, 84; *v* 37; *adj* 31, 50

total abstinence *n* 955

total destruction *n* 2

total eclipse *n* 421

totality *n* 50, 52

totally *adv* 31, 50, 52

to the eye *adv* 448

to the four winds *adv* 180

to the letter *adv* 19

to the minute *adv* 132

to the point *adj* 494

to the quick *adv* 375

totter *v* 160, 275, 314, 315, 659, 665

tottering *adj* 160

touch *n* 379

touch *n* 41, 375, 569; *v* 9, 197, 199, 375, 379, 824

touchable *adj* 316

touched *adj* 503, 821, 914

touching *n* 199; *adj* 199

touch on *v* 516

touchstone *n* 211

touchy *adj* 684, 901

tough *adj* 46, 323, 327

toughness *n* 327

tour *n* 266, 302; *v* 266

tourist *n* 268

tourniquet *n* 263

tow *v* 285

towage *n* 285

toward *adv* 278

tower *v* 31, 206, 305

towering *adj* 31, 192, 206

towing *n* 285

townsman *n* 188

toxic *adj* 657

trace *n* 551; *v* 230, 554

tracery *n* 219

trace to *v* 155

track *n* 627

tract *n* 181, 593, 595

tractability *n* 743

tractable *adj* 324, 705, 743

tractile *adj* 285, 324

tractility *n* 324

traction *n* 285

trade *n* 148, 625, 794, 796; *v* 148, 794, 796

trader *n* 797

tradesman *n* 797

trade wind *n* 349

tradition *n* 124

traditional *adj* 124, 983a

traffic *n* 794; *v* 794

tragedy *n* 619

tragic *adj* 619, 830

trail *n* 65; *v* 214, 275, 285, 286, 281
train *n* 65, 69, 214, 235, 271, 272, 281; *v* 285, 370, 537, 673
trained *adj* 698
training *n* 673
traipse *v* 275
trait *n* 448, 550
traitor *n* 742
trammel *v* 706
tramp *n* 268
trample on *v* 739
trample out *v* 162
trample upon *v* 649
trance *n* 993
tranquil *adj* 174, 265, 721
tranquilization *n* 174
tranquilize *v* 265, 723
tranquillity *n* 265, 721
transact *v* 680, 692, 794
transaction *n* 151, 625, 794, 796
transcend *v* 31, 33, 303, 648, 650
transcendence *n* 33, 650
transcendent *adj* 33
transcribe *v* 590
transcript *n* 21
transcription *n* 21
transfer *n* 783
transfer *n* 21, 270; *v* 185, 270, 783
transferable *adj* 270, 783
transference *n* 270
transference *n* 140, 783
transfiguration *n* 140
transfigure *v* 140
transform *v* 140
transformable *adj* 140, 149
transformation *n* 140, 144
transfuse *v* 41
transfusion *n* 41

transgress *n* 303, 742, 773, 945
transgression *n* 303, 773, 927
transience *n* 111
transient *adj* 111, 264
transit *n* 144, 270
transition *n* 144, 270
transitional *adj* 264
transitoriness *n* 111
transitory *adj* 111
translate *v* 522
translation *n* 522
translator *n* 524
translucent *adj* 425
transluscence *n* 425
transmissible *adj* 270
transmission *n* 270, 302, 783
transmissive *adj* 783
transmit *v* 270, 783
transmit light *v* 425
transmittable *adj* 270
transmutable *adj* 144
transmutation *n* 140, 144
transmute *v* 140
transparence *n* 425
transparency *n* 425
transparent *adj* 337, 425, 518
transpire *v* 532
transplant *v* 270
transplantation *n* 270
transport *n* 270, 827; *v* 270, 829
transportable *adj* 270
transportation *n* 272
transporter *n* 271
transporting *adj* 977
transposal *n* 218
transpose *v* 148, 185, 218, 270
transposition *n* 140, 148, 185, 218, 270
transverse *adj* 217, 219

trap *n* 530, 545, 667
trappings *n* 225
trash *n* 643
trashy *adj* 209, 575, 643
travail *n* 686
travel *n* 266; *v* 266
traveler *n* 268
traveling *n* 266; *adj* 264, 266
traverse *v* 266, 302
travesty *n* 21, 523; *v* 19, 523
trawler *n* 273
treacherous *adj* 544
treachery *n* 545
tread *n* 264
tread down *v* 749
tread upon *v* 649
treasure *n* 648; *v* 991
treasurer *n* 801
treasury *n* 802
treat *v* 595, 829
treatise *n* 593, 595
treatment *n* 662
treat well *v* 906
treaty *n* 23, 721, 769
treble *v* 93; *adj* 93
trebly *adv* 93
tree *n* 367
trellis *n* 219
tremble *v* 149, 160, 315, 383
tremendously *adv* 31
tremor *n* 315
tremulous *adj* 149, 315
trench *n* 259
trenchant *adj* 171, 253, 572, 574, 642
trend *n* 176, 278, 516
trendiness *n* 123
trendy *adj* 123
trepidation *n* 860
trespass *n* 303; *v* 303, 945
trestle *n* 215
triad *n* 92

trial n 463, 675, 686, 828, 830, 969
triality n 92
tribe n 72, 75
tribunal n 966
tributary n 348; adj 784
trice n 113
trick n 545; v 545
trickle n 348; v 295, 348
trickly adj 348
tricky adj 545, 702
trifle n 32, 451, 643; v 499
trifling n 499, 643; adj 4, 32, 477, 499, 643, 880
triform adj 92
trill v 407
trim n 231, 240; v 27, 231; adj 652
trimming n 231
trinity n 92
trio n 92, 415, 416
trip n 266, 302, 306; v 306, 309
tripartition n 94
triple v 93; adj 93
triplet n 92
triplicate adj 93
triplication n 93
triplicity n 93
tripling n 93
triply adv 93
trip the light fantastic toe v 309
trip up v 495
trisect v 94
trisection n 94
trite adj 496, 598, 613
triumph n 731, 733, 838; v 731, 838
triumphant adj 731, 838, 884
trivial adj 32, 209, 499, 517, 643, 880

triviality n 32, 209, 643, 736, 880
troll n 980
trollop n 962
troop n 72
trophy n 733
tropical adj 382
troubadour n 597
trouble n 59, 686, 704, 735, 828, 830; v 61, 828, 830
troublemaker n 913
trouble oneself about v 682
troublesome adj 59, 704, 830
trough n 252, 259, 350
trove n 480a
truant n 623
truce n 142, 721, 723
truck n 271, 272; v 264
trudge v 275
true adj 1, 17, 246, 246, 494, 543, 648, 772, 922, 604
true faith n 983a
truelove n 897
true to life adj 17
truism n 496
truistic adj 496
truly adv 31
trump card n 731
trumped up adj 546
trumpery n 643
truncate v 201, 241
truncation n 241
trunk n 50
truss n 215
trust n 484, 507, 805, 858; v 858
trusted adj 484
trustee n 758, 801
trusting adj 484, 486, 547

trustworthy adj 474, 484, 543, 664
trusty adj 474
truth n 494
truth n 1, 474, 543, 922, 983a
truthful adj 494, 543
truthfulness n 543
try v 463, 480, 675, 677
try a case n 967
trying adj 841
tube n 350, 351
tubed instruments n 417
tuck n 258; v 258
tuck in v 300
tug n 285; v 285
tugboat n 273
tumble n 306; v 162, 306, 315
tumid adj 194
tumult n 59, 315, 825
tumultuous adj 59, 173, 404, 825
tundra n 344
tune n 413, 415; v 413
tuned out adj 452
tuneful adj 413, 597
tunefulness n 413
tuneless adj 414
tune out v 452
tunnel n 350; v 252, 260
turbulence n 173, 315
turbulent adj 59, 173, 825
turf n 388
turgid adj 194, 577, 579
turgidity n 579
turkey n 493
turmoil n 59, 173, 315
turn n 7, 134, 138, 140, 176, 245, 311, 621,

698; *v* 49, 140, 245, 248, 279, 311, 312

turn about *v* 218

turn a circle *v* 311

turn a deaf ear to *v* 419

turn and turn about *adv* 148

turn around *v* 311

turn aside *v* 140, 279, 616

turn away *v* 297

turn away from *v* 623

turn back *v* 145, 283

turncoat *n* 607

turn color *v* 434, 435

turn down *v* 764

turned *adj* 397

turned off *adj* 452

turning *n* 311

turning point *n* 8, 67, 134, 145, 153, 210, 233

turn into *v* 144

turn off the brain *v* 452

turn of speech *n* 566

turn of the tide *n* 145, 218

turn one's hand to *v* 625

turn on the juice *v* 274

turn out *v* 151, 297

turn over *v* 218, 270, 784

turn pale *v* 429

turn tail *v* 623

turn the scale *v* 28

turn the stomach *v* 395

turn the tide *v* 28, 145

turn to dust *v* 360

turn to profit *v* 775

turn topsy-turvy *v* 61, 218

turn up *v* 151, 156, 446

turn upside down *v* 14, 61

turquoise *adj* 438

tutelage *n* 537, 539, 749

tutor *n* 540, 753; *v* 537

tutorship *n* 537

twaddle *n* 584

twain *adj* 89

twang *n* 402, 408

tweak *v* 378

twelve *n* 98

twenty *n* 98

twenty-five *n* 98

twerp *n* 493

twice *adv* 90

twilight *n* 126

twin *n* 17; *adj* 17, 88, 89, 90

twine *v* 219, 248

twine round *v* 227

twinge *n* 378, 828; *v* 378

twinkle *v* 113, 422

twinkling *n* 113

twins *n* 89

twirl *n* 248; *v* 248, 311, 312

twist *n* 243, 248, 503; *v* 43, 219, 243, 248, 279, 311

twisted *adj* 248

twister *n* 315, 349

twist the meaning *v* 523

twit *v* 856

twitch *n* 378; *v* 378

twitter *n* 315; *v* 315, 412

two *n* 89; *adj* 89

two-faced *adj* 544

twofold division *n* 91

two or more *n* 100

two-sided *adj* 89

type *n* 5, 17, 22, 75, 550, 591; *v* 240

typical *adj* 82, 550

typify *v* 550

typographical *adj* 591

typography *n* 591

tyrannical *adj* 739

tyrannize *v* 739

tyrant *n* 739

U

ubiquity *n* 186

ubiquitous *adj* 186

ugliness *n* 846

ugliness *n* 243

ugly *adj* 846

ukase *n* 741

ulterior *adj* 121

ulterior motive *n* 615

ultimate *adj* 67

ultimately *adv* 117, 121, 133

ululation *n* 412

umbra *n* 421

umbrage *n* 900

umbrageous *adj* 421, 422

umbrella *n* 223, 424

umpire *n* 967; *v* 174

unable *adj* 158, 699

unaccompanied *adj* 87

unaccountable *adj* 964

unaccustomed *adj* 614

unachievable *adj* 471

unacquaintance *n* 491

unadorned *adj* 576, 849

unadulterated *adj* 42, 960

unadvisable *adj* 647

unaffected *adj* 578, 823, 849

unallied *adj* 10

unalterability *n* 141

unalterable *adj* 150

unanimity *n* 23, 709

unanimously *adv* 709, 714

unanswerable *adj* 964

unanticipated *adj* 508

unapplied *adj* 678

unapproachable *adj* 196

unappropriate *adj* 923

unartificial *adj* 703
unassailable *adj* 664
unassuming *adj* 849, 879, 881
unassured *adj* 475
unatoned *adj* 951
unattached *adj* 44
unattended *adj* 87
unattended to *adj* 460
unauthorized *adj* 925, 964
unavailing *adj* 645
unavoidability *n* 601
unavoidable *adj* 601, 744
unavoidableness *n* 601
unaware *adj* 508, 823
unawareness *n* 491
unbearable *adj* 830
unbegotten *adj* 2
unbeliever *n* 485
unbelieving *adj* 485, 487, 989
unbend *v* 246, 687
unbent *adj* 246
unbiased *adj* 942
unblemished *adj* 650
unborn *adj* 2
unbound *adj* 748, 927a
unbridled *adj* 748
unbroken *adj* 50, 69, 729
uncanny *adj* 980
uncanonical *adj* 984
uncared for *adj* 460
uncaring *adj* 823
unceasing *adj* 104, 112
uncertain *adj* 139, 475, 485, 520, 605, 704
uncertainty *n* 475
uncertainty *n* 111, 139, 485, 519, 520, 605
unchained *adj* 748
unchangeable *adj* 5, 150
unchangeableness *n* 150

unchanged *adj* 16, 141
unchanging *adj* 16, 141, 150
unchartered *adj* 964
unchaste *adj* 961
unchecked *adj* 748
uncivil *adj* 895, 911, 929
uncivilized *adj* 876
unclad *adj* 226
unclean *adj* 653, 961
uncleanness *n* 653
uncleanness *n* 961
unclear *adj* 426
unclose *v* 260
unclosed *adj* 260
unclouded *adj* 420
uncolored *adj* 429
uncomfortable *adj* 378, 828
uncommon *adj* 83, 137
uncommon *adv* 31
uncommunicative *adj* 528, 585
uncommunicativeness *n* 585
uncompleted *adj* 53
uncompliant *adj* 742
uncomplicate *v* 849
uncompromising *adj* 82
unconceived *adj* 2
unconcern *n* 456, 458, 866
unconcerned *adj* 866
unconditional *adj* 52, 748
unconfined *adj* 748
unconformable *adj* 83
unconformity *n* 83
uncongenial *adj* 24
unconnected *adj* 10, 44, 70
unconquerable *adj* 159
unconscious *adj* 823
unconsciousness *n* 376, 491
unconsolidated *adj* 47

unconstitutional *adj* 964
unconstrained *adj* 748
uncontaminated *adj* 960
uncontrite *adj* 951
uncontrollability *n* 606
uncontrollable *adj* 173, 606, 825
uncontrolled *adj* 748, 825
unconventional *adj* 83
unconventionality *n* 83
uncopied *adj* 20
uncorroborative *adj* 468
uncorrupted *adj* 960
uncouth *adj* 579
uncover *v* 226, 260, 480a, 529
uncovered *adj* 260
uncovering *n* 529
uncreated *adj* 2
unctuosity *n* 355
unctuous *adj* 355
unctuousness *n* 355
uncurbed *adj* 748
uncurl *v* 246
uncurved *adj* 246
uncustomary *adj* 83
undated *adj* 115
undecided *adj* 475
undefiled *adj* 960
undefined *adj* 447
undeniable *adj* 474
undependability *n* 475
undependable *adj* 475
under *adv* 34, 207
under a cloud *adj* 735
underage *adj* 127
under consideration *adv* 454
under control *adj* 749
undercover *adj* 528
undercurrent *n* 526
undercut *v* 179
underdeveloped *adj* 193
underestimate *v* 481, 483

underestimated *adj* 483

underestimating *adj* 483

underestimation *n* 483

underfoot *adv* 207

undergo *v* 151

undergo pain *v* 378

underground *adv* 207

underlie *v* 207, 526

underline *v* 550, 642

undermine *v* 179, 659

undermost *adj* 211

underneath *adv* 207

under obligation *adj* 926

under one's nose *adj* 446

under one's very nose *adv* 715

under protest *adv* 603

underrate *v* 483

under restraint *adj* 751

underscore *v* 550, 642

undersized *adj* 193

understand *v* 450, 490, 498, 518, 522

understandable *adj* 518

understanding *n* 23, 450, 480, 490, 498, 714, 822, 842; *adj* 498, 822

understand one another *v* 714

understructure *n* 211

understudy *n* 634

undertake *v* 622, 625, 676, 768

undertaking *n* 676

undertaking *n* 620, 622, 625, 768

under the circumstances *adv* 8

under the conditions *adv* 8

under the head of *adv* 9

under the pretense of *adv* 617

under the stars *adv* 338

under the sun *adv* 180, 318

under the weather *adj* 655

undertone *n* 405

undervaluation *n* 483

undervalue *v* 483

under way *adv* 264

under wraps *adj* 754

underwrite *v* 768, 771

undesirability *n* 647

undesirable *adj* 830

undetermined *adj* 475

undeviating *adj* 278

undevout *adj* 989

undiminished *adj* 50

undirected *adj* 279

undiscerning *adj* 442

undiscriminating *adj* 465a

undisturbed *adj* 265

undiversified *adj* 16

undivided *adj* 50, 52

undo *v* 145, 162, 179

undone *adj* 732

undoubtedly *adv* 474

undraped *adj* 226

undress *n* 226

undress *v* 226

undressed *adj* 226

undulate *v* 248, 314

undulating *adj* 248

undulation *n* 248, 314

undulatory *adj* 314

undutiful *adj* 927

unearth *v* 363, 480a

unearthly *adj* 317, 976, 980, 981

uneasiness *n* 828, 832

uneasy *adj* 828, 832

uneducated *adj* 491

unembellished *adj* 849

unemotional *adj* 383

unemployed *adj* 678

unendurable *adj* 830, 982

unenlightened *adj* 491

unenlightenment *n* 491

unentitled *adj* 925

unequal *adj* 15, 28

unequaled *adj* 18, 33

unequivocal *adj* 31, 246, 570

unequivocally *adv* 31

unessential *adj* 643

unestablished *adj* 185

uneven *adj* 16a, 28, 243, 256

unevenness *n* 16a, 28

uneventful *adj* 643

unexciting *adj* 174

unexpected *adj* 132, 508

unexpectedly *adv* 132, 508

unfaded *adj* 428

unfading *adj* 112

unfailing *adj* 474

unfaithful *adj* 544

unfashioned *adj* 241

unfathomable *adj* 208, 519

unfathomable space *n* 208

unfathomed *adj* 208

unfavorable *adj* 135, 708, 735

unfeasibility *n* 471

unfeasible *adj* 471, 704

unfed *adj* 956

unfeeling *adj* 381, 383

unfetter *v* 750

unfettered *adj* 748

unfinished *adj* 53, 730

unfit *adj* 158, 647, 699, 923

unfitness *n* 647

unfitted *adj* 158

unfixed *adj* 149, 475

unfocused *adj* 447

unfold *v* 246, 313

unfolding *n* 313
unforeseen *adj* 508
unforeseen occurrence *n* 508
unforgettable *adj* 505
unforgiving *adj* 919
unforgotten *adj* 505
unformed *adj* 241
unfortunate *adj* 135, 735
unfounded *adj* 546
unfriendliness *n* 889
unfriendly *adj* 708, 889
unfrozen *adj* 382
unfruitful *adj* 169
unfruitfulness *n* 169, 645
unfulfillment *n* 509
unfurl *v* 313
ungenerous *adj* 32, 819
ungentlemanly *adj* 895
ungodliness *n* 989
ungodly *adj* 989
ungovernable *adj* 173, 825
ungoverned *adj* 748
ungraceful *adj* 579
ungracious *adj* 895
ungrammatical *adj* 568
ungrammatical usage *n* 568
ungrateful *adj* 917
ungrounded *adj* 4
unguarded *adj* 460
unguent *n* 356
unhallowed *adj* 989
unhandy *adj* 699
unhappy *adj* 828, 837
unharmonious *adj* 410
unhealthiness *n* 657
unhealthy *adj* 655, 657
unheard of *adj* 137, 508
unheeded *adj* 460
unheedful *adj* 452
unheeding *adj* 419, 458

unhewn *adj* 674
unhindered *adj* 748
unhinge *v* 61
unhinged *adj* 173, 503
unhip *adj* 246
unholy *adj* 989
unhoused *adj* 185
unhurried *adj* 275
unhurt *adj* 670
unification *n* 48, 87
unified *adj* 46, 48
uniform *v* 225; *adj* 16, 42, 58, 80, 242
uniformity *n* 16
uniformity *n* 17, 23, 58, 80, 87, 150, 242
uniformly *adv* 16, 82
uniforms *n* 225
unimaginable *adj* 471
unimaginative *adj* 598, 843
unimitated *adj* 20
unimpaired *adj* 50, 670
unimpeachable *adj* 474
unimportance *n* 643
unimportance *n* 32, 175a
unimportant *adj* 32, 34, 643, 736
unimpressionable *adj* 823
unimproved *adj* 659
uninfluential *adj* 175a
uninformed *adj* 491
uninjured *adj* 670
uninquiring *adj* 456
uninquisitive *adj* 456
uninstructed *adj* 491
unintellectual *adj* 450a
unintelligent *adj* 450a
unintelligibility *n* 519
unintelligibility *n* 533, 571
unintelligible *adj* 519, 571
unintentional *adj* 621
unintentionally *adv* 621

uninterested *adj* 456, 841
uninteresting *adj* 843
uninterrupted *adj* 69, 112, 143
unintoxicated *adj* 958
union *n* 23, 43, 46, 48, 178, 709, 714, 903
unique *adj* 18, 20, 79, 83, 87, 870
uniqueness *n* 18, 20, 123
unison *n* 87, 714
unite *v* 41, 43, 48, 72, 87, 178, 290, 709, 712
united *adj* 46, 903
uniting *n* 37
unity *n* 87
unity *n* 13, 23, 50, 52, 714
universal *adj* 78
universality *n* 78
universalize *v* 78
universe *n* 180, 318
university *n* 542
unjust *adj* 923
unkempt *adj* 653
unknown *n* 233; *adj* 533
unlawful *adj* 964
unlawfulness *n* 923, 964
unlearn *v* 506
unlearnedness *n* 491
unless *adv* 8, 83
unlettered *adj* 491
unlicensed *adj* 964
unlike *adj* 15, 18
unlikelihood *n* 473
unlikely *adj* 473
unlikeness *n* 18
unlimited *adj* 31, 104, 180, 748
unlimited space *n* 180
unload *v* 185
unlooked for *adj* 508
unlovely *adj* 846

vegetable *adj* 367
vegetable kingdom *n* 367
vegetable life *n* 365
vegetable oil *n* 356
vegetable physiology *n* 369
vegetal *adj* 367
vegetarian *n* 953
vegetate *v* 367
vegetation *n* 365
vegetative *adj* 365, 367
vehemence *n* 173, 825
vehement *adj* 173, 382, 574, 825
vehicle *n* 272
vehicle *n* 271, 631
veil *n* 424, 530; *v* 424, 528
veiled *adj* 447, 526
veiling *n* 528
vein *n* 176, 205, 602
veined *adj* 440
velocity *n* 274
velocity *n* 264
velvety *adj* 255, 256
venal *adj* 211, 819
venality *n* 819
vend *v* 796
vendible *adj* 796
vendition *n* 796
vendor *n* 796
veneer *n* 223; *v* 204, 223
venerable *adj* 124, 128, 928
venerate *v* 860, 928, 987
veneration *n* 860, 928, 987
vengeance *n* 718, 919
vengeful *adj* 718, 919
vengefulness *n* 919
venom *n* 663, 907
venomous *adj* 649, 657, 663, 907
vent *n* 260, 351

ventilate *v* 338, 349, 652
ventilation *n* 338
venture *n* 621, 675, 676; *v* 621, 665, 675, 861
venturesome *adj* 621, 675
veracious *adj* 494, 543
veracity *n* 543
veracity *n* 494
verbal *adj* 562
verbal interchange *n* 588
verbiage *n* 573
verbose *adj* 573, 584, 641
verbosity *n* 573, 584, 641
verdant *adj* 367, 435
verdict *n* 480, 969
verdure *n* 367, 435
verdurous *adj* 435
verge *n* 231, 233; *v* 176, 278
verification *n* 478
verify *v* 478
veritable *adj* 494
verity *n* 494
vermilion *adj* 434
vernacular *n* 560; *adj* 560
versatile *adj* 149
versatility *n* 149
verse *n* 590, 597
versification *n* 597
versifier *n* 597
versify *v* 597
versus *adv* 708
vertex *n* 210
vertical *adj* 212, 246
verticality *n* 212
vertically *adv* 212
verve *n* 159, 515, 574
very *adv* 31
very best *adj* 648
very much *adv* 31

vespers *n* 126
vessel *n* 191, 273
vestal virgin *n* 960
vestige *n* 551
vestments *n* 999
veteran *n* 130
veteran *n* 700
veterinary science *n* 370
veto *v* 761
vex *v* 828, 830
vexation *n* 828, 830, 835
vexatious *adj* 830, 901a
vibes *n* 314
vibrate *v* 314
vibration *n* 138, 314, 408
vibrato *n* 408
vice *n* 945
vice *n* 649, 923
vice versa *adv* 148
vicinity *n* 186, 197
vicious *adj* 907, 945
vicissitude *n* 111, 149
victimize *v* 649
victorious *adj* 731
victory *n* 731
vie *v* 648, 720
view *n* 441, 448, 453, 484, 620; *v* 441
viewpoint *n* 441
vigilance *n* 459, 682, 864, 920
vigilant *adj* 459, 507, 682, 864, 920
viginal *adj* 960
vignette *n* 594
vigor *n* 574
vigor *n* 157, 159, 171, 359, 364, 604, 654, 682
vigorous *adj* 159, 171, 359, 574, 654
vile *adj* 207, 211, 395, 649, 830, 846, 874, 898, 930

vilification n 934
vilify v 934
vilifying adj 934
villager n 188
villain n 941, 949
villainous adj 649
vinculum n 45
vindicate v 717, 919, 937
vindicated adj 937
vindicating adj 937
vindication n 937
vindication n 717
vindicator n 919, 937
vindictive adj 919
vindictiveness n 919
vinegariness n 397
vinegary adj 397
vintage adj 124
violate v 742, 773, 927
violate the law v 964
violation n 773, 927
violation of custom n 83
violence n 173
violence n 825
violent adj 59, 173, 382, 825
violently adv 31, 173
violet adj 437
virgin n 904, 960; adj 66, 123
virginal adj 123, 946
virginity n 960
virility n 159
virtually adv 5
virtue n 944
virtue n 648, 922, 939, 946, 960
virtuous adj 881, 939, 944, 946, 960
virtuousness n 944, 946
virulence n 649
virulent adj 649, 657
virus n 663
visage n 448
viscid adj 352
viscosity n 352

viscous adj 327, 352
visibility n 446
visible adj 446, 525
vision n 441
vision n 443, 515, 980
visionary n 504; adj 2, 4, 441, 515
visit often v 136
visor n 530
vista n 448
visual adj 441
vital adj 359, 642
vital flame n 359
vitality n 159, 359, 364, 654
vitalize v 359
vital spark n 359
vitiate v 659
vivacious adj 359, 515, 682, 829, 836
vivacity n 359, 515, 682, 836
vivid adj 171, 375, 420, 428, 505
vivify v 159, 359
vocabulary 562
vocal adj 415, 416, 580
vocal group n 416
vocalist n 416
vocality n 580
vocalization n 580
vocalize v 416, 566, 580
vocal music n 415
vocation n 625
vociferate v 411
vociferation n 411
vociferous adj 404, 411
vociferousness n 404
vogue n 613, 852
voice n 580
voice n 402; v 566, 580, 582
voiceless adj 581, 583
void n 2, 4, 187; v 2, 297, 756; adj 2, 187
volatile adj 149, 320, 336

volatility n 149, 320, 334
volcanic adj 173, 384, 825
volition n 600
volitional adj 600
volubility n 584
voluble adj 334, 584
volume n 25, 31, 102, 192, 590, 593
voluminous adj 192
voluntarily adv 600
voluntary adj 600
volunteer v 676
voluptuary n 954a, 962
voluptuous adj 377, 829
voluptuousness n 827
vomit v 297
voodoo n 993
voracious adj 957
voracity n 957
vortex n 312, 315, 348
voucher n 807
vow n 768
vowel n 561
voyage n 267, 302
voyager n 268
V-shaped adj 244
vulgar adj 579, 851, 876, 895
vulgarity n 851
vulgarity n 579, 895
vulgarize v 851
vulnerability n 177

W

wad v 224
wadding n 224, 263
waddle v 275
wade through v 539
waft v 320, 349
wag n 844
wager n 621; v 621
wages n 775, 812
wage war v 722
waggle v 315
wagon n 272

waif *n* 268
wail *n* 411, 839; *v* 411
wailing *n* 411, 839
wait *v* 133, 265, 681
wait for *v* 507
waiting *n* 507, 681
wait on *v* 88, 746
waive *v* 624, 678, 782,
   609a
waiver *n* 624, 782
waiving *n* 624
wake *n* 65, 235, 363
wakefulness *n* 459, 682
wake up *v* 824
walk *n* 266; *v* 264
walker *n* 268
walk over *v* 649
wall *n* 212, 232
wall in *v* 229
wallop *v* 315
wallow *v* 207
wallow in *v* 377, 954
wan *adj* 429, 430, 435
wander *v* 264, 266, 279
wanderer *n* 268
wane *n* 36; *v* 36, 195,
   287, 659, 732
waning *adj* 128, 195
want *n* 804, 865; *v* 34,
   304, 640, 804, 865
wanting *adj* 53, 187,
   499, 640
want of elasticity *n* 326
want of intellect *n* 450a
want of intelligence *n*
   499
want of skill *n* 699
wanton *adj* 83, 149,
   608, 748
wants *n* 630
war *n* 722; *v* 722
warble *v* 416
ward *n* 862
warden *n* 664
warder *n* 753
wardrobe *n* 225
wares *n* 798

warfare *n* 722
warfare *n* 173
wariness *n* 487, 864
warlike *adj* 720, 722
warm *v* 382, 384; *adj*
   382, 434, 664, 824,
   892
warmed *adj* 384
warm-hearted *adj* 822
warmth *n* 382, 382,
   574, 821, 897
warn *v* 616, 668, 669,
   695, 864
warning *n* 668
warning *n* 512, 665,
   695, 864
warp *n* 243, 279; *v* 140,
   217, 243, 279, 659
warped *adj* 651
warrant *n* 737, 760,
   924, 937; *v* 737, 760,
   768, 771
warranted *adj* 937
warranty *n* 768, 771
warrior *n* 726
wary *adj* 451, 457,
   459, 487, 664, 864
wash *n* 345, 428; *v* 337,
   428, 652
wash out *v* 429
waspish *adj* 684
waste *n* 638
waste *n* 162, 180, 679,
   818; *v* 162, 195, 638,
   659, 679, 818
waste an occasion *v* 135
waste away *v* 655
wasted *adj* 124, 160,
   203, 638, 659, 959
wasteful *adj* 638, 818
wastefulness *n* 169, 818
waster *n* 165; *v* 776
waste time *v* 106, 135,
   681, 683
wasting *n* 638
wastrel *n* 893

watch *n* 114; *v* 441,
   664, 668
watchdog *n* 664, 668
watch for *v* 441
watchful *adj* 457, 459,
   507, 864, 920
watchfulness *n* 457,
   459, 920
watchman *n* 668
watch over *v* 717
water *n* 337
water *v* 337
water down *v* 160, 203
watergate *n* 350
waterish *adj* 203, 337
waterpower *n* 388
waters *n* 341
watershed *n* 210
watertight *adj* 261
watery *adj* 203, 333,
   337, 339
wave *n* 248, 314, 348; *v*
   248, 314
waver *v* 149, 422, 475,
   485, 605
wavering *adj* 485
waves *n* 341
wavy *adj* 248
wax *n* 356, 356a; *v* 255
waxy *adj* 324, 356a
way *n* 260, 302, 302,
   613, 627, 632
wayfarer *n* 268
wayfaring *n* 266; *adj*
   266
ways *n* 692
ways and means *n* 632,
   800
wayward *adj* 149, 606,
   608
weak *adj* 32, 158, 160,
   175a, 203, 337, 391,
   477, 499, 575, 605,
   651, 655, 738
weaken *v* 158, 160,
   468, 732
weak foundation *n* 667

whiz *v* 409
whole *n* 50
whole *adj* 50, 52, 729
wholeness *n* 52
whole number *n* 84
wholesale *adj* 31; *adv* 50
wholesome *adj* 656
wholesomeness *n* 656
wholly *adv* 31, 50, 52
whoop *v* 411
whoosh *v* 409
whooshing *n* 409
whopper *n* 192
whopping *adj* 192
whore *n* 962
wicked *adj* 923, 940, 945, 961
wickedly *adv* 923
wickedness *n* 923, 940, 945
wicker *n* 219
wide *adj* 202
wide apart *adj* 15
wide awake *adj* 682
widely *adv* 31
widen *v* 194, 202
wide of the mark *adj* 732; *adv* 279
wide-open *adj* 260
widespread *adj* 31, 73, 78, 180, 194
wide world *n* 180, 318
width *n* 202
wield *v* 677
wife *n* 903
wild *n* 180; *adj* 173, 503, 606, 825
wild animals *n* 366
wilderness *n* 59, 180
wildness *n* 606
wile *n* 545
wiliness *n* 702
will *n* 600
will *n* 150, 604; *v* 600, 604

willful *adj* 150, 600, 696
willfully *adv* 600
willfulness *n* 606
willing *adj* 602, 831
willingly *adv* 602
willingness *n* 602
will power *n* 600
willy nilly *adv* 601
wilt *v* 306
wily *adj* 702
win *v* 775
wince *v* 378
wind *n* 349
wind *n* 338; *v* 248, 279
wind around *v* 629
windbag *n* 884, 887
windfall *n* 618
winding *n* 245, 248, 629; *adj* 248
winding sheet *n* 363
windpipe *n* 351
windpower *n* 388
winds *n* 417
windup *n* 261
windy *adj* 334, 338, 349
wine-colored *adj* 434
winged being *n* 977
wink *v* 443
winning *adj* 897
winnings *n* 775
winning ways *n* 829
winnow *v* 42, 55
winsome *adj* 836
winter *n* 126
wintry *adj* 383
wipe *v* 340
wiped out *adj* 162
wipe off the face of the earth *v* 2
wipe out *v* 162, 552
wire *n* 205
wiry *adj* 205
wisdom *n* 498
wisdom *n* 480, 490, 698, 842

wise *adj* 490, 498, 698, 842
wisecracker *n* 844
wise man *n* 492, 500
wish *n* 600, 858, 865, 865; *v* 865
wish for *v* 865
wishful *adj* 865
wish well *v* 906
wishy-washy *adj* 175a, 391, 575
wit *n* 842
wit *n* 698, 844, 856
witch *n* 513, 994
witchcraft *n* 992
witchery *n* 829, 992
witching hour *n* 126
with *adv* 37, 41, 88
with a flourish *adv* 882
with a heavy hand *adv* 739
with a high hand *adv* 739
with all one's heart *adv* 602
with a long face *adv* 837
with a vengeance *adv* 31
with bated breath *adv* 507
with consummate skill *adv* 698
with downcast eyes *adv* 879
withdraw *v* 38, 283, 287, 293, 893
withdrawal *n* 38, 283, 287, 624, 893
withdrawn *adj* 893
wither *v* 195, 360, 659
withered *adj* 160
with flying colors *adv* 731
withhold *v* 781, 819
within *adv* 221
withindoors *adv* 221

wrathful *adj* 900
wreak *v* 739
wreath *n* 247
wreathe *n* 219
wreck *n* 162; *v* 162
wrecker *n* 165
wrench *n* 301; *v* 44,
285, 301
wrest *v* 243
wretch *n* 949
wretched *adj* 649, 828
wretchedly *adv* 32
wretchedness *n* 735
wriggle *v* 315
wring *v* 248, 378
wring from *v* 301
wrinkle *n* 258; *v* 248,
258, 259
wrinkled *adj* 128
writ *n* 590, 969
write *v* 569, 590
write down *v* 590
write prose *v* 598
writer *n* 590, 593
write to *v* 592
writhe *v* 243, 315, 378
writing *n* 590
writing *n* 593, 598
written *adj* 590
wrong *n* 923
wrong *n* 173, 619; *v*
649, 923; *adj* 481,
495, 544, 649, 923,
945
wrongdoer *n* 913, 949
wrongheaded *adj* 481
wrongly *adv* 923
wrong side out *adj* 218
wrought up *adj* 824

Y

yacht *n* 273
yachting *n* 267
yank *n* 285; *v* 285
yap *v* 412
yard *n* 232
yarn *n* 549
yawl *n* 273
yawn *v* 260, 688
yawning *n* 688; *adj*
208, 260
year *n* 106, 108
year after year *adv* 104
yearning *n* 276, 865,
897
years *n* 128
years ago *adv* 122
yeast *n* 320, 353
yell *n* 411; *v* 411
yell out *v* 411
yellow *n* 436
yellow *v* 435; *adj* 435
yellowish *adj* 435
yellow streak *n* 862
yelp *v* 410, 412
yesterday *n* 122
yesteryear *n* 122
yet *adv* 30, 106, 116,
122
yield *v* 82, 324, 360,
488, 624, 725, 762,
782, 812
yielding *n* 624, 725,
782

yoke *n* 749; *v* 43, 89
yon *adj* 196
yonder *adj* 196
young *adj* 123, 127,
129, 435
younger *adj* 127
youngster *n* 129
young years *n* 127
youth *n* 127
youth *n* 123, 129

Z

zany *n* 501
zeal *n* 171, 382, 604,
682, 821
zealot *n* 606
zealotry *n* 606
zealous *adj* 171, 606,
682
zenith *n* 206, 210
zephyr *n* 349
zero *n* 101
zero *n* 4
zest *n* 394
zigzag *n* 279; *adj* 279,
629; *adv* 314
zip *n* 101; *v* 409
zipping *n* 409
zone *n* 181, 204, 247
zonkers *adj* 503
zonko *adj* 503
zoography *n* 368
zoological *adj* 366, 368
zoologist *n* 357
zoology *n* 368
zoology *n* 357

FOR GIFT GIVING

WEDDING ANNIVERSARY SYMBOLS

	TRADITIONAL	MODERN
1st	paper	clocks
2nd	cotton	china
3rd	leather	crystal, glass
4th	books	electrical appliances
5th	wood	silverware
6th	sugar, candy	wood
7th	wool, copper	desk sets
8th	bronze, pottery	linens, laces
9th	pottery, willow	leather
10th	tin, aluminum	diamond jewelry
11th	steel	fashion jewelry
12th	silk, linen	pearls, colored gems
13th	lace	textiles, furs
14th	ivory	gold jewelry
15th	crystal	watches
20th	china	platinum
25th	silver	silver
30th	pearl	diamond
35th	coral	jade
40th	ruby	ruby
45th	sapphire	sapphire
50th	gold	gold
55th	emerald	emerald
60th	diamond	diamond
75th	diamond	diamond

BIRTHSTONES

January	Garnet
February	Amethyst
March	Bloodstone or Aquamarine
April	Diamond
May	Emerald
June	Pearl or Alexandrite
July	Ruby
August	Sardonyx or Peridot
September	Sapphire
October	Opal or Tourmaline
November	Topaz
December	Turquoise or Zircon

WEIGHTS AND MEASURES

Cubic Measure

1.728 cubic inches	1 cubic foot
27 cubic feet	1 cubic yard
128 cubic feet	1 cord (wood)
40 cubic feet	1 ton (shipping)
2,150.42 cubic inches	1 standard bushel
231 cubic inches	1 U.S. standard gallon
1 cubic foot	about ⁴/₅ of a bushel

Dry Measure

2 pints	1 quart
8 quarts	1 peck
4 pecks	1 bushel

Liquid Measure

4 gills	1 pint
2 pints	1 quart
4 quarts	1 gallon
31½ gallons	1 barrel

Imperial Liquid Measure

1 U.S. gallon	0.833 Imperial gallon
1 U.S. gallon	3.785 liters
1 Imperial gallon	1.201 U.S. gallons
1 Imperial gallon	4.546 liters
1 liter	0.264 U.S. gallon
1 liter	0.220 Imperial gallon

Long Measure

12 inches	1 foot
3 feet	1 yard
5½ yards	1 rod
40 rods	1 furlong
8 furlongs	1 statute mile
3 miles	1 league

Mariner's Measure

6 feet	1 fathom
120 fathoms	1 cable length
7½ cable lengths	1 mile
5,280 feet	1 statute mile
6,080.2 feet	1 nautical mile

Square Measure

144 square inches	1 square foot
9 square feet	1 square yard
30¼ square yards	1 square rod
40 square rods	1 rood
4 roods	1 acre
640 acres	1 square mile

Avoirdupois Weight

27¹¹/₃₂ grains	1 dram
16 drams	1 ounce
16 ounces	1 pound
25 pounds	1 quarter
4 quarters	1 cwt
2,000 pounds	1 short ton
2,240 pounds	1 long ton

Troy Weight

24 grains	1 pwt
20 pwt	1 ounce
12 ounces	1 pound

Used for weighing gold, silver and jewels

METRIC EQUIVALENTS

Linear Measure

1 centimeter		0.3937 inch
1 inch		2.54 centimeters
1 decimeter	3.937 inches	0.328 foot
1 foot		3.048 decimeters
1 meter	39.37 inches	1.0936 yards
1 yard		0.9144 meter
1 dekameter		1.9684 rods
1 rod		0.5029 dekameter
1 kilometer		0.621 mile
1 mile		1.609 kilometers

Square Measure

1 square centimeter	0.1550 square inch
1 square inch	6.452 square centimeters
1 square decimeter	0.1076 square foot
1 square foot	9.2903 square decimeters
1 square meter	1.196 square yards
1 square yard	0.8361 square meter

```
1 acre . . . . . . . . . . . . . . . . . . . . . . . . . . . . . . . . . . . . . . . . . . . 160 square rods
1 square rod . . . . . . . . . . . . . . . . . . . . . . . . . . . . . . . . . . . . . 0.00625 acre
1 hectare . . . . . . . . . . . . . . . . . . . . . . . . . . . . . . . . . . . . . . . . . 2.47 acres
1 acre . . . . . . . . . . . . . . . . . . . . . . . . . . . . . . . . . . . . . . . . . . 0.4047 hectare
1 square kilometer . . . . . . . . . . . . . . . . . . . . . . . . . . . . . 0.386 square mile
1 square mile . . . . . . . . . . . . . . . . . . . . . . . . . . . . . . . 2.59 square kilometers
```

Weights

```
1 gram . . . . . . . . . . . . . . . . . . . . . . . . . . . . . . . . . . . . . . . . . 0.03527 ounce
1 ounce . . . . . . . . . . . . . . . . . . . . . . . . . . . . . . . . . . . . . . . . . 28.35 grams
1 kilogram . . . . . . . . . . . . . . . . . . . . . . . . . . . . . . . . . . . . . 2.2046 pounds
1 pound . . . . . . . . . . . . . . . . . . . . . . . . . . . . . . . . . . . . . . . 0.4536 kilogram
1 metric ton . . . . . . . . . . . . . . . . . . . . . . . . . . . . . . . . 0.98421 English ton
1 English ton . . . . . . . . . . . . . . . . . . . . . . . . . . . . . . . . . 1.016 metric tons
```

Measure of Volume

```
1 cubic centimeter . . . . . . . . . . . . . . . . . . . . . . . . . . . . . . 0.061 cubic inch
1 cubic inch . . . . . . . . . . . . . . . . . . . . . . . . . . . . . . 16.39 cubic centimeters
1 cubic decimeter . . . . . . . . . . . . . . . . . . . . . . . . . . . . . 0.0353 cubic foot
1 cubic foot . . . . . . . . . . . . . . . . . . . . . . . . . . . . . 28.317 cubic decimeters
1 cubic meter . . . . . . . . . . . . . . . . . . . . . . . . . . . . . . . . . 1.308 cubic yards
1 cubic yard . . . . . . . . . . . . . . . . . . . . . . . . . . . . . . . 0.7646 cubic meter
1 stere . . . . . . . . . . . . . . . . . . . . . . . . . . . . . . . . . . . . . . . . 0.2759 cord
1 cord . . . . . . . . . . . . . . . . . . . . . . . . . . . . . . . . . . . . . . . . . 3.624 steres
1 liter . . . . . . . . . . . . . 0.908 dry quart . . . . . . . . . . . . 1.0567 liquid quarts
1 quart dry . . . . . . . . . . . . . . . . . . . . . . . . . . . . . . . . . . . . . 1.101 liters
1 quart liquid . . . . . . . . . . . . . . . . . . . . . . . . . . . . . . . . . 0.9463 liter
1 dekaliter . . . . . . . . . . . . 2.6417 gallons . . . . . . . . . . . . 1.135 pecks
1 gallon . . . . . . . . . . . . . . . . . . . . . . . . . . . . . . . . . . . 0.3785 dekaliter
1 peck . . . . . . . . . . . . . . . . . . . . . . . . . . . . . . . . . . . . . 0.881 dekaliter
1 hektoliter . . . . . . . . . . . . . . . . . . . . . . . . . . . . . . . . . . 2.8375 bushels
1 bushel . . . . . . . . . . . . . . . . . . . . . . . . . . . . . . . . . . 0.3524 hektoliter
```

APPROXIMATE METRIC EQUIVALENTS

```
1 decimeter . . . . . . . . . . . . . . . . . . . . . . . . . . . . . . . . . . . . . . . . 4 inches
1 liter . . . . . . . . . . . . . . 1.06 quarts liquid . . . . . . . . . . . . . . . 0.9 quart dry
1 meter . . . . . . . . . . . . . . . . . . . . . . . . . . . . . . . . . . . . . . . . . . . 1.1 yards
1 kilometer . . . . . . . . . . . . . . . . . . . . . . . . . . . . . . . . . . . . ⅝ of a mile
1 hektoliter . . . . . . . . . . . . . . . . . . . . . . . . . . . . . . . . . . . . 2⅝ bushels
1 hectare . . . . . . . . . . . . . . . . . . . . . . . . . . . . . . . . . . . . . . 2½ acres
1 kilogram . . . . . . . . . . . . . . . . . . . . . . . . . . . . . . . . . . . . . 2⅕ pounds
1 stere, or cubic meter . . . . . . . . . . . . . . . . . . . . . . . . . . . ¼ of a cord
1 metric ton . . . . . . . . . . . . . . . . . . . . . . . . . . . . . . . . . . . 2,204.6 pounds
```

States and Territories of the United States with Their Post Office Abbreviations and Capitals

Alabama (AL) .... Montgomery
Alaska (AK) .... Juneau
Arizona (AZ) .... Phoenix
Arkansas (AR) .... Little Rock
California (CA) .... Sacramento
Colorado (CO) .... Denver
Connecticut (CT) .... Hartford
Delaware (DE) .... Dover
District of Columbia (DC)
Florida (FL) .... Tallahassee
Georgia (GA) .... Atlanta
Hawaii (HI) .... Honolulu
Idaho (ID) .... Boise
Illinois (IL) .... Springfield
Indiana (IN) .... Indianapolis
Iowa (IA) .... Des Moines
Kansas (KS) .... Topeka
Kentucky (KY) .... Frankfort
Louisiana (LA) .... Baton Rouge
Maine (ME) .... Augusta
Maryland (MD) .... Annapolis
Massachusetts (MA) .... Boston
Michigan (MI) .... Lansing
Minnesota (MN) .... St. Paul
Mississippi (MI) .... Jackson
Missouri (MO) .... Jefferson City
Montana (MT) .... Helena
Nebraska (NE) .... Lincoln
Nevada (NV) .... Carson City
New Hampshire (NH) .... Concord
New Jersey (NJ) .... Trenton
New Mexico (NM) .... Santa Fe
New York (NY) .... Albany
North Carolina (NC) .... Raleigh
North Dakota (ND) .... Bismarck
Ohio (OH) .... Columbus
Oklahoma (OK) .... Oklahoma City
Oregon (OR) .... Salem
Pennsylvania (PA) .... Harrisburg
Rhode Island (RI) .... Providence
South Carolina (SC) .... Columbia
South Dakota (SD) .... Pierre
Tennessee (TN) .... Nashville
Texas (TX) .... Austin
Utah (UT) .... Salt Lake City

Vermont (VT) .... Montpelier
Virginia (VA) .... Richmond
Washington (WA) .... Olympia
West Virginia (WV) .... Charleston
Wisconsin (WI) .... Madison
Wyoming (WY) .... Cheyenne

American Samoa (AS) .... Pago Pago
Guam (GU) .... Agana
Puerto Rico (PR) .... San Juan
Virgin Islands (VI) .... Charlotte Amalie